An Ounce of Prevention

*Integrated Disaster Planning for Archives,
Libraries, and Record Centres*

Second Edition

Johanna Wellheiser and Jude Scott

With the assistance of John Barton

The Scarecrow Press, Inc.
Lanham, Maryland, and London
and
Canadian Archives Foundation
2002

SCARECROW PRESS, INC.

Published in the United States of America
by Scarecrow Press, Inc.
4501 Forbes Boulevard, Suite 200, Lanham, Maryland 20706
www.scarecrowpress.com

4 Pleydell Gardens, Folkestone
Kent CT20 2DN, England

British Library Cataloguing-in-Publication Information Available

Library of Congress Cataloging-in-Publication Data

Wellheiser, Johanna G.
 An ounce of prevention : integrated disaster planning for archives, libraries and record centres.—2nd ed. / Johanna Wellheiser and Jude Scott.
  p. cm.
 Rev. ed. of: An ounce of prevention / John P. Barton, Johanna G. Wellheiser, editors. 1985.
 Includes bibliographical references and index.
 ISBN 0-8108-4176-2 (alk. paper)
  1. Libraries—Canada—Safety measures. 2. Archives—Canada—Safety measures. 3. Emergency management—Canada. 4. Libraries—Safety measures. 5. Archives—Safety measures. 6. Emergency management. 7. Library materials—Conservation and restoration. 8. Archival materials—Conservation and restoration. I. Scott, Jude, 1951– . II. Canadian Archives Foundation. III. Title.

Z679.7 .O95 2002
025.8'2—dc21   2001049905

To our personal "mud angels" – Ian, Marjorie and Edward, and Conor and Roderick for their encouragement and understanding, and especially for being there when minor incidents appeared to be major disasters.

Table of Contents

Chapter 1

Chapter 2

Chapter 3

Chapter 4

Chapter 5

Chapter 6

Chapter 7

Chapter 8

Chapter 9

Chapter 10

Appendix 1

Appendix 2

Appendix 3

References

Index

Foreword

The 1985 edition of *An Ounce of Prevention: A Handbook on Disaster Contingency Planning for Archives, Libraries and Record Centres*, published by our predecessor organization, the Toronto Area Archivists Group (TAAG) Education Foundation, received acclaim throughout the archival and library communities. The Society of American Archivists, in awarding The Waldo Gifford Leland Commendation to John Barton and Johanna Wellheiser, recognized their work as an "outstanding contribution in the field of archival history, theory or practice". The manual was considered to be "comprehensive, unpretentious and superbly organized coverage of a subject of wide interest" and a "contribution to the professional literature".

While the first edition has been out of print for some years, there has been a continued and growing demand for information on disaster planning. In addition to requests for reprints, there have been many appeals for a new publication that takes into account advancements in disaster planning and recovery, and our use of information technology.

A decade later, the Canadian Archives Foundation, under the presidency of my predecessor, Richard Juneau, and in concert with Johanna Wellheiser (Manager, Preservation Services, Toronto Reference Library, Toronto Public Library) and Jude Scott (editor, the *Museum and Archival Supplies Handbook* published by the Ontario Museum Association and the Toronto Area Archivists Group) with the assistance of John Barton (Manager, Conservation and Reproduction Services, Archives of Ontario) agreed to proceed with a new edition. To Johanna and Jude in particular, as well as John, and to those others who served as expert readers and advisors, the Foundation acknowledges its inestimable debt of gratitude. The Foundation also wishes to acknowledge the financial support of the Government of Canada through the Canadian Council of Archives.

It is our belief that this new edition meets a number of the currently identified needs for practical information on disaster planning. It is intended as a further contribution to the art and science of preservation management and to the protection of recorded information and documentary heritage. This publication will also assist the Canadian Archives Foundation in achieving its various objectives. These include: promoting the education and training of practitioners of archival science at both the professional and non-professional levels; promoting the development of management skills in archival managers and administrators; promoting public education regarding the cultural importance and use of our documentary heritage; promoting research and publication in support of the training and public education functions; and promoting the proper care and preservation of our archival heritage.

James Lambert
President
Canadian Archives Foundation

Acknowledgments

We would like to acknowledge the Canadian Archives Foundation (CAF) for responding to the need for a revised and expanded edition of the original "Ounce". This led to the development of an entirely new publication – *An Ounce of Prevention: Integrated Disaster Planning for Archives, Libraries and Record Centres.* In particular, our thanks go to Mark Hopkins, Richard Huyda, James Lambert and Garron Wells of the CAF Board of Directors for their assistance throughout the project. Our colleague, John Barton, we thank for his key role in early development of the project and his valued assistance, as well as that of Ian Wilson, Archivist of Ontario.

We would like to thank Frances Schwenger, former Chief Executive Officer, Metropolitan Toronto Reference Library and Syd Jones, Director, Marketing and Communications, Toronto Public Library for their long-term support.

We want to express our gratitude and special appreciation to our professional readers for undertaking the arduous task of draft review and commentary:

- Paul Baril, Fire Protection Advisor, Preventive Conservation Services Division, Canadian Conservation Institute
- Mary Chalker, Associate University Librarian, Memorial University of Newfoundland
- Ann Douglas, Conservator, Toronto Reference Library, Toronto Public Library
- Jennifer Hutson, former Preservation Officer, National Library of Canada
- Nancy Marrelli, Archivist, Concordia University Archives
- Toby Murray, University Archivist and Preservation Officer, McFarlin Library, University of Tulsa
- Claude Ouellet, Planning Officer, National Archives of Canada
- Lucie Roy, Administrator Disaster Control, National Library of Canada
- David Tremain, Conservator, Preventive Conservation Services Division, Canadian Conservation Institute
- Brian Thurgood, Coordinator, Picture Conservation Section, National Archives of Canada
- and Betty Walsh, Conservator, British Columbia Information Management Services.

Our thanks also go to the following people for their valued advice and guidance:

- Ellen Demerais, former Director, Conservation Treatment Division, National Archives of Canada
- Karen Lenk, Conservator, Toronto Reference Library, Toronto Public Library
- and Don Macleod, Information Policy Analyst, Archives of Ontario.

In addition, we thank

- Eric Mills, for first draft copy-editing
- and the City of Toronto, for final inputting and formatting.

Permissions

The publisher and authors gratefully acknowledge all those who gave permission to reprint or otherwise use their material:

William A. Anderson and Shirley Mattingly. From Chapter 12 "Future Directions" in *Emergency Management: Principles and Practice for Local Government* (page 316). Thomas E. Drabek and Gerard J. Hoetmer, eds. Copyright © 1991 International City/County Management Association, 777 North Capitol Street NE, Suite 500, Washington, D.C. 20002. All rights reserved. Excerpts reprinted with permission.

Robbie Atabaigi. From "F.Y.I. Facts and Stats About Disaster Causing Phenomenas" in *Disaster Recovery Journal* Apr/May/June:38-39. Copyright © 1996 Systems Support, Inc. Excerpts reprinted or adapted and printed with permission.

J. Brett Balon and H. Wayne Gardner. From "Disaster Contingency Planning: The Basic Elements" in *Records Management Quarterly* 21(1):15. Copyright © 1987 Association of Records Managers and Administrators, Inc. Excerpt reprinted with permission.

Bruce Blythe citing Clouse and Riddell. From "Mental Health Plan. Trauma Intervention Supports Company Well-Being" in *Contingency Planning and Management for Business Preparedness and Recovery* 1(4):20. Copyright © 1996 Contingency Planning & Management for Business Preparedness and Recovery. Excerpt reprinted with permission.

Sally A. Buchanan. From *Disaster Planning: Preparedness and Recovery for Libraries and Archives: A RAMP Study with Guidelines*. PGI-88/WS/6 (page 71). Copyright © 1988 United Nations Educational, Scientific and Cultural Organization. Excerpt reprinted with permission.

Canadian Conservation Institute. From *Planning for Disaster Management: Hazard Analysis. CCI Notes N14/3* and *Emergency Preparedness for Cultural Institutions: Identifying and Reducing Hazards. CCI Note N14/2*. Copyright © 1988 and 1995 Government of Canada. Excerpts adapted and printed with permission of the Canadian Conservation Institute, Department of Canadian Heritage.

Rebecca Cesa. From "Don't Let Disaster Linger. Eliminating Odor Makes Sense" in *Contingency Planning & Management for Business Preparedness and Recovery* 1(2):19-21. Copyright © 1996 Contingency Planning & Management for Business Preparedness and Recovery. Excerpt adapted and printed with permission.

John N. DePew. From Chapter 8 "Disaster Preparedness and Recovery" in *A Library, Media and Archival Preservation Handbook* (page 257). Copyright © 1991 John N. DePew. Excerpt reprinted with permission of the publisher ABC-CLIO, Inc.

Thomas E. Drabek. From "The Events of An Emergency" in *Perspectives on Natural Disaster Mitigation: Papers Presented at 1991 AIC Workshop* (page 35). Copyright © 1991 American Institute for Conservation of Historic and Artistic Works (AIC). Excerpt reprinted with permission.

Emergency Preparedness Canada. From *A Summary of Federal Emergency Preparedness in Canada* (<http://hoshi.cic.sfu.ca1/epc1/EPCsum.html>). Copyright © 1996 Minister of Supply and Services. Excerpt adapted and printed with permission.

Claire England and Karen Evans. From *Disaster Management for Libraries: Planning and Process* (page 64). Copyright © 1988 Canadian Library Association. Excerpt reprinted with permission.

Al Foster citing Lawrence T. Jackson. From "Mental Health Plan. Trauma Intervention Supports Company Well-Being" in *Contingency Planning & Management for Business Preparedness and Recovery* 1(2):33. Copyright © 1996 Contingency Planning & Management for Business Preparedness and Recovery. Excerpt reprinted with permission.

Lisa L. Fox. From "Management Strategies for Disaster Preparedness" in *ALA Yearbook of Library and Information Series* 14:2. Copyright © 1989 American Library Association. Excerpt reprinted with permission.

Thomas M. Hawkins Jr. and Hugh McClees abridging Quarantelli. From Chapter 13 "Emergency Management" in *Managing Fire Services* (page 322). Ronny J. Coleman and John A. Granito, eds. 2nd edition. Copyright © 1988 International City/County Management Association, 777 North Capitol Street NE, Suite 500, Washington, D.C. 20002. All rights reserved. Excerpt reprinted with permission.

Introduction

Much has changed in the intervening years since the publication of the original "Ounce". Our observation is that today's approaches to disaster planning, preparedness and recovery reflect advancements that have occurred in the field of preservation overall, where "big picture" preservation management strategies have supplanted the previous emphasis on single item conservation. Today's approaches have also begun to reflect global changes where technology and access to information in all forms have assumed critical and more defined roles. These changes have resulted in an emerging recognition of the value and necessity of the total disaster planning process, and its integration into the core responsibilities and functions of an organization and the broader community.

The aim of this publication is to provide planners with a pragmatic, broad-based approach to what we call "integrated disaster planning". This preservation management approach to planning emphasizes the importance of an ongoing integrated process, rather than the singular goal of compiling information for a disaster plan. In many organizations this will require a paradigm shift in their concept of disaster planning. It is our conviction that the process of disaster planning can only be successfully achieved by first acknowledging it as a broad organizational responsibility – one that must be encouraged, managed and coordinated. In addition, an organization must recognize the interdependence of all the phases of disaster planning – prevention, protection, preparedness, response, recovery, rehabilitation and post-disaster assessment. As a result, what was previously and predominantly viewed as solely a security or conservation function becomes a shared commitment across the entire organization. We hope that this publication may serve as a catalyst in this regard for planners who are working to successfully mitigate hazards, to prevent any emergencies from turning into disasters, to minimize the effects of disasters that cannot be prevented, and to maximize their organization's response and recovery efforts.

The book's focus is on the protection and preservation of collections and records in order to ensure continued access to our documentary and cultural heritage, and service to our various publics. The critical issues of human health and safety, as well as building design are not the focus of this book. We leave these issues to the experts in these fields. This book is written for those individuals in archives, libraries and record centres charged with the responsibility for disaster planning. A basic knowledge of collections preservation is assumed. As well, we wish to emphasize that this publication is not designed to turn the disaster planners into professional emergency service providers. The actual containment of an emergency or disaster remains the responsibility of specially trained professionals. Our role in an emergency or disaster is to assist these efforts where possible.

We recognize that the audiences for this book will come from a variety of situations. Each reader will need to evaluate and adapt this book based on their particular circumstances, resources and priorities. Regardless of the size of the organization, integrated disaster planning requires a top-down commitment and will take considerable time, staff and money. Each organization should consider the broad scope of disaster planning as outlined in this publication, and then direct and scale its efforts according to its mandate, collections and services. This publication is intended to be of most benefit when used at the outset of a disaster planning process or prior to the revision of any existing plans. This or any other planning manual, or disaster plan, should not be applied without careful thought and modification.

The book is structured to reflect the desired sequence of disaster planning in all its phases. Each planning phase has a separate chapter. Within each chapter, the respective process for planning is outlined, followed by the information needed to support its implementation. In this way, the steps for each process are clearly articulated. Thus, it is hoped that the reader may distinguish between the "what to do" and the "how to do it". This book outlines the planning processes involved for each planning phase as well as putting the reader "on location" at each of the three stages of a disaster (before, during and after), so that they may understand and anticipate what may be required at the time. In summary, we have provided a planning tool to manage the process, one that draws on a great number of resources, one that is process driven, but also supplies the content necessary for its execution.

We acknowledge that this structure requires the reader to work through the entire process of disaster planning. All the relevant information on a given topic cannot be found in a single chapter. Thus, all of the chapters are best read, considered and worked through in the formulation of a disaster plan – disaster planning is truly not for the faint of heart, nor the linear thinker!

This book acknowledges the inevitability of the unexpected, and the fact that you cannot plan for everything. It focuses on the effects of disasters, rather than their causes, so that generic workable plans may be developed and applied to a variety of situations, great and small.

Johanna Wellheiser
Jude Scott

Toronto/Beeton

Selected Acronyms

ACA — Association of Canadian Archivists

ACGIH — American Conference of Governmental Industrial Hygienists

AES — Audio Engineering Society, Inc.

AIC — American Institute for Conservation of Historic and Artistic Works

AIHA — American Industrial Hygiene Association

AIIM — Association for Information and Image Management

ANSI — American National Standards Institute

ARMA — Association of Records Managers and Administrators, Inc.

ASHRAE — American Society of Heating, Refrigeration and Air Conditioning Engineers

CAC — Canadian Association for the Conservation of Cultural Property

CAPC — Canadian Association of Professional Conservators

CCA — Canadian Council of Archives

CCEP — Canadian Centre for Emergency Preparedness

CCI — Canadian Conservation Institute

CCOHS — Canadian Centre For Occupational Health and Safety

CGSB — Canadian General Standards Board

CIHM — Canadian Institute for Historical Microreproductions

CLA — Canadian Library Association

CLIR — Council on Library and Information Resources

CSA — Canadian Standards Association

DRI — Disaster Recovery Institute

DRIE — Disaster Recovery Information Exchange

EPC — Emergency Preparedness Canada

EPIX — Emergency Preparedness Information eXchange

FEMA — Federal Emergency Management Agency

ICA — International Council on Archives

ICBS — International Committee of the Blue Shield

ICMA — International City/County Management Association

ICOM — International Council of Museums

ICOMOS — International Council of Monuments and Sites

IDNDR — International Decade for Natural Disaster Reduction

IFLA — International Federation of Library Associations and Institutions

IIC — International Institute for Conservation

IPI — Image Permanence Institute

ISO — International Organization for Standardization

LBI — Library Binding Institute

MIACC — Major Industrial Accidents Council of Canada

NAC — National Archives of Canada

NARA — National Archives and Records Administration

NFPA — National Fire Protection Association

NIOSH — National Institute for Occupational Health and Safety

NISO — National Information Standards Organization

NLC — National Library of Canada

OSHA — Occupational Safety and Health Administration

SCC — Standards Council of Canada

SMPTE — Society of Motion Picture and Television Engineers

UL — Underwriters Laboratory

ULC — Underwriters' Laboratories of Canada

UNESCO — United Nations Educational, Scientific and Cultural Organization

See also Appendix 3: Resources.

Chapter 1

1.0 Disaster Planning

1.1 Introduction

Books passed delicately from hand to hand. There were so many of these hands, thousands of them, a long chain that embraced, surrounded and helped Florence at her times of trial. These were the hands of the young and not so young people who flocked here from all over Italy and the world and plunged into the mixture of mud and oil that was left...when the [River] Arno retreated to its bed. These were the hands of the "Mud Angels." (Pintus and Messeri 1996)

The year 1996 marked the 30th anniversary of the flood in Florence, Italy, a pivotal point in disaster planning and recovery for archives, libraries and record centres, and indeed the entire field of preservation. Response to the flood and recovery of the damaged collections of the Biblioteca Nazionale generated new thinking, collaborative approaches and a wealth of innovative advances that continue to be used and adapted worldwide.

Since 1966, the library and archival community's response to disasters has reflected the experience gained from the successful handling of a wide range of natural, technological and social events: floods and hurricanes, power failures and chemical spills, and war and arson. Our concept of disaster planning has shifted and broadened, and our response reflects a vastly changed and changing world. As preservation professionals, we now make consistent and better use of expertise and practices from other industries and occupations. In the future, we expect to see further collaboration among those responsible for cultural heritage and those who practice emergency management as a profession. The services of professional disaster recovery companies with archives and library experience are now also more widely available. And national and international preservation initiatives, many of which are now undertaken cooperatively, have increased.

In addition, there has been a dramatic shift from collection and information warehousing to collection and information management, as we have gained understanding of the balance between the needs of preservation and those of access. More recently, the new information technologies have changed the very nature of the services we provide. Disaster planning now recognizes our increasing use of and dependence on electronic resources. The Y2K phenomenon has underscored the magnitude of this reality. And our care of collections and records is now, more than ever, irrevocably linked to the care of our online catalogues and database records. Our responsibility also includes mixed format collections of greater diversity, and more recently digital collections. With this evolution, or rather revolution, from collections-based to information-based management, continued and enduring access is recognized as the pre-eminent goal of preservation.

The concept of "business resumption planning," conceived in the business world, has also recently come to be considered by planners in archives, libraries and record centres. Business resumption planning concentrates more on identifying and maintaining essential services than on detailing responses to specific disasters. Its purpose, that of implementing pre-established plans to resume vital functions as swiftly as possible, reflects, in part, the changes that have taken place in preservation overall.

During the past decade in particular, awareness of the need for disaster planning has increased substantially. Many more organizations have formulated plans and integrated planning into their ongoing operations, training opportunities have grown in frequency and scope, disaster planning activity has increased in many professional organizations and has come to be required for some types of funding. While not yet acknowledged as indispensable by all, disaster planning has become a key management responsibility in many institutions and organizations.

The question remains: are we now better prepared to respond to emergencies and disasters?

1.2 Disaster Planning in Practice

Hard data on the state of disaster planning in the preservation literature is limited. Surveys of some communities do indicate a reasonably healthy state of disaster preparedness, while others dramatically point to the need for increased efforts.

The following overview of published survey data is neither comprehensive nor conclusive, and the surveys themselves are not directly comparable. However, several observations can be made.

The vast majority of the libraries surveyed did not have disaster plans. Of those who reported not having a plan in place, an alarming number in some surveys indicated that they had already experienced a disaster. In general, archives would seem to be better prepared than are libraries. This may be due in part to the respective differences in their mandate, collections and services. The inherent nature of archival collections and the need to preserve unique materials of cultural value provides a compelling argument for disaster planning. On the other hand, the public libraries included in a number of the surveys are presumed to have circulating collections, many of which would not be unique, and as a result present quite different long-term preservation needs.

It appears that the current reality is that many organizations, despite their good intentions, have yet to realize these intentions in the form of a disaster plan or integrated disaster planning.

On a more positive note, recognition of the necessity and value of disaster planning has increased overall. This is demonstrated by the great strides that have been made in certain areas such as the growing body of disaster planning literature, improved technical expertise in the recovery of various media, increased training opportunities, the formation of local support networks and, in some instances, the development of national disaster management initiatives.

- **Britain**

  In 1986, just 9% of university and polytechnic libraries in Britain responding to a national survey reported that they had a disaster control plan (Mowat 1987, 39).

  A survey of preservation management and policy in all types of British libraries was sponsored by the Leverhulme Trust and done at the University of Loughborough in 1994. Nearly 42% of the 488 respondents reported having a member of staff responsible for the management and implementation of disaster control planning, and almost 30% had a disaster control plan. (Eden, Feather and Matthews 1994, 6)

  In a further 1995/96 survey sponsored by the British Library and carried out at the University of Loughborough, 20% of the 388 responding libraries (academic, public, national and special) reported having a written disaster control plan (Matthews and Eden 1996b, 7).

- **New Zealand**

  A 1995 New Zealand survey of emergency planning covered 475 institutions (museums, libraries and archives) and 75 conservators. Roughly 13% of the 137 institutional respondents reported having a written emergency policy, and 26% reported having an emergency response team. Of the 27 conservator respondents, 59% reported contributing to an emergency preparedness plan. (Clarke 1995, 38-39)

- **United States**

  A 1987 Florida state disaster preparedness survey of 196 academic and public libraries determined that just over 50% had experienced collections-related incidents as a result of natural disaster, human-initiated water damage, fire, etc. in the last five years. Close to 80% of respondents reported that they did not have a disaster plan. (DePew 1989, 8 and 16)

  The first nationwide study of U.S. archival practices was undertaken in 1989, covering a wide range of archives such as academic, local, religious, museum and state. Of the 320 respondents, 56% reported having a disaster plan in place or in the planning stages. (Conway 1990, 219)

  In 1991, the Regional OCLC (Online Computer Library Centre, Inc.) Network Directors' Advisory Committee (RONDAC) undertook a preservation needs assessment survey. Of 161 respondent libraries, 19% reported having a disaster response plan and 17% reported working on a plan. (Kahn 1993, 73)

  In 1992 a similar survey to that of RONDAC above was carried out by the AMIGOS Library Services. Of 239 respondent libraries, 75% said that they "had no disaster plan to speak of, despite the fact that 25% of the institutions had suffered some sort of calamity in 1992" (Kahn 1993, 73-74).

  A 1992 survey examined emergency planning and management in U.S. college and small university libraries. More than half (57%) of the 175 respondents reported they had never experienced a disaster. Of the 43% who had experienced a disaster, half had a disaster manual. (George 1994, 1-2)

- **Canada**

  The Canadian Council of Archives provided grant funding for the preparation of disaster plans in 15 archives (municipal, academic, religious, library, etc.) across the country from 1991-96 (Ostiguy 1997).

The Canadian Council of Federal Libraries Committee on Conservation and Preservation of Library Materials conducted a library disaster survey in January 1993. Of 146 respondents, 20% reported that they had a plan or were developing one, while 27% had suffered at least one disaster. (Council of Federal Libraries 1994, Section 15)

In 1994, Le Comité de préservation du Réseau des archives du Québec surveyed 104 members on the status of preservation and preservation management. Of the respondents, 44% reported that written disaster plans were in place, in development or planned. (Emond 1994, 31)

1.2.1 The Purpose of Disaster Planning

The refrains "it can't happen here" and "it can't happen to us" have a hollow ring to those who have seen the catastrophic consequences wrought by floods, arson and hurricanes, or even by procrastination and negligence. Such denial creates a dangerous and false sense of security. Disaster planning is founded on the premise that emergencies and disasters can and will occur. No amount of precaution can reduce this risk to zero. Therefore, disaster planning must consider not only how disasters can be prevented, but also how their impact can be contained and minimized.

There are no hard and fast definitions as to exactly what constitutes an emergency rather than a disaster. This determination depends largely on the organization or community itself.

- An **emergency** can be defined as an adverse event that does not have widespread impact nor requires the use of extraordinary or prolonged resources to return conditions to normal.

- A **disaster** can be defined as an adverse event of organization-wide or community-wide impact resulting in significant damage and loss that requires the use of prolonged or extraordinary resources to return conditions to normal.

> Disasters are qualitatively different from...emergencies...In short, a disaster is not simply a large-scale accident or emergency. Organizations must recognize that during crisis situations the environment changes quickly and drastically and that their disaster preparedness planning and response strategies must give consideration to this important fact. (Quarantelli abridged by Hawkins and McClees 1988, 322)

The purpose of integrated disaster planning is to ensure the continued delivery of service by avoiding losses and damage to the organization's collections, records, facilities and systems. This is achieved by undertaking all the phases of disaster planning. The disaster plan that results is an essential tool, providing staff the necessary resources to successfully respond to an emergency or a disaster and to prevent, where possible, the former from turning into the latter. However, this document cannot stand alone. It must be supported by appropriate education and training, so that staff develop the necessary knowledge and skills, and have an opportunity to test the plan before it is required.

> *Effective disaster planning is systematic.* Good plans are purposeful, methodical and above *all built on a firm foundation.* (Jablonowski 1997, 18)

However, disaster planning neither begins nor ends with the plan. All the steps leading up to producing the plan and all those that follow are required for an institution to be able to say: "we do disaster/recovery planning – on a systematic and continuous basis. Learning the process is the key, not just having a manual." (Bologna cited in Hunter 1984b, 4)

The disaster plan enables the organization to effectively prepare for and respond to disasters. To be fully effective, disaster planning must be seen as a core responsibility, integrated into the overall operations of the organization, and taken into account when other planning exercises are considered. It is now recognized that collections and records can only be responsibly protected within the context of the mandate, goals and services of the entire organization.

Integration is fundamental to the success of planning and ultimately that of recovery and rehabilitation, for organizations have come to understand that it is not possible to extinguish the fires or contain the floods and quickly return to normal operations. There is now a recognition of the ripple effect that disasters generate, an effect that may involve all operations and services and may, in some circumstances, require extraordinary efforts and resources. For archives, libraries and record centres, successful protection and safety of staff, the public, the facility and its resources allow us to fulfil our goals of continued preservation and access to collections and information.

1.2.2 The Phases of Disaster Planning

Our concept of disaster planning has broadened to include not only the phases of preparation and response, but also those of prevention, protection, recovery, rehabilitation and post-disaster planning. Each phase has its own aims and process. Each phase is generally the result of the preceding one, and usually determines the requirements of the next. Effectively undertaking the full spectrum of pre-disaster planning activities may eliminate the need for post-disaster response and recovery or, at least, reduce the effects of the disaster.

Planning in and of itself is a critical activity and encompasses all stages of a disaster. It must take place for each of the three stages – before, during and after. Planning is the activity that provides a continuous link and makes the phases work in synergy. Planning itself is a continuous process.

Stage of Disaster	Phase of Planning
Before	Prevention, Protection and Preparedness
During	Response
After	Recovery, Rehabilitation and Post-Disaster Planning

1.2.3 The Principles of Disaster Planning

A comprehensive, integrated approach to disaster planning involves virtually all the operations in an organization. As such, the task can be complex and multifarious. Disaster planners may find it useful to articulate a set of principles to focus their thinking and development of goals and objectives at the outset of a planning process, or to verify the direction of ongoing planning efforts.

Disaster Planning Principles
Plan ahead.
Plan for people.
Plan realistically and plan for resistance.
Plan for change.
Plan for the worst and hope for the best.
Plan for the effects, not the causes.
Plan for all possible effects.
Plan for adequate, ongoing education and training.
Plan for self-reliance and for expert help.
Plan for the aftermath.
Plan for public concern.
Plan for the emotional impact.
Plan for the financial impact.
Plan for return to normal operations.
Plan for the next disaster.
(Based in part on Boozer cited by Nelson 1991, 77-78)

1.2.4 Health and Safety

Whether it be a flood, a fire, an earthquake or a hurricane, a disaster may result in injury, death and destruction. To deal effectively with this threat to life and property, planning must aim to keep losses to a minimum and articulate a clear course of action for staff. Above all, the safety of human life must take precedence: no collection or record is worth more than a human life.

Evacuation plans and emergency safety procedures for staff and the public must be established before any disaster planning for the collections and records. While planning for human safety will overlap with the planning for safety of property, the respective safety and emergency/disaster plans should be kept distinct.

Although our discussions of disaster planning include issues of human health and safety, it is beyond the scope of this publication to deal comprehensively with them. Each organization has a responsibility to comply with applicable legislation and establish appropriate measures, systems and procedures for the security and safety of staff, users and visitors.

1.2.5 The Human Factor

Ultimately, a disaster plan is a people plan. As Stasak (1996, 29) observed: people develop it, people test it, people maintain it, and people put it into practice when needed. Committed, trained, knowledgeable and informed personnel are the organization's most valuable resource. In an archives, library or records centre, the nature of the collections and records will determine the nature of the planning, but people will determine its effectiveness.

Disaster research on the social science issues is providing useful and extensive information on the psychological impact of disasters. Studies have dispelled the assumption that people either go into shock or flee the scene. Trained personnel rally in the face of disaster and go to extraordinary lengths to help:

> Their [Response Action Team (RAF) of the National Library of Canada] devotion to the collections, concern for the damage they suffer, pride in their jobs, and keen sense of responsibility, are all magnificent (Michaels 1994, 2).

Experience with community-wide disasters has shown that it is unreasonable to expect people to give top priority to the organization unless some provisions have been made for the well-being of their families. Such provisions, sometimes called a "family assistance function" (Stasak 1996, 31), can include measures to allow staff to prepare for disaster at home as well as at work, such as communication links, training in first-aid and access to emergency supplies. This also underscores the importance of having alternates to fill in when principal disaster team members are unavailable. Establishing that loved ones are safe and provided for will allow staff to redirect their focus to the disaster in the workplace and then initiate the necessary response and recovery operations.

Understanding the psychological factors will help the emergency manager plan and prepare for the people who deal with disasters as well as the collections, records and buildings *(see also Chapter 10)*.

1.3 Disaster Planning Worldwide

Disasters can befall any community in the world, and archives, libraries and record centres have had their share. Irreparable damage and tragic losses can result from all forms of disasters.

Natural disasters are random and will always be with us. Science has increasingly provided ways of predicting and measuring them, but nothing can prevent their occurrence. All we can do is prepare as best we can and deal with their after-effects.

Technological disasters and those of social origin are not always random, and they too will likely always be with us. Some of the most ruinous disasters visited upon nations have been the result of intentional, purposeful destruction. In these cases, archives, libraries, museums and other cultural and educational institutions have repeatedly been targeted for destruction by those wishing to eradicate the cultural and documentary legacy of a nation or people.

In recent years, there has been growing concern in the preservation and conservation community worldwide over tragic losses of cultural heritage, both as a result of natural disasters (e.g., Hurricane Hugo on the eastern seaboard of the United States and the earthquake in Kobe, Japan) and of armed conflict (e.g., wars in the Persian Gulf, Africa and the former Yugoslavia). Cultural and emergency agencies and organizations, both governmental and non-governmental, have introduced many initiatives aimed at reducing losses, preparing for and responding to these threats to our cultural and documentary heritage.

The following are selected key initiatives:

1.3.1 The International Decade for Natural Disaster Reduction

In 1989, the United Nations General Assembly proclaimed the 1990s as the International Decade for Natural Disaster Reduction (IDNDR). The objective of the Decade is to reduce substantially by the year 2000 (especially in developing countries), loss of life, property damage and social and economic disruption caused by natural disasters such as earthquakes, windstorms, tsunamis, floods, landslides, volcanic eruptions, wildfires, insect infestations and drought. This is to be accomplished through concerted international action and each member state of the United Nations is to implement the Decade as it feels appropriate. The IDNDR encourages cooperative planning between private and public sector groups. *(See also 1.4.3)*

In summary, the five goals of the IDNDR are (UN General Assembly 1989):

· To improve each country's capacity to effectively mitigate the effects of natural disasters, paying particular attention to assisting developing countries.
· To devise appropriate guidelines and strategies for applying scientific and technological knowledge.
· To foster scientific and engineering endeavours to reduce loss of life.
· To disseminate existing and new technical information.
· To develop programmes of technical assistance and technology transfer, demonstration projects and education and training.

The member countries' agreed-upon targets by the year 2000 are (EPC 1996, 23):

· Comprehensive national risk assessments.
· Mitigation plans at national and local levels, including long-term prevention, preparedness and community awareness.
· Ready access to global, regional, national and local warning systems and their broad dissemination.

1.3.2 The 1954 Hague Convention

The Hague Conventions are a series of international treaties that were issued from conferences held at The Hague in the Netherlands. The 1954 Hague Convention was developed under the auspices of the United Nations Educational, Scientific and Cultural Organization (UNESCO). Called the *Convention for the Protection of Cultural Property in the Event of Armed*

Conflict, it is an instrument of international humanitarian law. Its purpose is to create a world system to protect the physical heritage of humanity in times of war and other armed conflict. The Convention includes general provisions for protecting cultural property, reporting mechanisms and procedures to be invoked during armed conflict.

One means of protection is to effect adequate peacetime preparations to protect heritage. A recent example of preparation for war hazards included:

· microfilming of inventories

· safe storage of valuable documents

· preparation of packing materials for transport

· verification of employees indebted for transport in case of evacuation

and in accordance with the Hague Convention,

· provision of employee identification cards to facilitate continued work in case of war

· provision of flags and emblems with distinctive blue and white shield emblems for protective marking of valuable buildings and objects.

(Croatian archives report cited in van der Hoeven and van Albada 1996, 37)

The 1992 general conference of the International Council of Museums (ICOM) in Quebec City adopted a resolution urging implementation of the Hague Convention. In addition, the resolution stated that protection of cultural heritage should be a task of UN peacekeeping missions, as part of humanitarian aid, and should also be included in disaster aid. To date, over 90 member states of the United Nations have ratified and adopted the 1954 Hague Convention as national law. Canada has recently ratified the Convention.

The UNESCO publication, *A Review of the Convention for the Protection of Cultural Property in the Event of Armed Conflict* (Boylan 1993), concluded that the 1954 Hague Convention is still valid and relevant; however, issues of application remain to be resolved.

A 1994 resolution passed at an International Expert Meeting held by the Central Board of National Antiquities (Sweden), the Swedish National Commission for UNESCO and the International Council of Monuments and Sites (ICOMOS Sweden) resolved that deliberate war damage to cultural heritage (being but one part of a strategy of domination through destruction) is to be condemned as a war crime according to the Hague Convention. When carried out in extremis, as in former Yugoslavia, such damage is deemed to be a specific form of genocide, namely, ethnocide. (UNESCO 1994, 1)

In 1997, UNESCO commissioned the International Council on Archives to develop emergency programmes for the protection of vital records in the event of armed conflict. The project was based on case studies of three countries in different continents: Costa Rica, Croatia and Gambia. Emergency programmes were produced for each of the country's archives, as well as a general guide for use in other countries (see UNESCO 1998).

In 1998, the International Committee of the Blue Shield (*see 1.3.6*) and UNESCO organized the Radenci (Slovenia) Conference. Participants adopted a *Declaration on the Protection of Cultural Heritage in Emergencies and Exceptional Situations* encouraging that strategies be developed to improve prevention, intervention and recovery measures.

For international conventions and other instruments see the UNESCO website *(See Appendix 3.1 Sources of Information: Armed Conflict).*

1.3.3 The UNIDROIT Convention on International Return of Stolen or Illegally Exported Cultural Objects

UNIDROIT (the International Institute for Unification of Private Law) is an independent intergovernmental organization with 56 member states, including Canada and the U.S. The 1970 UNESCO Convention on the Means of Prohibiting and Preventing the Illicit Import, Export, and Transfer of Ownership of Cultural Property was recognized to have limited effectiveness. In 1986, UNIDROIT began work, at the request of UNESCO, on a more comprehensive convention intended to establish a uniform international private law code for the protection of cultural property.

The resulting 1995 convention, known popularly as the UNIDROIT (one law) Convention, was written to provide recourse in the courts for the owners (individuals or institutions) of stolen cultural property. Neither Canada or the U.S. has ratified this convention. Coverage of cultural objects by the convention is broad and includes prints and drawings, manuscripts, incunabula, books, documents, publications of special interest and archives (including sound, photographic and cinematographic). (Convention on Stolen or Illegally Exported Cultural Objects 1995 and Technology & Conservation 1995, 6-8)

1.3.4 G7 Declaration on Terrorism

In June 1996, the world's leading industrial countries, known as the Group of Seven (G7), issued a declaration condemning terrorist activities in all forms and agreeing on a general plan to combat terrorism (The Toronto Star 1996, A14).

The countries agreed to:

· strengthen the sharing of government information about terrorist groups.

· improve protection of transportation links against terrorism.

· urge states to refuse to meet the demands of hostage-takers and to ensure that those responsible are brought to justice.

· promote extradition in order to make it more difficult for terrorists to commit crimes.

1.3.5 Memory of the World Programme

In 1992, the United Nations Educational, Scientific and Cultural Organization (UNESCO) launched its ambitious Memory of the World Programme, aimed at protecting the documentary heritage of the world, democratizing access and raising awareness of its significance and the need for its preservation. "The documentary heritage residing in libraries and archives throughout the world constitutes a major portion of the memory of the world – and much of it is currently at risk" (Foster et al. 1995, 1).

One of the key elements of the Programme planning in 1994-95 was to specifically identify library collections and archive holdings that have already suffered irreparable damage in the 20th century. The report that resulted, *Lost Memory: Libraries and Archives Destroyed in the Twentieth Century* (van der Hoeven and van Albada 1996), attempts to list the major disasters during this century that have destroyed or caused irreparable damage to libraries and archives and their collections. The listings cover accidental and purposeful destruction such as floods, earthquakes, arson and war, but the impacts of vandalism, environmental control and insects were not included.

1.3.6 International Committee of the Blue Shield

In 1992, the International Council on Monuments and Sites (ICOMOS) convened an international round table to examine how international agencies and organizations, both governmental and non-governmental, could together improve the response to disasters. Several important initiatives from the resulting action plan are described below (based on 1er Sommet 1996, 1-2 and Stovel 1996, 1-5).

In February 1995, the round table led an evaluation of UNESCO activities related to protection of cultural heritage. An Inter-Agency Task Force was established among the permanent members of the round table to promote cooperation and to identify and undertake projects of common concern. In April 1996, ICO-

MOS, ICOM, the International Council on Archives (ICA) and the International Federation of Library Associations and Institutions (IFLA) agreed to join forces to establish the International Committee of the Blue Shield (ICBS) to coordinate the action in the case of emergencies. The ICBS took its name from the emblem of the Hague Convention (1954) on the protection of cultural property during armed conflict. The ICBS programme is intended to develop local resources for cultural emergencies and disasters (natural or manmade) through involvement at a national level. In addition, national ICOMOS committees such as those of Sweden, Sri Lanka, Japan and Canada will examine their national models for disaster response.

As part of Canada's participation in these initiatives, ICOMOS Canada with support from the Cultural Heritage Division of UNESCO and others organized the "First National Summit on Heritage and Risk Preparedness in Canada" in 1996 *(see 1.4.7 and Appendix 1)*.

See Blue Shield Preparedness and Emergency Response Program under *Appendix 3.1 Sources of Information: Conservation and Disasters.*

1.3.7 U.S. National Disaster Task Force on Emergency Response

In the United States, a National Disaster Task Force on Emergency Response was formed in 1995 by the Federal Emergency Management Agency (FEMA), the Getty Conservation Institute and the National Institute for the Conservation of Cultural Property (NIC). The task force is a partnership of 29 federal agencies, national service organizations and private institutions, including the American Institute for Conservation of Historic and Artistic Works (AIC). Its members are dedicated to safeguarding U.S cultural heritage from the damaging effects of natural disasters and other emergencies, and providing coordinated, expert assistance to the general public in case of disaster. Activities to date have focussed on developing information and training tools for cultural institutions and the public.

In 1995, the U.S. National Fire Protection Association issued its first national standard on disaster planning, *NFPA 1600-1995. Recommended Practice for Disaster Management.*

1.4 Disaster Planning in Canada

Canada's ten million square kilometres contain virtually every geological and ecological feature found in the world. Combined with its varied climates and diverse economic activities, Canada is in a unique position to experience a wide range of disasters. Emergency Preparedness Canada (EPC 1996, 3-4) has identified roughly 60 types of emergencies that might affect Canadians, ranging from severe storms to nuclear war: "From 1982 to 1992, there were approximately 67 major disasters in Canada causing 498 deaths, 1,417 injuries, 48,407 evacuations and $2.9 billion in damage" (Duguay 1994, 16).

In North America, our experience with disasters has frequently involved those considered natural, such as floods, hurricanes and earthquakes. Scientists are warning that:

> With global warming...it is likely that planners will have to deal with more climate-induced problems...Others are also saying that Canada – and in fact the world – may be entering a time of more frequent weather-related catastrophes (Cliche cited in Corelli 1996, 24).

Recent examples of natural disasters in Canada include the 1996 Quebec Saguenay region flood and the 1997 Manitoba Red River flood. These floods are estimated to have cost $4 million each. The most expensive natural disaster in Canadian history, the 1998 winter ice storm, devastated much of Quebec and eastern Ontario. Total recovery cost may exceed $1 billion.

North American disasters of technological and social origin – such as arson, bombings, chemical spills and nuclear power plant leaks – have also occurred. However, Canada has not, to date, experienced the widespread destruction endured by nations that have directly suffered the ravages of prolonged armed conflict.

Emergency planning in Canada rose to prominence after World War II. Government took the lead with its focus on preparation for nuclear war, and educated the population on how to respond to emergencies at home, school and work. In Canada, the management of disasters is a shared responsibility among all three levels of government. Emergency preparedness is ultimately an individual personal responsibility. As a crisis extends beyond individual or organizational capabilities, its management shifts to one or more appropriate levels of government. First response is usually at the local level; if the emergency escalates, regional, provincial and federal governments may become involved.

A significant Canadian disaster recorded in the professional library literature was the 1952 Library of Parliament fire in Ottawa. This fire marked the first known use of vacuum freeze-drying to recover water-damaged books, an innovation that has since been widely used and developed over the years. Ironically, the Library had survived intact an earlier 1916 fire that destroyed the centre block of the Parliament Buildings. (Hamilton, 1953)

In Canadian archives, libraries and record centres, current strategies reflect our growing knowledge of and experience with disaster planning, response and recovery, and that of the international community. Recently, Canada has been involved in a number of national developments and international initiatives including the following:

1.4.1 The Emergency Preparedness Act and the Emergencies Act

In 1988, new comprehensive federal emergency legislation was passed. The *Emergency Preparedness Act* establishes preparedness as a function of government. The *Emergencies Act* provides the means for a national emergency to be declared and establishes jurisdictions and means for response. *(See Appendix 2)*

1.4.2 Emergency Preparedness Canada

Emergency Preparedness Canada (EPC) has the primary federal responsibility to advance emergency preparedness in Canada, in cooperation with the provinces, and to provide financial compensation to individuals and organizations that suffer in the event of a federally declared emergency. Amongst its programmes are education and training, publications, facilitation and coordination of activities including international initiatives with the provinces, other countries and agencies. *(See Appendix 2)*

1.4.3 Canada and the IDNDR

Canada was a co-sponsor of the United Nations resolution that established the 1990s as the International Decade for Natural Disaster Reduction (IDNDR). Canada's participation in the IDNDR was based, in part, on the following:

- Canada's tradition of providing humanitarian aid to disaster victims.

- Canada's engineering expertise, products and technology, such as remote sensing technologies for the monitoring of floods and forest fires.

- Canada's skills in training and education for emergency providers.

A Canadian National Committee has been established under the auspices of the Royal Society of Canada and the Canadian Academy of Engineering to develop an action programme to mitigate the effects in Canada and abroad of natural disasters. The United Nations IDNDR World Wide Web site was developed and is maintained by the Simon Fraser University EPIX project as a contribution to the IDNDR *(See Appendix 3.1 Sources of Information: Education and Training).*

1.4.4   Canada and the United States

At the Shamrock Summit in 1986, Canada and the United States reaffirmed their long-standing bilateral cooperation in comprehensive civil emergency planning and management in an agreement signed by Emergency Preparedness Canada and the U.S. Federal Emergency Management Agency.

1.4.5   Canada and Standards Development

Canada has assumed a leadership role in the international community of disaster planning and standards development. In 1991, Canada became one of the first countries to develop a national standard on disaster planning, *CAN/CSA-Z731-91, Emergency Planning for Industry.* Prepared by the Canadian Standards Association (CSA) and the Major Industrial Accidents Council of Canada, the first edition focused on disaster planning for industry. The second edition, *CAN/CSA-Z731-95. 1995. Rev. ed. National Standard of Canada. Emergency Planning for Industry*, covers disaster planning for a broad range of businesses, industries and facilities. Its importance lies in the establishment of minimum criteria for emergency or disaster planning, and guides owners and operators of private and public facilities in developing a plan for effective disaster preparedness and response.

In 1995, Canada first presented this national standard as an international draft and basis for the development of an international ISO (International Organization for Standardization) standard.

1.4.6   Major Industrial Accidents Council of Canada

The Major Industrial Accidents Council of Canada (MIACC) was formed in 1987 as a result of the world's most devastating chemical accident, in Bhopal, India, in 1984. Its mandate is to reduce the frequency of major industrial accidents involving dangerous substances by examining Canada's potential for a Bhopal-like accident; by reviewing existing measures taken by industry and government to prevent industrial accidents; and by reviewing the collective ability of industry and government to respond to these accidents.

1.4.7   ICOMOS Canada

In September 1996, ICOMOS Canada with the support of UNESCO's cultural heritage division, the National Capital Commission of Quebec, ICOM Canada, the Department of Canadian Heritage and the University of Montreal organized the First National Summit on Heritage and Risk Preparedness in Canada in Quebec City. The objectives were to improve the state of risk preparedness for Canadian cultural heritage and to work on the development of a national model for the International Committee of the Blue Shield Risk Preparedness Scheme.

The summit issued what is called the Quebec Declaration *(see Appendix 1)*, in which the participants agreed to pursue a number of objectives covering a wide range of issues associated with risk preparedness:

· awareness-building

· collaboration

· development of local resources

· development of an action network

Subsequent to the Quebec Summit, a Steering Committee of the Canadian Blue Shield was established. The committee consists of representatives from the archive, library, museum, conservation, historic buildings and sites, and emergency preparedness and the Federation of Canadian Municipalities communities.

Chapter 2

2.0 The Disaster Plan

A disaster plan is a document that outlines an organization's strategies for dealing with emergencies and disasters. The plan is a critical tool, providing both a framework and a series of prepared and practised actions to protect the organization from disasters and minimize their impact.

A comprehensive disaster plan is not just one plan, but a set of separate yet interrelated plans or strategies – administrative, technical and personnel. It results from the entire process of planning that takes into account the organization's particular vulnerabilities, its strengths and its resources at a given point in time. For these reasons, each organization should custom-tailor its plan to fit its own circumstances and needs.

There is a growing trend towards purchasing a ready-made disaster plan or generic disaster planning software, or hiring an outside consultant to produce your disaster plan. Whatever approach is considered, staff must be closely involved because they will be responsible for implementing the plan and for ongoing disaster planning. If a consultant is used, it is critical that this person completely understand your organization's particular mandate, environment, needs and resources.

The plan is not a finite document to be filed away, nor is its preparation a one-time duty. Rather, the plan should be considered a "working" document. Disaster planning is an ongoing responsibility, and the organization should recognize this commitment by making it an integral part of its overall strategic development.

The disaster plan should be a concise yet comprehensive document. Its format and content will vary from organization to organization, but some components are common to all. Its design and layout should facilitate both access and ease of use.

Our approach to disaster planning begins with a discussion of the disaster plan itself. But we emphasize that a plan is the tangible result of having undertaken planning in all its phases. The plan will not take shape until these phases – prevention, protection, preparedness, response, recovery and rehabilitation and post-disaster planning – have all been considered. This process of planning is the key to producing the plan. As Fox (1989, 2) notes, much of the library disaster planning literature produced in the last 20 years is "...content-oriented...Most emphasize the *content* of disaster preparedness, but do not adequately address the *process* by which a coherent whole is formed...the result is a compendium of solid information, but not actually a plan."

This chapter provides guidelines for production of a disaster plan. They are presented in the basic order in which they should be approached. Some of these steps take place concurrently and some overlap, but all should be considered.

2.1 The Purpose of the Disaster Plan

The purpose of a disaster plan is to enable the organization to continue to provide services by avoiding losses to the facility, collections and records, and information systems. DePew (1991, 257) stresses the importance of continued access:

> The plan should also be geared to the needs of the users. All too often policies are developed that address the library's needs and forget the mission of the institution. A disaster plan is written and implemented expressly for one underlying purpose: to provide the users *access* to the information in collections as soon as possible after the catastrophe is over. The objectives of the plan must be developed to meet this goal.

Archives, libraries and record centres are repositories for information, collections and records, and thus bear the larger responsibility of ensuring that the heritage of human knowledge is safeguarded and passed on to future generations. Some materials must be protected, preserved and retained in their original format, while others have value for their informational content only. This distinction has major implications for the direction and requirements of disaster planning.

An effective disaster plan enables people to overcome the confusion and turmoil created by a disaster, and provides preplanned and rehearsed courses of action. It also equips the staff responsible to work cooperatively with emergency officials.

2.1.1 The Realities of Planning

What is the incentive for disaster planning? All too often, it takes an actual disaster to trigger the impetus:

> Disasters have not been known to inquire about one's state of readiness before striking (Murray 1987a, 12).

The need for integrated disaster planning is often a hard sell, and formulating a disaster plan is no easy task – it costs time, resources and money. Management and staff must recognize that the time required may be considerable. In large and complex organizations, such a project may take several years and is prone to both planning inertia and planning tedium. The concept of a formal project management process, coupled with broad staff involvement, can be daunting. It "requires staff who are dedicated to the preservation of materials and are persistent in the face of the amused tolerance that their colleagues will display at the absurd fears they express!" (Wright 1979, 255).

Disaster planning can be a long-term project with few obvious short-term benefits. Reluctance in the organization and sometimes downright opposition are common. There may be the will to provide lists and telephone numbers, but this is not fully realized disaster planning. The planners, while promoting the necessity and benefits of disaster planning, must acknowledge the challenges and costs involved. In the corporate sector, "programs with longer-term pay-offs [such as disaster planning] are generally viewed as more expendable than programs with direct contributions to short-term profits" (Anderson and Mattingly 1991, 323).

So why undertake such a labour-intensive project, which concerns a topic that most of us would rather not think about, that produces a document or a programme that we hope never to have to use? Certainly, disaster planning has in the past been considered a luxury and even an extravagance. However, with today's downsizing, staff cutbacks and reduced funding overall, disaster planning may prove essential for survival. An ill-prepared organization may simply not be able to recover effectively from even a moderate disaster. At minimum, image and reputation, perhaps hard won over a long period of time, may suffer profoundly.

> Lack of preparedness, lack of prevention, will mean a heavier expenditure than necessary of financial and human resources – thus further hurting the operations of the institution (Wright 1989, 283).

2.1.2 Ancillary Benefits of Planning

Disaster planning does mean spending money by making necessary repairs, upgrading the facility or retraining staff. However, it can also save the organization money by preventing costly damages to the facility and by reducing insurance premiums. Improvements can be as basic as relocating or isolating library bookdrops in order to reduce the opportunity for arson, or as complex as installing a state-of-the-art fire detection and suppression system. Capital costs can be phased in, with higher priority given to expenditures that will reduce the most imminent hazards.

As a result of undertaking all the phases necessary to produce a plan, staff in the organization will have gained confidence in their ability to respond appropriately and effectively. Webb (1995, 260) stresses that you must be clear about your objectives, know your procedures and use your initiative – he calls this the best and most empowering planning of all.

In addition to the direct and obvious advantages of avoiding disasters and being well prepared for response and recovery, ancillary benefits can also result from the disaster planning process:

- Efficiencies or innovations may be identified when undertaking risk hazard analyses, or collections and operational assessments that contribute to the overall services of the organization. In some instances, lower costs can result, such as those for energy and system maintenance.
- Disaster planning cuts across the normal hierarchy of the organization, and can help build teams amongst people who may ordinarily not have a reason or opportunity to work together.
- Involvement of a cross-section of staff, along with individuals from other organizations and agencies, creates a network that can serve to benefit other operations.
- Staff morale and commitment can improve as a result of team-building, shared experiences, group training and common work towards a critical organizational goal.
- Awareness and knowledge of safety issues can be raised.

The group responsible for disaster planning in your organization may wish to identify some of these outcomes as specific secondary goals of the planning process.

2.1.3 Why Write the Plan Down?

In an emergency, there is no time to undertake, let alone contemplate, aspects of planning such as researching resources and prioritizing collections for recovery. An emergency demands action. In order to respond to the needs of the disaster – which invariably occurs at 4:00 a.m. on a long weekend with the key players absent – all designated personnel must be able to follow a written plan that allows them to act quickly, decisively and effectively. In the absence of a written disaster plan, tactical rather than preplanned, strategic decisions will likely be made.

A formal written plan that clearly outlines authority, roles and actions – and that has formal approval – also signifies that disaster planning is an integral part of the organization's management process and responsibilities. It serves as a tangible record of the organization's commitment to protecting staff, users, collections and other assets. The act of producing a written document tends to elicit its own process of review, discussion, amendment and approval. It also focuses the organization's commitment, decision-making, assignment of authority, determination of priorities and allocation of resources. The plan can and should serve as a critical training tool.

2.2 The Process for Developing a Disaster Plan

The process of developing a disaster plan should be given the same consideration as any other major project that the organization undertakes. That is, choose the best people for the task, provide them with the necessary support, and integrate the project into the organization's project management structure.

The process of developing a plan includes the activities described below. These activities are intended to be logical and sequential, but not rigid. The process outlined is intended to expedite the process of planning, *the goal being to plan the best plan, not to plan the best process.*

The Disaster Plan: Process at a Glance

· Develop a project proposal.
· Get agreement in principle.
· Define the project and get approval to proceed.
· Form the teams.
· Train the teams.
· Consult and conduct research.
· Do cooperative planning and form networks.
· Draft the plan.
· Review and revise the draft plan.
· Issue the draft plan.
· Train the staff at large.
· Test and practice the draft plan.
· Revise the draft plan again.
· Adopt the plan as policy.
· Maintain the plan.

The process of preparing the plan provides opportunities for all concerned to work together towards a common goal. This will serve the organization well if the plan must be activated.

2.2.1 Develop a project proposal

In many cases, the idea for developing a disaster plan comes from the staff responsible for collections care and management. In other instances, the organization's governing body recognizes the need and initiates the process. In either case,

> Contingency planning needs to be in the hands of someone who thoroughly understands the [organization's] business, has the respect and support of senior management and has a demonstrated track record of managing large, complex projects (Schreider 1994, 25).

The first step is to outline a project proposal for management approval. Experience has shown that proposals that follow a project management structure are more likely to be granted approval and the needed resources. At a minimum, the proposal should include rationale, purpose, goals and objectives, methodology, personnel requirements, and a rough schedule and cost estimates. The proposal should recommend establishing two distinct groups, i.e., a Disaster Planning Committee (DPC) and a Disaster Action Team (DAT). The process can begin with appointment of a DPC coordinator, and perhaps also a DAT coordinator.

2.2.2 Get agreement in principle

Approval of the project proposal by management and, where necessary, a governing body such as a board of directors is critical. Unfortunately in these times, projects frequently compete with one another for scarce resources and funding. And as Rothstein (1996, 6) notes, "the art of eliciting top management support is not taught in 'Disaster Recovery 101'." However, approval of the proposal depends on your ability to do just that. You must be an advocate for disaster planning in its entirety. Your case for priority status and required resources must be carefully, thoroughly and realistically prepared, documented and presented.

While the need for disaster planning may be easily demonstrated in emotional terms, the project must also be justified in practical terms. You must be prepared to explain the consequences of doing nothing or delaying. Management needs to know what the organization will and will not get for spending the requested time and money, how long it will take, what effort is required and how effective the project will be. In the business community, experience has shown that a proposal emphasizing enhanced recovery as well as continued service quality and service delivery is most successful. (Rothstein 1996)

In addition, it must be understood that the disaster planning process will likely identify the need for improvements and changes to the facility, its systems and staff practices.

Your proposal must make clear the commitment you seek for the time and resources to research, coordinate, prepare and implement the plan. Management's commitment must be genuine and explicit and, once made, communicated across the organization.

2.2.3 Define the project and get approval to proceed

Once agreement in principle has been obtained, the project should be defined with detailed work plans, staffing plans, scheduling requirements and resources. At this point, many organizations form a Disaster Planning Committee (DPC). In other cases, one individual may define the project in consultation with other key players. Approval of the project by management and the governing body will be needed, and again your case must be carefully prepared, documented and presented. Benefits and costs, as well as the limitations of the proposal, must be made fully clear.

Overall management of the disaster planning project should not vary significantly from that of other suc-cessful cross-departmental projects. In short, the project should suit the organization's structure, culture and capabilities. The planning and the plan itself should be based on an organization's existing structure, and should depend wherever possible on its current and familiar chain of command and operations. While the plan will define necessary and temporary changes of priorities and practices, the most effective plan will be rooted in the established infrastructure.

> The solution is not, as some suggest, to create a separate (and inevitably inexperienced) emergency organization, but for the existing... organization to move smoothly into a previously planned "emergency mode" (CCI 1984, 2).

Management planning literature describes many project models that can be used to help define and organize the project's goals and objectives. The aim is to become adequately prepared in a reasonable amount of time. A schedule (milestones and sequence) must be detailed, as well as the assignment of responsibilities, reporting schedule, decision-making process and communications. Good communication will be essential throughout the project, both to elicit full participation and to avoid conflict.

> Finally, set a deadline for the group to report. Sooner or later, contingency planning can become a "black hole" that can trap your potential plan in the group development process forever. (Miller 1988, 357)

In other words, the planning process must be well-managed and not unduly hamper other essential services and operations over extended periods.

2.2.4 Form the teams

It is generally recommended that two groups or teams be formed: one responsible for the planning process and developing the disaster plan, and the second for implementing and activating the plan. In this publication, the teams are called the Disaster Planning Committee (DPC) and the Disaster Action Team (DAT). Each team has its own particular role to play, but the final outcome depends upon their combined efforts.

Disaster planning and disaster response are two distinct functions that call into play different skills, experience, and probably, temperament of the people involved. Some skills are common to both teams, such as being resourceful, organized and able to anticipate problems and solutions, while other skills are more team-specific. Planning team members need to excel at defining problems and formulating a set of separate but interrelated strategies. Action team members need to be able to think clearly amidst tumult and translate planning into quick, decisive action.

Coordination of the two teams can be done by one individual (i.e., the coordinator of both the DPC and the DAT) who possesses an unusual combination of skills, knowledge and experience. The two groups may be appointed by management, or the DPC may be appointed first and take on the task of determining DAT membership.

2.2.5 Train the teams

> Having a plan does not in itself enable a community to respond effectively to a disaster. Experience shows that if responders do not fully understand procedures or responsibilities, serious problems will arise during efforts to respond to an incident. (Daines 1991, 184)

Disaster planning workshops and seminars should be held at the outset for the DPC and the DAT. The scope and nature of the instruction will depend on the needs of the organization and the existing level of staff awareness and knowledge. Training provides a good opportunity to develop commitment, build teams and start gathering information. Training for staff at large should be undertaken after the plan is completed *(see 2.2.12)*.

Training should begin by educating the teams regarding the purpose and importance of disaster planning. This should be followed by training as to the purpose, application and activation of a plan. Training on the details of your plan should be undertaken once the plan has been drafted and reviewed at least once. At this time, staff should go through the sequences of actions outlined in the plan to practice their duties. Key steps such as evacuation, notification of authorities and putting the plan into action should be stressed and practiced.

Hands-on, mock-disaster workshops should also be held, and may be considered part of testing the plan. While it is critical that the teams come out of the training with an understanding of their team responsibilities and actions, all members must also become familiar and comfortable with their individual roles. If done at the testing stage, recommendations for critical plan revisions may result from staff input.

Courses in first aid and cardiopulmonary resuscitation (CPR) also help prepare the staff for emergency

duties and increase the number of people who could help in an emergency. Support from outside agencies such as the Red Cross, St. John Ambulance and emergency management representatives can be useful in developing in-house training programmes. As well, crisis management professionals can offer pre-disaster workshops to prepare staff for any post-traumatic reactions *(see Chapter 10)*.

2.2.6 Consult and conduct research

Consultation and research are needed in order to confirm or acquire information necessary to the disaster planning process, such as facility design, the number and location of sprinklers, and current staff practices. In addition, you will need to seek cooperation from personnel to identify strengths and weaknesses within the organization. As well, consultation with external experts and service providers will be necessary. This requires investigation of many distinct but related areas of expertise, from fire safety to data recovery.

Lack of staff participation has been identified as a stumbling block in producing a disaster plan. "Because other staff members are not given an opportunity to develop a sense of 'ownership' toward the disaster preparedness effort, they develop no sense of responsibility for its success" (Fox 1989, 3).

The DPC should consider the following when consulting and conducting research:

Internal

· Define the functions essential to your organization's viability and determine the relevant operations. Identify who is responsible for what. This is especially important in a multi-use facility.

· Determine if any disaster plans (full or partial) exist. All previous plans should be reviewed to see if any portions can be used.

· Identify any existing departmental reports, data etc. that may be useful. Does the purchasing department maintain an up-to-date list of suppliers? Has the security department recently undertaken a risk hazard analysis?

· Investigate how your organization handled past emergencies or disasters. Are they likely to happen again, or have remedial measures been taken?

· Identify internal staff expertise related to collections development and management functions, systems operations and overall administration, as well as disaster-related activities that may be useful.

External

- Consult with the appropriate authorities, such as the fire department, federal and provincial emergency agencies and your insurance company. Prior consultation is especially important with the fire department, as their mandate is to first preserve lives, second put out the fire and only then, protect property.

- Invite local public authorities – police, fire department and emergency preparedness agencies – to a planning meeting. Face-to-face contact, as well as their assessment of the risks facing your organization and their practical advice, may be invaluable.

- Contact Emergency Preparedness Canada (EPC) concerning the federal government's role in disaster planning, training and aid *(see Appendices 2 and 3)*.

- Investigate local and provincial legislation regarding such concerns as insurance, fire regulations, and building design. Be aware that in the event of a major catastrophe, authorities can designate your organization as an evacuation shelter.

- Consider ideas from other organizations' disaster plans *(see References)*. While wholesale adoption of another organization's disaster plan is not recommended, there are always content, structural and design features that could be adapted.

- Seek information and advice on technical parts of the plan such as recovery techniques for paper-based records and electronic databases.

- Find out about the availability and costs of emergency supplies and services. Request references and tours of facilities, such as full service records management companies.

- Use Internet sources such as the Emergency Preparedness Information eXchange (EPIX), a Canadian forum on all aspects of disaster planning. Many organizations, governmental and non-governmental, publish extensive information on their operations and services on the Internet, and have hyperlinks to other related sites *(see Appendix 3)*.

- Seek advice from those responsible for disaster planning in other organizations, especially those who have recently gone through the disaster planning process.

- Explore the professional literature for disaster case studies *(see References)*.

2.2.7 Do cooperative planning and form networks

In addition to obtaining information and advice from other organizations, the DPC should also consider mutual aid, cooperative planning and forming networks. Cooperative planning can occur between departments in different locations, amongst related or neighbouring organizations, or amongst owners/tenants of a common facility. Could they assist you in time of need? Could you use their facilities, supplies or equipment? Could they use yours?

Ad hoc disaster planning networks could undertake joint research, acquisition of supplies, provision of aid, procurement of speakers, training workshops, etc. In Toronto, for example, several major libraries and archives cooperate in ongoing development and maintenance of external supply and service resource lists.

Networks are more formal arrangements, generally among similar organizations, such as archives, libraries and record centres. In order to ensure that reciprocal arrangements are clearly understood and will function when needed, some networks have formalized their agreements. One such network is California's Inland Empire Libraries Disaster Response Network (IELDRN). The *IELDRN Mutual Aid Agreement* (1990) covers a wide range of disaster recovery issues, such as shared purchase of supplies and assistance by disaster recovery teams (including arrangements regarding authority, wages and compensation).

Development of a network for outside supply and service assistance is crucial to implementing the disaster plan. Contacts must be established with essential services, suppliers of materials, equipment, services and facilities, as well as other recovery and treatment specialists. Working arrangements should be reviewed at least twice a year, preferably quarterly, to make sure each company is still in business and can provide the required services. Alternatives should be investigated in case a disaster is widespread and services are out of commission or resources have been commandeered elsewhere. Seasonal availability of supplies and equipment must also be confirmed. For example, bakers trays are generally not available from commercial sources during the summer barbeque season.

Disaster plans should be explained in detail, where necessary, to individuals and organizations that are contacted for inclusion in the plan. Their possible role in the event of a disaster at your organization should be outlined and permission received to include their name and other pertinent information. Such information would include the name of the company or organization, the contact person and a back-up should your contact be unavailable, address of the organization, telephone numbers for normal office hours and after hours, and other details such as availability of services and costs. This information should be updated regularly.

2.2.8   Draft the plan

While the disaster plan is being drafted, questions may be raised (probably not for the first time) as to whether the full project can be completed in the time allocated or whether an interim plan should be considered. The latter's role is to swiftly establish a contingency program that will apply until the final plan is completed and implemented. This interim plan usually concentrates on immediate responses to disasters judged most likely to occur. If you decide to develop an interim plan, the full plan should be completed as quickly as possible to avoid giving the organization a false sense of security. In some cases, it may be necessary to phase in the full plan as resources permit.

In all cases, it is advisable to take immediate measures to make your organization a safer place.

2.2.9   Review and revise the draft plan

This may be the planning committee's first opportunity to view the plan in its entirety. This draft should incorporate all contributions submitted by any working subcommittees. At the draft stage, input should be sought, in particular, from the staff who will be responsible for activating and implementing the plan, as well as from relevant members of the administration. Evaluation should concentrate on the plan's workability, the role of staff, and any training needs.

External review should also be sought, perhaps from some of the people whom the planners consulted earlier. This is also a good opportunity to review the planning process in order to confirm objectives, resources, schedule, roles and responsibilities, as well as the committee's goals, methodology, and the results to date.

Based on the outcome of the review, evaluation and consultation, the Disaster Planning Committee should make any changes necessary to improve the draft plan. A more accessible, workable or comprehensive plan should be the result *(see also 2.5)*.

2.2.10   Issue the draft plan

Once finalized and approved in draft form, the plan must be issued to all key personnel in the organization, as well as to appropriate external parties. Because some of the information contained in the plan is confidential, distribution should be restricted *(see 2.6.4)*.

2.2.11   Train the staff at large

In addition to training the DPC and the DAT, training the staff at large is also essential, as there is no way of predicting who will be onsite or available when a disaster hits. The likelihood of effective response and recovery will increase with a larger base of trained staff. Staff at large who have been apprised concerning the reasons for the plan and how it will work, should feel a greater sense of security and commitment to its development and execution.

Staff should be knowledgeable about procedures for evacuation and notification of authorities, as well as their own role in a disaster. The staff would also benefit from training in mock-disaster workshops and first aid courses *(see also 2.2.5 and 4.12)*.

See Lopes 1997, Powell 1997 and Powell and Appy 1997 for further information on training and education.

2.2.12   Test and practice the draft plan

> The middle of a disaster is no time to find that you've forgotten something (Daley 1991, 5).

It is essential to organize and run a test of the disaster plan before it is needed. Testing lifts the plan from theory into reality, albeit a controlled reality. It allows those who will have specific assigned duties an opportunity to exercise and experience their roles and responsibilities beforehand. The DPC should consider conducting a test without the aid of the key person or persons, as they may be unavailable in a real emergency or disaster.

The objective of testing is not to produce a flawless test score, but to discover problems and unforeseen gaps well in advance of a disaster, so that they may be corrected. Routine practice of the plan keeps it fresh in the minds of the teams and staff, and functions as a tool for further training and evaluation.

The U.S. Federal Emergency Management Agency (FEMA) suggests three progressive exercises (based on Scanlon 1991, 98 and Daines 1991, 187):

1. A low-stress tabletop exercise, which involves devising a scenario and working through the response on paper.
2. A functional exercise involving a small-scale simulation, e.g., pretending there is a localized fire.
3. A full-scale exercise in a high-stress environment in which the actions called for in the plan must actually be taken, e.g., a fire drill requiring evacuation.

2.2.13 Revise the draft plan again

After testing, the Disaster Planning Committee should meet with the Disaster Action Team and other key members of staff for a post-mortem. These sessions should provide ample opportunity for examining the plan's effectiveness, as well as re-assessing the roles and responsibilities assigned. Based on this evaluation, the DPC should then revise the draft plan.

2.2.14 Adopt the plan as policy

To complete the process of integrating the disaster plan into the organization's operations, the plan should be submitted and presented for approval to the director or chief executive officer, and then to the governing body for adoption as policy. Further revisions may result from this submission.

The approved plan should then be re-issued to personnel within the organization, and appropriate external parties.

2.2.15 Maintain the plan

> Maintenance should be considered when the plan is being developed, not when the plan has been completed (Schreider 1994, 25).

We began this chapter by calling a disaster plan a "working" document. This means it must remain open to revisions and updates in order to be fully functional when needed. If the plan simply gathers dust at the back of a filing cabinet, all the efforts that went into its preparation will have been to no avail. This risk should be considered the most serious pitfall of all. Indeed, there is a danger that having a plan may lead to a sense of preparedness that may prove illusory when disaster strikes.

> An out-of-date plan may be worse than no plan at all if time is wasted in trying to put it to work (Kreps 1991, 34).

The plan should not be a fixed entity cast in stone. It must change with changing times and circumstances. The plan must be periodically updated to reflect changes in administration, the collections, the building and its equipment, personnel, suppliers, technology and legislation. New collections will be acquired, old policies will be revised and recovery priorities may change. The building may undergo alterations and new equipment may be acquired. Organizations may cut staff and personnel may retire or their responsibilities change. Suppliers may go out of business or relocate. Technological progress may render certain conservation and recovery techniques obsolete. New laws and regulations that affect the plan may be passed. To take these changes into account and keep the document valid, someone within the organization must be responsible for making key changes as needed, as well as systematic revision of the plan. This person must also ensure distribution of revised plans and destruction of outdated copies.

2.3 The Disaster Planning Committee (DPC)

2.3.1 The Purpose of the DPC

The purpose of this committee is to develop the disaster plan. It will also be charged with identifying the needed preventive, protective and preparedness measures. The DPC is not responsible for executing the plan.

The DPC should be a standing committee. It will be involved in a wide variety of disaster planning activities, including assessing risks, recommending improvements to the facility, systems and staff practices, prioritizing the collections and records, consulting external resources, and investigating the suitability and availability of recovery options and costs. The committee may be divided into subcommittees or working groups as necessary.

DPC members must transcend the comfortable world of the office and situate themselves in the frenzied chaos that prevails when disaster strikes. This group must predict the unthinkable, anticipate the unforeseen, and expect the unexpected.

2.3.2 Coordinator, Disaster Planning Committee

One person from the organization should be appointed to head the Disaster Planning Committee and oversee formulation of the plan. The DPC Coordinator's role is to direct the process of planning and make it happen, not to write the entire plan.

This person must fully understand their organization's objectives for disaster planning, i.e., that it establishes the function of disaster planning within their organization for now and in the future. This individual should be fully familiar with the organization's operations, collections and services, its management style and staff responsibilities. This knowledge will help ensure that the plan is workable within the organization's existing structure and climate.

Schreider (1994, 24) describes disaster planning as "mission-critical," and further warns of the pitfall of choosing an unqualified disaster planner:

> Management often assigns responsibility for contingency planning to whomever is viewed as having extra time for the endeavour. All too often, it may be used as a final test or special project for someone who is winding down a career or on the way out the door.

The person who occupies this key position must have the planning skills and the authority to guide the process through to completion. The coordinator must have the experience to manage a multitask project, as well as formidable leadership and coordination skills. This individual must be able to direct the determination and evaluation of the organization's state of preparedness and its ability to prepare for and respond to disaster.

The DPC Coordinator does not have to be a conservator, but should have a basic knowledge and understanding of preservation and access issues relevant to the library, archives or record centre and its collections and records. This person may, depending on the organization, be an archivist, librarian, records manager, administrator, etc.

2.3.3   DPC Composition and Responsibilities

There are advantages to soliciting interested members of staff to participate on this committee, but specific staff appointments may be necessary to ensure a representative and qualified group.

> The size will vary depending upon the size of the organization, but it should be large enough to represent all major functional components and small enough to achieve coherence and consensus (Fortson 1992, 84).

People should be chosen as befits their ability to effectively plan and organize, their willingness and ability to commit to the project and their skill in working with staff and external contacts at all levels. Knowledge and experience of disaster planning, expertise and perhaps temperament will be factors in their selection. The planning committee could also include outside experts – such as staff from other archives, libraries and record centres, or representatives of local disaster support agencies – either as full members or as resource contacts. Above all, the planners must know and understand all aspects of the organization, warts and all. For as Wright (1989, 289) warns, "to avoid isolating the planners from the rest of the archives, I would argue against hiring someone to come into your institute to develop [the]...plan...particularly because it involves evaluating the comparative worth of collections and setting priorities."

As noted, the number of team members will vary according to the size of the organization. What is important is that key functions are covered. Heads of the following departments should be considered for membership on the DPC:

· Administration – for knowledge of personnel, financial and insurance requirements.

· Facilities/building operations – for knowledge of building structure, utilities, fire and security systems, etc.

· Preservation and conservation – for knowledge of preservation and conservation issues. If in-house expertise is lacking, external expert advice should be sought.

· Bibliographic services and registration – for knowledge of the holdings and the associated online records.

· Collections – for knowledge of collections' value, importance and use.

· Systems and computer operations – for knowledge of hardware, software, networks, telecommunications, etc.

· Communications – for knowledge of staff, public relations and fundraising.

Job descriptions for DPC members are not outlined in this publication. The structure, size and existing lines of authority in an organization would usually drive the duties of this committee.

2.3.4   Training for the DPC

Members of this committee would benefit from training courses in disaster planning, such as those offered by Emergency Preparedness Canada, and its local affiliates. Some of this training could be undertaken in concert with DAT training. *(See also 2.2.5 and 2.2.12)*

2.4 The Disaster Action Team (DAT)

2.4.1 The Purpose of the DAT

The purpose of this team is to respond to a disaster and activate the disaster plan. It is charged with implementing the recovery and rehabilitation strategies. The DAT is not responsible for developing the plan, although some DAT members may participate extensively in this process. The DAT should be a standing team, and like the DPC, may be divided into work groups as necessary.

This team must function smoothly as a unit during stressful times, such as evacuation of the facility and response to the disaster. These responsibilities continue through recovery and rehabilitation, which in some cases may be prolonged. Depending on the disaster, the DAT may need to substantially amend existing strategies, and develop alternative approaches. This group may be called upon to face the unthinkable, respond to the unforeseen and recover from the unexpected.

2.4.2 Coordinator, Disaster Action Team

Responsibility for overall disaster coordination, allocation of resources and decision-making rests with the DAT Coordinator. In an emergency, from response through to rehabilitation and post-disaster planning, this person's authority takes precedence over all routine lines of command.

The DAT Coordinator's role is to direct the processes of response, recovery and rehabilitation, and make them happen, not to actually undertake them.

The DAT Coordinator should possess strong leadership, facilitation, organizational and administrative skills. More important, these skills must have been successfully demonstrated in a team environment. He or she must be intimately familiar with the entire disaster plan, and may in fact have been intimately involved in its development.

The DAT Coordinator is responsible for creating and maintaining an effective team. The coordinator needs to create credibility by providing what the team needs and by keeping things moving. In addition, the coordinator should create a climate where conflict is openly addressed. Unsolved problems will lead to apathy, frustration and anger in an already stressful situation.

It may seem logical to select as DAT Coordinator the staff member responsible for preservation of the collections. Such a decision would, however, depend on the structure of the organization, as well the individual's management and technical abilities and experience. The ideal candidate would be skilled in both. In some organizations, DAT coordination is a shared responsibility between several individuals.

Suitable alternates must also be appointed to increase the likelihood that a designate will be available when disaster hits.

2.4.3 DAT Composition and Responsibilities

The composition of the Disaster Action Team will likely overlap with that of the Disaster Planning Committee. The size of the DAT depends upon the organization. The oft-suggested number is four or five, but more important is that all the principal functions should be covered. In a smaller organization, these functions may be handled by a few individuals. Many individuals holding the positions previously listed for potential DPC membership *(see 2.3.3)* would also be appropriate for the DAT. Key individuals who have been fully involved at the planning stage would be especially effective members.

In addition to having particular expertise and experience, DAT members need to be able to think clearly and decisively and act quickly, while achieving a delicate balance of both taking direction and making necessary decisions in the midst of upheaval. They must be capable of multitasking, and of working in a team environment under a strong leader. Perseverance, practicality and initiative are important attributes.

> Emergency managers must...not only be committed to, but also live up to, the responsibility placed on them... The real proof ultimately is in the doing. Good intentions are not enough. (Roberts and O'Donaghue in Anderson and Mattingly 1991, 334)

Disaster response and recovery operations can involve long and irregular hours. This may be impossible for some people with family or other obligations, and should be considered when choosing team members. Staff's obligations to the organization in the event of a disaster need to be clarified well in advance. The counsel of human resources personnel and health and safety coordinators, and legal advice pertaining to labour laws should be sought as necessary.

The best approach to forming the DAT is to establish job descriptions based on functional requirements. This allows you to choose the best people for the jobs and to move beyond the existing organizational hierarchy. In small organizations with few staff, personnel from other organizations could be invited to be members. Organizations without a conservator should include an outside conservator on the action team.

The following job descriptions outline principal functions of the DAT.

DAT Coordinator

- Responsible overall for activating and executing the disaster plan.
- Oversees and coordinates those responsible for the response, recovery and rehabilitation strategies and operations in conjunction with any ongoing service delivery.
- Responsible overall for the decisions made regarding disaster and damage assessment and setting priorities.
- Responsible overall for allocation of personnel and other resources.
- Responsible overall for staff training.
- Responsible overall for liaison with all internal and external authorities and services.
- Responsible overall for return to normal operations.
- Reports to the Director, Chief Executive Officer or governing body as appropriate.

Administration Coordinator

- Responsible for tracking personnel.
- Authorizes all expenditures including staffing, supplies, equipment and services.
- Responsible for ordering, receipt and distribution of supplies, equipment and services.
- Responsible for insurance and liability.
- Reports to the DAT Coordinator.

Collections Recovery Coordinator

- Responsible for estimating damage to collections and records, and determining recovery and rehabilitation strategies.
- Responsible for collections-related staff training.
- Establishes action priorities for collections recovery and rehabilitation.
- Determines treatment areas onsite or offsite.
- Determines requirements for collections-related supplies, equipment and services.
- Responsible for contacts for external collections-related supplies, equipment and services.

- Advises the Building Recovery Coordinator and the Computer Systems Coordinator of the sequence and methods of collections recovery, and coordinates activities.
- Responsible for operations of collections-related external services.
- Reports to the DAT Coordinator.

Building Recovery Coordinator

- Responsible for estimating damage to facility, utilities and systems, and determining recovery and rehabilitation strategies.
- Responsible for security of the building and collections.
- Responsible for building-related staff training.
- Establishes action priorities for facility recovery and rehabilitation.
- Determines requirements for building-related supplies, equipment and services.
- Responsible for contacts for external building-related supplies, equipment and services.
- Advises the Collections Recovery Coordinator and the Computer Systems Coordinator of the sequence and methods of building recovery, and coordinates activities.
- Responsible for operations of building-related external services.
- Reports to the DAT Coordinator.

Computer Systems Coordinator

- Responsible for estimating damage to hardware, software, telecommunications, etc., and determining recovery and rehabilitation strategies.
- Responsible for systems-related staff training.
- Establishes action priorities for systems recovery.
- Determines requirements for systems-related supplies, equipment and services.
- Responsible for contacts for external systems-related supplies and services.
- Advises the Building Recovery Coordinator and the Collections Recovery Coordinator of the sequence and methods of systems recovery, and coordinates activities.
- Responsible for operations of systems-related external services.
- Reports to the DAT Coordinator.

Communications Manager

· Responsible for internal communication in all forms to DAT members and the staff at large.

· Responsible for communications-related staff training.

· Responsible for external communication in all forms to users, external emergency providers, the general public, media, etc.

· Determines requirements for communications-related supplies, equipment and services.

· Responsible for set-up and operations of communications centre.

· Reports to the DAT Coordinator.

Documentation Manager

· Responsible for documentation strategies throughout response, recovery and rehabilitation, including damage, relocation of collections and records, treatment operations, etc.

· Responsible for documentation-related staff training.

· Determines requirements for documentation-related supplies, equipment and services.

· Maintains records on all damaged materials for evaluation and insurance purposes.

· Responsible for operations of documentation-related external services.

· Reports to the DAT Coordinator.

2.4.4   Training for the DAT

Training must be mandatory for Disaster Action Team members. It will include intensive instruction in the use of the disaster plan, as well as in response and recovery hazards (including applicable legislation) and procedures. Training in handling wet and damaged collection materials is also recommended. Some organizations organize mock disasters, where staff and sometimes outside personnel participate in response and recovery exercises. These hands-on experiences are extremely valuable in determining DAT readiness.

In addition to providing theoretical grounding in the different phases of the disaster plan, training enables the DAT to work as a team and develop the practical skills necessary to carry out their roles and responsibilities effectively. Depending on the organization, training to be a team may be needed. DAT members need to have a sense of common destiny, a cohesive understanding of objectives and a shared commitment to those objectives, which can lead to common action. Team-building exercises should help to develop these characteristics. The opportunity to work together in a non-threatening test scenario should

also encourage active participation, mutual respect and the willingness to consider alternative approaches during an actual disaster.

One approach to practical skills training starts with visualizing the tasks associated with a disaster response and recovery operation. The skills required should then be identified and appropriate staff selected. Skills in some areas may be lacking. Modes of training delivery should be investigated to meet these deficiencies as well as overall identified requirements.

Some courses are already available, such as in first aid and CPR, but others will have to be developed and provided by the organization. It is the responsibility of the DAT Coordinator to ensure that all needed training occurs. Training opportunities exist in the professional heritage community and the professional emergency provider sector (see Appendices 2 and 3).

Practical training should include hands-on demonstrations of procedures and equipment, their use and limitations; courses in workplace health and safety that relate to emergency response; the use of protective clothing and equipment; safety issues associated with health, such as exposure to mould and preventive care; as well as training in crisis counselling (see Chapter 10). The DAT should also have up to date vaccinations.

Note: The Workplace Hazardous Materials Information System (WHMIS), legislated by both federal and provincial jurisdictions, provides employers and employees across Canada with information on hazardous materials used in the workplace. The training of emergency personnel for incidents involving hazardous materials is covered by NFPA 472-1997. Standard for Professional Competence of Responders to Hazardous Materials Incidents, accepted by the industry and fire departments across the United States and Canada. In the U.S., OSHA (Occupational Health and Safety Administration) requires workers to be trained before being assigned work with either hazardous materials or locations, as well as documentation of this training (see Rossol 1998, 4).

2.5   The Characteristics of the Disaster Plan

The disaster plan should be a concise, comprehensive document, both easy to read and easy to follow. As DePew (1991, 258) notes, it will be used "during a time of chaos, in poor light, by people who may not be very familiar with it".

In a disaster, human emotions and the confusion created can be overwhelming. Thus the plan must be designed to function effectively in such circumstances. Many disaster plans look good on paper, but prove unworkable. In addition to the administrative and technical aspects of response, recovery and rehabilitation, the plan must consider the human elements of imagination, leadership and cooperation.

Hunter (1983, 257) summarizes the chief characteristics of a disaster plan as follows:

> The written plan should be characterized by flexibility, simplicity, detail, and adaptability. The plan should be *flexible* to allow for changes in your staff, in the availability of outside help and recovery supplies, and in the threats to which the museum may be vulnerable. The plan should be *simple* enough to be easily understood and quickly executed. Yet it must be *detailed* enough to minimize the number of decisions that must be made during an emergency. The plan should be *adaptable* to any situation that it may not be specifically designed to cover. [italics added for emphasis]

2.5.1 Customizing the Plan

As well as being tailored to fit the particular circumstances of your organization, the disaster plan should also conform to the culture of the organization. For example, introduction of an informal document in a highly structured environment will likely prove to be unworkable. The key to success is familiarity with the organization and the working environment.

Fill-in-the-blanks plans and commercial software are available for creating a plan. However you choose to proceed, the important thing to remember is that your plan must be custom-designed. Similarly, the guidelines provided in this publication must be adapted to take into account the needs and circumstances of your organization: its structure, personnel, collections, hazards, resources, etc.

2.5.2 Designing the Plan

The plan should convey the most critical information at the front, such as emergency instructions and DAT contacts. Lists and supplemental information can be included in the appendices. All text should be presented clearly, perhaps in point form using large typefaces. Many organizations use a binder format for ease of use and replacement of individual pages or sections that are outdated.

Each page should be numbered and dated, e.g., "08/18/96; 3 of 26 pages." Some organizations dif-

ferentiate various emergencies or actions by using a tabbed format or distinctive design such as paper size and weight. The use of colour to readily distinguish the disaster plan from other organizational manuals is recommended.

2.6 The Components of the Disaster Plan

This section of the book outlines the basic components of a final (but not finite!) disaster plan. Based on a review of the literature, no ideal plan exists, although a number of components are common to all. Each organization must decide for itself the detail necessary according to the its needs and resources. No plan can cover every possible situation, mode of operation, time of year, etc. "A plan must be based on a set of assumptions and where there is no experience how is it possible to predict the unthinkable?" (Waters 1996, 246).

The plan should focus on disaster effects, not their causes, and specify basic response, recovery and rehabilitation measures to be taken. If additional support information is needed, it should be provided in the appendices.

2.6.1 Introduction and Statement of Purpose

The introduction should briefly outline why the plan was created, its purpose and for whom it is intended. It should document who put it together, when it was written and when it will be updated. A table of contents helps orient the reader.

2.6.2 Scope of the Plan

The scope statement should outline which emergencies and disasters the plan covers. It could start with the events most likely to occur or those most likely to have serious effects as determined by the risk hazard analysis *(see 3.3)*. Remembering that the plan is to be used at the time of an emergency, decisions must be made on what situations – fire, flood, bombing, earthquake, etc. – will and will not be covered. Users of the plan must also know if it applies to all or any of the following issues: human health and safety; collections and records recovery; building recovery; and building assets such as furniture, office equipment and computers. For example, "the plan is limited to disaster prevention and preparedness for library collections, and deals essentially with damage caused by fire and water" (Library of Parliament 1994, 1).

It should also specify that the plan is in effect and covers the organization 24 hours a day. This coverage applies irrespective of the "mode of operation" of the building (Paulhus 1983, 122):

Mode 1:   Supervised by security and occupied by staff.

Mode 2:   Supervised by security and occupied by staff and public.

Mode 3:   Supervised by security and occupied by public.

Mode 4:   Supervised by security alone.

This part of the plan should then outline how it relates to any pre-existing or associated plans. These can include internal fire protection and evacuation plans, emergency procedures for patrons, or external plans such as those developed by local emergency preparedness organizations. State whether your organization is part of a complex and whether the other tenants have their own disaster plans, as well as any agreements on coordinated responses. It must also be clear whose plan takes priority in an emergency, and how the plans should work together.

2.6.3   Authority

Several types of authority for the plan should be included:

- **Authority for producing and implementing the plan.**

  Outlines the authority for developing the plan and implementing preparedness, prevention and protection measures.

- **Authority for activating the plan**

  Outlines the authority necessary for response and recovery, so it is clear who is in charge during and after an emergency (including alternates if key members are absent). A transfer of the regular authority of the organization from the Director or CEO to the DAT Coordinator must be indicated first and foremost. Lines of authority must be laid out, detailing who reports to whom.

  Hunter (1983, 258) makes a useful distinction between implementation and execution of the plan: A plan is *implemented* when the DPC fulfils measures called for by the plan in advance of disaster, such as acquiring supplies and equipment, training staff, and assigning priorities for recovery. A plan is *executed* when an emergency occurs and the DAT responds with the response, recovery and rehabilitation actions laid out in the plan. Note: the term *activation* of a plan is used instead of *execution* in this publication.

- **Authority for external coordination**

  Outlines who is in charge during a disaster in relation to outside agencies. For example, in case of a fire, the fire chief is in charge. Outlines how internal and external operations are to work together.

2.6.4   Distribution, Review and Update

Distribution of the plan must be documented. Members of the Disaster Action Team, in particular, must always have up-to-date copies. Copies should be kept onsite, as well as offsite in the homes of key personnel. It is also wise to leave extra lists of essential telephone numbers with the security and facility maintenance departments.

This part of the plan should outline the responsibility for and frequency of review and update. The mechanism for distributing revised plans and collecting and destroying outdated plans should also be described.

Most plans contain confidential information such as unlisted phone numbers (only with the employees' knowledge and assent) and the locations of the most valuable collections and records. These copies should have controlled distribution. Abridged copies of plans, without the confidential information, can be distributed to other personnel. Additional copies of the plan should be kept in key-accessible locations. Fire-resistant and waterproof containers should be used to protect these plans.

The best disaster plan in the world is useless if the building has been evacuated and your plan remains inside. Key personnel should be assigned to take copies of the plan outside upon evacuation. Some organizations include the plan in emergency packs containing immediate supplies such as cameras and rubber boots *(see 5.11)*. If the disaster plan has not been recently updated, the organization's telephone listing (internal and external) and local telephone directory should also be taken outside upon evacuation.

Appropriate parts of the plan should also be given to the authorities who assisted with its formulation and will be involved in response and recovery operations: fire department, insurance company, police, etc.

2.6.5   Emergency Instructions

The disaster plan of any organization must outline how staff should immediately respond when faced with an emergency. Of critical concern are procedures for safely evacuating all staff, users and visitors from the building, sounding the alarm and notifying the authorities, and special provisions for evacuating disabled and/or elderly persons *(see 6.4)*.

These instructions must be clear and concise, and should be conspicuously located at the front of the plan. Instructions for various emergencies should be developed, as appropriate, and this information linked to the disaster response operations *(see 2.6.9)*.

2.6.6 Contacting the DAT

This part of the plan must outline how to contact the Disaster Action Team and how to activate the disaster plan. This information should also be conspicuously located at the front of the plan.

It must be clear who is to respond during various modes of operation *(see 2.6.2)*. These instructions may be in the form of a telephone tree, and should include work and home telephone numbers. In order to ensure that someone with authority is onsite, it is essential that each key position have a designated alternate. Basic description of the DAT roles and responsibilities may be provided in the appendices.

The use of a telephone tree enables DAT members to be contacted in a pre-determined sequence. The first names to call on the list are usually the DAT Coordinator and designated alternate(s). These instructions should also figure prominently in the plan.

2.6.7 Preparations for Disaster

This part of the plan should outline the organization's prevention, preparedness and protection measures and systems that have been implemented as a result of the hazards survey and risk hazards analysis. Outstanding tasks related to these issues can also be included and as such may be viewed as planning priorities. Some sources consider the inclusion of this part of the plan optional. Additional information, such as contact lists for supplies, equipment, facilities and services, can be included in the appendices. *(See Chapter 5)*

2.6.8 Forewarning of Disaster

This part of the plan should include information, perhaps in the form of checklists, to be used when there is forewarning of disaster. It should concentrate on human safety and other measures that can minimize the impact of a disaster before it occurs, such as moving collections from a basement in advance of a flood. *(See 6.3)*

2.6.9 Disaster Response Operations

This part of the plan should outline the immediate actions to be taken in a variety of situations, such as flooding, fire, earthquake, and power failure. It focuses on the effects, not the causes, of the disaster, and should cover the basics for disaster containment measures; protective measures for the collections, records and systems; assessment of damage to the collections, records, facility and systems; assessment of recovery options including costs; and development of the recovery strategy and the required support operations, including personnel, security, documentation and communications. *(See 6.4)*

2.6.10 Disaster Recovery Operations

This part of the plan is generally the largest and most carefully prepared section. Instructions and procedures for the recovery of collections, records, data, the facility, etc. should be clear and straightforward so that personnel can understand and carry them out under pressure with perhaps only minimal training. They should include enough detail to be useful, but not be so complicated that the instruction is confusing or frustrating. Some organizations are now supplementing text information with charts that permit rapid access to and comprehension of basic guidelines.

Most plans have separate parts dealing with the major collections categories (bound volumes, fine art, microfilm, etc.). It is also a good idea to provide guidelines for a number of options that may be necessary.

After a disaster, a recovery strategy specific to the situation will need to be developed. The framework and much of the information you need should be found in your existing disaster plan. However, it is usually necessary to modify and/or expand the existing instructions. *(See 6.5, 6.6 and Chapter 7)*

2.6.11 Disaster Rehabilitation Operations

This part of the plan should outline instructions and procedures for the rehabilitation of collections, records, data, the facility, etc. Specific strategies will need to be developed post-disaster based on the situation, the resources available and the organization's priorities. Some of these strategies may be implemented over the long term. *(See Chapters 8, 9 and 10)*

2.6.12 Appendices

The appendices should cover essential support information that would be too cumbersome to include in the main body of the disaster plan. Appendices also include lists and other data that need periodic updating.

Appendices could include the following:

A) DAT Roles and Responsibilities

Specific roles, responsibilities and duties must be clearly defined for the Disaster Action Team and other staff responding to a disaster. Assignment of responsibilities should be linked with the authority to carry them out. For example, the DAT Coordinator's authority takes precedence over that of all other DAT and staff members.

B) Collections, Records and Systems Priorities

This appendix should list recovery priorities for collections and records, as determined during the planning phase, and should have limited distribution for security reasons. It includes records essential to the operations of the organization (personnel, financial, etc.), as well as priority collections holdings in all formats. Their locations should also be marked clearly on floor plans. Names of associated specialists such as curatorial staff and human resources staff could also be included.

This appendix should also include associated systems and computer-related priorities in order to retain access to essential electronic information. External arrangements such as hot and cold sites would be listed in Appendix F.

C) Floor Plans

Accurate and up-to-date floor plans of the entire facility should be used as an organizational tool and an aid to recovery. Using these plans as base maps, additional information may be annotated, or if already recorded on the map, may be emphasized using colour codes and representative symbols. Whatever coding system is chosen, it should be simple, easily understood and legible in dim lighting.

In the event of a disaster, this information may be extremely useful to the police and fire departments, and may reduce the risk to both personnel and the collections. The location of essential collections and records with designated recovery priorities should be marked on priority removal maps. This information is confidential and should have limited distribution.

At least one set of these coded plans should be stored in a secure location in the building and be accessible by the DAT Coordinator. At least one other back-up set should be stored securely offsite in an easily accessible location. Due to the confidential nature of the information on some of the plans, access should be restricted to selected personnel.

D) Temporary Collections and Records Relocation

This appendix may list two types of temporary storage: onsite and offsite. Onsite refers to potential safe relocation areas within the facility; offsite refers to buildings or facilities that have been designated as possible alternate sites. Offsite options could include sister organizations, vacant office spaces, arenas, gymnasiums and other facilities. In case of a widespread disaster, such alternate arrangements may be needed. Strategies for tracking all materials moved within the facility or offsite should have been made during development of the plan.

E) Internal Emergency Equipment and Supplies

This appendix should contain lists and locations of essential emergency supplies and equipment that are stored in emergency depots, either onsite or offsite. These may be used for dealing with a small disaster or for use at the outset of a larger emergency until further supplies and equipment can be obtained. These supplies and equipment will, however, be of little use if the disaster renders them inaccessible. *(See 5.11)*

F) External Emergency Facilities, Equipment, Supplies and Services

This appendix should list external suppliers of disaster supplies, equipment, facilities and services that the organization may need to purchase, borrow or rent. These include companies that already provide services to the organization, such as utilities, fire and security systems, offsite data storage, insurance and elevator repair. This list should include names and telephone numbers for each supplier with day, night and weekend contacts. *(See 5.11)*

G) External Resource Contacts

This appendix should list professional resources that the organization can contact for assistance, advice and information. This list may include collections specialists, data recovery experts, conservators, archivists and librarians with disaster experience, as well as institutions with conservation or preservation departments that may be able to provide aid *(see 5.11.3)*.

Chapter 3

3.0 Disaster Prevention Planning

The reality is that disasters do happen and emergencies can turn into disasters. While disasters cannot be totally prevented, useful measures can be instituted to reduce their effects. An emergency contained does not become a disaster. Prevention is ultimately less costly than response and recovery; clearly, an ounce of prevention is worth a pound of cure.

At this point in the disaster planning timeline, the Disaster Planning Committee (DPC) and the Disaster Action Team (DAT) have been formed and the DPC should be ready to initiate the process for disaster prevention planning in order to determine the vulnerability of the organization to disaster, and to minimize the hazards identified.

The ideal way to cope with disaster is to prevent it from happening. Admittedly, some disasters such as flash floods and earthquakes are difficult, if not impossible, to predict, let alone avoid. However, in many cases the root cause of a disaster is not misfortune but human negligence. Fire, in particular, can result from poor security practices, faulty wiring, imprudent storage of flammable materials, etc.

Minor disasters such as burst pipes are not only more likely to occur, but do so with greater frequency than major disasters. The resources necessary to remedy damages associated with frequent minor disasters can approach the costs associated with a large disaster. As a result, the possibility of such incidents should never be dismissed.

3.1 The Purpose of Disaster Prevention Planning

The purpose of disaster prevention planning is to prevent incidents, emergencies and disasters wherever possible, and to contain or reduce their effects when the best preventive measures fail. Effective prevention must be done on a systematic and planned basis. The organization should routinely identify hazards and deficiencies, correct those it must, and plan to rectify others in progressive stages.

3.2 The Process for Disaster Prevention Planning

Disaster prevention planning includes identifying hazards, correcting hazards in the short term and doing so in the longer term where necessary.

The process for disaster prevention planning includes the following activities:

Disaster Prevention Planning: Process at a Glance

- Seek expert help.
- Survey building and environs.
- Identify existing and potential hazards.
- Undertake risk hazard analysis.
- Determine priorities for hazard prevention and reduction.
- Assess hazard prevention and reduction options.
- Assess costs.
- Recommend hazard prevention and reduction strategies and get approval to proceed.
- Minimize existing hazards.

3.2.1 Seek expert help

The organization's Disaster Planning Committee (DPC) *(see 2.3)* should consult outside experts such as members of the police and fire departments, the insurance company and commercial services such as security companies in order to supplement expertise within the organization as necessary. Many such contacts may already have been made and some experts called in if your plan is already under development or review.

At this point, you will be initiating or furthering specific requests for advice or hands-on aid to undertake a thorough survey of the building and its environs. The resulting knowledge of the facility and surroundings, as well as experience with survey practice, are essential for present and future disaster planning.

3.2.2 Survey building and environs

A critical step in planning for disaster prevention is to undertake a systematic survey of the building and its environs. A hazards survey designed for your organization and tailored to your region will identify problems that need to be remedied, as well as issues that require emphasis in formulating your disaster plan.

> ...Few...disasters have a single cause, and many result from a multiplicity of small failures, both human and structural (CCI N14/2 1988c, 1).

Staff, preferably members of the DPC including the building manager, and outside experts should survey the building inside and out to identify existing and potential hazards. Checklist sheets that are part of a regular inspection programme can be used for this purpose. One such form is the "Fire Prevention Checklist", in the *Fire Protection Handbook (Higgins 1997, 3.371).*

> The staff must know why information is being gathered about the collection, equipment and facilities. When staff are kept fully informed, they often will volunteer information about problems threatening the collection that may not be obvious to others, e.g., flooding, fire hazards, mold, etc. (DePew 1991, 259-260)

Although this survey will not predict disasters, it will identify potential problems that could cause a disaster, or could aggravate a disastrous situation. This survey serves as the basis for analyzing identified problem areas.

Survey Procedure

1. Start with the external: topography, climate, location and building structure.
2. Move to the internal: internal operations, staff practices, hazardous materials, environmental hazards, security hazards and other issues *(see 3.4.8, 3.5.1 to 3.5.9).*

Checklists are helpful for identifying potential problems in a systematic and comprehensive manner *(see 3.3.1).*

3.2.3 Identify existing and potential hazards

Once the survey of existing hazards inside and outside your building is completed, identify which of those are a potential threat to your organization.

Disasters are usually divided into two types: natural (floods, earthquakes, etc.) and those caused by people (arson, bombs, acts of war, etc.). The DPC should cast its net wide when considering what type of emergency or disaster could occur. Each kind of event should be listed, starting with the most serious (see Stewart and Tremain 1994 and Hunter 1984). This is followed by the risk hazard analysis – an assessment of the probability, vulnerability and criticality of each *(see 3.3).*

Each organization must decide for itself what constitutes an emergency and a disaster *(see 1.2.1)*, and provide ways to respond to each. Being aware, informed and knowledgeable about the probability of different types of hazards is key.

3.2.4 Undertake risk hazard analysis

In this part of the planning process, the DPC must consider the range of possible emergencies and disasters, and then assess the likelihood of their occurrence. Next, the DPC should estimate the impact of each possible disaster on the organization. In this way, resources and efforts can be directed to planning, preventing, protecting against and preparing for the most probable disasters without summarily dismissing the less likely or even freak occurrences.

3.2.5 Determine priorities for hazard prevention and reduction

Once the DPC has identified what measures need to be taken to minimize risks, it will probably come up with a lengthy 'wish' list, such as facility deficiencies and poor staff practices. This list must then be prioritized and resources allocated to minimize risks prior to a disaster.

> A universally acceptable level of risk does not exist (Stewart and Tremain 1994, 22).

Priorities for hazard prevention and reduction are set according to urgency, resources, timing and costs. Assessing and determining these priorities is essential to the entire disaster prevention process and the selection of strategies.

Human safety is the overriding priority for any decisions made on implementing measures to prevent disaster. Resources must be found when fire detection systems or other measures are needed to protect human life and to comply with building and fire code requirements.

3.2.6 Assess hazard prevention and reduction options

The assessment of hazard prevention and reduction options will be predicated on the nature and extent of the hazards, the resources and services available, and the organization's ability to support the costs.

With small hazards, the options are quite straightforward. With medium and larger hazards, several options may exist that could solve the same problem. Considerable research may be required, such as on code requirements, and a variety of service providers could be contacted for their expert input and ideas.

3.2.7 Assess costs

After the organization has determined its priorities and investigated options and costs for hazard prevention and reduction, staff should assess the costs. For some organizations, cost will be critical to the decision to proceed with some courses of action. A decision to develop short-, medium- and long-term objectives may result from this assessment of costs.

The following should be considered for any course of action:

· personnel requirements
· estimated time frames, scheduling and costs
· training requirements
· quality control and supervision
· supply, equipment and service needs

3.2.8 Recommend hazard prevention and reduction strategies and get approval to proceed

The DPC must now recommend the strategies for the collections, records, systems and facility, based on the priorities determined, assessment of options and costs, and available resources. The DPC must then seek any necessary approval by the organization's governing body.

The strategies may cover:

· retrofits to existing systems
· purchase and installation of new equipment and systems
· purchase of new services
· repairs to the facility
· renovations to the existing facility
· construction, i.e., new additions
· revision or development of new policies and procedures
· renewed enforcement of existing policies and procedures
· staff training

3.2.9 Minimize existing hazards

Once approval has been granted and the funds made available, the DPC can implement its plan to minimize hazards. Some hazards can be eliminated immediately with minimal expense, such as housekeeping improvements. Interim measures to protect the collections from known hazards should be taken until long-term remedies are possible. Other hazards may be reduced through specialized training for staff, such as building inspection programmes.

3.3 The Risk Hazard Analysis

Risk hazard analysis is the identification and estimation of the impact of any and all risks to the facility, collections and records. *Hazards* are natural, technological or civil threats to people, property and the environment. *Risk* is the probability that a hazard will occur during a particular time period. *Vulnerability* is susceptibility to injury or damage from hazards.

The DPC is responsible for analyzing hazards, identifying risks, and reducing the organization's vulnerability. A risk hazard analysis involves undertaking the hazards survey *(see 3.3.1)* and subsequently assessing the probability and degree of risk *(see 3.3.2)*.

> ...The risk of disaster is a combination of environmental hazards plus the vulnerabilities of buildings, mechanical systems, and collections. An institution-wide risk survey is the best way to assess these factors (Lindblom and Motylewski 1993, 2).

3.3.1 Hazards Survey Checklists

The checklists below are intended to be used as a guide, and should not be viewed as a comprehensive analysis. Each organization is unique and has its own particular needs and circumstances.

These lists, except where noted, are based on the work done by the Canadian Conservation Institute (CCI Notes N14/2, 1995b and N14/3, 1988d). As well, Buchanan (1988, 26-36, and appendices A.1-2) and Stewart and Tremain (1994, 10-21) include comprehensive checklists that you may wish to consult.

a) Site

Topography

· Is your building situated by a lake, river or ocean? Is flooding a possibility? Is the river tidal?
· Is your basement below the water level or water table?
· Is your region prone to avalanches or landslides? What is the gradient? Is your building in a valley?
· Is your region subject to earthquakes or volcanic action? What is its seismic rating?

Climate

· Is your region subject to extremes or to sudden changes in temperature (e.g., chinooks) and relative humidity (RH)?

- How soon after your heating or cooling system fails will the temperature and RH in your building reach unacceptable levels?
- Which materials in your collections are most sensitive to extremes and fluctuations of temperature and RH?
- Is your region subject to heavy or prolonged rainfall or snow?
- Is your region subject to severe weather, i.e., hurricanes, tornados, severe electrical storms, ice or high winds? Could severe weather interrupt access, essential services or communications?

  It is best not to make assumptions about weather patterns typical to your region. Freak climatic occurrences happen.

Location

- Is your organization located near industry that produces, stores or transports hazardous materials such as radioactive waste, chemicals and fuels?
- Is your organization located near industrial or government buildings with a history of demonstrations and riots? Does your region have a history of war or terrorism?
- Is your facility located near subways, railways or major highways, or under an air flight path that could cause significant vibrations?
- Are trees on the property a potential hazard? Consider roots, loose branches and the threat of brush fires.
- What are the adjacent structures?
- What is the access route for both evacuation and emergency vehicles?
- Where are the fire hydrants?
- How far away is the nearest fire station?

b) Facility, Structure and Systems

Survey from the top down.

- How old is the building? Additions?
- What are the structural materials? What is their general condition and level of repair?
- Has the building a flat roof, skylights, roof access doors or internal roof drains? Are there signs of water damage?
- Are the eavestroughs and downspouts free of debris and in good repair?
- Do water pipes run through collection areas? Have the pipes ever leaked?

- Are the drains and sewage system adequate and well maintained?
- Are the foundations sound? Are there cracks and/or signs of leakage inside or out?
- Are the egress routes complicated and/or blocked?

c) Construction and Renovation

Regardless of how well a facility measures in the survey, certain activities such as construction and renovation are particularly hazardous. Accounts in the literature attest to the dangers inherent in these activities. After arson, "the next most common cause of library fires (25% by some [U.S.] estimates) is construction or renovation. (Motylewski 1994, 2)

- Are you familiar with the hazards and precautions associated with construction and renovation?
- Are the facility's unique precaution and protection requirements – regarding fire, dust, dirt, water and mechanical damage – clearly and fully specified in the construction or renovation contracts?
- Have the precautions and protective measures been communicated fully to staff? Who is responsible for implementing and monitoring them?
- Are applicable fire and safety regulations being adhered to?
- Are the fire detection and suppression systems, security systems and water alarms operational?
- Are security measures adequate to protect collections from vandalism, theft and accidents?
- Are collections secure from vandalism, theft and accidents?
- Do collections need to be relocated, or can they be sealed off effectively from the work area(s)?
- Are there security procedures for work crews? Do staff make routine checks of the work area(s)?
- Is ventilation adequate to prevent dust and fumes from creating a fire hazard, exposing staff and workers to health hazards, or damaging collections?
- Are preparations adequate to deal with accidents?
- Are emergency supplies available and accessible?
- Do you need to review evacuation and other emergency procedures?

(Based on Motylewski 1994, 5-7.)

d) Operations and Services

Essential Services

- Do you have a regular maintenance and inspection programme for plumbing, electrical, fire alarm, fire detection, fire suppression, water detection and security systems? Is it adequate? Is it documented?

- Do you have up-to-date plans and structural/mechanical drawings of all the above, and are duplicates stored safely offsite?

- Do you know which services (e.g., heating and other fuel sources, electricity, water, sewers and septic tanks) are the responsibility of the organization rather than the municipality?

- Have you up-to-date plans and drawings of service access locations, including master switches, standpipes and valves?

- Is there a back-up for any or all of these services?

- Is the water pressure adequate for fire fighting?

Security

- What training programmes are there for security personnel and other staff?

- Is there a visible security presence, i.e., do security staff do regular walkabouts at irregular times?

- Are security policies posted in public? How often are they reviewed?

- Are emergency service numbers (i.e., internal security, police, fire, ambulance) posted on telephones?

- Are access control procedures adequate for both opening and closing, for staff and users?

- Are "staff only" areas secure and clearly marked?

- Are user identification and registration procedures adequate?

- Are staff responsible for the confidentiality of their computer access codes?

- Are the computer system security policies and procedures adequate? How often are they reviewed and updated?

- Is there a need to install surveillance cameras?

- Is the security system adequate? Is it regularly serviced?

Staff Practices

- Are there inspection and maintenance procedures for the facility, collections and services? Are they performed routinely according to need and are they documented?

- What are the procedures for maintenance or repair requests? How are they monitored?

- How is garbage disposed of? How are flammable materials dealt with?

- Is there a policy for food and drink? Is it enforced?

- Is there a policy or legislation regulating smoking? Is it enforced?

e) Hazardous Materials

The disaster plan should identify all hazardous materials in the building that pose direct or indirect risks. In Canada, refer to the Canadian Occupational Safety and Health Regulations, the Canada Labour Code and the Workplace Hazardous Materials Information System (WHMIS). WHMIS is a Canada-wide system designed to provide employers and employees with information on hazardous materials used in the workplace. It covers material safety data sheets (MSDS), container labelling and education programmes. In the United States, refer to the U.S. Occupational Safety and Health Act and Occupational Safety and Health Administration (OSHA) standards *(see Appendix 3.1 Sources of Information: Health and Safety).*

- Get expert advice on the identification of any unknown materials that may be hazardous.

- Are hazardous materials such as gas cylinders, solvents and paints handled, used and stored in the building in accordance with applicable safety regulations and standards?

- Are staff trained in the correct handling, use, storage and disposal of hazardous materials? Are appropriate equipment and protective clothing provided and used?

Hazards in the Collections

- Identify potential hazards such as live ammunition.

- Identify pesticides and other toxic materials that may be found in collection items (such as arsenic, DDT and mercury on taxidermy mounts).

- Identify any cellulose nitrate-based film. In addition to its high combustibility, cellulose nitrate slowly decomposes under normal storage conditions, releasing gases harmful to people and collection materials, especially paper and film.

- Familiarize yourself with the literature and the standards for the safe handling, storage and destruction of nitrate-based films.

The storage and handling of nitrate-based films are governed by a National Fire Protection Association standard (see *NFPA 40-1997. Standard for the Storage and Handling of Cellulose Nitrate Motion Picture Film*). This standard is not law in Canada; however, the fire department or local building and electrical inspectors may require compliance with it. *(See also 3.5.7c)*

· Store cellulose nitrate-based film properly and apart from other collections including other cellulose nitrate-based films.

· Be aware that cellulose nitrate-based films deteriorate in five stages. In the early stages of deterioration they can be photographically reproduced, but not in the later stages.

Kodak recommends that cellulose nitrate films that have reached the third stage of decomposition, or that have no historical value, be destroyed at an authorized facility (see Eastman Kodak Co. 1995, 2).

· Consult with the fire department on safe disposal of the original films after reproduction.

· Be aware that cellulose nitrate-based films are classified as hazardous materials or hazardous waste when shipped for storage, projection, duplication, repair or destruction, and are subject to various restrictions.

3.3.2 Assessment of the Probability and Degree of Risk

This stage of risk hazard analysis combines knowledge of the hazards facing the organization with an assessment of its particular vulnerability to those hazards. Disaster planning considers these factors and lays out the actions and resources necessary to counter them.

> Risk evaluation is not the bugaboo many opponents insist it is, or, at least, it doesn't have to be that. The risk evaluation process is...a learning experience for both users and...professionals, if they realize the calculations are at best approximations. It is the *process* of risk evaluation and the *development* of the recovery plan that follows the analysis, which are most important. The plan itself is not set in concrete and will, without question, be changed as new conditions and situations warrant. (Bologna cited in Hunter 1984, 4)

Many methodologies in various professional fields have been developed for measuring risk quantitatively. Sources that have particular application to the field of preservation of collections include Stewart and Tremain (1994, 22-33), Hunter (1983, 243-246), and CAN/CSA (1995, 52-54). These methods can provide a framework to guide an organization in measuring risks, thereby planning more effectively to eliminate risks or mitigate any effects of disaster. However, this field is constantly evolving, and no mathematical formula can supplant a thorough knowledge of an organization and the attendant risks. Judgement, priority-setting and ultimately decision-making are still the main tools of risk hazard analysis.

The following methodology developed by J. L. Paulhus (1983, 123-124) is one very clear and useful model for measuring risk. While designed to measure security needs, Paulhus' approach can be used to prioritize needs in the arena of disaster planning. This is done by determining how critical each danger is relative to the risks and the organization's vulnerability.

· **Risk (R)** is defined as the possibility of an event occurring that may adversely affect the normal functions of the institution.

The likelihood of occurrence (Risk) can be rated...

Absolute occurrence	76-100%
Highly likely to occur	51-75%
Likely to occur	26-50%
Least likely to occur	0-25%

· **Vulnerability (V)** is defined as any event or activity that affects the normal operation of the institution.

The levels of effect (Vulnerability) can be rated...

Disastrous effect	76-100%
Critical effect	51-75%
Serious effect	26-50%
Tolerable effect	0-25%

· **Criticality (C)** is the correlation of the probability of an occurrence (risk) and the degree of its impact (vulnerability) expressed as RV = C. The following table shows how criticality is determined and gives rise to priorities among security needs.

Event	Risk (R)	%	Vulnerability (V)	%	Criticality (C)	Priority
Fire	Least likely to occur	5	Disastrous effect	80	400	1
Theft	Least likely to occur	5	Critical effect	65	325	2
Leaks	Highly likely [to occur]	60	Tolerable effect	5	300	3
Injury	Likely to occur	45	Tolerable effect	5	225	4

The preceding table indicates that a programme to eliminate or reduce the danger of fire is the priority need, followed by theft, leaks and injury. However, the measures taken to satisfy one priority may alter the risk in others and change their criticality, and therefore, priority. Recalculating the criticalities at each step is a good measure of the process of analysis (Paulhus 1983, 123-124).

The impact of a particular disaster varies broadly according to its scale, severity, area affected, etc. The impact on unique and irreplaceable collection materials is vastly different from that on widely available, readily replaceable materials. Not all disasters are equally disastrous. Some losses can be replaced. In other cases, collections are irreplaceable by reason of their uniqueness or rarity, or by their existence in a particular community.

The risk hazard analysis provides the basis for priority-setting by the DPC. Events that are most likely to occur and would have the greatest impact on the organization should be planned for first and resources allocated accordingly. A longer-term timetable for implementing counter-measures can be established for events classified as lower priority.

Risks, however, do not remain fixed. They will shift as conditions change, and it is wise to schedule periodic risk analysis reviews.

Plan for degrees of disasters

Each organization must determine what constitutes an emergency and/or a disaster, and then anticipate, plan and implement measures for expected effects. Plans should cover as many contingencies as possible. The DPC should weigh the potential effects and the likelihood of each, and allocate resources accordingly.

Severity	A slow leaking pipe, for example, or a frozen and burst pipe.
Scale	Area affected (one bay, floor, building, block, etc.).
Scope	Minor, moderate, major or catastrophic. Affecting just your facility or the whole region?
Size	Ten books, hundreds or thousands?

Secondary effects can include those from a domino effect, i.e., events triggered by a chain reaction. Regardless of the many forms a disaster may take, the actual damage to materials is usually caused by fire or water. Even when not the primary cause, fire and flooding almost invariably arise as secondary effects. An earthquake, for example, can cause gas mains to rupture and water pipes to burst. Similarly, a breakdown in law and order following a major disaster creates ideal conditions for arson and vandalism. Flooding and damage also often result from the efforts required to put out a fire.

3.4 Disaster Profiles

The following profiles are intended to help the DPC better understand the overall nature and effects of disasters, in order to effectively plan for prevention, protection, preparedness, response and recovery.

3.4.1 Fire

Fire can come from many causes: lightning, explosions, earthquakes, arson, careless smoking, faulty wiring and equipment and even from hazards within the collections themselves, such as nitrate film. One source considers fire "a probability rather than a possibility" (Nelson 1991, 61). The Fire Commissioner of Canada's statistics on fire losses in Canadian museums, art galleries and libraries from 1982 to 1991 report 264 fires with 31 injuries and over $16 million of property losses excluding collection damage and loss or business interruption (cited in Baril 1995, 4).

According to a 1983-1993 survey, the leading cause of fire in U.S. libraries and the second leading cause in museums was arson or "suspicious causes." Failures in the electrical distribution system was the second leading cause in libraries and the leading cause in museums. Together these account for well over half of the reported fires in the U.S. (Bush and McDaniel 1997, 9.92 - 9.93).

Fire can consume collections, buildings and all who get in its way, creating intense heat, smoke and gases. Ironically, the agent used to fight fire – water – can be as damaging to collections and other property.

a) Triangle of Fire

Basic to fire prevention and protection measures is an understanding of the Triangle of Fire, which defines the components required for fire to occur:

1. Fuel	Any substance capable of burning.
2. Oxidizer	Air is the most obvious and is ever present.
3. Ignition source	A flame, spark or heat alone as a supply of energy.

All three components must be present for a fire to start. Lack or removal of any of these components will prevent or stop fire. In all organizations, fuel and air are ever present – paper being an excellent fuel. Thus, the ignition source is the one area where the risk may be reduced or eliminated.

b) Classes and Stages of Fire

Fires are classed according to the type of burnable substance.

Classes of Fire

Class A	Combustible materials (cellulose materials such as wood and paper, cloth, rubber and many plastics)
Class B	Flammable or combustible liquids (gasoline, methane, oil, lacquers, oil-based paint, paint thinners, cooking fat, etc.)
Class C	Live electrical equipment
Class D	Combustible metals (magnesium, titanium, sodium, potassium, etc.)

Although Class A fires are the most common in archives, libraries and record centres, any class of fire can occur. Class D fires are rare.

The type of burnable substances (class of fire) determines the selection of the extinguishing agent for given areas in a facility *(see 4.6 and 4.7)*.

An understanding of fire's four-stage development process demonstrates the importance of arresting it in its earliest stages.

Stages of Fire

1.	Incipient Stage	No visible smoke or flame, low to moderate heat. This stage can last from minutes to days.
2.	Smouldering or Smoke Stage	No visible flame, but smoke is now present. Heat is still low to moderate.
3.	Flame Stage	Flames are now evident. Temperature is climbing; heat stage is imminent.
4.	Heat Stage	The characteristic "fire" – flame, smoke and heat. Most dangerous and destructive stage; toxic gases are produced.

c) Effects of Fire on Collections and Computer Equipment

Although shelved books or packed paper files burn slowly, all paper exposed to high temperatures becomes so brittle that it will crumble when touched – even though it does not appear burnt. Books and papers that do not burn become discoloured by soot and smoke. Heat shrinks vellum and leather. Heat and flames dry out and contort photographs; the emulsion shrivels. Audiovisual materials and microforms usually do not survive a fire or are damaged irreparably.

Computer hardware, software and electronic records are extremely sensitive to heat, steam and smoke, and thus easily damaged even when not directly in the fire. Some plastic casings, covers and housings melt into amorphous blobs when exposed to even moderate temperatures.

> "Non-paper records media tend to be more susceptible to damage than paper"
> (Goonan 1997, 3.277)

The type and severity of damage will depend on the nature of the material and how it is stored, its length of exposure to fire (flame, heat, smoke, gases), the temperatures reached and other factors such as exposure to high humidity.

Temperatures at Which Damage to Materials Starts

Above 120°F (49°C)	Permanent damage to computer equipment and data starts
125°F (52°C)	Floppy disks, magnetic tapes, etc. start to lose information
150°F (66°C)	Hard disk damage
174°F (79°C)	Computer equipment components failure
225°F (107°C) and high humidity	Microfilm, microfiche damage
300°F (149°C) and low humidity	Microfilm, microfiche damage
300-500°F (149-260°C)	Major computer equipment components failure
302°F (150°C)	Polypropylene softens
350°F (177°C)	Paper products damage
420°F (216°C)	Paper chars
650-750°F (343-399°C)	Polystyrene cases, reels degrade

(Based largely on Pearce 1997, 9.206)
(Reprinted with permission from *Fire Protection Handbook*, 18th edition, Copyright © 1997 National Fire Protection Association, Quincy, MA 02269)

The temperature generated by burning wood and other combustible construction materials in a building fire can well exceed 538°C (1000°F). This heat is transmitted throughout the building by radiation, conducted through walls, floors and ceilings, and often through the heating and ventilation ducts. (Cunha 1992, 594)

3.4.2 Water

Most major disasters to libraries and archives involve water (Buchanan 1988, 71).

Accounts in the literature have focussed extensively on the recovery of water-damaged collections. Generally, wet collection material can be more effectively recovered than fire-damaged material. In addition, our experience with water-based conservation treatments has made us more familiar with the effects of water on paper and related materials.

Water may be the primary cause of a disaster, or a secondary effect of a disaster of another type, such as a hurricane or fire. The source of the water will, to a great extent, determine the response required. Dirty, contaminated water can pose a major health hazard and will further complicate the response effort. Weather may also play a critical role when, in the case of a severe and prolonged storm, response may be delayed or hampered.

a) Effects of Water on Collections and Computer Equipment

In some fires, ironically, most damage is caused not by the fire itself, but by the efforts required to put it out.

The smallest line used by the fire department, a 1-1/2" hose, puts out at least 90 gallons of water a minute, enough pressure to throw collections into total disarray. The more commonly used 2-1/2" line discharges 250 to 350 gallons of water a minute. (Trinkley 1993a, 1)

The effects of water on the collections and equipment may be further compounded by deposits of ash, soot and smoke and other debris.

Books, documents and other materials may lay submerged in water for hours, sometimes days, before building entry is permitted and recovery can begin. Mould will rapidly begin to form in damp conditions. Paper absorbs water at various rates depending on its age, condition and material composition. In general, pre-1840 books and documents absorb water to an average of 80 percent of their original weight. This compares to the 60 percent absorption of modern books, excluding those on the most brittle paper.

Water can cause leather and parchment to warp, wrinkle or shrink. It can also cause gelatinization of parchment. Audiovisual materials, photographs, microforms, magnetic and other media are also vulnerable to water damage. The deformation of book covers and text blocks may be irreparable. The type and severity of damage will depend on the nature of the material and how it is stored, its length of exposure to water, the temperature of the water and other factors such as contaminants present.

Computer hardware and software damaged by water may or may not be recoverable. Much depends on the contamination present in the water. Corrosion can easily result from high levels of humidity *(see 9.4)*. Even when equipment is recoverable, the cost of repair can exceed the replacement cost.

b) Floods

Floods have been classified as "the most common and widespread of all natural hazards" (FEMA 1990, 4). In Canada, floods are most common during spring runoff, especially along northward-flowing rivers whose still-frozen lower reaches are unable to cope with the rush of water from upstream. Low-lying areas near glaciers or water or those areas downstream from dams are also prone to flooding. In some places, floods are caused by local storms, spring thaws, the remnants of tropical storms from the Gulf of Mexico, or earthquakes (tsunamis). Flash floods may occur almost anywhere at any time. Storm surges are weather-driven floods and have been described as a "combination of water pushed by the wind, high tides and low atmospheric pressure that allows seacoast water levels to rise to unthinkable heights" (Nelson 1991, 60).

Full-scale flooding can quickly outpace efforts to sandbag and protect property from its leviathan nature. When a flood tips the scales and human safety comes to the forefront, evacuation is the only recourse. Clean-up and recovery come later. Flooding is a prime example of a disaster that can devastate a whole community and put extraordinary demands on local authorities, supplies and the population. Its secondary results can include health threats and looting.

c) Tsunamis

Tsunamis (literally "great harbour wave") are the watery spawn of large underwater earthquakes or, less frequently, volcanic eruptions. These series of long-period waves can travel as fast as 960 km/h (600 mph). They are imperceptible in deep ocean water, but can reach heights of three storeys by the time they reach shallower coastal waters. Their effects are catastrophic: "In the United States in this century alone, more people have died in tsunamis than in earthquakes" (Jervis 1990, 14).

While the possibility of a tsunamigenic event is ever present along the Pacific Coast of North America, no coastal area is exempt. For example, two and a half hours after a 1929 earthquake struck 350 km off the south coast of Newfoundland, a tsunami assaulted that coast and Nova Scotia, and was recorded on tide gauges as far away as Bermuda and the Azores:

...Around 7:30 p.m., a calm, wind-less, moonlit sea drained silently out of all the harbours along the south coast of Newfoundland's Burin Peninsula. It then returned about 10 minutes later with a thunderous roar. Over the next half-hour, three main pulses of tsunami assaulted the... coast. (Ruffman 1996, 25)

3.4.3 Hurricanes, Tornadoes and Severe Weather

a) Hurricanes

Known as hurricanes in the Atlantic, typhoons in the Pacific and cyclones in the Indian Ocean, these storms are characterized by heavy rains and winds blowing in a wide circle around a central eye. Hurricane winds reach more than 160 km/h (100 mph), and the after-effect can produce tornadoes and flash flooding. In fact, much of the damage caused by hurricanes comes from flooding, including storm surges that combine high water flooding with a high tide in coastal communities.

As described by Nelson (1991, 58), buildings that are not secured to another building and/or to the ground are more likely to fail. The strong, seesawing winds of a hurricane can rip through roofs or peel metal roofs off and allow wind and water to surge into the building. Detached structures such as porches, downspouts, roofs and even trees, shrubs and lighting fixtures can hurtle through the air, killing people and damaging structures.

Less common than tornadoes, hurricanes reach eastern Canada from the Atlantic seaboard between June and November (the hurricane season), with September being the peak month. By the time they enter this country, heavy rain and flooding generally pose a greater danger than high winds. Hurricanes are rare in other parts of Canada. Hurricanes are slower moving than tornadoes, so there is generally time to seek shelter and take precautionary measures.

The following hurricane information is based on the Saffir/Simpson Hurricane Scale (Atabaigi 1996, 38):

Category	Winds	Storm Surge
I	74-95 mph (119-153 km/h)	4-5 ft (1.2-1.5 m)
II	96-110 mph (155-177 km/h)	6-8 ft (1.8-2.4 m)
III	111-130 mph (179-209 km/h)	9-12 ft (2.7-3.7 m)
IV	131-155 mph (211-249 km/h)	13-18 ft (4.0-5.5 m)
V	155+ mph (249+ km/h)	18+ ft (5.5+ m)

Regardless of the precautionary measures taken, Class III or worse hurricanes pose a very real threat to buildings (DePew 1994, 57).

b) Tornadoes

The U.S. has more tornadoes than any other country (FEMA 1984, 7). In Canada, tornadoes occur in all areas except those with an Arctic climate. They are relatively frequent in the interior, from New Brunswick to the Rocky Mountains, and are most common in Ontario, which averages 25 per year (Ebbs 1995a, 8), followed by Manitoba. Class F4 tornadoes (see Fujita-Pearson Scale) have occurred in Regina (1912), Barrie, Ontario (1985), and Edmonton (1987). The Edmonton tornado has been called "the greatest single storm loss in Canadian history" (Canadian Encyclopedia 1988, 2168).

In Canada, tornadoes most commonly occur from April to October, peaking in June and July. A tornado is most likely to occur in the mid afternoon to early evening, and to approach from the west or southwest.

Tornadoes are the most violent of atmospheric storms. One is recognizable by a twisting, funnel-shaped column that points downward from the base of a cloud bank and touches the ground for up to 20 minutes, leaving destruction in its path. Tornadoes move rapidly, at speeds of up to 500 km/h (300 mph). If the column does not touch the ground, it is referred to as a funnel cloud. If it touches down on water, it is called a water spout. Twisters are small tornadoes usually restricted to damage covering about 100 metres (328 feet) of ground.

As described by Nelson (1991, 59), a tornado can tear a roof from a building or even lift a wooden building and hurl it through the air. The rapid reduction in air pressure produced by a tornado can extract the contents from the building or even cause the building to explode from internal high pressure.

The following tornado information is based on the Fujita-Pearson Scale (Atabaigi 1996, 38):

Class	Wind	Damage
F0	40-72 mph (64-116 km/h)	Light
F1	73-112 mph (117-180 km/h)	Moderate
F2	113-157 mph (182-253 km/h)	Considerable
F3	158-206 mph (254-331 km/h)	Severe
F4	207-260 mph (333-418 km/h)	Devastating
F5	261-318 mph (420-512 km/h)	Incredible

c) Severe Weather

Severe weather can take many forms, such as thunderstorms and depressions. Depressions have intense winds that manifest as blizzards in the winter. A storm's production of water, hail, sleet, ice or snow, combined with high winds, can have significant consequences. The weight of ice and snow on roofs, or ice and snow on trees and power lines, can cause structural damage to buildings. In severe cases, building roofs can collapse. Water and snow, forced by high winds, may enter openings. Power outages can also result.

Blizzards are fierce winter storms characterized by winds above 40 km/h (25 mph), temperatures below -10°C (14°F) and visibility of less than 500 metres (546 yards) in falling or blowing snow.

Wind Speed

The force of the wind is normally combined with its description. For example, a storm is called a Force 10 storm and the word "wind" does not appear. The Beaufort descriptions are commonly used to describe wind speed and force level.

Beaufort Descriptions

Description	Force Level	Wind Speed	
calm	Force 0	less than 1 km/h	(1 mph)
light air	Force 1	up to 5 km/h	(up to 3 mph)
light breeze	Force 2	6–11 km/h	(4–7 mph)
gentle breeze	Force 3	12–20 km/h	(7–12 mph)
moderate breeze	Force 4	21–29 km/h	(13–18 mph)
fresh breeze	Force 5	30–39 km/h	(19–24 mph)
strong breeze	Force 6	40–50 km/h	(25–31 mph)
near gale	Force 7	51–61 km/h	(32–38 mph)
gale	Force 8	62–74 km/h	(39–46 mph)
strong gale	Force 9	75–87 km/h	(47–54 mph)
storm	Force 10	88–101 km/h	(55–63 mph)
violent storm (rarely on land)	Force 11	102–116 km/h	(64–72 mph)
hurricane	Force 12	more than 117 km/h	(more than 73 mph)

(Based on McFarlane and Clements 1996, 389-390)

Freezing rain or ice storms are forms of precipitation that fall first as rain and then freeze upon contact with power lines, trees and the ground. Sleet is a mixture of rain and a frozen form of precipitation (snow, snow pellets, ice pellets or hail).

Hail Size Estimates (Based on Atabaigi 1996, 39)

Hail is generally described in common terms such as golf ball and baseball and is reported in sizes ranging from pea – .25″ (.64 cm) to grapefruit – 4.00″ (10.2 cm).

3.4.4 Earthquakes

For the most part, earthquakes in Canada have not occurred in highly populated regions. They occur most frequently along the Pacific Coast, the Ottawa River and the St. Lawrence Valley. Recent predictions from seismologists, however, point to the likelihood of a sudden and catastrophic earthquake in British Columbia:

> ...The next great earthquake in Cascadia [the area from northernmost California to southern B.C.] will generate extremely large seismic waves lasting for as long as several minutes. After the shaking ceases, most coastal sites will be one to two meters lower and five to 10 meters seaward of where they started. (Hyndman 1995, 75)

During an earthquake, it is not the actual movement of the ground that causes most deaths and injuries. Rather, the danger to human life comes from the effects of its vibrations on structures. Unreinforced buildings collapse; old wooden structures can bounce completely off their foundations, and foundations built on landfill and flood plains can fail when the apparently solid soil liquifies. (Nelson 1991, 56)

Secondary damage includes debris falling off damaged buildings, glass flying from broken windows, fires caused by broken chimneys and gas lines, and flooding due to ruptured water mains. The most serious flooding associated with earthquakes is caused by damage to dams or by tsunamis (a series of huge seismic sea waves). Conversely, earthquakes can also sever water mains and leave an affected area without water with which to fight fire.

Secondary damage inside buildings can result from wall shelves (both bolted and unbolted) and storage units toppling and tossing their contents to the floor. Fixtures, ceiling tiles and structural supports can also fall. Unsecured computer equipment can vibrate off desks. In addition, water from broken pipes can soak the collections, and fire may pose a further threat.

Earthquakes themselves are of surprisingly short duration – the powerful 1989 earthquake at Loma Prieta, California, measured 7.1 on the Richter Scale but lasted only 15 seconds. However, once the tremor has passed, aftershocks of decreasing severity may follow within the next few hours or even days.

Earthquake magnitude is generally measured using the Richter Magnitude Scale, while earthquake intensity is measured using the Modified Mercalli Intensity Scale.

Richter Magnitude Scale Measure (Atabaigi 1996, 38)

Magnitude	Earthquake
4	Minor
5	Moderate
6	Strong
7	Major
8	Great

Each whole number increase in magnitude corresponds to a release of energy approximately 30 times as great.

Natural Resources Canada can provide information on the seismic rating for local areas *(see Appendix 3.1 Sources of Information: Earthquakes).*

3.4.5   Explosions

Explosions may result from various circumstances such as leaking gas, faulty heating equipment and flammable vapours. They may also be caused by deliberately set explosive devices arising from civil unrest, military conflict or vandalism. In particular, library bookdrops have been noted to be easy access points for unpleasant deposits and occasionally even explosive devices. Secondary effects of explosions are fire and flooding, resulting from ruptured gas mains, electrical systems and sewers and firefighting efforts.

3.4.6   Power Failure

In Canada, electric power interruptions occur most often after winter storms, when the weight of ice and snow causes power lines to snap. Similar interruptions may occur during summer thunderstorms. Power reductions in the form of blackouts or brownouts also take place during the summer, particularly during heat waves, when air conditioner use causes power demand to exceed supply. In recent years, growing dependence on computer technologies has made power failures a critical concern.

3.4.7   Civil Disturbances, Terrorism and Military Conflict

Civil disturbances such as strikes, riots and demonstrations, as well as terrorism and military conflict, are possibilities that cannot be ignored. Although Canada has participated in wars in other countries, armed conflict on Canadian soil has been rare. However, to dismiss this threat altogether would be naive.

Compared with many countries, Canada has had relatively little experience with civil unrest or terrorist activities. However, the 1996 protest at Ontario's Legislative Assembly and the events involving the Front de Libération du Québec (FLQ) in the 1960s and '70s, as well as the British Columbia Direct Action group's bombings indicate that Canada is by no means exempt.

> The actions required to meet riots and civil disturbances vary with geographical location and social attitudes from no more than closing the main entrance to the complete mobilization of all resources (Paulhus 1983, 130).

In the case of military conflict, history has shown that libraries and archives can be specifically targeted for destruction. An archive or library with politically or socially sensitive collections and/or exhibitions can also become a focal point for protest action.

During war, the effects of disaster may be similar to those resulting from fire and water by natural means. However, an organization's ability to respond can be rendered useless by circumstances. It is difficult to fully prepare for and prevent damage in the case of war or other armed conflict. *(See also 1.3.2)*

> The Geneva (1949) and Hague (1954) Conventions afford some degree of protection for museums and other cultural institutions against bombing, shelling, looting and vandalism by enemy troops. Under the terms of these conventions, however, cultural properties located near strategic targets will not necessarily be spared (Hunter 1986, 240).

3.4.8   Infestation

Infestation is a problem faced by all archives, libraries and record centres. Collections of all types are subject to damage and deterioration by mould (the common term for the growth caused by fungi), insects, and sometimes rodents and other animals. Damage to collections may take many forms, as materials may be a food source, a source of nesting material or an obstruction to movement. Materials may be consumed, shredded, weakened, soiled and stained. Prevention is critical, as much of this damage is irreversible.

> Libraries and archives...are not unlike the setting in agriculture where huge quantities of foodstuffs are stored for long periods of time ... a banquet for insects, rodents and mould (Parker 1988, 7).

Integrated Pest Management (IPM), recognized as the safest and most effective approach to preventing pests in libraries, targets the source of the problems by concentrating on excluding pests from a facility. As Parker (1988) has described, the strategy focuses on continual awareness of potential problems and the use of a variety of control techniques, in addition to immediate response to infestations. The use of chemicals is considered a last resort due to health and safety concerns for both people and collections. In the case of an infestation, the prevention programme should be thoroughly evaluated to avoid reoccurrence.

For the purposes of disaster planning, the outbreak of mould is the significant issue. While infestations of insects and vermin can cause extensive damage, they are not generally classified as disasters. This section is not intended to be a comprehensive guide to pest management, but to provide basic directions on responsible collections care. Extensive information on the characteristics and behaviour of insects, animals and mould, and on identification and their control, is widely available in the literature. Readers are also encouraged to consult professional pest control firms familiar with the needs of library and archival facilities and collections.

a) Mould

Of all the microbiological agents, moulds constitute the major risk for collections. Other microorganisms such as bacteria can cause deterioration and decomposition of materials; however, damage caused by mould is most often reported in the literature. See Florian (1997) for comprehensive discussion of fungi: description, activity, prevention and control, and McCrady (1999) on assessment and health issues.

Mould spores (conidia), active and dormant, are present everywhere in our surroundings and require only suitable nutrients and environmental conditions to proliferate. They tend to establish their own microclimate and feed solely by digesting their host. Mould participates in the decomposition of organic materials of plant or animal origin (even those that have been fumigated) as well as many human-made materials.

Mould affects both the physical and chemical properties of materials. Some species of mould can cause irreversible structural damage and discolouration to paper. Others attack the starches, gums and gelatins found in bookbindings, sizes, adhesives and paints. In addition, dust, dirt and stains contain spores and nutrients that support mould growth, even on materials such as plastics and glass.

Mould can grow locally on a few items in a collection. Often it affects many items in a particular area, result-

ing in what is known as mould bloom, a white or coloured velvet-like growth. In either case, the growth results from an environmental shift that has enabled germination.

The temperature range for optimal growth and reproduction of mould is variable and species specific, but is approximately 15°C to 35°C (60°F to 95°F). The average optimum temperature is approximately 30°C (86°F), with a relative humidity of 75% to 100% (Wessel 1970, 55). Optimum temperature range for germination is 20°C to 26°C (68°F to 79°F) and in general, germination is limited by minimum temperatures of 0°C to 10°C (32°F to 50°F) and a maximum of 34°C to 36°C (93°F to 97°F) (Florian 1997, 128). Many species can endure long periods of freezing or sub-freezing temperatures, and others may tolerate long periods of extremely high temperatures. Their growth will be halted, but spores remain dormant.

Moisture is required for mould growth. In general, the higher the relative humidity or RH (measure of the moisture in the air) the more readily mould will grow. Sustained conditions of 70% RH will almost surely produce mould. Many species of mould, however, will grow in moderate RH, as low as 45% (Nyberg 1987, 2). This is because moisture necessary to mould growth can also exist in or on the surface of the item where the mould is growing and in the mould itself. Collection materials and mould contain moisture that exists in equilibrium with their surroundings. Their water content may be higher than that of the air. Different materials also have different capacities to retain moisture, which may explain localized mould growth. (Florian 1993a, 1997, 124-127 and Glaser 1994, 2)

A principal means of preventing mould germination and growth is to control the environment. A maximum RH of 65% is often recommended; however, 55% is preferable, and lower (within reason) is better if possible. Temperature should not exceed 21°C (70°F). Both temperature and RH should be monitored constantly.

The mould species most common to library and archival materials germinate and proliferate when the relative humidity reaches or exceeds 65% for several days. With wet materials, germination can occur within a very short time – 24 hours (Craig-Bullen 1996, 34). Once mould has germinated, other factors such as high temperatures, stagnant air and poor sanitation will assist and accelerate its growth. The affected materials should be immediately isolated and the relative humidity reduced to 45%. In most cases, mould growth then ceases and becomes inactive or dormant, but desiccated mould growth and spores remain viable.

Multi-stage, particulate air filtration systems are best for reducing the entry and movement of spores in a building. Moderate air circulation is recommended to eliminate stagnant air pockets.

Environmental control measures must be accompanied by a programme of building inspection, maintenance, sanitation and cleaning that limits the sources of mould spores and their spread. Routine inspection and maintenance of collections should also be undertaken. Staff training is essential for effective control.

Florian (1993b, 869, 1994, 7-8 and 1997, 120-121) warns that some conservation treatments may activate dormant spores: mild heat treatment of 40°C to 75°C (104°F to 167°F) for various periods from five minutes to five hours; freezing, low temperatures or freeze/thaw cycles; and the use of chemicals such as alcohols, certain acids, detergents and some alkaline materials in specific amounts (though alcohol in larger amounts is lethal to mould). Thus, mould spores could be activated by heat from a fire, exposure to freezing temperatures for the purposes of insect eradication, or certain chemical treatments. Further research is required to confirm the actions and circumstances that make materials more susceptible to mould growth.

Mould Identification Guidelines

Stains, cobwebs and residues of dust or dirt can sometimes be mistaken for mould. While it may not always be necessary to identify the species of mould, confirmation of its presence is necessary, as is determination of its state, active or dormant.

The following is based on the guidelines of Olcott Price (1994, 2):

- **Does it look like mould?** Examine under magnification. Early stages of mould appear as a fine web of filaments (hyphae) on the surface of, or within, the structure of the host material. Later stages appear as a bushy growth, and the fruiting bodies containing spores are clearly visible. Mould can be many colours. Examined under ultraviolet light, microorganism growth appears luminescent.
- **Does the material feel damp?**
- **Does the material smell musty?**
- **Is the mould dormant (dry and powdery) or active (soft and smeary)?** Test with a soft brush. Active mould continues to grow and damage the collection, while dormant mould causes no further damage unless the RH is again elevated.

- **What are the temperature and RH in the suspected affected area?** Mould is active and grows only in conditions of elevated RH and remains there for some period of time. Elevated temperatures increase the rate of growth.
- **Is it foxing?** Foxing (red-brown spots or splotches) on paper is a closely related phenomenon that can be confused with mould. Foxing will demonstrate no visible hyphae or mould structure, but like mould, occurs in high relative humidity.

Health hazards posed by mould have recently started to be seriously discussed in the preservation literature. Moulds can cause serious illness, and some can cause toxic and pathological diseases. Moulds are strong sensitizers, and exposure through inhalation or contact can lead to serious allergies in some people not previously prone to allergic reactions. Staff who have a history of allergy problems or are asmatic should not be exposed. To maximize the safety of staff and others who use the collections, a mycologist should be brought in to assess the species (and relative quantities) present, and protective containment procedures must be implemented (see 6.4.9). Minor outbreaks of mould are fairly easily handled and contained. Major outbreaks and those involving highly toxic species require immediate outside professional assistance.

Mould growth is of particular concern following a disaster when damp, wetted or soaked collections remain in conditions of high temperature and relative humidity. Immediate action is critical, as mould will likely develop in 48 to 72 hours or less. Mould places collections and the people handling them at risk. Its presence also complicates disaster response and recovery efforts (see 6.5.8 and 7.2.3). It is best to seek expert advice.

b) Insects

More than 70 species of insects have been identified as threats to library and archival materials. Not only do such insects cause severe damage when conditions are favourable, they may also rapidly produce large numbers of young. In their life cycle, all insects grow through metamorphosis, where growth proceeds in a series of stages. Egg, larva, pupa and adult constitute a complete metamorphosis. Generally, larvae cause the most damage to collections while feeding. Insects not only consume materials, but cause damage by their nesting and burrowing activities, body secretions and excrement.

Of the species that infest collections, some are omnivorous and some are selective. Cockroaches consume all forms of paper and binding materials, especially those with pastes and glues, as well as food remains and dead insects. Bookworms including the Furniture, Drugstore and Death-Watch Beetle consume and damage most collection materials, including paper, cardboard and adhesives. Silverfish and firebrats consume carbohydrates (paper size, adhesives) in binding materials, magazine papers and photographs. Flies and their corrosive droppings pose a threat mainly to art collections. Other insects considered hazardous include clothes moths and beetles, which can damage not only collections but also shelving, storage furniture and building structures.

In general, the optimum temperature for insect development and reproduction is 20°C to 30°C (68°F to 86°F). Most insects prefer a relative humidity of 60% to 80%. Insects also need moisture, which some species obtain by converting foodstuffs within their bodies.

As with mould, infestations can largely be prevented through environmental control. While mould and insects can thrive in various conditions, most prefer high humidities. Environmental management should, of course, be but one facet of an integrated control programme. Proper sanitation, housing, monitoring and inspection of the facility and collections can all play crucial and interdependent roles.

There has been considerable advancement in using non-chemical treatment to control insects, as part of an IPM approach. Many successful uses of alternative means – such as deep-freezing, modified atmospheres and thermal control – have been reported effective and safe (Brokerhof 1989, Florian 1997 and Wellheiser 1992).

c) Animals

The most common animal pests encountered are rodents (mice, rats and squirrels), small mammals (bats, raccoons, porcupines), and birds. These pests are cosmopolitan, and can be a threat in both urban and rural locations. Some can damage building structures. Once inside, they damage collections by eating them, shredding them for nesting material and staining them with wastes. Nests and dead animals also attract insects, which can spread to the collections. These animals may also carry diseases that are transmitted though contact with nest materials, wastes and parasites.

Mice, in particular, tend to be a persistent seasonal problem in Canada. They often enter buildings in the fall to overwinter. As with other pest problems, it is critical to recognize the signs of such infestation, such as droppings and nests of shredded material, because the mice may not show themselves.

The most effective animal control programmes focus on prevention by exclusion. Preventive measures should be implemented in the facility as well as on the exterior and around the perimeter. Measures to consider include control of sanitation, sealing of entry points, screening of louvres and vents, installation of door sweepers, and removal of exterior plantings. Trapping, combined with exclusion methods, can be an effective means of eliminating a problem. If required, a professional pest control firm should be contacted. Local humane societies can provide information on live trapping. Chemical control should be employed only by trained personnel. Some chemicals, such as single-dose rodenticides, are restricted to licensed pest control operators. Aside from direct hazards from toxic chemicals, poisoned animals frequently die in inaccessible locations, and then attract insects that threaten collections.

3.5 Disaster Prevention Guidelines

The following guidelines are intended to aid the Disaster Planning Committee in minimizing existing hazards and mitigating potential hazards. All those charged with responsibilities for the care of the facility and its collections will recognize these as the common sense tenets of good management.

3.5.1 Environmental Management

Recently, significant changes to established thinking on environmental guidelines have been suggested by the scientific community. These continue to be debated. Reports on these new concepts (and the resultant dialogues) are available in the literature *(see References)*. This section outlines the basic issues associated with environmental management and thus is not intended to be a comprehensive discussion.

Experience and research have demonstrated that appropriate environmental management can significantly contribute to the long-term preservation of collections and records. Environmental control can also play an important role in minimizing the effects of disasters, principally those involving water, where reduction of temperature and relative humidity can help to prevent or reduce the growth of mould.

Recent years have seen extensive work done on the development of models for predicting the deterioration of various materials, such as paper, photographic materials and magnetic tape. In addition, new approaches were investigated where practical climate control took precedence over perfect climate control. As a result, a number of new approaches can be used to consider and assess environmental control. These include the well-known Isoperm Method, which quantifies the effect of temperature and relative humidity (RH) on the life expectancy of paper-based collections (Sebera 1994) and the newer Time Weighted Preservation Index (TWPI) that measures how temperature and RH changes affect the preservation quality of storage environments (Reilly, Nishimura and Zinn, 1995).

As a result of this and work at the Canadian Conservation Institute (CCI), the Conservation Analytical Laboratory (CAL) of the Smithsonian Institution and elsewhere, there has been a trend overall towards acceptance of broader acceptable limits for temperature and relative humidity across the seasons while continuing to limit extremes:

- For collections dominated by rigid organic materials (wood and paint)...overall, high risk begins outside the range of 25%-75% RH ... If tight control sacrifices long-term reliability of the 25%-75% limits...I believe it is counter-productive to the total well-being of most collections. (Michalski 1993, 628)

- Conservation research scientists at CCI have shifted from defining a single, simplistic standard to identifying degrees of correctness or, more precisely, degrees of incorrectness. (Michalski 1994, 6)

- ...There can be as much as plus or minus 15 percent fluctuation in relative humidity and as much as 10 degrees Celsius (50°F) difference in temperature. Within that range ...'Mona Lisa' or an installation of Jeff Koons' vacuum cleaners may be safely stored or placed on exhibit... (Smithsonian Institution cited by Druzik and Banks 1995, 1)

Past guidelines provided very narrow RH and temperature ranges, such as 50% ±2% RH and 21°C ±1°C (70°F ±2°F). Often these ranges have been impossible to achieve owing to equipment limitations and climate. In addition, control may have been unreliable and/or attained only at great cost. Research continues on these new findings and recommendations. However, this loosening of recommendations for RH and temperature has immediate and clear economic advantages – lower energy, capital, building renovation and system maintenance and replacement costs.

An international standard for archive and library collections is in development (see *ISO/DIS 11799 Information and Documentation – Document Storage Requirements for Archive and Library Materials*). There is as yet no Canadian or Americian standard. However, the National Information Standards Organization (NISO) has published a technical report on environmental guidelines for the storage of paper records (Wilson 1995), which acknowledges much of the new thinking of recent years. ISO (International Organization for Standardization) and ANSI (American

National Standards Institute) have published standards on the storage of photographic materials. Standards on the life expectancy of compact discs and the storage of polyester base magnetic tape have recently been issued by ANSI in conjunction with ISO and NAPM (National Association of Photographic Manufacturers) – now PIMA (Photographic and Imaging Manufacturers Association).

Overall, organizations are coming to recognize that they may have varied collection storage needs and requirements, based on factors such as retention periods, type of use, frequency of use, etc. Organizations that retain collections in the short term for information purposes only probably do not require special facilities. On the other hand, if indefinite storage is required, special facilities would be necessary.

a) Evaluation of Existing Environmental Control

Any evaluation of environmental control must consider the nature and needs of the collections (material type, value, retention goals, use patterns). Such analysis must also include the needs and comfort range of staff and users in no-, low- and high-use areas, as the environment most suitable for collections is not necessarily suitable for people. Local climate will also be a critical determining factor. Building age, design and construction should be considered, and of course, cost.

> The fundamental issue of climate control comes down to system costs versus risk to collections and buildings (Weintraub 1996, 23).

The environment – including temperature, relative humidity, light and pollution – should be carefully studied and monitored in order to clearly identify problems. Regular inspection and maintenance of the heating, ventilation and air conditioning (HVAC) system and lighting controls, as well as good housekeeping practices, are essential to any environmental management programme.

b) Temperature and Relative Humidity

> Inherent chemical deterioration in organic materials is an ever-present threat because it is the material itself that undergoes the reactions of decay – neither external pollutants nor exposure to light are required...Some level of thermal energy and some moisture are always present, and these are the environmental factors that govern the rate of chemical deterioration (Reilly, Nishimura and Zinn 1995, 2).

Temperature and relative humidity play the crucial roles in the chemical processes of deterioration of collection materials. The damage done by hydrolysis, oxidation and photochemical action is accelerated by both factors. Higher temperatures and humidities are damaging to hygroscopic materials such as paper, parchment, leather and textiles, as well as to hydrophobic materials like magnetic tape. Heat in combination with moisture also encourages corrosion, growth of mould and infestations of insects. Excessive dryness causes embrittlement as well as yellowing and shrinkage in paper, paint layers, adhesives and photographic and film emulsions.

Cooler and drier (to a point) conditions are recognized as better for collections. An organization with mixed collections should consider either providing different environments for different groups of materials or determining a balance between the needs of the different materials (and those of the staff and users). Specialized microclimates for materials with unique requirements are not feasible for all libraries and archives, because the majority of collections are housed in common storage areas.

For the purposes of disaster planning, the important environmental management issue is to control temperature and relative humidity after a flood or a fire. Implementation of effective measures will help minimize damage, and prevent or reduce the growth of mould (*see 3.4.8a*).

c) Light

Deterioration can result from the action of visible light, as well as ultraviolet (UV) and infrared radiation (IR). This action, basically photochemical in nature, results in bleaching or darkening, fading, discolouration, embrittlement, deformation and insolubility. This process of deterioration is essentially irreversible. When combined with adverse relative humidity and pollution, it is accelerated.

> The deteriorating effects of light... depend on the intensity of the radiation; the time of exposure; the spectral characteristics of the radiation; and the intrinsic capacity of individual materials to absorb and be affected by the radiant energy...(Stowlow 1966, 302).

Damage is a function of total exposure to light – low-intensity light over a prolonged period can cause as much damage as high-intensity light over a short period.

UV radiation is especially harmful to materials found in archives, libraries and record centres. The principal sources of UV are fluorescent lights and sunlight. Light from these sources should be filtered, or low UV-output fluorescent lights can be used. Curtains, blinds and other window covers can also reduce UV by decreasing the overall level of sunlight.

Visible light from other lighting sources, though less damaging, still endangers collection materials. Dimmer switches, motion- or noise-activated lights and timer lights can help reduce overall light exposure.

Heat generated by long exposure to IR causes damage such as embrittlement, desiccation and differential expansion. Produced mainly by tungsten spot lamps and sunlight, infrared light can be reduced by using filters or by positioning lamps so that their light first reflects off a ceiling or wall.

Light levels can be measured using a variety of monitoring equipment. The Canadian Conservation Institute has developed a light damage slide rule (CCI 1988a). This device correlates light intensity, amount of exposure and degree of fading.

d) Pollution

Atmospheric pollution is extremely hazardous to all collections. Pollutants can bleach, darken, discolour, embrittle and decay materials such as paper, film, leather, textiles and adhesives. Sulphur dioxide, for example, is absorbed from the air by paper, reacts with moisture and is catalyzed by copper and iron impurities to form sulphurous and sulphuric acid.

Sources of both gaseous and particulate pollution, outdoor and indoor, are countless. Industrial pollution in combination with gasoline exhaust and other pollution generates a number of harmful gases. Other damaging pollutants include nitrogen oxides, hydrogen sulphide and ozone. Particulate pollution (abrasive aerosols) absorbs and carries gaseous pollution to exposed collection materials, thus encouraging chemical reactivity as well as mechanical deterioration. Dust and dirt are also hygroscopic, thus promoting the damp conditions necessary for mould growth.

A central air conditioning system with specialized purifiers and filters is the most common approach to effective control of pollution, and that of temperature and relative humidity. Window air conditioners, portable humidifiers and dehumidifiers can also be used but are generally less effective. Electrostatic air purifiers and precipitators must be avoided because these units produce ozone, which accelerates the deterioration of many collection materials including film, paper and leather.

Pollution levels can be monitored with gas detectors and test strips. Specialist companies can be contracted to analyze particulate and gaseous pollution levels.

In the event of fire, air handling systems can be used to limit and handling the spread of smoke and soot-laden air, and thus minimize the damage to collections *(see 4.8).*

Refer to standards on ventilation and indoor air quality such as those published by the American Society of Heating, Refrigerating, and Air Conditioning Engineers (ASHRAE). Note: New temperature and relative humidity guidelines are soon to be issued by ASHRAE.

e) Summary of Environmental Management Guidelines

The following tables of environmental guidelines are examples from the literature that acknowledge developments of recent years. As noted in 3.5.1, environmental management for collections and records continues to be debated, and readers should always seek the most current standards and practices.

Criteria for the Conservation Environment (Lull with the assistance of Banks 1995, 14)

RELATIVE HUMIDITY (RH)

Paper:	30-40% RH*
Film:	Generally 30% RH, but can vary with material**

TEMPERATURE

Paper:	16°C-18°C (60°F-65°F) for storage
	18°C-21°C (65°F-70°F) for occupied areas
Film:	Same, or lower if possible**

Temperature goals should generally be subordinated to humidity goals and stability.

LIGHT

Storage:	10-50 Lux (1-5 Footcandles)
Display:	50-150 Lux (5-15 Footcandles), the lower the better
Reading and work areas:	300-500 Lux (30-60 foot-candles), but only short exposures for paper and other light-sensitive materials
UV content:	< 75 microwatts per lumen, < 2-4% UV
IR content:	Limit with light levels or dichroic reflector lamps

PARTICULATE CONTAMINATION

Remove problem particulates; where soot is present, filter to remove better than 50% of 0.5 micron particles.

GASEOUS CONTAMINATION

	$\mu g/m^3$	ppb
Sulfur Dioxide (SO_2):	1-10	0.38-3.8
Oxides of Nitrogen (NO_x):	5-10	2.5-5.0
Ozone (O_3):	2-25	1.0-12.8

*See **Sebera, Donald K.** 1989. A Graphical Representation of the Relationship of Environmental Conditions to the Permanence of Hygroscopic Materials and Composites. In *Proceedings of Conservation in Archives, International Symposium (Ottawa, May 10-12, 1988)*. Paris: International Council on Archives. 51-75

See **ANSI PH1.43-1985. 1985. *American National Standard for Photography (Film) — Storage of Processed Safety Film*. New York, N.Y.: American National Standards Institute.

Reilly, James M. 1993. *IPI Storage Guide for Acetate Film*. Rochester, N.Y.: Image Permanence Institute, Rochester Institute of Technology.

For paper-based records, Wilson suggests a broader range of RH than Lull and Banks for all types of storage areas, and varied temperatures for different types of storage areas:

Suggested Values for Temperature and Relative Humidity
(Wilson 1995, 2)

	Temperature	Relative Humidity
Combined stack and user areas	70°F maximum[a] (21°C) maximum[a]	30-50%[b]
Stack areas, minimal human entry	65°F maximum[a] (18°C) maximum[a]	30-50%[b]
Optimum preservation stacks	35°-65°F (2°-18°C)[c]	30-50%[b]
Maximum daily fluctuation	±2°F (±1°C)	±3%
Maximum monthly drift	±3°F (±2°C)	±3%

[a] These values assume that 70°F (21°C) is about the maximum comfort temperature for reading, and 65°F (18°C) the minimum for light physical activity. Each institution can make its own choice.
[b] A specific value of relative humidity within this range should be maintained ±3%, depending on the climatic conditions in the local geographic area, or facility limitations.
[c] A specific temperature within this range should be maintained ±2°F (±1°C). The specific temperature chosen depends on how much an organization is willing to invest in order to achieve a given life expectancy for its records.

Suggested Guidelines for Exposure to Light
(Wilson 1995, 2)

· Filter light from windows, skylights and fluorescent lamps to eliminate wavelengths below 415 nm. However, if incandescent lamps are the sole source of light, the necessity for filters is questionable. Also use appropriate filters on user reading station lights to remove wavelengths below 415 nm.

· Where the ultimate in lighting control is impossible, the first choice is incandescent lamps with low wattage. The second choice is fluorescent lamps with the smallest UV output available.

· Avoid sunlight through window glass and unfiltered skylight due to substantial UV component.

Suggested Maximum Levels of Gaseous Pollution
(Wilson 1995, 3)

	Parts/billion/volume
Sulphur dioxide	5-10
Nitrogen dioxide	5-10
Ozone	5-10

Suggested Guidelines for Removing Particulates by Air Filtration
(Wilson 1995, 3)

	Level of Filtration (%)
Combined stack and user areas	60-80
Stacks areas, users excluded except for retrieval	90-95
Optimum preservation areas	> 95

The National Media Lab has summarized the recommended conditions from various sources (1982-1996) for the storage of magnetic tape:

Recommended Storage Conditions for Magnetic Tape
(National Media Lab 1997)

Agency/Researcher	Year	Temperature	Relative Humidity
Cuddihy	1982	65°F ± 3°F (18°C ± 2°C)	40% ± 5%
SMPTE (RP-103)	1982	70°F ± 4°F (21°C ± 2°C)	50% ± 20%
NARA	1990	65°F ± 3°F (18°C ± 2°C)	40% ± 5%
SMPTE (RP-103)	1995		
Operating[1]		63°F to 77°F (17°C to 25°C)	30% to 70% ± 5%
Storage <10 years[1] (medium term)		59°F to 73°F ± 4°F (15°C to 23°C ± 2°C)	40% to 55% ± 5%
Storage >10 years (long term)		63°F ± 4°F (17°C ± 2°C)	30% ± 5%
ANSI/AES	1996		
Medium Term		73°F (max) ± 4°F[3] (23°C [max] ± 2°C)	20% to 50% ± 10%[4]
Extended Term[2]		68°F (max) ± 4°F[3] (20°C [max] ± 2°C)	20% to 30% ± 5%[4]
		-or-	-or-
		59°F (max) ± 4°F[3] (15°C [max] ± 2°C)	20% to 40% ± 5%[4]
		-or-	-or-
		50°F (max) ± 4°F[3] (10°C [max] ± 2°C)	20% to 50% ± 5%[4]

[1] For operating or storage less than 10 years, the center point for temperature and humidity can be selected anywhere within the allowable range, but the variation cannot exceed the allowable range.

[2] For ANSI/AES Extended-Term Storage, a lower storage temperature can compensate for a higher humidity to provide the same life expectancy and a wider relative humidity range can be tolerated. For this reason, several relative humidity-temperature combinations can be used for an extended-tem storage environment as specified above.

[3] Storage of tape below 8°C (46°F) may cause lubricant separation from the tape binder. The manufacturer should be consulted to determine if this is a potential problem.

[4] The moisture content of the tape to be stored shall not be greater than the tape in moisture equilibrium with these relative humidities.

See also *ANSI/PIMA IT9.23-1998. American National Standard for Imaging Materials - Polyester Base Magnetic Tape – Storage.*

3.5.2 Housekeeping

In addition to an environmental management system, a comprehensive housekeeping programme should be established. Its benefits extend far beyond the need for cleanliness and order, contributing significantly to preventing hazards such as fire from combustible trash. Good housekeeping maintains a comfortable environment for staff and users and extends the lifespan of collections materials. It also serves a second purpose: to eliminate conditions and circumstances likely to result in a disaster.

Housekeeping measures that should be considered include approved dust control methods; cleaning of carpets, drapery, etc.; restrictions on smoking; and methods for use and storage of janitorial supplies, paints, chemicals and solvents. Unless the facility has a sophisticated zoned environmental management system, the dust, smoke and fumes created in one area will be circulated throughout the building. Where collections contain significant amounts of brittle paper, much of the dust will be paper.

Regular inspection routines should be established. Some should take place daily, some weekly or monthly, and some annually. Each organization must determine what routine is required based on the hazards identified in the survey, size of staff, etc. Ideally, staff would be assigned responsibility for inspection and then undertake the correction of deficiencies.

See Higgins 1997 for a discussion of housekeeping practices.

a) Housekeeping Checklist

While not an exhaustive list, the guidelines below cover areas of good housekeeping that relate to disaster prevention and preparation. Many of these guidelines are simply common sense. A clean, tidy and orderly environment can significantly aid the control and containment of a disaster.

· Keep exits, aisles, corridors, and stairwells unobstructed.

· Ensure that internal fire-rated doors are kept closed.

· Ensure that emergency equipment (e.g., fire hoses, fire extinguishers, first-aid kits and rescue equipment) is accessible and in good working order. Do not place furniture, display cases, coat racks, etc. in front of firehose cabinets, fire extinguishers, or manual box fire alarm systems.

· Never store collection materials directly on the floor.

· Avoid leaving any materials, especially original documents, out on desks or on tables overnight. Close drawers of storage cabinets when not in use.

· Do not use the stacks as a storage place for empty boxes, supplies, etc.

· Maintain a stable environment in areas where collections are stored, housed and exhibited (*see 3.5.1*).

· Store cellulose nitrate-based film apart from the rest of the collection and other cellulose nitrate-based film. Be aware of standards for its safe handling, use, storage and destruction (*see 3.3.1e*).

· Ensure that books and boxes are not shelved too tightly. This measure not only prevents damage to the bindings or containers when they are retrieved, but also ensures that in case of flooding, water will not cause the books to swell to the point where they burst from their shelving units. This applies to a lesser degree to other materials.

· Shelve materials a short distance back from the edge. This precaution prevents wear of the materials and inhibits the vertical spread of fire between shelves (*see also 4.11.1*).

· Ensure that staff maintain appropriate housekeeping standards and procedures (such as for dust control), and are provided with appropriate supplies and equipment.

· Use waste-paper baskets made from non-combustible materials and empty them regularly. Have separate safety receptacles for flammable materials such as rags soaked in solvent, and establish proper procedures for handling and disposal (*see also 3.3.1e*).

3.5.3 Infestation

Regular programmes of building and collections maintenance, inspection and good housekeeping are necessary to minimize the growth of mould and the attraction of insects and rodents, and to provide early warnings of any infestations. The following guidelines summarize measures to prevent infestation (*see 3.4.8*).

a) Facility Checklist

· Maintain relative humidity below 55%.

· Maintain temperature of less than 21°C (70°F).

· Install a multi-stage particulate filtration system.

· Maintain adequate air circulation.

· Implement a heating, ventilation and air conditioning (HVAC) system maintenance programme (inspection and cleaning of heat-exchange coils, drip pan and ductwork, filter changes).

· Implement a building maintenance programme to minimize the risk of dampness and water leakage.

· Implement interior and exterior exclusion and non-attractant measures (door sweepers, non-organic mulches).

· Modify building facilities for efficient cleaning (smooth floors, space allowances under and behind equipment).

· Maintain proper sanitation (general cleaning, garbage disposal).

· Establish internal detection programme (insect trapping, routine inspections).

b) Staff Checklist

· Ensure staff understand both the health risks to themselves and the potential damage to the collections.

· Get outside professional help when necessary (mycologist, pest control service).

· Establish evaluation and documentation procedures for your prevention programme.

· Train staff in pest identification, safe handling of mouldy, insect-infested materials, etc.

· Communicate your prevention programme across the organization.

· Be prepared to respond if prevention is unsuccessful.

c) Collections Checklist

· Examine incoming materials (acquisitions or loans) at the point of entry for signs of dormant or active infestation.

· Avoid storage in potentially damp areas or where water accidents may occur.

· House collections in protective storage enclosures (envelopes, folders, boxes).

· Routinely clean collections and shelving using vacuums with High Efficiency Particulate Air (HEPA) filters.

· Routinely inspect storage, use and exhibition areas.

· Quarantine collections where necessary in clean isolation areas with relative humidity below 45%.

· Avoid collections overcrowding to reduce potential for damage (handling, spread of fire).

3.5.4 Staff Practices

Staff practices (smoking, kitchen use, etc.) should be surveyed in order to identify potential hazards, and to establish and enforce rules for smoking and food and beverage consumption, safe equipment operation safe egress routes, and for unauthorized access to work areas, storage facilities, etc. *(see also 3.5.6).*

Staff Practices Checklist

· Restrict smoking to a designated area. Many workplaces have declared their premises smoke-free. Check local bylaws and enforce them.

· Ensure that staff do not leave fire doors open for air circulation or ease of movement.

· Ensure that staff do not block corridors, stairwells with equipment, etc.

· Restrict eating and drinking to a designated area, not where collections are used, stored or exhibited.

· Never let water run unattended.

· Ensure that electrical appliances such as tacking irons, hot plates and kettles are placed on noncombustible surfaces, well maintained and operated at a safe distance from combustible materials. They should be listed by an independent testing laboratory.

· Unplug electrical workshop machinery when not in use.

· Establish procedures for the safe operation of all electrical appliances and equipment.

· Establish day's-end closing routines such as turning off equipment, locking doors, etc.

· Provide support and ongoing training for a safe workplace environment.

3.5.5 Facility Maintenance

Facility maintenance should be integrated into the overall management of the organization. Improvements in maintenance can help to prevent disasters.

Inspection routines appropriate to the facility's environmental management systems and the security, fire detection and suppression systems should be established. Serious deficiencies should be corrected immediately.

The following checklists can aid in formulating the disaster plan, as well as identify needed facility maintenance routines. All inspection and service measures should be thoroughly documented.

a) Building Structure Checklist

· Inspect the roof for missing shingles, damage and leaks (more often in the case of flat roofs).

· Inspect windows and skylights for damage and leaks.

· Inspect the foundation for cracks, leaks and any signs of dampness.

· Make sure the eavestroughs are functional and free of debris.

· Ensure that floor plans and structural drawings are up-to-date and accessible. Store duplicates offsite.

b) Essential Services Checklist

· Perform regular maintenance and inspection for plumbing (e.g., locate and check all drains), and environmental management, security, electrical, fire detection and fire extinguishing systems.

· Ensure that plans and mechanical drawings are up-to-date and accessible. Store duplicates offsite.

· Have up-to-date manuals for service installations, including master switches.

· Arrange for emergency back-ups for essential services.

· Ensure that water pressure is adequate for fighting fires.

c) Fire and Water Damage Prevention Checklist

· Have an electrician regularly check the distribution system (wiring, boxes, lighting fixtures, receptacles switches, etc.) heating and other equipment, and appliances.

· Ensure that the transformers in fluorescent light ballasts are thermally protected.

· Do not allow open flames unless precautionary measures have been taken.

· Use non-flammable paints whenever possible. Oil-based paints on drywall do not increase fire spread substantially; however, oil-based varnishes are more hazardous as they are usually applied to large combustible surfaces such as wood floors. Fire-retardant paints are often recommended for combustible materials such as plywood display cases (Baril 1997). Ensure that freshly painted areas are well ventilated.

- Examine the building in consultation with the local fire department and your insurance company's engineers, to determine all construction and furnishing materials and their fire rating.

- Assess the safety of heating, air conditioning and ventilation systems.

- Ensure that ducts are made of galvanized metal and have automatic fire dampers. Clean ducts and vents at least every five years.

- Avoid using polystyrene or polyurethane foam insulation, due to their flammability and emission of large quantities of smoke (see Spafford and Graham 1993a,b). Burning polyurethane foam also emits toxic fumes.

- Avoid/replace interior finish materials with high flame spread rates. Flame can spread in low density fiberboard and acoustic ceiling tile as fast as people can run. (Bush and McDaniel 1997, 9.95).

- Use non-flammable carpeting.

- Use non-flammable fabrics such as fibreglass where possible. Have other fabrics treated to reduce their flammability where possible. Synthetic fabrics vary greatly in their flammability; many melt when hot and form a molten plastic that can cause serious burns.

- Select the fire extinguishing agents appropriate to the type of burnable substances in given areas *(see also 4.6 and 4.7)*.

- Check the fire detection and extinguishing systems and equipment regularly.

- Check service pipes regularly and install flow/pressure alarms to warn of trouble.

- Install automatic shut-off sink taps.

- Install floor alarms in susceptible areas to indicate water leakage. Ideally, these alarms should be connected to a central alarm system *(see also 4.9)*.

- Monitor areas where pipes and windows may be subject to condensation.

d) Mould Checklist

- Do regular heating ventilation and air conditioning (HVAC) system maintenance, including regular inspection and cleaning of heat-exchange coils, drip pans and ductwork where mould can breed.

- Change high-efficiency air filters frequently to reduce dust.

- Maintain good air circulation, especially where HVAC humidity control is inadequate or non-existent. Fans, including "whole-house" fans that keep air moving through a building, can be very effective.

3.5.6 Facility Construction and Renovation

During construction and renovation, collections are subject to increased risk of loss. Many hazards can be predicted, and every effort should be made to anticipate dangerous circumstances so as to prevent damage.

Construction and Renovation Checklist

- Consult the local fire department at the outset of any construction or renovation project regarding specifications, firefighting plans, etc.

- Include in any construction or renovation contracts specifications that take into account the unique protection requirements of the facility and collections, such as from fire, dust, dirt, water and mechanical damage.

- Assign a staff representative to liaise with the contractor and ensure that protective measures and precautions are implemented and maintained.

- Ensure that the contractor understands and meets your requirements for strict safety compliance, i.e., welding operations.

- Ensure that fire detection and suppression systems, security systems and water alarms remain operational.

- Review existing evacuation and other emergency procedures, and amend as necessary.

- Ensure that emergency supplies are stocked and accessible.

- Move, wrap or otherwise protect collections with barriers as necessary.

- Implement and maintain cleaning routines regularly throughout and after the project.

- Communicate all changes to normal operating practices and procedures to staff. Keep everyone involved up-to-date with revised schedules etc.

- Be prepared to respond if precautions fail or an accident occurs.

(Based on Motylewski 1994, 5-7)

3.5.7 Storage

Good storage practices are a cornerstone of collection preservation. As well, proper storage methods can reduce hazards that could lead to fire and water damage. The following section covers storage as it relates to disaster prevention, rather than storage as a comprehensive topic.

Well-planned and well-designed storage is critical. Books stored off the floors or away from overhead pipes are at less risk from water damage. Collections stored near windows can face a triple threat from light deterioration and water damage as well as loss from theft. Relocating or reorganizing a storage area can be a relatively low-cost preventive measure.

a) Storage Location Checklist

· Avoid basement storage. When flooding occurs, water seeks the lowest level. Basements often have uninsulated outside walls, which leads to problems with dampness and eventually mould.

· Avoid attic storage. Attics are also often uninsulated, prone to leaks and subject to infestations.

· Avoid storage near or below service pipes.

· Separate storage areas from washrooms, darkrooms, labs, kitchens and workshop areas.

· Storage areas should never be next to the physical plant operations due to the risk of fire.

· If basement storage is unavoidable, use it for collections that the organization considers less valuable.

· Store more valuable collections on main and upper floors.

b) Collection Storage Checklist

· Never store collections directly on the floor, even temporarily.

· Store collections at least 15 cm (6") above the floor.

· Store collections on the top shelf of hooded shelving units only.

· Place more valuable, vulnerable or irreplaceable collections on lower shelves but not the bottom shelves. For example, photographic media, which are susceptible to heat, could be housed on lower shelves. Disaster experts have noted that materials on top shelves are often burned beyond recovery, while those on bottom shelves are in good condition. Easily replaceable volumes could be placed on top shelves. (Buchanan 1988, 55)

· If shelving cannot be relocated away from water hazards, cover it with plastic sheeting. This should only be done as a temporary measure, and the collections monitored for conditions of elevated humidity.

· Install shelving at least 5 cm (2") away from inside walls and 30 cm (12") away from outside walls to avoid damage from condensation, burst pipes within walls, etc.

· Consider orienting files within boxes perpendicular to their shelves *(see 4.11.1)*.

· Avoid using carpet in storage areas. Carpets retain water, hamper drainage and hinder efforts to stabilize the relative humidity of the storage area after flooding.

c) Hazardous Supply Materials and Collections Storage Checklist

The following storage guidelines aid in preventing fire. They apply not only to employees within the organization, but also to outside contractors. If the work involves flammable materials and sources of heat, the fire risk will be greatly increased.

· Store flammable and combustible supply materials in a safe, cool place out of sunlight, inside fireproof containers and cabinets.

· Store hazardous supply materials such as gas cylinders, solvents and paints in accordance with safety regulations and standards.

· Provide training for staff in the correct handling, use, storage and disposal of hazardous supply materials according to applicable legislation *(see also 3.3.1e)*.

· Remove potential hazards such as live ammunition from the collections.

· Store hazardous supply materials in properly marked containers.

· Do not store large containers of hazardous supply materials on high shelves from which they may fall and break. "Shelf-lips" may be installed to help prevent materials from accidentally falling off.

· Keep all chemical and solvent containers closed, even during use, to minimize the escape of flammable and toxic vapours and dusts.

· Store and dispose of cellulose nitrate-based film according to applicable standards *(see 3.3.1e)* and fire regulations. CCI recommends either storing it at low temperature – 10°C (50°F) – and 30-40% RH or having it copied by an experienced firm and disposing of the original (Stewart and Tremain 1994, 39). Kodak recommends a vault temperature of 2°C (35°F) and RH of between 20-30% for long-term storage, and a vault temperature of no greater than 21°C (70°F) and RH below 50% for extended-term storage (Eastman Kodak Co. 1995, 3). This film can be retained, however, if proper conditions for its handling, use and storage are complied with (see Eastman Kodak 1995). Failing the means to do this, some sources recommend immediate copying and storage of the original outside the facility.

· Enclose storage areas with fire separations (any wall, ceiling or floor that effectively retards the passage of heat and smoke).

· Keep all fire-rated doors closed.

d) Shelving and Cabinets

Steel shelving and cabinets coated with a baked enamel finish are generally recommended for library and archival storage. However, it has been suggested that organizations consider the use of sturdy wooden shelving due to its stability until consumed by fire – "...metal shelves buckle and eject their contents at temperatures of 400°C-500°C [752°F-932°F], which can be reached in minutes" (Society of Archivists - Scottish Region 1996, 3.5).

The type of wood used for storage is a consideration, as some woods offgas more then others. Oak, for example is not generally recommended. If wooden shelving is used, a coating should be applied as a barrier to the off-gassing of acid and other compounds from wood fibres, as well as any adhesives/binders present. Options include acrylic latex paint, acrylic urethane latex paint and some acrylic urethane clear varnishes (Tétreault 1998). Use of a semi-gloss or gloss finish will result in less wear and tear on books or containers. Some sources suggest lining shelves with polyester film as an added barrier. Any coating applied should be allowed to offgas and cure completely before being used for collections storage. *(See also 4.3.3 and 4.11.1)*

See Tétrault (1999) for technical information on display and storage coatings.

e) Vital Records Storage

Some larger organizations store vital records offsite in separate fire-resistive buildings. Equipment and furnishings for such buildings should also be fire-resistant. These facilities have environmental controls (temperature, relative humidity, lighting and ventilation), and appropriate security, fire detection and suppression systems.

Failing the means to provide a separate building for vital records, other offsite locations could include: a commercial storage facility, a branch company office or a cooperative arrangement (jointly owned and operated between other similar organizations).

While governments operate remote facilities, and some large corporations utilize branch plants for remote storage, most smaller organizations find that privately owned commercial record centres provide the most cost-efficient method of protecting and providing records services.

Commercial Records Storage Checklist

· What types of storage are provided: bulk and general storage, privately operated records storage rooms, special vaults for microfilm and magnetic tape, and private vaults built to client specifications?

· Does it provide offsite centres for emergency operations?

· Are the environmental storage conditions appropriate?

· Are the security conditions adequate? Personnel must be qualified and have security clearance, and access to the storage area must be tightly controlled.

· What is the turnaround time for records retrieval? Does it offer service guarantees?

· Are specialists available for consultation?

· How long has the company been in business? Is it financially stable?

· Does the company have a disaster plan? In the event of disaster, a record storage centre requires not only an offsite storage vault, but also an offsite computer facility that is fully compatible with its own.

· Is the facility located close enough for reasonable convenience, but far enough away to escape the effects of a large-scale disaster?

3.5.8   Security of Collections

Security in the broadest sense includes all measures to prevent disaster and protect a facility and its staff, users, collections, information systems, etc. These measures would include theft and vandalism deterrence, staff education and training for problem patrons, staff safety programmes, security policies, security software, controlled access to work stations and telecommunications devices, control of the environment, protective storage, collections care and handling practices, insurance, and disaster prevention and preparation.

Security is discussed here only in brief and focuses on the deterrence of specific crimes: arson and theft. Arson is the leading cause of fire in libraries in the United States *(see 3.4.1 and 3.5.8a)*, and theft and vandalism of collections have become over the years an increasingly serious and costly issue. Security as it relates to construction and renovation projects is covered in sections 3.3.1c and 3.5.6. Security of records, data and information technology is addressed in section 3.5.9.

Most organizations have come to recognize that security is a basic responsibility, one that must be considered systematically as an integral component of managing the facility, personnel, collections and information. Appropriate security measures balance the need to safeguard collections and information with the need to make them accessible.

> The most effective security programme is the almost free byproduct of a well-planned and well-run institution (Paulhus 1983, 124).

The key to successful security for collections, records, data and information technology is access control. This control will aid in the prevention of loss and damage, and includes all the policies, procedures and systems used to identify and monitor people, collections, information, equipment, materials and vehicles entering and leaving the facility. The security programme must cover all operations: routine, during renovations, and in case of emergencies or disasters. See Kelly (1999) for technical information on security planing and practices. *(See also 6.6.2.e)*

An effective security programme must take into account a wide range of factors, their interrelationships and their impact on security. Many planning sources emphasize that damaged collections tend to stimulate vandalism and therefore such items should be promptly repaired.

Security Checklist

Major categories to be considered include:

- location of facility
- neighbourhood characteristics
- organizational characteristics
- facility design
- perimeter control
- entry and exit control
- interior facility control
- building systems control
- computer system and network control and back-up
- management of collections and information
- management of supplies, equipment and other contents
- management of personnel

a) Arson

"Arson accounted for 71 percent of the average annual property loss due to fires in U.S. libraries during the years 1980 through 1993..." (NFIRS and NFPA survey cited in Bush and McDanie 1997, 9.92). It may be impossible to prevent all incidents of arson; however, a security programme must still include measures to reduce or discourage deliberately set fires. A visible security presence is essential.

Arson Checklist

- trained staff and established procedures for monitoring and response.
- a central guard station and patrols with monitored routes.

- surveillance throughout the facility at variable intervals.
- security mirrors and closed-circuit surveillance video cameras.
- thorough security and safety procedures upon opening and closing.
- adequate exterior lighting.
- locked windows and doors, as appropriate (emergency exit doors have panic hardware that allows exit but not entry).
- alarms on windows and doors, and perimeter motion detectors.
- contained or isolated library bookdrops, or none at all.
- smoke and fire detection, alarm and suppression systems *(see Chapter 4)*.

A microcomputer-based Arson Information Management System (AIMS) has been developed in the United States *(see Appendix 3.1 Sources of Information: Fire)*. This software is widely used in the U.S. for recording, sharing and tracking down incidents of arson.

b) Vandalism

Vandalism is the unpredictable and malicious or ignorant destruction of property. Personal gain is not necessarily a strong motivating factor as it is in theft. Spite, vengeance or simple thoughtlessness are often the reasons behind acts of vandalism. Documents may be destroyed or defaced because they deal with sensitive or controversial social, religious or political issues. People may seek to alter or destroy embarrassing or incriminating personal or organizational information in archives or record centres.

c) Theft

Theft is motivated by personal gain and may take many forms. Valuable items such as drawings and manuscripts may be stolen and resold for profit. Other materials, such as periodicals, disks and electronic data may be removed for studies or research at home. Materials may also be displaced or made unavailable to other users, as some people intentionally mis-shelve or conceal materials in the facility for their exclusive use. Increasingly, theft is non-professional in nature and occurs during normal operating hours. While distressful to consider, theft by staff does occur, and studies in the business community indicate it is occurring at an alarming rate.

Clearly, the total prevention of collections theft or vandalism in any organization is an unreasonable expectation. However, the implementation of realistic practices that are fully supported by management will yield positive results. It is also important to remember that laws regarding theft and vandalism vary according to jurisdiction; legal counsel should be sought when security policies are being formulated.

d) Staff Responsibility and Training

• Surveillance and Supervision

An organization in which responsive, caring and vigilant staff provide efficient service creates a positive impression and sets the tone for the user.

> ...Unreliable, untrained, or disgruntled staff can be a liability...by failing to enforce the ...[organization's] rules and regulations. This laxness creates an atmosphere conducive to theft and/or mutilation... (Trinkaus-Randall 1995, 26).

Responsibility for security rests to varying degrees with all staff, not only with security personnel. Users are most often exposed to non-security staff who are on the front line for safeguarding the collections. Observant staff can significantly enhance security, especially when established practices are consistently enforced. Enforcement is facilitated when responsibilities and procedures are clear, there is support from the top, and basic facility needs (such as clear sight lines) have been addressed.

• Awareness and Training

Priority should be given to developing and maintaining a comprehensive staff and user education programme. Staff training on security issues, policies and procedures should be mandatory. In addition to increasing the level of security awareness overall, such training will result in enhanced staff commitment.

On a day-to-day basis, public awareness and education is the responsibility of all staff who interact with users, visitors and contractors. Security measures for users may also be reinforced through instructional flyers, bookmarks or posters, or a media campaign that addresses a wider audience. Rules and regulations of the organization that contain statements on security should be clearly posted in public.

e) Theft Detection Systems

The introduction of electronic theft detection systems was a significant advance for library security. When a detection strip or tag concealed in the library materials is sensed at the check-out/exit desk, it activates an alarm and in some cases causes the exit gate to lock. These systems are generally available in two modes: the "circulating" system, in which the strips can be desensitized for borrowing purposes and the "bypass" system, in which materials to be borrowed are passed around the sensing gates.

These systems cannot eliminate loss, but they have been proven to substantially reduce loss by theft, both casual stealing and serious theft attempts. However, they should be considered in conjunction with other control measures in the facility, such as perimeter and intrusion alarms, locks, security patrols, and identification and key programmes.

f) Ownership Identification

Labelling, embossing, perforating, or stamping materials with a permanent mark identifying ownership is a standard procedure in most organizations for many collections and records. Not only can marking identify materials before they leave the premises, it makes resale of stolen material difficult and also identifies the rightful owner when such materials are recovered. On the other hand, some forms of permanent marking can disfigure, if not damage, the very items that they are meant to protect. The type and scope of identification depend on the nature and needs of the organization; however, conservation of the collection materials should always be a consideration. A National Information Standards Organization (NISO) standard, *Adhesives Used to Affix Labels to Library Materials*, is currently in preparation.

3.5.9 Security of Electronic Records, Data and Information Technology

Recent studies in the U.S. covering federal government and private sector computer systems concluded "that computer crime is on the rise, current security procedures and policies are deficient, computer users are inadequately educated and that the majority of attacks go unreported" (Vouglas 1996, 1).

Many situations can limit or prevent the use of electronic records and data, and the ability of information technology (IT) to deliver services. These can range from disasters such as fires and earthquakes to accidents during renovations such as severing a communications cable. The impact can also result from a disaster nearby. For example, a 1980 train derailment in Mississauga (near Toronto) forced a large data centre to close for a week.

The three primary objectives of a broad-based information security plan are:

1. To secure electronic records, data and computer programmes against unauthorized or inappropriate use, alteration, copying, disclosure or destruction.

2. To ensure the integrity, completeness and authenticity of electronic records and data.

3. To ensure that critical electronic records, data and IT resources are reliably and continuously available.

The first two objectives relate largely to access control and need to be specifically addressed by an IT security plan. The third objective should be addressed by establishing a comprehensive disaster plan for records, data and IT disaster protection, response and recovery *(see 5.2.6, 5.8 and 9.4)*.

a) Information Technology (IT) Security Plan

Information technology can process a great volume of information very rapidly and efficiently...When an accident disables a computer, it is usually not possible to substitute human labour, and often difficult to access the information quickly (Ontario Management Board of Cabinet 1991, 7-3-10).

The rationale for an IT security plan includes the following:

· Records and data such as the on-line catalogue and accounts receivable are means to manage the assets of the organization, while others themselves comprise the assets of the organization.

· Records, data and computer programmes facilitate critical operations such as acquisitions, cataloguing and on-line searching.

· Some information is confidential (such as personnel and financial records) or proprietary. The Canada Health Act and the Ontario Freedom of Information and Protection of Privacy Act are examples of laws that require confidentiality of certain information.

· Invalid, illegitimate or erroneous records or data can cause delays or failure of operations and services that cannot be readily accomplished by other means.

A comprehensive discussion of an IT security plan to protect records, data and computer programmes is beyond the scope of this publication. However, the following actions are basic to this protection:

IT Security Checklist

· Identify information that requires confidentiality protection, and establish rules of conduct for personnel who handle such information.

· Establish and document precautions for collecting, processing, communicating, disseminating, storing and disposing of data.

· Determine access requirements and establish controls to authorize user access; limit the type of access (creating, reading, changing or deleting data), limit the conditions of access (time of day, specific terminals, etc.), identify users attempting to access data, allow only authorized access, and document denied accesses.

· Restrict physical access to workstations, storage media, etc.

· Systematically test computer programmes and systems.

· Establish and maintain "change controls" to maintain the integrity of data and processes when the IT environment (hardware, network, programmes, etc.) is modified.

Chapter 4

4.0　Disaster Protection Planning

The preceding chapter discussed the means for identifying the hazards, risks, and disasters that could threaten archives, libraries or record centres. This phase of planning outlines the measures and associated equipment needed to protect human life and property, and to minimize the effects of a disaster. The primary focus is on fire protection including detection, alarm and suppression systems.

> A balance between prevention and protection is the key to a sound defense against fire...Effective fire prevention requires motivation and a genuine belief that fire can happen anytime to anyone (Baril 1997, 1).

This chapter covers fire detection, alarm and suppression, water detection, data and systems protection, protective storage and the all-important issue of trained staff. These measures are intended to provide protection against fire, as well as mitigation of the effects of other disasters such as earthquakes, hurricanes and floods. This chapter does not cover facility design or renovation and their related construction and fire-resistant requirements. We leave these issues to the experts in these fields.

Adherence to fire and building code requirements during any construction, reconstruction, alteration, upgrading or renovation project is essential to protection *(See Canadian Commission on Building and Fire Codes and Canadian Standards Association in References and Appendix 3.1 Sources of Information: Fire, Standards)*. Readers should also refer to applicable provincial fire codes. Two sources in the professional literature of note are *Planning Academic and Research Library Buildings* (Metcalf 1986) and *Libraries and Archives: Design and Renovation with a Preservation Perspective* (Swartzburg, Bussey and Garretson 1991).

This chapter's descriptions of fire detection, alarm and signalling systems, and extinguishing and suppression systems are largely drawn from the National Fire Protection Association's (NFPA) *Fire Protection Handbook*, (18th edition, Arthur E. Cote ed., 1997). NFPA codes, standards, guides and recommended practices cover fire-related issues including control, equipment, construction, facilities and systems. Some are specific to the needs of archives, libraries and record centres, i.e., *NFPA 909-1997. Standard for the Protection of Cultural Resources Including Museums, Libraries, Places of Worship and Historic Properties, NFPA 232-1995. Standard for*

Protection of Records and *NFPA 232A-1995. Guide for Fire Protection for Archives and Record Centers.*

NFPA standards are often made law in Canada by their reference in national and provincial building codes. Readers should refer to appropriate NFPA, Underwriters Laboratory (UL) or Underwriters' Laboratories of Canada (ULC) standards.

4.1　The Purpose of Disaster Protection Planning

The purpose of disaster protection planning is to put in place measures to guard and shield human life and safety, and that of the facility, collections, systems and operations. Protective efforts will not entirely prevent fire, flood, etc.; however, effective measures can thwart their escalation and spread, as well as reduce damage.

At this point in the disaster planning timeline, the Disaster Planning Committee (DPC) should have identified the specific protection needs of the organization, based on the results of the hazards survey and the risk analysis *(see Chapter 3)*. Now the DPC must determine the appropriate means and resources to best meet those needs, and then plan for their implementation.

4.2　The Process for Disaster Protection Planning

The DPC may decide to form a subcommittee to investigate the various protection systems available. The subcommittee must carefully research the systems and measures available, and evaluate their suitability to the specific situation.

The process for disaster protection planning includes the activities described below:

Disaster Protection Planning: Process at a Glance

- Seek expert help.
- Determine protection objectives and priorities.
- Assess protection options and costs.
- Determine a protection strategy.
- Recommend the strategy and get approval to proceed.
- Implement the protection strategy.

4.2.1 Seek expert help

Due to the increasingly sophisticated nature of fire and computer protection systems, expert professional assistance should be sought. Fire and building code requirements will need to be met, and specialists in fire and systems protection should be involved at every stage of the process.

4.2.2 Determine protection objectives and priorities

The protection needs of the organization must be prioritized. The organization's objectives for protection must take into account human life and safety, the value of its collections, records and databases, and its obligations to provide continued service and access.

4.2.3 Assess protection options and costs

The DPC must assess options and costs for protection from fire and water damage, and power failure. The costs of protection will vary tremendously, depending on the needs, resources and circumstances of the organization. Options for protection systems, their installation or retrofit, may be readily affordable. For options that are prohibitively expensive, long-term funding plans must be made.

Fire protection per se is not optional: building and fire codes must be adhered to according to legislation. However, there are options to choose from in meeting the fire protection objectives of the organization.

The professional fire protection literature recommends a "systems" approach to fire safety whereby decision-tree analysis and other techniques establish the level of fire protection that should contain a fire within acceptable limits (see *NFPA 550-1995. Guide to the Firesafety Concepts Tree*). This approach recognizes that fire protection requires an integrated and balanced strategy, using different measures, features and systems that support one another and also perform in the event of the failure of any one.

4.2.4 Determine a protection strategy

Based on the protection objectives, priorities and the available resources, the DPC must determine a protection strategy that covers human life and safety, property and the continuity of operations. The strategy should include fire detection, alarms, communications, manual and automatic suppression systems, protective storage, protection of the computer systems and staff training.

4.2.5 Recommend the strategy and get approval to proceed

The DPC should submit its protection strategy for management approval. In the case of major facility and system deficiencies requiring large expenditures, a phased implementation may be necessary.

4.2.6 Implement the protection strategy

The approved protection strategy should be implemented as planned. The strategy may include the following:

- purchase and installation of new systems
- systems' retrofits
- security and storage improvements
- staff training

When major projects are undertaken, operational support strategies will need to be developed. These will include security, documentation and communications, and should provide for ongoing modifications.

4.3 Fire Protection Issues

The fire protection issues associated with archives, libraries and record centres are particular to their mandate for preservation and continued access to the collections, records and information. Bush and McDaniel (1997, 9.92) note that "library...collections include large quantities of combustible, highly valuable, often irreplaceable materials...their extraordinarily high fuel loads are more typical of warehouse occupancies." Thus, protection must consider not only fire control and loss prevention. The suppression system itself should not cause 'significant' harm to the collections and records being protected.

Collections and records are usually housed in dense storage situations. Some organizations house millions of items. Paper, cardboard and related paper-based materials are readily combustible, and magnetic media and their containers can be a concern when stored in large quantities. Polystyrene cases and reels pose a severe fire hazard; however, acetate and polyester-based tapes generally pose a hazard similar to that of paper (Goonan 1997, 3.276).

The degree and nature of public access in the organization also play critical roles. Large stack areas where there are no access restrictions present particular risks, i.e., arson. Non-public access storage areas can also be problematic, as the presence of staff may be infrequent.

The level of protection desired, the type of systems best suited to the situation and the funds available will all be determining factors in selecting systems and measures. In addition, systems must conform to local building and fire codes.

However, sole reliance on code provisions may not adequately provide for the preservation of building contents, especially high-value collections. Additional fire protection features...may be needed over and above the minimum requirements imposed by local codes. (Bush and McDaniel 1997, 9.96)

In the U.S., roughly 50% of library fires occur during off-hours when few people are present to sound an alarm or extinguish them in their initial stages. From 1980-1993, 24 percent of U.S. library fires occurred between the hours of 9 p.m. and 9 a.m., and another 23 percent between 5 p.m. and 9 p.m. (NFIRS and NFPA survey cited in Bush and McDaniel 1997, 9.96-97). The potential for loss is great if the organization relies solely on preventive measures and manual means of fire suppression. This reality underlines the necessity of automatic fire detection, alarm and suppression systems.

A complete early fire detection and alarm system is a key component of a fire protection system. Such a system allows for safe evacuation and facilitates response by the fire department. When coupled with an appropriate automatic suppression system, it can also reduce the extent of fire damage. All systems must be designed, installed, inspected and maintained by qualified licensed fire equipment specialists. All inspection and maintenance programmes should be well documented and verified.

4.3.1 Effects of Fire Suppressants on Collections

In general, the effects of fire suppressants on collections are not well understood, either alone or in combination with heat, smoke, fire and other combustion products. The NFPA Technical Committee on the Protection of Cultural Resources has been seeking assistance to conduct further research in this area.

Perhaps best understood and documented in the preservation literature are the effects of water on collections (see 3.4.2). Some of the effects of other fire suppressants are known. For example, dry chemical powders are caustic, adhere to hot surfaces and are extremely difficulty to remove from metal. Foam fire suppressants, due to their high water content, dampen exposed materials and can loosen identification labels. And halon can damage electronic media and damage or delete data, when it reaches 900°F (482°C) and decomposes into acidic chemicals (Conroy 1996, 8).

Note: Technical bulletins on clean-up are available from most manufacturers.

The mode of application of a suppressant can also effect collection materials depending on their size and weight, as well as their orientation and proximity to the discharge. Sources often caution that lightweight materials or boxes may be knocked off shelving when suppressant systems are activated.

4.3.2 Arson

The leading cause of fire in libraries in the United States has been identified as arson. Arson accounted for 71 percent of the average annual property damage costs due to fires in libraries from 1980 through 1993, (NFIRS and NFPA survey cited in Bush and McDaniel 1997, 9.93). From 1950-59, electrical fires were identified as the primary cause of library fires, while arson accounted for 18 percent (Morris 1986, 30).

The professional literature describes a number of deliberately set fires including the 1976 Saint Louis Military Records Center fire, the 1986 Los Angeles Central Public Library fires and the 1988 U.S.S.R. (now Russian) Academy of Sciences Library fire in St. Petersburg.

In the case of the Los Angeles fire, the arsonist set a second fire three weeks after the first one. The fires completely destroyed nearly 400,000 volumes, 700,000 books were damaged by the effects of water, and virtually all the remaining books in the 2.1 million-item collection suffered smoke damage. Damage to the uninsured building and contents (books, artwork, other contents) totalled over $22 million [U.S.]. Except for the basement, the library did not have a sprinkler system. (Butler 1986a, 1)

While it is impossible to prevent all deliberately set fires, effective security measures can reduce their occurrence (see 3.5.8), and compartmentalized fire barriers and appropriate protection systems can minimize the damage.

4.3.3 Compact Storage

Space-saving compact storage is commonly used in archives, libraries and record centres today as a means to increase shelving capacity. These modular shelving ranges are mounted on carriages that move upon tracks, enabling the shelving ranges to be moved (either manually or electrically) snugly against one another, thus minimizing the space taken up by aisles. The flexibility of compact storage systems affords a large measure of earthquake protection which is further enhanced by their built-in, anti-tip features. An aisle for access to a particular shelving range is created when and where it is needed. Adequate load-bearing floors are required. (see also Novak 1999)

However, this method of storage can result in an excessive fire load situation, which may lead to structural collapse. Dense storage environments may conceal a smouldering fire that could spread through the shelving. Heat or smoke generated by a fire in the centre of the shelving could be trapped, thus delaying detection. Suppression may be more difficult.

The NFPA recommends the use of automatic sprinkler systems for compact storage areas. Water mist fire suppression tests have shown promise for such areas. Testing has also shown that a compact storage design that leaves a gap between ranges can enhance fire detection and suppression (Bush and McDaniel 1997, 9.105).

4.3.4   Multi-Tier Storage

Multi-tier storage has been used for many years in libraries, archives and record centres. The tiers are supported by metal columns or beams, and openings between each tier serve to heat the areas by convection of air currents. These openings can serve as flues to speed the spread of fire to the tiers above. Modern versions of these systems are still sold, but without the vertical openings.

Smoke barriers should be installed in these vertical multi-tier openings to facilitate smoke detection on the tier of the fire's origin.

4.4   Fire Detection Options

The detectors commonly used in archives, libraries and record centres are activated by heat or smoke. Many kinds of smoke detectors are available to suit specific situations. Smoke detectors are preferred because fire produces smoke before there is any appreciable rise in temperature.

A detection system is essential as a communications tool – it does not control or extinguish fire. The effectiveness of any detection system depends upon both the placement and the density of the fire detectors. While more detectors are needed in fire-prone areas, the entire building must be protected since fire may break out anywhere. The detection system must be connected to an audible alarm system linked directly to the fire department, to a 24-hour security service, or to a central onsite security post.

See Moore 1997 for discussion of automatic fire detectors.

4.4.1   Flame Detectors

Flame detectors respond either to visible or invisible radiant energy generated by a flame. This radiant energy can be either infrared or ultraviolet.

- **Infrared Detectors**

  Infrared detectors filter out unwanted wavelengths in the light generated by a flame, focusing the infrared energy onto a photoelectric cell that then triggers the alarm.

- **Ultraviolet Detectors**

  Ultraviolet detectors use a sensoring element or detection tube that is triggered by ultra-violet light, which is typically present in a flame.

Flame detectors have limited use where a fire is more likely to smoulder before flames are produced, and are generally used only in high-hazard areas where explosions or very rapid fires may occur. They are not suitable for general use in archives, libraries or record centres, but may be used in conservation laboratories or any other area where volatile, flammable materials are stored. These detectors must be strategically located so their sensors are not obstructed by ductwork, shelving units, etc.

4.4.2   Heat Detectors

Heat detectors are triggered when the heat from a fire reaches a "trigger" temperature or temperature change rate set by the manufacturer. There are two basic types: fusible link and bimetal strip or disk.

- **Fusible Link Detectors**

  In this detector, a fusible link in the detector melts at a set temperature, completing an electrical circuit that triggers the alarm.

- **Bimetal Strip or Disk Detectors**

  In this detector, a bimetal strip or disk flexes or distorts, completing an electrical circuit that triggers the alarm. A variation of the bimetal heat detector is the "rate of rise" heat detector. In this detector the alarm is triggered when the temperature change exceeds certain parameters.

Heat detectors are the least costly and most commonly used detectors in public buildings, as they are usually the minimum required by local building codes. They have the lowest false alarm rate but are also the least sensitive, as they are triggered only when the fire has become serious. While the preset trigger temperature can be as low as 57°C (135°F), the core of the fire will probably have to reach above 315°C (599°F) before the detector is triggered. By then, serious damage will have taken place. Heat detectors are best used to protect confined spaces or directly over hazards where flaming-type fires would result.

4.4.3 Smoke Detectors

These detectors will usually detect fire much more rapidly than heat detectors. They are identified by their operating principle.

Recent technological advances have led to the development of analog sensors. The sensitivity of these sensors can be custom-adjusted for specialized environments and they provide an absence of false alarm incidents.

- **Ionization Smoke Detectors**

  Ionization detectors use a small quantity of radioactive material inside a chamber to ionize the air, making it conductive, which allows an electrical charge to flow between two electrodes. Smoke particles entering the chamber attach themselves to the charged ions, thereby reducing their conductivity and triggering the alarm.

  Ionization detectors respond faster to open flame fires that produce large numbers of smaller smoke particles than they do to smouldering fires.

- **Photoelectric Smoke Detectors**

  Photoelectric smoke detectors work on the principle of scattering or obscuring the light passing through air.

  Light-scattering detectors contain a light source (beam) and a photosensitive cell. The light source is placed so that the beam does not fall on the photosensitive cell. When smoke particles enter the beam they scatter the light onto the photosensitive cell, triggering the alarm.

  Light-obscuring detectors are similar to light-scattering detectors, but direct the light beam at the photosensitive cell. When smoke passes through the beam it reduces or obscures the light hitting the photosensitive cell, triggering the alarm.

Light-obscuring detectors are usually used to protect large, open areas where the beam can be projected across a wide space to a photosensitive cell or receiver. This type of detector should be used only in areas where nothing obstructs the beam (shelving, boxes, books, etc.).

- **Air-Sampling Type Smoke Detectors**

  Cloud chamber smoke detectors draw an air sample into a high-humidity chamber. When smoke particles are present, the density of the resultant cloud of condensation is measured by a photoelectric principle, triggering the alarm.

  Continous air-sampling detectors actively and continously sample air which is irradiated by an intense light source. The device can sense smoke particles in extremely low concentrations, and will trigger the first three levels of alarm.

In general, ionization smoke detectors react faster to open-flaming fires (smaller smoke particles). Photoelectric smoke detectors tend to react faster to smouldering fires, as these generally produce larger smoke particles. Continous air-sampling detectors can provide constant low concentration smoke detection. Smoke detectors are more expensive than heat detectors, but respond faster because they react to the smoke generated by a fire.

4.4.4 Gas-Sensing Fire Detectors

During a fire, detectible levels of gases are reached after smoke is detected but before a heat detector would be triggered. There are two types of gas-sensing detectors: semiconductor and catalytic element.

- **Semiconductor Detectors**

  This gas-sensing fire detector responds to a conductivity charge from a semi-conductor caused by the oxidizing or reducing gases of the fire, thereby triggering the alarm.

- **Catalytic Element Detectors**

  This gas-sensing detector uses a catalytic element that does not change in itself, but accelerates oxidation of the combustible gases. This results in a temperature rise that triggers the alarm.

Gas-sensing detectors are not usually recommended for use in archives, libraries and record centres as they can be triggered by aerosols or hydrocarbon solvents causing a false alarm.

4.4.5 Selection of a Fire Detection System

Flame detectors are generally used only in areas such as conservation labs where there is a risk of explosion. These detectors also are used where flash fires are likely to break out with little or no smouldering, such as in gasoline transport and loading terminals, and in storage depots for flammable liquids and gases.

Heat detectors are the least expensive, but are not ideal for archives, libraries and record centres. By the time the alarm is triggered, a fire would have already caused serious damage.

Smoke detectors, both ionization and photoelectric detectors (light-scattering and light-obscuring), are suitable for archives, libraries and record centres. A combination of both is ideal as they each react to different aspects of fire: an ionization detector more quickly to an open-flaming fire and a photoelectric detector to a smouldering fire. In most of these organizations, the bulk of stored material is paper (either packed in boxes or in books on shelves), making a smouldering fire more likely unless the fire was deliberately set using an accelerant.

In addition, continous air-sampling smoke detectors, with their sensitive detection capabilities are an effective option. These systems are used in applications such as electronic data processing areas and museums.

Gas-sensing fire detectors are not usually used in archives, libraries and record centres because false alarms are likely.

4.5 Automatic Fire Alarm and Signalling Options

When an automatic fire detector is activated, it triggers an alarm or signal. That signal can set off an audible alarm alone, as a home stand-alone detector does, or set off both an audible alarm and alert a monitoring system. The detector can also trigger a suppression system. In some systems fire detectors trigger water valves to fill sprinkler piping, allowing water to discharge when sufficient heat reaches the sprinkler. In other systems, detectors actually trigger the automatic suppression system.

Fire alarm systems can be activated *manually* at fire alarm stations, usually located near the exterior exit doors. They can be activated *automatically* by fire detectors when heat, smoke or flame is detected, and by automatic sprinkler systems when water begins to flow.

The basic features of alarm or signalling systems are:

· a central control unit

· a power supply

· a back-up power supply

· circuits that may connect to a manual fire alarm, sprinkler water flow alarm, automatic fire detectors, other alarms and public address and life safety systems and/or an offsite alarm.

4.5.1 Local Alarm Systems

A local alarm system sounds an alarm to evacuate the building. This system does not automatically relay a signal to the fire department or a monitoring company; once the alarm is triggered, someone must still notify the fire department. This system is effective only if the building is occupied at all times, either by staff or security personnel. In their absence, a local alarm system does not provide any protection.

4.5.2 Auxiliary Signalling Systems

An auxiliary signalling system connects the local alarm system to a municipal fire alarm system, and from there to the local fire department. This system is primarily used for building protection, and may or may not have an evacuation alarm.

4.5.3 Proprietary Systems

A proprietary system is monitored and operated by the property owner or contracted supplier, who is responsible for calling the fire department. This system, automatically and constantly monitored from a central location either onsite or from another location, is often used in large commercial or industrial situations. Sophisticated computer-controlled systems can also provide smoke and elevator control, as well as climate control and energy management.

4.5.4 Remote and Central Stations Systems

These systems are similar to proprietary systems, but the signal is transmitted to a remote or central station that is monitored by a private company 24 hours a day. This company is then responsible for calling the fire department.

4.5.5 Selection of an Alarm or Signal System

Local alarm systems require someone, either staff or security, to be present in the building at all times; they are not fully effective otherwise.

Auxiliary, proprietary, remote and central station systems are directly connected to either the fire department or a monitoring station. These systems are effective in buildings that are sometimes vacant.

4.6 Automatic Fire Suppression Options

> Lack of an automatic suppression system is the foremost contributing factor to large-loss fires in museums and libraries. Sprinkler systems are the single most reliable and effective means for minimizing the risk of large-loss fires in these cultural heritage institutions. (Wilson cited in Bush 1991, 8.65)

In addition to an automatic detection system, the building should have an automatic fire suppression system that can put out or limit the spread of incipient fires and avoid the delays involved in calling in the fire department. Regardless of the sophistication of the system, the fire department should always be called in the event of a fire.

The type of burnable substances (class of fire) determines the selection of the extinguishing agent for given areas in an organization. The choice also depends on other factors including cost, effectiveness and safety.

The more common extinguishing agents are listed below (See also 3.4.1).

When installing a new system or upgrading an existing system, a competent specialist and the local fire department should always be consulted. Selection of a specialist should be based on documented experience and referrals.

Of note, recent comments in the fire protection industry appear to support the theory that "portable radios (walkie-talkies) can cause microprocessor-based fire alarm systems to activate. Older relay-type fire protection systems appear to be safer from this problem" (Baril cited in Tremain 1996).

4.6.1 Water-Based Extinguishing Systems

Water can extinguish a fire by cooling (reducing temperature to below that necessary for combustion) and smothering (reducing or eliminating the amount of air – oxygen – necessary for the fire to burn). The traditional way to put out a fire is to direct a stream of water at the base of the fire. A more effective way is to apply water in the form of spray. This increases both the cooling effect and the reduction of water to steam, two key factors in extinguishing a fire. Sprinkler systems do this very well. The speed at which the fire is put out depends on how soon and how much water is applied and how it is applied.

4.6.2 Automatic Sprinkler Systems

Automatic sprinkler systems provide an effective and economical way of extinguishing most fires in their early stages. Standard sprinkler systems also automatically initiate an alarm (onsite or offsite) that alerts authorities. (See Bush and McDaniel 1997, 9.106 for listing of museums and libraries with automatic sprinkler protection).

Some archivists, librarians and records managers still believe that sprinklers, in particular automatic wet-pipe sprinkler systems, are as damaging to collections as fire and are also fearful of accidental discharge. Shepilova (1992, 17-18) offers a convincing rebuttal to these concerns:

· Sprinklers as a method of fire control involve a minimum not a maximum of water.

· Sprinklers open individually: the operation of one does not cause another to operate. Only sprinklers in the heat of the fire will discharge water.

· With properly maintained systems, the probability of accidental sprinkler discharge is negligible.

· Virtually all wet collections are recoverable with prompt and appropriate attention. Burned collections are generally not recoverable.

Class of Fire		Extinguishing Agent
A.	Combustible material (wood, cloth, paper, rubber and many plastics)	Water, halogenated agent, dry chemical (if multipurpose Class A:B:C), most foams
B.	Flammable or combustible liquids (gasoline, oil, paint, cooking fat, etc.	Carbon dioxide, halogenated agent, dry chemical, some foams
C.	Live electrical equipment	Dry chemical, halogenated agent
D.	Combustible metals (magnesium, titanium, sodium, potassium, etc.)	Dry powder

Where there is no suppression system in place to control the development of a fire, firefighters will need to use fire hoses. A typical sprinkler discharges 95 to 260 litres (25 to 70 U.S. gals.) of water per minute while a 63.5 mm (2.5") fire hose discharges, on average, 570 to 950 litres (150 to 250 U.S. gals.) per minute. Studies indicate that the majority of fires are extinguished by four or fewer sprinklers, discharging far less than one 63.5 mm hose. The local fire department, using one such hose can pump more than 56,760 litres (roughly 15,000 U.S. gals.) of water an hour onto a fire, more water than held in an average-sized backyard swimming pool! In addition, hoses and water discharge can knock materials to flooded floors.

Some on/off sprinkler systems shut themselves off once the fire has been extinguished and the temperature has returned to normal, thus reducing the volume of water used. However, caution should be exercised when considering such systems, as some have been plagued with numerous problems, and their use generally adds little or no benefit.

The most appropriate fire suppression system for archives, libraries and record centres is an automatic sprinkler system. It is the simplest and least expensive to install. It is reliable when properly designed, installed and maintained, and the extinguishing agent, water, is discharged immediately when the sprinkler is activated – "the reliability of automatic sprinkler systems is in excess of 96% and can be as high as 99%" (Richardson cited in Baril 1995, 5). Bush and McDaniel (1997, 9.99-9.100) note that "most fires in buildings with automatic sprinklers are controlled with fewer than five sprinklers opening…less water per minute than one hose stream." In addition, insurance statistics indicate a failure rate of approximately one head failure per 16 million sprinklers installed per year (Artim 1995, 26).

Sprinkler systems usually consist of a grid system of pipes and sprinklers connected to a reliable water supply and the equipment necessary to keep pressure in the system constant regardless of the number of open sprinklers. Sprinklers must be placed and spaced so as to limit the fire damage and must be configured for the specific site. In most sprinkler systems, each sprinkler on the grid opens individually, but in a deluge system all sprinklers are open all the time.

When a system has been discharged, either by a fire or accidentally, the system must be refurbished and checked by a qualified, licensed fire equipment specialist.

All water-based suppression systems must be protected from freezing if they are exposed to below-freezing temperatures. Antifreeze is often used for this purpose. Water-based systems used in organizations covered in this publication should not be exposed to below-freezing temperatures because antifreeze could stain and damage the collection on discharge. Should there be a need to protect sprinkler piping against freezing, a dry-pipe sprinkler system should be selected instead of an antifreeze system.

Every sprinkler system should have a waterflow alarm with an audible alarm inside and outside the building to indicate that the system has been activated.

Readers should refer to appropriate standards, e.g., *NFPA 13-1999. Standard for the Installation of Sprinkler Systems*. (See also Solomon 1997)

The most common types of automatic sprinkler systems are:

• **Wet-Pipe Systems**

The sprinklers are attached to pipes that contain water under pressure at all times. The sprinklers open individually at a pre-set temperature, usually 57°C to 77°C (135°F to 171°F). When the fire is out, the water has to be shut off manually by closing the valve for that branch line.

Wet-pipe systems are the most common sprinkler systems. Their simplicity of design makes them reliable and relatively inexpensive to install, modify and maintain. In addition, these systems generally require the least work to refurbish after a fire.

• **Dry-Pipe Systems**

The sprinklers are attached to pipes that contain air or nitrogen under pressure at all times. The sprinklers open individually at a pre-set temperature, reducing pressure in the pipe to the point where water pressure on the other side of the water flow valve forces the valve open to allow water to flow into the pipe. When the fire is out, the water has to be shut off manually by closing the valve for that branch line. This system is normally used in cold, unheated areas where water-filled pipes could freeze and burst.

One problem with the dry-pipe system is the delay between the opening of the sprinkler and the discharge of the water. This delay, of up to one minute, may result in the spread of the fire and the opening of more sprinklers. Quick-opening devices can be installed to reduce the time it takes to discharge the air or gas from the pipe or to open the water control valve.

Another problem with dry-pipe systems is corrosion which can require extensive maintenance. Non-corrosive piping, such as galvanized piping, should be used to prevent rust and sediment build-up from damaging collections.

• **Pre-Action Systems**

Pre-action systems are similar to the dry-pipe systems, but the air in these systems may or may not be under pressure. A separate fire detection system activates the water flow valve and releases water into all the pipes before the sprinkler is activated by the heat of the fire. No water is released from the sprinkler until activated by the heat of the fire directly below. When the fire is out, the water has to be shut off manually.

The principal advantage of pre-action systems over wet-pipe and dry-pipe systems is that their dual action design adds protection against accidental discharge. The water flow valve is opened by a separate fire detector and not by the sprinkler itself. These systems are often used where water-sensitive materials are located, such as fine art storage vaults and computer rooms.

A major drawback with pre-action systems is their total reliance on the smoke detection systems. When the detection system does not perform, the sprinkler system is rendered useless. Pre-action systems are complex and are more expensive to install, modify and maintain.

• **Combination Dry-Pipe and Pre-Action Systems**

These types of systems combine the features of dry-pipe and pre-action systems. Like the dry-pipe system, the pipes contain air or a gas under pressure. Like the pre-action system, this system has a supplementary detector system to open the water flow valve that fills the pipes. If the supplementary detection system fails, the system will open as a conventional dry-pipe system would. When the fire is out, the water has to be shut off manually.

Combined dry-pipe and pre-action systems are primarily used where more than one dry-pipe system is required because of the size or capacity of the space and when it is impossible to install the supply piping for each supply pipe valve by way of a heated or protected space, such as in large cold-storage warehouses. Solomon (1994, 20) advises that "these are special application systems and should not be used merely for large areas in an ordinary building".

• **Pre-Action Recycling Systems**

These systems are a variation of the pre-action systems, where the water flow valve is controlled by a device activated by a heat detector. But in this case, when the fire cools to below the heat detector's trigger temperature, the water supply valve is automatically closed after a brief delay, stopping the

water flow. If the fire rekindles and the temperature rises and again triggers the detector, the water flow resumes.

Caution should be taken when considering recycling sprinkler systems, as some have experienced many problems. Their use, like that of on/off sprinklers, generally adds little or no benefit.

• **Deluge Systems**

In a deluge system, all the sprinklers are open at all times and there is no water in the pipes. When a fire detector is activated, a water flow valve is opened and water is discharged through all sprinklers in the system zone controlled by that valve.

This system is not recommended for use in archives, libraries and record centres, as large amounts of water are discharged over a large area regardless of the extent of the fire.

• **Water Mist Systems**

One of the significant new technologies is the water mist system, which is proving in many circumstances to be a good replacement for halon systems *(see 4.6.5)*. See *NFPA 750-1996. Installation of Water Mist Protection Systems.*

This system discharges limited amounts of water at a pressure that creates a micromist of water droplets of less than 20 microns in diameter. This provides extremely high-efficiency cooling and fire control with little water. Testing has indicated that a fire can be extinguished using less than 25 litres (6.6 U.S. gals.) of water, sometimes in less than one minute and usually within five minutes. Installation costs are expected to be far lower than halon gas replacement systems and less than standard wet-pipe systems. (Artim 1995, 27)

Another advantage of this system is its 'compactness', i.e., its small diameter piping.

See also Mawhinney and Solomon, 1997 and Bush and McDaniel 1997, 9-101.

• **Fast Response Sprinkler Technology**

This sprinkler technology, in development over the past twenty years, provides improved fire protection. Fast-response sprinklers respond to heat at an earlier stage of fire development than other standard sprinklers. There are a number of types: quick-response sprinklers, quick-response early suppression sprinklers, early suppression fast-response sprinklers, etc.

Quick-response sprinklers are being installed to protect collections in a number of major institutions, such as the National Library of Canada, the Library of Congress, the U.S. National Archives and the new British Library. (Bush and McDaniel 1997, 9.98)

See also Cote and Fleming, 1997.

4.6.3 Sprinkler Types

Sprinklers are available in many designs to suit a variety of application and installation needs. Where technically feasible, sprinklers can be made less conspicuous if installed in ornamental ceiling finishes, inside the ceiling itself or in the wall's woodwork.

The three more common types of sprinklers for the organizations covered in this publication are upright, sidewall and concealed sprinklers. All three are activated by heat. The trigger temperature which depends on specific use and code requirements is set by the manufacturer.

• Upright Sprinklers

Upright sprinklers are installed so that the water discharge is directed upwards against a deflector. They are attached to the top part of the sprinkler piping, and are thus somewhat protected from accidental mechanical damage such as being struck by a ladder.

Upright sprinklers are most often used in open pipe installations where appearance is not a factor. They are ideal for storage rooms of any kind.

• Sidewall Sprinklers

Sidewall sprinklers are installed on walls usually about 30 cm (1 foot) below the ceiling. They have special deflectors that are designed to discharge most of the water away from the wall, with a small portion of the discharge being directed at the wall behind the sprinkler. One sprinkler can cover a large area, and they are also useful in buildings where ceiling-mounted sprinklers cannot be installed without major renovations. Where historic integrity of the facility is important, brass finish sidewall sprinklers can be used.

These sprinklers have also been used in open pipe runs to protect archival material stored on regular fixed shelving. For instance, the National Research Council of Canada designed such an installation for a low ceiling environment at the National Archives/National Library of Canada (see Lougheed et al 1994). This successful design, achieved after extensive testing, was praised by the fire protection community (Baril 1996).

• Concealed Sprinklers

Concealed sprinklers are pendant sprinklers (attached under the sprinkler piping) installed in the ceiling space and recessed inside a metal body covered with a plate. The cover plates release and drop when the room temperature approaches the sprinkler's operating range. As the manufacturer can paint the cover plates to match a ceiling finish, they are ideal for areas where aesthetics are important. Concealed sprinklers are also well protected from accidental mechanical damage.

4.6.4 Selection of an Automatic Sprinkler System

Pre-action systems are often preferred by archives, libraries and record centres because there is no water in the pipes, thereby reducing the chance of accidental discharge if the sprinkler is damaged. The downside of pre-action systems is their total reliance on the automatic smoke detection system. If it fails to detect fire, the sprinkler system is rendered useless.

Rust, scale and sediments usually found in dry-pipe sprinkler systems can be avoided by using galvanized or copper piping. The cost of stainless steel piping would be prohibitive, and thermoplastic is not approved for dry-pipe systems.

Unlike dry-pipe or pre-action systems, wet-pipe systems discharge water as soon as the sprinklers are activated. In addition, the wet-pipe system is simple, relatively inexpensive to install and easy to maintain. As already mentioned, with modern, well-maintained systems, the chance of accidental discharge is minimal. "Wet-pipe systems offer the greatest degree of reliability and are the most appropriate system type for most heritage fire risks" (Artim 1995, 28).

And as already noted, experience with water mist suppression technology appears to be very positive. Further testing is being done to determine its effectiveness on fast-developing and deep-seated fires and its impact on collections (Bush and McDaniel 1997, 9.101).

With all these automatic sprinkler systems, when the fire is out, the water has to be shut off manually.

4.6.5 Total Flooding Gas Systems

A total flooding system develops a uniform concentration of extinguishing agent throughout a room, for the purpose of extinguishing fire within regardless of its location.

In these systems, liquified gas (under pressure) is held in steel canisters connected to a piping grid with open nozzles. These systems are activated by a signal from the automatic detection system that opens a valve at the cylinder head.

A total flooding gas system allows only one opportunity to put out a fire. Once the cylinders are empty and the gas has been depleted, there is no reserve to fight the remains of the fire or a rekindle fire.

See also Taylor 1997 for discussion of halogenerated agents and systems.

- **Fluorocarbon Gas Systems**

In the past, halons have provided an acceptable, albeit expensive, alternative where the risk of water damage could not be taken. Rare collections and other water-sensitive materials (e.g. computer equipment) were placed in separate, enclosed rooms protected by halon. Another advantage of halon is its effectiveness against chemical and electrical fires that cannot be extinguished by water. The disadvantages are:

- depletion of the earth's ozone layer and global warming
- human toxicity (above certain concentrations for certain periods of time)
- corrosive nature (decomposition products) at very high temperatures
- high cost of recharging depleted gas supplies

Under the 1987 Montreal Protocol, amended in 1992, signatory countries agreed to phase out the use of ozone-depleting substances by the year 2000 because of the damage caused to the ozone layer and the environment. Fluorocarbons fall under this agreement. In November 1992, the United Nations Environmental Program proposed that the production of Halon 1301 cease by the end of 1993. In Canada and the United States, production of Halon 1301 was banned as of January 1, 1994 with most other countries following suit in 1995. Environment Canada's goal is to phase out the use of halons by the year 2000.

Existing halon installations can still be used but it will become more difficult to obtain replacement gas in the event of a discharge. In the U.S., the Halon Recycling Corporation facilitates the disposal of halon and the trade of recycled halon *(See also Appendix 3.1 Sources of Information: Professional Associations)*.

- **Halon 1301 Alternatives**

A number of substitutes for Halon 1301 are now available, including halocarbon compounds and inerting agents and water mists *(see 4.6.2)*. In 1997, over a dozen clean agent alternatives existed and more are in development. There are two main categories: halo-carbon compounds (containing carbon, hydrogen, bromine, chlorine, fluorine and iodine), and inert gases and mixtures. The halocarbons share a number of characteristics: all are clean agents, all are electrically non-conductive, and all are liquefied gases or exhibit analogous behaviour. (See DiNenno 1997, and Keafer 1998 for a discussion of alternatives to halon fire protection).

In some cases retrofits to existing halon systems may be possible. In other cases, totally new systems will be needed. *NFPA 2001-1996. Standard on Clean Agent Fire Extinguishing Systems* covers the design, installation, inspection, test and use information on halocarbon and inert gas alternatives. See also *NFPA 750-1996. Installation of Water Mist Protection Systems.*

Note: Under its Significant New Alternatives Policy (SNAP) programme, the U.S. Environmental Protection Agency (EPA) is required to evaluate alternative chemicals and processes intended to be used in place of ozone-depleting substances to ensure that they are acceptable from a human health and environmental perspective. The EPA's list of acceptable substitutes does not provide information on the suitability of a substitute for a given situation. (See Environmental Protection Agency 1997).

- **Carbon Dioxide**

Carbon dioxide (CO_2) is not recommended for use in the fire extinguishing systems of the facilities covered by this publication, since the high concentrations needed to extinguish a fire would cause asphyxiation. Moreover, since pressurized CO_2 cools the air when discharged, condensation forms and engenders some risk of water damage.

4.6.6   Selection of a Total Flooding Gas System

Fluorocarbon gas systems can no longer be installed, and carbon dioxide gas systems are not recommended. Substitutes for halon gas systems are now available, including the halocarbon compounds, inerting agents *(see 4.6.5)* and water mists *(see 4.6.2)*. The water mist system with its provision of inexpensive, high-efficiency cooling combined with it being safe for people and the environment make it a particularly attractive option.

4.6.7   Other Systems

The following fire suppression systems are **not** recommended for use in the facilities addressed by this publication.

• **Foam Systems**

Foam systems are normally used in buildings having large spacious interiors, such as airplane hangars or warehouses. Owing to foam's low water content, the water damage to materials is minimal but the problem of clean-up remains. Specific foams must be used in specific situations.

• **Dry Chemical Systems**

Dry chemical systems are used where rapid extinguishment is essential and re-ignition sources are not present, such as in flammable liquid storage rooms, and areas where flammable liquid spills may occur.

4.7 Manual Fire Suppression Options

4.7.1 Standpipe Systems

Most institutions are required by law to have standpipe systems on every floor. The standpipe system can be accessed at one of the two connections within a fire-hose cabinet. The 38.5 mm (1.5") connection is normally already connected to a fire hose and should be only be used by thoroughly trained staff, and even this is not usually recommended. The 63.5 mm (2.5") connector is reserved for fire department use only.

See *NFPA 14-1996. Standard for Installation of Standpipe and Hose Systems.*

4.7.2 Portable Fire Extinguishers

Extinguishers are selected mainly according to the nature of the fuel present. Other factors are then considered: personnel who will use the extinguisher, the physical environment in which the extinguisher will be placed, and whether any chemicals present will react adversely with the extinguishing agent.

If staff are present when a fire breaks out, they may be able to extinguish it with a portable fire extinguisher. However, they should attempt such action only if the fire is small and only if they have been thoroughly trained in the use of the extinguisher. Staff can be at risk due to their lack of experience and knowledge, as well as the lack of breathing equipment and other protective wear.

The choice of extinguisher depends upon the material on fire. It is essential that the extinguisher used be the proper type for the identified hazard(s). While water can extinguish burning paper or wood, if applied to electrical equipment the user can be electrocuted. Many organizations provide only multipurpose extinguishers in order to ensure that the wrong class of extinguisher is not used on a particular fire.

The following are the more common extinguishing agents used for portable fire extinguishers and the class of fire *(see 3.4.1b)* to which they apply:

Class of Fire	Extinguishing Agent
A	Water
A, B:C	Halon
A:B:C	Multipurpose dry chemical (ammonium-phosphate-base)
B:C	Dry chemical (bicarbonate-base or potassium chloride)
B:C	Carbon dioxide
A, B	Aqueous film-forming foam
D	Dry powder

All portable fire extinguishers should be appropriately located, clearly visible and inspected regularly. Their locations must be communicated to staff.

The following portable extinguishers are now obsolete and should **not** be used: soda-acid, cartridge-operated water, foam and vaporizing liquid (carbon tetrachloride).

See *NFPA 10-1998. Standard for Portable Fire Extinguishers.*

4.8 Smoke Control Options

Smoke generated by a fire can, of course, be suppressed with sprinklers. However, in modern building fires, a great deal of smoke is produced before there is sufficient heat to set off the sprinkler system. Successful smoke containment in the fire zone and its exhaust to the outside enables a safe, smoke-free evacuation, facilitates response and reduces the overall damage caused by smoke and soot. There are several options for smoke control.

See *NFPA 92A-96. Recommended Practice for Smoke-Control Systems.*

4.8.1 Smoke Damper Systems

These "passive control" systems are based on the concept of compartmentalization. They automatically turn off the fans and close the ductwork dampers upon detection of smoke in order to contain the smoke. Exhaust from the fire zone is otherwise directed out of the building.

4.8.2 Zoned Smoke Control and Pressurization Systems

Some building control systems can be used to contain smoke and exhaust. This "active control" of smoke uses the buildings heating, ventilation and air conditioning systems to prevent the movement of smoke from the fire area to other areas in the building and to exhaust it to the outside. Air supply to the fire zone is decreased, and the exhaust with smoke and soot is moved from the fire zone directly out of the building. The system can also generate positive pressure by supplying air to unaffected neighbouring rooms, thereby preventing the movement of smoke into these areas.

4.9 Water Detection Options

As accidental water damage to collections is a major concern, it is important that any flooding or water problems be identified immediately. Unwanted water can result from many sources: sweating or leaky pipes, malfunctioning air conditioning systems, damaged windows and roofs, burst pipes or water mains, poorly maintained fire protection systems or flooding due to earthquake or weather conditions.

Basements are especially vulnerable as water travels downward and accumulates there, and floor drains can back up. Water detection systems are a must in any vulnerable area within the building, particularly where valuable collections, records and equipment are housed. Compact storage makes visual inspection difficult and water may go unnoticed.

Water detection devices and systems are available as either stand-alone purchases or part of an overall protection package.

4.9.1 Stand-Alone Water Detection Devices

Stand-alone devices, such as cables or turtle-shaped units, have an audible alarm, but ring only locally. If the building is not staffed 24 hours a day, they are effective only when staff are present to respond. Some units can be set to provide audible alarms for as long as three days, so that a water problem may be detected immediately when staff return. Even during business hours, in a large facility the alarm may not be heard. Some of these devices are battery-operated, so they should be checked regularly as prescribed by the manufacturer.

4.9.2 Water Detection Systems

Some devices can be connected to a central monitoring station. This is far more effective than the stand-alone units, particularly when the building is large and/or unstaffed for part of the day. This type of system is more costly but may pay for itself in the event of severe flooding.

Detectors should be placed in strategic locations throughout vulnerable storage areas. It is best to also place them near any floor drains as these are normally the lowest parts of the rooms and where the water will likely accumulate.

Regardless of the type of detectors being used, they must be checked and maintained according to a regular schedule. Such inspections and maintenance should be documented.

4.9.3 Water Pressure Alarms

Water pressure alarms should be installed on all the major water supply pipes, whether they are part of the water mains or the fire extinguishing system. Low pressure indicates a leak somewhere in the system. Legislation usually dictates that fire extinguishing systems incorporate low water pressure alarms, for these systems cannot function with pressure below a certain point. These alarms should also be connected to a central monitoring system.

4.10 Protective Measures for Electronic Data, Computer Systems and Equipment

Records in electronic format can be altered or deleted more readily those in the more traditional formats (paper and film). Therefore, the DPC must consider protecting data and systems not only from the effects of natural and other disasters, but also against the threat of electrical power complications (interruptions, fluctuations and overload) and security violations.

This section provides a basic introduction to the particular measures for the protection of electrical power, as well as that for computer equipment. Preventative measures for security to ensure continued access, confidentiality, integrity, authenticity and completeness of information requires an information technology security plan *(see 3.5.9)*.

See *NFPA 75-99. Standard for Protection of Electronic Computer/Data Processing Equipment,* and Pearce 1997.

4.10.1 Electrical Power Protection

To protect the organization from loss of any data, measures must be taken to ensure that there will be no computer systems downtime. To ensure this, the following is needed: an emergency generator for back-up electrical power in the event of a power outage, another site with duplicate equipment, operating systems and software, and continuous back-ups.

No downtime and no data loss is an expensive proposition, one that many organizations cannot afford. Other strategies must therefore be considered *(see 5.8)*.

According to Schreider (1994, 24), the most likely cause for extended downtime of a computer system is power complications – "59 percent of all computer disasters are caused by or result in power failures." These power complications can be prolonged or transient such as surges, line dips and other fluctuations and interference.

To protect the system and the stored data from these power complications, installation of an uninterruptable power supply (UPS) is recommended. A UPS is essentially a rechargeable battery-powered back-up to utility-provided power. It keeps the system running until regular or emergency power is returned. The UPS should provide enough power to perform a controlled shutdown. A generator may be required in conjunction with the UPS to sustain needed power. Expert advice should be sought when selecting a UPS. The UPS and back-up systems must be routinely checked to ensure they are working.

A controlled shutdown involves closing all active files and programmes, backing up all files if there is sufficient time, removing back-up tapes to an offsite location, shutting down the LAN/WAN (local area network/wide area network), and turning off all computer components and equipment. All equipment should then be unplugged from the power source and covered to prevent damage from water, smoke and debris, etc.

Surge suppressors should be installed on the system, and spike protectors on the telecommunication lines, to protect them from intermittent power surges that can interrupt the system and cause downtime.

4.10.2 Protection of Computer Equipment

Computer equipment should be safely secured to desks, workstations, etc. by means of special fastener devices. These devices help to minimize theft and the possibility of equipment falling to the floor in the event of an earthquake. Equipment should ideally be covered when not in use as protection from dust and water damage.

In addition, measures taken in earthquake-prone regions to secure the facility overall will also help ensure that the equipment can withstand the tremors of an earthquake.

Computer installations such as mainframes are generally located in a separate secure and protected room with a controlled environment, and appropriate fire detection, alarm and suppression systems. Raised-floor systems are used to house the electrical wiring and act as air plenums, and also serve to protect the equipment from flood waters.

"Most fires damaging computer rooms do not originate in the specialized equipment itself", either inside or outside of the computer room (Pearce 1997, 9.205). To minimize this risk, the design, construction, operation and maintenance of the room and surrounding areas should be carefully planned.

4.11 Protective Storage Measures

Storage practices are discussed in Chapter 3. This section outlines storage enclosures, containers and equipment as protective measures in the event of a fire or flood. The issue of "conservation quality" storage (i.e., the design of enclosures and their material composition) is not included. For this refer to the professional literature and seek expert advice.

4.11.1 Storage Enclosures and Containers

One of the best ways to protect collections and records is to house them in suitable storage enclosures and containers. The diversity of available storage enclosures and containers reflect the broad range of media and formats found in archives, libraries and record centres. Although usually viewed as general organizational and preservation measures, boxes, cases, envelopes, folders and wrappers can act as a safeguard against an onslaught of water. Smoke and soot damage from a fire can be minimized. Boxed materials are more difficult to ignite and boxes can help shield their contents from flames.

> The key is to remember that placing as many barriers between the collections and the disaster-causing event will buy time and reduce damage (Buchanan 1988, 53-54).

It has been reported that plastic jackets have protected books from smoke and heat damage, and to a much lesser extent, fire damage. Paper dust covers on books can also offer a small measure of protection from water damage. Boxes are, of course, designed to provide more substantial protection. In recent years, as phased conservation has been implemented in many organizations, there has been discussion as to the relative merits and risks of the use of various cardboard boxes versus those manufactured from various plastic materials. These discussions have centred not only on the conservation storage issues for archive and library materials, but also on disaster concerns.

For example, in the early 1990s, the National Library of Canada investigated the suitability of corrugated plastic, corrugated board and solid fibreboard for the storage of their collections. As to fire protection, solid fibreboard was considered preferable to corrugated cardboard as it is less likely to catch fire because of its density. Corrugated board has air pockets that might aid fire. Fibreboard was also considered preferable to corrugated board in its resistance to water damage. The potential for damage to collections by melting corrugated plastic in a fire was considered to be an unacceptable risk. (Bullock 1997)

A National Archives of Canada project analyzed options for the selection of a new record storage box. In fire simulation tests, it was found that solid card boxes protected their contents the longest, and corrugated card measured somewhat better than corrugated plastic boxes which melted very quickly. However, the plastic was not found to soak into the file folders or coat the surface of the documents. In a water sprinkler test (corrugated boxes only), it was found that the plastic did not protect the contents from water as well as the paper-based box. It appears that when the card absorbs water and swells, leakage to the interior is prevented. (Kulka 1993, 1-2, 13)

Both cardboard and plastic boxes can offer good protection but both have disadvantages. Closed-style boxes of course offer better protection than do open-style designs. Cardboard boxes ignite at lower temperatures and, depending on their component materials, finish and design, can absorb significant amounts of water resulting in structural weakness or collapse of the container, as well as contents damage. On the other hand, plastic containers and enclosures can melt and fuse to the materials if exposed to high temperatures. For example, polypropylene softens at about 150°C (302°F), melts at about 165°C (329°F) and ignites at about 600°C (1112°F). Polypropylene as a copolymer of polyethylene melts at a range of lower temperatures. However, plastics are impermeable, not generally damaged by water and the weight increase from absorption is minute. Thus, it may be possible to clean, dry and reuse the boxes. The use of corrugated plastic or cardboard materials also raises additional issues of water and fire-resistance. Other factors to consider include joint construction (glued, stapled, pressure-held), use of water-soluble components (adhesives, water-soluble dyes in book cloths), hand holes (penetration of water, aid to fire), type of identification labelling, etc.

Protection of film, magnetic and optical media is usually provided by storing them in a variety of containers such as film cans, microfilm boxes, cassette cases, jewel boxes, and disk boxes. As for books and documents, these containers can shield the contents from water, smoke and, to a point fire, depending on their design and component materials (cardboard, plastic, metal).

The orientation of materials in their containers can also be important. The results of fire tests conducted in 1974 (General Services Administration 1977) on the orientation of boxed document files in open shelf storage showed that the rate of fire growth was dependant on the release of these files into the aisle, after the rupture of the cardboard cartons. When the files were oriented parallel to the aisle within the boxes, an intense fire resulted. When the files were oriented perpendicular to the aisle they tended to exfoliate onto the shelves and thus the fire spread slowly and did not develop in intensity.

Enclosures and containers also afford some protection if collections and records fall off shelving during an earthquake.

4.11.2 Storage Facilities and Equipment

Fire-resistive facilities (vaults and file rooms) and fire-resistant equipment (safes and cabinets) are used to protect the vital and other important records or collections of an organization. The extent of the protection needed depends on the kinds of media that need protection (paper documents, magnetic tapes, etc.), mandated or legislated specifications, accessibility needs and of course, cost. The extent of the protection provided depends first on the design and construction of the facility or equipment, as well as its use within the organization. For example, a safe of vital records should be in a secure location free of fire hazards and protected by fire detection, alarm and suppression systems.

Fire protection requirements and fire resistance test methods are provided in several standards. *NFPA 232-1995. Standard for the Protection of Records* covers requirements for records protection facilities (vaults and file rooms), equipment (safes and cabinets) and records-handling techniques including design, location, supporting structure, floors, roof, doors, electrical service, heating and ventilation, fire suppression, and signalling equipment and operating practices. *NFPA 232A-1995. Guide for Fire Protection for Archives and Record Centers* covers facilities larger than those covered in NFPA 232 and applies to record collections in file rooms exceeding 1,416 m³ (50,000 ft³) and to all archives and record centres. It includes fire characteristics, fire control, systems, construction, equipment and facilities.

Standard tests for fire resistance related to such facilities and equipment are covered by *UL 155-1995. Tests for Fire Resistance of Vault and File Room Doors* and *UL 72-1995. Test for Fire Resistance of Record Protection Equipment.* These tests are intended to demonstrate the performance of record protection equipment during exposure to fire, but are not intended to determine acceptability for use afterwards. These tests are conducted on materials considered common such as newsprint, and coated and uncoated magazine paper. The materials are considered "useable" after the tests, if they are legible and can withstand ordinary handling. UL 72 test methods are used to evaluate products covered by Underwriters Laboratories, Inc. and are recognized by insurance companies across Canada and the U.S.

It should be noted that resistance to forced attack and burglary is covered in standards and guides, jointly with fire protection for some applications and separately for others. Readers should refer to appropriate NFPA, UL or ULC standards.

The following information is based on the specifications and requirements from the above-mentioned standards.

• **Vaults and File Rooms**

Vaults and file rooms are used for the storage of larger volumes of records. Vaults are defined by NFPA 232 as completely fire-resistive enclosures used exclusively for records storage. They should be used for the storage of vital records. File rooms, on the other hand, are defined as fire-resistive enclosures that provide less protection than vaults. They should be used for the storage of records, but not those deemed vital. The volume of records in file rooms should not exceed 1,416 m³ (50,000 ft³).

Facilities below grade should be avoided due to the risk of damage from fire above (accumulated smouldering debris), flooding and water leakage. Fire-resistive construction and the use of noncombustible materials are essential. Automatic sprinklers are considered to provide the best protection, and all fire detection, signalling and suppression systems should be provided in accordance with the appropriate standards such as *NFPA 10-1998. Standard for Portable Fire Extinguishers, NFPA 13-1999. Standard for the Installation of Sprinkler Systems* and *NFPA 14-1996. Standard for the Installation of Standpipe and Hose Systems.*

• **Safes and Cabinets**

Records protection equipment is defined by NFPA 232 as moveable and includes fire-resistant safes and cabinets. They are intended to provide protection for various types of records for various durations of fire exposure by isolating them from surrounding fire exposure. This equipment should be selected according to the requirements of the organization and should have a label from an independent testing agency such as UL.

Safes and cabinets are tested, rated and classified according to their design and fire-resistance characteristics. Fire-resistant equipment is specifically designed to resist fire, and consists of a metal shell filled with fire-resistant insulation. The preservation community has come to advise against the use of fire-resistive equipment for valuable collections and records, especially photographs, and instead recommends the use of uninsulated cabinets in concert with fire-resistive vaults and file rooms. This is because insulation, while it works well to protect the contents from the heat of a fire, can also create high and damaging levels of relative humidity within the safe or cabinet.

Under the requirements of UL 72, record protection equipment is exposed to a fire endurance test and an explosion test, and where applicable, a fire and impact test. The equipment is classified in terms of an interior temperature limit and a time expressed in hours. The complete rating means that the specified interior temperature and humidity limits are not exceeded when the equipment is exposed to a standard test fire for the specified length of time. Three temperature and humidity limits are used and form the basis for the three classes of devices: 125°F (52°C) with 80% RH (considered limiting conditions for flexible computer disks); 150°F (66°C) with 85% RH (considered limiting conditions for photographic, magnetic or similar nonpaper records); and 350°F (177°C) with 100% RH (considered limiting conditions for paper records). The time limits used are 4, 3, 2, or 1/2 hour.

There are three classes of devices for records protection (UL 72-1995):

1. Class 350 rated devices – intended to protect paper records.

2. Class 150 rated devices – intended to protect paper and non-paper records such as EDP media (magnetic tapes) and photographic records.

3. Class 125 rated devices – intended to also protect flexible computer disks.

UL classifications of record protection equipment cover a variety of devices of differing sizes and designs, such as insulated records containers, insulated filing devices, insulated file drawers, media boxes and mixed media containers (for descriptions of these devices see Hunter 1993a).

• Selection of a Safe or Cabinet

This equipment should be selected according to the requirements of the organization and should have a label from an independent testing agency such as UL.

Based on the protection of the media, Hunter (1993a, 5-6) advises that:

· Paper records are best stored in equipment with a Class 350 rating, where the internal temperature is maintained below 350°F (177°C) for the rated time in order to keep the contents below 420°F (216°C), the charring point of paper. They do this during a fire by releasing steam from the insulation to the inside of the unit. As a consequence, the internal RH of the unit can be at or approach 100%.

· Photographic, magnetic or similar nonpaper records are best stored in equipment with a Class 150 rating, where the internal temperature is maintained below 150°F (66°C) and the RH below 85% for the rated time in order to maintain the dimensional stability of the plastics.

· Computer floppy diskettes are best stored in equipment with a Class 125 rating, where the internal temperature is maintained below 125°F (52°C) and the RH below 80% for the rated time in order to maintain the dimensional stability of the particularly sensitive media.

A collection containing paper and plastic media can be protected in a mixed-media safe or cabinet which has separate compartments rated for paper records and for plastic records *(see also 3.5.7e)*.

4.11.3 Shelving and Earthquake Protection

Earthquakes can cause shelving and cabinets to pitch their contents to the floor or even collapse with their entire load. Even tremors and vibration can dislodge shelving units, boxes and books.

Archives, libraries and record centres rely on shelving to house their collections. Yet shelving can be the "weak link" during an earthquake, and tall shelving units are the most vulnerable. It is important to thoroughly understand this complex topic, especially if earthquakes have been identified as a major threat in your area. The advice of a structural engineer should be sought as proper shelving selection, installation and maintenance are crucial.

Extensive information is provided in Shelton's *Manual of Recommended Practice Seismic Safety Standards for Library Shelving* and Weber's *Library Buildings and the Loma Prieta Earthquake Experience of October 1989*. The former reference recommends specifications and standards for shelving (fixed, flexible and compact) that will withstand the range of earthquakes found in California. The latter discusses these issues in a less technical manner. As well, both Fortson (1992, 38-43) and DePew (1991, 264-267) include good information on this topic.

Even facilities not located in earthquake zones are never completely free from tremors, as vibration from demolition projects, subways or airline flight paths can damage collections.

Storage Checklist

· Install "shelf-lips" to help prevent material from falling off shelving. This must be weighed against the reduced ease of material removal.
· Tilt shelves back to reduce the chance of books "walking off".
· Use restraints at the front of shelves to hold materials in place. Possibilities include nylon webbing, guard rails, retention bars, bungee or elastic cords.
· Avoid free-standing shelving units. Bolt shelving to structural supports such as the floor, ceiling or a wall, or to other shelving units. Shelving bolted to the walls must be attached to the studs of bearing walls, not just to the drywall.
· Use metal shelving units with welded frames, ideally with solid back and end panels. Units with only bolted corners can collapse as a unit.
· For shelving without solid back or end panels, Fortson (1992, 39) advises using cross-bracing or x-bracing to prevent buckling. She further notes that tall units require more than one cross-brace, which should be welded in place or securely bolted. Hooked braces detach easily in an earthquake. Top tie channels and welded bottom spreaders are essential if the installation of adequate cross bracing is not possible.
· Bolt stacked map cabinets or other drawer units to each other. The drawers should have automatic latches. If not, use a piece of doweling pushed through the handles.
· Consider using compact shelving units. While more than 750,000 volumes fell to the floor at the Stanford Library during the 1989 Loma Prieta earthquake, "no material fell from any compact shelving installation on movable carriages over a raised safety floor" (Weber 1990, 16). This can be attributed in part to the flexibility of the units, as well as to the support provided by books in these closely connected units.

4.12 Trained Staff as a Protective Measure

One of the best and most cost-effective forms of protection is the staff of the organization, including contracted custodial and security personnel. Their vigilance, powers of observation and their very presence throughout the facility provide a first line of defence in the protection of lives and collections. Ongoing education and training is key to heightening the awareness of personnel. It is irresponsible, or at the least unrealistic, to rely upon untested and untrained staff. Methods to be used for staff training can include seminars and group discussion, hands-on simulation exercises and role playing, on-the-job training and case study evaluation *(see also 2.4.4)*.

The following issues should be considered for inclusion in any training programme:

- evacuation procedures including mustering locations
- protective measures, systems, equipment and supplies
- use of fire extinguishers
- housekeeping practices
- health and safety education (applicable legislation and regulations, CPR, first aid, recovery hazards, etc.)
- the organization's overall disaster planning, fire planning, earthquake planning, etc.

A staff member, by spotting and reporting any suspicious activity could protect the organization from a deliberately set fire. A security guard on rounds who alerts the facilities department to a leaking pipe may protect the facility from a widespread flood. The goal of training is to effectively prepare staff to take on the responsibility for protecting the organization. With proper training staff will know how to recognize a potential threat, what to do when a problem is identified, how and when to report a problem and how and when to activate the disaster plan.

The means to achieve effective protection is by providing all staff with the information, support and instruction needed:

- to recognize existing and potential hazards
- to take immediate and appropriate action before an incident develops into an emergency or escalates into a disaster
- to take immediate and appropriate actions to protect other personnel and users
- to take immediate and appropriate action to protect the collections, facility, etc.
- to activate the disaster plan as appropriate *(see 6.4.2g)*.

See *NFPA 101-1997. Life Safety Code.* Also Lopes 1997, Powell 1997, and Powell and Appy 1997.

Chapter 5

5.0 Disaster Preparedness Planning

Plan for a secure operation, but prepare for a disaster (Buckland 1991, 166).

At this point in the disaster planning timeline, the Disaster Planning Committee (DPC) should have addressed planning for the identification, prevention, and reduction of hazards, as well as that for various disaster protection measures. Now the DPC should focus their planning efforts on preparedness activities and strategies. Reviewing existing internal programmes, forming external liaisons and arranging for future provision of external supplies and services, should collectively result in an integrated framework that will help to prepare the organization for the very real possibility of disaster.

5.1 The Purpose of Disaster Preparedness Planning

Disaster preparedness acknowledges that disasters can and do occur. An organization in a state of readiness is better prepared and equipped to minimize the effects of disaster and to facilitate response and recovery. Therefore, the purpose of disaster preparedness planning is to develop organizational capabilities that may be required when disaster strikes.

5.2 The Process for Disaster Preparedness Planning

It has been assumed that many of the programmes covered in this chapter are undertaken as part of an organization's general operations. Here, the process emphasizes programme review and modification from a disaster planning perspective. The actions to be undertaken will vary according to the organization and its existing programmes and external liaisons.

Disaster Preparedness Planning: Process at a Glance

- Liaise with external agencies.
- Survey the collections and records.
- Review identified materials of intrinsic value.
- Review the vital records programme.
- Review the insurance coverage.
- Review preparedness strategies for electronic data and systems.
- Set priorities for collections and records recovery.
- Review strategies for relocating and/or duplicating collections and records.
- Make arrangements for disaster-related equipment, supplies and services.

As a result of the above process, staff education and training related to each specific issue will have occurred, and thus serve to enhance overall organizational preparedness. Training specific to other stages of planning is covered in other chapters.

5.2.1 Liaise with external agencies

During disasters, organizations are forced into more and different kinds of interactions with other groups (Quarantelli abridged by Hawkins and McClees 1988, 322).

As part of disaster prevention and protection planning, the DPC should have consulted with external agencies to obtain information, assistance and advice. Contact should now be broadened for the purposes of developing partnerships, establishing lines of communication and/or reciprocal arrangements. It is wise to remember that interorganizational arrangements may break down in times of crisis. In addition, organizations may be forced to relinquish some measure of their autonomy where emergency service providers assume control. The organization's disaster plan should also be coordinated with any community-wide plans already in effect:

> ... so that it does not count on using outside resources that may be committed to higher priority disaster operations elsewhere. Likewise, it is important that the police and fire departments, the civil defense organization, and other public protection organizations know of the plans the museum is making so they can coordinate efforts to support the museum appropriately in time of disaster (Hunter 1983, 243).

In addition to contacting local service authorities and businesses, it may be necessary to pursue contacts with various levels of government. Just as it is critical to maintain the disaster plan, contacts with local agencies must also be maintained to apprise them of any changes made in your disaster planning as well as to keep abreast of changes in their roles and services.

5.2.2 Survey the collections and records

The DPC should survey the collections, for as Murray (1987, 89) notes, "you cannot protect anything unless you have control over it." This survey will provide the DPC with an overview of the various collections and records. This overview will enable the organization to knowledgeably set priorities, appropriately insure the collections, and adequately plan response and recovery procedures.

A survey should determine:
· the number of collections and records
· the material types found in the collections and records
· the vulnerability of each material type.

5.2.3 Review the identified materials of intrinsic value

Materials of intrinsic value are rare or unique collections and records used for historic, artistic and scholarly research purposes. These materials would generally be identified (and maintained in their original format) as part of the organization's regular operations.

It remains for the DPC to review and modify the identification of these collections and records in order to assign their priority for recovery *(see 5.9)*. Their protection and, in the event of a disaster, their recovery and rehabilitation would take precedence over that of materials not having intrinsic value, i.e., materials held for their information value only.

5.2.4 Review the vital records programme

It is assumed that the organization has in place a vital records programme. This section outlines the process for programme review by the DPC within the context of overall disaster planning, in order to ensure that vital records are integrated into the organization's disaster plan.

a) Definitions

In general, the term 'vital' records may be used interchangeably with the term 'essential' records. The term vital records has been selected for use in this publication, except where quoted from other sources.

There are two categories of vital records:
· The vital records of the organization, which contain information considered essential to its operations. These are necessary to re-establish or continue the organization's responsibilities and functions in the event of an emergency or disaster. They can include the catalogue, finding aids, personnel records, legal records, financial records and correspondence.

· The vital records held by the organization. These are records that are acquired, either through purchase or donation, i.e., the collections. Some have intrinsic value; others are retained for their information content only.

The sections in this publication covering vital records apply to the operational records of the organization. The records held by the organization are covered in the discussions on collections *(see also 5.9)*.

b) The Review Process

The purpose of the review is to confirm that the vital records programme is valid and current, and that the identified records are adequately maintained and protected. Modifications to the programme should be made as necessary.

The review process consists of the following:
· Review the organization's key responsibilities and confirm that the records classified as vital are up-to-date. Criteria for the selection of vital records can be found by consulting the references for this chapter, in particular, Emergency Preparedness Canada (1996) and National Archives and Records Administration (1996).
· Review the existing protective measures, such as duplication and dispersal, protective storage, and the use of hot and cold sites for computer systems.
· Review the records retention schedules, i.e., the schedules that determine where, for how long, and in what form records are retained.
· Review the procedures for maintaining an up-to-date inventory of the vital records in offsite storage.

5.2.5 Review the insurance coverage

The DPC should review the organization's existing insurance so that coverage may be modified to meet needs in case of emergencies and disasters. This applies even if the organization is part of a larger complex and has coverage through its parent body. Insurance coverage does not preclude the need for disaster planning, and a disaster plan does not exclude the need for insurance; the two go hand in hand.

> Having an insurance policy is not enough...You must be insured under the terms and conditions that will provide your organization with financial protection during your disaster recovery and restoration efforts (Luongo 1996, 15).

Archives, libraries and record centres present special problems for insurance companies, as these organizations store large quantities of information and collection materials that are frequently difficult or even impossible to replace. A comprehensive risk management programme should involve putting in place measures to reduce the possibilities of loss, as well as having an insurance policy. Insurance coverage is necessary because it is impossible to eliminate all sources of loss, but all too often "the importance of insurance is frequently recognized only after a major loss" (Myers 1991, 46).

a) The Review Process

The insurance review process requires an investigation of both the organization's needs and the insurance options available:

- **Understand the existing insurance policy.**

  DPC members should familiarize themselves with the existing insurance coverage. Consultation with comparable organizations to discuss their coverage may also be useful before initiating a dialogue with your and/or other insurance brokers.

  Discussion of the existing policy with the broker will identify any strengths and weaknesses of your coverage and help both parties better understand the issues particular to your organization. For example, the use of volunteers in a recovery operation can be an insurance problem and coverage must be negotiated for their specific inclusion. Marrelli (1996) suggests postulating three or four hypothetical disasters and querying what would happen in each with the existing coverage – Does the policy cover the costs involved in recovery, i.e., outside conservator's fees, professional building cleaning, etc.? Any terms used in the policy must be clearly understood to avoid assumptions made by the organization as to what would be covered (or not covered), under what circumstances and up to what amount.

  So important is the understanding of the liabilities in the insurance policy, that Wright (1979, 255) considers it "the first step in contingency planning".

- **Preplan with the insurance broker.**

  A copy of the existing disaster plan should be provided to the insurance broker. The broker and the organization share a common interest in both the planning and the recovery effort. Trust and cooperation between the two parties is essential to formulating the policy and the disaster plan and when necessary, the settlement of a claim. By developing well-prepared prevention, protection,

preparedness, response and recovery plans, an organization can minimize losses and thus keep the insurance claim to a minimum. Similarly, an institution with a comprehensive disaster plan that can demonstrate mitigation strategies taken should, all other things being equal, be assigned a lower premium rate.

- **Understand the insurance options available.**

  Consultation and discussions with other brokers should be undertaken. This will enable the DPC to understand the various policies available and their applicability to the organization's particular needs. Insurance for electronic data and systems should be carefully considered (see 5.8.3).

- **Modify the insurance coverage.**

  The DPC is now prepared for and in a better position to recommend any adjustments in the insurance coverage, such as removal of exclusions, upgrading of policies, etc. This may involve getting extended coverage, updating inventories, changing policies, or even changing brokers and companies.

  Policies may be extended to cover almost any scenario the DPC can visualize; the issue is whether the organization is willing and able to pay the corresponding premium. However, premiums are not the only criterion for selecting a broker and the DPC must consider that different insurance companies have different records of settlement, approaches to working with clients, etc. Insurance is a competitive industry, and the goal is to obtain the broadest coverage possible at the lowest possible price.

- **Prepare the organization to meet its contractual obligations.**

  In order to meet the contractual obligations outlined in the insurance policy, the organization should implement the planned mitigation strategies.

  Strategies for prevention and protection include those outlined in Chapters 3 and 4, such as fire and water detection systems, fire alarm and suppression systems, general housekeeping practices, facility management and security programmes.

  A copy of the revised disaster plan should be provided to the insurance broker. This will demonstrate the organization's commitment to minimizing losses and document, in part, your fulfilment of the insurance requirements.

5.2.6 Review preparedness strategies for electronic records, data and systems

Computer systems are now considered essential to the operations of most organizations. Not only does the creation, maintenance and storage of data rely upon them, but we depend on electronic data systems for access to information on a daily basis.

> In some industries...loss of computing power would bring an organization to a complete halt (Buckland 1991, 2).

Electronic databases including online public access catalogues (OPACS) have taken the place of manual card catalogues in many organizations, and few organizations continue to maintain both. Inability to access the collections and records databases, as well as financial, operational and personnel records, would be disastrous for many organizations and could result in lost revenue or business and a crisis of patron trust. As a result, it is crucial to get the computer systems functional as soon as possible after a disaster strikes.

a) The Review Process

Preparedness planning for data and systems is known in the business community as 'business resumption planning' *(see 5.8)*. This planning process mirrors that of overall disaster planning. The same steps apply: defining the project, getting management approval, testing and maintaining the plan, etc. In addition, the organization must identify key responsibilities, determine which activities are time-critical, and develop the measures necessary to restore these activities in the event of a disaster. This section draws on concepts from business resumption planning by focusing on strategies that allow the DPC to link the electronic data and systems plan with the overall disaster plan.

The process for review of the preparedness strategies for electronic records, data and systems consists of the following:

- **Review existing operations and preparations**

    This organization-wide review should include: existing hardware, software and network configurations; established practices and procedures for data back-up and systems recovery *(see 5.8)*; and existing insurance coverage *(see also 5.2.5 and 5.7)*.

- **Identify critical functions and determine consequences for varying degrees of downtime**

    Based on the functions identified as critical to an organization's mission and the consequences of any service disruption, goals should be set based on the organization's priorities for recovering data, hardware and functional operations. It is important to determine which functions must resume immediately and which can withstand some downtime.

- **Determine system requirements necessary to support the critical functions**

    Identify the minimum system resources needed to support the operation of essential systems: utilities, communication requirements, hardware, software, databases, staff resources, etc.

- **Assess protection options and costs**

    This assessment should include: data back-ups to assure the availability of records and information created and stored on software after a disaster; systems back-ups to assure minimum disruption; and facilities back-ups such as reciprocal arrangements with similar organizations, cold sites, hot sites and offsite storage.

- **Develop a proposal for modification to data and systems preparedness**

    The proposal should detail the recommended strategy or strategies. It could also outline strategies considered and rejected.

- **Get approval and funds**

    Costs associated with data and systems strategies are legitimate and necessary costs. The process of getting approval for these strategies and the necessary funding parallels that of obtaining overall management approval for the disaster planning process *(see 2.2.3)* and the plan itself *(see 2.2.14)*.

- **Implement the plan for data and systems back-up**

    The plan may include: the creation of back-ups for data and software, and establishment of routines for their duplication and offsite storage; arrangements for site strategies; documentation of procedures for creating copies of data and software and establishing a systematic method of keeping accurate records of their storage.

- **Test and maintain the electronic data and systems plan**

    The plan should be tested on a semi-annual basis. This should include a controlled shutdown *(see also 6.4.7)*. The electronic data and systems plan must also be kept current to take into account changes in operations, hardware, software, etc. It must be integrated into the organization's overall disaster plan.

5.2.7 Set priorities for collections and records recovery

Based on the survey of collections *(see 5.2.2)* and the identification of materials of intrinsic value *(see 5.2.3)* and vital records *(see 5.2.4)*, the DPC should proceed to determine priorities for collections and records recovery. The purpose of setting priorities is twofold. First, this identification of the relative importance of the collections and records directs the protection and preparation efforts (storage, insurance, etc.) for items that contribute most to the continued operations of the organization. Second, in the event of a disaster, this identification focuses the response and recovery operations on these most important assets.

> Without setting priorities in advance, effort may be wasted on trying to protect or save low value objects at the expense of those that deserve the most attention (Hunter 1990, 10:12).

Considerable thought, effort and perhaps compromise will go into developing lists of priorities for collections and records. In the event of a disaster, the organization will have to make rapid decisions about what to save, recover or discard. This is a difficult task, both in theory and practice. "Many of the questions to consider cut to the heart of library priorities and staff allegiances: Which will we save first, the reference books or the special collections?" (Fox 1989, 3).

At the time of the disaster, the collections and records priorities developed during the planning phase and documented in the disaster plan will be revisited, and recovery priorities may need to be adjusted based on the realities at hand. Financial resources will be a major consideration *(see 6.5.9)*.

5.2.8 Review preparedness strategies for relocating and/or duplicating collections and records

As a result of the risk hazard analysis *(see Chapter 3)* and the priority-setting exercise above, it may be decided that the risk facing the collections and records is great and that current strategies are inadequate. If so, existing strategies for their relocation and/or duplication will need to be modified.

Based on an assessment of the various options (relocation, duplication, dispersal, etc.), and a comparison of the associated costs, an appropriate strategy should be developed; one that will prepare the organization to both protect the records and collections and preserve access to them wherever housed.

5.2.9 Make arrangements for disaster-related equipment, supplies and services

Suppliers of disaster-related equipment and supplies should be contacted to verify availability, price, minimum order, account requirements, etc. Some supplies should be purchased in advance and stored onsite in emergency entry cabinets and supply depots. However, an onsite depot will be of little use if the disaster renders it inaccessible. For this reason, some supplies ought to be stored offsite as well.

As a preparedness measure, the DPC should also research and contact companies and individuals that provide disaster recovery services, such as transportation, collections drying, clean-up and conservation. The organization's potential needs should be outlined to ensure that what may be required can be provided. Alternate service providers should also be identified in the event of a widespread disaster.

Pre-approved service contracts and supply/equipment accounts should be established and documented in the disaster plan. This should include which supplies, equipment and services the companies or individuals provide, whom to contact (especially after hours), and service rates plus any restrictions, such as on hours of service *(see also 5.11)*. This list should be updated semi-annually.

Planning should also include a rough determination of when, during the response and recovery stages of a disaster, external service providers should be called in and how best to use their services. Such deliberations may save valuable time and money.

5.3 Liaisons with External Agencies

The development of close ties with external agencies, both governmental and non-governmental is critical to both the disaster response and recovery operations. The plan must clearly outline how the two spheres of organization, internal and external, are to work in concert. For example, in certain disasters, the external agency would take charge of the organization. All disaster planning efforts should be carefully coordinated with those charged with responsibility for the safety of people during a disaster, such as fire and police departments.

Liaisons with external agencies usually begin at the local level and then broaden to include regional, provincial, and federal resources and when necessary, international organizations. Working partnerships should be developed that link the organization with the necessary government and service agencies.

At the local level inquiries should be made such as:

· What plans exist for emergencies and disasters?

· What disaster-related supplies or other resources exist?

· How does the organization participate in any reciprocal arrangements?

· What provisions for temporary relocation during a disaster are available?

· What arrangements have been made by local emergency preparedness agencies for area evacuation, first aid, food and water, and sanitation?

· Would the facility be designated as an evacuation centre in the case of a widespread disaster?

Then, the DPC should contact the appropriate provincial or territorial emergency measures organization to determine its role in a disaster situation. Emergency Preparedness Canada (EPC) should be contacted to determine the role of the federal government in a nationally-declared disaster *(see Appendices 2 and 3.2).*

5.4 The Collections Survey

A "big picture" survey of the collections should be undertaken in order to assess the holdings and set priorities for recovery. The goal of the collections survey is to determine gross numbers by format, i.e., books, documents, photographs, microforms, and magnetic media. When feasible, the survey should further categorize the collections formats, i.e., photographs – black and white prints, colour prints, etc.

Many sources suggest that the people responsible for collection areas undertake that area's particular survey. Their expertise is especially valuable at the initial stages, but broader input by the DPC in consultation with top management will be essential to develop overall organizational priorities *(see 5.9).*

After determining gross numbers and the various formats, the DPC should now assess the vulnerability of the collections. A similar assessment will have been carried out as part of the risk hazard analysis and should have covered the facility, its location, its services and operations, as well as hazards specific to the collections *(see Chapter 3).* Here, the DPC focuses on the vulnerability of the collections.

The purpose of the collection assessment is threefold: it identifies collections requiring specialized environmental controls or storage practices; it identifies priorities based on the collections' vulnerability to various threats such as fire and water; and it identifies collections that may require either further

research or external resources to develop appropriate response and recovery procedures.

Points to consider:

· Which formats are most vulnerable to water damage, changes in relative humidity and temperature, etc. resulting from emergencies or disasters, such as power failure, fire or flood? Some materials are very sensitive to water damage, for example, early colour starch photographic prints will not survive immersion.

· Does the organization have in-house expertise to recover some or all of the formats found within the collections? What outside assistance would be necessary? The advice of external conservators should be sought if in-house expertise is lacking.

· Have all the internal hazards in the collections such as cellulose nitrate-based film been identified? *(See also 3.3.1e)*

5.5 Materials of Intrinsic Value

Establishing a programme for the management of materials of intrinsic value (often termed Special Collections) parallels the process of establishing a vital records programme. Both require definition, identification, programme responsibility, protective measures, etc. While detailing this process is beyond the scope of this publication, the DPC should ensure that the programme is linked to the disaster planning process.

It is difficult to arrive at a precise definition for materials of intrinsic value that would apply universally to all organizations. The U. S. National Archives and Records Service (NARS) staff information paper defines intrinsic value in relation to archival materials and may provide a useful starting point for the DPC's discussion of such materials.

In general, record materials having intrinsic value possess one or more of the following qualities or characteristics, (National Archives and Records Service 1982):

· physical form that may be the subject for study if the record provides meaningful documentation or significant examples of the form

· aesthetic or artistic quality

· unique or curious physical features

· age that provides a quality of uniqueness

· value for use in exhibits

· questionable authenticity, date, author, or other characteristic that is significant and ascertainable by physical examination

- general and substantial public interest because of direct association with famous or historically significant people, places, things, issues, or events

- significance as documentation of the establishment or continuing legal basis of an agency or institution

- significance as documentation of the formulation of policy at the highest executive levels when the policy has significance and broad effect throughout or beyond the agency or institution.

5.6   The Vital Records Programme

A vital records programme ensures that vital records and electronic information systems are identified, protected and readily accessible and where necessary allows the organization to resume normal operations after a disaster. Vital records can be found in many forms such as: paper records (memos, letters, reports); photographs; maps; electronic records including those stored on computer disks and tapes; videotapes; and audiotapes.

Detailed descriptions of vital records programmes are well documented in the professional literature. Our purpose here is to provide a basic understanding of vital records that enables the DPC to integrate the programme into the organization's disaster planning process.

5.6.1   Authority and Responsibility

Federal and some provincial and municipal governments and associated libraries and record centres have mandated authority and responsibility for the establishment of vital records policies and programmes. The protection of vital records is a critical component of that responsibility. Failure of government to discharge this duty may have devastating consequences, such as the loss of birth, citizenship, taxation, health and employment records. Disaster planning provides the means to ensure the protection of, as well as, continued access to those records considered essential to the continuity or resumption of operations.

In Canada, the *Emergency Preparedness Act* requires federal government departments and agencies to have emergency plans. The National Archives of Canada is responsible for the administration of secure sites for vital records storage for government departments and agencies, and for the provision of advice on other aspects of vital records. In addition, the *Government Security Policy* sets out security standards for federal government organizations. For municipal governments, the need for records, data and informa-tion security is mandated to enable municipalities to fulfil their fiduciary responsibilities, contracts, etc. For example, the *Municipal Freedom of Information and Protection of Privacy Act, Regulation 517/90* legislates this mandate in Ontario.

Any organization whose viability depends on the continued availability of essential information, must recognize the need to preserve vital records. This includes public service organizations such as hospitals, police and fire departments, and the business sector. Without these records, accounts receivable may be uncollectible, ownership rights may not be fully exercised, vulnerability to litigation may be increased, and insurance claims may be denied or delayed. Dissolution may result and the organization may not be able or permitted to resume operations. (EPC 1996, 2)

5.6.2   Identification of Key Responsibilities

The process of determining key responsibilities of the organization should develop from an examination of the organization's governing legislation, mission statement and collection policies.

These responsibilities must be determined by clearly assessing roles and operations, including operations that affect other organizations. An assessment then must be made of those activities deemed most critical and a determination made as to which records support these responsibilities.

5.6.3   Identification of Vital Records

When determining which records are to be defined as vital, stringent judgement must be exercised in order to properly identify, prioritize and protect those records or electronic information systems that are truly "time-critical". This means that a service or function is considered essential and that non-performance would significantly impair the effective operation of the organization.

Sources vary on the percentage of records that fall into the "vital" category; estimates range from 1 percent to 7 percent. EPC (1996, 6) suggests that these records make up no more than 10 percent of an organization's total records.

Determining the key responsibilities and identifying the supporting records is an organization-specific exercise. This identification starts with an inventory of the total holdings *(see 5.2.2)*. Inventoried records must then be classified as static (undergoing little or no change) or active (constant change), and assessed relative to their values or costs in the event of loss.

Criteria to be used to identify records series or electronic information systems that contain essential information will need to be determined. While no standards exist that could apply to every organization, EPC suggests the following guidelines (based on EPC 1996, 4):

· Select records essential to the viability of your organization.

· Choose records that fulfil the mandate of the organization.

· Select records that are essential to ensure the continued delivery of programs and services.

· Select records in consultation with the key users of the information.

· Select records in the form most appropriate to their anticipated use.

· Select records that are not appropriately preserved elsewhere.

· Identify and locate records essential to your organization that are housed elsewhere and conversely, records you hold have that are vital to another organization.

· Exclude records that are available elsewhere and are therefore easily replaceable.

Records that may be identified as vital can include payroll records, leases, union agreements, constitution and by-laws and employee records, etc. Comprehensive checklists of records that may be vital are provided by Emergency Preparedness Canada (1996, 6-8) and National Archives and Records Administration (1996, 6).

5.6.4 Vital Records Maintenance

Vital records must be kept current through a process of records maintenance. Records should be reviewed and deleted from the vital records programme when they have been superseded or are no longer applicable according to the records retention schedule. This process should also identify any missing or excluded vital records. Records maintenance also covers the addition of newly designated vital records. Proper storage for vital records must also be maintained.

5.6.5 Vital Records and Disaster Planning

Vital records must be accorded high priority where disaster prevention, protection and preparedness measures are being considered. Response and recovery planning must also acknowledge their significance, so that resources can be allocated accordingly.

The DPC must integrate the vital records programme with the organization's overall disaster planning

process and ultimately the disaster plan. This is accomplished by documenting the following measures in the plan:

· Identification of the vital records, including their formats and locations.

· Identification of personnel who have authorized access to the vital records.

· Identification of potential or assigned relocation sites *(see 5.10)*.

· Identification of back-up strategies for electronic data and systems *(see 5.8.2a)*.

5.7 Insurance Coverage

Insurance is a contract between an organization and its insurance underwriters; it can be described as the distribution of the losses of the few over the contributions of the many. In exchange for the payment of premiums, the insured party is protected against the risk of loss or damage up to a monetary limit specified in the contract. For large organizations, this risk is usually so great that it must be shared among several insurance companies. Consequently, the organization must takes out its policy through the intermediary of a broker who divides the risk among several underwriters or re-insurance companies either on a package basis or separately, according to the kind of risk in which each insurer specializes.

We suggest that the DPC refer to the work of England and Evans (1988) for a comprehensive overview of insurance. As well, Wright's 1979 article discusses fully the need for an understanding of the liabilities of both the insured and the insurer. Readers consulting U.S. insurance sources should note that the U.S. industry is similar to Canada's.

5.7.1 Authority and Responsibility

The responsibility for insurance in the organization rests with the governing body which usually delegates this task to the director, risk manager or other individual. That person would then negotiate with the insurance broker for suitable coverage. For the purpose of disaster planning, the responsible person should be considered for membership on the DPC, or consulted fully throughout the planning process.

Insurance is a complex field. The individual responsible should not expect to become expert in all of its facets, except when insurance is their primary function in the organization. Rather, the goal should be "...to become equal partners with the insurance firms in developing an insurance program to meet the present and to anticipate the future hazards facing their libraries" (Ungarelli 1984, 62).

5.7.2 Options for Coverage

While there are many types of insurance that an archives, library or record centre should consider, this section focuses on insurance coverage for collections, records and buildings.

The most common form of insurance taken out by archives, libraries and record centres is Physical Damage Cover Insurance, which is available as Named-Peril or All-Risk. Named-Peril is generally not recommended, since it provides protection only from the disaster named. An organization insured only against fire, for example, is not protected from flood.

All-Risk coverage, on the other hand, provides protection for all kinds of disasters and then proceeds to exclude this protection for certain cases, i.e., explosion, riots, hail, etc. By paying a higher premium, most of these exclusions can and should be removed. Damages resulting from war or radioactive contamination are excluded by law from insurance coverage. If a national disaster has been declared, the federal government may also compensate for losses *(see Appendix 2)*.

All-Risk coverage can apply to both buildings and contents. The general holdings should be put under a collective coverage based on the total number of items and their fair market value. Special collections and other particular risks should be individually covered in addition to the all-risk coverage.

Standard policies may be written to include extended coverage for valuable papers and records. Similar to a "Records" clause, it covers "the cost of reproducing books of account, abstracts, drawings, card index systems or any other records, including but not limited to film, tape, disc, drum, cell, magnetic recordings or any other storage media" (England and Evans 1988, 64).

Separate coverage for special papers in archives, libraries and record centres can be obtained as Valuable Papers and Records insurance for "...written, printed or otherwise inscribed documents and records, as books, maps, films, drawings, abstracts, deeds, mortgages and manuscripts" (England and Evans 1988, 64).

Fine Arts Floater coverage is usually intended for museums and art galleries, but can also include rare books and manuscripts held by libraries and archives.

Self-Insurance is an option selected by some organizations, especially government agencies. Instead of purchasing commercial insurance, a sum of monies is put aside annually to cover minor losses or damage. Alternatively, organizations can opt for a combination of commercial and self-insurance. A 1990 survey conducted by the Association of Research Libraries found that for buildings, over 41 percent of member respondents carried commercial insurance, 37 percent were self-insured and 33 percent used a combination of commercial and self-insurance (Myers 1991, 45).

5.7.3 Requirements for Risk Management Planning

The insurer requires the insured to preplan in order to meet the terms of the insurance contract. Gordon Wright identified the requirements for disaster planning that result from the statutory conditions for insurance policies that apply in Canada, except for Quebec, as follows. These requirements remain valid today.

1. To know and understand the liabilities of the institution as defined by the insurance policy.

2. To establish a sound policy for the maintenance of an adequate inventory and to ensure [that] these inventories are secure from damage. Microfilm and databases are key to being able to produce an inventory of the collections.

3. To ensure that technical details and plans of the organization are up to date and secure.

4. To establish with the insurer the cost parameters under which the organization will prepare its claim for loss.

5. To obtain the agreement of the insurer on the availability of expert advice.

6. To maintain a continuous dialogue with the insurer or the insurer's assessor to clarify the liabilities of both parties in the event of a claim.

7. To know the items insured, the location of the most expensive and irreplaceable items, and the cost and location of preservation facilities and services.

8. To isolate all those items which should be available to the organization to assist in mitigating loss.

9. To consider security of the area during salvage operation and the space required to salvage the material.

10. To assess the types of disasters and emergencies that may occur with particular reference to your locality.

11. To develop a procedural chart showing lines of communication and responsibilities for dealing with the emergency.

12. To develop a mechanism for periodic review and updating of the plan.

(Based on Wright 1979, 255-259)

The prescient reader will recognize that these activities parallel the process of disaster planning. Requirements 2 and 7 underline the necessity of maintaining up-to-date records in order to settle any claims after a disaster, as well as knowing which collections have top priority.

5.7.4 Evaluation of Property

Careful consideration must be given to an accurate and realistic assessment of the value of all property *before* any disaster happens. The following kinds of property should be evaluated for coverage: buildings, renovations, furniture, fixtures, equipment, collection materials, vital records, employees' property (at work) and equipment or collection materials on loan to the institution. The sheer number of items makes the evaluation of individual items difficult. Many organizations divide their collections into categories and then determine an average value for each category. As G. Myers (1977, 21) notes, "the greater the number of categories into which the library's collection can be divided, the more accurate and reliable will be the final value."

The insurance company will meet only the liabilities stated in the policy. In the case of fine art or valuable papers insurance, for archives and libraries, the insurer agrees in advance on the value for purposes of loss settlement. In other cases, property losses are settled on the basis of replacement cost (actual cost with no depreciation deduction) or actual cash value (fair market value or replacement cost less depreciation). In some circumstances, settlement may be based on a combination of the above. Of course, the cost of replacing an item may be considerably more than its assigned value.

Although it may be tempting to undervalue the holdings in order to avoid high premiums, it is inadvisable to do so, since most policies have a co-insurance clause which makes the organization a co-insurer. This clause reduces the insurance company's liability in proportion to the difference between the real value and that given by the policy. For example, if an item worth $1,000 is valued at $800 and the loss incurred is $600, the compensation will not be $600, but $600 multiplied by $800/$1,000 = $480. In effect, the insured, by undervaluing, co-insures the item for the difference of $120.

Conversely, there is a danger of valuating the object over its market value to the point where the value of the collection exceeds the insurance coverage. Where a damaged item is assessed as having lost 100 percent of its market value it may have to be surrendered to the insurance company irrespective of the settlement received.

After a disaster the organization will be required to furnish an assessment of damages and proof of loss *(see 10.2.7 and 10.7)*. The DPC must consider this requirement during the planning process.

5.8 Data and Systems Preparedness Strategies

The purpose of preparing strategies for data and systems is to minimize any damage and disruption to services resulting from a disaster in order to resume normal operations in a timely fashion.

> Forget about the computer, the goal is to keep the library running (Miller 1988, 357).

As noted in Chapter 1, there exists a parallel programme to disaster planning in the business community. The process of "planning to ensure the continued availability of essential services, programs, and operations, including all the resources involved" is known as business resumption planning (EPC 1995, 2). In general, the emphasis in business resumption planning (BRP) lies in its focus and speed. BRP endeavours to restore services with a minimum of delay rather than concentrating on the cause of the disruption (Daley 1991, 3), and thus concerns itself with many critical data, records and systems issues.

According to a study by the University of Texas Center for Research on Information Systems:

> 90% of all data losses with resulting partial or complete business disruption are attributable to the following incidents: power failures, water leaks, loose cables, user mistakes, hardware, software, and human errors (Tydlaska 1996, 25).

It is beyond the scope of this publication to describe fully the establishment of a comprehensive resumption plan; however, we outline the basic process as it applies to protecting electronic data and systems. We refer the reader to additional business resumption planning sources in the references: *The Disaster Recovery Handbook* (Buckland, 1991), which provides an extensive analysis of alternative recovery strategies and *Business Resumption Planning – A Guide* (Emergency Preparedness Canada, 1995).

5.8.1 Goals

The goals for data and systems protection should be based on level of service disruption deemed acceptable by the organization and the measures needed to achieve this level. The following chart outlines various possible goals for data protection in descending order of cost.

Planning Goals for Data Protection

Potential Goal	Comment
No downtime ever	Requires redundancy and live secondary sites. Requires continuous onsite and offsite back-up. Requires generator for prolonged power outage.
Minimal downtime	Requires contingency planning for alternate sites. Requires current onsite and offsite back-up.
Never lose access to any data	Requires current onsite and off site back-up. Requires back-ups for all users.
Never lose access to critical data	Requires current onsite and off site back-ups. Requires back-ups for critical systems.
Never lose much data	Requires periodic onsite or off site back-ups. Not a recommended goal.

(Software Partners cited in Tydlaska 1996, 23).

5.8.2 Options

A review of the professional literature indicates that the preparedness strategies most often considered include: data back-ups and offsite storage, system and facility back-ups (cold sites, hot sites, and reciprocal arrangements), and adequate insurance coverage, or any combination of the above. In addition to these strategies, an organization might consider a reduction or delay of services, especially those determined to be non-essential or discretionary. Instant recovery, where data processing occurs at another location on demand, is an option rarely considered by archives, libraries and record centres due to the prohibitive cost.

a) Data Back-Ups

The importance of back-ups is obvious to anyone whose work depends on computers and the "failure to have them is inexcusable negligence and incompetent management" (Cunha 1992, 593). Power outages, drive, tape or disk failures and the resulting loss of data and service, and wasted staff time underline the need for a systematic approach to back-ups and their assured availability.

The most cost-efficient way to prevent loss of data is to continually create and store back-up copies in secure locations. Back-ups of electronic databases, applications software, financial information and any other records essential to the organization should be stored and maintained offsite. The emphasis should be on a considered and consistent approach with back-ups in more than one site. Storage of back-ups with the originals or even in the same building may result in the loss or damage of both, or render the information inaccessible in the event of a disaster. A comprehensive back-up strategy will return the effort expended when compared with the labour, tedium and costs involved in regathering and recreating an entire database. "Studies have shown that it takes about eight hours to replace every hour of lost data" (Krohe cited in Kahn 1994a, 23).

Number and Frequency of Data Back-Ups

Determination of the number and frequency of back-ups and their storage is dependent on the significance of the information, the vulnerability of the data, the size and complexity of the databases, and associated costs. Some organizations base the frequency of back-ups and number of copies to be created on the vital records retention schedule. Data with, say, a retention period of two years may warrant three back-ups. Data with an extended retention period of say, 30 years may warrant five back-ups. The business community generally recommends making three copies of critical data.

Many sources suggest doing daily back-ups for data files, and backing up the software applications when any changes have occurred. Each organization must decide what type and level of risk to data is acceptable to them.

Offsite Storage of Back-Ups

Multiple copies of data and software applications should be made. Daily data back-ups could be stored both onsite, and offsite, so that the loss of any one set of back-ups does not prevent recovery. Some organizations store a duplicate set in another city in case the disaster is widespread and their site is inaccessible.

Weekly back-ups should be stored offsite, ideally with a contracted commercial records storage centre that provides scheduled pick-ups and delivery for tapes and disks and that stores them in climate-controlled, protected facilities. Record storage centres are in business to assure the security of data for their clients. As a client, it is up to the organization to thoroughly investigate that the company is able to do just that. Vouglas (1996, 25) provides an extensive checklist related to the selection of a commercial records storage centre.

It is advisable to document and back-up the systems' operating and recovery procedures.

Maintenance of Data Back-Ups

As well as maintaining an inventory of stored data back-ups, it is important to schedule regular quality checks and any subsequent copying of the disks, tapes, etc. held in storage, as they deteriorate over time. The technology (operating and application systems and equipment) needed to read the information must be available or the data will be inaccessible.

Changes made to the master files must also be made to the back-ups or the information will be out of date.

b) Systems Back-Ups

LANs and WANs

Local area networks (LANs) and wide area networks (WANs) allow multiple users to work concurrently on a computer system. In addition to the standard systems back-up procedures, individual users who have their customized programmes, databases, etc. must document and adequately back-up these applications as well.

The frequency of back-ups should vary according to the situation. Continuous or daily back-ups are considered standard. Onsite secure LAN storage is only appropriate in the short term. Offsite storage is preferable because in the case of major disaster, the facility may be inaccessible and the data damaged.

Most LANs are well protected by back-up procedures. But a 1994 survey of the biggest companies in the U.S. (including government agencies and non-profit organizations) showed that when all the data stored on the network (both clients and servers) is considered, only about half of the data is protected by back-up procedures. This dramatically increases LAN vulnerability. (Tydlaska 1996, 26)

Stand-Alone PCs

Arrangements for the back-up of personal computers (PCs) are relatively straightforward. Generally, stand-alone PCs are not backed up with the same regularity as other computer systems. The goal should be to recover the system in about one day after a disaster. Preparedness measures for PC systems include: having offsite back-ups for data and software; recording the hardware, software and telecommunications requirements; making arrangements ahead of time to replace the hardware; and then reconfiguring the software for the new system.

Hardware Checklist

A list of PC hardware should be prepared including:

- supplier (original vendor and current supplier)
- make, model and serial number
- configuration, e.g., 8 Mb RAM etc.
- boards added, e.g., modem board
- drives e.g., one 3.5 inch, one 5.25 inch and one CD-ROM
- memory e.g., 200 Mb disc
- any other specialized additions, e.g., such as cables and peripherals

In addition, the make, model, serial number and blocking factors for the hard drive(s) should be recorded. (Turner 1994, 39)

Software Checklist

A list of all PC software should be prepared including:

- supplier
- name of package
- version
- your registration number
- help line telephone number
- alterations made to files such as the "autoexec" or "config.sys" files in order to run the program

In addition, a record of your computer or server directory organization should be maintained so that the directory paths can be restored. (Turner 1994, 39)

c) Facility Back-Ups

Facility back-ups were once considered the domain of the private sector. Increasingly, public sector organizations such as archives, libraries and record centres that rely on mainframe computers and networks to provide service are using facility back-ups.

Providing services with as little disruption as possible is the goal of disaster preparedness. This would prove difficult if the facility is severely damaged or inaccessible. In order for the organization to have a functioning computer system as soon as possible, it may be necessary to plan for the use of alternative sites.

Temporary accommodations and systems arrangements must be planned well in advance. Back-ups will be of little use if equipment and software are unavailable, unworkable or incompatible.

Site Strategies

Temporary sites and arrangements may include reciprocal arrangements and alternative sites (cold and hot). As part of disaster planning, the DPC should identify facility sources with adequate capacity for the computer applications deemed essential.

Reciprocal Arrangements

Smaller organizations might consider making reciprocal arrangements with organizations nearby that would not only be willing, but would also have the required space and equipment and systems configurations to accommodate your computer systems. This arrangement should be formalized in advance. All details should be clearly understood by both parties, and adequate preparation time provided to test the systems' compatibility.

Alternate Sites

- **Cold sites** are usually commercially owned buildings, or spaces in buildings controlled by the organization that can be set up with computer and telecommunications systems when necessary. The space is maintained unequipped but with power, air conditioning, etc. When disaster strikes, the organization staffs and equips the space, provides the hardware, software and any data back-ups. This type of site is usually operational days after the disaster.

- **Hot sites** are commercially operated computer facilities that are fully equipped with hardware, software and telecommunications equipment. These facilities are staffed at all times and can have the organization functional in a matter of hours. This service must be previously contracted and is costly.

  After a disaster, the organization brings its data back-ups and staff to the hot site and begins operations. In general, six weeks is the maximum time for access to a hot site. DeLuca (1996, 22) recommends having access to both hot and cold sites, with the cold site being used after the contract with the hot site ends.

Hot Site Checklist

When negotiating with hot-site providers, the following comparisons should be made:
- monthly cost
- contract term
- test time allocated
- early cancellation requirements/cost
- vendor compensation if contract not fulfilled
- activation cost
- usage cost
- number of subscribers
- availability of other sites
- networking capability/capacity
- technical expertise and assistance available
- installed base for hardware/software
- upgrade criteria
- long term viability of hot site provider
- experience specific to your industry
- number of actual disasters declared and successful activations
- references (positive and negative)
- startup manuals provided
- other services provided

(Jackson cited in Foster 1996, 33)

Current literature points to controversies involving the use of these sites. Miller (1988, 356-357) cautions that aside from the overhead costs, their usefulness depends on being able to restart your system on different hardware and he concludes "that the cost and the effort for either approach is beyond the means of most libraries". Related issues include, being able to re-establish network connections and deal with data security, and data integrity in an unfamiliar environment.

Schreider (1994, 24) points out that "nearly 50 per cent of all companies that recover at a hot site stay there less than 48 hours" and suggests that what may be needed is, "a back-up power strategy rather than a back-up computer site." He concludes that organizations should "exhaust all options before forcing the company to move from its present location." *(See also 4.10.1)*

5.8.3 Costs

The costs associated with backing up electronic data and systems and offsite storage are much less than the costs of either attempting to recover the hardware and software or regathering and recreating the information after a disaster. However, protective measures such as hot sites for data and systems involve heavy expenditure. The DPC must carefully weigh the costs associated with recovering data and systems against the organization's need to provide continued service. The need for complete and instant recovery is often overstated. The length of time between the disaster and full restoration of service can be extended in many instances without serious repercussions. A temporary reduction in the level of service may be acceptable.

The following factors should be considered when costing a plan for data and systems protection:

· the size and complexity of the electronic data systems

· the level of service and length of downtime the organization is willing to accept after a disaster

· the probability of emergency or disaster happening

· the potential financial impact of loss

· the cost of disaster preparedness measures including overhead costs for sites

· the existing insurance coverage (see 5.2.5).

Insurance can provide some compensation to replace computer hardware, software, etc. This type of insurance is commonly known as EDP (electronic data processing) coverage and can also cover expenses such as computer rental. Other costs involved – such as for temporary sites, equipment rental, staff time and "proven loss of revenue" – can be covered with business interruption insurance. However, this type of insurance does not cover any costs incurred in recreating databases.

In a 1991 Association of Research Libraries survey, only 4 percent of respondents carried special insurance for their electronic data (Myers 1991, 46).

The following table shows that recovery time has a significant impact on the costs. The options in this table are presented in descending order of cost. The table is not intended to reflect incremental cost between the options.

The instant recovery with "no downtime and no data loss" option is the ideal. It is also the least used and by far the most expensive option and, depending on the type of operation, it may not be necessary to restore every function immediately. For example, one or several day's downtime or loss of data might be acceptable to some organizations and this decision would result in significant savings. The aim is to find the option that meets the goals for data and systems protection at the least cost.

5.8.4 Review and Modification of the Strategies

Based on a determination of the goals, and assessment of the options and costs, a strategy should be undertaken and modified as necessary to prepare and implement data and systems' protection. The strategy may be as simple as frequent back-ups with offsite storage or may involve outside agencies and contracted hot sites. Buckland (1991, 25) suggests determining the essential services of the organization and starting with, "a short-term, high-impact plan to get sufficient procedures in place that will handle the most pressing needs...". This strategy would help cover the organization's critical functions in the short term, thereby allowing it to develop a full plan to reintroduce the remaining function. It also necessitates additional expertise and resources, and while usually less costly, the risks are greater if not well planned.

5.8.5 Testing the Strategy

Testing the strategy should be conducted in much the same way as testing the overall disaster plan (see 2.2.13). As well, in order to ensure the resumption of critical functions, it is essential to conduct connectivity tests, i.e., testing the programmes at the pre-arranged sites on the available systems within a prescribed time. It is use-

Effect of Recovery Time on Cost of Disaster Planning

Option	Description	Recovery Time
Instant recovery [most expensive]	"Mirror-image" processing takes place in another site on demand	Minutes to hours
Hot site	Alternate, fully equipped and operational data centre on standby	Hours to a few days
Cold site	Data centre "shell" ready to receive equipment	A few days minimum
No alternate site [least expensive]	Original data centre to be recovered	From days to months

(Ontario Management Board of Cabinet 1991, 7-3-13).
(Copyright © Queen's Printer for Ontario, 1991. Reproduced with permission. From *Information Technology Security: A Managers Guide. Ontario Management Board of Cabinet Guideline 7:3.*)

ful to conduct a test without the aid of the organization's most technically adept staff.

5.8.6 Maintenance

Data and systems preparedness strategies should be maintained in the same way as the disaster plan. In addition, any changes in the critical functions of the organization as well as in the hardware, software or network configurations to support these functions must also be integrated into the plan and tested. This means that back-up media in all formats must be properly scheduled and removed to secure storage, and that back-up sites must be maintained in operable condition. In addition, the viability of these strategies should be evaluated and reported to the DPC twice a year.

5.9 Collections and Records Recovery Priorities

Overall collections and records recovery priorities for the organization should be based on the outcome of reviews previously outlined in this chapter for existing programmes or strategies, including those for materials of intrinsic value, vital records, insurance coverage, and electronic data and systems.

Setting recovery priorities organization-wide is labour-intensive and demands an objective big-picture approach. It is impractical to consider collections and records on an item-by-item basis. Instead, related parts of collections or related collections should be grouped for the purpose of setting priorities. Some decisions will be obvious, while others may require considerable discussion and consultation. The DPC must involve staff from all relevant departments, so that it can determine where best to put the organization's efforts and resources into both protection (to mitigate the possibility of a disaster) and recovery (after a disaster).

> ...each library must establish its own priorities based on its own situation and needs. It can be disastrous, or at the very least, embarrassing, if the staff has not agreed about which materials and/or records *must* be removed from the building or protected (DePew 1991a, 257).

This organization-specific process requires input from and the cooperation of many departments and individuals. A coordinated assessment process for departmental and functional priorities will be needed to develop the organization's overall priorities in a balanced way.

5.9.1 Recovery Priority Considerations

The determination of collections and records priorities involves a large number of disparate factors. The following considerations may be used in guiding deliberations:

- the importance of the collections and records to the mandate, programmes and services of the organization, and to the wider community. This would encompass not only the unique and inherently valuable collections and records, but also those that are high-use and/or vital to core operations.

- the historical, cultural or scholarly value of the collections and records, e.g., materials in their original format that have intrinsic value, rare and out-of-print items, and items the organization is legally obliged to protect.

- the monetary value of the collections and records.

- the availability, ease and cost of replacement for the collections and records. Alternative formats should be explored, such as reprints, microforms and digital images. If available elsewhere, the cost implications need to be considered.

- the collections and records that could be considered for discard in the event of disaster. These might include reference works that are updated yearly, and embrittled materials of which copies have been made according to accepted standards.

- the potential for recovery of the collections and records. Determinations should be made as to whether the organization could provide in-house treatment or whether external expertise and services would be required in the event of a disaster. Items that are already damaged or fragile will complicate the recovery effort. These materials must be identified and protected using measures such as secure storage and duplication.

There are no standard criteria for measuring the relative importance of one collection over another or for establishing priority categories; however, guidelines in the professional literature can be used as a starting point for discussion. The following recovery priority categories are based in part on DePew (1991a, 273-274). He drew upon the work of the Inland Empire Libraries Disaster Response Network (IELDRN) and the University of California at Los Angeles Biomedical Library, which had developed sets of recommendations to establish salvage priorities.

5.9.2 Recovery Priority Categories for Collections

In order of descending priority:

1. Bibliographic records of the collections (shelflists, card catalogue or electronic storage). Personnel

and financial records, acquisition and cataloguing tools and any other records vital to the organization's operations. All of the above *must* be protected, duplicated or backed-up and stored off-site to prevent their irretrievable loss.

2. Collections and archival records that support the organization's current programmes and services, and that cannot be replaced. These could include reference collections, high-use current materials, special collections with intrinsic value and materials that are too costly to replace or are irreplaceable.

3. Collections and records that support the organization's current programmes and services, and that are replaceable, i.e., the information could be acquired in the same or another format. If these were lost, the strength of the collection as a whole would be jeopardized and the impact on users would be considerable.

4. Collections and records that support the collecting and information goals of the organization, but can be more easily and less expensively replaced than recovered. Such materials, if heavily damaged, could be replaced after a disaster.

5. Collections and records that do not need to be recovered or replaced and could be discarded, such as, older editions that have been superseded by newer versions and have no historical value.

5.9.3 Summary of Factors to Consider when Setting Collections Recovery Priorities

The mandate and mission of the organization will drive decisions made when setting collections recovery priorities.

Once consensus is reached and the recovery priorities are finalized, this information must be appended to the disaster plan, and the locations of these collections and records clearly marked on floor plans. Where confidentiality of this information is an issue, distribution of marked plans should be limited. The Disaster Action Team members must be completely familiar with these priorities and the location of the high priority material as well as their respective access routes. Staff training plans must include clear communication of these priorities.

Importance of Collection and Impact of Loss	Value of Collection	Replaceability of Collection	Recoverability of Collection
Consider collection - importance and impact of loss to the organization and public:	Consider various values of the collection:	Consider potential replaceability of collection and resources required:	Consider potential recoverability of the collection and resources required:
· Mandate and mission · Provision of core services · Provision of support services · Usership · Use and demand · Access provided · Community support · Funding and revenue · Image and reputation · Relationship to other collections · Relationship to other organizations	· Intrinsic · Documentary · Informational · Research · Reference · Scholarly · Cultural · Historical · Artistic · Popular · Legal and administrative · Monetary · Sentimental	· Discard · Irreplaceable · Theoretically replaceable · Readily replaceable · Method of replacement · Availability · Replacement format · Copyright issues · Overall ease of replacement · Replacement timeline · Cost of replacement	· Nature and size of collection · Existing damage · Fragility · Media and material sensitivity to loss · Protective and secure storage issues · Type and degree of treatment required · Available expertise · Estimated success of treatment · Treatment timeline · Cost of treatment

5.10 Relocation Sites and Duplication/Dispersal Strategies

As a result of the risk hazard analysis *(see 3.3)* and the priority-setting exercise above, it may be decided that the risks facing the collections and records are high and that current protection strategies are inadequate. If so, existing strategies for their relocation and/or duplication will need to be modified.

5.10.1 Relocation Sites

Relocation sites can mean either a location where collections and records can be stored as a general protective measure or a location to which items can be moved in advance when disaster threatens. These relocation sites can be in a safer location within the building or at a site external to the facility.

a) Relocation Within the Building

Permanent relocation of collections and records to secure storage, such as rooms, vaults or safes within the building is an option, especially for materials in need of additional protection that cannot be taken offsite for reasons of access, security, cost, etc. Temporary relocation may be necessary prior to or after a disaster where the risk of damage is high.

b) Relocation Offsite

The relocation of collections and records to another site may be considered as part of a general ongoing protective strategy, and is sometimes referred to as decentralization. Offsite relocation should also be considered when there is sufficient advance warning of a wide-scale disaster or when a repository has been damaged and the collections must be moved to protect them.

Removing the collections to another location can be risky due to factors such as security, damage in transit, and exposure to different environmental conditions. In order to reduce these risks, the relocation of the collections must be planned well in advance.

Relocation Checklist

· Determine the suitability of the site: its accessibility, size, security and environmental control.
· Make arrangements beforehand (contracts with movers and storage).
· Ensure insurance coverage for the collections while in transit and offsite.
· Maintain an up-to-date inventory of the relocated collections.
· Train the staff responsible in proper packing methods and arrange for adequate supplies and equipment.
· Document relocation arrangements in the disaster plan as necessary.

(Based in part on Hunter 1983, 251).

5.10.2 Duplication and Dispersal

Duplication and dispersal are measures that can be taken to ensure the protection of vital or high priority materials in the event of a disaster. The intrinsic value of some materials requires that they be retained and protected in their original form. In other cases, however, it may be appropriate and possible to duplicate the originals. In instances where duplication is legally acceptable, and where the information, not the medium, is vital, duplication and dispersal of copies may prove the simplest, most cost-effective means of protection. See National Standard of Canada *CAN/CGSB -72.11-93. Microfilm and Electronic Images as Documentary Evidence*, as well as *ISO/Technical Report ISO/TR 10200: 1990. Legal Admissibility of Microforms.*

a) Record Duplication Versus Record Recovery

An assessment of options and costs involved in the duplication of records needs to be undertaken. Decisions will then be made on the cost effectiveness of duplicating the records versus their recreation or recovery after the disaster.

Questions to consider:
· Is the material considered vital to the organization's mandate?
· Does the material exist elsewhere? In the same format? Is it accessible and how?
· Can or should the records be replaced or reconstruct?
· What would be the replacement cost in comparison to costs required to recreate the destroyed records?

One organization weighed the pros and cons this way:

> ...it was clear that offsite storage of certain types of records and the duplication of other records was preferred to the costs of either salvaging the records or trying to re-gather the information. In other instances, where the cost of duplicating the records was more than the estimated value of the information itself, the City decided to gamble on the possibility of disaster occurring. (Balon and Gardner 1987, 15)

b) Dispersal of Duplicate Records

Dispersal is the means by which the records are protected by sending copies offsite. To an extent, dispersal may already be built into standard operations. Organizations that normally function at more than one location may have copies of records such as payroll, minutes and directives, that are issued to all locations. Many of these records will be classified as vital. Duplicate copies of land title, patent and other records are maintained in government land registry or patent offices. Banks and insurance companies also maintain duplicates of vital corporate records. Of concern, however, is the ready availability of and access to these records in the event of a disaster.

Duplication of the records may be achieved at the time of creation, at point of acquisition or subsequently, through various methods: photocopying, microfilming, or electronically. The use of microforms or electronic media has the added benefit of minimizing storage space, and of being more easily and economically reproduced and dispersed.

Some sources make the case for selecting collections based on the value, condition, age, provenance, etc. and duplicating and/or storing them offsite as part of the regular archival processing procedure. For many organizations this would not be feasible.

Whichever duplication and dispersal options are chosen, they should be documented in the disaster plan.

c) Storage of Duplicate Records

Duplicate or back-up records must be stored offsite. These should include back-ups for electronic databases, card catalogues and any other records vital to your organization's operations *(see 5.8.2a)*.

5.11 Disaster-Related Equipment, Supplies and Services

The DPC will need to consider the organization's requirements regarding disaster-related equipment, supplies and services. Some equipment and supplies should be purchased in advance and stored onsite and/or in a nearby location. The availability, ordering requirements, costs, etc. of services, and other supplies and equipment should be determined so that needs may be swiftly met after a disaster. The DPC should also consider alternatives to direct purchase. Some equipment, supplies and services may be available through parent organizations and the loan of equipment from other organizations may be an option.

Some response and recovery supplies, such as plastic sheeting, blotting paper and other non-perishables should be kept onsite in protective storage, commonly known as emergency depots. Hunter (1990, 10:15) advises against storing "perishable materials, expensive equipment, and larger quantities of non-perishable supplies."

Some essential supplies can be kept in what the National Archives and National Library of Canada call an "entry cabinet." This cabinet should be as close as possible to a building entrance. It would contain an emergency pack with one or more copies of the disaster plan, essential keys, and other supplies. These supplies could include protective clothing, flashlights, caution tape, etc. Subsequent to safety clearance, they would allow the Disaster Action Team to quickly initiate any needed inspection and assessment of damage. In addition, DAT members should also store any planned-for supplies, equipment and personal protective wear at home.

5.11.1 Disaster Funds

It is impossible and impractical to stock every supply that may be needed for use after a disaster. For this reason, provision should be made for the prompt purchase of supplies not on hand. Accounts with local businesses should be established in advance and purchase orders or a credit card included in the entry cabinet. For items that can be purchased only with cash, a disaster account could be established with a nearby bank and the bank card included in the entry cabinet. Appropriate security measures for authorization, use and storage of these cards and purchase orders should be established.

5.11.2 Equipment and Supply Checklists

The following equipment and supply checklists anticipate a variety of disaster-related needs. Each organization must anticipate its own requirements and plan accordingly. Housekeeping procedures related to the maintenance of the supplies should be established such as: creating a master supplies list; appointing a staff member to periodically verify supplies and ensure that these supplies are not used for other purposes.

Provisions for People Checklist

In the event of a major or community-wide disaster, people may be trapped in the workplace or be without transportation, and thus not be able to return home for some time. The organization should be prepared to function as an emergency shelter for several days. Note: Emergency Preparedness Canada has compiled a comprehensive emergency shelter supplies list.

More often, supplies are needed to sustain personnel who are working long hours throughout response and recovery operations. This list outlines minimal basic requirements.

- first-aid supplies and equipment that meet legislated requirements
- safety supplies and equipment that meet legislated requirements (see General Supplies Checklist)
- identification badges
- drinking water
- refreshments and snacks
- a list of twenty-four hour restaurants and food delivery services
- blankets
- battery-powered radios
- washrooms and telephones
- secure storage for personal belongings
- rest areas with chairs and tables

(See also 6.6.2g and 6.6.3f)

General Supplies Checklist

Clean-up and Repair
- wet and dry vacuum cleaners and hoses
- hand/electric pumps to remove water
- a source of clean running water
- janitorial supplies: cleansers, disinfectants, mops, sponges, scrub brushes, squeegees, brooms, buckets, clear plastic trash bags
- emergency repair tools and supplies such as hammers, pliers, nails, plywood, etc.
- towels, hand cleanser, soap

Protective Wear
- dust masks, respirators, goggles and safety glasses
- rubber, leather and latex gloves
- rubber boots, safety boots
- hard hats, disposable aprons, waterproof smocks and coats

Protective Materials
- tarpaulins and polyethylene sheeting (in rolls) to protect collections, to insulate windows and to cover tables during recovery operations
- dust sheets to protect furniture and equipment from debris
- tape, rope, bulldog clips

Absorbent Materials
- disposable diapers, sand bags, sawdust, spill control packs

Equipment and Supplies for Collections and Records Pack-Out Checklist

- paper towels, blotting paper, sponges
- interlocking plastic milk crates and cardboard boxes of standard sizes for packing collection and records materials
- bakers bread trays for packing large volumes, maps, blueprints, etc.
- plastic pails, buckets, tubs, resealable bags and sponges for wet-stabilization packing of films and tapes
- book trucks, trolleys, and conveyor systems to transport and move materials
- pallets and hydraulic pallet movers
- sheets of polypropylene, masonite, cardboard, etc. for supporting materials
- packing materials: freezer paper, blank newsprint, file folders, sealing tape, utility knives and blades, scissors, waterproof marking pans, labels, etc.
- elasticized bandages for wrapping books

Supplies for Collections and Records Recovery Checklist

- absorbent paper (rolls and sheets) for covering tables: blank newsprint, blotters, paper towels, etc.
- interleaving supplies: blank newsprint, blotters, freezer paper, wax paper (white florist paper is absorbent, household paper is not), spunbonded polyester fabric sheets
- washing trays, washing tanks or large plastic garbage containers in which mud and dirt deposits can be washed from certain collection materials
- polyester and polyethylene sheeting/sheets
- bubblepack, felts
- lint-free cloths
- weights of various sizes and types, i.e., glass, bricks, etc.
- collections supports, i.e., book ends, etc.
- garbage bags and cans

Equipment Checklist

- emergency lighting (floodlights, flashlights of various sizes and lightsticks with extra batteries)
- fans and dehumidifiers to promote drying of the materials and reconditioning of the environment
- generators to power equipment (lights, air conditioners, fans, etc.)
- waterproof and grounded heavy-duty extension cords
- moisture meter to measure moisture content of wet materials *(see 6.5.6)*
- equipment for monitoring/recording temperature and relative humidity of damaged areas, treatment areas, and rehabilitated areas, i.e., thermohygrometer, thermohygrograph, battery-operated psychrometer, dataloggers, etc.
- camera, video camera and film/tape to document damage and recovery
- PCs, portable computers with software, disks, battery chargers
- barcode scanner equipment

Include copies of operating manuals or instructions for all equipment.

Both batteries and film have a limited shelf life. Check and replace as needed, as part of the supplies inventory.

Communications Equipment and Supplies Checklist

- telephones (portable or cellular) and walkie-talkies to coordinate the Disaster Action Team
- portable battery-operated radios for use in a major disaster. Special receivers are required for weather radio broadcasts *(see 6.3.5)*
- megaphones, especially if public address system has no back-up
- electronic pagers especially for large or complex buildings
- photocopier and paper or access to a photocopying service
- portable flip charts with paper and markers
- notice boards

Miscellaneous Equipment and Supplies Checklist

- general office supplies: paper, notebooks, pencils, permanent markers (waterproof), scissors, plastic paper clips, staplers, masking tape, measuring tapes, clip boards, etc.
- furniture: folding tables, chairs, etc.
- stanchions and spools of caution tape to cordon off the disaster areas

5.11.3 Services and Networks

As discussed in Chapter 2, a network of individuals and organizations that can provide advice, assistance, equipment or services should be established as part of the planning process. This may include companies with pre-existing contractual obligations to the organization, as well as professional service providers and individuals in related organizations.

a) Building and Systems Service Providers

- services for internal building systems (security, public address, fire detection, alarm and suppression, etc.)
- building and equipment maintenance and repair services (carpenters, electricians, plumbers, glaziers and locksmiths, HVAC, elevator, custodial services, etc.)
- insurance broker
- computer system services (hardware, software, network, offsite information storage)
- utility services (telephone, electricity, gas, hydro)
- pest control services

Current maintenance contracts should be checked to see if any contractual obligations apply in an emergency.

b) Emergency Facilities and Service Providers

· full recovery services
· transportation and storage services
· rental facilities (office, warehouse)
· freezer truck services
· freezer and cold storage facilities
· collections drying services
· photo and film recovery services
· data recovery services
· equipment recovery services
· furniture recovery services
· hot and cold site facilities
· pest control services
· sterile cleaning services

c) Professional Resource Network

Professional colleagues may be able to provide hands-on assistance or advisory support over the phone in times of emergency. This may include individuals from similar organizations or government agencies. To prepare for this, a frank discussion of your expectations will be necessary as other organizations will have limits as to the amount of time and resources they can provide. Permission should be obtained before including their names, home phone numbers, etc. in the disaster plan.

d) Conservators in Private Practice

Conservators in private practice are likely to be required for the recovery of specialized collections. Inquiries should be made ahead of time. Experience, qualifications, references, rates, etc. should be discussed. In addition, disaster-specific issues such as: direct disaster experiences, availability (short notice, evening or weekend and extra costs for same) and emergency conservation equipment needed (or provided) should be covered. Any arrangements made should be clearly outlined in the disaster plan.

e) Canadian Conservation Institute (CCI)

The CCI, an agency of the Department of Canadian Heritage, plays an important role in the ongoing development of disaster preparedness planning for archives, libraries, museums, galleries, etc. CCI staff have also successfully aided many organizations with their recovery efforts. CCI advises that its phone number should be posted in the organization for ready access in the case of disaster, and further that:

For Canada only –

In the event of an emergency where the safety of collections is at risk, contact CCI immediately for advice. Make sure you inform the CCI operator that you have an emergency. You may call at any hour of the day or night, seven days a week. During working hours, your call will be immediately connected with someone who can advise you. If you call during non-working hours, be prepared to give the CCI operator the following information:

· your name
· the name and location of your institution
· the phone number where you can be reached
· the size and nature of collections affected
· the type, extent and severity of damage
· what action has been taken so far

This information will be conveyed to a CCI staff member by means of a call-up list, and you will be contacted as soon as possible. Do not put off doing this. The sooner you are able to stabilize the condition of your collections, the less damage they will ultimately suffer.

(Stewart and Tremain 1994, 53-54)

In certain disaster situations, onsite assistance by CCI staff may be possible *(see Appendix 3.2 Sources of Assistance: Disasters and Conservation for CCI entry).*

Chapter 6

6.0 Disaster Response Planning

An organization's response to a disaster sets in motion strategies developed by the Disaster Planning Committee (DPC) during the planning phase and documented in the existing disaster plan. Response will also include the development of a recovery and operational support strategy for collections, records and the facility in reaction to the specific disaster. The strategy for the collections and records is addressed later in this chapter, and that for the facility in Chapter 9.

> Response is any action taken immediately before, during, or directly after an emergency occurs to save lives, minimize damage to property, and enhance the effectiveness of recovery (FEMA 1984, I-8).

Depending on the type of disaster and the capabilities of the organization, successful response may also depend upon the assistance of external resources. In the event of a major disaster, extraordinary effort and resources will be needed. This assistance will be complicated where a whole region is a disaster area, due to flooding, earthquake, armed conflict, etc., and when external services and facilities are not readily available. In the case of an earthquake of moderate severity, the organization should be prepared to be self-sufficient for a number of days. Some sources say 72 hours.

A disaster can strike with or without forewarning. Even if preventative, protective and preparedness measures were undertaken, they may prove unsuccessful in containing the emergency and preventing damage. Response is the first phase of reaction to a disaster, and puts to the test all those carefully prepared plans.

Appropriate immediate response to disaster can make the difference between successful recovery and severe loss. The better organized the response effort, the greater the likelihood will be of saving collections and records, preventing further damage, keeping costs to a minimum and ultimately returning to "normal" operations. The planning done in advance provides a framework of options and guidelines for response from which the Disaster Action Team (DAT) can make decisive, informed and rehearsed decisions in order to prepare and implement an effective recovery operation. A measured response is the primary goal. Speed is secondary.

6.1 The Purpose of Disaster Response Planning

The purpose of disaster response planning is for the DAT to develop the necessary resources to ensure human life and safety, to arrest an emergency and to limit the extent of a disaster, to retain or re-establish control of the facility and collections, and then to provide the basis for a successful recovery operation.

Response comprises the preplanned activities that enable personnel onsite to take quick action by sounding the alarm, calling the proper authorities, evacuating the building, activating the disaster plan if necessary, and then mobilizing personnel and assistance, containing the effects of the disaster, and moving into the recovery preparation phase. The latter forms the bridge to overall recovery. The existing disaster plan outlines recovery and associated support operations. These would be implemented and modified as necessary at the time of the disaster.

6.2 The Stages of Disaster Response Planning

In this chapter, disaster response planning has been divided into four distinct stages as follows:

Stage I   Disaster forewarning

Stage II   Immediate emergency response

Stage III   Recovery strategy: collections and records

Stage IV   Recovery strategy: support operations

The reason for this division is to clearly articulate for the planners the sequence of events that they would encounter during the course of a disaster, so that they may understand and anticipate what may be required at the time, and plan accordingly.

The sequence and activities outlined for each of the four stages are intended to provide a pragmatic framework that enables the DPC to plan the response section of the disaster plan. Actual response measures will vary according to factors such as the nature, scope and timing of the emergency or disaster, and the availability of internal and external sources of assistance. In some circumstances, actions will be limited to immediate response to an incident, such as an overflowing sink, while in other cases, full activation of the plan and extensive recovery operations will be required.

6.3 Stage I: Disaster Forewarning Planning

At this point in the disaster timeline, forewarning of a impending emergency/disaster may be imminent.

> In 1969 in China, [staff of] a large city zoo observed that a tiger was depressed, pandas screamed, yaks did not eat, turtles were restless, and swans stayed away from the water. Within just a few hours, there was a 7.4 earthquake (Weber 1990, 54).

Due to advances in science, technology and communications, we now have an increased ability to predict the occurrence of many types of natural disasters. The DPC should familiarize themselves with these means of prediction and their practical application. Disasters are not always unforeseen, but response begins with or without forewarning. In the event of a hurricane, flood, fire in a nearby building or civil disorder, forewarning may provide a critical period of time in which to prepare and take precautionary measures. Other disasters such as industrial explosions come with no warning. In all cases, safety of personnel and the public takes first priority.

In some cases, planning may be based on the increasing likelihood of an event, such as a major storm, and outline a series of steadily escalating actions. For example, the emergency manual of Mystic Seaport, an historic maritime site in Connecticut, includes action plans at four different levels in response to the most likely threat of hurricanes (Nelson 1991, 104-105):

Condition Watch There is persuasive indication of severe storm threat within 48 hours. Emergency plan is activated. Command center is established and preparedness tasks are initiated.

Condition I Storm is predicted to arrive within 36 hours. Long lead-time preparations continue. Site closure is minimal.

Condition II High winds and tides are expected within 12-18 hours. Major preparations begin: site is closed, emergency communications networks are activated, etc.

Condition III The storm is imminent. Preparedness measures are completed. Power is turned off. All staff members who have not volunteered for storm duty are dismissed.

When the storm has passed, the Mystic Seaport emergency plan goes into reverse. The command center evaluates the weather conditions and readiness is reduced down to Condition Watch and further as appropriate.

6.3.1 The Purpose of Disaster Forewarning Planning

> One of the most serious problems in disasters is not panic, but *unwillingness to believe and react even to obvious signs of danger* (Scanlon 1991, 91).

The purpose of disaster forewarning planning is to develop the resources and measures to alert people to the danger of possible impending disaster so that they may protect life and property. Forewarning provides a period of time, albeit varied, in which to prepare for the arrival of whatever disaster is forecast. This time can be profitably used for evacuation, if necessary, and the protection of human life and safety, as well as that of the organization and collections. The organization may already be on alert and in a state of readiness. In cases of severe weather disasters, activation of the disaster plan may proceed in stages.

6.3.2 The Process for Disaster Forewarning Planning

A common process is followed when forewarnings are issued by the authorities: the problem is detected; the threat is evaluated; a decision is made about what to do and then implemented; and a public warning is issued. In the case of a major or widespread disaster, personal survival preparation is critical.

Disaster Forewarning Planning: Process at a Glance

Prepare to:
- Follow instructions – if any were issued.
- Evacuate as necessary.
- Stay informed by staying tuned to radio, television, etc. for updates.
- Protect the facility, collections and records as much as possible.
- Perform a controlled shutdown of the computer system.

The decision whether to issue a warning is not always easy, such as in the case of an earthquake of low probability. The aim of forewarnings is to alert people to possible danger – about what to do and who is being warned, as well as identifying the agency that is issuing the warning. It is recommended that people familiarize themselves with what constitutes forewarning in their community, i.e., the various signals and terms used in warnings.

In general, authorities issue forewarnings for disasters of magnitude. As part of the organization's planning process, the DPC will have investigated the wider community's existing plans and will have established reciprocal links as appropriate. When a warning is issued, the organization's response should be coordinated with the community's response.

6.3.3 Fire Warnings

In general, there will be no advance warning of a fire. In some instances, such as a fire in a nearby building or a forest fire, forewarning may occur. A forewarning might also be issued in the case of arson, the leading identified cause of fires in U.S. libraries *(see 4.3.2)*.

The most common immediate warning of a building fire will be an audible fire alarm, manually set off at a fire alarm station in the building, or by the central monitoring station, after automatic systems detect a fire or activate the sprinkler system. This generally results in evacuation of the premises and arrival of the fire department.

6.3.4 Flood Warnings

Floods may develop over a period of days, as a result of heavy, prolonged precipitation. Or flash flooding can quickly result in raging waters from, for example, a storm surge, dam failure or a tsunami following an earthquake. Coastal areas and other low-lying regions are always vulnerable.

Under the British North America Act, the atmosphere in Canada falls under federal jurisdiction, whereas water resources are a provincial responsibility. Consequently, Environment Canada issues warnings for tornadoes, heavy rain and high winds, while flood warnings are issued by provincial agencies. As heavy rains can lead to flooding, the federal and provincial governments cooperate extensively whenever flood conditions arise.

The provincial body that issues flood warnings varies, although the procedures followed in each province are similar. In Ontario, the Atmospheric Environment Service of Environment Canada supplies weather forecasts to the Aviation, Flood and Fire Management Branch (AFFMB) of the Ministry of Natural Resources. The AFFMB, in turn, provides information to local conservation authorities and the Ministry's district offices which assess the local flood threat and issue warnings as required. Environment Canada and some provincial ministries issue flood risk maps for certain areas *(See Appendix 3.1 Sources of Information: Weather)*.

Flood condition terms:

- A *flood advisory* is issued when water levels, snow survey conditions, etc. indicate that flooding *may* occur.
- A *flood warning* is issued when conditions indicate that flooding *will* occur. The anticipated time and location is provided. Low-lying areas would be ordered evacuated.

If the provincial government is unable to cope with the flood emergency, assistance through Emergency Preparedness Canada can be requested *(see Appendices 2 and 3.2 Sources of Assistance: Disaster Planning and Recovery – National. Provincial and Territorial)*. This federal body has regional directors in every province and territory who coordinate emergency planning with their respective provincial governments.

6.3.5 Severe Weather Warnings

Weatheradio Canada is a national public service provided by the Atmospheric Environment Service (AES) of Environment Canada. It is a specialized VHF-FM (Very High Frequency-Frequency Modulated) radio network that broadcasts continuous, 24-hour-a-day, 7-day-a-week weather information. Weatheradio Canada maintains a cross-country network of main stations that serve main urban areas, as well as repeater stations. The service provides continuously updated weather reports, both current conditions and forecasts, as well as any weather warnings in effect.

Weatheradio Canada stations broadcast throughout the country on an eight-minute cycle on one of the three assigned frequencies in the VHF-FM band: 162.40 MHz, 162.475 MHz and 162.55 MHz. In most cases, special radio receivers are needed to receive these transmissions. AES maintains a list of approved Weatheradio Canada receivers across Canada. Many of the approved radios incorporate special visual and audible signals to automatically alert listeners to severe weather conditions.

Severe weather can also be monitored on AM radio or television (i.e., The Weather Network/Channel). Radio and TV stations will stay on the air unless power is lost, in which case it is generally easier for radio stations to switch to backup generators. Now is the time to use your battery-powered radio.

Many Internet sites focus on the weather and Environment Canada maintains a number of regional sites *(see Appendix 3.1 Sources of Information: Weather)*. The WeatherNet site maintained by the University of Michigan covers most major centres in Canada, in addition to the United States, and provides hundreds of hyperlinks to weather sites around the world.

In the United States, a new warning system, the Emergency Alert System (EAS), has been developed to cover everything from severe weather to war. Information is transmitted from broadcasting stations and cable systems to televisions, radios, pagers, etc.

a) Blizzards

Blizzards are severe winter storms accompanied by very heavy snowfall, high winds and often extreme cold. Visibility is usually severely reduced, and power failures can occur. Sleet (a mixture of rain and frozen snow or ice pellets and hail) may result.

Winter storm terms:

· A *winter storm warning* is issued when heavy snow, sleet or freezing rain is anticipated.

· A *blizzard warning* is issued when heavy snow and winds in excess of 35 mph (56 km/h) are anticipated.

· A *severe blizzard warning* is issued when very cold temperatures below 14°F (-10°C), heavy snow, visibility less than 500 metres (547 yards) and winds in excess of 45 mph (72 km/h) are anticipated.

(Based on FEMA 1990, 116 and McFarlane and Clements 1996, 388)

b) Hurricanes

These severe cyclonic storms are known as hurricanes in the Atlantic, typhoons in the Pacific and cyclones in the Indian Ocean. Hurricanes originate in the Caribbean and tropical Atlantic.

A hurricane begins as a disorganized storm system over warm waters. When it becomes more organized, it is classified as a "tropical depression". It is reclassified as a "tropical storm" and given a name when the winds reach 40 mph (61 km/h). The storm is upgraded to a "hurricane" when the winds reach 75 mph (121 km/h). (Yatcom 1995a, 1)

Hurricanes are severe storms, generally relatively slow moving over water at 10-15 mph or 14-16 km/h, permitting forewarning as to when and where the storm will make landfall. However once over land, hurricanes move more quickly. Hurricanes are now monitored by satellite, and advisories may be issued days in advance. Radio and television broadcasts will issue preparedness instructions. Particular attention should be paid to weather alerts during hurricane season (June to November).

Hurricane terms:

· A *hurricane watch* is issued when hurricane conditions pose a threat to an area normally within 24 hours of the start of the watch. There will be bad weather at a minimum, possibly gale-force winds of 30+mph (48+km/h), possibly high waters and flash flooding, and maybe tornadoes.

· A *hurricane warning* is issued when hurricane conditions are expected within 24 hours. Low-lying areas would be ordered evacuated. There will probably be 75+mph (121+km/h) winds plus high waters, tidal surges, flooding and tornadoes.

(Based on FEMA 1990, 118 and Yatcom 1995b, 2)

c) Tornadoes

Tornadoes are very violent, destructive storms, and are more localized than hurricanes. Radio and television broadcasts will issue preparedness instructions. When approaching, tornadoes make a very distinctive sound, like that of a roaring train (Yatcom 1995e, 1). A very small tornado is called a twister. According to the Fujita-Pearson Scale, the winds of a tornado range from 40-318 mph (64-512 km/h) *(see 3.4.3b)*.

Tornadic storms can be detected using Doppler radar, however radar cannot always determine when the tornado is in contact with the ground. In the future, seismic signals generated by ground-contact tornadoes may be used to detect and warn of imminent tornadoes.

Tornado terms:

· A *tornado watch* is issued when tornadoes and/or severe thunderstorms are likely to strike an area.

Stay tuned to radio and television reports for local information.

· A *tornado warning* is issued when the funnel of the tornado has been sighted in the area.

Shelter should be sought immediately.

(Based on FEMA 1990, 119)

6.3.6 Earthquake Warnings

The ability of experts to forecast specific earthquakes is constantly improving; however, earthquakes are still characterized by their lack of predictability. For example, the 1994 Northridge earthquake (near Los Angeles), like others, such as that near Loma Prieta, "demonstrated that damaging earthquakes do not always occur on well-known, mapped faults..." (Brown 1994, 105). In addition to measurement of earthquake activity by seismograph, other methods are being developed to improve mapping of earthquake hazards. These include land surveying, tide gauges, gravity variation measurement and the satellite-based Global Positioning System.

In the mid 1980s, the U.S. Geological Survey and the Geological Survey of Canada began predicting that giant earthquakes could strike the coast from northernmost California to southern British Columbia (Hyndman 1995, 68-69). In response, the B.C., Alberta, and Canadian governments in conjunction with non-governmental agencies put together the National Earthquake Support Plan for British Columbia. In the case of a major earthquake, mobilization and coordination of federal support of emergency response authorities in that province would be managed under this plan, which has been tested in earthquake simulation exercises, provincially (Operation Thunderbird I) in 1993 and nationally (CANATEX 2) in 1994.

After an earthquake, aftershocks of decreasing severity may follow within a few hours or even days. Following a powerful earthquake, large aftershocks are a recognized threat during the recovery period, as they may initiate the collapse of buildings weakened by the mainshock.

Warning of tsunamis, generated by underwater earthquakes or volcanoes, is provided on the west coast by the Tsunami Warning System. This international program is designed to provide timely and effective information and warnings about tsunamis generated in the Pacific Basin. The B.C. Provincial Emergency Program is responsible for warning and evacuating the public *(see Appendix 3.2 Sources of Assistance: Disaster Planning and Recovery – National, Provincial and Territorial)*.

On the Internet, some sites provide information on earthquakes within hours of their occurrence. The Earthquake Information Gopher serves as a link to the available information services on earthquakes *(see entry for U.S. Geological Survey, Appendix 3.1 Sources of Information: Earthquakes)*.

6.3.7 Explosion Warnings

Explosions can be intentional, as in the case of controlled blasting from nearby construction sites and from deliberate acts of violence or terrorism, such as a bomb or other incendiary device. They can also occur accidentally from leaking gas or as the secondary result of a disaster such as an earthquake. Forewarning of an explosion is generally rare, except in the case of planned construction activities or a bomb threat *(see 6.3.12)*. As Buckland (1991, 108) notes: "More than 95 percent of all written or telephoned bomb threats are hoaxes. However, there is always a chance that a threat might be authentic".

6.3.8 Power Failure Warnings

Aside from accidents and catastrophic events, power failure most often results from severe weather conditions or excessive power consumption. Warnings of power reductions are sometimes issued and consumers are requested to reduce their power consumption. Power failures tend to be more frequent in outlying rural areas.

6.3.9 Civil Disturbance, Terrorism and Military Conflict Warnings

Fortunately, civil disturbance, terrorism and military conflict have been rare in Canada. Forewarning of these actions can take many forms such as radio and television broadcasts, newspaper coverage, community notifications, etc. In many instances, there is no forewarning. Staged demonstrations are generally preplanned and well publicized in the media. Other civil disturbances, such as protests, may have been carefully planned but occur without warning.

In the case of terrorism and military conflict, advance notice of an attack may be given or a military alert issued where forces are mobilized and moved to strategic locations. It is the responsibility of the federal government to take the required measures in responding to war and other armed conflict.

6.3.10 Disaster Forewarning Checklist

The following checklist outlines general actions that the organization should plan for in advance and be prepared to implement upon receiving forewarning of the afore-mentioned events. Specific actions will depend on the immediacy, severity and nature of the threat.

Disaster Forewarning Checklist

Be prepared to:
- alert/advise authorities within and outside of the organization.
- ensure the safety of all people in the building.
- activate the disaster plan.
- establish a command centre and communications.
- initiate preparedness measures.
- follow community emergency action plans.
- respond to community warning signals.
- evacuate the building and close the facilities as appropriate.
- assemble at designated mustering locations.
- follow community evacuation routes.
- evacuate to designated community evacuation centres.

6.3.11 Evacuation Planning Checklist

The following checklist outlines activities and issues that the DPC should consider when developing a general evacuation plan.

Evacuation Planning Checklist

- Use only one type of signal for the evacuation order.
- Identify evacuation routes, as well as alternate means of escape. Keep the routes unobstructed.
- Establish safe mustering locations for staff to gather for head counts, to ensure that everyone has left the danger zone.
- Make provisions to assist the elderly, children and the disabled.
- Identify means to distinguish staff, especially those with training in CPR and first aid.
- Consider installing evacuation aids such as fluorescent light strips, textured exit information on the floor, etc.
- Ensure that illuminated exit signs are functional.
- Plan to carry out evacuation procedures simultaneously with efforts to contain the emergency *only* where safe to do so.
- Plan to contain the extent of the property loss *only* when all staff and users are safe.
- Plan for alternate sources of medical aid when normal facilities may be in the danger zone.
- Assign individuals to carry an emergency pack including copy(ies) of the disaster plan and other essential supplies outside when evacuated.
- Provide training for all staff.

6.3.12 Bomb Threat Checklist

A bomb threat should always be taken seriously. A checklist format is very useful for recording essential information for the authorities.

Bomb Threat Checklist

If a bomb threat telephone call is received:
1. Remain calm.
2. Be polite and listen carefully.
3. Try to keep the caller talking to learn more information.
4. Pass a note to a colleague to call authorities, or as soon as the caller hangs up call them yourself immediately.
5. Write down as much information as possible (use a checklist format).
6. Do not discuss threat with other staff.
7. Follow instructions issued by security staff.
8. Plan to evacuate as directed.

Questions to ask caller:
- When is the bomb set to explode?
- What does it look like and where is it?
- What kind of bomb is it?
- Did you place the bomb? Why?
- What is your name? Your address?

Note:
- Number at which telephone call was received.
- Length of telephone call. Time and date.
- Language of the caller.
- Sex of the caller.
- Distinguishing characteristics of the caller's voice (tone, emotion, accent, etc.).
- Background sounds or noises.

(Based on Smithsonian Institution 1993, 9-10)

6.4 Stage II: Immediate Emergency Response Planning

6.4.1 The Purpose of Immediate Emergency Response Planning

The purpose of immediate emergency response planning is to develop the necessary resources and measures to ensure the safety of the people in the building, and to bring the emergency under control. In terms of the disaster timeline, the emergency/disaster has occurred, with or without any forewarning. Response can occur at the outset of an emergency, during an emergency or subsequent to the event. Actions will depend upon the scope of the event, the timing of the event, the timing of its discovery and in most cases, the effectiveness of the disaster planning.

When disaster strikes, the organization should be prepared to convert what writer George Steiner calls the "unthinking immediacy of response" into an effective coordinated effort. In any type of emergency, the best advice is to stay calm. Panic will only aggravate the situation and prevent or hinder those responsible from taking effective action. Preplanning and training can do much to displace fear and indecision, thereby facilitating an organized and productive reaction.

6.4.2 The Process for Immediate Emergency Response Planning

The immediate emergency response process will be determined by the nature, scope and timing of the emergency or disaster. Depending on the situation and the threat to human life and safety, it may be possible for staff to try to contain the effects of the flood, fire, etc. and to protect the building, systems and collections. However, it is the responsibility of the emergency service providers to actually contain the emergency or disaster, and regain control of the facility.

The sequence of activities outlined is intended to provide a structure that enables the DPC to plan the immediate emergency response section of the disaster plan. Some response actions take place concurrently and some overlap, but taken together they roughly form the sequence to be followed.

Immediate Emergency Response Planning: Process at a Glance

Prepare to:
· Sound the alarm and
· Alert the authorities and the Disaster Action Team (DAT) coordinator.
· Evacuate the building as required.
· Eliminate hazards.
· Get safety clearance.
· Inspect the site.
· Activate the disaster plan and contact the DAT.
· Brief the DAT.
· Access supplies, equipment and services.
· Protect collections, records and systems.
· Stabilize the environment.
· Prevent or stabilize mould growth.

---

a) Sound the alarm

The aim is to alert staff, users and visitors in the facility to danger. The method of sounding the alarm will depend on many factors: the nature and timing of the emergency, who is onsite to discover the situation, the design and sophistication of the public address (PA) system, fire alarm and other alarm systems, and

the emergency instructions laid out in the plan. If the emergency is small, a local alert only may be required. Evacuation is always necessary where human health and safety is threatened.

b) Alert the authorities and the Disaster Action Team (DAT) Coordinator

Designated staff must alert the appropriate authorities as outlined in the plan. In a small emergency, internal personnel only may be involved. In a larger-scale emergency or where human safety is threatened, external authorities must be contacted. This may include the fire and police departments, mobile rescue units and emergency medical services.

The Disaster Action Team (DAT) coordinator may already be onsite. If not, the coordinator or alternate(s) must be contacted. When the DAT coordinator is notified, he or she should return immediately to the site.

Staff assigned the task of contacting the authorities must remain close to the scene to help advise and direct the firefighters, police, etc. upon their arrival, as well as to communicate with any onsite personnel. The role of onsite staff is to first notify these authorities and then to work in concert towards common goals. Contact with the insurance company may be required at this point. It may also be necessary to notify offsite building owners and managers, external agencies and resources, such as municipal and regional government departments and the Emergency Preparedness Canada provincial counterpart.

c) Evacuate the building as required

The evacuation process must be clearly laid out in the disaster plan. In addition, evacuation route and exit location diagrams should be posted in prominent positions throughout the building. All personnel must be trained to respond appropriately to follow established evacuation procedures.

When the emergency involves no threat to life, staff may be able to retain access to the building, and try to limit the damage to collections and the facility *(see 6.4.2j)*.

d) Eliminate hazards

The DAT should work in conjunction with the emergency service providers such as the fire chief and public works department to ensure safe re-entry, working conditions and movement of personnel within the building.

Major hazards such as structural, electrical, sewage, chemical spills and asbestos must be eliminated. Personnel must also be advised to watch for nails, glass and other debris. Good safety practices will be essential, in concert with the provision of appropriate safety gear.

The elimination of hazards would usually be entirely or largely carried out by the fire department or other emergency response personnel. In minor disasters, DAT members and the organization's facilities personnel may do the majority of this work.

Rossol (1998, 1) cautions:

> Many conservators have a romantic notion that they will rush into a damaged building after a disaster and heroically get right to work salvaging the collection. Today, it is more likely that firefighters, hazardous materials (HAZMAT) responders, and professional abatement workers will do the preliminary work.

She further advises that regulations enforced by safety, building and firefighting authorities will require employers to keep conservators out of the building until it meets safety standards.

e) Get safety clearance

If the building has been evacuated, appropriate authorities (usually the fire marshal and other emergency personnel) must give full safety clearance before staff may re-enter. Access will be denied until the emergency or disaster is totally contained; fire, building and safety codes and requirements are met; and in cases such as arson, until a cause is pinpointed. However, with the cooperation of the fire marshal, it may be possible to access those areas containing particularly valuable or vulnerable material prior to total building clearance, especially if provisions to this effect were made during planning. Employer's responsibility for training and liability in cases of staff or volunteer's entry to a disaster area must have been investigated in advance.

In situations requiring total evacuation, considerable time can pass before the facility is declared safe to re-enter and recovery commences. This period of time can be profitably used by staff both to assist, where permitted, those who are "fighting" the emergency, and to prepare for partial or full activation of the disaster plan. Firefighting and other emergency personnel are responsible for and will do most of the containment or suppression of the emergency. Facilities personnel and other staff should provide assistance only where it is safe to do so. Firefighters or police should be provided with details of the layout of the building, the location of valuable materials, computer facilities, chemicals and flammable materials.

f) Inspect the site

Once safety clearance has been obtained, the DAT coordinator and DAT members as available, should inspect as much of the disaster area as can be reasonably done. Appropriate protective clothing and safety equipment should be used for the building walkthrough. Onsite inspection by your insurance company may also be required before any recovery operations start.

Depending on the circumstances, it may be possible to identify hazards, and determine which collections have been damaged and which are further threatened. If possible, photographs or videos should be taken to document damage. Comprehensive damage assessment however, will likely have to wait. At this point, it is critical to determine what immediate actions need to be taken such as: activating the plan, eliminating hazards, protecting the collections, etc.

g) Activate the disaster plan and contact the DAT

After a swift considered assessment, the DAT coordinator must decide whether to "stand down" or proceed with partial or full plan activation. The decision to activate the plan is an on-the-spot judgement made by the DAT coordinator. Depending on the situation, this decision may be straightforward or complex. Activation should proceed according to instructions laid out in the disaster plan, where the organization has determined what constitutes, at least on paper, a disaster. Activation of the plan must often proceed even when the severity of the disaster or severity of damage is not fully known.

The field of emergency management generally distinguishes between an "emergency" and a "disaster". As outlined in chapter 1 *(see 1.2.1)*, emergencies are adverse events that do not have broad impact, nor do they require the prolonged and ample use of uncommon resources. On the other hand, a disaster is an adverse event of organization-wide or community-wide impact that requires the use of extensive or extraordinary resources to return conditions to normal. Exactly what constitutes a disaster depends largely on the organization or community, and their ability to cope.

The DAT coordinator may already be onsite. Assuming the plan is to be activated, all other DAT members should now be called in the sequence outlined in the plan. It is expected that the DAT will have taken a copy of the full plan with them if evacuated from the building or will bring their copy with them if contacted at home. The onus must be on the DAT coordinator or designate to contact members of the team and not the reverse. This should be done as the plan instructs without delay. If the phones are not working, or the emergency occurs after hours, alternate arrangements must be made. Cellular phones, pagers or direct contact can be used when necessary and the plan should include different instructions to account for varied staffing levels *(see 2.6.2)*, as well as varied specialist collection expertise.

DAT members should also bring with them, any supplies, equipment and personal protective wear that were planned for and is required by the situation.

h) Brief the DAT

Once assembled, the DAT coordinator must brief the DAT members on the situation in conjunction with the authorities, as necessary. Roles and responsibilities must be swiftly confirmed, and decisions made about immediate response and the resources required.

i) Access equipment, supplies and services

Access to emergency response equipment and supplies, as well as services may be required. Supplies needed immediately may include those stored in entry cabinets and/or emergency depots such as personal protective equipment and clothing, plastic sheeting, etc. or supplies required by facilities staff such as tools and equipment *(see 5.11)*. Once the recovery plan is determined, additional supplies, equipment and services will be needed *(see 6.6.2j)*.

Emergency services may be required for electrical power and telephones. Carpenters, electricians, plumbers, and glaziers may be needed for immediate building repairs. Depending on the disaster and the severity and type of damage, vendors of various recovery services should be alerted. Contacts should be made as outlined in the disaster plan *(see 5.11.3)*.

j) Protect collections, records and systems

Where the emergency situation involves no threat to life or where forewarning allows, staff may be permitted to remain in the building and work to protect the collections, records and systems from initial or further damage. Critical collections and equipment should be covered wherever possible to prevent damage from water and debris. Undamaged and threatened collections, records, equipment, etc. should be protected first. A controlled shutdown of the computer systems should be performed *(see 4.10.1)*, and back-ups removed offsite when necessary. These measures will vary widely, depending on the nature of the emergency and available time and resources. Protection also includes stabilization of the environment *(see 6.4.2k)*.

As mentioned, when evacuation has taken place, protection of the collections, records, etc. will take place *only* after safety clearance has been obtained. In some circumstances, the fire department may help to protect collections and other property, i.e. by providing tarpaulins to cover and protect collections and computer equipment.

k) Stabilize the environment

Action must be taken to stabilize the environment (temperature and relative humidity) in the building and thus the condition of the collections, records, equipment and other assets *(see 3.5.1)*. Steps taken will vary according to the nature of the disaster, as well as the size and design of the building. A large and complex building can be an advantage, as it may retain its original levels of temperature and relative humidity for longer periods of time. Weather will, of course, be a critical factor.

Before taking action, the environment should be assessed carefully by personnel familiar with the building design and systems, as well as by staff familiar with collections preservation and the effects of high temperatures and relative humidity (RH) on materials. Sustained high RH that may initiate mould growth is of particular concern. Raising the temperature will lower the humidity (if no additional moisture is added to the air) but can, however, also accelerate mould growth.

In buildings with automated heating, ventilation and air conditioning (HVAC) systems that remain operational, it may be possible to accurately determine building conditions and make corrections with relative ease. In other cases, temperature and RH monitoring and recording equipment will be required, such as hygrothermographs (best calibrated with a battery-operated psychrometer). Dataloggers could be used, although they do not provide readings at a glance – these portable monitors need to be connected to a computer to access the readings. Equipment such as fans and dehumidifiers may also be needed.

Once the environmental conditions have been determined, corrective measures will need to be undertaken. Assistance from a commercial company specializing in disaster recovery may be required. Stabilizing the environment is not a one-time event. Ongoing onsite monitoring and control is necessary throughout response and recovery operations. This includes any offsite areas used for collections, records and computer equipment storage and recovery.

l) Prevent or stabilize mould growth

The occurrence of mould growth on collections and records usually results from conditions of high RH and high temperatures *(see 3.4.8a)*. By reducing RH and temperature, as well as increasing air circulation, this risk can be reduced, thus avoiding a complicated and sometimes persistent problem.

Mould may occur:

· At the outset of response, if immediate remedial action was not possible.

· During response, if stabilization of the environment was neither possible nor successfully achieved.

· During the recovery process, if stabilization of the environment was not achieved, or was improperly or inadequately monitored.

· After recovery, subsequent to drying, if collections, records and equipment were inadequately dried or were returned to conditions suitable for mould growth.

Ongoing monitoring and control of RH and temperature are critical to preventing and stabilizing mould growth.

If mould growth has already occurred, it is best to identify the species due to the potential human health risk. The relative quantities of species should also be determined. Mouldy materials will need to be isolated. Intensive efforts must be made immediately to control the environment to reduce further opportunities for mould germination and growth, both for the collections and records overall and those already isolated. Protective clothing must be worn and proper containment procedures followed to reduce the risk to staff and other onsite personnel. *(See 3.4.8a and 6.4.9)*

6.4.3 Alarm and General Evacuation Checklist

This checklist is intended to serve as a guideline for the DPC in developing disaster plan alarm and evacuation instructions.

Alarm and General Evacuation Checklist

· Sound the alarm.
· Alert the authorities.
· Leave the building.
· Direct other people to do same. Do **not** risk your life if people refuse to leave.
· Assist people if your safety is not threatened.
· Close fire doors.
· Use all exits to speed up evacuation.
· Use stairs (not elevators).
· Gather at your pre-determined external mustering location.
· Remain as close to the site as safety allows.
· Do not re-enter the building.
· Advise firefighters, police, etc. if staff, users and visitors still remain in the building.
· Ensure that entry and movement of the fire department and their equipment is not hindered by staff or the public. Stay out of the way.
· Wait for further instructions.

6.4.4 Action Checklists: Specific Emergencies

The following checklists and discussions outline actions that should be taken in the event of specific emergencies. They are intended to serve as guidelines for the DPC when formulating disaster plan action checklists.

a) Fire

Fire Checklist

1. Remain calm.
2. Sound the alarm.
3. Call the fire department. State the address of your institution, the part of the building affected, and the number of people, if any, trapped inside.
   It is a dangerous misconception to assume that your fire alarm system has successfully automatically alerted the fire department, either directly or through the security company.
4. Do not attempt to extinguish the fire unless it is very small and self-contained, such as in a waste basket. Only trained personnel should use fire extinguishers and standpipe systems.
5. Evacuate the affected area or the entire building.
6. Muster outside for head counts.
7. Advise authorities of any persons remaining in the building.

b) Flooding

Flooding Checklist

1. Remain calm.
2. Follow Fire Checklist steps 2-3 as appropriate.
3. Evacuate the affected area or the entire building as appropriate.
4. Make sure that electrical power is turned off.
5. Prevent persons from walking through any water until the area has been declared safe.
6. Determine the location and cause of the flooding.
7. Call immediately all persons who can help: facilities staff, etc.
8. Turn off manual cutoffs if drains are below ground level.
9. Ensure that sewage lines are intact before running water or flushing toilets.
10. If the flood is major, listen to a battery-powered radio for further instructions.

c) Earthquake

Once the earthquake has passed, aftershocks of decreasing severity may follow within the next few hours or even days. Keeping this danger of further tremors in mind, take the following measures.

Earthquake Checklist

1. Remain calm.
2. Follow the Fire Checklist steps 2-4 as appropriate.
3. Stay indoors, preferably within the inner core of the building away from windows. Seek shelter within a doorway, a room corner or archway, in a narrow corridor or under a heavy table, bench or desk. Avoid shelter near windows, skylights, other structural hazards or near anything that could fall (e.g. shelving).
4. Do not go outside, due to hazards of falling debris, etc.
5. Do not attempt to use the exits or the stairways.
6. Do not use elevators or escalators.
7. Assist, where personal safety permits, those who have been trapped or injured by falling debris, glass, etc.
8. Shut off utilities at main valves or meter boxes. Turn off appliances.
9. Check for broken water pipes, shorting electrical circuits, and leaking gas or heating fuel. Do not use a match or candle to find your way, since flammable gas may be present.
10. Do not use the telephone, except where absolutely necessary. The lines should be kept free for rescue operations.
11. Ensure that sewage lines are intact before running water or flushing toilets.
12. Listen to a battery-powered radio for further instructions.

d) Severe Weather

Upon receiving warning of severe weather, the following actions should be taken.

Severe Weather Checklist

1. Remain calm.
2. As appropriate, seek shelter in the basement or an inner hallway or small inner room away from windows and walls. In the case of a tornado, the rapid decrease in air pressure may result in explosion of the building.
3. Do not seek shelter in large open facilities such as arenas and armouries because their roofs can collapse from high winds or heavy snow and ice.
4. Turn the electrical power and utilities off.
5. Close shutters and board up or tape windows to reduce danger from flying glass.
6. Close doors.
7. Listen to a battery-powered radio for further instructions.

e) Power Failure

If the power failure is of short duration, little will need to be done beyond ensuring that no one is trapped in the elevators. Irrespective of the duration, security, computer, fire systems, etc. will subsequently need to be checked to ensure their continued operation.

In the event of a long-term power failure, the following steps are recommended.

Power Failure Checklist

1. Remain calm.
2. See if anyone is trapped in the elevators. Contact the fire department or facilities staff to free any trapped people.
3. Inform the local electric authority. Telephone lines may not be operational.
4. See if neighbouring buildings are affected.
5. Evacuate the public and non-essential personnel from the building. This may not be necessary if it appears that the power interruption will be short. It may be necessary to switch to emergency power.
6. Institute security measures to replace any automated security systems.
7. Listen to a battery-powered radio for further instructions.

The impact of a power failure on an organization's holdings will depend on the difference between climatic conditions inside the building and those prevailing outside. In winter, flooding may result if water pipes freeze and burst.

To prevent this sort of flooding:

· Turn off the main electrical power source.
· Turn off the water main where it enters the building. Protect the valve, inlet pipe, and meter or pump with blankets or insulating material.
· Open all water taps and flush toilets several times, to drain the water system.
· Water supply lines that might not drain should be blown out.

If flooding occurs in winter as a result of burst pipes, it may be best to leave materials frozen and deal with affected areas over time, so that further damage is minimized. In other seasons, steps must be taken to control RH and temperature *(see 3.5.1 and 6.4.2k,l).*

f) Explosion

After an explosion, the following measures should be taken.

Explosion Checklist

1. Remain calm.
2. Call in the police and fire department to determine the source of the explosion.
3. Determine whether the building is still structurally sound.
4. At the same time, evacuate all uninjured personnel from the building. Attend to seriously injured personnel in place until medical help arrives.
5. If the explosion has ruptured water or gas pipes, turn these pipes off at the point where they enter the building. The layout of these pipes must be included in the disaster plan.
6. Listen to a battery-powered radio for further instructions.

g) Civil Disturbances and Military Conflict

Due to the variety of situations that may occur, a checklist is not provided here. Readers are referred to the previous checklists for response to specific circumstances. Staff must work with the appropriate authorities, i.e., local police, the RCMP and the military, and prepare for response as necessary.

Civil disturbances and military conflict may result in threats of varying severity, such as explosions, fires, etc. Safety of staff, users and other personnel in the building will be the paramount concern. Security issues must be addressed, such as vandalism, theft, as well as access to and from the building.

6.4.5 Hazard Elimination

Once safety clearance for building re-entry has been obtained, a number of hazards may need to be eliminated before response efforts can safely begin.

General Hazards Elimination Checklist

· Turn off the electrical power supply.
· Turn off the main water valve.
· Turn off the gas.
· Have the authorities check the building structure.
· Check shelving and fixed wall units.
· Examine pipes for damage.
· Drain or pump out any standing water.
· Activate portable generators and alternate light sources.
· Clear debris from aisles and stairwells.

a) Water

One of water's main hazards is its ability to conduct electricity. In addition, standing water can obscure other hazards such as glass shards and nails, as well as structural damage. Even after water is drained, debris or mud can conceal these hazards. Other hazards include contamination from sewage, oil or other fuels, chemicals. In winter, water may freeze and pose a safety hazard.

b) Electricity

See water-related hazards above. Wet or damp areas are not safe unless the electrical power has been turned off because it could unexpectedly become operative causing serious injury or even death.

c) Structural

The building could have sustained unseen structural damage and should be checked thoroughly. Floors, stairs, ceilings and walls could have been undermined by fire damage and water absorption. Shelving and wall units will need to be checked for stability and in the case of compact storage, checked to ensure its safe operation.

d) Health

Disasters may result in a variety of health hazards that can make the response and recovery operations dangerous for workers. Hazards can include: unsafe building structure conditions, electrical hazards, explosive gases, slippery surfaces and broken glass, as well as physical and mental strain.

- **Chemicals**

  Containers of chemicals may have been damaged, and leaked or spilled their contents. Appropriate protective clothing – including respirators with the proper filters, supplies and equipment must be used – and the chemical waste safely disposed of according to local legislation. Spill control specialists must be involved in all major incidents.

- **Sewage**

  Sewage contamination can result from backed-up sewers, broken stack pipes, flooding, etc. Contaminated items must be handled with gloves, protective clothing, and the proper masks to reduce health risks. Before response and recovery begins, it is best to seek the advice of a health professional.

- **Asbestos**

  Buildings constructed prior to 1980 may have asbestos in insulation, ceiling or floor tiles. The disaster may have dispersed invisible asbestos particles throughout the building. Air quality inspection and evaluation by a qualified consultant is required.

Personnel working in a disaster area may come in contact with soot, bacteria, mould *(see 3.4.8a)*, lead, etc. Many of these substances are carcinogenic and toxic. Other potential health issues include respiratory problems (especially for people with allergies and asthma), infections, eye and skin irritations, and poisoning. Appropriate precautions must be taken to protect workers from inhalation and skin absorption of all hazardous contaminants. Disaster preparedness must include protective clothing and equipment, and an up-to-date list of people who have first aid training. All major injuries must be treated by health care professionals. For further detail on health and safety issues readers are referred to Rossol (1998).

Local legislative health requirements must be met and specialists called in to assist where necessary *(see 3.3.1)*.

6.4.6 Protection of Collections and Records

The nature and severity of the disaster will determine what measures can and should be taken to protect the collections and records. The following checklist outlines the general measures to be considered when time and safety permit.

Collections and Records Protection Checklist

- Protect or remove undamaged collections and records first and then proceed in order of established priority for damaged collections and records.
- Relocate collections to a safe room within the building, or remove them to a safe place offsite as necessary.
- Cover collections and records that cannot be moved with heavy-grade plastic or tarpaulins. The coverings should extend to the floor and not be left in place unattended for more than 24 hours (due to the danger of mould growth). Prevent water from collecting on top of the coverings.
- Keep collections above ground level.
- Move materials from lower shelves.
- Raise cabinets off the floor with bricks.
- Secure loose objects and move them away from windows or glassed-in areas.
- Board up windows and skylights.
- Use sandbags or other barriers to direct water away from materials.

6.4.7 Computer Data and Systems Protection

Damage and loss of computer data and systems can have serious consequences on the recovery and resumption of normal operations. In addition to the preparedness strategies already put in place *(see 5.8)*, if not done prior to evacuation, a controlled systems shutdown should be undertaken.

Controlled Systems Shutdown Checklist

- Close all active files.
- Back up all files.
- Remove back-ups offsite.
- Shut down LAN/WAN and all computer components and equipment.
- Unplug all equipment.
- Cover equipment to prevent damage from water and debris.

6.4.8 Environmental Control

The following measures can be used to stabilize the environment in the affected building.

Environmental Control Checklist

- Monitor and record temperature and relative humidity (RH) on an ongoing basis.
- Reduce the RH to less than 65%, 50% is better.
- Reduce temperature to less than 21°C (70°F).
- In winter, turn off all heat. Ensure that pipes are protected from freezing.
- In summer, reduce the temperature and RH as much as possible.
- Keep air conditioning systems operational where possible. Use portable air conditioners where necessary.
- In warmer weather, insulate single-pane windows by placing polyethylene sheeting on the interior, and use window shades or other coverings to help regulate the temperature.
- Increase air circulation and expel humid air from the building by opening windows and doors (only if humidity outside is lower than inside) and using fans, taking care not to blow materials or mould spores around.
- Use dehumidifiers to reduce RH.
- Remove standing water with mops, squeegees and pumps.
- Remove all wet debris and remove or dry all sources of humidity, such as water-soaked carpeting, drapes and furniture.
- Dry all structural sources of humidity, such as drywall.

6.4.9 Mould Control

The measures outlined in the environmental control checklist above will assist in preventing and stabilizing mould growth. Where mould has already occurred the following measures should be undertaken. Protective equipment and clothing must be worn and safe handling and cleaning procedures must be established and followed. Success of the control measures taken should be determined by air monitoring (swab test kits or air sampling).

Mould Control Checklist

- Intensify efforts to control the environment – reduce the temperature and RH, increase air circulation, remove wet debris, etc.
- Monitor effectiveness of environmental control measures.
- Consult experts, such as a mycologist. This is the safest approach, as moulds pose health hazards. Some reactions to mould can be severe even fatal.
- Reduce staff exposure to mould as much as possible.
- Prevent spread of contamination as much as possible.
- Seal mouldy materials in plastic bags and remove them to a separate isolation work area where treatment decisions should be made promptly. If the materials are damp or wet they must be frozen immediately to prevent further mould growth. The isolation work area must have a controlled environment.
- Wear protective clothing and equipment – disposable protective smocks, latex gloves, goggles and face masks (capable of filtering particulate matter of 1 micron).
- Use established procedures for safely handling mouldy materials – wash hands with antibacterial soap, clean work surfaces with 2% chlorine bleach solution, seal and dispose of used, contaminated, disposable clothing, etc.
- Use established procedures for cleaning mould contaminated areas – use a 2% chlorine bleach solution for cleaning and 5% chlorine bleach solution for mops and pails, seal and dispose of used, contaminated, disposable clothing, etc.
- If contamination is large-scale, seal off contaminated areas (use taped polyethylene sheeting isolation barriers) and ensure that spores are not escaping (use a HEPA exhausted negative air unit, air locks or decontamination room). Undertake clean-up and HEPA-vacuum prior to removal of isolation barriers. Do air monitoring to ensure clean-up was effective and the area is safe. Check heat-exchange coils and filters in the HVAC system.

(Based largely on the internal procedures of the National Archives of Canada, 1996)

6.5 Stage III: Recovery Strategy Planning: Collections and Records

What makes disaster recovery planning so unique is that you are solving problems that don't yet exist (DeLuca 1996, 21).

The Disaster Planning Committee (DPC) must plan carefully for this response stage as it prepares for and sets the scene for actual recovery operations. In terms of the disaster timeline, the existing disaster plan will have been activated, and the Disaster Action Team (DAT) and other emergency service providers would be working on securing the facility, and continuing to control the environment and protect the collections. At this point, the situation must be assessed and decisions made in order for the DAT to organize and develop the recovery strategy and make preparations for its implementation. Requirements for operational support must also be determined *(see 6.6)*.

This section outlines the development of a recovery strategy for collections and records. Many of the same principles also apply to building structure, systems and other contents – their recovery and rehabilitation are covered in Chapter 9.

Although decision paths based on a range of variables would have been considered at the planning stage, the DAT coordinator with the DAT must now decide on a specific course of action for recovery of the collections and records. They must consider alternative actions by weighing such factors as: the climate inside and outside the building; the severity of the damage; the number and nature of items affected; the value and importance of these collections and records; the availability of dedicated and knowledgeable assistance and; last but not least, the cost factor.

6.5.1 The Purpose of Recovery Strategy Planning: Collections and Records

The purpose of recovery strategy planning is to develop a recovery strategy for collections and records specific to the situation at hand. Theory and broad guidelines will have been formulated and documented in the written disaster plan. No plan can, however, address all eventualities. Based on the existing plan, a situation-specific recovery strategy must now be developed.

6.5.2 The Process for Recovery Strategy Planning: Collections and Records

Information contained in the existing plan provides the basis for and is used to assist with the following activities: assessing the severity of the disaster and the damage, determining priorities, assessing recovery options and costs, and developing specific plans for the particular situation. Where this plan does not adequately cover the situation, it will need to be enhanced, modified and amplified. Collectively, these activities form the basis for your recovery strategy.

Some recovery preparation actions must occur in sequence, as they depend on the results of previous tasks. Others can take place concurrently.

> **Recovery Strategy Planning: Process at a Glance**
>
> Prepare to:
> - Get expert help.
> - Assess severity of the disaster.
> - Assess severity of the damage.
> - Assign recovery priorities.
> - Assess recovery options.
> - Assess costs.
> - Determine the recovery strategy and get approval to proceed.

a) Get expert help

Professional advice from external conservators, consultants, organizations and commercial services should be sought in order to supplement expertise within the organization, and to determine the necessity, availability and costs of external assistance, services and other resources. Much of this legwork will have already been done as part of the planning process, thus saving time and avoiding costly mistakes. Some assistance may already have been called in as part of the initial emergency response or plan activation. At this time however, the DAT will make further specific requests for advice or hands-on aid, or seek information on the purchase or rental of supplies and equipment, or arrange for services. It is best to be well-prepared when making these contacts, so your needs and situation are clearly understood, duplication is avoided, and time and money are not wasted.

b) Assess severity of the disaster

The scale and extent of the disaster needs to assessed, in order to gauge the level of continued response and subsequent recovery measures required. In the case of widespread disaster, supplies and services may not be readily available. Once the severity of a disaster has been determined, the DAT can decide on the type and level of assistance and resources that will be needed.

Some information needed for the assessment can be obtained from emergency service providers, working with the DAT during the building walk-through (subsequent to obtaining safety clearance). This assessment of disaster severity is then coordinated with the damage assessment to help formulate the recovery strategy.

The following assessments should be made:

- What type of disaster is it: fire, flood, earthquake, explosion, etc?
- What are the secondary effects: fire, flood, explosion, power outage, etc?

· Is the disaster contained fully, in part, or is it ongoing?

· How long did the disaster last?

· What are the current and predicted weather conditions?

· What was or is the threat to human life and safety?

· What was or is the threat to assets and other property?

· Is the disaster localized or widespread across the organization, immediate area or the region?

· Are the effects minor, moderate, major or catastrophic?

· What is the impact on availability of staff and external resources?

c) Assess severity of the damage

Damage assessment follows assessment of the disaster. This is done by surveying the building and its contents as fully as possible after safety clearance is obtained. This chapter focuses on damage to the collections and records. Damage assessment of the building is covered in Chapter 9. Professional help (engineering, building system, insurance, conservation, computer, etc.) should be sought, as needed, in order to accurately determine the extent, degree and nature of the damage. Protective clothing, safety equipment, emergency lighting, etc. may be required for the inspections.

The damage assessment, in concert with the disaster assessment, provides the basis for assigning recovery priorities, which in turn provides direction for the recovery strategy.

d) Assign recovery priorities

The assessment and assignment of recovery priorities for collections and records after a disaster is essential to the entire recovery process. These priorities drive the assessment of recovery options and costs, and the determination of a recovery strategy for a specific situation. Priorities must be clearly articulated and communicated, otherwise the recovery of all collections will assume equal status. A focused and effective recovery process is impossible when there is no order of precedence and no urgency to do one thing before another. Further loss of collections will surely result from a frantic effort to recover everything.

The assignment of recovery priorities is determined not only by the priorities recorded in the existing plan and the collections damage assessment, but also by the damage sustained by the facility. Access to critical areas may be not immediately possible and alternative plans may be needed.

e) Assess recovery options

All recovery options have pros and cons. These must be carefully considered in order to determine those most appropriate to the collections and records, and the resources available. The assessment of options will be defined first by the size, nature and extent of the disaster; second by the resources, facilities and services available; and third by the organization's ability to support the associated costs.

In the event of a small or localized disaster, recovery options will likely be quite straightforward. As the magnitude and complexity of the disaster situation increases, so do the number of factors and options. This will require the involvement of more people and may complicate the decision-making process. The goal is to come to the best decisions possible in the shortest period of time. However, it is generally wise to sacrifice a small measure of time in the interests of getting the decisions right at the outset. *(See 6.5.5)*

f) Assess costs

Based on the damage assessment, assignment of priorities, recovery treatment options and estimates provided by staff and external service providers, overall recovery cost estimates can be developed.

> Too often the assumption is that it is necessary to try to save everything when the objective is to save what can be saved within the desired cost parameters (Wright 1979, 258)

For some organizations, these estimates will be critical to the decision to proceed with some courses of action; for others this may be less of an immediate issue. The need to develop short-, medium- and long-term recovery objectives may result from this assessment of costs.

A critical component of cost assessment will be the existing insurance coverage. Proof of loss will need to be established before a claim can be settled *(see 5.7 and 10.7)*.

g) Determine the recovery strategy and get approval to proceed

The DAT must now determine the recovery strategy for the collections and records based on the disaster plan, as well as recovery priorities, damage assessments, assessment of recovery options and costs, and available resources. This must be done in conjunction with the recovery of the facility *(see Chapter 9)*. The DAT must then seek approval from the governing body as appropriate for their recommended strategy.

The DAT must recognize and make clear to them that on-going modifications to the strategy in terms of time, resources and costs may be necessary.

This strategy will cover:
· recovery priorities assignment
· recovery methods and procedures to be used
· personnel requirements (internal and external)
· estimated timeframes, scheduling and costs
· team composition and assignments
· training requirements
· quality control and supervision requirements
· supply, equipment, offsite facility and service needs

Operational support strategies will also have to be developed so that recovery can be effectively implemented. These include coordination, staff mobilization, security, documentation, communications, personnel welfare needs, etc. *(see 6.6).*

6.5.3 Damage Assessment of Collections and Records

The disaster site should be surveyed by the DAT with the assistance of experts as required, such as the fire marshal, insurance agent, collection specialists and recovery specialists. For efficiency, the team should be divided into working groups by floor, wing, collection or whatever seems logical. There is nothing to be gained by impetuous decisions at this stage. The best advice is to proceed carefully and methodically, documenting wherever possible.

The extent, character and degree of damage must be examined and an accurate assessment made in order to initiate further protective measures, to prepare the recovery strategy and to support any insurance claim *(see 10.7).* Full settlement of a claim cannot be reached until all damaged materials have been recorded and their values established. The extent and potential success of recovery and rehabilitation must also be estimated. The insurance company may require onsite inspections before the start of any practical work. Documentation should be ongoing.

a) Extent of Damage
The organization will need to identify and evaluate the extent of damage to the collections and records. If there is no preservation department or conservator, external expertise should always be sought. Scale and scope of the damage must be determined, as well as the impact on the organization.

The following provides some rough overall benchmarks for the DAT when determining the extent of damage in a mid- to large-sized organization:

- **Minor Damage**

  Up to 500 books or 50 record centre boxes of documents could likely be dealt with by an in-house preservation department with some assistance by the rest of the organization.

- **Moderate Damage**

  Up to 10,000 books or 1,000 record centre boxes of documents could perhaps be dealt with by a large in-house preservation operation. Assistance by the rest of the organization will be required, as well as external resources.

- **Major Damage**

  Up to 100,000 books or 10,000 record centre boxes of documents will necessitate the use of extensive, even extraordinary, internal and external resources.

- **Catastrophic Damage**

  More than 100,000 books or 10,000 record centre boxes of documents will require the use of extraordinary internal and external resources.

The estimated number of damaged books or documents, in concert with established priorities and assessment of the nature and degree of damage will determine the number of staff, supplies and other resources needed, such as the space required for processing, sorting and air-drying. Syracuse University Library (1995, 4) estimates that it takes roughly 30 minutes for 2 people to wrap and box 100 volumes (@10 volumes per box).

b) Nature and Degree of Damage
While a quantitative evaluation of damage is important, the nature and degree of damage must also be assessed in order to formulate the recovery strategy.

The immediate external appearance of the collections may indicate the nature and degree of damage, as in the case of water-soaked materials lying in flooded aisles, or appearances may be deceptive, such as storage containers that seem undamaged but whose contents are harmed. Materials on shelves and in cabinets will be damaged to different and varying degrees depending on the nature of the disaster: soaked, partially wet, damp, charred, smoke-damaged, debris-covered, etc.

Generally, if any books on a shelf are wet, the whole shelf should be treated as wet. The rate of water absorption by collection material will vary according to age, nature and condition of their components. This will affect the immediate and ongoing damage sustained by materials and the drying time required.

The damage to collection materials should be appraised without handling whenever possible, as further irreparable damage may result. A realistic and thorough assessment must be made quickly, efficiently, and safely.

6.5.4 Priorities for Recovery of Collections and Records

a) Overall Priorities

Priorities assigned for recovery of collections and records will be largely based on determinations made when the original disaster plan was developed. These determinations must now factor in the nature and extent of damage, the overall recovery effort required and available resources.

The recovery priorities established for collections and records when the plan was developed were based on value and importance of the materials to the organization or wider community, as well as other factors such as replaceability *(see 5.9)*. Added to these factors now are the physical condition of the collections and the facility, time constraints and the availability of resources and services, both inside and external. Decisions must be made as to which materials to recover, or attempt to recover, which to discard and which to replace. These recovery decisions are not easily made and must take a number of factors into account.

Collections-related factors to consider include:
· Importance of the material to the organization.
· Value of the material.
· Options and costs for recovery.
· Time required for recovery.
· Availability of replacement material.
· Time required for material replacement.
· Cost of replacement (acquisition and staff costs).

Institutional implications include:
· Mandate of the organization.
· Service resumption, usership and users.
· Staff and volunteers.
· The insurance claim.
· Funding (current and maybe future).

· Public relations.
· Recovery of the facility.
· Overall rehabilitation (short- and long-term).

In other words, the decisions must be made carefully based on full knowledge and understanding of the organization's needs, operations and capabilities.

b) Situation-Specific Priorities

Most disasters involve water, and soaked materials are generally given high priority. Removal of wet materials will also assist in lowering the RH of the affected area. Generally, if a top priority category collection is beyond recovery, efforts should be redirected to lesser-priority materials that are viable candidates for recovery.

Overall Priority Factors for Wet Materials

1. Undamaged but threatened collections.
2. High-priority collections and records: soaked, wetted and damp.
3. Medium-priority collections and records: soaked, wetted and damp.
4. Low-priority collections and records: soaked, wetted and damp.
5. Undamaged, unthreatened collections.

It is generally held that wet magnetic (Van Bogart 1996b, 3) and film media can remain wet for a period of time, if only wet from clean water or if rinsed. Priority should be given to paper-based materials.

Additional Priority Factors for Wet Materials

· Materials that were fragile or damaged prior to the disaster.
· Materials that have already developed mould, providing they are not expendable.
· Materials on coated paper, and coated linen plans, blueprints, blueline prints and brownline prints. The coatings or impregnations of these materials become soluble in water and then fuse to adjacent pages or sheets, if allowed to dry in contact with each other without attention (most sources cite six to eight hour time limit). They will form irreversible solid blocks of paper. (See Tremain 1998).
· Magnetic and film-based media, if wet from contaminated water or if wetted and now drying. They deteriorate rapidly and should be attended to as soon as possible.
· Leather, vellum and parchment require prompt attention and special handling.

· Books, prints, drawings, maps, etc. with water-soluble components require prompt attention and special handling to avoid loss or feathering of inks and dyes.

· Works of art with friable media (such as gouache, pastel, chalk, crayon) or multiple components (such as collage and chine appliqué) also need prompt attention and special handling.

· Certain photographic materials cannot withstand immersion (such as early colour process starch prints) and others require immediate attention (such as wet collodion and silver glass plate negatives).

See Chapter 7 for details on the particular recovery needs of these media.

Additional Factors to Consider

· Was the water clean?
· Was salt water involved?
· What other contaminants are present?
· Has mould started to develop?
· How many materials are wet?
· What types of material are wet?
· How wet are the materials?
· How long have the materials been wet?
· Have any of the materials started to dry?
· How quickly do the materials need to be dried?
· Are there any constraints as to where the material can be dried?
· Are materials also smoke-, or soot-covered or charred?
· What environmental controls are in place? Is the weather affecting this environment?

The assigned priority list is a working document. Priorities may have to change as response and recovery proceeds.

6.5.5 Collections and Records Recovery Options

The Disaster Planning Committee should thoroughly investigate options for the recovery of collections and records as part of the planning process. Alternatives for service provision and their availability should be spelled out in the plan. When developing a recovery strategy, the Disaster Action Team will need to revisit these alternatives, at least in part, and modify them as necessary to meet the needs of the specific situation. It must be remembered that when disaster strikes, the overall organization will shift into disaster-mode, and the decisions made regarding collections and records should reflect this shift (*see also 7.0*).

The focus in the following section is on recovery options for water- and fire-damaged collections and records. Other disasters such as earthquakes and explosions also generally result in fire or water damage. In these cases, severe mechanical damage or destruction can also result from collapsed shelving, structural components, etc.

While there is significant knowledge and successful experience in the recovery of paper- and film-based media, problems with the mass treatment of paper-based materials remain. Vacuum freeze-drying is still the preferred mass drying method, however, the process does not permit distorted materials to dry flat. Dehumidification-drying is proving effective, although it is best suited to damp or slightly wetted materials. Fumigation remains a difficult issue as the health and safety of people and the safety of the collections are put at risk by the fumigants most effective at eradicating mould spores.

The recovery of computer data and systems is an emerging field, and further research is needed to fully confirm the safety and effectiveness of mass treatments. Vacuum drying at ambient temperatures and dehumidification-drying are showing great promise. However, back-ups remain the best protection.

Unfortunately, a disaster of any consequence will result in materials which are damaged beyond salvage and must be discarded. Each organization must determine its own criteria for discard. These decisions are linked to the recovery priorities set during planning.

6.5.6 Water-Damaged Collections and Records Recovery

This section is intended to assist the DPC in its investigation of collections and records recovery options. Most disasters to libraries and archives involve water. The cause of the disaster may not be water per se, but water damage will surely be a consequence or secondary effect of fire or earthquake. Major concerns involving water are growth of mould on damp, wetted or soaked collections and records; blocking of coated paper; distortion; and water-sensitive media and components. All wet materials should be considered fragile and must be handled with care.

> If there is one clear rule for response to water damage it is this: **the faster the correct action, the better the result.** The key word is "correct". Once wet, paper and film emulsion will swell, bindings distort, leather and vellum react. The quicker they can be brought under control, the less disastrous your emergency will be. (Buchanan 1988, 71)

As the majority of the damage to materials takes place in the first hours after a disaster, immediate action must be taken to control the environment, and to stabilize the wet collections. Decisions must then be made about appropriate recovery techniques to be used. Where few items are involved, immediate decisions can usually be made. Larger amounts of wet material will require more extensive assessment and a larger recovery effort.

Some materials will pose particular problems. Wet coated paper, films and magnetic tapes, for example, are susceptible to total loss and must not be allowed to dry out unattended. And collections of differing media require different techniques for recovery.

An understanding of the effects of water on various collections and records materials is essential to planning a successful recovery operation. This is because paper and other materials absorb water at varying rates and to differing degrees, depending on their nature, condition and age. The affected collections will probably contain a mixture of wet, wetted and damp materials.

Paper absorbs water quickly, causing swelling and other problems. The percentage of water absorption can also be very high. Uneven wetness of paper is a particular problem: such materials are unlikely to dry without distortion. Except for lengthy immersion situations, boxed materials will likely survive with less damage than shelved book materials, as the boxes will protect the contents. The level of protection will depend on the material of the box (type of board or plastic) and its design. Tightly shelved materials can, however, ward off considerable water.

Where large numbers of books are involved, the quantity of water to be extracted in the drying process can be estimated based on an average per book dry weight and an appropriate water absorption percentage. In general, pre-1840 books and documents will absorb water to an average of 80% of their original dry weight, although some may absorb as much as 200%. More modern books, except those with brittle paper, will absorb an average of up to 60% of their original dry weight. (Waters 1993, 2)

Waters (1993, 2-3) stresses that recovery action should be determined by the water content of the material, and not by the relative humidity of the environment. The water content of the materials may stay dangerously high, even when the area's RH has been successfully lowered. He suggests using a moisture meter, or if one is not available, a mirror placed within, but not touching, the textblock. Condensation will form on the mirror's surface if

moisture is present. Less than 7% water content is considered dry.

Waters (1993, 12) also stresses that any drying service contracts drawn up must specify that the acceptable water content of all the book's **composite** materials be less than 7%. An average reading of water content is not acceptable, as some composite materials may be far less than the desired 7% and other materials, such as book cover boards, may exceed this percentage.

Other materials, such as magnetic tapes, are not affected by water in the same way as books and other paper materials. Paper can absorb water quickly and fully, while tapes are hydrophobic and thus, water absorption is both low and slow. Tapes are more sensitive to damage by extremes of heat and cold. Newer tapes are more resistant to damage by moisture than older tapes. Moisture and water cause tapes to fail when absorbed by the tape binder, causing it to become soft and gummy. However, a wet tape is not immediately in danger, unless the water contains organic or corrosive components, such as sea water and sewage, that may degrade the tape. As stated previously, the recovery of wet paper should take precedence over wet tape. (Van Bogart 1996a,b)

Photographic materials vary in their resistance to water damage. Starch prints (early colour photographic processes) will not survive immersion and thus, prevention of water damage is essential. For other materials, such as wet collodion glass plate negatives, immediate appropriate action is critical to successful recovery. *(see 7.4.7)*

a) Cleaning Wet Materials

Wet paper-based materials can be cleaned, however, it is usually best to do so once the materials are dried. No cleaning should be done of wet, rare or valuable materials, fragile materials or materials with water-sensitive or friable media or components. All mouldy materials must be dried before being cleaned. Cleaning of wet, fire-damaged materials is not recommended.

Wet, film-based materials, some photographic materials and computer media should be rinsed in clean water as part of the recovery process. Dirt, mud and other debris and contaminants should not be allowed to dry on these materials.

The cleaning of mouldy or sewage-covered materials requires the use of protective equipment and clothing as well as special precautions *(see also 6.4.5 and 6.4.9)*.

b) Wet-Stabilization

Wet-stabilization is an interim measure, an option to be used only for a limited period of time until treatment can be undertaken. Materials (such as coated paper, some film and magnetic materials) once wet, should be stabilized by wet-packing until they can be freeze-stabilized or dried as appropriate, either in-house or at an external recovery company. This is to prevent materials from sticking together (blocking) permanently in a solid block as they dry and to prevent debris from drying onto their surfaces. If the water was contaminated however, materials such as films and magnetic tapes should first be rinsed before wet-packing. Wet-packed materials should be kept cool to avoid or reduce the opportunity for mould growth. Materials cannot be kept wet indefinitely – six to eight hours is the general rule of thumb for coated papers, and 48 hours for film-based materials. However, this will depend on the nature and condition of the materials. Already damaged materials are extremely vulnerable to further damage. Immediate freezing is preferable for wet coated paper, followed by vacuum freeze-drying.

Note: Wet-stabilization packing methods are different for paper- and film-based materials (*see 7.3.5*).

Wet-stabilization has many advantages:

· It prevents coated paper from blocking.
· It prevents film-based materials from sticking to one another or their enclosures.
· It prevents debris from drying onto film-based materials.
· It provides a period of time, albeit limited, in which to organize systematic drying operations, carry out further damage assessments, etc.

Wet-stabilization also has disadvantages:

· It is labour intensive.
· The bags containing paper-based materials must be removed prior to drying.
· Further damage to materials may result, such as increasing solubility of paper coatings.
· Loss of identification markings or labels may result.

c) Freeze-Stabilization

Freezing is the preferred method for the stabilization of large quantities of water-damaged, paper-based, library and archival materials prior to drying (often by vacuum freeze-drying or vacuum thermal-drying methods). Freeze-stabilization can also be used for smaller quantities that will later be air-dried. Many materials, including vellum, can be safely frozen (*see 7.4.2*). However, some materials, such as paintings and some photographs, can be further damaged by freezing. Further research needs to be done on some materials, such as magnetic tape, where the professional literature is not clear on the risks associated with freezing. Further research is required overall to more fully understand the physical and chemical reactions in materials.

However, paper-based library and archival materials, once frozen, can be stored indefinitely in that state without damage, while decisions are made as to how to dry them. It may be best to freeze everything that you might want to recover, rather than discarding at the outset.

Refrigeration of wet materials (at approximately 4°C or 39°F) should only be used as a temporary measure when other treatment options are not available. The rate of mould growth will be reduced, but heavy, persistent pigmentation will result. (Florian 1997, 149).

Prolonged freezing will dry paper through a natural sublimation process, like the dehydration which materials undergo in the freezer compartment of a frost-free refrigerator. Drying time will depend on the efficiency of the freezer unit, volume and wetness of the material, the freezer temperature and air circulation.

Freeze-stabilization has many advantages:

· Freezing arrests the condition of materials, preventing further distortions and blocking of coated paper. Saturated volumes swollen by immersion will increase slightly more in thickness during freezing; however, this has not been found to contribute further significant damage.
· Further damage caused by the diffusion of water-soluble components is prevented by freezing. Inks, dyes, etc. would otherwise continue to spread by the action of wicking, if left wet or if dried by conventional means from the wet state. Inks and dyes can run if air-dried from the frozen state.
· Freezing reduces mould growth by inducing the dormant state in the spores (conidia). It also kills germinating conidia and hypae, but not dormant or activated conidia (Florian 1997, 155). Materials infested by mould should be either cleaned and returned to controlled environmental conditions or if absolutely necessary, further treated.
· Freezing provides time in which to organize systematic drying operations, carry out further damage assessments and determine replacement requirements, estimate recovery costs and plan for rehabilitation of the building.

(Based largely on Waters 1993, 8)

Freeze-stabilization also has limitations and disadvantages:

· Moisture in materials remains high.

· Further damage to materials may result as a result of ice crystal formation, increased thickness and porosity.

· Some materials cannot be safely frozen, e.g., some types of photographs.

· Costs can be significant depending on the volume of collections to be frozen and the length of treatment.

· As compared to manual drying and cleaning alone, mouldy materials once frozen and dried may be susceptible to reoccurrence of fungi as the spores may have entered a dormant state and thus be potentially viable *(see 6.5.8a)*.

· Materials still need to be dried (unless frozen long-term for the purpose of drying).

Wet books and documents should be packed and frozen as rapidly as possible *(see 7.4)*. This will minimize the size of the ice crystals formed within the materials and limit swelling and deformation. It is best to straighten out distortions before freezing, if that can be done safely.

The best freezing option is blast freezing (with rapidly circulating air) at a commercial facility, which freezes materials swiftly. The British Library blast freezes at -25°C (-13°F) (Parker 1993, 176). Once frozen, it is generally recommended that cold storage temperatures be maintained at -20°C (-4°F) or less. If this temperature cannot be achieved, then maintain at whatever frozen state is possible. Commercial freezers can also be used – they generally operate at -10°C to -30°C (14°F to -22°F). Household freezers can also be used for smaller quantities of materials, although temperatures do not usually go below -10°C (14°F).

The type of transportation to the freezer facility will depend upon the particulars of the situation. If the freezer facility is close at hand and prepared for arrival of the material, transport by regular truck may be the best option. Refrigerated or freezer trucks are generally less available and considerably more expensive than regular trucks. Refrigerated trucks will only chill materials or keep already frozen materials from thawing. Freezer trucks do provide freezing temperatures, but do not offer blast freezing. In cold winter conditions, materials may be frozen outside in a secured area.

Florian (1997, 130) notes that if frozen wet materials are slowly thawed in a refrigerator, the vegetative growth of germinated fungi and a high percentage of hydrated conidia will be killed.

Note: The procedure used for freeze-stabilization of water-damaged materials is different from the freezing treatment used specifically for the treatment of insect-infested dry materials.

d) Drying

Many factors will determine which of the various methods of drying is best in a given situation. The type, number, nature, condition, value, importance and frequency of use of the water-damaged items, as well as time constraints, should all be taken into account. The use of a number of different drying methods for different collections may need to be considered. The focus in this section is on the mass drying of paper-based materials. *(See also 6.5.6e and 7.4)*

General Guidelines for Drying

· Mass chamber or mass *in situ* drying methods are generally not suitable for rare or special collections. Vacuum freeze-dried books and paper documents can show good results (excluding leather, parchment and vellum).

· Air-drying is most suitable for smaller numbers of damp or slightly wetted books and documents. Blocking of bound coated paper may be a problem.

  It is the preferred method for works of art on paper, paintings, most photographic materials and smaller numbers of other non-paper media. It has the highest staff labour costs.

· Dehumidification-drying is most successful when used on damp or slightly wetted, rather than soaked, materials including books, documents, some microforms, computer media and some sound and video recordings. It is generally faster than freezer-drying, vacuum thermal-drying or vacuum freeze-drying, except where major structural drying is being done *in situ* at the same time.

· Freezer-drying is most suitable for smaller quantities of water-damaged book and paper-based material.

· Vacuum drying at ambient temperatures can be used to dry computer media, some microforms, some sound and video recordings and electronic hardware.

· Vacuum freeze-drying is considered the best overall option for water-damaged, paper-based library and archival materials, subsequent to freeze-stabilization. Coated paper is best recovered by this treatment. It is more expensive than vacuum thermal-drying.

· Vacuum thermal-drying is less expensive than vacuum freeze-drying and air-drying for larger numbers of paper-based materials. However, blocking of coated paper, distortion of books, etc. often results. Materials that have already suffered major damage may be the best candidates for this option. Some materials must not be treated by this method, such as parchment and vellum, photographic materials, microforms, etc.

· "There is only a 50% success rate in drying clay or coated paper, no matter what drying method is used" (Munters Corp., Moisture Control Services Division and MBK Consulting 1996, Section II).

· Costs for all types of mass chamber or *in situ* drying provided by an external service company are roughly the same: generally from $50-70 Can. per cubic foot or $6-11 Can. per book, depending on the handling required. A large number of materials would cost less per unit.

· It is best to know the risks associated with each drying method and select accordingly for the materials that require treatment. Availability may also vary depending on timing and geographic location.

· Where weather suits, consider the low-tech option of natural freeze-drying outside (see Palmer Eldridge 1999)

The drying methods described below are listed in alphabetical order.

• **Air-Drying**

Air-drying in a controlled, well-ventilated environment is the preferred method when the wet materials are manageable in number and/or in unbound form or are edge wet only or merely damp or if other drying techniques cannot be used. The process consists of separating the individual wet sheets or fanning out book materials and laying them on paper-covered tables where they dry by evaporation. Absorbent papers can be used to encourage wicking of moisture from items. If only damp, pamphlets and thin volumes may be hung on support lines to dry. Drying outside in the open air may be an option depending on the time of year and weather. Irrespective of the technique used, ongoing monitoring of the items and the environment must be done. *(See also 7.3.7)*

Air-drying is the preferred method for most photographic materials, magnetic tapes, compact discs and phonographic records.

The advantages of air-drying are:

· It is a low-tech option.

· The cost is relatively low if the number of items is not large.

· Sorting and manipulation of the materials can be carried out as necessary.

· It allows for control of individual material characteristics.

· Other associated treatments can be carried out by conservators.

· The state of the materials being dried can be easily assessed.

· It is next to impossible to over-dry materials.

· Large quantities of freeze-stabilized items can be air-dried in batches.

· The drying costs are less than replacement costs.

The principal drawbacks of air-drying are:

· It is impractical for enormous numbers of items.

· For large numbers of items that require ongoing attention, it is very labour-intensive.

· The cost can be high (labour and supplies).

· Staff training is required.

· Considerable space is needed if large numbers of materials need to be dried. And the dedicated space may be required for a long period of time.

· Controlled environmental conditions must be maintained.

· Some wet materials cannot be successfully air-dried, i.e., books with coated paper (pages may block), and water-soluble inks, pigments, etc. (may bleed or offset).

• **Dehumidification-Drying**

Dehumidification-drying has been used for many years to dry buildings and ships' holds. It has recently been used in the library and archives community to dry rooms and their contents *in situ*, and even entire facilities. A room onsite can also be set up as a drying chamber for collections. There are two types of dehumidification-drying: desiccant and refrigerant.

Desiccant dehumidification is drying whereby moisture is trapped and absorbed by a desiccant. A room (or building) is sealed to create a "chamber" and the HVAC system is locally deactivated. Dry air is then continuously circulated through the room and ducted through portable, desiccant dehumidification equipment, situated in or outside the building. The equipment extracts the moisture to the outside, and dry air is returned into the wet areas for moisture pick-up and subsequent moisture removal.

Depending on the equipment, this type of dehumidification can be effective in small or large spaces, as well as in cold temperatures. The air can be dried down to 10% RH, so careful monitoring is required. The temperature should remain below 21°C (70°F) to prevent damage to materials. "If handled and controlled properly, desiccant dehumidification can be just as effective as vacuum freeze-drying" and is reported to be "excellent for drying photographs, film, negatives, X-rays, microfilm/fiche and mylar" (Munters Corp., Moisture Control Services Division and MBK Consulting 1996, 7&9).

Refrigerant dehumidification is drying whereby moisture is condensed on coils, then collected and flushed into a drainage system. This method uses portable equipment and is effective for small-sized applications and local control. The air can be dried down to 20% RH, and careful monitoring is required of temperature and the removal of water from the drainage system. Refrigerant dehumidification lowers the RH more quickly and to a lesser degree than does desiccant dehumidification.

In either case, the process continues until the room and its contents are dry and the desired level of ambient humidity is achieved. Library and industrial buildings, books, documents, carpeting and equipment have been successfully dried in this way. Books and documents are best treated before any swelling or blocking has occurred. Water-damaged tapes may also be dehumidification-dried (Van Bogart 1996b, 3). The drying time averages seven to 10 days, where structural drying is not a significant issue. Monitoring of the items and the environment must be done on an ongoing basis.

The advantages of dehumidification-drying are:

· Labour costs are minimized.
· There is no need to pack and transport materials if done *in situ*. Documentation needs are minimized.
· It is relatively fast.
· It reduces risks to health from bacteria, viruses and mould.
· The drying costs are less than replacement costs.
· Materials can be treated from the frozen or wet state.

The disadvantages of dehumidification-drying are:

· It is not suitable for soaked materials.
· It is not suitable for some materials, i.e., photographic materials, parchment and vellum.
· Inks, dyes, etc. can run.
· Paper can cockle and wrinkle.
· Coated papers can stick or become distorted.
· Adhesives in bound volumes can release.
· Materials can be over-dried.

Dehumidification-drying can cause the above-noted problems, because the items stay wet until the moisture is removed. Thus, damp or slightly wet materials will generally show better results than soaked materials.

• **Freezer-Drying**

As mentioned in the discussion on freeze-stabilization *(see 6.5.6c)*, water-damaged materials will dry over time in a freezer. An alternative for drying up to 200-300 books is to use a commercial freezer that has been specifically modified for the purpose of drying library and archival materials. The Hussman freezer modified for this purpose is also capable of insect extermination (Smith 1984). No experience of using this equipment for drying documents is reported in the literature: however, there is no technical reason why this could not be undertaken.

Prepared books are placed onto racks in the freezer. They are first stabilized by blast-freezing and then dried by temperatures just under freezing. The water moves as a gas from the frozen books in the book compartment (temperature approx. -7°C to -2°C or 20°F to 28°F) to the evaporator component of the freezer, at temperatures well below -40°C, preferably between -45°C to -50°C (-49°F to -58°F). On average, wetted books take two to four weeks to dry. Individual books can be removed when they are dry, and distorted books may be reshaped during the freezer-drying. (Smith 1984)

This method would be used onsite with your own equipment or offsite with that of a sister organization. If small numbers of materials are involved, these may also be dried over time in the freezer compartment of a frost-free refrigerator or a regular freezer.

The advantages of freezer-drying are:

· The unit allows for good control of the process because of accessibility.
· Wetted books can be straightened during the freeze-drying.
· Major relocation of materials is not required.
· Drying costs are less than replacement costs.

The disadvantages of freezer-drying are:

· Limited treatment capacity.
· Capital cost of equipment.
· No reported experience of use with documents.

• **High-Frequency Radiation Drying**

Microwave and other forms of high-frequency radiation drying are not generally recommended. This is because of problems associated with the metal inclusions and attachments found in documents and books in the form of staples, clips, stamping, security strips, etc. which can cause burning of materials.

- **Manual Freeze-Drying**

Following the 1989 fire at the USSR (now Russian) Academy of Sciences Library, a process termed "manual freeze-drying" was developed by the USSR Ecological Safety Research Centre for drying some 200,000 books.

Shapinka et al (1991, 221-223) described the process as follows. Subsequent to freezing, groups of 10 to 15 books of similar size were parcelled together and tightly wrapped with absorbent cloth. Each parcel had an outside pocket on each of its six sides, each of which was filled with sawdust. No special requirements were established for the cloth or sawdust. The still-frozen parcels were then moved in lots of about 300 to shelves in a drying room in which air was vigorously circulated and continuously exhausted to the outside by ventilating fans. There was a 3,000 to 4,500 book capacity per cycle. Drying occurred at 25°C-35°C (77°F-95°F) and 25-35% RH. Books were normally dry after one week. If not, they were returned to the drying room for a second week.

The advantages of manual freeze-drying identified by Shapinka are:
- Books dry evenly from inside to outside.
- Books tightly tied together cannot move or change direction as they dry.
- Books can be straightened out after drying because they are not absolutely bone dry.
- There is no mould growth.

Aside from the onsite equipment needs, the apparent disadvantage of manual freeze-drying is that it is very labour intensive. The costs of this drying method are unknown.

- **Vacuum Drying**

Vacuum drying is a drying method where materials are dried in a vacuum chamber generally at ambient or near-ambient temperatures. Freezing or high temperatures are not used. The progress of drying is determined by weighing. The process may need to be halted and the chamber opened. This method is reported to be very successful for the drying of magnetic tapes and electronic hardware.

The advantages of vacuum drying are:
- Materials are not likely to be over-dried.
- Drying costs can be less than air-drying for larger quantities of material.
- Drying costs can be less then vacuum freeze-drying.
- Drying costs are less than replacement costs.

The disadvantages of vacuum drying are:
- Availability and size of chambers is limited.
- Books may distort during drying.
- Coated papers generally block.
- Inks and pigments can run.
- There is a danger of mould development during drying.
- Some materials cannot be successfully vacuum dried, i.e., photographic materials, parchment and vellum.

- **Vacuum Freeze-Drying**

Vacuum freeze-drying is considered the least damaging and most successful method for drying large quantities of water-damaged library or archival materials. Frozen materials are dried in a vacuum chamber, and do not thaw out as they dry, thus greatly reducing certain types of damage. This is the important difference between vacuum freeze-drying and vacuum thermal-drying.

In the vacuum freeze-drying process, pre-frozen materials are placed in a chamber at a commercial facility from which the air is removed to create a vacuum. Then carefully controlled heat is applied. Because of the lowered air pressure (vacuum), the water sublimates directly from the solid to the gaseous state (i.e. from ice to vapour), thus eliminating further damage by the liquid phase of water. As water in the ice phase (ice in the frozen books) passes into the vapour phase (sublimation), heat is lost. If this heat is not replaced, the temperature of the material is continually lowered, thus slowing the drying process due to evaporative freezing. Extreme care must be taken to ensure that the materials are neither under- nor over-dried. Excess water removal will result in embrittlement of the materials being dried. The progress of drying is determined by weighing. The process may need to be halted and the chamber opened.

Waters (1993, 11) recommends that the internal temperature of a chamber (vacuum freeze- or vacuum thermal-drying) be no greater than 100°F (38°C). This is considered a safe temperature. For sensitive materials, he suggests lower temperatures be used to dry the material slowly and under carefully monitored conditions. The costs can be high. Waters (1996, 247) further advises that the materials must remain completely frozen throughout the drying cycle (below 0°C [32°F] and preferably lower to reduce the size of the ice crystals), and the vapour pressure must be below 4.5 torr.

Blast-freezing and vacuum freeze-drying experiments have been carried out by the British Library on a variety of library materials including books, documents, vellum, computer and audio tapes and microforms. Detailed descriptions of temperatures and pressures, as well as results are provided in a number of published articles (Parker 1989, 1991 and 1993, and Ward and Copeland 1992). Parker (1989, 6) concludes that vacuum freeze-drying can be used successfully on a wide variety of library materials. Some problems have been experienced with some coated papers (early clay loaded art papers), parchment and vellum materials. Parker (1989, 5) says a vacuum freeze-drying temperature of 30°C (86°F) produces good results, but is too hot. He indicates that future drying will be done at a maximum of 20°C (68°F), which will take longer but leave the materials less brittle.

The British Library has test-frozen and vacuum freeze-dried a number of materials in recent years (Parker 1993, 183-185). A great many materials were considered successfully dried (i.e. various papers, computer tapes, various bindings, diazo microfiche, etc.). Materials considered to be unsuccessfully dried or resistant to the procedure were reels of microfilm (silver halide positives), art/glazed/machine finished paper, liquid toner type photocopy paper and illuminated vellum.

The advantages of freeze-stabilization followed by vacuum freeze-drying are:

· It is suitable for large numbers of materials.

· Frozen materials may be selectively chosen for vacuum freeze-drying.

· Expansion and distortion of the materials being dried is minimal.

· Wicking of the materials' water-sensitive or water-soluble components is minimal.

· Rate of mould growth is reduced and germinating conidia and hypae are killed. The effect on dormant or activated conidia is not clear (Florian 1997, 155).

· Results are good for coated papers and drafting linens. There is minimal blocking.

· Dirt and silt are pulled to the materials' surfaces more effectively than with vacuum thermal-drying, allowing for more effective post-treatment cleaning.

· Mobile units are available.

· Drying costs are less than replacement costs.

The disadvantages of vacuum freeze-drying are:

· The cost is more than that of vacuum thermal-drying due to the use of sophisticated equipment.

· Materials can be over-dried, as for any vacuum method.

· Some materials cannot be successfully vacuum freeze-dried, such as some photographic materials.

· Limited availability. As many vacuum freeze-drying facilities in Canada are associated with food-processing plants, timing can be an issue. To prevent contamination, frozen collections must be kept separate from food being stored or processed.

• **Vacuum Thermal-Drying**

Vacuum thermal-drying offers a less expensive alternative to vacuum freeze-drying for the treatment of large numbers of wet materials. Vacuum thermal-drying uses a vacuum to pull the water out, after which warm, dry air is pumped into the chamber to complete the drying. If frozen materials are vacuum dried, some water will sublimate from ice to vapour. Most of the water, however, will first pass through the liquid state before vaporizing. As a consequence of the heat and reintroduction of water, materials will show distortion. Damp or slightly wet materials will generally show better results than soaked materials. Adhesives may release resulting in the need for rebinding. Inks and dyes may run and coated papers may stick together. In addition to the process limitations, there is a problem with the limited capacity and availability of facilities currently available in Canada.

As previously mentioned, the disadvantage of any vacuum method is that some of the material can be over-dried. Waters (1993, 11) recommends that the internal temperature of a chamber be no greater than 100°F (38°C). As the progress of drying is determined by weighing, the process may need to be halted and the chamber opened.

The advantages of vacuum thermal-drying are:

· It can be used for large numbers of materials.

· Frozen materials may be selectively chosen for treatment.

· If an onsite mobile unit is used, there is no need to pack materials for distance travel.

· Drying costs are less than replacement costs.

The disadvantages of vacuum thermal-drying are:

· Wet or wetted materials do not show as good results as damp materials.

· Materials may be distorted.

· Inks and dyes may run.

· Coated papers may block.

· Binding adhesives may release.

· Materials can be over-dried.

· Some materials cannot be successfully treated, such as many photographic materials, leather, parchment, vellum, computer media and microforms.

e) Summary of Recovery Options for Water-Damaged Collections and Records

In recent years, knowledge of recovery treatments and their effect on a variety of materials has increased dramatically. A great deal of the work and experience is well documented; however, further research and confirmation by experience in the field is needed.

The following summary of recovery options (*see chart-page 136*) is drawn from the literature including case studies and experimental research, as well as reports from commercial recovery services, published and unpublished. It is intended to be used as a general planning guide to recovery options for water-damaged collections and records by material type. It is not intended to prescribe the specific applications, limitations or availability of the options, or their suitability for a given disaster. Where situation-specific factors must be considered, i.e. degree and nature of wetness and other damage, water-soluble media, number of items, etc., it is always best to seek expert advice.

Discussion of each of the stabilization and drying options is provided earlier in this chapter. Recovery treatments for specific material types are outlined in Chapter 7.

6.5.7 Fire-Damaged Collections and Records Recovery

Fire can be the most destructive of disasters because with fire also comes smoke, soot, and water. Many materials simply cannot be successfully recovered after a fire and its secondary effects, no matter how sophisticated or extensive the recovery effort.

Little can be done with collections and records that have been severely burned, although in some cases, partial rehabilitation is possible. For example, the charred edges of books can be trimmed and the covers replaced by library binders. Magnetic tape and other computer media may be recovered if the temperature of the fire was not excessive. Tape reels and cassette housings can be replaced, and soot can be vacuumed from tapes or cassettes.

Any materials that have been exposed to high temperatures should be assumed to be fragile. If also wet, they will be even more delicate and must be handled with extreme care. Extra physical support is often necessary; cardboard or polyester film can aid in packing or transport.

Protective housings (folders and boxes) may have warded off some water, smoke and soot. However, smoke is very penetrating and deposits will have carried with them the materials consumed in the fire, including plastic residues that are often impossible to remove. Soot-covered and smokey-smelling materials can sometimes be successfully treated.

Careful consideration should be given to replacing rather than rehabilitating collections exposed to a major fire. Not only is the cost of recovery high, but once burned or exposed to extremely high temperatures, books and documents cannot be returned to their pre-fire state. Reformatting by filming or photocopying, purchase of microfilm or reprints, acceptance of gifts, and purchase of new editions are all good alternatives. Replacement is generally not an option for rare or special collections: however, it may be possible to undertake reformatting so that access to the information is not totally lost.

a) Cleaning of Smoke- and Soot-Covered Materials

This is generally considered to be a rehabilitation measure (*see Chapter 8*).

b) Wet-Stabilization

Some materials, if wet as well as burned, should be kept wet. Coated paper materials should be wet-packed. Immersion of burned films and tapes will surely result in further loss; however, even further damage will result if left to dry as is (*see 6.5.6b*).

c) Freeze-Stabilization

If materials are wet as well as burned, they should be stabilized by freezing (*see 6.5.6c*).

d) Drying

If materials are wet as well as burned, a number of drying options are available (*see 6.5.6d*).

6.5.8 Mouldy Collections and Records Recovery

The occurrence of mould on collections and records after a fire, flood or other disaster will depend in part on the weather. In warm humid weather, mould can appear in as little as 24 hours. However, mould can appear in any weather where conditions are moist and warm, and ventilation is poor. If active mould is present on the collections, the immediate response measures to the mould outbreak have not been successful and efforts must now be intensified to control the environment. If not already done, the mouldy materials must be immediately isolated, confined and stabilized.

Coated paper stock and materials such as leather and vellum bindings can be most severely damaged by

Summary of Recovery Options for Water-Damaged Collections and Records

Material Type	Wet-Stabilize	Freeze-Stabilize	Air-Dry	Freezer-Dry	Dehumid-ification-Dry	Vacuum Dry: (Ambient Temp)	Vacuum Freeze-Dry	Vacuum Thermal-Dry
Books, Periodicals, Pamphlets								
• Uncoated paper	No	Yes	Yes	Yes	Yes	Yes	Yes	Yes
• Coated paper	Yes	Yes	Yes	Yes	Yes	No	Yes	No
• Leather bindings	No	Yes	Yes	No	No	No	No	No
Parchment and Vellum								
• Documents	No	Yes	Yes	No	No	No	Yes*	No
• Bindings	No	Yes	Yes	No	No	No	Yes*	No
Paper Documents								
• Uncoated paper	No	Yes	Yes	Yes*	Yes	Yes	Yes	Yes
• Coated paper	Yes	Yes	Yes	Yes*	Yes	No	Yes	Yes
Plans and Maps								
• Uncoated paper	No	Yes	Yes	Yes*	Yes	Yes	Yes	Yes
• Coated/drafting linen	Yes	Yes	Yes	Yes*	Yes	No	Yes	No
Works of Art on Paper								
• Uncoated paper	No	Yes	Yes	No	No	No	Some	No
• Coated paper	Yes	Yes	Yes	No	No	No	Some	No
Paintings	No	No	Yes	No	No	No	No	No
Photographic Materials								
• Black-and-white prints	Some	Yes	Yes	No	Some*	No	Some	No
• Colour prints								
Chromogenic	Yes	Yes	Yes	No	Some*	No	Yes*	No
Dye transfer	No	No	Yes	No	No	No	No	No
• Negatives								
Wet collodion glass plate	No	No	Yes	No	No	No	No	No
Gelatin dry plate glass	Yes	Yes	Yes	No	No	No	Yes*	No
Polyester-based film, nitrates and acetates	Some	Yes	Yes	No	Some*	No	Yes*	No
• Transparencies								
Lantern slides, silver gelatin	No	Yes	Yes	No	No	No	No	No
Additive colour	No	No	Yes	No	No	No	No	No
Chromogenic colour transparencies, mounted slides, sheet film	Yes	Yes	Yes	No	No	No	Yes*	No
• Motion picture film	Yes	No	Yes	No	No	No	No	No
• Cased photographs (tintypes, ambrotypes, etc.)	No	No	Yes	No	No	No	No	No
Microforms								
• Roll film	Yes	Yes*	Yes	No	Yes*	No	No	No
• Aperture cards, jacketed film	Yes	Yes	Yes	No	Yes*	Yes*	Yes*	No
• Diazo and vesicular fiche	No	Yes	Yes	No	Yes*	Yes*	Yes*	No
Computer Media								
• Open reel magnetic tape	Yes	Yes*	Yes	No	Yes	Yes	Yes*	No
• Cartridge/cassette tape	Yes	Yes*	Yes	No	Yes	Yes	Yes*	No
• Cased and floppy disks	No	No	Yes	No	No	No	No	No
Compacts Discs (CD-ROM, etc.)	No	No	Yes	No	Yes	No	No	No
Sound and Video								
• Open reel tapes	Yes	Yes*	Yes	No	Yes*	Yes	Yes*	No
• Cassette tapes	Yes	Yes*	Yes	No	Yes*	Yes	No	No
• Phonograph records (shellac, acetate, vinyl, etc.)	No	No	Yes	No	No	No	No	No

Notes: This is a general planning guide. <u>Seek expert advice before taking any action.</u> See introductory commentary (6.5.6e).
Rare and special collections are best treated on an individual basis rather than by mass chamber drying.

Yes	=	Treatment option has been successfully used and is well documented.
Yes*/Some*	=	Qualified yes. Experimental research and anecdotal evidence indicates treatment can be successfully used.
No	=	Treatment option is not recommended due to further damage caused to materials OR its effects are unknown.

mould. In general, the exposed bindings and edges of shelved books will be attacked by mould first. Undisturbed collections in boxes may not be so rapidly affected, unless they are saturated. Photographic, film and tape materials may also be attacked, although protective storage containers may reduce this risk.

Mould must be taken seriously, both in terms of preservation of the collections as well as human health and safety *(see 3.4.8a and 6.4.9)*.

In the past, solid, liquid and gaseous fumigants of various types have been used to treat outbreaks of mould, both small and major. However, due to the identified hazards, previously accepted practices are being phased out and chemical fumigation should be considered only where absolutely necessary.

Research and case studies in the professional literature document our increasing knowledge and awareness of both the hazards and the effectiveness of chemical fumigation, such as ethylene oxide and thymol. Concern for human health and safety, and for the environment, is reflected in increasingly stringent legislation. Impacts on the collections, in the form of deleterious effects, are also now more widely known. In addition, a number of fumigants while identified as being able to stop or retard the growth of mould, have been proven to not be fully effective in preventing germination of spores.

According to Florian (1997, 149 and 155), dehydration at room temperature or higher"…is probably the best way to stop fungal activity". She says that temperatures above 40°C (104°F) are lethal to most hydrated states of fungi, and that room temperature or temperatures up to 30°C (86°F) kill all but dormant or activated states. While such drying would be expected to result in further damage to wet material, she cites several examples where, by using restraint, drying was successfully completed with minimal or no change (soaked book example) to the items. This mould treatment and others, such as altered atmospheric gases, require further research to ensure their effective and safe application.

Other treatments such as gamma radiation can be effective in killing mould. However, such radiation facilities are not widely available and major negative effects on collection materials will result.

Effective treatments, chemical or nonchemical, can be either fungicidal or fungistatic. Fungicidal treatment means that the mould and the spores are killed; however, most fungicides do not have a residual effect, and reinfestation may occur. Fungistatic treatment means that germination is halted, but the spores are not killed. Florian (1997, 149) notes that the trade names under which many commercial fungicides are sold present problems. As product formulations may change over time trade names can be misleading. Therefore the generic name of the fungicide must be identified. The sale and use of fungicides and fumigants are controlled by the Pest Control and Products Act in Canada, and the Environmental Protection Agency in the U.S.

The treatment of mould-infested materials is an issue for which there are no easy answers. Active mould on a few materials may be fairly easily handled; however, a major outbreak on a large number of items demands that difficult decisions be made.

The benefits of treatment must be weighed against the risks. The safest advice is to bring the mould to an inactive state. Thereafter, the materials must be isolated from the rest of the collections for a minimum observation period of six months. The materials must be subsequently stored in conditions of low relative humidity.

a) Freeze-Stabilization and Drying

Freezing and various drying techniques can be used to bring mould to an inactive state, but these will not kill all the spores. Multiple freezing treatments, however, can reduce the population significantly. For example, blast-freezing books and documents at -40°C (-40°F) results in an 11% survival rate of fungi and a second blast-freezing treatment at the same temperature results in a 1% mould survival rate (Florian cited in DePew 1991, 78). According to probability theory, 100% kill may be impossible. See Florian (1997, 129-130, 155) for a discussion in the effects of freezing on a number of microorganisms.

Stabilization of paper-based materials by freezing can be used to retard the growth of mould. There is, however, a downside:

> …if fungal-infected material is dried, cleaned with vacuum (HEPA type filter), and then stored at 50-60% RH and constant …temperature there is little chance for most fungal spores to germinate. This seems to be due to the fact that the spores will not enter dormancy. If [however] spores are frozen and dried, they may enter a dormant state and thus be potentially viable years later (ICOM International Committee for Conservation 1994, 1).

This means that after equilibration and under the proper conditions, mould can reoccur on books after freezing. *(See also 3.4.8a)*

Various of the drying methods described previously *(see 6.5.6d)* can be used to dry damp or wet mouldy materials. Whatever method is chosen, the mouldy items must be packed separately and kept apart from the other collections.

Drying of mouldy materials should be followed by cleaning, treatment as appropriate, isolation from other collections, monitoring, and storage in a climate-controlled environment. This is even more critical where the mould has not been killed, but brought to an inactive state.

b) Fumigation

Fumigation should be undertaken only in extreme circumstances. All fumigation is strictly regulated and must be done only by fully trained and licensed personnel in licensed facilities, onsite or offsite. It is best to seek expert advice and offsite commercial fumigation. Fumigation treatment should not be undertaken on rare materials or others such as film and tape materials.

c) Cleaning and Treatment of Mould-Covered Materials

Cleaning and other mould treatments should be undertaken on dry materials only and are considered to be rehabilitation measures *(see Chapter 8)*.

6.5.9 Cost Factors

The costs of recovery and rehabilitation, of course, vary tremendously. In the event of a minor disaster, determining costs may be quite straightforward, if internal expertise and resources are sufficiently large for prompt response and recovery. After a major disaster the costs will be enormous, regardless of the size, nature and resources of the organization. In 1992, Cunha estimated the recovery cost of a 100,000-volume library of fire- and water-damaged books after a major disaster to be U.S. $3.2 million (Cunha 1992, 542). This figure did not include costs for in-house staff processing of replacement purchases or those for rehabilitation of the building or for repair and replacement of furniture and equipment.

The experience of organizations that have recovered from disasters hold significant implications for disaster planning, and recovery requirements in particular. It is essential to know what your recovery options are, both in theory and in practice – which methods, services and facilities would be appropriate, given your collections and location, what is actually available to you and what you could reasonably afford.

Factors to consider when determining costs:

- The costs associated with discard can be significant. These include the staff time required for decision-making and database changes. Discarding applies to general library collections and rarely to special library or archives collections, except where duplicate copies exist.

- Some materials should not be recovered or replaced, such as older editions of general reference type materials that are available elsewhere.

- Generally, it is less expensive to replace severely fire- or water-damaged materials that are not unique or have no intrinsic value, than to attempt recovery. Libraries with large holdings of current collections will often be able to replace these materials if funding is available. But special libraries and archives often hold unique materials, the majority of which have not been duplicated and cannot be replaced.

- For replacement, in-house processing costs must be considered. Repurchase may be difficult and long-term, and costs may be high depending on the nature of the collections. Reformatting may be an option, albeit an expensive one.

- Costs for freeze-stabilization can be significant if large numbers of materials must be frozen for extended periods.

- In a major disaster, the majority of collections in an organization with large paper-based holdings will require 'restoration' to some degree. Sometimes a high percentage of the collections will need intermediate treatment.

- The costs associated with the recovery and rehabilitation of archival material versus that of library material may vary enormously. Boxed material may, in some cases, suffer less direct damage and be less costly to recover and rehabilitate. However, boxed archival material can be very mixed in terms of media, and may require significant staff time if pre-treatment sorting is desirable. Alternatively, the potential for damage to some materials may be considered an acceptable risk and the materials may be treated by mass means without sorting.

- The successful recovery of damaged electronic data is an increasingly important issue. Copies and back-ups are essential to keeping these costs to a minimum.

- A well-planned and well-rehearsed response and recovery effort will keep costs to a minimum.

Cost Recovery and Rehabilitation Tables

The following tables summarize the estimated costs for recovering and rehabilitating fire- and water damaged library and archival materials after major disasters. Both assume that the collections have suffered various levels of damage. It should be noted that the storage space required by the library of 100,000 books corresponds roughly to that of the archives of 10,000 record centre boxes. However, the damage sustained by books stored on shelves would be different from that sustained by documents stored and protected in boxes. Discard and replacement in the library situation would be more extensive than in the archives situation, where original documents would rarely be discarded and replacement less possible, and therefore less frequent. The unit costs per book or box also vary considerably, depending on whether the decision is to discard, replace or treat.

Costs will also vary depending on the level of in-house staff needed for various activities and the duration of recovery and rehabilitation. Costs of external assistance will depend on the nature of that assistance (conservators, mycologists, recovery company personnel, etc.). The hourly rate for specialist work is, of course, more expensive than for basic packing, removal and recovery activities.

The costs provided in the tables are estimates only; every situation will be different. However, these tables do serve to underline the very high costs of collections recovery and rehabilitation versus those of disaster prevention, protection and preparedness. The tables are based on the work of Cunha (1992, 542) and have been expanded and revised to include archival materials, as well as to reflect current Canadian costs.

Estimated Cost for Recovering and Rehabilitating Fire- and Water-Damaged Books After a Major Disaster at a Library of 100,000 Books

Decision	Percent Damaged	Number of Books	Per Book Cost* (Can $)	Total Cost (Can $)
Discard[1]	20	20,000	5	100,000
Replacement[2]	20	20,000	50	1,000,000
Treatment				
Minor[3]	10	10,000	5	50,000
Medium[4]	48	48,000	50	2,400,000
Major[5]	2	2,000	1,000	2,000,000
Total Cost[6]				**$5,550,000**

Notes:
* Assumes both general and rare material collections, each fairly homogeneous.
[1] Staff cost for withdrawing books (@$5 for handling, record-keeping and deleting database records).
[2] Cost of purchasing replacement books (@$35) and minimum staff costs for in-house processing after purchase (@$15).
[3] Cost of minor-level treatment (@$5 for onsite cleaning of soot-covered books and drying of damp-only books including handling, documentation and processing).
[4] Cost of medium-level treatment (@$50 for freeze-stabilization, vacuum freeze-drying and commercial rebinding including handling, documentation, transportation and processing).
[5] Cost of major-level treatment (@$1,000 for freeze-stabilization and vacuum freeze-drying followed by professional conservation of textblock and binding including handling, documentation, transportation and processing).
[6] This estimate does not include any costs for rehabilitation of the facility or repair and replacement of furniture and equipment.

Estimated Cost for Recovering and Rehabilitating Fire- and Water-Damaged Documents After a Major Disaster at an Archives of 10,000 Record Centre Boxes

Decision	Percent Damaged	Number of Boxes	Per Box Cost*(Can $)	Total Cost (Can $)
Discard[1]	2	200	20	4,000
Replacement[2]	8	800	120	96,000
Treatment				
Minor[3]	30	3,000	45	135,000
Medium[4]	55	5,500	200	1,100,000
Major[5]	5	500	4,500	2,250,000
Total Cost[6]				**$3,585,000**

Notes:
*   Assumes 500 documents per box and a fairly homogeneous collection of documents and manuscripts (not maps, prints and drawings).
[1]   Staff cost for withdrawing box of documents (@$20 for handling, record-keeping and deleting database records).
[2]   Cost of microfilm replacement produced in-house (@$.10/frame for processing, verification and quality control; plus handling, preparation of originals, i.e, drying and documentation).
[3]   Cost of minor-level treatment (@$45 for onsite cleaning of soot-covered documents, drying of damp-only documents and rehousing including handling, documentation and processing).
[4]   Cost of medium-level treatment (@$200 for freeze-stabilization, vacuum freeze-drying, rehousing and minor conservation including handling, documentation, transportation and processing).
[5]   Cost of major-level treatment (@$4,500 for freeze-stabilization and vacuum freeze-drying followed by professional conservation including handling, documentation, transportation and processing).
[6]   This estimate does not include any costs for rehabilitation of the facility or repair and replacement of furniture and equipment.

Estimating recovery costs is a complex and arduous task. In addition to the collections and records, costs for the recovery for systems, furniture and equipment and the facility will need to be estimated *(see Chapter 9)*.

Costs for collections and records recovery may be estimated as follows:

• Paper- and Film-Based Collections and Records

The number of books, boxes and items to be discarded, replaced and treated needs to be roughly determined. For each category, an estimated unit cost must be assigned. Staff costs should be included when decision-making, research, database changes, rehousing and other processing are involved. Mass treatment costs for general materials should be kept separate from costs for unique or rare items requiring custom-designed treatment. In-house costs should be kept separate from estimates for external services and facilities.

• Computer-Based Collections and Records

The costs of computer data recovery will depend, in part, on the strategy selected and implemented during the planning process: cold site, hot site, etc. Additional costs will be incurred where substantial changes need to be made. *(See 5.8.3)*

Estimated costs for in-house or external professional recovery of tapes, disks, etc. need to be calculated as for paper- and film-based collections and records.

Once options have been assessed and costed, decisions on the recovery strategy will need to be made. Discussion and negotiation will need to take place with the insurance company.

6.6   Stage IV: Recovery Strategy Planning: Support Operations

The Disaster Planning Committee (DPC) must plan carefully and fully for this latter stage of response. At this point in the disaster timeline, the recovery strategy for the collections and records, as well as that for the facility, systems, etc. *(see Chapter 9)* would have been developed by the Disaster Action Team (DAT) or is in the final stages of development. However, before this strategy can be implemented, the framework and logistics for support operations need to be determined. While much of this work will have been done at the initial planning stage for the disaster plan, modifications and enhancements will be required to meet the needs of the current situation.

Immediate emergency response actions, such as stabilizing the environment, may be ongoing.

6.6.1   The Purpose of Operational Support Strategy Planning

The purpose of operational support strategy planning is to develop the necessary resources and measures to ensure effective implementation of the overall recovery strategy. This support strategy should cover all the operations that enable and facilitate recovery.

Components of this strategy may continue throughout rehabilitation.

Coordination and flexibility will be key, as many different operations will need to be planned, organized and integrated. People, equipment, supplies, systems and external services will all need to come together at the right times. Forthright and timely communication will also be critical. Staff and external service personnel will need to be clear on the working conditions, schedules and expectations.

6.6.2 The Process for Operational Support Strategy Planning

The existing disaster plan should be used as a basis for developing the operational support recovery strategy. This would include a variety of operations such as coordination, communications, documentation, security and workforce deployment. Some may be initiated during immediate emergency response, when time and safety factors allow. Collectively, these operations form the support strategy necessary to implementation of the recovery strategy.

Operational Support Strategy Planning: Process at a Glance

Prepare to:
· Establish a coordination strategy.
· Establish a command centre.
· Get the computer system operational.
· Establish a communications strategy.
· Establish a security strategy.
· Establish a documentation strategy.
· Establish a personnel strategy.
· Mobilize the staff at large.
· Communicate the recovery strategy and instruct the recovery teams.
· Order supplies and equipment, and contract with outside services.

---

a) Establish a coordination strategy

The DAT coordinator must make sure that the necessary activities are carried out in the proper sequence, link the team members and activities where appropriate, and oversee and expedite the allocation of personnel and other resources, both internal and external.

Coordination of specific activities may be assigned to individuals in addition to the DAT, such as work teams responsible for particular tasks. A set of agreed-to objectives will be important to decision-making, timing and workflow. Every detail cannot be planned for, and creativity will play a critical role. The focus is on moving the plan forward by matching needs with assistance and resources.

Leadership shown by the coordinator(s) sets the tone for the response and recovery operations. A professional, well-coordinated, ordered and organized approach will encourage the same in other team members and personnel.

> Everyone must be reminded that a crisis management team is not democratic; the intention of the team is not to manage the event by committee (Environment Canada 1993, 25).

Coordination will be of particular importance where several organizations or agencies must work together. Overlapping lines of authority and responsibility can produce conflict, stress and frustration and result in lower productivity, less effective recovery operations and higher costs.

b) Establish a command centre

The command centre serves as the base for the overall disaster operation (coordination, communications, security, etc.), as well as ongoing response measures (collections protection, stabilization of the environment, etc.), subsequent recovery operations (collections removal, drying, etc.), and possibly rehabilitation operations. All decisions must be made, recorded, implemented and communicated through this location. This is the base of operations for the DAT, staff at large, emergency response personnel, external service providers and government agency representatives. Lines of authority and responsibility must be clear and articulated, otherwise miscommunication, stress and conflict can occur. The centre should be near to the affected area to permit smooth and rapid communications, but far enough removed to be safe, and to avoid disruption of or by working personnel.

c) Get the computer system operational

The ability to rapidly get the computer system operational will depend on both the nature and extent of the disaster, as well as the adequacy of the advance planning. The computer system can facilitate the response and recovery process in many ways, such as by providing access to the online collections databases, personnel records, etc. An operational system will be a priority in most circumstances, either onsite or at an external location (hot site, cold site, etc.). This service may be furnished by previously-contracted service providers.

d) Establish a communications strategy

The function of communications is to facilitate the response and recovery efforts and to avoid confusion and delays. In larger organizations a communications officer will be part of the DAT, responsible for the issuing of all information and reports concerning the disaster, both internal and external. In other situations, personnel, such as the director, may be appointed to fulfil this role. All communications should be centralized in the command centre and issued through or by the designated communications person.

It is important to communicate frequently with a number of groups: administration, response and recovery staff, staff not directly involved in these efforts, users, the general public and the media. Many of these individuals will be stakeholders of the organization and their information needs will vary, and should be met using mechanisms appropriate to the intended audiences, i.e., e-mail, memos, meetings, press releases, interviews, etc.

• Internal Communications

Internal communication needs will be diverse, and will continue throughout response, recovery and rehabilitation and post-disaster planning. These include responses to queries from staff, handouts, signage, bulletins, notification of debriefings and meetings, and progress reports.

> In a massive disaster, morale and productivity will drop after a day or two. Communication helps to overcome some problems by keeping people informed, by noting progress, by expressing appreciation (Buchanan 1988, 67).

Internal communications will also include information needed by external personnel such as the fire and police departments, medical and rescue services, and recovery specialists who will be working onsite. Depending on the size of the organization and physical layout of the premises, this may require extensive planning and coordination.

Timely dissemination of information and news will be a key factor in the effectiveness of the response, recovery and rehabilitation efforts.

• External Communications

Since a disaster is bound to attract widespread attention, the communications officer should manage all queries from users, the public at large and the media. As Gordon Wright observed after the 1977 fire at the University of Toronto, the presence of the media was an unforeseen complication:

> Salvage operations are interrupted for exclusive interviews, everyone on the scene is approached for eyewitness accounts. Quite apart from the inevitable distortion of facts, few people are conversant with the kind of decisions that must be made based on the best available judgement (Wright 1979, 258).

News coverage can generate considerable goodwill or can have extensive negative impact. Publicity can be used to your advantage when it is anticipated, organized and controlled, and when information is accurate and current. It can aid when external assistance is required in the form of volunteers, supplies and services. Positive news coverage can also help with financial support and fundraising.

> The press were not contacted quickly, nor did they respond quickly. This was definitely a missed opportunity. Early, favourable press coverage can be useful if financial appeals are to be made. It may also be good publicity for the organizations responding to the disaster (Henderson 1995, 54).

At the outset, the communications officer should quickly advise the media of the disaster, explain that a previously prepared and comprehensive recovery programme is under way, and inform them that regular reports will be issued. The media will later expect information on how the building and collections are being rehabilitated, when services will resume and where users can obtain replacement services in the interim.

Be sure to make public what outside assistance you are seeking, if any, and how individuals and other organizations could make contact. The aim is to match needs with offered resources, not to waste the valuable time of internal resources or external individuals, institutions and businesses.

In the case of a major disaster, ongoing and regular communications will be important when a phased return to normal operations is required, possibly over a long period of time. Kahn (1994, 24) stresses that it is important to "market the resumption of your services, tout the quality of services provided in the alternate location and the..[organization's]...importance. Now is the time to provide the best and most efficient service possible". Effective communication helps the organization maintain its usership when it reopens for business.

e) Establish a security strategy

After the disaster, the facility may be widely vulnerable due to damage, inoperable systems, and the access needs of emergency personnel. Windows may be broken, doors may be open and normal security systems may be inoperable. Security measures must be implemented to protect personnel, the facility, its systems and, of course, the collections (*see 3.5.8*). Security of the command centre must also be considered.

Security measures are needed as part of immediate response, when emergency personnel may be entering and exiting the building, and evacuation may still be under way. After the emergency is contained, security measures will need to be enhanced to accommodate access by staff and other external personnel. Authorized personnel only should be permitted to enter the building. Disaster and recovery areas should be offlimits to non-designated staff or other personnel, and the public.

Security will be a continuing issue throughout response, recovery and rehabilitation operations. Protection and safety are the critical concerns.

f) Establish a documentation strategy

All activities associated with the response, recovery and rehabilitation effort should be documented carefully (written, photographic, video, etc.). Appropriate record-keeping hand in hand with good communications will provide the information needed to coordinate and keep the recovery strategy moving, make the right decisions, get the best results, make the best use of resources and allow flexibility.

Good record-keeping in concert with good communication can:

- facilitate and focus the overall planning and co-ordination of the response, recovery and rehabilitation efforts.
- provide necessary information for insurance purposes (proof of loss and replacement) or for assistance from government agencies in the event of a declared disaster.
- expedite the response, recovery and rehabilitation processes.
- identify what is working well and what is not.
- assist with post-disaster analysis to prevent or mitigate future disasters.
- document whom you need to thank for specific contributions.

g) Establish a personnel strategy

Personnel requirements will have been established as part of the recovery strategy. However, specific deployment (work teams) and scheduling will need to be determined. Access to personnel records (paper or electronic) might not be immediately possible, and arrangements to access back-up information may be necessary. Rapid access is critical – otherwise mobilization of the staff will be delayed.

Staff will need to know:

- whom to report to and when.
- where to report.
- what hours they are expected to work.
- what tasks they have been assigned.
- what the safety and security procedures are.
- how and where to access supplies and equipment.
- what the documentation procedures are.
- what the response, recovery and rehabilitation priorities and procedures are.

The coordination and organization of human resources will involve assigning tasks to staff within the organization, and in many cases, hiring external service personnel. Coordination and supervision of these internal and external workforces will be critical. Quality-control decisions will need to be made. Shiftwork arrangements will likely be required, and work assignments for individuals with physical limitations may need to be considered.

It is essential to acknowledge that even in the case of small scale disasters, people will be worried and upset. Emotional and physical stress will be more significant in the event of a major disaster. In a region-wide event, where people may be distraught over the safety of their families and homes, their ability to participate may be severely limited, thus jeopardizing recovery operations. Cunha (1992, 568) stresses the importance of cooperative disaster planning whereby "recovery team positions would be filled by principals and alternates from several libraries instead of one, but rarely with principals and alternates for any position being from the same library".

Many of the response, recovery and rehabilitation activities may be exhausting, dirty and demoralizing. People's energy and optimism will decline, adrenalin will wear off and the reality of the problems may appear insurmountable. People may feel overwhelmed to the point of ineffective action or sheer inactivity. Advance planning and training will help to reduce these effects, but will not eliminate them. Effective supervision will be critical at all levels.

Timely provision of the proper equipment and supplies, as well as work breaks and refreshments will facilitate not only productivity, but also safety and morale.

The welfare and morale of personnel must be a prime consideration. Communicating information and news will help foster teamwork and a positive environment. Celebrating small achievements can be very important.

Work schedules must be reasonable. It is unrealistic to expect people to work effectively for more than one and a half hours straight. After that, people are increasingly less effective, mistakes will happen and accidents can occur. A routine of adequate rest breaks with refreshments and snacks must be established and maintained.

In order to plan effectively, the DAT should be familiar with the emotional phases of a disaster: heroic, honeymoon, disillusionment and reconstruction phases *(see 10.4.3).*

h) Mobilize the staff at large

When contacted, staff should be instructed to assemble at the mustering point(s), either the pre-arranged location or alternate as necessary (confirm the location at time of contact). This mustering point may or may not become the command centre for the disaster operations. If the location is inside the building, team members must be instructed which entrance to use, and a staff member must be stationed there to direct personnel as they arrive. A contact list is recommended to document who was contacted and when, as well as who has arrived on the scene.

In the event of a major or widespread disaster, members of the public may want to become involved. The use of volunteers may be a contentious issue. On the positive side, volunteers are genuinely interested in helping and may be able to offer valuable assistance. Concerns regarding the use of volunteers centre on training, supervision, insurance and liability issues, as well as the nature, value and confidentiality of the collections and records being recovered.

i) Communicate the recovery strategy and instruct the recovery teams

Once assembled, the staff should be briefed on the situation: the nature and scope of the disaster, the response measures already taken, the nature and progress of measures to stabilize and protect collections, assessments of damage, etc. The plan and objectives for recovery are then communicated, and work teams are established, assignments allocated and further specific instruction provided. Each staff member must be clear about their role and responsibilities (such as contacting outside suppliers and resources) before beginning work.

All personnel, internal and external, must be briefed on lines of authority and procedures (safety, security, recovery, etc.). Instruction on media contacts and the use of volunteers must be provided. This briefing is not a one-time event. Ongoing communication in the form of progress reports, plan modification updates, etc. is essential to the morale of the workforce and to effective recovery.

As part of the disaster planning process, training for some disaster scenarios will have taken place; however, not all eventualities can have been covered. Onsite training for volunteers and to supplement existing staff expertise may be required.

j) Order equipment and supplies, and contract with outside services

Equipment and supplies will need to be borrowed, purchased or rented. Contracts may need to be drawn up, such as for drying services or the rental of space offsite for drying and other recovery operations. Sources for most of these requirements should be in the resources section of your disaster plan. Advance arrangements that you have made will expedite the process.

When supplies and equipment are received, they should be prepared and distributed as needed. Work stations or areas (onsite or offsite) will also need to be prepared for the packing, removal and treatment of damaged collections.

6.6.3 Support Operations Checklists

These checklists are intended to support and facilitate the recovery and rehabilitation strategies by indicating critical factors that should be considered.

a) Coordination

Coordination Checklist

- Establish the command centre.
- Define clearcut lines of authority and responsibilities, including inter-organizational relationships.
- Establish strategies and actions required.
- Organize staffing.
- Determine and acquire needed resources.
- Organize regular reporting processes.
- Establish a communications centre and strategy.
- Establish safety and security strategies.
- Initiate needed training and supervision.
- Establish a plan for the welfare and morale of personnel.
- Document activities and costs.

Coordinator's Checklist

- Be visible and accessible.
- Work with your team.
- Acknowledge success.
- Recognize human limitations (including your own).
- Foster a calm and positive outlook.
- Maintain a big-picture approach.
- Stay current with developments.
- Call meetings only when necessary.
- Get the information needed to make decisions.
- Communicate decisions clearly.
- Monitor and communicate progress.
- Set realistic priorities and timelines.
- Delegate where appropriate whenever possible.
- Remember that small problems require small solutions.
- Encourage creative solutions.
- Solve problems quickly.
- Be prepared for the unexpected.
- Keep your sense of humour.

b) Command Centre

Command Centre Checklist

- Is the location convenient?
- Is the location easily accessible?
- If the location is offsite, for how long is it available?
- Can access be controlled with minimum staffing?
- Is the location well protected and secured?
- Does it have electrical power? operational computers? telephones?
- Does it have furniture? administrative supplies?
- Is other needed equipment and furniture available?

c) Communications

Communications Checklist

- Coordinate all communications through the command centre.
- Arrange for needed communications supplies and equipment (computers, telephones, pagers, walkie-talkies).
- Establish protocols and procedures for communication.
- Provide communications staff with contact information they need (names and telephone numbers).
- Ensure that all information issued is current, accurate and consistent.
- Communicate regularly with response, recovery and rehabilitation personnel.
- Communicate availability of services to your public.
- Use a variety of mechanisms to communicate.
- Issue information to media regularly.
- Be responsive to changing needs for information.

d) Security

Security Coverage Checklist

Establish coverage for:
- Staff, volunteers and other personnel.
- The disaster site.
- Offsite working and storage locations.
- Computer systems.
- Collections and records.
- Other assets.
- The command centre.

Security Checklist

- Establish and communicate security measures.
- Establish access control for building and offsite locations.
- Establish an identity badge system and a worker registration system.
- Get security systems operational as soon as possible.
- Effect building repairs that affect security.
- Modify security measures as needs change.

e) Documentation

Documentation of the following activities, locations, etc. can assist with determining needs, priorities and resources. It can also form the basis for post-disaster reports and help with the preparation of the insurance claim.

Documentation Checklist

- Immediate emergency response:
  Nature and scope of emergency
  Personnel contacted and when
  Measures taken

- Collections and records:
  Quantity, nature and severity of damage
  Tracking relocation (internal and external)

- Facility and contents:
  Quantity, nature and severity of damage
  Tracking relocation (internal and external)

- Environmental conditions
  Monitoring process
  Locations and readings

- Human resources:
  Staff
  External (emergency personnel, contractors, volunteers)

- External assistance, services and supplies:
  Purchase
  Rental
  Loan

- Communications:
  Internal
  External

- Costs for all of the above

f) Personnel Welfare

Personnel Welfare Checklist

- Provide a safe and secure workplace.
- Provide training as needed.
- Make expectations and reporting relationships clear.
- Set realistic work schedules.
- Provide identification badges or tags.
- Provide frequent breaks.
- Establish a refreshment and rest area.
- Provide refreshments and snacks.
- Communicate progress, news, etc. frequently.
- Provide clothing, equipment and supplies when needed.
- Provide access to restrooms and telephones.
- Arrange for security of people's personal belongings.
- Arrange for minor medical emergencies.
- Modify personnel plans as needed.

Chapter 7

7.0 Disaster Recovery Planning for Collections and Records

Recovery can be described as shorter-term activity intended to limit further damage to the collections and records and to return them to a useable state. In some cases, recovery activity will render them minimally useable, and in others fully useable. Any further treatments required, whereby damaged collections and records are rendered fully useable and accessible, are generally termed rehabilitation *(see Chapter 8)*.

This chapter focuses on the actions taken to recover collections and records including stabilization, cleaning, removal and drying. At this point in the disaster timeline, the Disaster Action Team (DAT) is ready to implement the recovery strategy, based on the strategies developed by the Disaster Planning Committee (DPC) and documented in the disaster plan, and the modifications made to meet the needs of the particular disaster situation *(see Chapter 6)*. A command centre has been established, and staff and volunteer work teams have been mobilized, debriefed and instructed. External experts have been contacted and outside contractors have been hired and briefed; as well, safety and security measures are in place, and the necessary supplies and equipment received and distributed. Secure work areas for collections and records (onsite and/or offsite) have been established and prepared. Stabilization processes for the environment and facility are likely ongoing.

In a disaster situation, it is the responsibility of conservation professionals to provide expert guidance and assistance related to the recovery and rehabilitation of collections and records. Just as the overall organization has shifted to disaster-mode, the decisions made regarding collections must be made in light of practical realities. The desire to recover everything according to normal operating procedures may simply be unrealistic, and may in fact lead to greater losses. The Canadian Association for the Conservation of Cultural Property (formerly International Institute for Conservation – Canadian Group) in its *Code of Ethics and Guidance for Practice* (IIC-CG 1989, 12) (currently under revision) acknowledges that, in emergency situations, it may not be possible to adhere fully to the *Guidelines for Practice*. Other associations including the American Institute for Conservation of Historic and Artistic Works *Code of Ethics and Guidelines for Practice* (1994) also acknowledge this reality.

7.1 The Purpose of Disaster Recovery Planning for Collections and Records

The overall purpose of disaster recovery planning is twofold: to minimize the damage and prevent further losses to collections and records, and to ensure maximum opportunities for rehabilitation and resumption of operations. The recovery phase sets in motion the strategies developed during the response phase. The strategy for collections recovery, such as removal and drying, is put into effect and modified as necessary, as recovery proceeds. It is supported by the strategies for communications, security, personnel, etc. and by external resources as necessary.

For collections and records, the goal is to prevent or reduce the effects of:

- mould growth
- dimensional changes (warping, swelling, distortion, splitting, delamination, etc.)
- solubilization/transfer of water-sensitive or water-soluble components (inks, dyes, sizes, adhesives, etc.)
- staining from flood waters, debris, etc.
- contamination from sewage or chemicals in flood waters
- sticking or fusion of adjacent components or items (such as coated paper or film emulsions on drying)
- corrosion of metal components
- hardening of parchment, leather, etc. on drying.
(Based on Stewart and Tremain 1994, 61-62)

A further goal throughout the recovery process (handling, packing, removing and drying of collections and records) is to prevent or reduce the effects of:

- mechanical damages (tearing, smearing, scratching, etc.) to wet paper, bindings, film, disks, etc.
- transfer of mud, smoke and soot deposits, plastic residues, etc.
- over-drying or under-drying of materials
- loss of identification markings and labels from collections and housings.

7.2 The Process for Disaster Recovery Planning for Collections and Records

At this point in the disaster timeline, undamaged but threatened items should have been or continue to be removed to safe and secure areas either within the building or offsite. Undamaged items not at risk should have been left as they are. Now, the systematic removal of the damaged collections and records can begin. This work should proceed according to the priorities determined for the recovery strategy, although circumstances may dictate on-the-spot rethinking. Further expert help should be obtained whenever necessary. Progress must be monitored regularly, and plans for personnel, communications, security, etc. modified as needs change. The actions involved in recovery will vary according to the circumstances; however, some are common to all recovery efforts.

This is a period of intense activity, both emotionally and physically, with a number of varied tasks happening simultaneously. Time may be a critical factor, as collections must be stabilized and perhaps removed before the onset of mould and other further damage. Difficult, and perhaps unpopular, decisions need to be made, communicated and implemented. Here is when planning and training should really come together. An organized and rehearsed recovery operation will be the most effective and least stressful.

Collections and Records Recovery Planning: Process at a Glance

Prepare to:
- Document damage to and relocation of collections and records.
- Sort collections and records according to urgency and treatment.
- Isolate collections and records with active mould.
- Rinse debris-covered and contaminated wet materials as appropriate.
- Pack damaged materials.
- Transport materials to external facilities for treatment.
- Move and treat materials onsite or nearby offsite.
- Receive treated materials.

After treated materials are returned from external facilities or onsite treatment areas, any further required treatment and processing as necessary would be undertaken as part of rehabilitation (*see Chapter 8*).

7.2.1 Document damage to and relocation of collections and records

It is critical that collections and records are identified before removal. Damage must be documented, as well as any relocation either onsite or offsite. Records can be written by hand or input on a portable computer, and may be usefully augmented by photo or video documentation. If the collections are barcoded, it may be possible to use portable scanning equipment to identify and track materials. If the online database is available and includes an item status or tracking module, movement of the collections may be further detailed.

It is essential that accurate records be kept of all materials during packing, removal and relocation. Boxes should be numbered, and boxes and quantities tracked. Box content listings are a valuable tool, only when accurate, complete and current. This information will be essential for insurance and replacement, as well as for resumption of normal operations. Other recovery activities and associated costs should be documented throughout.

Recovery procedures should be designed to prevent the damage or loss of existing identification labels and markings. Should it be necessary to mark collection material containers, waterproof labels with soft pencils or waterproof markers are recommended. No attempt should be made to mark the actual wet or otherwise damaged collection materials. Materials with defaced labels or no labels could be assigned special numbers, although this is time-consuming and it may be better to just keep a running total. In the case of materials or containers with badly defaced or missing labels/markings, it is best to note the location where the materials were found (i.e., on floor x, near bay y) as an aid to later identification.

7.2.2 Sort collections and records according to urgency and treatment

Based on the damage assessment and the priorities set for the recovery operation (*see 6.5.3 and 6.5.4*), and prior to removal, collections and records should be sorted according to the urgency of treatment and the nature of that treatment. This sorting is critical as respective timing, handling and packing requirements will vary. Materials may be damp only, edge-wetted or saturated. The presence of dirty or contaminated water will complicate the situation. Some materials may also be covered in smoke-residue and soot, while others may be charred.

Some materials, such as coated paper, items with water-soluble media, items with known low recovery rates and mouldy items are best treated immediately.

Wet coated paper is best frozen within six to eight hours. Other materials will need to be treated within 24 to 48 hours. Depending on the nature and condition of the collections, more than one drying treatment may be used. Materials to be discarded, replaced, etc. will also need to be identified.

The type, number and condition of damaged materials will determine how much time can be spent in preparation for packing, transportation, freezing and drying.

Sorting can be time-consuming and labour intensive; however, it is, in most cases, worth the effort. Proper sorting eliminates unnecessary treatment and reduces the potential for damage caused by under-drying of wet material, over-drying of damp materials or the drying of sensitive materials by inappropriate means. This will result in cost savings during the drying operation and later rehabilitation.

7.2.3 Isolate collections and records with active mould

Mould may develop during the recovery process where the environment has not been effectively stabilized and collections and records have not been adequately monitored. Ongoing control of relative humidity and temperature is a must *(see 3.4.8a and 6.4.2k)*, and all collections with active mould must be isolated from the other collections. Larger numbers of mouldy, water-damaged materials should be immediately bagged and frozen, or immediately dried by mass means. Mould on paper-based materials must be dry before any cleaning is attempted.

Due to health risks, appropriate precautions must be taken when handling mouldy materials *(see 3.4.8a, 6.4.2l and 6.4.9)*.

7.2.4 Rinse debris-covered and contaminated wet materials as appropriate

It is preferable to remove mud or other debris from wet, paper-based material once dried, so that mud or silt is not forced into the paper fibres. However, in some circumstances, onsite cleaning is necessary. The rinsing of mud, sewage, etc. prior to drying is **essential** for materials such as film and magnetic tape. These materials, even when wetted by clean or contaminated water or effluent, must not be allowed to dry out unattended, and should be treated immediately, either dried or wet-stabilization packed and kept cool.

The extent and character of the cleaning operations will depend on the nature of the materials and the resources available. Where there are large numbers of

paper-based materials involved, or there is risk of damage, mud or other debris should be left as is, until drying is completed. Washing must not be attempted on opened books, or any fragile, mould-damaged, water-sensitive, or friable material. Many materials should be neither rinsed nor washed; it is best to seek expert advice.

No attempt should be made at this point to rinse, wash or otherwise clean smoke and soot residues.

Proper precautions must be taken when handling mouldy materials or those damaged by sewage *(see 3.4.8a and 6.4.9)*.

7.2.5 Pack damaged materials

Damaged collections and records should be removed and packed according to the nature and location of the upcoming treatment. The order of packing and removal should be organized according to the urgency of treatment. Priority materials should be dealt with first.

Materials that will be treated onsite, or nearby offsite, may require minimal packing prior to their relocation. Others will need to be packed for transport to external facilities for freezing, drying, etc. Other materials may be packed for treatment nearby in a mobile facility. Some materials need to be wet-stabilization packed to prevent further damage and facilitate their recovery and rehabilitation.

7.2.6 Transport materials to external facilities for treatment

Packed materials will need to be moved to the loading area, stored on pallets and loaded onto vans or trucks for transport to external facilities for freezing, drying, etc. Pallets, pallet movers and forklifts should be used to move boxes and crates wherever possible. The stacking of cartons more than three high should be avoided, as they may collapse. Wetted or wet partially-filled cardboard boxes will be particularly fragile.

If the loading dock is inaccessible, alternate routes and arrangements will need to be made. Crates and boxes must be moved and stacked carefully. Water-filled containers holding damaged materials, such as films, must be transported with minimal disturbance. To avoid congestion and maximize efficiency, personnel should be assigned to coordinate the safe and systematic stacking and loading of all materials.

Prior arrangements should have been made regarding the responsibility for unloading packed collections and records on arrival at the external treatment facility.

If unloading is your responsibility, sufficient staff must accompany the material.

Materials that are being freeze-stabilized will need to be transported again after freezing, once decisions on further treatment are confirmed, i.e., air-drying, vacuum freeze-drying, etc.

The progress of treatment of the collections undertaken at external facilities must be monitored to ensure its safety and effectiveness, and to ensure that any contractual specifications are being met. Treatment conditions and results should be fully documented. Expectations of the results of various mass drying treatments must be realistic, based on appropriate research (see 6.5.6d).

7.2.7 Move and treat materials onsite or nearby offsite

Packed materials may need to be moved to various treatment sites, either in the building or nearby. In some cases, mobile facilities from external companies will be used. Materials may be treated onsite where freezers are accessible and functional. Nearby external work sites may have been set up to dry wetted or damp materials, or as a triage location for soaked materials. Handcarts, booktrucks, pallet movers, etc. should be used as necessary for onsite relocation.

7.2.8 Receive treated materials

Treated materials may be returned from external treatment facilities over a period of time during the course of recovery and into rehabilitation. Other materials may have been dried onsite or nearby. Some freeze-stabilized materials may be kept frozen indefinitely and released as resources become available for their treatment.

This return of materials should be scheduled and organized to allow for their safe and efficient handling. Staff, equipment and appropriate secure work and storage spaces must be available. Documentation should be ongoing (see 8.2.2).

Once dried materials are returned, strategies for their rehabilitation will need to be developed and implemented (see Chapter 8).

7.3 General Disaster Recovery Guidelines

The disaster recovery effort may involve large numbers of damaged materials and large numbers of personnel. Activities to recover collections will be proceeding at the same time as work is proceeding to deal with damage to the facilities, systems and other contents. These activities, such as handling and packing, must be carefully coordinated and managed, and should be guided by appropriate knowledge, experience and training.

The following guidelines cover a range of recovery operations (based in part on Waters 1993, 6-13).

7.3.1 Operations and Work Practice Guidelines

· Safety of the people involved in the recovery operation is paramount. Protective equipment and clothing must be made available and used whenever necessary. Established safety procedures must be followed and assignments rotated.

· Morale and well-being of the workforce are critical. Needed information should be communicated in a timely manner and milestones should be celebrated. Routines for rest breaks, refreshments, etc. must be maintained.

· Required instruction and training of staff and other workers must be completed before any work commences.

· Consider media- or format-specific team instruction and training for collections care and handling, packing, cleaning, etc.

· Continued security of staff and other workers, the collections and records and the site must be ensured.

· All communications should continue to be issued from the command centre.

· Adequate documentation of collections packing and relocation must be ensured.

· Damaged materials sorted for discard or replacement should not be thrown out until documentation is complete and the insurance company has been consulted. If wet, however, they should be removed from the building.

· Generally, rehabilitation of collections and records should not be undertaken onsite concurrent with recovery. It may hinder the overall recovery process and if done incorrectly will add to the costs and difficulty of later treatment.

· All work areas should be kept as clean and neat as possible, and all debris, especially wetted or wet debris, must be disposed of immediately.

· Supervision and quality-control checks should be ongoing. Sloppy, careless work that hinders or endangers other workers and the recovery process should not be permitted.

· Work should proceed according to assigned priorities and tasks. Problems should be quickly resolved as per established authority and procedures.

7.3.2 Treatment Priority Guidelines

· Seek expert advice for the type of materials involved in the disaster.

· The general rule of thumb is that the wettest materials should be treated first, followed by the partially wetted, and then the damp. Removing wet materials will help to reduce the relative humidity in the affected areas; however, the situation and the needs of specific materials or collections may dictate that materials other than the wettest are removed first.

· The treatment of wet paper-based materials should take precedence over that of wet films and magnetic tapes, except where the film or tape has been contaminated by mud, sewage, sea water, etc.

· Wet coated paper must not be allowed to dry out. In most cases, the only chance of successfully recovering a large quantity of wet books and documents printed on coated stock is to freeze-stabilize or vacuum freeze-dry them immediately. The time between removal and freezing is critical, as soaked coated paper can stick together permanently within six to eight hours. Wet-stabilization packing may be necessary. Fortunately, coated paper in bound volumes is difficult to wet; often only the edges of these books will be affected. "There is only a 50% success rate in drying clay or coated paper, no matter what drying method is used" (Munters Corp., Moisture Control Services Division and MBK Consulting 1996, Section II).

· Wet photographic materials and magnetic tapes must not be allowed to dry out, or they will stick permanently to themselves or their housings, as will any debris that is present. Some photographic materials cannot withstand any immersion.

· As noted in section 7.1, water-soluble media, dyes, etc. and leather, parchment and vellum pose their own sets of problems and need to be treated with particular care.

· Materials with active mould should be swiftly isolated from other materials. Environmental control efforts must be intensified.

· The relative humidity (RH) and temperature of the site and all drying areas should be monitored on an ongoing basis. These RH readings, though, are not a measure of the actual moisture content of the collection materials. The normal water content of paper is 5-7% by weight. Materials that feel only slightly damp, may in fact, contain 10-30% water. Moisture meters may be used on books or layered paper-based materials, but the meter's probe must be inserted extremely carefully so as not to cause damage.

7.3.3 Care and Handling Guidelines

· Successful recovery of materials depends, in large part, on the extent and nature of their handling throughout the recovery process.

· Extreme care must be taken in the handling of all materials. Wet material is usually heavy, very fragile and will damage easily. Fire-damaged material will be very brittle and will crumble easily.

· Be aware of specialized handling needs, such as avoiding shocks with phonographic records.

· Special health precautions must be taken with mouldy or sewage-covered materials.

· Be alert to materials with water-soluble media, friable media, and those with fragile or damaged surfaces or components.

· Be alert to boxes and drawers of mixed materials, where some media are stable and others not.

· Wetted books, documents, etc. will be further damaged as water wicks into the paper. Materials should be removed from standing water as quickly as possible.

· Clear the floor first, then go to the top shelves, moving in order from left to right on each shelf. Keep materials in shelf order and avoid handling that may damage identification labels and markings.

· Wet materials should never be left piled or stacked on one other, as excessive water weight will cause irreparable damage.

· Items on the floor should be removed in the condition in which they were found, by human chain, cart or conveyor belt starting from the nearest accessible point to a nearby "dry" area for packing.

· No attempt should be made to write directly on wet material. Do not use staples, paper clips, adhesives or pressure-sensitive tapes.

· Do not use coloured paper, card stock, etc. of any sort for packing, transport or drying.

· Heavy and/or oversize materials will need to be handled by teams of two or more people.

7.3.4 Sorting Guidelines

· Sort items according to upcoming treatment and urgency of treatment based on recovery priorities and available resources and other applicable situation-specific factors.

· Handle all collections and records with care to avoid causing further damage (see 7.3.3).

· Some situations will allow for extensive sorting. Others will not, and decisions will need to be made on the best approach for the majority of materials.

- Proper sorting of materials can reduce recovery and post-recovery costs significantly. Training and supervision of the sorting teams are important factors.

The following sorting categories are suggested:

- Items of high intrinsic value and all fragile or water-sensitive rare or special collection material should be identified. Immediate examination by an experienced conservator is preferable
- Items requiring no treatment
- Items requiring new labelling or housing only
- Mouldy items requiring immediate isolation
- Items to be wet-stabilized and sent for external mass drying/recovery treatment (i.e., microforms, motion picture film, computer media, coated paper)
- Items to be freeze-stabilized (i.e., books, paper documents, some photographic materials)
- Items that can be air dried in-house (i.e., books, single sheet materials, photographic materials, microforms, computer media)
- Items to be sent directly for external mass drying treatment (i.e., books, paper documents)
- Items to be considered for discard (with or without replacement)

7.3.5 Packing Guidelines

- Handle all collections and records with care to avoid causing further damage *(see also 7.3.3)*.
- Careful packing of materials can reduce recovery and post-recovery costs significantly. Training and supervision of the packing teams are important factors.
- The selection of packing containers should have been considered at the planning stage. Where possible, it is best to use the containers suited to the upcoming drying treatment. For freezing and vacuum freeze-drying, one cubic foot dairy-type milk crates are preferred for large quantities of paper-based materials: they aid in freezing and sublimation, and their uniform size and strength makes them easy to handle and stack. Milk crates are traditionally made from high density polyethylene and have good low temperature impact strength. Other plastics may lose impact strength at lower temperatures. Collapsible plastic crates may be useful where storage space is a problem *(see Appendix 3.4 Sources of Supplies and Equipment: Emergency Recovery Supplies)*.

Corrugated cardboard boxes are acceptable for drying where sublimation does not occur. They are less expensive than plastic, easy to obtain and store (unassembled). The use of unperforated cardboard boxes can be problematic as they can insulate materials against freezing, inhibit the efficiency and rate of drying, and may fall apart after being filled with wet material. Wax-coated or waterproof boxes should not be used, as they will impede the drying process. Neither should grocery boxes, as they may have food residues or harbour pests. Overall, it is preferable to minimize the type and size of containers, and not mix sizes on pallets. It is best to use pallets of uniform size.

Note: Soaked and swollen contents may not fit well in new boxes of the same size as the originals, and documentation problems may result.

- Wet boxes should generally not be used. The contents should be repacked in new containers, and any information on the damaged storage box should be transferred to the new container. Wet boxes can be frozen as is if strong enough. This is a time-saver, although after treatment the boxes will need to be replaced.
- The professional literature does not agree on what should be used to separate books and other materials during packing prior to freezing or drying. Some sources suggest that no separator sheets are necessary. The Canadian Conservation Institute suggests wax or freezer paper. The National Library of Canada recommends blank newsprint as it doesn't block penetration of mass drying processes. A compromise would be to use wax or freezer paper, if materials are only being frozen only. If mass chamber drying will later be done, separate materials with blank newsprint. Double-sided silicone release paper can be used for some applications, but it is expensive and not suitable for all applications, as are spunbonded polyester fabrics.
- Wet coated paper materials should not be allowed to dry out before freeze-stabilization or drying. They should be wet-stabilized on an interim basis by being kept wet and cool. If they are subsequently going to be thawed and air-dried, the packing boxes can be lined with plastic bags – this approach has a low success rate. If they are subsequently going to be vacuum freeze- or vacuum thermal-dried, it is best to exterior bag the container in which they are packed. The bag must be removed prior to the drying, otherwise the materials will be prevented from drying. Clean, damp sponges can be included in the bag to help the materials from drying out.
- Wet films and tapes should not be allowed to dry out before recovery treatment can be undertaken.

They should be wet-stabilized by being kept wet and cool prior to in-house treatment or while in transit to an external recovery service. Some sources recommend that materials be immersed in clean water in plastic pails. Others recommend packing in plastic bags with clean, damp sponges. Containers of a manageable size (with handles and lids) should be used, and each should contain materials of only one format.

- As each range of shelves or cabinets is emptied, the boxes or containers should be coded and recorded according to the documentation plan (see 6.6.2f and 6.6.3e).

- Pack boxes to a maximum 3/4 full.

- Boxed materials must not be stacked directly on the floor or stacked in large piles while awaiting removal, as this will lead to mechanical damage and reduce air flow around each item. Pallets should be used, and the number/orientation of containers or boxes per pallet should be carefully planned (see Atwood 1999).

- Containers should be consistently identified with information, such as the name of the organization, the box/pail number, the number of items, the original location of the contents and the type of materials or collection name, call number range, etc. Information should be clearly written with a permanent water-proof marker on the end of the boxes, so it is visible when the boxes are stacked. Milk crates, with their perforated sides, are less easy to directly label – spunbonded polyester olefin tags (durable and unaffected by water) attached with nylon ties could be used.

7.3.6 Cleaning Guidelines

- Undertake media- or format-specific team instruction and training as required.

- Rinsing and washing should only be carried out if time, resources and facilities permit. The circumstances and the nature of the materials will determine whether immediate cleaning is necessary, feasible or appropriate.

- Cleaning book and paper materials is generally best left until the materials have been dried.

- Rinsing or washing other wet materials, such as magnetic tapes and some photographic materials, must be done prior to their being dried (whether dried directly or freeze-stabilized first).

- All rinsing and washing must be carried out by carefully supervised, competent personnel and only on materials that will not be further damaged by such treatment. Clean water only should be used, no detergents or bleaches – special treatments may be required for some materials, such as

tapes wetted by sea water. This process is obviously wet and messy and ideally should be carried out in a suitable area with good drainage. An experienced conservator must be consulted as to which materials can or cannot be treated.

- Cleaning of mould-, soot- and smoke-covered materials would not generally be an immediate priority during the recovery process. The recovery of wet materials would take precedence. These materials should be cleaned once they are dry.

7.3.7 Air-Drying Guidelines

A number of drying options for collections and records were described in Chapter 6 (6.5.6d). The following guidelines only cover air-drying activities which would be carried out in-house. Except for dehumidification-drying undertaken in situ, all other mass drying would be carried out by service providers at external facilities.

- Undertake media- or format-specific team instruction and training as required.

- Air-drying is most often used for smaller numbers of damp or wetted collection materials, but can be used for wet items in a triage situation.

- Air-drying of coated paper or linen plans has limited success (see also 7.3.2).

- The air-drying area should be: dedicated to drying alone, clean and secure, readily accessible, well appointed (large tables, good lighting, etc.) and available for the timeframe needed.

- Keep the temperature of the area under 21°C (70°F) – preferably 18°C (65°F).

- Keep the relative humidity of the area at less than 65% – 55% is good, 45% – 50% is better. Use dehumidifiers as necessary.

- Keep air circulating with fans, blowers or open windows to promote evaporation and discourage pockets of moist air, where mould can develop. Fans and blowers should be placed in strategic locations and set on low to medium speed with no heat. Ensure that the fans do not cause damage, i.e. blowing books over.

- Work tables should be sturdy and able to bear the weight of wet collections. The table surfaces should be covered with clean, blank newsprint. Additional coverings will be needed for the drying of some collection materials, i.e., blotters, polyethylene, padding, etc.

- Provide required treatment supplies such as blotters, polyester sheets, book supports, elasticized bandages, lint-free cloths, etc.

- Provide the required general supplies such as garbage cans, sponges, etc.

· Maintain safe work procedures and environment.

· Handle all collections and records with care to avoid causing further damage *(see 7.3.3)*.

· Dispose of all debris promptly, and wet or wetted debris immediately.

· Monitor the drying process carefully. Keep continual watch for signs of mould.

· Document progress and conditions of air-drying effort. Continue process of documentation for collections relocation.

7.4 Disaster Recovery Guidelines by Material

Collections and record series may be quite homogeneous or may contain a wide variety of formats and component materials, both natural and synthetic. The collections may be historic, contemporary or a combination of the two. Some are retained for their informational value, and others for their intrinsic value. These factors, as well as the severity and nature of the damage and cost parameters, will have guided the decisions already made for the recovery strategy – that is, which materials are going to be recovered, which need to be treated first and by what method(s) *(see also 6.5.4 and 6.5.5)*.

The following guidelines focus on recovery from water damage and are organized by material and further divided by activity. Treatment summaries are provided for each material to expand on the general information on treatment options previously discussed (see *6.5.6*). The activities cover preparation for drying by various methods including care and handling, cleaning, packing and removal. Guidelines for air-drying are provided. The discussion on the mass chamber drying processes that rely on specialized chambers or equipment is limited to preparatory requirements and some commentary on material-specific applications.

The treatment summary for each material type is based on the work and input of Walsh (1988, 1997). The sections on the recovery of paper-based materials rely on the work of many, including Waters (1993) and Kahn (1994b). The section on recovery of photographs relies heavily on the work of Hendriks 1991, Hendriks, Thurgood, Iraci, Lesser and Hill 1991 and Hess Norris (1996). The sections on the recovery of computer media rely heavily on that of Van Bogart (1996a,b) and Kahn (1994a, 1998). As well, specific acknowledgements are made within the chapter.

7.4.1 Books, Periodicals and Pamphlets

Books, periodicals and pamphlets are materials common to many collections. More current collections of periodicals will contain both bound volumes and single issues, almost exclusively printed on coated paper which requires prompt attention if wetted. Collections dating from the mid 19th century to recent times will include books, periodicals and pamphlets printed on acidic, embrittled paper – these fragile materials will need to be handled with particular care. Special collections will likely contain books printed on handmade paper, as well as fine bindings that will require expert attention.

Knowledge and experience of the recovery of water-damaged paper-based materials has advanced rapidly over the past several decades. A number of options are now available for drying large numbers of bound materials *(see 6.5.6d)*.

Treatment Summary: Books, Periodicals and Pamphlets

· Books, periodicals and pamphlets with stable media should be freeze-stabilized or dried within 48 hours. Drying options include air-drying (smaller numbers of books), freezer-drying, dehumidification-drying (damp or slightly wetted items), vacuum freeze-drying or vacuum thermal-drying. Vacuum drying (ambient temperature) could be attempted (uncoated paper and stable media only). See exceptions below.

· Books, periodicals and pamphlets with coated paper should be immediately freeze-stabilized or dried. If this is not possible, wet-stabilize as an interim measure. Vacuum freeze-drying is preferred over air-drying. Vacuum drying (ambient temperature) and vacuum thermal-drying are not recommended.

· Books, periodicals and pamphlets with water-soluble inks should be immediately freeze-stabilized or dried. Preferred drying options include air-drying and vacuum freeze-drying.

· Books with leather bindings should be immediately air-dried. Freeze-stabilization is best where there are large numbers of volumes, followed by thawing and air-drying. Vacuum freeze-drying could be attempted. Other drying methods are not recommended.

· Some books, periodicals and pamphlets (stable media, not severely damaged, etc.) may be rinsed prior to freeze-stabilization or drying. Seek expert advice.

· For parchment and vellum see 7.4.2.

Special Considerations

· Be alert to books with coated plates and non-coated text in the same volume. Treat as for books on coated paper.

· Be alert to books with hand-written notations and hand-coloured plates.

· Wet leather is often not recoverable.

· Plastic jackets can retard drying, and are best removed.

· Plastic-laminated covers and plastic-coated binders should be pricked before vacuum freeze-drying otherwise the plastic will inflate.

· Plastic-coated binders delay the drying of the contents. Prop open covers prior to vacuum freeze-drying using small blocks of ethafoam/styrofoam if practical. (Stewart and Tremain 1994, 88).

a) Care and Handling

· Minimize handling of books.

· Maintain original shelf order of books.

· Sponge water from shelving as work proceeds.

· Wet and/or fire-damaged books require careful handling. They may be very fragile and/or brittle.

· Rare materials and fine bindings require special consideration and should be kept separate from the rest of the materials being treated.

· Handling may be complicated by the presence of water-soluble or friable media.

· Wet books should not be opened. If already swollen open they should left as is.

· Distorted closed books, other than those with coated paper, may be gently, manually shaped (where possible) prior to freezing or drying.

· Heavy and/or large format items are best handled by a team of two.

· Do not remove covers from books, as they will provide support for the textblock during drying.

b) Cleaning

If necessary, and time and conditions allow, dirt and mud deposits may be removed from closed books and bound periodicals. If in any doubt that this can be safely done, do not clean.

· Use a clean, rustproof container (such as a plastic garbage can) with a securely-fastened hose to provide a low-pressure, slow, continuous water flow.

· Hold the wet book firmly shut and dip under clean, cold, running water.

· Remove the dirt, mud or sludge with a sponge, using a gentle, dabbing motion. Do not rub, scrub or brush.

· Leave stains or stubborn deposits for later treatment.

· Rinse the books with a gentle stream of water.

· Remove excess water from the book by squeezing gently with hands only, or pat lightly with a clean sponge, terry towelling, etc. No mechanical pressing should be done.

A more thorough process can be undertaken with a series of washing containers.

c) Packing

The method of packing will be determined by the type of drying treatment to follow. Special packing is necessary for extremely damaged, fragile, large or odd-shaped materials. These items should be supported on a sheet of sturdy cardboard, masonite, plywood or bakers trays covered in polyethylene. Books should be removed from shelves and packed in shelf order wherever possible. Adequate support for taller books in mixed-size boxes should be provided – scrunched-up, blank newsprint can be used for this purpose.

Coated paper must not be allowed to dry out. Newer, coated-paper materials will likely demonstrate more fusion/blocking problems than older materials. The best approach is to freeze materials rapidly. If it is necessary to wet pack large numbers of items, a bag around the outside of the box with a damp sponge inside is a practical approach. The materials should be kept cool and transported quickly. If materials are going for mass chamber drying after freezing, and the materials are placed in a bag lining the box or each item is bagged individually, you will have to repack them (and discard the bag) after freezing and before mass chamber drying.

For books that will be freeze-stabilized and later vacuum freeze- or vacuum thermal-dried:

· Excess water may be removed from books by draining and then lightly patting them with a clean sponge, terry towelling, blotting or paper towelling.

· Gently shape distorted books where possible.

· Separate books with blank newsprint to prevent them from sticking to one another. It is not necessary to fully wrap the books.

· Pack books spine down, in a single layer wherever possible, in plastic milk crates or strong, dry cardboard boxes. Spine-down placement will avoid distortion and separation of the textblock from the binding. It is best to pack to allow for some expansion but not a lot of movement, and materials must not be forced to fit in the crate or box. Fischer (1996, 66) recommends 'fist' spacing, where a fist can still be inserted between the books (or filed documents) at one point. Hutson (1996) recommends 'flat hand' spacing. On the other hand, Parker (1989, 4) says that "packing them [books] tightly can help to reduce distortion".

· Books may also be packed flat. Larger books should not be placed on top of smaller books.

· Mark the containers clearly with their content, original location and destination. Record information on inventory sheets. Tape cardboard boxes shut using freezer tape – other tapes may come off during treatment.

· Keep packed materials cool and transport rapidly.

Note: Packing for direct vacuum freeze-drying or vacuum thermal-drying (no freeze-stabilization) is the same as above. However, wet coated papers which must be kept wet cannot be vacuum treated in plastic bags. Any bags, if used, will have to be removed.

For books that will be freeze-stabilized and later air-dried:

· Excess water may be removed by draining and then lightly patting them with a clean sponge, terry towelling, blotting or paper towelling.

· Gently shape distorted books where possible.

· If books are few in number, put each in a plastic bag, withdraw the air and seal. Use resealable bags or seal bags with tape, and label. Otherwise wrap them fully with freezer or wax paper and seal. If the materials are likely to be frozen for a long time, special care should be taken with their packing.

· Alternatively, separate books with freezer paper and put multiple books in one bag (up to about 7.5 cm or 3 in. thick), withdraw air, seal and label.

· Pack bagged books spine down in boxes, as described above, for transport, or if being frozen onsite transport them spine down on book trucks. Mark the containers clearly with their content, original location and destination, and record this information on inventory sheets. Tape cardboard boxes shut.

· Strap books with leather, parchment or vellum bindings across the boards from spine to fore edge using elasticized bandages, cloth wrapping, etc. to minimize distortion.

· Keep packed materials cool and transport rapidly.

For books that will be air-dried:

· Drain and pack books spine down in boxes, as described above, for transport, or if being dried onsite, transport spine down on book trucks. Mark

the boxes clearly with their contents, original location and destination, and record this information on inventory sheets.

· Strap books with leather, parchment or vellum bindings across the boards from spine to fore edge using elasticized bandages, cloth wrapping, etc. to minimize distortion. These books may also be dried if not too wet, under weights with good air circulation.

For books that will be freezer-dried onsite:

· Insert spunbonded polyester fabric sheets between the book boards and flyleaves and periodically throughout the textblock. These sheets act as wicks, drawing water out by capillary action to accelerate drying. The sheets should stick out of the books about 2.5 cm (one inch) on all open sides.

· Gently straighten out books where possible.

· Place books between plastic boards, about 10 books between each, spine to fore edge. Use spunbonded polyester fabric sheets between the outside book covers and the plastic boards, and secure with rubber bands.

· Record bibliographic information on inventory sheets.

· Thermocouples are then usually placed inside some of the books.

See Smith (1984) for a description of the process.

For books that will be dehumidification-dried *in situ*:

This is best used for books that are damp or have slight edge wetting only:

· Remove as much standing water from floors as possible.

· Allow as much air circulation as possible, i.e., position mobile shelving so there are aisles between all the shelving units.

· Expose collection materials by opening boxes and drawers.

· Remove rare collections, coated paper or other materials that are to be dried by other means.

d) Freeze-Stabilization

As outlined in Chapter 6, freezing is one of the best ways to stabilize and prevent further damage to water-damaged books and other paper-based materials.

Rapid transportation to the freezer or freezing facility is essential. If the books are being frozen or freezer-dried onsite, transport should relatively straightforward. Once at the freezer facility, the crates, boxes, drawers etc. should be carefully stacked. Containers without perforated sides should be separated from one another with wood slats to prevent crushing and to promote air circulation. Although treatment is the responsibility of the external service provider, it is best to confirm that established conditions or arrangements are being met.

e) Drying

Drying options to consider for books, periodicals and pamphlets include air-drying, dehumidification-drying, freezer-drying, vacuum drying (ambient temperature) vacuum freeze- and vacuum thermal-drying *(see 6.5.6d)*. As outlined, each has its pros and cons.

It is likely that a combination of air-drying and mass chamber drying methods will be used for bound materials, depending on their nature and number as well as their condition, i.e., wet, wetted or damp. Materials, packed as described above, will be transported to freezer facilities and/or drying facilities for treatment.

• Air-Drying

Air-drying is generally used for smaller numbers of damp or wetted books, but can be used for wet books in a triage situation. Air-drying requires a controlled, well-ventilated environment *(see 7.3.7)*. The table surfaces should be covered with clean, blank newsprint.

- If drying bagged frozen books, remove the bag first, otherwise water will collect at the bottom of the bag upon thawing. Do not try to open frozen books. Only thaw what you can readily treat. Provide support and leave to thaw until the covers and outer pages start to open on their own. Various support methods can be used: book ends, acrylic stands, etc.

- Determine which books can be dried standing up throughout the entire drying process, which should be laid flat at the outset only, and which should be dried flat throughout (i.e., large or fragile books).

- Wet books will need to be drained. Stand the book on its head with the covers only slightly open and provide support where necessary. When the pages begin to dry and separate, interleave them.

- Books can be interleaved with white, blank absorbent paper sheets (thin blotters, paper towels or blank newsprint). The sheets should be cut larger than the book pages and inserted into the gutters throughout the books so that they project out from the fore edges and the top of the book when placed upright (not on the edge where the book stands). Do not try to peel apart pages that are stuck together and do not interleave too much (maximum about one third of the book's thickness), as this will damage the binding (i.e., concave spine) and will result in the book drying in a distorted shape. Separate the covers from the textblock with paper. Where the cover dyes may stain the pages, polyester sheets or aluminium foil may be used, although this will slow the drying.

Note: Blotters and paper towels are more effective at absorbing moisture than blank newsprint. But newsprint is thinner and causes less strain to bound materials.

- Stand the books upright on their driest end (head or tail) and gently fan open the pages to an angle less than 45 degrees.

- Books with plastic-laminated covers and jackets will need careful monitoring to ensure that mould does not start to form. It is best to remove the plastic jackets from the books with the paper dust covers and dry the dust covers separately. This will require careful organization to ensure that they are matched correctly with the books once dry.

- In general, air-drying of coated paper has a low success rate. The process demands special attention – for damp or wetted books, interleaving between each page, frequent fanning of the pages and careful monitoring – to ensure that the pages do not stick together. A gentle touch is necessary – printed information will easily smear. Blank newsprint or paper towels used as interleaving can stick to the coated pages. Wax or silicone release paper avoids this hazard but slows down the drying process. Wet books with coated paper are best immediately freeze-stabilized, and then sent for vacuum freeze-drying *(see 6.5.6d)*.

- Rotate books from head to tail at least every 12 hours to minimize distortion, and change the newsprint underneath as necessary.

- Change interleaving sheets as they become wet. To speed drying, vary the locations of the interleaving sheets. They may be dried and reused if not stained or cockled.

- Once books feel almost dry to the touch (back of the hand), remove all the interleaves. Gently close and manipulate the books back into shape. Books can then be laid flat with the spines extending over the edge of a table. Weight the covers until the books are fully dry to the touch.

- Keep material with active mould isolated from other materials. No attempt should be made to wipe off mould, as such treatment will only rub the spores and staining deep into the pages and covers. Dirt and mud should also be allowed to dry as is.

- If the book spine when viewed from the bottom has a concave shape, due to interleaving or to water swelling the leaves, the volume can be hung to finish drying while supported on three or more short monofilament fishing lines. Fragile books, books that are saturated with water or those weighing more than a pound should not be dried in this manner because the lines may cut through the bindings, and adhesives may migrate down between the pages.

- Books with leather bindings should, if the binding is in good shape, be bound around the cover from spine to fore edge with cloth or elasticized bandages to minimize distortion.

- Pamphlets can be dried open – pages should be gently turned often. Pamphlets can also be interleaved. Care must be taken not to interleave too much as this will cause damage.

- Monitor the drying process carefully.

- Once books are dried, sort out those requiring further treatment (i.e., flattening, repair). As necessary, relabel books that do not require further attention and move them to separate controlled storage.

7.4.2   Parchment and Vellum Material

Parchment and vellum materials would generally be found in special collections in the form of book covers, textblocks and single sheet documents, some with illumination. Expert advice should be sought.

Parchment and vellum dry more slowly than paper does. Drying is usually accompanied by dimensional changes (thickening, shrinking and cockling) and brittleness. Thus, considerable damage can occur if drying is not carried out under restraint, at a slow and controlled rate. This restraint must be occasionally released to promote safe and even drying. Composite materials may be particularly problematic.

Wet parchment and vellum swell and expand in thickness. Studies indicate that freezing can reduce this expansion, but will not return the material to its original thickness. Freezing also traps water and any distortions in place and the method of drying must be chosen carefully. Vacuum freeze-drying has been successfully undertaken on non-illuminated sheet materials (Parker 1993, 181-182).

Treatment Summary: Parchment and Vellum

- Parchment and vellum sheets should be immediately freeze-stabilized (later thawed and air-dried) or air-dried.
- Parchment- and vellum-covered books should be immediately freeze-stabilized (later thawed and air-dried) or air-dried. Alternatively, the covers can be removed and air-dried (or frozen and air-dried), and the textblock vacuum freeze-dried.
- Parchment and vellum can be vacuum freeze-dried; however, covers and textblocks will distort and gilded or illuminated pages and manuscripts will show serious loss. Single sheets with no illumination should show good results. Other drying methods are not recommended.

---

a) Care and Handling

Extreme care should be used when handling wet parchment or vellum, and handling should always be minimized.

- Parchment and vellum should be separated from the rest of the materials being treated for special consideration.
- Handling may be complicated by the presence of water-soluble or friable media and in the case of documents, by attachments such as seals.
- Illuminated single sheets or textblocks need to be handled with particular care to prevent water from flowing onto undamaged areas and to prevent offsetting of the illumination.

b) Cleaning

Cleaning should be attempted only by an experienced conservator.

c) Packing

The type of packing depends on the drying treatment and is similar to that for books (see 7.4.1c). Vellum and parchment textblocks will need to be strapped to prevent distortion, although this will be a problem for illuminated textblocks because offsetting can occur.

d) Freeze-Stabilization

Parchment and vellum can be frozen successfully, ideally at -25°C (-13°F). Freezing can reduce the expansion in thickness that occurs when parchment or vellum gets wet, but it will not return it to its original pre-wetted thickness.

e) Drying

Drying options to consider for vellum and parchment materials include air-drying and vacuum freeze-drying *(see 6.5.6d)*. As outlined, each has its pros and cons.

• **Air-Drying**

Air-drying of parchment and vellum requires considerable care, and must be done at a slow and controlled rate. Single sheets, covers and textblocks each have their own requirements. Illuminated materials need particular care. This work should be undertaken only by an experienced conservator.

· If drying frozen books, remove the bag first otherwise water will collect at the bottom of the bag upon thawing. Only thaw what you can readily treat. Do not try to open frozen books. Thaw flat with blotters placed on the outside and dry under weights – this prevents the binding from drying out while the textblock thaws (Hutson 1996).

· Separate the covers from the textblock with blotters. Interleave the book and lay flat. Place blotters top and bottom, and carefully place board and weights on top. Change the interleaving sheets as they become wet.

· Manuscripts are dried using blotters with weights or weights around the edges.

• **Vacuum Freeze-Drying**

A French study on freezing and vacuum freeze-drying under laboratory conditions indicated that leather can be vacuum freeze-dried with minimal risk, but that parchment poses particular problems. However, the thickening and stiffness of parchment can be reduced by subsequent relaxation and flattening under weights. (Fleider, Leclerc and Chahine 1978, 5-6)

The British Library has undertaken experimental research on the freezing and vacuum freeze-drying of parchment and vellum, among many other materials. It was concluded that parchment and vellum can be safely frozen, and that vacuum freeze-drying was partially successful. Non-illuminated sheets can be successfully vacuum freeze-dried. Problems remain with parchment and vellum covers, textblocks and illuminated manuscripts. Illuminated manuscripts show serious loss of pigments when freeze-dried and should probably be separated from other materials after freezing. Further research is planned for these materials. (Parker 1991 and 1993)

Note: Ibsen (1998) describes the treatment of leather and vellum bindings after vacuum freeze-drying.

7.4.3 Paper Documents and Manuscripts

Paper document and manuscript collections may include a wide variety of media and formats. They may be stored flat in folders in drawers, vertically or flat in folders in drawers or boxes, or rolled, etc. Documents may be printed on coated paper, some with handwritten notations. Manuscripts may include a wide variety of inks and papers. The inks may or may not be stable in water. Carbon copies, self-carbon papers, photocopies, thermofacsimiles and documents printed by other means (i.e., laser-printed) may also be found in the collections.

The contents of tightly stored boxes are likely to be damp or wetted rather than saturated, unless they have been submerged. The boxes themselves, however, may be soaked and will need replacement. Soaked contents may not fit well in new boxes of the same size as the original, and documentation problems may result. Boxes may contain a mixed variety of formats, and decisions will need to made as to whether extensive pre-treatment sorting can be done.

> **Treatment Summary: Paper Documents and Manuscripts**
>
> · Paper documents and manuscripts with stable media should be freeze-stabilized or dried within 48 hours. Drying options include air-drying (smaller numbers of items), freezer-drying, dehumidification-drying (damp or wetted items only), vacuum freeze-drying or vacuum thermal-drying. Vacuum drying (ambient temperature) could be attempted (uncoated paper and stable media only). See exceptions below.
> · Paper documents and manuscripts with coated paper should be immediately freeze-stabilized or dried. If this is not possible, wet-stabilize as an interim measure. Vacuum freeze-drying is preferred over air-drying.
> · Water-damaged paper documents and manuscripts with water-soluble media (such as inks and hand colouring) should be immediately freeze-stabilized or dried. Drying options include air-drying and vacuum freeze-drying.
> · Some documents and manuscripts (stable media, not severely damaged, etc.) may be rinsed prior to freeze-stabilization or drying. Seek expert advice.

a) Care and Handling

· Minimize handling of water-damaged documents and manuscripts.

· Separate out special collections and rare materials for special consideration.

· Maintain the original order of the documents.

· Single sheet materials that are stuck together should not be separated.

· Do not try to straighten out crumpled or wrinkled materials.

· Water should be sponged carefully from drawers or boxes before attempting to move or lift the materials.

· Do not blot water-soluble media.

· Support materials as necessary. Materials in folders should be handled in the folders.

· Coloured file folders should be discarded and replaced with manila folders or folders made of freezer paper, if time and volume permit. Note: some filing systems are based on colour-coded file folders. All information recorded on the old folder should be transferred in pencil to the new one.

· Watch for boxes of mixed materials, some may have stable media and others not. Different treatments may be required.

b) Cleaning

A folder or pile of documents covered in mud or other debris cannot be cleaned in the same manner as books.

· If absolutely necessary, a gentle stream of water could be run over a folder of documents. This should only be attempted on non-fragile items with stable media. If in any doubt, do not clean.

· If the items are not fragile and have stable media, water washing could be undertaken in trays using appropriate supports and precautions.

· Blot materials gently, do not rub.

· In general, the removal of mud and other debris from large numbers of items should be undertaken after drying.

c) Packing

As for books, the drying treatment selected determines the method of packing. Special packing is necessary for extremely damaged, fragile, large or odd shaped materials. These items should be supported on the appropriate size sheet of sturdy cardboard, masonite, plywood or bakers trays covered in polyethylene.

As for books with coated paper, documents on coated paper must not be allowed to dry out *(see 7.3.2)*.

For documents that will be freeze-stabilized and will be later vacuum freeze-dried or vacuum thermal-dried:

· Excess water may be removed by draining and then lightly patting with a clean sponge, terry towelling, blotting paper or paper towelling. Do not drain or blot materials with water-soluble inks, etc.

· Gently shape distorted documents where safe to do so.

· Keep documents in file folders. Separate folders or piles of loose documents with freezer paper to prevent them from sticking to one another. Separate into units not exceeding roughly 7.5 cm (3 in.) in thickness wherever possible. It is not necessary to fully wrap them, but a folder of freezer paper may make handling easier. Interleaving is not necessary if the materials are going for immediate vacuum freeze-drying.

· Pack folders spine down in the box or crate. Placing the container on its side will facilitate loading, as the materials will sit flat and will not slide or collapse. The materials should be packed snugly but not forced to fit tightly in the containers.

· Materials may also be packed flat in containers. Larger items should be placed flat, not on top of smaller items.

· Mark the boxes clearly as to their content, original location and destination.

· Keep packed materials cool and transport rapidly.

Note: Packing for direct vacuum freeze-drying or vacuum thermal-drying (no freeze-stabilization) is the same as above. However, wet coated papers which must be kept wet cannot be vacuum treated in plastic bags. Any bags, if used, will have to be removed.

For documents that will be freeze-stabilized and will be later air-dried:

· Excess water may be removed by draining and then lightly patting with a clean sponge, terry towelling, blotting or paper towelling. Do not blot materials with water-soluble inks, etc.

· Gently shape distorted documents where possible.

· Separate folders or piles of documents with freezer paper, put a stack maximum about 7.5 cm (3 in.) thick in a plastic bag, expel air and seal. Use resealable bag or seal bag with tape and label.

· Pack in boxes or crates as above and label as necessary.

· Keep packed materials cool and transport rapidly.

For documents that will be air-dried:

- Drain and pack documents with folder spine down in boxes as described above for transport, or if being dried nearby onsite, transport flat on carts. Do not pile high.

For documents that will be freezer-dried onsite:

There is no reported experience on the freezer-drying of documents, but the following could be attempted:

- Insert spunbonded polyester fabric sheets periodically throughout groups of documents to act as wicks to remove water by capillary action and accelerate drying. The sheets should stick out of the documents about 2.5 cm (one inch) on all open sides.
- Straighten out documents where possible.
- Place documents between plastic boards and secure with rubber bands.
- Thermocouples are then placed between some of the documents.

For documents that will be dehumidification-dried in situ:

Refer to packing as outlined for books, periodicals and pamphlets *(see 7.4.1c)*.

d) Freeze-Stabilization

Refer to packing and freeze-stabilization as outlined for books, periodicals and pamphlets *(see 7.4.1c and 7.4.1d)*.

e) Drying

Drying options to consider for paper-based documents and manuscripts include air-drying, dehumidification-drying, freezer-drying, vacuum drying (ambient temperature) vacuum freeze- and vacuum thermal-drying *(see 6.5.6d)*. As outlined, each has its pros and cons.

- **Air-drying**

The facility arrangements and set-up necessary for documents is the same as that for books *(see 7.3.7)*.

- Remove folders and packages from boxes one at a time, and keep in order.
- If drying bagged, frozen documents, remove the bag first otherwise water will collect at the bottom of the bag upon thawing. Only thaw what you can readily treat.
- If items are polyester-encapsulated, carefully open the encapsulation by cutting along the welded seams or taped edges. Double-sided tape seams sometimes separate readily when wet.

- Use polyester if necessary to separate wet documents. Place a sheet of polyester on top of the upper item and lift up carefully. Lay the item flat (polyester on top) on top of blotters preferably covered with spunbonded polyester fabric sheeting. Carefully remove the polyester in a rolling motion.
- Carefully blot excess water on documents with stable media.
- Materials with unstable media should not be blotted. If necessary, blot through spunbonded polyester fabric.
- Give rapid and special attention to coated paper. Materials will need to be separated or interleaved with spunbonded polyester fabric to ensure that sheets do not stick together. Unless there are few items, it is best to immediately freeze-stabilize and then vacuum freeze-dry these materials.
- Sort out thermofacsimile and self-carbon paper, as adjacent sheets will stick to one another.
- Dry materials flat face-up wherever possible. If materials cannot be laid out individually, lay the pile flat, and remove the top items as they dry. Alternatively interleave stacks of damp or wetted papers and turn frequently.
- Change interleaving sheets frequently. They may be dried and reused if not stained or cockled.
- Mouldy materials should be isolated from other materials. No attempt should be made to wipe off mould, as such treatment will only rub the spores and staining deep into the paper. Dirt and mud should be removed after drying.
- Monitor the drying process carefully.
- Once documents feel dry to the touch (back of the hand), remove all the interleaves and leave to further air-dry for several days if possible. Further flattening may be required. Then replace materials in new folders and relabel in pencil. Rebox and relabel as necessary.

7.4.4 Plans and Maps

Plans and maps come in a variety of media – printed, hand-drawn and -coloured, reproductive processes such as blueprints on various supports, etc. They are also produced on different support materials – paper, drafting linen and various plastics such as polyester.

Plans and maps are often large format or oversized. They are stored in a variety of ways, i.e., flat or folded in drawers (some may be polyester-encapsulated), rolled on tubes or poles and then placed on end or hung horizontally.

> ### Treatment Summary: Plans and Maps
>
> · Plans and maps with stable media should be freeze-stabilized or dried within 48 hours. Drying options include air-drying (smaller numbers of items), freezer-drying, dehumidification-drying (damp or wetted items only), vacuum freeze-drying or vacuum thermal-drying. Vacuum drying (ambient temperature) could be attempted (uncoated paper and stable media only). Air-drying or vacuum freeze-drying are preferred. See exceptions below.
> · Plans and maps with coated paper should be immediately freeze-stabilized or dried. If this is not possible, wet-stabilize as an interim measure. Preferred drying options are vacuum freeze-drying and then air-drying.
> · Plans and maps on drafting linen (starch coated cloth) should be immediately freeze-stabilized or dried. If this is not possible, wet-stabilize as an interim measure. Preferred drying options are air-drying and vacuum freeze-drying.
> · Plans and maps with water-soluble media (such as inks, hand colouring and photoreproductive processes particularly blueprints and diazos) should be immediately freeze-stabilized or dried. Preferred dry options are air-drying and vacuum freeze-drying.
> · Plans and maps on polyester should be immediately air-dried. Beware of water-soluble inks.
> · Some plans and maps (stable media, not severely damaged, etc.) may be rinsed prior to freeze-stabilization or drying. Seek expert advice.

a) Care and Handling

· Wet, large format and oversized materials are difficult to handle. Minimize handling.
· Maintain original order of the plans and maps.
· Large-format and oversized materials are best handled by a team of two.
· Water should be sponged carefully from drawers or boxes before the materials are moved or lifted.
· Rolled materials are best unrolled and dried flat.
· Maps and plans with water-soluble media, such as hand-colouring and the photoreproductive processes (blueprints and diazos), should not be blotted. Any pressure should be avoided.
· Drafting linens may stick together and should not be blotted. No pressure should be applied.
· Watch for drawers of mixed materials where some items have stable media, and some do not. Different handling and treatments will be required.

b) Cleaning

Cleaning of plans and maps is best done after the material has been dried.

c) Packing

As for books and documents , the drying treatment selected determines the method of packing. Special packing is necessary for extremely damaged, fragile, large or odd shaped materials. These items should be moved on the appropriate size support.

As for books and documents with coated paper, maps and plans on coated paper and drafting linen must not be allowed to dry out *(see 7.4.1c)*.

For plans and maps that will be freeze-stabilized and will be later vacuum freeze- or vacuum thermal-dried:

· Smaller items in folders can be handled in the same way as paper-based documents and manuscripts.
· Special packing is necessary for large and odd-shaped materials. Drawers, once removed from cabinets, can be stacked and shipped as is with wood slats inserted between each drawer. Pack loose, flat items on the appropriate size sheet of sturdy cardboard, masonite, plywood or bakers trays covered in polyethylene. Remove items in their folders from drawers. Use a sheet of polyester as support where necessary.
· If necessary, rolled plans and maps can be frozen rolled. Pack in adequate sized boxes to avoid crushing.
· Do not try to separate wet layered materials within folders.
· Keep plans and maps on coated paper and drafting linen wet by packing in map drawers, bread trays, flat boxes or placed on sturdy cardboard or plywood covered in polyethylene and then bag in polyethylene.
· Keep packed materials cool and transport rapidly.

Note: Packing for direct vacuum freeze-drying or vacuum thermal-drying (no freeze-stabilization) is the same as above. However, wet coated papers which must be kept wet cannot be vacuum treated in plastic bags. Any bags, if used, will have to be removed.

For plans and maps that will be freeze-stabilized and will be later air-dried:

Refer to packing as outlined for paper documents and manuscripts *(7.4.3c)*.

For plans and maps that will be air-dried:

· Pack maps and plans on the appropriate size sheet of sturdy cardboard, masonite, plywood or bakers' trays covered in polyethylene for transport to the drying site.

d) Freeze-Stabilization

Refer to freeze-stabilization for books, periodicals and pamphlets *(see 7.4.1d)*.

e) Drying

Refer to drying as outlined for paper documents and manuscripts, and that for works of art on paper *(see 7.4.3e and 7.4.5e)*.

7.4.5 Works of Art on Paper

Collections containing works of art can include a wide variety of media (prints, drawings, watercolours, various reproductive processes, multi-media, etc.) and supports (various papers and synthetic materials). Expert advice should be sought for identification as necessary.

Some works are extremely small and others can be oversized and multi-part. They may be stored flat in boxes or drawers in folders (matted or unmatted), or they may be stored in frames and hung on tracking systems or in slotted cabinets. They may also be on exhibition in display cases or frames.

Most works of art, by their nature, are considered to have high intrinsic value. These materials require particular consideration and are best air-dried.

An experienced conservator should be consulted as soon as possible to assess the extent of damage and to advise on possible conservation treatments. No attempt should be made to treat severely damaged or fragile works of art.

Treatment Summary: Works of Art on Paper

· Prints and drawings with stable media should be freeze-stabilized or dried within 48 hours. Air-drying is preferred over vacuum freeze-drying. Other drying methods are not recommended.
· Works on coated paper (such as posters and printed ephemera) should be immediately freeze-stabilized or dried. If this is not possible, wet-stabilize as an interim measure. Air-drying is preferred over vacuum freeze-drying.
· Works on paper with water-soluble media (such as watercolours and hand-coloured prints) should be immediately freeze-stabilized or dried. Air-drying is preferred over vacuum freeze-drying.
· Framed works should be unframed and unmatted prior to treatment.
· Some works of art (stable media, not severely damaged, etc.) may be rinsed prior to freeze-stabilization or drying. Seek expert advice.

---

a) Care and Handling

Extreme care should be taken when handling works of art on paper whether they are matted and framed, matted only, or stored as is in folders. The same principles apply as for paper documents and manuscripts *(see 7.4.3a)*. Be alert to water-soluble and friable media, and fragile supports.

b) Cleaning

Cleaning of works of art on paper should be undertaken only by an experienced conservator.

c) Packing

The same principles apply as for paper documents and manuscripts *(see 7.4.3c)*. Be alert to water-soluble and friable media, and fragile supports.

d) Freeze-Stabilization

If necessary, unframed works of art on paper can be frozen in the same way as paper-based documents and manuscripts. Framed works of art can be freeze-stabilized, if they cannot be treated within the appropriate timeframe, or if there is no other option. The wet framed item should be drained, blotted carefully and sealed in a large polyethylene bag such as a garbage bag, and frozen immediately.

e) Air-Drying

Air-drying is preferred for works of art on paper. Vacuum freeze-drying could be attempted in exceptional circumstances.

• Frame Removal Prior to Air-Drying

Extreme caution must be taken during removal of a damp or wet work of art from its frame. Additional damage may easily result where components have adhered to one another or where the method of original assembly is complex and difficult to determine. Consult a conservator if in doubt as to how to proceed, or if the work of art is particularly fragile with water-sensitive (some watercolours, inks, etc.) or friable (charcoal, pastel, etc.) media.

These guidelines are for removing works of art from their frames.

For glazing that is broken:

· If the glass is still intact, it may be held together with pressure-sensitive tape applied lightly over the breaks. The frame may then be laid face down and the work of art removed as outlined (see following guidelines for glazing that is not broken).

· If the glass is shattered and broken pieces have dropped behind the remaining glass, keep the frame vertical and using extreme care remove all loose pieces of glass. It may then be possible to safely remove the work of art from the back of the frame (see following guidelines). If the work of art has been damaged by the glass, a conservator should be consulted.

· Proceed with drying (see following guidelines).

For glazing that is not broken:

· Place the frame face down on a smooth, flat work surface covered with blotting paper or bubblepack. Cover with polyethylene as necessary.

· For wood frames, carefully remove all hanging hardware, dust seals, nails, glazier's points and brackets.

· For metal frames, carefully remove the corner hardware where necessary and hanging hardware.

· Ensure that the work of art is not adhered to frame's rabbet, liner or spacer.

· Lift the glazing, mat assembly (window mat, work of art and back mat) and backing board as a unit. Use a support if necessary.

· Place the unit face up on a smooth, flat surface.

· Ensure that the work of art is not adhered to the glazing. If adhered, place it, as is, between blotting paper under light weight and consult a conservator

before proceeding any further. If not adhered, carefully remove the glazing.

· Separate the mat assembly from the backing board, using a support where necessary, and place face up on a smooth flat surface.

· Ensure that the work of art is not attached directly either to the front or back mat. If so, place it, as is, between blotting paper under light weight and consult a conservator before proceeding further. If it is not attached, lift the window mat fully and detach the work of art from the back mat by carefully cutting the hinges. Leave the hinges attached to the work.

· Proceed to dry work of art as follows.

• Air-Drying After Frame Removal

For Prints and Other Works of Art on Paper with Stable Media (Non Water-Soluble, Non Friable)

· Support the item with a non-woven support (spunbonded polyester fabric) front and back to aid in safe handling.

· Place the item (still between the non-woven supports) on a smooth, flat surface between layers of clean, dry blotting paper.

· Place a sheet of glass or smooth board fully on top of the blotting paper. Use additional weights, placed evenly, as required.

· Change the blotters frequently, until the item is dry to the touch (back of hand).

· Change the blotters one final time and leave under light pressure for two to three days or until flat.

Note: If the item has a plate mark, use extremely light pressure so as to not press it flat.

For Prints and Other Works of Art on Paper with Unstable Media (Water-Soluble, Friable)

· Support the item from behind with a non-woven support (spunbonded polyester fabric) to aid in safe handling.

· Place the item on clean, dry blotting paper and allow it to air-dry. Do not attempt to blot the item since blotting may result in offset losses of water-soluble or loose pigments, inks, etc.

· Consult a conservator after air-drying.

7.4.6 Paintings

While not found in all libraries and archives, some organizations hold extensive collections of paintings. They may include a wide variety of media (oil, acrylic, etc.) and supports (canvas, various solid supports).

Some will be framed and glazed, some not. Storage practices may vary – they may be framed and hung on tracking systems or in slotted cabinets. If part of the organization's exhibition programme or corporate art collection, they may be on display.

The conservation of paintings is a specialized field and it is best to seek expert advice for identification and treatment.

Treatment Summary: Paintings

· Paintings should be immediately air-dried. Other drying methods are not recommended.

· Framed works should be unframed and unmatted prior to treatment.

· An extremely wet or damaged painting (with signs of softened, lifting, or flaking paint or ground layers or tears in the canvas) should be placed face up on a table and allowed to dry untouched in a controlled environment until it can be examined and treated by an experienced conservator.

The following guidelines apply to items (glazed and unglazed) in wetted or damp, but overall sound condition (based on Barton and Wellheiser 1985, 72-74; Canadian Conservation Note 10/5 (1989 and 1996); Keck 1972; Stewart and Tremain 1994, 93-96; and Weidner 1974, 28).

a) Care and Handling

All paintings should be handled with extreme care.

· Drain off water carefully by lifting the painting and tilting it to allow water to drain from one corner of the frame.

· Large items are best handled by a team.

· Carry horizontally by the frame, not the hardware.

· Work tables should be covered with felts or layered blotters and then polyethylene which can be wiped dry and clean.

· If paintings must be transported, pack face up without contact with the paint layer.

b) Cleaning

Where a painting is covered in loose dirt, it may be tempting to remove it, but it is best to consult a conservator.

c) Freeze-Stabilization

Freeze-stabilization of paintings is not recommended.

d) Air-Drying

Air-drying is preferred for paintings. The following is based on Barton and Wellheiser 1985, 72-74; Keck 1972; and Stewart and Tremain 1994, 93-96:

• **Frame Removal Prior to Air-Drying:**

· Broken glazing presents additional problems. For removal of glazing (intact or broken) (see 7.4.5e).

· Place the frame face down on a smooth, flat surface covered with clean, dry blotting paper or bubble pack where necessary.

· For wood frames, carefully remove hanging hardware, dust seal, nails, brackets and backing boards.

· For metal frames, carefully remove corner hardware where necessary, hanging hardware and backing boards.

· Ensure that the painting is not adhered to frame's rabbet, spacer, liner or glazing by gently lifting each side of the painting, one at a time, to ensure freedom of movement.

· Carefully lift the painting straight up and out of frame. Contact a frame conservator as necessary.

· Proceed to air-dry painting as outlined below.

• **Air-Drying Paintings on Canvas After Frame Removal:**

· Handle painting carefully.

· Do not remove the unframed painting from its stretcher.

· Place the painting face down on a flat, firm surface covered with layers of clean, dry, white blotting paper with Japanese tissue or blank newsprint next to the paint layer. For paintings with impasto, use sufficient layers of blotting paper to cushion the projections against possible breakage or flattening under pressure. Keep these layers absolutely flat and wrinkle-free, since creases may impress themselves into the damp paint. Check that paint or glazes do not adhere to the paper.

· Cover the back of the canvas between the stretcher bars with blotting paper. Cut the blotters to fit and do not overlap. Gently place blotters under the stretcher keys in the corners.

· Cover the entire back of the painting with a sheet of thick masonite or plywood cut to fit inside the stretcher. Cut the board smaller where necessary rather than forcing it under the stretcher keys.

· Weigh the board down evenly. Weights may also be needed at the corner joints of the stretcher to prevent warping or torquing.

· Change the blotting paper every 10 minutes or so at first, then every 30 minutes and then every hour until the blotters are dry. If the Japanese tissue or the blank newsprint next to the paint surface is damp or wet and can be removed, replace it carefully with a fresh protective layer when changing the blotters. If this layer is stuck, leave it in place for later removal by a conservator.

· Change the blotters one final time and let the painting stabilize under the weights for several days.

• **Air-Drying Paintings on Solid Supports (Cardboard, Masonite, Wood Panel, etc.) After Frame Removal:**

· Handle painting carefully.

· Place the painting face up, on several layers of clean, dry, white blotting paper or blank newsprint on a clean, flat surface.

· Cover the face of the painting with Japanese tissue or, if unavailable, use blank newsprint. Then place three or four layers of white blotting paper on top. For paintings with impasto, use sufficient layers of blotting paper to cushion the projections against possible breakage or flattening under pressure.

· Place a slightly larger sheet of masonite or glass on top of the painting.

· Weigh the board or glass down evenly.

· Change the blotting paper every 10 minutes or so at first, then every 30 minutes and then every hour or so until the blotters are dry. If the Japanese tissue or the blank newsprint next to the paint surface is damp or wet and can be removed, replace it carefully with a fresh protective layer when changing the blotters. If this layer is stuck, leave it in place for later removal by a conservator.

· Change the blotters one final time and let the painting stabilize under the weights for several days.

7.4.7   Photographic Material

Photographic materials are produced by a variety of processes and come in many formats i.e., still photographs on paper, glass plate negatives, film, etc. They are stored in many different ways, i.e., sleeves, envelopes, folders, reels, boxes, etc. either by format or as a collection, sometimes together with documents and other paper-based items.

In general, the damage that can be done to photographic materials by water depends on these factors:

· type of photograph.

· its physical condition.

· how it was processed, i.e., whether or not it was hardened.

· immersion time.

· water temperature and pH.

· contaminants in the water.

· handling during recovery.

Moor and Moor (1987, 321) note that because photographs are either alkaline or acid stabilized, the acidity or alkalinity of flood water can produce irreversible changes in colour, density, etc. and have a solubilizing effect on applied inks, emulsions, etc.

Immersion time is critical and should always be minimized. Some materials will not survive any immersion, while others may last up to four days. Therefore, the least stable materials should be treated first.

Stability and Maximum Immersion Time	Types of Photographic Materials
Will not survive immersion	Starch prints – early colour processes: Autochromes, Dufay Color, Paget, Finlay, Agfa Color
Less than 24 hours	Wet collodion glass plate negatives (including ambrotypes and tintypes) Silver gelatin glass plate negatives
Maximum of 48 hours	Color materials (contemporary) Silver gelatin prints Silver gelatin negatives Salted paper prints
3 to 4 days	Collodio-chloride prints Albumen prints

(Hendriks, Thurgood, Iraci, Lesser and Hill 1991, 424)

(Reproduced with the permission of the Minister of Public Works and Government Services, 1998 from *Fundamentals of Photograph Conservation: A Study Guide.* 1991. Copyright © 1991 Minister of Supply and Services Canada.)

Immediate air-drying after rinsing is the preferred drying method for most wet photographic materials (Eastman Kodak 1985, 87-88). If resources do not permit immediate drying, freeze-stabilization followed by thawing, rinsing and air-drying is the next preferable alternative. Hendriks and Lesser (1983) demonstrated that freezing, far from seriously damaging wet still photos, helps to retard further deterioration. In a later publication, Hendriks (1991, 19) advised that some materials cannot be frozen: materials made by the wet collodion process (wet collodion glass plate negatives, ambrotypes, tintypes) or colour lantern slides made by additive processes

(Lumière Autochrome plates, Agfacolor plates, Dufaycolor plates).

Vacuum freeze-drying should be avoided – it is the preferred treatment only for albums of documentary photographs (Hendriks 1991, 19). Vacuum freeze-drying can damage photographic materials, causing loss or changes in surface gloss, density loss and dimensional changes. Frozen photographic materials should never be thawed and vacuum-dried at temperatures above 0°C (32°F) as this can cause blocking and sticking of gelatin layers – "everything will stick permanently into a solid block!" (Hendriks et al 1991, 425 and Hendriks 1991, 19).

The results of recent experiments in Australia:

> ...suggest that significant physical alteration can occur when certain types of wet photographic materials are freeze-dried. Less damage occurs when the material is frozen and later thawed out and air-dried. This accords with the findings of Hendriks and Lesser. (Macgregor 1996, 109-110)

Macgregor also indicates that a form of freezing pre-treatment may help to reduce damage including that from ice crystal impressions on the surface and emulsion cracking. Experiments are being conducted to determine the effectiveness of rinse water additives, i.e., Polyethylene Glycol 400 or ethanol.

The treatment of black-and-white and colour microfilms and motion picture films can be undertaken in-house; however, as most organizations do not have the necessary equipment or expertise they are usually wet packed and sent to an external film-processing facility for treatment.

The conservation of photographic material is a specialized field. It is best to seek expert advice regarding identification and recovery treatment. Surfactants, cleaning agents, etc. should only be used on the advice of an experienced conservator.

Readers are referred to Hess Norris (1996) for practical observations and recommendations on the recovery of water-soaked historic and contemporary photographic materials based on hands-on recovery training workshops.

a) Black-and-White Prints

Treatment Summary: Black-and-White Prints

- Albumen prints should be freeze-stabilized (later thawed and air-dried) or air-dried within 48 hours. Air-drying (no freezing) is preferred.
- Collodion prints should be freeze-stabilized (later thawed and air-dried) or air-dried within 48 hours. Vacuum freeze-drying could be attempted.
- Silver gelatin printing out and developing out paper prints should be freeze-stabilized (later thawed and air-dried) or air-dried within 48 hours. Wet-stabilize as an interim measure. Air-drying (no freezing) is preferred. Vacuum freeze-drying could be attempted. Do not vacuum thermal-dry.
- Photomechanical prints (such as collotypes and photogravures) and cyanotypes should be freeze-stabilized (later thawed and air-dried) or air-dried within 48 hours. Air-drying (no freezing) is preferred. Vacuum freeze-drying may be attempted.
- Carbon prints and woodburytypes should be immediately freeze-stabilized (later thawed and air-dried) or air-dried. Air-drying (no freezing) is preferred.
- Some prints (stable media, not severely damaged, etc.) may be rinsed prior to freeze-stabilization or drying. Seek expert advice.
- Dehumidification-drying could be attempted for some black-and-white prints. Seek expert advice.
- Freezer-drying, vacuum drying (ambient temperature) and vacuum thermal-drying are not recommended for black-and-white prints.

Care and Handling

- Extreme care should be taken when handling photographic material to ensure that the emulsion or binder layer or support is not damaged. Note: photographic papers have very high wet strength.
- Maintain order of the photographs and keep identification information (such as enclosures) with the photograph where possible. Use slips of paper with pencil notes as needed.
- Do not touch emulsion or binder with bare hands. Handle at the edges.
- Keep photographs wet until separated from their enclosures, sleeves or each other. If wet photographic material has started to dry, it will likely stick permanently to whatever it is in contact with. If there is any sign of mould, there is a significant chance that the emulsions will also stick to adjacent materials and be damaged if they are again wetted.

Packing

For materials that will be freeze-stabilized and later thawed and air-dried:

· Excess water may be removed by draining. Do not blot.

· Separate groups of prints with freezer paper, put a stack maximum about 7.5 cm (3 in.) thick in a plastic bag, expel air and seal. Use resealable bag or seal bag with tape and label.

· Pack in boxes and label as necessary.

· Keep packed materials cool and transport rapidly.

For materials that will be freeze-stabilized and later vacuum freeze-dried:

· Excess water may be removed by draining. Do not blot.

· Separate groups of prints with freezer paper, stack maximum about 7.5 cm (3 in.) thick.

· Pack in boxes and label as necessary.

· Keep packed materials cool and transport rapidly.

Note: Packing for direct vacuum freeze-drying or vacuum thermal-drying (no freeze-stabilization) is the same as above. However, wet photographs which must be kept wet cannot be vacuum treated in plastic bags. Any bags, if used, will have to be removed.

For materials that will be air-dried or sent to an external treatment facility:

· Separate the prints carefully from their sleeves, envelopes, etc. where possible.

· If silver gelatin printing out and developing out paper prints are wet, wet-stabilize. Place the prints in cold, clean water in clean, resealable plastic bags or containers with tight-fitting lids – add ice to the cold water as necessary. If prints are fragile, place in sealed plastic bag to minimize drying and place in container of cold water.

· Proceed to clean and air-dry as below or transport quickly to external processing firm for treatment.

Cleaning and Air-Drying

If prints are damp only:

· Air-dry material in a controlled ventilated area *(see 7.3.7)*. Place the prints emulsion side up on clean blotters or blank newsprint. If the emulsion layers are quite hard, prints on paper can be placed face down to minimize curling or use edge weights. Change absorbent paper as needed.

· Monitor until dry, allowing at least 48 hours.

· Rehouse and relabel as necessary.

If prints are wet:

· Remove mud and dirt deposits by gently rinsing the prints in a tray of clean, cold water. Do not rub. Handle the edge of the prints only. A soft brush or dental cotton (Hess Norris 1996, 603) with a gentle touch can be used on the surface of some photographic materials.

Do not rinse prints where the binder has swollen and is beginning to separate from the support. If the emulsion shows any sign of softening, remove immediately.

Avoid washing carbon prints and woodburytypes if binder layer is lifting.

Some processes are very susceptible to abrasion, such as collodion chloride printing-out and glossy silver dye bleach papers (Hess Norris 1996, 607).

· Drain the rinse water off carefully.

· Air-dry material in a controlled ventilated area *(see 7.3.7)*. Place the prints emulsion side up on clean blotters or blank newsprint. If the emulsion layers are quite hard, prints on paper can be placed face down to minimize curling or use edge weights. Change absorbent paper as needed.

· Allow excess water to drain off the prints.

· If the prints are in good condition, blot carefully and gently with newsprint or blotter through spunbonded polyester fabric. Do not blot prints with badly swollen binder layers or ones that are tacky.

· Monitor until dry.

· Rehouse and relabel as necessary.

If drying bagged frozen photographs:

· Only thaw what you can readily treat.

· Remove the bag first otherwise water will collect at the bottom of the bag upon thawing. It may be necessary to re-wet the materials in cold water to ensure that they do not dry before being separated.

· Remove all enclosures carefully as materials thaw.

· Allow excess moisture to drain off the prints.

· Air-dry material in a controlled ventilated area *(see 7.3.7)*. Place the prints emulsion side up on clean blotters or blank newsprint. If the emulsion layers are quite hard, prints on paper can be placed face down to minimize curling or use edge weights. Change absorbent paper as needed.

· Monitor until dry.

· Rehouse and relabel as necessary.

b) Colour Photographs

> ### Treatment Summary: Colour Photographs
>
> · Chromogenic prints and negatives should be freeze-stabilized (later thawed and air-dried) or air-dried within 48 hours. Wet-stabilize as an interim measure. Air-drying (no freezing) is preferred. Vacuum freeze-drying could be attempted. Do not vacuum thermal-dry.
> · Dehumidification-drying could be attempted on some chromogenic prints. Seek expert advice.
> · Dye transfer prints should be immediately air-dried. Recovery rate is low. Dehumidification-drying, vacuum freeze-and vacuum thermal-drying are not recommended.
> · Freezer-drying and vacuum drying (ambient temperature) are not recommended for colour photographs.
> · Some colour photographs (stable media, not severely damaged, etc.) may be rinsed prior to freeze-stabilization or drying. Seek expert advice.

See Black-and-White Prints (*7.4.7a*) for guidelines on care and handling, packing, cleaning and drying.

c) Negatives

> ### Treatment Summary: Negatives
>
> · Wet collodion glass plate negatives should be immediately air-dried face up. Recovery rate is low. Do not freeze-stabilize.
> · Gelatin dry plate glass negatives should be freeze-stabilized (later thawed and air-dried) or air-dried within 48 hours. Wet-stabilize as an interim measure. Air-drying (no freezing) is preferred. Vacuum freeze-drying could be attempted.
> · Polyester-based film, nitrates and acetates in good condition should be freeze-stabilized (later thawed and air-dried) or air-dried within 48 hours. Wet-stabilize as an interim measure. Air-drying (no freezing) is preferred. Vacuum-freeze-drying could be attempted. Do not vacuum thermal-dry. Dehumidification-drying could be attempted for polyester-based films. Seek expert advice.
> · Deteriorated nitrates with soluble binders should be immediately freeze-stabilized (later thawed and air-dried) or air-dried. Recovery rate may be low. Air-drying (no freezing) is preferred. Vacuum freeze-drying could be attempted.
> · Deteriorated acetates should be immediately freeze-stabilized (later thawed and air-dried) or air-dried. Recovery rate is low. Air-drying (no freezing) is preferred. Vacuum freeze-drying could be attempted.
> · Freezer-drying, vacuum drying (ambient temperature) and vacuum thermal drying are not recommended for negatives.
> · Some negatives (stable media, not severely damaged, etc.) may be rinsed prior to freeze-stabilization or drying. Seek expert advice.

Glass plate negatives are often kept in boxes without envelopes or any interleaving. Consequently, it may be difficult to separate them without transferring gelatin from one plate to another. There is also the danger that any further immersion will loosen or separate the emulsion from the glass carrier.

See Black-and-White Prints (*7.4.7a*) for guidelines on care and handling, packing, cleaning and drying.

Air-Drying

· Glass negatives in good condition can be dried vertically in racks – emulsions should not touch rack. Negatives in poor condition (flaking emulsions or cracked) should be dried flat.

· Polyester-based film, nitrates and acetates in good to fair condition may be air-dried by hanging separately on lines with plastic clips.

· Sheet film negatives (gelatin layers) may adhere to absorbent paper. Vertical air-drying is preferred with negatives plastic clipped on lines (Hess Norris 1996, 605). If drying flat, place emulsion up on spunbonded polyester fabric-covered blotters.

d) Transparencies

> ### Treatment Summary: Transparencies
>
> · Lantern slides, silver gelatin should be freeze-stabilized (later thawed and air-dried) or air-dried within 48 hours. Air-drying (no freezing) is preferred.
> · Additive colour transparencies – most are glass – (Autochromes, Agfacolor, Dufaycolor) should be immediately air-dried. Recovery rate is very low. Do not freeze-stabilize.
> · Chromogenic colour transparencies, mounted colour slides and sheet films should be freeze-stabilized (later thawed and air-dried) or air-dried within 48 hours. Wet-stabilize as an interim measure. Air-drying in mounts (no freezing) is preferred. Vacuum freeze-drying could be attempted. Do not vacuum thermal-dry.
> · Some transparencies (stable media, not severely damaged, etc.) may be rinsed prior to freeze-stabilization or drying. Seek expert advice.
> · Freezer-drying, dehumidification-drying, vacuum drying (ambient temperature), vacuum freeze-drying (exception noted above) and vacuum thermal-drying are not recommended for transparencies.

See Black-and-White Prints (see *7.4.7a*) for guidelines on care and handling, packing, cleaning and drying.

Air-Drying

· Lantern slides should be dismantled to prevent the emulsion from sticking to the components. Dry as for glass negatives.

· Additive colour transparency mounts will need to be dismantled. Remove the binding tape and dry flat face up.

· Film transparencies in good to fair condition may be air-dried by hanging separately on lines with plastic clips.

· Sheet film transparencies (gelatin layers) may adhere to absorbent paper. If drying flat, place emulsion up on spunbonded polyester fabric-covered blotters.

· Colour slides should be removed from plastic storage pages or sleeves. Colour slides may be dried in their mounts if damp only. Larger numbers of wet slides will require that the slides be removed from their mounts. Careful record keeping will be needed. The film can be air-dried on lines or flat on absorbent paper.

· Colour transparencies may need a post-recovery stabilization treatment (Hess Norris 1996, 607).

e) Motion Picture Film

Treatment Summary: Motion Picture Film

· Motion picture film should be rewashed and dried by a film processor within 48 hours. Wet-stabilize as an interim measure. In-house air-drying could be attempted.

· Freeze-stabilization and other drying methods are not recommended.

Packing

If the film is wet, keep it wet and:

· Leave film in its container and fill with clean, cold water.

· Place containers in cold, clean water in clean, resealable plastic bags or plastic containers with tight-fitting lids.

· Transport film quickly to external processing firm for treatment within 48 hours. Do not leave film in water for more than 72 hours or it will deteriorate.

See Kopperl and Bard (1995) for discussion of film freezer storage.

f) Cased Photographs

Treatment Summary: Cased Photographs

· Ambrotypes, daguerreotypes and tintypes should be immediately air-dried. Recovery rate for ambrotypes and other collodion processes is low. Do not wet- or freeze-stabilize.

· Other drying methods are not recommended for cased photographs.

Cased photographs are best treated by an expert. Immediate drying is crucial.

Air-Drying

If expert help is unavailable, the following may be attempted:

· Handle the cased photograph with care. Glass supports, cover glass and the binders are fragile.

· Remove the assembly from the case.

· Carefully bend back the preserver frame, cut the sealing tape if any, and take the assembly apart.

· Place the photograph emulsion face up on clean, dry blotters. Keep the case components beside the photograph.

· Air-dry emulsion face up in a well ventilated area.

g) Microforms

Microfilm and microfiche are found in most archive, library and record centre collections. They come in a variety of types: silver halide, diazo and vesicular. Master negatives and positives (usually silver halide) are best protected by offsite storage. When stored onsite, they should be identified as recovery priorities. Damaged use copies (usually diazo or vesicular) with masters in good condition could be candidates for discard.

Storage of microforms can vary widely: paper envelopes and sleeves of various designs, boxes of cardboard or plastic, and metal tins.

Treatment Summary: Microforms

· Roll film should be rewashed and dried by a micro-film processor within 48 hours. Wet-stabilize as an interim measure. Freeze-stabilization could be attempted.

· Aperture cards and jacketed microfilm should be freeze-stabilized (later thawed and air-dried) or air-dried within 48 hours. Wet-stabilize as an interim measure. Air-drying (no freezing) is preferred.

· Diazo and vesicular microfiche should be freeze-sta-bilized (later thawed and air-dried) or air-dried within 48 hours. Air-drying (no freezing) is preferred.

· Dehumidification-drying, vacuum drying (ambient temperature) and vacuum freeze-drying could be attempted for some microforms. Seek expert advice. Freezer-drying and vacuum thermal-drying are not recommended for microforms.

· Some microforms (stable, not severely damaged, etc.) may be rinsed prior to freeze-stabilization or drying. Seek expert advice.

Readers are referred to a U.S. study that concluded "microfilm can be frozen as a disaster recovery mea-sure, but duplicated copies should be made from the salvaged roll for archival purposes" (Gavitt 1995, 279).

Packing

If the roll film is wet:

· Leave the film in the boxes.

· Place film in cold, clean water in clean, resealable plastic bags or containers with lids.

· Keep cool and transport film quickly to external processing firm for reprocessing.

Rehousing

If only the microfilm boxes are wet:

· Remove the reels of dry roll film from the boxes.

· Replace with new boxes and relabel.

Air-drying

· Remove the film from aperture cards. Wash and then air-dry film emulsion face up on blank newsprint or blotters.

· Cut the film strips from jackets. Wash and dry film and insert into new jackets.

· Remove film from enclosures. Wash and air-dry flat or hang to dry.

· Transfer all information from damaged aperture cards, jackets and enclosures to new ones.

h) Framed Photographs

Treatment Summary: Framed Photographs

· Water-damaged framed photographs should be removed from their frames and treated according to the type of photograph.

Refer to guidelines on frame removal for works of art on paper *(see 7.4.5e)*.

7.4.8 Computer Media

The recovery of computer media is a specialized and relatively new field, and in the case of major and extensive damage is best left to professional data recovery companies. Recovery can be limited, espe-cially if the materials have been exposed to high temperatures in a fire – permanent damage to data starts above 120°F (49°C). And in-house treatment of large numbers of wet materials may not be feasible. Results of research on freeze-stabilization and mass drying methods, such as vacuum drying at ambient temperatures, has only recently begun to appear in the literature. Back-ups remain the best protection. It should be noted that most recovery techniques have been developed so that data can be copied and the originals retained or discarded.

Magnetic tapes are not as susceptible as paper to per-manent damage from water, except where the water is contaminated (sea water, sewage, etc.). Such tapes must be rinsed as soon as possible and further treat-ment for sea water contamination may be needed. A wet tape that is rinsed in clean water and wet packed can sit for several days before drying (Van Bogart 1996b, 3, 4). Accompanying material, markings or labels may alter this time limit.

Contamination by water and other substances, such as smoke may be confined to the outermost layers of the tape. Magnetic tapes in cassettes are better pro-tected from contamination; cleaning only of the cassette exterior may be required.

In addition to factors of rarity and the existence of back-ups, prioritization of tape recovery efforts should be by age, backing and pigment type (Van Bogart 1996b, 9):

· Older tapes should take precedence over newer tapes.

· Paper-backed tapes should take precedence over acetate-backed tapes, and acetate-backed tapes should take precedence over PET (polyethylene terephthalate)-backed tapes.

- Metal-based tapes (ME – metal evaporated and then MP – metal particle) should take precedence over the oxide-based tapes, as they are more susceptible to corrosion.

A variety of recovery treatments for wet magnetic tape have recently been discussed in the literature:

- Small numbers of magnetic tape (computer and audio) have been freeze-stabilized and vacuum freeze-dried (Ward and Copeland 1992, Parker 1993).
- Van Bogart advises that it is best to avoid drying methods that use extreme heat or cold. He recommends air-drying, dehumidification-drying, and vacuum drying (ambient temperatures) for wet tapes. He advises against freezer-drying at -10°F (-23°C), vacuum freeze-drying at <32°F (<0°C) and vacuum thermal-drying at >75°F (>24°C). (Van Bogart 1996b, 3)

The Canadian Conservation Institute is currently undertaking a project on disaster recovery of modern machine-readable information carriers including optical discs, magnetic disks and magnetic tapes (CCI 1999).

Treatment Summary: Computer Media

- Recover data from back-ups if possible. All priority-designated media without back-ups should be treated as follows in-house or wet-stabilized and sent to a data recovery company for cleaning, drying and copying.
- Tapes (open reel, cartridge and cassette) should be air-dried, dehumidification-dried or vacuum dried at ambient temperature within 48 hours. Wet-stabilize as an interim measure. Freeze stabilization and vacuum freeze-drying and could be attempted. Do not vacuum thermal-dry.
- Tapes contaminated with mud, sewage or other debris should be immediately washed, rinsed and then dried. Those contaminated with sea water should immediately undergo a series of rinses and then be dried. Additional treatment may be required to remove tape debris.
- Cased and floppy disks should be air-dried within 48 hours. Wet- or freeze-stabilization or other drying methods are not recommended.

---

a) Open-Reel Computer Tapes

If there are back-ups, discard the water-damaged tapes. If being sent to an external recovery company, provide the necessary technical information, such as tape size, format, speed, back-up system and computer type. The copied tapes should be checked for readability as part of the recovery procedure. A deci-

sion can then be made whether to discard or retain the originals.

Care and Handling

Avoid damaging the edges of the tape. As most tapes are edge guided through the recorder, damage can result in mistracking.

Packing

If the tape is wet, it is important to keep it wet until treatment can begin. Dried deposits will be difficult, if not impossible, to remove from the tape.

- If the tape has been wetted by contaminated water, rinse it first in distilled water at room temperature.
- Place the tape in a clean, resealable plastic bag with a clean, wet sponge and keep it cool.
- Pack vertically in plastic crate or tub.
- If the tape is going to a data recovery company for cleaning, drying and copying, pack and label bags.
- Keep packed materials cool and transport rapidly.

Cleaning, Air-Drying and Copying

If the tape is wet from fresh water:

- Remove the tape canister and wraparound.
- Rinse the tape exterior with distilled water at room temperature.
- Gently blot the tape with a clean, soft, lint-free cloth if the tape is in good condition and tape pack quality is such that edge damage will not result.
- If the tape edges are fragile, separate the reel flanges with a rubber grommet (Geller 1983, 34).
- Air-dry at ambient temperature, away from heat and sources of contamination. Van Bogart (1996b, 4) suggests 20% RH or less.
- Cleaning the outer surface of the tape pack may be sufficient. Use of a winder cleaner may be necessary if there is debris between the layers of the tape.
- Copy the tape. A decision can then be made as to whether the original will be discarded or saved.

If the tape is wet from mud or sewage contamination, rinse it off as soon as possible (Van Bogart 1996b, 5):

- Use soapy water (dye-free and perfume-free dishwashing liquid) to remove debris as necessary.
- Rinse in distilled water and dry as above.

If the tape is wet from sea water contamination, rinse it off as soon as possible. Metal-based tapes are very susceptible to corrosion from the salts in sea water.

Oxide-based tapes are less so. If in doubt, rinse. (Van Bogart 1996b, 5)

· Immerse the tape in tap water as soon as possible.

· To remove calcium carbonate deposits (resulting from extended sea water immersion, drying out before rinsing, etc.) place the tape in a mild hydrochloric acid solution.

· Rinse the tape in tap water.

· Rinse the tape in distilled water and then dry as above.

Care must be taken during cleaning to ensure that the tape labels are not lost or put back on the wrong tapes. A wax crayon may be used to identify the tapes temporarily while they are being cleaned and dried.

b) Cartridge and Cassette Tapes

If there are back-ups, discard the water-damaged tapes. If being sent to an external recovery company, provide the necessary technical information, such as tape size, format, speed, back-up system and computer type. The copied tapes should be checked for readability as part of the recovery procedure. A decision can then be made whether to discard or retain the originals.

Handling, Packing, Cleaning, Drying and Copying

· Do not touch tapes with bare hands.

· Handle open reel tapes by the hub or reel.

· Wet pack in plastic bags and pack vertically in plastic crates or tubs.

· Keep packed materials cool and transport rapidly.

· If only the exterior of the cassette or cartridge is wet, blot with clean, soft, lint-free cloth.

If there are no other options, the following may be attempted, although there is no consensus in the current literature on the success of treatment. Cartridge and cassette tapes are not designed to be readily opened.

· Dismantle the case.

· Wash and rinse the tape as necessary *(see 7.4.8a)*.

· If the tape edges are in good condition, blot the sides of the tape with a clean, soft, lint-free cloth.

· Air-dry the tape by laying it flat on blank newsprint or support the tape and air-dry vertically.

· Use a tape cleaner if there is debris between the layers of tape.

· Place tape in new case and copy. A decision can then be made as to whether the original will be discarded or saved.

c) Cased and Floppy Disks

Disks are now commonly found in the collections and records of organizations, as well as being vital operational records. Disks are commonly stored in plastic or paper enclosures, within plastic boxes.

If there are back-ups, discard the water-damaged disks. If being sent to an external recovery company, provide the necessary technical information. The copied disks should be checked for readability as part of the recovery procedure. A decision can then be made whether to discard or retain the originals.

Handling, Cleaning, Drying and Copying

· Do not touch disk surface with bare hands.

· If immediate drying is not possible, keep disks wet by packing vertically in cold water in clean, resealable plastic bags or containers with lids.

If there are no other options the following may be attempted:

· Remove the disk from its sleeve.

· For 3.5″ disks – carefully open the shell or case by removing the screws or open the shell at the side with a microspatula, after removing the sliding metal door.

For 5.25″ disks, move the disk to one side of the jacket and cut open the far side of the jacket *carefully* (only 1.6 mm or 1/16″ between the disk and the jacket edge) with non-magnetic scissors.

· Remove the disk from its shell, case or jacket. Do not touch the surface or fold, bend or abrade the disk.

· Clean by dipping the disk in clean distilled water to remove any surface debris.

· Gently blot the disk surface with a clean, soft, lint-free cloth or air-dry on a clean, soft, lint-free cloth for about eight hours at ambient temperature, away from heat and sources of contamination.

· When dry, place the disk in a temporary shell or jacket.

· Copy the disk, remembering that there is risk of damage to your equipment.

· Check the copy for readable data.

· Label the disk with a waterproof marker.

· Discard the original.

(Based on Kahn 1994a, 18-20)

Wet floppy disks (and disk sleeve linings) have been dried by directing a stream of room temperature air from a hair dryer on "air" setting into the sleeves. The disks were then copied successfully. (Olson 1986, 634-636)

7.4.9 Compact Discs

Collections of CDs and optical discs (video or laser) and other multimedia products are becoming increasingly prevalent in archives and libraries. These formats may be among the many found in an organization's collections and records. Or the organization may be devoted to music recordings, where non paper-based formats would predominate. Except for optical discs which generally contain unique information, the majority of CDs are produced commercially and many may be replaceable.

CDs come in a variety of formats, some of the more familiar being CD-ROM (Read-Only Memory), CD-WORM (Write Once Read Many times) and Photo-CD. CDs are often stored in hinged plastic cases with accompanying paper or card enclosures, usually on coated paper.

Recovery treatments for these media are in development. Kahn advises that "all these CDs [CD-ROMs, CD-Is, CD-WORMs, Photo-CDs, CDs (usually audio only), video discs, laser discs and optical discs] are variations of the same format and should be treated the same way" (1998, 69).

Treatment Summary: Compact Discs

- Recover data from back-ups if possible. All priority-designated media without back-ups must be treated immediately as follows or media should be wet-stabilized and sent to a data recovery company for cleaning, drying and copying.
- Compact discs should be immediately rinsed and air-dried or dehumidification-dried. Do not freeze-stabilize. Other drying methods are not recommended.
- Discs contaminated with mud or sewage should be immediately washed, rinsed and then dried. Those contaminated with sea water should immediately undergo a series of rinses and then be dried.
- Paper enclosures should be treated in the same way as other paper-based material.
- Severely scratched or deformed discs should be discarded and replaced when possible.

Handling

- Particular care should be taken to avoid scratching. Permanent misread of CD-ROM data can result if the substrate side (shiny side) is scratched or degradation may be accelerated if the data layer (label side) is exposed. (Van Bogart 1996b, 11)
- All compact and optical discs are composed of five layers (label, sealcoat, metal layer, pits holding the encoded signals, and polycarbonate or substrate). Most vulnerable is the label layer. (Kahn 1998, 69)
- CD-ROMs and optical discs encoded on both sides and housed in cartridges are very vulnerable to damage, and should not be removed from their housing unless wet (Kahn 1998, 69).

Cleaning and Drying

(Based on Van Bogart 1996b, 12, Kahn 1994a, 28 and St. Laurent 1991, 11)

If the disc is wet from fresh water:

- Carefully remove the disc from its container so as not to bend or scratch it.
- Rinse debris off the disc in clean, distilled water at room temperature. Do not soak.
- Place the disc vertically in a rack and leave it to dry slowly at ambient temperature, away from heat and sources of contamination.
- Gently wipe the disc in a blotting motion if necessary with a clean, soft, lint-free cloth moving perpendicular to the grooves from the centre to the edge (radially), *not* in a circular motion (tangentially).
- Rehouse the clean, dry disc in a clean container and label.
- Check its playability and readability.
- Paper or card enclosures can be treated in the same way as any other paper-based material.

If the disc is wet from mud or sewage contamination, it is important to rinse it as soon as possible:

- Use soapy water (dye-free and perfume-free dishwashing liquid) to remove debris from the disc as necessary.
- Rinse it in distilled water and then dry as above.

If disc has been exposed to sea water contamination, it is important to rinse it off as soon as possible:

- Immerse the disc in tap water as soon as possible.
- Rinse it in distilled water and then dry as above.

7.4.10 Sound and Video Recordings

Sound and video recordings may be among the many formats found in an organization's collections, or the organization may be an archive of recordings, historical and contemporary. The collections could include a variety of formats, such as reel-to-reel tapes, cassettes and phonograph records. A variety of storage containers and devices may be in use, i.e., metal, plastic and paper-based. The identification of less familiar formats and materials is sometimes difficult. It is always best to seek expert advice.

Recent reports in the literature cover freeze-stabilization and vacuum freeze-drying and vacuum drying at ambient temperature:

- Van Bogart (1996b, 3-4) says that there is no need to freeze tapes, and it can actually cause more damage. Cooled tape packs can loosen, allowing water to enter between the tape windings and the tape backing can distort on freezing. Freezing can also cause migration of lubricants in the binder to the surface of the tape that may not be reabsorbed. He says that vacuum drying is acceptable at ambient temperatures.

- Ward and Copeland (1992, 4-5) reported on blast-freezing and vacuum freeze-drying experiments that have been conducted in Britain on magnetic tapes carrying audio material. They concluded that:

    The risk of physical damage caused by, say, the expansion of ice in the tape pack, seems less serious than the risks from decomposition and mould growth. The use of a vacuum chamber provides a new technique for bulk drying tapes which might otherwise have been discarded as irrecoverable.

    They also briefly cite a 1989 case in which studio master tapes were successfully dried in a vacuum chamber.

- Cuddihy (1994, 185) suggests vacuum drying at ambient temperatures and recommends slow drying – 12.7 mm tapes require two to three days for complete drying and 25.4 mm tapes require four to five days.

Temperature of the water in which tapes are submerged is a factor. Cuddihy (1994, 185) warns that if the water temperature is greater than 11°C (52°F), tapes may or may not be recoverable. If the water temperature is less than 11°C tapes submerged in water should not be degraded, and therefore can be recovered. He recommends that wet tapes be immediately placed in ice-water at nominally 0°C (32°F) – this arrests hydrolysis if the tapes were wetted by water warmer than 11°C.

Air-drying of videocassettes and audiocassettes can be attempted provided the cases are not screw-mounted – the cases can be broken apart and replaced (Macdonald referenced in Walsh 1996).

Treatment Summary: Sound and Video Recordings

- Recover data from back-ups if possible. All priority-designated media without back-ups should be treated as follows. Otherwise, media (except for phonograph records) should be wet-stabilized and sent to a recovery company for cleaning, drying and copying.
- Tapes (reel-to-reel and cassettes) should be immediately rinsed and wet packed, and then air-dried or vacuum dried at ambient temperature within 48 hours. Wet-stabilize as an interim measure. Freeze-stabilization, dehumidification-drying, vacuum drying (ambient temperature) and vacuum freeze-drying (open reel tapes) could be attempted. Vacuum thermal-drying is not recommended.
- Tapes contaminated with mud or sewage should be immediately washed, rinsed and then dried. Those contaminated with sea water should immediately undergo a series of rinses and then be dried. Additional treatment may be required to remove tape debris.
- Shellac and acetate records should be immediately cleaned and air-dried. Wet- or freeze-stabilization and other drying methods are not recommended.
- Vinyl records should be cleaned and air-dried within 48 hours. Wet- or freeze-stabilization and other drying methods are not recommended.
- Paper/card enclosures that accompany records should be treated in the same way as other paper-based material.

---

a) Reel-to-Reel Tapes

If there are back-ups, discard the water-damaged tapes. If being sent to an external recovery company, provide the necessary technical information, such as tape size, format, speed, etc. The copied tapes should be checked for readability as part of the recovery procedure. A decision can then be made whether to discard or retain the originals.

Handling, Packing, Cleaning, Drying and Copying

- Do not touch tapes with bare hands.
- Wet pack in plastic bags and pack vertically in plastic crates or tubs. Keep packed materials cool and transport rapidly.
- Wash and rinse the tape (while wound on its reel) as necessary (*see 7.4.8a*).

- If the tape edges are in good condition, blot the sides of the tape with a clean, soft, lint-free cloth.
- Air-dry the tape by laying it flat on blank newsprint or support the tape and air-dry vertically.
- Use a tape cleaner if there is debris between the layers of tape.
- Rerecord the tape. A decision can then be made as to whether the original will be discarded or saved.

b) Audio and Video Cassettes

If there are back-ups, discard the water-damaged tapes. If being sent for recovery by an external company, provide the necessary technical information should be provided, such as tape size, format, speed, etc.

Handling, Packing, Cleaning, Drying and Copying

- Do not touch tapes with bare hands.
- If only the exterior of the cassette or cartridge is wet, blot with clean, soft, lint-free cloth.
- If the inside is wet –

  wet pack in plastic bags and pack vertically in water in plastic crates or tubs. Keep packed materials cool and transport rapidly

  or

  dismantle the cassette case and air-dry as for reel-to-reel tapes.

- Replace the case and rerecord the tape. A decision can then be made as to whether the original will be discarded or saved.

c) Phonograph Records

Older phonograph records were made of a variety of materials such as shellac, acetate, metal and glass. Modern records are made of vinyl or plastic. Vertical storage in protective paper or plastic sleeves within cardboard jackets or boxes is the most common storage method.

Handling, Cleaning and Air-Drying

- Shellac and acetate records are sensitive to water and should be treated before vinyl. Washing, if necessary, should be kept to a minimum. (St. Laurent and Gibson in Walsh 1997, 20)
- Records are fragile – avoid shocks.
- Remove the record carefully from its enclosure(s) so as not to damage the playing surface.
- Hold records by their edges.

- Seek expert advice on the use of cleaning agents. Alcohol-based cleaners should not be used on shellac and acetate records (Kahn 1998, 71).
- Clean surface debris from records preferably using a record cleaning machine (St. Laurent 1991, 10). Alternatively, clean them by dipping in clean distilled water.
- Clean and dry vinyl records (1970s-1990s) with clean, soft, lint-free cloth – cloth may be dampened with slightly soapy water (using one tsp. mild detergent (i.e, Ivory) or 200:1 Kodak Fotoflow in one gallon lukewarm distilled water (Kahn 1998, 70). Clean and then remove water from both sides of the record by gently wiping counterclockwise in the direction of the grooves (not perpendicular as for CDs).
- Air-dry the records vertically while supported in a rack. Ensure that records and any paper labels are fully dry.
- Rehouse and relabel as necessary.
- Paper or card enclosures and separated labels can be treated in the same way as any other paper-based material.

Chapter 8

8.0 Disaster Rehabilitation Planning for Collections and Records

Rehabilitation can be described as longer-term activity intended to return collections and records to a fully useable and accessible state. This phase which follows disaster response and recovery is also dependent upon the nature and scope of the disaster, as well as the availability of resources. Thus, the Disaster Planning Committee (DPC) must anticipate and consider a variety of circumstances in order to plan for complete resumption of services.

This chapter outlines the major issues associated with the rehabilitation of collections and records. At this point in the disaster timeline, the Disaster Action Team (DAT) will have undertaken the recovery of all or part of the collections, either onsite or at external facilities. Data recovery may still be in progress or have been completed. Rehabilitation of collections and records must now be undertaken in coordination with the recovery and rehabilitation of the facility and systems *(see Chapter 9)*. In some circumstances, it may be feasible to resume limited services to users. Alternatively, the organization may decide to focus all its resources on the rehabilitation effort.

> The onus is on you to be thorough and creative. About the only sure thing is the unlikelihood of having vast amounts of money to simply buy your way back to normal (Miller 1988, 358).

Depending on the nature and severity of the disaster, rehabilitation may be accomplished relatively swiftly or may require long-term planning and substantial commitments of time, money and resources. Priorities will be established, in part, by the service demand placed on the organization. As a result, strategies documented in the disaster plan must be revisited and modified as necessary.

8.1 The Purpose of Disaster Rehabilitation Planning for Collections and Records

The overall purpose of rehabilitation planning is to enable the organization to successfully complete any work initiated during recovery, and undertake restorative treatments, refurbishment and rehousing in order to render collections and information usable and accessible so that services and normal operations

can resume. Decisions will be needed as to which materials should and can be successfully further resuscitated and by what means. In other cases, losses will have to be accepted and alternatives for the provision of services will need to be examined.

The aims of collections and records rehabilitation planning are:

· to return the collections and records operations to normal by restoring, rehousing, discarding, duplicating and replacing materials as appropriate

· to ensure the successful treatment and safe return of materials from offsite facilities and service providers

· to prevent or limit post-recovery problems

· to eliminate contamination and odours from mould, smoke, sewage, chemicals in flood waters, etc.

· to ensure that the card catalogue or online database and any physical relabelling accurately reflects any collections and records relocation and disposition

· to return the collections to clean, safe and stable storage with operational climate control.

8.2 The Process for Disaster Rehabilitation Planning for Collections and Records

As with other phases of disaster planning, rehabilitation planning must acknowledge that activities will vary according to the specific situation. Now, the systematic rehabilitation of the collections and records can begin. This work should proceed according to the priorities determined for the recovery strategy *(see 6.5)*, although the results of drying and other treatments may require that modifications be made. Some rehabilitation activities may have already been initiated during the recovery phase, where collections have been sent for external treatment.

Further expert help should be obtained when necessary. Staff training will be critical, particularly where extensive inhouse rehabilitation of collections is undertaken. Progress should be monitored regularly, and the strategies for personnel, communications, security, etc. modified as needs change.

Collections and Records Rehabilitation Planning: Process at a Glance

Prepare to:

· Get expert help.
· Receive treated collections and records, and continue documentation.
· Assess recovered collections and records, and revisit priorities.
· Assess rehabilitation options and costs.
· Determine short- and long-term rehabilitation strategies.
· Modify ongoing support operations.
· Order supplies and equipment.
· Brief and train staff.
· Perform in-house treatments.
· Send collections and records for external rebinding and restorative treatments.
· Receive remaining treated collections and records. Return all collections and records to storage

---

8.2.1 Get expert help

Further expert help may be required to assist the DAT with rehabilitation decisions and treatment of the collections and records. Conservators, bookbinders, systems professionals, etc. specializing in materials, such as rare books, photographs, fine art and electronic media should be consulted as necessary to assess options for collections in their dried state, to determine the best alternatives for still frozen materials, and to assist with costing and planning short- and long-term objectives.

8.2.2 Receive treated collections and records, and continue documentation

Collections and records may have been dried at external treatment facilities, or onsite or in a nearby location. Treated materials may be returned over a period of time. Some materials may be left frozen *(see 6.5.6c)* and their drying and further rehabilitation will continue as resources permit.

Temporary storage and rehabilitation areas will be needed for assessing, sorting, and storing these materials apart from the rest of the holdings, and for their repair, rehousing, etc. Waters (1993, 12) recommends providing about twice the number of bookshelves that would be normally needed. This will compensate for swollen, expanded materials and allow materials to regain their equilibrium moisture content over a week or two. Newly returned, packed collections must never be allowed to sit unattended for more than several days maximum. Some materials may not be fully dry (i.e., boxes of mixed formats and media),

while others may be too dry and will need to acclimatize to the stable environment to which they will be returned. Ideally, all treated materials should be stored apart from the rest of the holdings for at least six months.

Waters (1993, 12) recommends that the rehabilitation area for paper-based materials be maintained at a relative humidity (RH) of 30% to 40%, with a temperature of less than 18°C (65°F). The RH and temperature of the rehabilitation area(s) must be controlled and may be gradually adjusted to duplicate conditions in the storage areas to which the materials will be returned. Acceptable RH and temperature levels must be achieved and maintained in the storage areas before any materials are returned.

Documentation of the relocation and disposition of collections and records should continue. Inventory verification of collections returned from offsite treatment or storage must be undertaken immediately to confirm that the correct number of boxes, crates, etc. have been returned. For large numbers of materials, this verification will be more easily accomplished by automated means. In addition, ensure that all contractual obligations have been met, such as the drying and cleaning of materials.

8.2.3 Assess recovered collections and records and revisit priorities

Materials returned from drying need to be unpacked, and their condition assessed, and then sorted according to whatever further treatment is required. A clean and environmentally stable area is needed for these activities. The DAT should ensure that staff are made aware that materials returned from vacuum drying processes may be particularly brittle and should be handled with care.

In addition, staff should be made aware that paper-based collections treated by mass means will either be dry or returned frozen for drying, but will not be magically restored. Distorted volumes will still be distorted, and mud-covered documents will still be mud-covered. However, film-based materials or computer media will be returned cleaned and dried, in usable condition or copied after recovery by a full service provider.

Decisions regarding collections rehabilitation are organization-specific. Broad guidelines will be laid out in the existing disaster plan. However, priorities may need to be revisited based on the nature of the damaged collections, the results of recovery (primarily drying), the need and urgency to resume some or all services, and of course, available resources. Collections

---

and records with intrinsic value must be distinguished from those that are being retained for their information content only. In general, priorities would follow those established for the recovery phase; however, circumstances may dictate modifications.

The following categories of materials should be considered:

· items to be returned directly to storage
· items requiring relabelling or rehousing
· items requiring further minor treatment
· items requiring further major treatment
· items to be copied and the original discarded
· items to be replaced and the original discarded
· items to be discarded

Dried, mouldy materials should still be stored separately from other collections in a controlled environment and carefully monitored.

Where materials do not appear to require drying but must be packed and moved to another area or site, be sure that they are, in fact dry before packing them, so that mould will not develop. When in doubt, allow them to air-dry in a stable, controlled environment for a week before packing. A controlled environment should also be provided in the area or site to which they are being moved.

8.2.4   Assess rehabilitation options and costs

The collections assessment described above will yield gross numbers of materials designated for a variety of rehabilitation treatments. The costs of these treatments will then need to be assessed by the DAT. Difficult decisions and sacrifices may need to be made, especially for materials that require extensive and costly restorative treatment. Some, perhaps many decisions, for discard and replacement will already have been made during the recovery operations.

The costs of rehabilitation will vary enormously as outlined in the discussion of overall cost factors in Chapter 6 *(see 6.5.9)*. Restorative treatment costs for books differ from those for documents. In addition, damage sustained by shelved materials versus materials stored in boxes or cabinets will not be the same. Unboxed shelved materials will likely be more severely damaged.

Full settlement of an insurance claim cannot be reached until an evaluation of the losses has been completed *(see 10.7.2)*. It is best to work closely with experienced conservation and insurance professionals to determine which materials can and cannot be

rehabilitated, regardless of apparent condition, and at what cost. The potential success of any further treatments must be estimated, and the consequences of failure identified. In addition, the collective impact to the organization should be considered.

8.2.5   Determine short- and long-term rehabilitation strategies

Based on the assessment of the condition of recovered collections and records, along with options and costs, the DAT will need to determine strategies for their rehabilitation. In some cases, rehabilitation will be confined to rehousing and some minor repair and cleaning. If large numbers of collections were severely damaged, more extensive and long-term plans will be needed.

The framework and guidelines in the existing disaster plan provide the basis for these deliberations; however, the determination must also be based on the situation at hand. Users and the public should be advised when full services are expected to resume, or where and when partial services will be available.

8.2.6   Modify ongoing support operations

Depending on the nature and scope of the rehabilitation strategies, support operations developed during response for personnel, communications and security will have to be modified by the DAT *(see 6.6.)*. The progress and schedule for the recovery and rehabilitation of the facility and systems may require that further ongoing modifications are made. Working conditions will change and the number of personnel required may vary. The tasks, while perhaps less physically and emotionally demanding than during recovery, can still be exhausting and labour-intensive. Security measures will need to be modified as the collections are returned and building repairs proceed.

Communications, both internal and external, will continue to be important to staff, onsite and offsite contractors, users, the media and the public. Here again, users and the public should be advised when full services are expected to resume, or where and when partial services will be available.

8.2.7   Order equipment and supplies

Based on the rehabilitation strategies for collections and records, equipment and supplies required for in-house treatments, such as repair, relabelling and rehousing, should be ordered. It may be possible to make use of equipment and supplies stored onsite, if undamaged and accessible. Work areas, additional to those established for recovery operations, may be needed for rehabilitation. See NISO Z39.77-2000. *Guidelines for Information about Preservation Products.*

8.2.8 Brief and train staff

The DAT will need to brief and instruct the staff-at-large on the rehabilitation strategies for collections and records. Team appointments, supervisory assignments and training will be needed. Training undertaken as part of planning may need to be modified *(see 2.4.4)*, and that developed as part of response and recovery may prove useful *(see 6.6.3i)*. Quality control measures should be put in place. Health and safety issues, such as those involved in cleaning of mouldy materials, must be addressed *(see 3.4.8a)*.

8.2.9 Perform in-house treatments

The nature and scope of in-house rehabilitation treatments would be determined by the nature of the collections affected, and the resources, time and expertise available. More extensive in-house treatments may be undertaken if the organization has an established preservation or conservation programme.

In-house treatments may include:

· cleaning of mouldy, soot-covered, smoke-covered, mud-covered materials

· flattening and other minor repairs

· relabelling

· rehousing

· binding preparation, such as trimming of charred edges

· rebinding and restorative treatment

· data verification (disks, tapes).

8.2.10 Send collections and records for external rebinding and restorative treatments

Some collections, which have already been dried or otherwise treated, may also require rebinding or other restorative treatment. Unique materials for which there is no in-house expertise, are best sent out during the recovery phase. Depending on the volume of materials involved, a tender process may be necessary. The treatment and relocation of rebound and restored collections will need to be documented. External contractors should provide documentation of their treatment of collections and records.

8.2.11 Receive remaining treated collections and records. Return all collections and records to storage

Collections and records, once returned from rebinding or other external restorative treatments, should be received and processed according to established procedures. Documentation should be ongoing.

Once recovery and rehabilitation of the facility is completed and the environment stabilized, the treated collections and records may be returned to storage. This transfer must be carefully organized by the DAT and responsibilities clearly outlined to all personnel.

Ideally, all dried, cleaned and restored materials, whether fumigated or not, should be retained in a rehabilitation area apart from the rest of the holdings for at least six months. Monitoring, follow-up and random checking of collections and records should be done on a routine basis to prevent the reoccurrence of mould.

Collections' Return Guidelines:

· No materials that were mass chamber-dried should be returned to the stabilized disaster area before they are thoroughly acclimatized to the facility's normal environment. Materials should be unpacked, laid out individually and left for several weeks. Handle them with care, as the material is liable to be brittle.

· No materials should be returned until the shelving, cabinets, etc. have been rehabilitated and the storage environment meets and is able to hold desired levels of RH and temperature.

· No materials should be returned to storage until *thoroughly* dry.

· No materials should be returned without careful examination by trained personnel.

· No dry materials should ideally be returned before necessary treatments, such as repairs, have been completed.

· No materials should be returned before ensuring that identification markings are correct.

· No materials should be returned before ensuring accurate record-keeping is complete.

Returning materials to proper sequence in storage can be laborious, either for books or sheet materials in boxes, folders, etc. Computers have been used to assist with putting books back into call number sequence (Lundquist 1986, 51-54). If a warehouse approach for random inventory storage is used, sequencing is not an issue.

Consideration should also be given to the possibility that the size and format of some materials may have been altered. Less space may be required if materials are discarded and not replaced, but treated materials often require extra storage space, such as vacuum freeze-dried materials that have swollen.

8.3 Collections and Records Rehabilitation Options

Each organization must determine its own decision-making criteria for rehabilitation of collections and records. These decisions are linked to the priorities set during planning and the recovery operations, and to the results of recovery treatments.

Sometimes the costs of restorative treatment or replacement *(see 6.5.9)* cannot be justified. In these cases, it may be better to accept the loss, rather than attempt to rehabilitate or repurchase the item. However, no item should be discarded without sober second thought. Discarded items must be carefully recorded and their values (either individual or unit) established in order to substantiate any insurance claim. Where duplicates, other editions or formats of the material may have survived undamaged, treatment or discard decisions of the damaged originals may be made swiftly.

No mass, chamber-based rehabilitation remedies exist. Decisions and tasks related to repair, rehousing, restorative treatment, etc. must be made on an item-by-item basis. Copying by various means and commercial rebinding, while carried out in a production environment, are still labour-intensive as items are handled one by one. In-house treatment is also labour-intensive and requires additional, specialized staff training and careful supervision. Materials such as rare books, works of art, photographs, etc. should be treated only by experts.

a) General Rehabilitation Guidelines

The following guidelines (based in part on Buchanan 1988, 60-62) outline options for collections and records rehabilitation, such as repair, and alternatives to rehabilitation, such as reformatting. If reformatting is being considered, it must be ensured that you can copy materials without violating use restrictions.

- **For General Materials and Records Collections**

These are defined as materials of information value only used for reference, research, education and entertainment purposes. Includes circulating library collections.

- Clean and repair in-house.
- Rebind using commercial binding services.
- Discard and replace with copies or reprints through purchase or donation.
- Discard and replace with other formats (photocopy, microfilm, online access, etc.) through purchase, donation or lease.
- Accept losses and discard.

- **For Special and Vital Records Collections**

Special collections are defined as materials of intrinsic value that are rare or unique, and used for historical and scholarly research purposes. Vital record collections may have intrinsic value or be held for their information content only. Some vital records must be retained in their original format for legal reasons.

- Undertake partial or full restorative treatments.
- Rehouse after stabilization until funds are available for restorative treatment.
- Accept damages and rehouse as necessary.
- Copy information (photocopy, scan, microfilm, etc.) and rehouse the originals.
- Accept loss, but discard only in extraordinary circumstances.

- **For Vital Operational Records**

These are defined as materials essential to the operation of the business and systems of the organization, some of which may need to be retained in their original format.

- Undertake partial or full restorative treatments.
- Copy information (photocopy, scan, microfilm, etc.) and rehouse or discard the originals.
- Accept losses and discard only in extraordinary circumstances.

8.3.1 Water-Damaged Collections and Records

Depending on the nature and extent of the water damage and the results of drying treatments, collections and records may require further minimal treatment or extensive restorative treatments. Some materials may need cleaning, repair or other preparation prior to treatment, either in-house or by external conservators and bookbinders. Materials that were freeze-stabilized will be returned as resources allow for drying, cleaning and other treatment. These materials must be dry prior to undertaking further treatment. It is best to seek expert advice before proceeding.

a) Cleaning

Some materials (some photographic materials, films and magnetic media) should not have been allowed to dry out and should have been rinsed and cleaned while still wet during recovery *(see 7.4)*. Dried mud-, debris- or sewage-covered paper-based materials can be cleaned using a variety of manual techniques, such as brushing and vacuuming. Works of art and other valuable materials, fragile materials and those with stains should be treated by a conservator. Due to the health hazards, serious consideration should be given to discarding sewage-covered materials. If they are to be retained and cleaned, proper safety precautions must be taken.

b) Repairs and Rebinding

Flattening and repair of minor mechanical damages to paper-based materials can be done in-house. Loose textblocks can be repaired where the page attachment is still sound. Materials with damaged protective covers can be resewn into new pamphlet binders. Large numbers of books from general or circulating collections are generally sent out to commercial binding firms.

c) Restorative Treatments

Restorative treatments – stain reduction of works of art, rare book binding, chemical resuscitation of photographs, etc. – should be left to experts. Restorative treatment is generally reserved for items of intrinsic value, when it is essential to maintain the original format and integrity of the item.

d) Rehousing

Wetted or otherwise damaged boxes, folders, envelopes, cases, sleeves and mounts should be replaced as necessary. Some boxes may be reuseable. Enclosures must be discarded if mould or sewage is present. Plastic cases and boxes used to store tapes and disks may be cleaned and reused, but if there is any doubt of contamination, they should be discarded. All identification information should be carefully copied.

Dried, water-damaged materials should be rehoused in new, conservation-quality, protective enclosures as necessary. Some materials may already have been restored; others may be later rehabilitated or copied to another format when funding and/or expertise is available. Enclosures and materials should be relabelled as appropriate and their disposition reconciled with card catalogue or online database records.

e) Data Verification

Tapes and disks may have been treated onsite or shipped to an external recovery company for cleaning, drying and perhaps copying. In either case, the original or copied data should be checked and verified for readability. Copied originals are generally discarded. *(See 7.4.8)*

8.3.2 Fire-Damaged Collections and Records

Depending on the extent of the fire damage and the results of any drying treatments, collections may require further minimal treatment or extensive restorative treatment. Some may need cleaning (smoke and soot), repair or other preparation prior to treatment, either in-house or by external conservators and bookbinders. Materials that were freeze-stabilized will be returned as resources allow for drying, cleaning and other treatment. These materials must be dry prior to treatment.

a) Cleaning Smoke- and Soot-Covered Materials

Smoke is a combination of solid, liquid and gas materials that have been completely combusted. Soot is a liquid and solid product of combustion, an oily residue containing carbon and other compounds.

Smoke and soot on the surfaces of dry materials can be reduced and sometimes successfully removed by a variety of manual techniques, such as using vacuums, dry-chemical sponges, dry- cleaning powder and erasers. Wet cleaning methods should be used only by experts.

b) Smoke Odour Removal

Collins (1996, 44-46) described the use of ozone to remove smoke odour from paper materials after a school library fire. After drying and soot removal, the materials were treated with ozone. The process converts smoke odours into carbon dioxide and water vapour as follows: air is drawn into an ozone generator where oxygen molecules are split into free atoms by an electrical discharge, forming an oxidizing agent that attacks odours, mould and certain bacteria. Collins reported that odour removal was successful; however, he identified ozone as being responsible for accelerating the deterioration of paper fibre. Kahn (1998, 75) also warns of the adverse effects of ozone on a host of other materials, such as: photographs, microfilm, motion picture film, magnetic media, compact discs, and laser and optical discs.

Ozone is considered to be very effective at removing odours (and mould using high concentrations), and is used by a number of disaster recovery companies. It is no doubt suitable for certain situations, where mass treatment of materials may be required or in the case of an empty facility, however:

> Ozone is a strong photochemical oxidant that will react irreversibly with most organic and some inorganic materials and should therefore never be used in museums, libraries, archives, or other irreplaceable collections (Pruesser 1994).

Smoke odour can also be reduced by other means although many of the accounts in the literature are anecdotal in nature. The methods cited include: outside airing, and the use of baking soda, activated carbon, activated charcoal, zeolites, kitty litter or liquid deodorant. The smoky-smelling collections are placed in an enclosure or enclosed container with, for example, baking soda. The baking soda or other materials should not come in direct contact with the materials being treated.

c) Rehabilitation of Charred Materials

Damage caused by high temperatures is irreversible, and severely charred materials cannot be restored. Sometimes however, the information written, printed or drawn on such materials can be retrieved by forensic sciences laboratories. Such treatment is expensive and should only be undertaken in exceptional circumstances. No attempt should be made to open fragile charred books or documents. Such handling will result in further irreparable damage.

d) Repairs and Rebinding

Where the condition of the materials permits, repairs and rebinding to fire-damaged collections and records can be carried out as for water-damaged materials. In the case of burnt material, charred edges can be trimmed and the materials repaired or rebound, although the brittleness of materials may preclude the use of some treatments. All materials must be handled extremely carefully.

e) Restorative Treatments

As with water-damaged materials, restorative treatments of fire-damaged collections and records should be left to the experts. Restorative treatment is generally reserved for materials of intrinsic value, when it is essential to maintain the original format and integrity of the item.

f) Rehousing

As with water-damaged materials, dried, fire-damaged materials should be rehoused as necessary. Paper-based materials may be very brittle and particular care should be taken with their handling and the design of their protective storage.

Tape reels and cassette shells that are warped or otherwise severely damaged should be replaced. Soot often can often be successfully removed from plastic housings by vacuuming and damp cleaning.

8.3.3 Mouldy Collections and Records

Mouldy materials should remain isolated from other collections in an appropriate climate-controlled environment. They must be handled with care due to the health hazards they pose *(See 3.4.8a)*. Non-chemical means that bring the mould to an inactive state are preferred over chemical treatment. *(See 6.5.8)*

Mould can be removed from dry materials by a variety of means including vacuum, dry-chemical sponges, dry-cleaning powders and soft brushes. Mouldy materials can be very fragile, and a gentle touch is required. It is best to seek the advice of a conservator.

8.4 Basic In-House Rehabilitation Options for Collections and Records

The definition of "basic" collections and records rehabilitation treatment will vary depending on the expertise available in the organization. This section is limited to cleaning, minor repairs and preparation for commercial binding of materials that do not have intrinsic value. Regardless of the nature of the treatment, all in-house work should be carried out under the supervision of a conservator; anything beyond "basic" should be undertaken by a conservator.

Wetted materials must be dry before any of this work is carried out, and treatment of fragile materials that risks further damage should be avoided. Appropriate health and safety precautions must be taken, particularly with soot-, sewage- and mould-covered material.

8.4.1 Cleaning

Soot-, sewage- and mould-covered materials pose health risks. Appropriate health and safety procedures must be enforced and proper equipment and supplies must be provided. Personnel must wear protective clothing and gloves, and use filter masks or respirators with High-Efficiency Particulate Air (HEPA) filters that screen out exhaust of particulate matter down to .3 microns. It is best to work in a fume hood.

a) Cleaning Mud-Covered Materials

Mud on paper-based materials should only be cleaned after the material is dry. Mud on films, magnetic tapes, etc. should have been rinsed off while the materials were still wet as part of recovery.

Some incrustations on books and documents may be loose and may be manually removed. Surface cleaning can be undertaken using a vacuum, dry-cleaning powders, soft brushes, etc. *(see 8.4.1b)*. If the mud has firmly adhered to the material, it is best to seek the advice of a conservator.

b) Cleaning Smoke- and Soot-Covered Materials

Spafford and Graham (1993b, 421) advise that removing soot is not the same as removing dirt and other accretions. Soot agglomerations are easily broken into minute carbon particles that will "pigment" or become a part of the smoothest surfaces. The completeness of the soot removal depends on the first stages of soot "disruption."

> An indisputable necessity in the thorough removal of minute soot particles is a progressive cleaning technique using direct vacuuming (this stage, if properly carried out, removes almost all of the soot), dry methods that lift more particles from the surface, and, lastly, wet methods if appropriate (Spafford and Graham 1993b, 421).

Materials should be treated only after they are dry. Time may also be a factor, as cross-linking of soot compounds may occur.

Materials should be vacuumed using a vacuum cleaner that does not exhaust soot back into the room, i.e., it should be fitted with a HEPA filter. Lowest effective vacuum suction should be employed. The use of protective screening on the nozzle or brushing into the vacuum should be avoided as it has been found to cause ingraining of soot that could not later be removed (Spafford and Graham 1993b, 422). Once completed, the vacuum cleaner bag, gloves and other contaminated materials should be bagged and disposed of outside.

Soot may also be vacuumed from magnetic tape packs and compact discs. Direct contact with the tape pack should be avoided. Use of a winder cleaner may be necessary.

Commercial companies use dry-chemical sponges to clean soot from furniture and walls. These sponges have also been successfully used to remove smoke residues and soot from collection materials, as in the Dalhousie University Law Library fire (Matthews 1986). They are good for removing loose deposits, but not baked-on soot. They are more effective on larger, flat surfaces than on smaller, uneven surfaces. Analysis of these sponges indicates that the components are similar to that of other eraser products, that residue is the most serious drawback of their use and that residues deposited during treatment should be carefully removed (Moffat 1992, 9-10). Sulphur-containing residues make their use on some materials like photographs unsuitable. The Canadian Conservation Institute has analyzed four products sold for cleaning smoke- and soot-damaged materials – see *CCI ARS (Analytical Research Services) Reports Nos. 2445* (Moffat 1986), *2928* (Moffat 1991) and *4000* (Moffat 1992).

Opinions in the literature vary as to the use of these sponges. Some sources suggest that parts of the sponge, once dirty, should be cut off and discarded, while others suggest that the sponges may be washed, dried and reused.

After sponge cleaning is completed, further cleaning aids (such as dry-cleaning powders, erasers, molecular trapping action products, press room plate cleaning fabrics) can be used, depending on the condition, nature and surface of the material.

Smoke- and soot-covered rare materials, film-based materials, photographic materials, magnetic and optical media and works of art are best treated by experts.

- **Procedures for Cleaning Smoke- and Soot-Covered Items**

Books

Hold the book shut at the fore edge and vacuum the soot from:

> Head and tail from spine to fore edge and fore edge from head to tail
>
> Front and back covers, and spine
>
> Inside front and back covers near the spine.
>
> Repeat the process using a dry-chemical sponge, followed by erasers. A final wipe can be done with a soft cotton fabric such as those used to clean press room plates.

Paper Documents

> Soot-covered documents, pamphlets, etc. can also be vacuumed if done very carefully at minimum

effective suction. Attempt only if item is not fragile. This may be followed by cleaning with dry-chemical sponges, dry-cleaning powder, soft brushes and plastic erasers.

Compact Discs

Hold the compact disc only by the edge and:

> Vacuum or soft brush large soot from the surface of the disc
>
> Do not scratch the surface of the disc
>
> Wipe remaining soot from the surface of the disc with a soft cloth dampened with distilled water
>
> Wipe and brush radially from the centre of the disc to its edge. Do not wipe or brush in a circular motion as this may irreversibly obscure large portions of a track.
>
> (Van Bogart 1996b, 12)

See Van Bogart and Merz (1996) for description of cleaning of 12″ optical discs after hurricane damage (rain, sea water and sand).

Magnetic Tapes

Hold the tape pack carefully and:

> Vacuum soot without directly contacting the tape pack. Avoid damage to tape edge
>
> Brush remaining soot from the tape pack
>
> Wipe soot from the cassette with damp cloth
>
> Use cleaner winder to remove remaining soot.
>
> (Van Bogart 1996b, 6)

c) Cleaning Mould-Covered Materials

Mould is hazardous to human health, and precautions must be taken when handling affected materials *(see 3.4.8a and 6.4.9)*. The spread of contamination must be prevented, and it is best to sterilize work areas, work surfaces and any equipment and tools used – 70% ethyl alcohol or 0.5% bleach solution (Florian 1997, 155).

Materials should be treated only when dry and the mould is dead or dormant (can still contain allergens and toxins). Dormant mould is dry and can be easily brushed or otherwise removed generally without causing further damage. Active mould is soft and smeary, and is difficult to remove successfully and safely; it is best done by a conservator using mechanical means.

Severely mould-damaged materials may be very fragile and should be treated by a conservator. Eradication of mould using fungicides should be a last resort and done only by or under the close supervision of a conservator.

Materials can be vacuumed using a vacuum cleaner that does not exhaust spores back into the room, i.e., it should be fitted with a HEPA filter. Protective screening on the nozzle should be used along with the lowest effective suction. Once vacuuming is completed, the vacuum cleaner bag, gloves and other contaminated materials (i.e., the storage box) should be bagged and disposed of outside. Ideally they should be incinerated.

Dry-chemical sponges can also be used to remove mould *(see 8.4.1b)*.

Mouldy rare materials, film-based materials, photographic materials, magnetic and optical media and works of art are best treated by experts. Mould may be vacuumed from magnetic tape packs and compact discs. Tapes and discs may need to be copied.

- **Procedures for Mould-Covered Items**

Do not blow on mouldy materials. This will just spread the contamination. Clean only if the item is not fragile.

Books

Hold the book shut at the fore edge and vacuum mould from:

> Head and tail from spine to fore edge, and fore edge from head to tail
>
> Front and back covers and the spine
>
> Inside front and back covers near the spine.
>
> Repeat the process above using a dry-chemical sponge.
>
> (Based on Munters Corp., Moisture Control Services Division and MBK Consulting 1996, Section III).

Note: In the case of a major library mould cleanup project, Florian recommended a 70% solution of ethanol and distilled water (after HEPA vacuuming). The books were thoroughly wiped, and then bagged with solution-saturated absorbent cloth pieces. (Page 1998)

Paper Documents

> Documents, pamphlets, etc. can also be vacuumed if done very carefully at minimum effective suction. This may be followed by cleaning with dry-chemical sponges, dry-cleaning powder, soft brushes and plastic erasers.

Compact Discs

Hold the compact disc only by the edge and:

> Vacuum or soft brush mould from the surface of the disc
>
> Do not scratch the surface of the disc
>
> Wipe the disc surface with a soft cloth dampened with distilled water
>
> Wipe radially from the centre of the disc to its edge. Do not wipe or brush in a circular motion as this may irreversibly obscure large portions of a track.

(Van Bogart 1996b, 12-13)

Magnetic Tapes

Hold the tape pack carefully and:

> Vacuum mould without directly contacting the tape pack. Avoid damage to the tape edge
>
> Brush remaining mould from the tape pack
>
> Wipe mould from the cassette with a damp cloth
>
> Use a cleaner winder to remove remaining debris
>
> Transcribe the tape. Simple cleaning is not sufficient to prevent further mould growth in the right conditions – mycelia will still be present in the tape binder. Thoroughly clean recorder afterwards.

(Van Bogart 1996b, 7)

8.4.2 Flattening and Other Minor Repairs

Flattening and other minor repairs can be undertaken onsite. The extent of treatment will depend on the expertise available. Materials of significant intrinsic value should only be treated by a conservator. Minor treatments on other materials can be undertaken with appropriate staff training and supervision.

This work might include:

· flattening of cockled or distorted sheets, pages or textblocks
· repair of tears
· repair of loose hinges and covers
· replacement and resewing of pamphlet bindings

8.4.3 Commercial Binding Preparation

If the organization has a longstanding relationship with a commercial binding firm, the firm should be very familiar with your particular needs. This combined with your knowledge of their operations will assist in decision-making and expedite the preparation process. Condition of the dried materials will be critical to any decisions. Materials that are extremely damaged, distorted or fragile will need particular attention. If the cost of full treatment is prohibitive,

there may be minimum treatments that could restore the usability of the book. It is best to seek expert advice. Rare materials should only be sent to a commercial binding firm, if the company is equipped and experienced in this area.

Routine preparation for binding includes documentation by the organization. Organizations that normally transmit data to their binding firm via disk or telecommunications will need to ensure that their systems and binding software and/or databases are fully operational post-disaster. Other preparation activities may include:

· collation
· replacement of severely damaged or lost pages with copies on permanent paper
· tipping-in of loose pages
· flattening and minor repair of pages
· trimming of charred or soot-covered page edges – the covers will need to be removed
· protective wrapping of fragile materials

The type of binding treatment will need to be considered:

· Recase if the cover is loose or detached and its condition is acceptable, the page attachment is intact and the cover will still fit. Water-damaged textblocks may be very swollen.
· Rebind if the cover is damaged, will not fit and/or the page attachment is damaged.
· Rebind in hardcover if the softcover binding is damaged.
· Rebox or box in a protective clamshell box, phasebox, etc. if the material is too fragile or damaged to rebind or funds are not available for further treatment.

Typical external binding costs (excluding full restoration binding) will be in the range of $6 to $30 Can. per item, depending on its condition, size and type of binding selected. Particularly fragile and oversize items will cost more.

8.5 Alternatives to Collections and Records Rehabilitation

Decisions made regarding alternatives to rehabilitation will differ according to the overall mandate and responsibilities of the organization, as well as individual circumstances. A variety of methods and treatments are now available to recover and rehabilitate collections and records materials. The decision whether to proceed with recovery and restorative treatment depends on the feasibility of treatment (can it be done) and the advisability of treatment (should it be done). Factors include the value of the materials to the organization, their nature and condition, the projected success of treatments and the costs involved *(see 8.3)*.

In some cases, materials may be damaged beyond any kind of conservation or restorative treatment. These materials should be considered for discard. In many instances, recovery and rehabilitation is more costly than replacing the damaged item. As well, many damaged items simply cannot be replaced. Some materials may need to be replaced, others may not. Regardless, all materials designated for discard should be documented and held for insurance review.

Discarding should be considered for materials damaged beyond reasonable repair, or that are non-essential, easily replaced, etc. Special, rare materials and vital records would only be discarded in extraordinary cases.

Replacement of items by copying the damaged originals may be an option. Ensure that where this is done by an external firm they have experience in handling such materials. Decisions need to be made whether the original will then be discarded or retained.

Replacement alternatives to rehabilitation include:

Gift

Replacement copies, reprints or other editions may be available from individuals or other organizations through collections exchange or donation programmes.

Purchase

Replacement copies, reprints or other editions may be available for purchase from publishers or other organizations. The material may be available in the same format or in an alternative format. For example, contact the Canadian Institute for Historical Microreproductions (CIHM) *(see Appendix 3.1 Sources of Information: Microreproduction)*.

Photocopying

Depending on the severity and nature of the damage, materials may be replaced by photocopying the originals. This service is offered by some commercial binders. The materials are generally copied on permanent paper and given a library-quality binding. See relevant standards, i.e., *ANSI/NISO Z39.48-1992 (R 1997). American National Standard for Permanence of Paper for Publications and*

Documents in Libraries and Archives and *ANSI/NISO/LBI Z39. 78-2000. American National Standard for Library Binding (June 1998)*. Note: A Canadian standard for permanent paper is in the final stages of development.

Microfilming

Damaged materials may be also be replaced by microfilming the originals (See Canadian Cooperative Preservation Project 1993 and Fox 1996). Service bureaus offer this service or it could be done in-house. The materials should be filmed according to preservation microfilming standards.

Digital Scanning

Replacement of damaged materials by digital scanning may be a possibility, after which the information can be made available online and/or in hard copy format (See Kenney and Chapman 1996 and Conway 1996). Service bureaus and some binders offer digital scanning services for damaged book materials. This could also be done in-house. Refer to appropriate standards and guidelines for practice.

Online Access

The availability of online information is rapidly increasing. This applies mostly to serial material that is available in full-text form through various commercial services, as well as on compact discs available for purchase.

Chapter 9

9.0 Disaster Recovery and Rehabilitation Planning for Facilities and Systems

Preservation and conservation literature has little to say concerning the recovery and rehabilitation of facilities, their contents (other than collections and records), essential services and systems, and therefore we remain heavily reliant on the knowledge and experience of private industry.

This chapter provides a brief overview of basic planning requirements and covers the building structure, essential services, building contents such as furniture and equipment, and computer hardware. All of these are referred to collectively throughout this chapter as facilities and systems. At this point in the disaster timeline, it is assumed that the emergency service providers have successfully contained the disaster, the site has been declared safe for re-entry and hazards have been cleared. Recovery and rehabilitation of facilities and systems are specialized fields and, except for very minor incidents and contained disasters, should be left to the professionals, such as full service recovery companies, systems experts and reconstruction specialists.

Facilities-related actions depend on the nature and scope of the disaster, as well as the availability of resources. Thus, the Disaster Planning Committee (DPC) must anticipate and consider a variety of circumstances, such as the effects of water, heat, soot and smoke. Recovery and rehabilitation operations may be undertaken quite quickly, or in the case of a major disaster, long-term planning and substantial commitments of time, money and resources may be required. Buildings and systems may be restored or replaced; however, structural changes may require substantial rethinking of current services. For example, a fire may result in the destruction of a major building annex that the organization cannot afford to rebuild. Your temporary accommodations may well become long-term accommodations. On the positive side, this may provide an opportunity for the organization to rectify pre-existing design flaws, substandard storage conditions, etc.

The existing disaster plan will provide a general framework for the Disaster Action Team's (DAT) decisions on recovery and rehabilitation of the facilities and systems. However, these plans will need to be modified to meet the requirements of the particular situation. Recovery and rehabilitation plans for the facilities and systems must be fully coordinated with those for the collections and records to ensure the smoothest possible return to normal operations.

9.1 The Purpose of Disaster Recovery and Rehabilitation Planning for Facilities and Systems

The overall purpose of recovery and rehabilitation planning for facilities and systems is to enable the organization to successfully render them useable and accessible, and ultimately to resume normal operations. The purpose and process for this recovery and rehabilitation planning parallels that undertaken for the collections and records, as outlined in Chapters 7 and 8.

The purpose of facilities and systems recovery is to prevent further damage and reduce the effects of moisture, mould, corrosion, etc. The purpose of facilities and systems rehabilitation is to complete any necessary reconstruction, repair, refurbishment and/or replacement.

The aims of facilities and systems recovery and rehabilitation planning are:

- to minimize the need for replacement
- to minimize repair and reconstruction
- to eliminate contamination and odours from smoke, sewage, chemicals in flood waters, etc.
- to prevent or eliminate mould growth and corrosion
- to limit post-disaster effects
- to minimize costs overall
- to return the workplace environment to normal.

9.2 The Process for Disaster Recovery and Rehabilitation Planning for Facilities and Systems

As ongoing efforts are made to stabilize the environment and prevent further damage, the DAT should begin a systematic assessment of the extent and nature of the damage to the facilities and systems. The recovery and rehabilitation work should proceed according to the priorities determined for the building structure, building systems, equipment, computer systems and furniture that were documented in the organization's disaster plan. Circumstances may demand considerable on-the-spot decision-making. Ongoing progress must be monitored, and plans and arrangements for personnel, contractors, security, communications, etc. modified as needs change.

This chapter assumes that collections have been removed or otherwise protected before any work on the facilities begin. The actions involved in recovery and rehabilitation will vary; however, a number are common to all efforts.

Facilities and Systems Recovery and Rehabilitation Planning: Process at a Glance

Prepare to:
· Get expert help.
· Prevent further damage and stabilize the environment.
· Continue documentation.
· Assess damage to the facilities and systems.
· Determine priorities for recovery and rehabilitation.
· Assess options and costs.
· Determine recovery and rehabilitation strategies.
· Recommend, get approval for and implement strategies.
· Monitor implementation and coordinate with collections and records recovery and rehabilitation.
· Restore services.

9.2.1 Get expert help

Expertise found within the organization may be sufficient for incidents and minor disasters. However, if in doubt or in the case of a major disaster, it is best to seek professional help as outlined in the disaster plan.

A number of companies now specialize in facility and property recovery services after a flood, fire, etc. and also provide drying and restoration of collections and data. Emergency services are generally available 24 hours a day, seven days a week. Many will provide free estimates. Alternatively, there are individual companies which specialize in salvage, cleaning, systems, etc. Selection of any company should be based on its experience and appropriate referrals.

9.2.2 Prevent further damage and stabilize the environment

It is essential to prevent further damage to the facility and systems (see 6.4), and stabilize the environment (see 3.5.1). A major source of damage may be water resulting from flooding, firefighting efforts or other sources. Excessive moisture and standing water can cause many problems including warping, delamination, swelling, structural weakness, mould growth (see 3.4.8a) and corrosion. Fire may have caused severe damage to the facility, as well as smoke and soot deposits. Prompt and appropriate action is especially critical in the case of major struc-

tural damage, as well as for equipment and computer systems where irreparable damage can occur.

9.2.3 Continue documentation

The extent and nature of the damage to the facilities and systems should be thoroughly documented. While recovery service companies can offer this service, it is wise to augment their documentation with your own so that the organization's particular needs can be fully met and coordinated with the overall recovery and rehabilitation efforts, and the final settlement of the insurance claim.

9.2.4 Assess damage to the facilities and systems

Property damage may be a lot worse than it appears – or nowhere near as bad. In the immediate aftermath, the verdict hinges on proper assessment (Moore 1996, 17).

The DAT, with the necessary professional assistance, should survey the building, systems and its contents in coordination with that done for the collections and records, as fully as possible after safety clearance is obtained in order to accurately determine the extent and nature of damage. Protective clothing, safety equipment, flashlights, etc. may be required for these inspections. Critical areas may not be immediately accessible, and an alternative course of action may be needed. Emergency repair estimates, as well as specialty damage evaluations, may be required.

If the disaster was caused by a weakness in the facility, or if such weakness contributed to the severity and escalation of the disaster; this must be thoroughly documented and measures must be identified and taken to improve facility standards, thereby reducing the possibility of a reoccurrence.

The organization may wish to adapt various administrative tools developed by other organizations to facilitate their own damage assessment. For example, a damage assessment form created from those used after Hurricane Hugo and the Loma Prieta earthquake (Nelson 1991, 114-115), and a post-earthquake safety evaluation procedure using a tag system (Nelson 1991, 117-119).

9.2.5 Determine priorities for recovery and rehabilitation

The assessment and assignment of priorities for the facilities and systems following a disaster is essential to the entire recovery process and later rehabilitation efforts. These priorities drive the assessment of recovery and rehabilitation options and costs, and the determination of the strategies appropriate to the situation.

Priorities are determined by the damage sustained by the facilities and systems, as well as by those documented in the pre-existing disaster plan. Funding must be found where measures are needed to comply with insurance obligations and building and fire code requirements.

9.2.6 Assess options and costs

The DAT and any necessary external experts must assess the recovery and rehabilitation options available and their associated costs. Existing insurance coverage will need to be carefully examined. These options will be defined first by an assessment of the size, nature and extent of the disaster, secondly by the resources, facilities and services available, and thirdly by the organization's ability to support the associated costs.

For a small or localized disaster, options are not apt to be complicated. But a major disaster will involve many factors and many people from the organization, as well as external assistance, perhaps both governmental and non-governmental. Time constraints may also be an issue, such as in the case of a severely damaged facility where severe weather conditions continue.

Costs are estimated based on the damage assessment, assignment of priorities, recovery and rehabilitation options and estimates provided by in-house and external experts. For some organizations, these estimates will be critical to their ability to proceed with recovery and rehabilitation. It is beyond the scope of this publication to attempt to detail all the options to be considered and their associated costs. Professional advice should be sought. Selected options are discussed for facility-related issues *(see 9.3)* and for computer systems *(see 9.4)*.

Recovery and rehabilitation options for facilities and systems are similar to those available for collections and records. Outright discard may be appropriate in some cases, such as for equipment, if the damage is too severe or too costly to repair. Replacement of equipment, systems and structural features may be necessary in some instances. In other cases, repair, refurbishment, reconstruction or rebuilding are the best alternatives.

In the case of a major, community-wide disaster, extensive work and planning will be necessary to identify and secure the needed funding. Archives, libraries and record centres are considered part of public community life, and their recovery must be integrated with that of the community-at-large. Therefore, any repair or reconstruction will be undertaken in the context of the broader community's reconstruction, which would

include the resumption of essential services, i.e., water, sewer, electrical, phone, transportation, etc. In the world of professional emergency planning vis-a-vis community-based reconstruction, there is increasing attention paid to the concept of "pre-event planning for post-event recovery (PEPPER)" (Anderson and Mattingly 1991, 313-314).

9.2.7 Determine recovery and rehabilitation strategies

The DAT will need to determine which building components, systems, equipment, etc. can be recovered, repaired, reconstructed or rehabilitated in the short term. Major structural damage will necessitate the development of medium- or long-term strategies. These plans must ensure that the physical structure of the building, and the support systems and essential services will be safe and operational. Support strategies will also need to be addressed and integrated with those developed for the collections and records recovery and rehabilitation efforts, such as scheduling, communications and security.

9.2.8 Recommend, get approval for and implement strategies

The DAT should recommend its facilities and systems recovery and rehabilitation strategies for approval by the governing body as appropriate. Both the DAT and the governing body must recognize that ongoing modifications to these strategies may be necessary.

These strategies will cover:

- assignment of priorities
- recovery and rehabilitation methods and procedures to be used
- personnel requirements
- human health and safety requirements
- security requirements
- communications requirements
- documentation requirements
- training requirements, if any
- quality control and supervision
- supply, equipment and service needs
- estimated timeframes, scheduling and costs

Contracts will need to be drawn up to cover recovery and rehabilitation work whether done by a single full service recovery company or by a number of external companies. Specifications should be included and all work that must meet building or fire code requirements, or other standards or conditions, must be clearly stipulated.

9.2.9 Monitor implementation and coordinate with collections and records recovery and rehabilitation

The recovery and rehabilitation of facilities and systems should be monitored by the DAT to ensure that implementation proceeds according to the plans made, while recognizing that adjustments will be inevitable. Timing and costs will be critical, and coordination with the collections and records recovery and rehabilitation efforts must be ongoing. The disaster area should be made safe and stable, both structurally and environmentally, before any collections and records are returned. The same holds true if a comprehensive recovery service company is contracted to do the work.

As part of the communication plan for the broader recovery and rehabilitation effort, staff, users and the general public should be kept informed on progress made towards resumption of operations, as well as the availability of interim services.

9.2.10 Restore services

As recovery and rehabilitation of the facilities and systems (and collections and records) nears completion, the organization's focus should shift to the practical considerations of restoring operations and services to normal or near-normal. Disaster-related activities should wind down over time as the short- and longer-term goals for service restoration are met. It should be recognized that organizations may fail or services may change, either on a temporary basis or in some cases permanently, depending on the impact of disaster. According to Datapro Research, a division of McGraw-Hill, (cited by Shut in Pember 1996, 200), "43% [of organizations that suffer a major disaster] never re-open and a further 29% 'go under' within two years."

At first, it may only be possible to provide basic levels of service at less than full, normal hours of operation. Full resumption of services to pre-disaster conditions may need to be phased in over time in conjunction with the further repair and reconstruction of the facility, as well as rehabilitation of collections and records.

Final facility and systems inspections will need to be carried out and existing policies and procedures related to service resumption may need to be revisited. Reporting relationships should return to their pre-disaster configuration and staff will return to their routine responsibilities at the appropriate time. Plans will need to be made regarding hours of operation, levels of service to be provided, staffing needs, security issues, etc. These plans and arrangements should be communicated to staff and the public through bulletins, notices and signage as appropriate. Reopening the facility also provides

the organization with an opportunity to celebrate the successful resumption of services *(see 10.9)*.

9.3 Selected Recovery and Rehabilitation Options for Facilities

During their preliminary planning, the DPC would have investigated options for recovery and rehabilitation. Many different professions and trades may be needed in order to carry out the necessary repairs, reconstruction, restoration, rebuilding, or redesign of the facilities.

As previously mentioned, some recovery companies can undertake full cleaning and rehabilitation of a local disaster area, or the whole building if necessary *(see Appendix 3.3 Sources of Facilities and Services: Recovery Services – Full Service)*. This might include drying and cleaning of walls, ceilings, carpets etc., replacing walls or a major restoration of the complete building and the heating, ventilation and air conditioning (HVAC) system and ductwork. No collections or records must be returned to storage until safe to do so.

The DPC's planning and the DAT's planning and implementation should consider the following facilities and systems recovery and rehabilitation issues as appropriate:

· structural inspection
· emergency corrosion control for computer and other electrical equipment
· temporary barricades and repairs
· extraction of standing water
· climate control to prevent mould, bacteria and corrosion
· demolition and clearing of debris
· removal and discard or temporary storage of contents offsite
· decontamination of the HVAC system, elevator shafts, etc.
· hazardous material decontamination
· drying of the structure and contents (*in situ*, onsite or offsite)
· cleaning and sterilization of the structural components and built-ins, such as shelving
· cleaning and sterilization of contents (*in situ*, onsite or offsite), such as carpets, draperies, furniture, shelving, storage cases and cabinets
· fumigation (only in extreme cases)
· structural reconstruction and repair
· recovery and recertification or replacement of electrical, gas, plumbing, elevator, etc. utilities and services
· recovery and recertification or replacement of HVAC, security, fire alarm, detection and suppression systems, etc.

· smoke and soot removal

· odour control

· recovery and recertification or replacement of tele-communications, computer systems and equipment

· recovery and repair of microfilm readers, microfilm, scanning and photography processing equipment, photocopiers, vendacard machines, etc.

· restoration of floors, walls, doors, etc.

· restoration of furniture

· restocking of depleted disaster supplies.

9.3.1 Dehumidification-Drying

Dehumidification-drying has revolutionized the recovery and rehabilitation of facilities and their contents after disasters involving water. The major full service recovery companies report that dehumidification-drying can dramatically reduce replacement and reconstruction costs and shorten disruptions *(see 6.5.6d)*.

Dehumidification-drying for facilities can:

· eliminate or reduce the need for reconstruction, as structural components including plaster walls, wallboard, insulation, masonry block, concrete, studding, etc. can be dried in place.

· eliminate or reduce moisture-related deterioration including swelling of wallboard, warping of wood, corrosion of wiring, peeling of paint, etc.

· reduce costs and disruption by drying carpeting, drapes, furniture and equipment in place.

· inhibit growth of mould and bacteria.

However treated, the disaster area must be fully dried and checks for recurring mould should be undertaken. Any refurbishing and restoration such as new drywall, plaster, paint and carpets should not be undertaken until the temperature and relative humidity (RH) have stabilized. Newly applied plaster, paint and other finishes, as well as newly laid carpet (where glued) must be thoroughly cured before the staff and collections are reintroduced.

9.3.2 Fumigation

Control of the environment in the disaster area or building should be established as quickly as possible, to avoid or limit the growth of mould, bacteria and corrosion *(see 3.5.1)*. Mould *(see 3.4.8a and 6.5.8)* and bacteria can pose major health risks. Expert advice should be sought and isolation measures implemented immediately.

Mould infestation in the facility requires swift action. Due to the human health hazards and potential hazards to returned collections, fumigation should be undertaken *only* in extreme cases, and may have to be followed up by more intensive cleaning and sterilization.

Fumigation of the area or building should be undertaken *only* by a licensed professional fumigator. Staff or collections should not return to the area or building until it has been declared safe.

9.3.3 Cleaning and Sterilization

The affected area, or in some cases the entire facility, will have to be cleaned and sterilized before staff, users, and the collections and records can safely occupy the premises.

Cleaning and sterilization can be done by in-house personnel but outside specialists are generally recommended for this type of work. The cleaning crew should wear appropriate protective clothing and follow appropriate safety precautions.

Cleaning and Sterilization Checklist

· Remove any debris and incidental materials from the affected area.

· Remove all equipment for recovery and recertification.

· Remove all draperies and upholstered furniture. Have them cleaned, and sterilized if necessary.

Then,

· Thoroughly vacuum (with a HEPA filter) the affected area.

· For mould, isolate the affected area and clean with 2% chlorine bleach solution. Use a 5% chlorine bleach solution for mops and pails. Seal and dispose of contaminated disposable clothing. (See 6.4.9)

· Remove soot using dry-chemical sponges and a degreaser manufactured for that purpose. Other techniques have been used to clean cases, etc. (See Spafford and Graham 1993a,b).

· Thoroughly wash the floors, ceilings, walls, doors, shelving, and any other hard furniture or fixtures with a germicidal cleaner, such as hospitals use to sterilize isolation rooms. The underside, corners and backs of furniture and shelves must be included.

· Clean and sterilize the entire HVAC system including coils and filters, and ductwork; otherwise mould can be distributed throughout the building. Disposable wipers should be used to avoid the spread of contamination.

· Do air monitoring to ensure that cleaning procedures were effective and that the area is safe for staff, users and the collections and records.

9.3.4   Odour Elimination

Even after cleaning and sterilization of the facility is complete, the odour of mould, smoke, soot, etc. may still linger overall or remain pervasive in some areas. Odour elimination is best left to qualified specialists. Your concerns for the health and safety of the staff and collections should be made clear to any contractors.

Common methods used by the professional service companies include the following (Based on Cesa 1996, 19-21):

· **Deodorizing sprays** eliminate airborne odour by chemical absorption using an odour-killing chemical that bonds with the odour particles, causing them to drop to the floor where they can be removed during cleaning. This has to be done on a regular basis until the odour is eliminated.

· **Deodorizing gel blocks** are usually installed in the return air ducts of the HVAC system. They combine activated charcoal and a fragrant gel that conceals odour, and last about 30 days.

· **Thermal fogging** is very effective for odours in hard-to-reach places. This method uses a petroleum-based product to create a fog that can penetrate walls and surfaces. This product can, if exposed to an open flame, cause an explosion and can leave an oily residue that makes soot etc., removal more difficult. If thermal fogging is used, any residue must be cleaned off before the collection or staff return to the area.

· **Encapsulation** is a method where encapsulants are fogged into an area. They attach themselves to odour particles and dry into a smooth finish on the surface areas.

· **White pigment sealers** can be sprayed onto wall and ceiling surfaces to seal off sources of odour that cannot otherwise be removed or cleaned.

· **Ozone**, an oxidizing agent, combines with a substance to modify its structure and eliminate the smell. Ozone is a toxic gas and is most effectively used in an enclosed chamber. On exposure to ozone, rubber and rubber-based products can decompose, and dyed fabrics can fade (see 8.3.2b).

Small odour problems may be minimized or reduced by using charcoal or baking soda to absorb the odour. Trays of either may be placed in the affected area.

9.4   Computer Systems Recovery and Rehabilitation Options

As discussed in Chapter 5, the key to survival of your electronic records is a disaster plan that includes the back-up of system programmes and files, and arrangements for offsite facilities – hot and cold sites. Planning should also have included strategies for rebuilding the operating system, reloading of application software and recovery of application data. The system should be reinstalled to default configuration.

Opinions differ on the advisability of attempting recovery and rehabilitation of systems hardware. Many consider that the salvage of hardware that has been through a disaster to be a futile exercise, one that is not "...worth the effort when insurance is available at affordable prices" (Cunha 1992, 593).

Kahn (1994a, 30) suggests removing covers from the hardware and other equipment, and draining any water and gently rinsing off any debris with distilled water. The equipment should then be dried in a clean room with a temperature of 10°C to 16°C (50°F to 60°F) and a relative humidity of 40% to 50%. She alternatively suggests sending the equipment to a disaster recovery company who would then undertake drying and cleaning.

There is no right or wrong answer. Each situation must be evaluated by a technical expert. If funds permit, this may also be the ideal opportunity to replace and upgrade your system.

· **Corrosion Control**

Corrosion processes start immediately after a disaster as a result of water and the by-products of fire. Building components such as polyvinyl chloride (in water piping and electrical insulation) when heated, produce hydrogen chloride gas which combined with water produces the highly corrosive hydrochloric acid. Other plastics when heated, produce corrosive sulfates and chlorides.

As electronic and other electrical equipment is highly susceptible to damage by corrosion, rapid emergency treatment (within 24 - 48 hours) is critical. Equipment can be sprayed with a water-displacing corrosion inhibitor and corrosion may be effectively halted for about two weeks indoors. Decisions can subsequently be made regarding restoration of the equipment which can involve: disassembly, removal of contamination, rust removal, protective coating, reassembly and testing. (Gordon 1994, 72)

Chapter 10

10.0 Post-Disaster Planning

As part of pre-disaster planning, the Disaster Planning Committee (DPC) must anticipate the state of the organization after a disaster, and consider the reality of functioning, in some cases after having suffered serious loss. The impact of this on the ability of the organization to provide continued service and the physical and emotional toll on staff should be taken into account.

This chapter focuses on outstanding issues that must be addressed in order for the organization to fulfil its legal, financial and other responsibilities, and to also enable the people affected to complete emotional recovery. At this point in the disaster timeline, recovery of the collections and records, facilities and systems is finished, rehabilitation is near completion, and services have returned to normal or near normal. This stage of planning is the calm after the storm. It takes shape over time, thereby giving the people involved time to reflect, assess and move forward. Collectively, the DPC and the Disaster Action Team (DAT) should now review and assess all aspects of the emergency or disaster.

10.1 The Purpose of Post-Disaster Planning

The purpose of post-disaster planning is to assess what went right and what went wrong, in order to remedy the original disaster plan, and to rectify deficiencies identified in the plan as well as the facility and its operations. In short, the goal is to avoid making the same mistakes and suffering losses. Post-disaster planning should help the organization mitigate any future vulnerability to disaster.

It is at this post-disaster stage that the people involved try to make sense of what they and the organization have gone through. This reflection and assessment allows them to analyze the events leading up to and causing the disaster in order to learn lessons, acknowledge successes and finally to move forward.

The time following a disaster allows for what has been called a window of opportunity:

> There is a time window, albeit narrow, during which proposals for mitigation and preparedness activities will be viewed favourably. Your building may not even suffer damage when a tornado strikes, but risk awareness may not be higher for several years. As part of your planning process, build

in some time to analyze the recommendations you will make when that window of opportunity is raised (Drabek 1991, 35).

10.2 The Process for Post-Disaster Planning

The process for post-disaster planning brings together the debriefing sessions, assessments, strategies and modifications for facilities and operations, etc. to prepare the insurance claim and the final disaster report, and to plan for the future. The evaluation takes into account all of the factors involved in the disaster and must consider fully their impact on the staff involved. Evaluating the effectiveness of the disaster plan is a critical step in post-disaster planning, one that must not be overlooked in the desire to resume normal operations.

Post-Disaster Planning: Process at a Glance

Prepare to:
- Hold post-disaster debriefing sessions.
- Identify the need for staff counselling.
- Do a post-disaster assessment.
- Identify the need for facility and operational modifications.
- Assess priorities, options and costs for modifications.
- Determine short- and long-term strategies.
- Prepare and file the insurance claim.
- Prepare and submit an internal disaster report.
- Recognize and thank all those who helped.

10.2.1 Hold post-disaster debriefing sessions

Collectively, the DPC and the DAT should determine the extent of evaluation appropriate to the disaster experienced. Levels of review could range from examining how personnel responded to a minor incident up to a full-scale investigation of the cause(s) and management of a major disaster.

Then, at the earliest opportunity, the DPC and the DAT should convene post-disaster debriefing sessions in order to evaluate the organization's response, recovery and rehabilitation actions. All teams, staff, volunteers and external service providers should attend. The purpose of these sessions is to gather data, identify problems that occurred, acknowledge creative problem-solving and innovations that occurred and solicit opinions on the type and nature of future planning needed.

10.2.2 Identify the need for staff counselling

In the case of a major or severe disaster, staff will have experienced substantial emotional stress and trauma. People will be exhausted and may feel overwhelmed once the urgency of the situation has passed. While the needs of staff should have been addressed throughout the disaster, in practical terms, such consideration is seldom fully realized. Thus, sessions separate from the debriefing should be held at the earliest opportunity for staff involved in the disaster. The purpose of these sessions is to identify personnel in need of professional counselling. Plans can then be made to provide such assistance.

10.2.3 Do a post-disaster assessment

A post-disaster assessment is an essential component of the organization's overall recovery process. As stressed throughout this publication, disaster planning is an ongoing process, not a finite product. Analysis of the disaster can be best undertaken by those who were most intimately involved.

The post-disaster sessions will have produced information necessary to assess the effectiveness of the disaster plan (prevention, protection, preparedness, response and recovery) and all its supporting strategies, i.e., administration, communications, security and cooperative arrangements.

10.2.4 Identify the need for facility and operational modifications

As a result of the post-disaster assessment, strengths and weaknesses involving all aspects of the organization's facility and operations will have been identified.

Consideration should be given to:

· revision of operational and staff practices and procedures
· retrofit to the facility
· replacement or upgrading of systems and equipment
· replacement of supplies
· provision of additional staff training

As part of this process, the disaster plan should be reviewed and amended where necessary to remedy any inadequacies in practices and operations, and any facility weaknesses and problems that were identified as contributing to or exacerbating the disaster.

Necessary replacement equipment or supplies should be purchased, and plans made to upgrade existing systems, such as fire detection, alarm and suppression systems, and security systems.

The post-disaster assessment will also help to identify weaknesses in staff training. This provides an opportunity to plan for continuing education by developing workshops and other training to bring all staff collectively to a point of adequate disaster preparedness.

10.2.5 Assess priorities, options and costs for modifications

The post-disaster assessment may identify a variety of mitigation projects, some of which may be critical and some merely desirable. The immediate, intermediate and long-term need for these projects should be considered, along with options for their implementation and a breakdown of associated costs. Difficult decisions and choices may need to be made, as current levels of funding may not cover all that needs to be done.

10.2.6 Determine short- and long-term strategies

Determining strategies begins again the process of hazard analysis and hazard reduction as outlined in Chapter 3. Generally, priorities would follow those previously established in the original disaster plan, but circumstances may dictate that the strategies be modified based on the present condition of the facility, and available funds and other resources.

10.2.7 Prepare and file the insurance claim

The organization's insurance claim must be prepared and filed. A claim cannot be fully settled until all damaged materials and property have been recorded and evaluation of their loss is complete. The insurance company may require further onsite inspections and discussions to clarify losses claimed. Insurance adjusters will review the claim based on the documentation furnished by the organization. Photographs or videos should be provided to support the recorded damage information as necessary.

All materials damaged beyond repair must be listed, as well as those materials awaiting rehabilitation. The potential success of further conservation treatment for these latter materials should be estimated.

10.2.8 Prepare and submit an internal disaster report

The DPC, after consultation and input from the DAT, should prepare a summary report on the disaster. This report should include the observations and conclusions of staff, as well as reports from outside agencies such as the fire department, insurance adjusters, etc. This report should also include recommended strategies for modifications to the facility, its operations, staff practices, etc.

This internal disaster report should be submitted to senior management and the governing body for their review and approval. This report is the official record of the disaster and the organization's response, and acknowledgment of all who provided assistance.

The recommendations in the report would either be approved, or may require further amendment, before implementation can proceed.

10.2.9 Recognize and thank all those who helped

Appreciation should be expressed to all individuals, within and external to the organization, who helped during and after the disaster. Acknowledgment should given to those people for their specific efforts and dedication.

10.3 Post-Disaster Debriefing Sessions

Any emergency, up through a full-fledged natural disaster, provides a learning experience, from evaluating the effectiveness of a formal emergency plan to assessing how everyone performed under pressure. In fact, a post emergency critique should be part of the recovery process... (Nelson 1991, 158).

Debriefing sessions should be held with staff, volunteers and external emergency personnel. These sessions are an opportunity to gather information and generate ideas. The focus should be on both the cause and the effects of the disaster. A critique of the organization's response, the effectiveness of the disaster planning and the disaster plan itself will result in ideas from all those involved on how to improve the plan and how to modify the facility and organizational operations and practices.

10.4 Staff Counselling

Full recovery and rehabilitation includes not only the collections and the facility, but must also address the needs of the people who were directly affected by the disaster. In sessions separate from the disaster debriefing, external professionals should be brought in to facilitate sessions that focus on people's emotional needs, encouraging discussion and shared reactions. In cases of widespread and traumatic disaster, attendance at these sessions should be mandatory. They are designed to reach all of those involved, to make people aware of possible emotional health symptoms arising from the disaster, and to outline support and treatment available.

Human behaviour in the event of disaster is an emerging field that is rapidly becoming recognized as an integral part of disaster planning. Accordingly, the DPC must consider not only the administrative and technical aspects of a plan, but also mental health and emotions. Krell (Pember 1996) and others refer to this behaviour as the P-S factor or the psycho-social factor. As Pember (1996, 201) notes "intervention should be constructive and prompt, and to be so [it] must be pre-planned".

The DPC should familiarize themselves with the emotional impact of disasters in order to recognize the need for immediate traumatic stress intervention, as well as the need for any ongoing professional help. Ideally, the DPC should have consulted with external crisis management professionals before any disaster occurs for advice and basic training in psychological first aid *(see Appendix 3.1 Sources of Information: Human Resources)*. If the disaster has involved death or major injuries, mental health professionals should be brought onsite to conduct the rehabilitation sessions. Employees identified as being at risk should have subsequent access to individual counselling. As Lystad (1991, 19) says "inattention to individual symptoms could result in overlooking very distressed individuals within an otherwise normal population".

Included here is an overview of the main areas to be considered; further resources from the health care field can be found in Pember's article (1996).

10.4.1 Critical Incident Stress Debriefing (CISD)

A CISD is a psychological and educational group process designed specifically for emergency workers with two purposes in mind. First, the CISD is designed to mitigate the impact of a critical incident on the personnel. Second, the CISD is designed to accelerate normal recovery in normal people who are experiencing the normal signs, symptoms, and reactions to totally abnormal events. (Anderson and Mattingly 1991, 316)

These debriefing sessions are ideally held 24 to 72 hours and typically only "after powerful events – not after routine situations" (Anderson and Mattingly 1991, 316). They are conducted by mental health professionals (or a trained CISD team), who lead the group in sessions designed to allow personnel to express their feelings and reactions to the disaster. These sessions are separate from the critique and assessment of the disaster plan.

10.4.2 Acute Stress Disorder

Acute stress disorder is a new medical diagnostic category in which reactions occur immediately after the event as opposed to the more cumulative reactions of post-traumatic stress disorder. The DPC must recognize this type of trauma in order to provide for staff in the disaster plan and then to respond appropriately.

Clouse and Riddell (Blythe 1996, 20) outline the cognitive and emotional reactions of people with acute stress disorder. These reactions include:

Cognitive Reactions

· disorganization and sluggishness in thinking and decision-making
· confusion/uncertainty
· lack of awareness of immediate events
· decreased concentration
· hypervigilance

Emotional Reactions

· fear
· rage
· depression/sadness
· euphoria
· panic
· reckless feelings of invulnerability

Clouse and Riddell emphasize the importance of recognizing these first wave reactions "as highly predictive of later onset of post-traumatic stress disorder."

10.4.3 Post-Traumatic Stress Disorder (PTSD)

PTSD is a long-recognized medical diagnostic category in which cognitive and emotional reactions occur subsequent to the event for a minimum of a month.

Individuals suffering from this disorder need to be identified and offered treatment to prevent any long-term after-effects. Their recovery depends on successful assessment and treatment programmes.

Phases of the Recovery Process

Vossler (1987, 11) outlines four emotional phases of disaster recovery: the heroic phase, the honeymoon phase, and longer-term, disillusionment phase and the reconstruction phase.

· The **heroic phase** takes place when the disaster hits. People may risk their lives to save the lives of others and property. In the heat of the moment, people do not question the advisability of these actions, and often do not put on protective clothing nor wait for safety clearance.

· The **honeymoon phase** follows the event and can last as long as six months. Expectations are high, reality has not yet set in and people believe that the readily available support and resources will soon return everything back to normal. This is a very productive phase, and the disaster planner should harness this optimism and the shared sense of common purpose.

· The **disillusionment phase** can occur as early as two months after the event and can last up to two years. The enormity of the situation is understood at a time when outside support may be dwindling. This phase can be characterized by anger, disappointment, anxiety, grief and physical illnesses, which may show up in the workplace as increased absenteeism, depression and employee dissatisfaction.

· The **reconstruction phase** can occur from six months to several years after the disaster. Rebuilding may be lengthy, insurance claims may drag on and people feel no sense of resolution. This phase is characterized by burn-out and loss of efficiency.

10.5 The Post-Disaster Assessment

Collectively, the DPC and the DAT should determine what scale of post-disaster assessment is required. If a full-scale investigation of the disaster is required, then considerable time and effort should be devoted to the planning and implementation of this process.

The post-disaster assessment is an analysis of the whole disaster event, focussing on the disaster planning in general and the effectiveness of the disaster plan in particular. Any recommendations identified during evaluation of the disaster, the immediate emergency response and the plan's strengths and weaknesses should be brought forward for discussion.

> The plan and the performance of all participants in disaster operations should be subjected to a candid critique as soon as possible after operations have returned to a semblance of normality... Observation of what kinds of damage actually happened (possibly different from what was believed would occur) will permit revisions to the plan and will permit mitigating actions to be implemented. (Hunter 1990, 10:16-17)

This assessment should take place after any incident, emergency or disaster that causes the plan to be fully or partially executed. The assessment would:

· Discuss lessons learned. This would serve to alert management to potential policy or operational issues that need to be addressed. It would also identify which actions and procedures facilitated, slowed down or obstructed the response, recovery and rehabilitation operations.

· Evaluate the success of any cooperative or interorganizational arrangements.

· Provide direction for follow-up action, such as facility upgrades.

· Evaluate the supply, equipment and service operations and external providers.

· Identify overall strengths or deficiencies and any need for new arrangements.

Post-Disaster Assessment Checklist

The J. Paul Getty Museum in earthquake-prone Malibu, California has developed the following set of questions for a post-emergency critique (The J. Paul Getty Museum 1992, VII:1). These questions could be adapted for use during a post-disaster assessment.

Cause
· What were the major contributing factors [of the emergency or disaster]?

Notification
· Were you given timely notice of the emergency? Of your assigned role?
· How were you notified and by whom?
· Were you given accurate and adequate information?
· How can notification procedures be improved?

Communications
· What methods of communication were used: telephones, runners, radios, other?
· If a Manager or Supervisor, did you receive a radio? Did you use it?
· Were the communications effective?

Collections Management
· Did the damage mitigation procedures and ...[recovery] operations reduce or prevent water damage, fire damage, etc.?
· How could these operations be improved?
· Were conservation efforts well coordinated and prioritized?
· Were adequate personnel available? Were they effectively deployed?
· Were...[collections] movement and temporary storage arrangements well planned and well handled?
· What kinds of specialized conservation tools and supplies were needed that were not available? Were they obtained? Did the delay play a significant role in the outcome of the incident?
· Was...[collection] damage and...[collection] movement documented in a timely manner? Were photos taken? Was the incident videotaped?

Control Room Operations
· Were operations effective?
· Were Control communications clear and concise? Were communications timely?
· Were events documented?
· Were appropriate personnel assigned to the Control Room immediately?
· How can procedures be improved?

Protective Services
· Were the security and safety of staff and visitors properly considered?
· Was the appropriate pool of equipment and supplies established?
· Were adequate personnel available? Were personnel well deployed?
· Were all operations conducted in a safe manner? Did personnel use safe methods and equipment?
· What kinds of equipment or supplies were needed that were not available? Were they obtained? Did the delay play a significant role in the outcome of the incident? Did all equipment operate properly?
· Was security of collections, buildings and ground maintained?

Media Relations
· Were the media contacted?
· Did the media contact the...[organization]?
· Did those staff in contact with media give only appropriate information?
· How can such contacts be improved?

Action Checklists
· Did you use an action checklist? Was it useful?
· How can it be improved?

Unexpected Contingencies
· Were there any special circumstances or serious unexpected problems? Were they handled appropriately?
· What other problems could have arisen? How could they have been handled?

Overall Effectiveness of Emergency Plan
· Was an emergency declared and did someone take charge?
· Was a chain of command established, clearly understood and followed?
· Were duties delegated to the appropriate people, and the necessary adjustments made?
· Were major decisions and activities documented?

Recommendations and Conclusions
· How could the incident have been avoided? Damage lessened?
· What...policies and procedures need re-evaluation?
· What specific lessons were learned in this incident?

(Reprinted by permission of The J. Paul Getty Trust)

10.6 Modifications to the Disaster Plan and Operations

> Change can come quickly if the timing is right, and the time is most often right in the immediate aftermath of a disaster (Anderson and Mattingly 1991, 319).

In the post-disaster period, pressure will likely be considerable for immediate action to prevent future disaster. The DPC should channel this support for action into carefully prepared plans.

Drawing on the post-disaster assessment and report, the organization will need to identify and plan modifications to the facility and operations. Priorities, options and costs will need to be assessed. Some of these modifications will be carried out in the short term and some will have to be planned for and implemented in the long term, depending on the severity of the disaster and the time, staff and resources that management commits to improvements. The disaster plan should then be revised accordingly.

If the post-disaster assessment identified lack of coordination with local agencies as a major stumbling block, the organization should take steps to integrate itself more fully into the local community infrastructure. This can include increased communication with local emergency agencies and attending local government meetings when policy decisions affecting your organization are on the agenda.

10.7 The Insurance Claim

Full settlement of a claim cannot be reached until all damaged materials have been recorded and their values established *(see 10.7.2)*. The extent and potential success of any further rehabilitation measures must also be estimated.

10.7.1 Assessment of Damages

The character and degree of damage must be fully assessed and documented to support the insurance claim. The insurance company and the organization share a mutual interest in minimizing costs. Recovery of irreplaceable collections and records is essential. In general, recovery costs less than replacement. In all Canadian provinces except Quebec, the laws are similar regarding responsibility for recovery and the mitigation of further loss:

> 9.(1) The insured, in the event of any loss or damage to any property insured under the contract, shall take all reasonable steps to prevent further damage to such property so damaged and to prevent damage to other property insured hereunder including, if necessary, its removal to prevent damage or further damage thereto.
>
> 9.(2) The insurer shall contribute pro rata towards any reasonable and proper expenses in connection with steps taken by the insured and required under sub-paragraph (1) of this condition according to the respective interests of the party.
>
> (*Statutes of Ontario* 1981 Chap. 218 Sec. 125/2)

In Quebec, the law appears to be less clear:

> When property insured is only partially damaged, no abandonment of the same will be allowed except with the consent of the company or its agent; and in case of removal of property to escape conflagration, the company will contribute to the loss and expense attending such act of salvage proportionately to the respective interests of the company or companies and the insured.
>
> (*Statutes of Quebec* 1974 Chap. 70 #5)

In spite of the significance of the statutory conditions for insurance policies, the terms and conditions of a policy will be designed in the context of applicable local laws, as well as the nature, needs, financial resources and risk management philosophy of the specific organization. An insurance policy is an integral part of risk management; however, the most important component is risk avoidance.

10.7.2 Proof of Loss

If the organization has experienced losses, then the insurance company requires a proof of loss form. This form outlines the circumstances of the loss, together with evidence of the loss and a declaration that the loss did not occur through any intentional act on the part of the insured. Inventory or database records are the usual evidence needed for proof of loss.

The onus is on the insured organization to fulfil the following obligations (a sample of the statutory conditions for insurance) in order to meet "proof-of-loss" provisions and start the claim procedures. As Wright (1979, 255) outlines:

> 1. Upon occurrence of any loss of or damage to the insured property, the insured shall, if the loss or damage is covered by the contract in addition to observing the requirements of conditions 9 [Salvage], 10 [Entry, Control, Abandonment] and 11 [Appraisal] of the statutory conditions [for insurance policies applying in Canada, except for Quebec]:
>
> a.) forthwith give notice thereof in writing to the insurer [on forms provided by the insurer].

b.) deliver as soon as practicable to the insurer a proof of loss verified by a statutory declaration:

    i.   giving a complete inventory of destroyed and damaged property and showing in detail quantities, costs and actual cash value and particulars of amount of loss claimed.

    ii.   stating when and how the loss occurred, and if caused by fire or explosion due to ignition how the fire or explosion originated so far as the insured knows or believes.

    iii. stating the loss did not occur through any wilful act or neglect or the procurement means or connivance of the insured.

    iv. showing the amount of other insurance and the names of other insurers.

    v.   showing the interest of the insured, and of all others in the property with particulars of all liens, encumbrances and other charges upon the property.

    vi. showing any changes in title, use, occupation, location, possession or exposures of the property since the issue of the contract.

    vii. showing the place where the property insured was at the time of loss.

c.) if required to give a complete inventory of undamaged property showing in detail quantities, cost, actual cash value.

d.) if required and if practicable produce books of accounts, warehouse receipts and stock lists, and furnish invoices and other vouchers verified by statutory declaration, and furnish a copy of the written portion of any other contract.

2. The evidence furnished under clauses (c) and (d) of sub-paragraph (1) of this condition shall not be considered proofs of loss within the meaning of conditions 12 [When Loss Payable] and 13 [Replacement, Repair] of statutory conditions...

In order to provide such proof of loss documentation careful, comprehensive pre-planning is necessary. A full inventory of loss reflecting current fair market values must be furnished by the organization. Being prepared in advance will facilitate successful recovery and rehabilitation operations. Not being prepared may result in the inability of the organization to continue its operations following a disaster, should its insurance claim be substantially or wholly denied.

(See also Appendix 3.1 Sources of Information: Insurance)

10.8 The Internal Disaster Report

Following the post-disaster assessment, the DPC and the DAT should collaborate on the preparation of the final written report, using information gathered through reports, the debriefing sessions, interviews, etc. It should summarize the disaster including observations, conclusions and recommendations for change.

The final report should:

· describe the disaster; a narrative time frame sequence could be used.

· detail any critical decisions that were made.

· outline the recovery and rehabilitation strategies chosen.

· detail any management approvals sought and received during response, recovery and rehabilitation.

· recommend modifications to the disaster plan.

· recommend modifications to the facility and operations and staff practices.

· include a detailed breakdown of costs, including those covered by the insurance claim.

· acknowledge all those who assisted throughout the disaster.

Documentation that should accompany the report could include:

· written reports from staff or external emergency and service providers.

· damage assessments.

· news releases and internal communications.

· photographs, slides and video tapes of the disaster, work in progress, recovery treatments, etc.

· receipts, invoices, etc.

· other correspondence.

This report and its accompanying documentation will aid in seeking assistance from government agencies if a disaster has been declared. It will also serve as a training aid for present and future staff and volunteers. The organization may wish to submit a written account of the disaster to a professional journal, to add to the body of knowledge on disaster planning and recovery.

10.9 Recognition and Appreciation

In the desire to return to "business as usual", the organization should take time to consider the human element. It is critical to recognize that the staff members who may have now fully returned to their routine responsibilities were the same individuals who shared and participated in a stressful and perhaps lengthy and dangerous event. As a result, a strong sense of personal and organizational purpose and commitment will likely have developed. It is prudent to acknowledge and build on this momentum, especially where the organization must implement long-term rehabilitation strategies, and also to effect overall organizational recovery.

Just as the plan was drawn up and implemented by people, people may have given 'above and beyond' in support of their organization. As Stasak (1996, 29) says:

> A [disaster]...plan is really a people plan. People design it, people test and maintain it and it's people who make the plan work when needed.

The dedication and hard work of all involved should be acknowledged including staff, volunteers, and personnel from emergency services and external companies. Appreciation can take many forms and organization-wide events can provide a venue for collective recognition of local heroes, as well as for the necessary commemoration of losses.

Acknowledgement should also be expressed on an individual basis. Such credit and appreciation recognizes people for their specific sacrifices, dedication and contributions. For ultimately, the organization owes its successful recovery to all those individuals who came to its aid in the time of disaster.

Appendix 1: First National Summit on Heritage and Risk Preparedness in Canada, Quebec City, Quebec. September 1996. Final Declaration

Given the following

Challenges

The ever present and increasing vulnerability of Canadian and world cultural heritage in the face of disasters and other events threatening the continuing life of that heritage;

The generally poor state of preparedness for the protection of Canadian cultural heritage in times of emergency;

The administrative obstacles limiting effective coordination among authorities responsible both for cultural heritage and for emergency response at federal, provincial and municipal levels, and

Opportunities

Existing emergency response infrastructure and mechanisms in Canada capable of integrating concern for cultural heritage, and the evident interest shown by officials responsible for emergency response to respond to concerns for increasing care and attention given to cultural heritage;

The leadership of some Canadian institutions (e.g. National Archives of Canada) in developing preparedness models of value and interest for other groups and institutions;

The focus offered by the existing international Blue Shield initiative for improving the situation in Canada, given:

- The key role played by Canadians in the international movement (that is in the Inter-Agency Task Force Round Tables on the subject initiated by ICOMOS in 1992, and held regularly in Paris since then);
- The interest of UNESCO and ICOMOS in developing a "Canadian model" of risk preparedness;
- The potential offered by the creation of the International Committee of the Blue Shield whose first act was to respond to the Saguenay floods.

Therefore, we the participants of the First National Summit on Heritage and Risk Preparedness in Canada held at the Musée de la Civilisation in Québec, on September 16-17, 1996, agree to pursue

Awareness

Increase appreciation of the nature and value of cultural heritage among those responsible for heritage and emergency response, and increase knowledge and understanding of potential risks and associated impacts of disasters of natural, technological and social origin threatening heritage;

Increase mutual awareness of emergency response management concerns and cultural heritage management concerns:

- Affirm importance of cultural heritage for those threatened by loss;
- Recognize strong link between effective heritage protection and clear identification of heritage values in the built environment;
- Better continuing appreciation of the concerns of the public, the youth and the media;
- Improve understanding of local authorities of concerns for cultural heritage protection.

Collaboration

Establish permanent structural links among all those involved with cultural heritage conservation (archives, libraries, museums, built environment) and with emergency response authorities (civil security, emergency response, public security, defence):

- Identification of potential partners (governments, institutions, corporations and individuals) and their interests;
- Developing network(s) for exchange among those concerned with these issues at a local, national and international levels;
- Ensuring effective communication among network members (e.g. electronic mail newslists);
- Providing occasional forums for exchange among network members, including follow-up to this Summit meeting;
- Developing Task Force/Working Group to guide collaboration following the Summit.

Appendix 1: First National Summit

Building local capacity

Clarify roles and responsibilities of local authorities in heritage protection (decision-making structures in times of emergency; policies for territorial environmental planning and management);

Improve capacity of local authorities, services and local institutions to improve care for cultural heritage threatened by disasters:

·   Integrate concern for cultural heritage in existing structures for risk management and emergency response (for example, in methods of risk assessment, intervention planning and implementation);

·   Improved knowledge of appropriate "models" in other contexts;

·   Improved training for responsible officials and managers;

·   Increased opportunities for volunteer participation.

Strengthening enabling framework for heritage protection

At local, regional, provincial, national and international levels:

·   Develop and install early warning detection and surveillance systems;

·   Improved databases of experiences and success models for consultation; improve accessibility to databases;

·   Ensure commitment of authorities concerned to mobilization of appropriate professional experience in times of disaster;

·   Development of emergency response mobilization plans.

From Tremain, David. 1996. The Blue Shield Programme in Canada. *IIC-CG Bulletin* 21(3):40-42.

Appendix 2

Appendix 2: Emergency Preparedness Canada (EPC)

1.0 Introduction

Emergency Preparedness Canada is a public service agency operating within the Department of National Defense that co-ordinates federal emergency preparedness for peace and war. Emergency preparedness within the federal government is based on coordinated efforts of all federal departments and agencies, under the guidance and stimulus of Emergency Preparedness Canada.

EPC provides direct support to the Minister Responsible for Emergency Preparedness. EPC staff report to the Deputy Chief of the Department of National Defence.

It has a staff of 98, 56 based at headquarters in Ottawa, 18 at the College in Arnprior with the remaining 24 allocated among EPC's regional offices located in each provincial capital.

1.1 Background

Emergency Preparedness Canada began as a civil defence organization in 1948, when civil defence measures were reinstituted in most countries that are now part of NATO. In 1951 in was transferred from the Department of National Defence to that of National Health and Welfare. In 1959, it was absorbed into a second civil emergency planning organization, known as the Emergency Measures Organization (EMO), created two years earlier in the Privy Council Office to ensure continuity of government in Canada through a nuclear attack on North American. EMO thus assumed sole responsibility for all civil aspects of defence policy.

Following a 1966 Cabinet decision giving it the additional responsibility of providing and co-ordinating the federal response to any peacetime disaster, EMO was moved from the Privy Council Office to a succession of different departments, returning to that Office in 1974 as Emergency Planning Canada (EPC). This latest change also signalled a shift in emphasis from wartime to peacetime emergencies.

The Minister of National Defence was named Minister Responsible for Emergency Planning (MREP) in 1984. On July 1, 1986, Emergency Planning Canada's name was changed to Emergency Preparedness Canada. In 1988, the *Emergency Preparedness Act* made EPC a separate agency reporting to Parliament through the MREP, but the organization was returned to the fold of the Department of National Defence as a result of government streamlining measures announced in the 1992 Budget.

1.2 Mandate

Emergency Preparedness Canada's role, on behalf of the Minister Responsible for Emergency Preparedness, is to advance civil preparedness in Canada for emergencies of all types, including the four types of national emergencies set out in the Emergencies Act. This is accomplished by facilitating and coordinating, among government institutions and in cooperation with provincial governments, foreign governments and international organizations, the development of civil emergency plans and assisting when required, in their implementation.

In addition to it's mandate for coordination of preparedness and response, EPC has the primary federal responsibility to advance the state of emergency preparedness in Canada in cooperation with provinces and to provide financial programs for the attainment of a reasonably uniform standard of national preparedness and alleviating costs of post disaster recovery.

1.3 Authority

Emergency preparedness and response in Canada are shared responsibilities of individuals, corporations and governments. The division of responsibility amongst these shareholders is established in a wide range of legislation, regulations and by-laws, as well as custom and practice. The division of responsibility between governments is founded on the *Constitution Act of Canada*.

This *Act,* amongst other things, defines the areas in which federal and provincial governments can enact legislation. Existing federal legislation and cabinet decisions define the regulatory, organizational, and procedural framework within which federal preparedness and response is conducted.

Prior to the passage in 1988 of new, comprehensive emergency legislation, Canada did not have such legislation at the federal level. There were a few federal laws in place that included provisions for emergency response to particular circumstances, such as oil shortages and spills of hazardous materials. The only general instrument of emergency empowerment available to the federal government was a piece of legislation called the *War Measures Act.* As its name implies, this piece of legislation was designed for a wartime contingency and gave the government virtually unrestricted powers to manage the resources of the nation, both human and material, and to take whatever action it thought necessary to control the situation. Those powers and the implication of an extension of such powers in the hands of an unrestrained government raised strong fears in the minds of many Canadians concerned with the preservation of civil liberties. Provincial governments were also concerned about potential federal intrusions into provincial areas of jurisdiction. A lengthy debate ensured that finally led to the passage of new, comprehensive emergency legislation in 1988.

The new legislation which is contained in two Acts (The *Emergencies Preparedness Act* and The *Emergencies Act*) sets out Emergency Preparedness Canada's responsibilities for emergency preparedness and response. Further responsibilities may be designated by cabinet decisions related to crisis management.

1.3.1 The Emergency Preparedness Act

This Act, spells out what the federal government and its institutions need to do to ensure that they are always ready to discharge their responsibilities in emergencies. It does this by defining the responsibilities of Emergency Preparedness Canada, and charging every Minister of the Crown with a responsibility to make plans for events that may fall under his/her mandate as well as to make plans to provide services and expertise in assistance to other governments and federal departments.

The responsibilities, as fulfilled by EPC on behalf of the MREP are:

· Advance civil preparedness.

· Develop policies and programs.

· Encourage and support provincial and local preparedness.

· Provide education and training.

· Enhance public awareness.

· analyze and evaluate risks and conduct preparedness research.

· Coordinate and support development and testing of civil emergency plans by government institutions.

· Develop arrangements for the continuity of constitutional government.

· Monitor and report on civil emergencies.

· Support plans implementation and federal assistance.

1.3.2 The Emergencies Act

This second Act, is contingency legislation that provides the means whereby:

· a *national emergency* may be declared;

· provides for extraordinary regulations and orders that may be authorized to deal with it;

· specifies the consultation that must occur with provincial authorities;

· lists the safeguards and constraints on Government actions in declaring and acting in a national emergency; and,

· details the provisions for compensating persons or organizations that suffer loss as a result of invocation of the *Act*.

It is a multi-part statute that carefully describes four types of national emergencies *(see 2.3)* and appropriate exceptional powers that *may* be authorized subject to democratic safeguards, for limited periods, where all other legislation is found to be inadequate to meet the demand for federal government action in a *national emergency.*

The Emergencies Act envisages that provincial governments would be responsible for managing most national emergencies of the public welfare and public order type, and thus federal government planning concentrates on supporting them in that role.

1.4 The Principles of Emergency Preparedness in Canada

Emergency preparedness and response in Canada are based on the following four basic principles:

· Lowest level competent to respond

· All-hazards approach to planning

· Emergency plans and arrangements based on existing organizational structures and procedures

· Centralized direction and coordination – decentralized implementation and response

First, each and every Canadian is charged with their own personal emergency preparedness. As a crisis expands beyond individual capability the responsibility devolves, as appropriate to the situation, on local (municipal) governments, the provincial jurisdictions or, and usually only in the direst circumstances, on the federal government.

Second, through the so-called "all-hazards" approach to emergency preparedness EPC strives to optimize planning and response resources by basing our planning effort on the *effects* of disasters, rather than the *causes*. This enables us, where possible, to develop a generic set of plans that has applicability in more than one circumstance.

Third, planning is developed on a building-block approach whereby emergency plans and arrangements are built, to the extent possible, in a graduated fashion upon existing plans, organizations and arrangements, thereby creating as little change as possible in time of emergency.

Finally, through Emergency Preparedness Canada and its Provincial Emergency Measures counterparts, elements of centralized coordination are provided to the sectoral expertise resident in Departments and Ministries that facilitates planning and response for emergencies that are multi-dimensional in nature.

1.5 How the System Works

Following the practice that has evolved in Canada, and in keeping with the country's legal and constitutional framework, responsibility for initial action in an emergency lies with the individual – who should be prepared to do what is reasonable possible to protect life and property. The different orders of government only step in as their resources and response capabilities are needed to control and mitigate the situation:

- If the individual cannot cope, the municipal services respond. Mayors and other elected heads of local governments are responsible for ensuring that emergency plans exist within their municipalities and that they are exercised regularly. Most emergencies occur within, and are dealt with effectively by, a municipality;

- If the municipality cannot manage to respond effectively, the province or territory is expected to come to its aid. Provincial and territorial governments are responsible for coordinating the interface with the municipalities; and

- If a province or territory needs help, the federal government's aid is formally requested, usually – but not necessarily – through **Emergency Preparedness Canada**. The federal government intervenes only when asked or when the emergency clearly impacts on areas of federal jurisdiction (e.g., floods or fires on federal lands, air crashes on federal airports), or in a national emergency.

2.0 Types of Emergencies

Emergencies comprise a spectrum of incidents progressing from the small to the large, the slightly consequential to the catastrophic. They also progress from localized to multi-jurisdictional involvement. The categorization of the types of emergency described below is based upon jurisdictional responsibility and not upon the relative severity of the emergency.

2.1 Provincial Emergencies

It is within the jurisdiction of the provincial government that most emergencies occur. The Emergency Preparedness Act defines a provincial emergency as:

> "an emergency occurring in a province if the province or a local authority in the province has the primary responsibility for dealing with the emergency".

Such emergencies tend to be events affecting only a single province and can usually be dealt with by the application of municipal and/or provincial resources, (fire, police, health, social services, etc.). Provinces may request federal assistance as circumstances warrant to supplement their own response capabilities.

2.2 Federal Emergencies

Emergencies are not "provincial" in nature when they occur outside a province (e.g., in Canadian territorial waters or in other countries) or if they impact *primarily* on areas of federal jurisdiction (e.g. federal property, clientele, entrusted natural resources and statutory or regulatory authority). Overall responsibility for managing such situations belongs to the appropriate federal authorities. The definition of a provincial emergency is also exceeded by emergencies which affect more than one province at a time. While there is no comparable definition for these non-provincial emergencies in the Emergency Preparedness Act, they may conveniently be thought of as "federal emergencies".

2.3 National Emergencies

At the highest extreme of the emergency spectrum will be situations so severe as to necessitate measures which exceed both provincial competencies and the normal authorities of the federal government. These "national emergencies" involve the concerted and closely coordinated efforts of all levels of government as well as the private sector.

The Emergencies Act authorizes the taking of "special temporary measures to ensure safety and security during national emergencies". It defines a national emergency as "an urgent and critical situation of a temporary nature that:

- seriously endangers the lives, health or safety of Canadians and is of such proportions or nature as to exceed the capacity or authority of a province to deal with it, or

- seriously threatens the ability of the Government of Canada to preserve the sovereignty, security and territorial integrity of Canada and that cannot be effectively dealt with under any other law of Canada."

The Act specifies four carefully circumscribed types of national emergencies, as follows:

Public Welfare Emergencies: are the more than 60 kinds of natural or human-made disasters from floods to nuclear accidents including severe natural disasters or major accidents affecting public welfare, that are beyond the capacity or authority of a province to manage.

Public Order Emergencies: which constitute threats to the internal security of Canada, such as insurrection or acts of terrorism; again beyond provincial authority or capacity.

International Emergencies: external acts that threaten Canada's sovereignty, security or territorial integrity, or those of its allies.

War Emergencies: real or imminent armed conflict against Canada or its allies.

The first two categories fall mostly within provincial jurisdiction, the federal government intervening only when invited or when the situation impinges directly on its own jurisdiction. However, the federal government would have the lead role in any international or war emergency, as these would involve such key areas of federal jurisdiction as defence, foreign affairs and national security.

3.0   Federal/Provincial Cooperation

Policy liaison between the Federal and Provincial governments is maintained by annual meetings both at the Ministerial and senior official levels. This liaison paves the way for staff level cooperation and the detailed development of national emergency arrangements. Cooperation between the two orders of government has been formalized through the signature of individual Memoranda of Understanding with each province which detail the respective areas of responsibility.

Provincial emergency planning is led by provincial emergency measures organizations which are, by and large, very similar to the federal model. Each of the provinces and territories have their own emergency legislation that comprehensively deals with emergency management issues within their boundaries. This includes the stipulation of local government responsibilities as well as those of the provincial government and its various Ministries. They vary somewhat from province to province, with some such

as that in Alberta, Quebec and British Columbia being quite mandatory in nature (e.g., all towns and municipalities *must*, by law, have an emergency plan and exercise it on a regular basis), to others such as that of Ontario that offer guidance (towns and municipalities are encouraged to have an emergency plan).

A common operating practice in responding in support of emergencies under provincial jurisdiction is for a federal lead agency with representation from supporting departments to establish themselves as part of, or collocated with, the provincial operations centre.

4.0   Financial Assistance

The federal government, and specifically EPC, assists the Provincial efforts in a number of ways. First there are three financial contribution mechanisms:

4.1   Disaster Financial Assistance Arrangements (DFAA)

Since 1970, the federal government has provided financial assistance in accordance with a formula based on provincial population at the request of the province or territory. The program was established to assist the provincial governments with the cost of dealing with a disaster where those costs would place undue burden on the provincial or territorial economy.

Generally payments are made to restore public works to their pre-disaster condition and to facilitate the restoration of basic, essential, personal property of private citizens, farmsteads, and small businesses.

EPC administers the Disaster Financial Assistance Arrangements for the federal government. When cost-sharing is arranged with a province, the EPC regional director is usually designated as the representative of the federal government. Their responsibilities include: arrangements for damage assessment, detailed interpretation of guidelines, a general surveillance of private damage claims and the development of joint federal-provincial teams to review claims for agricultural and public sector damage.

4.1.1   The Funding Formula

Under the formula, no sharing occurs unless provincial expenditures *exceed* an amount equal to $1 per capita of the provincial population. When a province's expenditures exceed this level, the amount of federal financial assistance payable to a province is determined as follows: 50% of the next $2 per capita of provincial expenditures eligible for cost sharing; 75% of the next $2 per capita and 90% of the remainder.

Federal Post-Disaster Financial Assistance (per Capita sharing)	
Provincial Eligible Expenditures	Federal Share
First $1 per capita	Nil
Next $2 per capita	50%
Next $2 per capita	75%
Remainder	90%

4.2 Joint Emergency Preparedness Program (JEPP)

The Joint Emergency Preparedness Program is a jointly-funded federal/provincial program, administered by EPC. The federal government cost-shares projects with provincial governments (and through them, local governments) to do planning and training and to acquire emergency equipment.

Through the JEPP program, the federal government provides financial contributions to provinces and territories to assist in meeting the costs of projects aimed at enhancing the national emergency response capability. JEPP was conceived to encourage and support co-operation among the federal and provincial/territorial governments in working toward a national capability to meet emergencies of all types with a reasonable uniform standard of emergency response. The program envisages a series of cooperative ventures with each party assuming its emergency responsibilities through appropriate contributions.

In order to keep current with amendments in the program, it is recommended to consult the JEPP Annual Update Instructions available through the EPC regional offices.

4.2.1 The Funding Formula

A funding formula has been developed to ensure that each province has access to the program to help develop a minimum emergency preparedness capability. These funds are not allocated to the provinces to manage directly, but are set aside or "earmarked" for projects within their jurisdiction with final approval remaining with the EPC Executive Director. Funds are determined by adding 10 cents per provincial capita to a base fund of $150,000. Provinces are advised of the earmarked amount annually through JEPP instructions. In addition to the earmarked funds earmarked for individual provinces, an amount is also available, for funding other projects on a national comparative merit basis (referred to as "regular" funds).

4.2.2 Project Proposals

Projects proposed for JEPP funding must meet rigorous requirements, the first of which are to meet the following federal objectives:

- achieving an appropriate and reasonably uniform level of national civil preparedness for emergencies;
- encouraging and supporting provincial civil preparedness and through the provinces, community civil preparedness;
- providing education and training related to civil preparedness for emergencies;
- enhancing public awareness and understanding of matters related to civil preparedness for emergencies;
- analyzing and evaluating civil preparedness for emergencies and conducting related research.

A series of national priorities are established from time to time through consultation with provincial officials and these priorities are used to guide determination of the relative merit of individual projects.

4.3 Workers Compensation Protection

The federal and all of the twelve provincial/territorial governments have undertaken to extend Workers Compensation protection to volunteers engaged in emergency response. These agreements which have been in effect since the 1960s, provide for sharing the cost of compensation paid to registered emergency services workers who are injured or die performing their duties. The federal government reimburses 75% of payments made by the Provincial/Territorial Workers' Compensation Boards. New agreements are currently being negotiated.

5.0 Other Resources

- **EPC Regional Offices** EPC maintains regional offices in the provincial capitals as focal points for the development of cooperative and compatible crisis management procedures in concert with their federal and provincial colleagues, as well as with federal and state authorities in adjacent parts of the United States. *(See Appendix 3.2 Sources of Assistance: Disaster Planning and Recovery – National, Provincial and Territorial Government Organizations)*

- **Government Emergency Book (GEB)** is a key document in the framework for federal emergency preparedness and response in Canada, providing the link between federal emergency legislation and policy and the development and implementation of specific plans and arrangements. EPC maintains the GEB on behalf of the federal government.

This reference document is used to help provide operational guidance for those emergencies that may require federal Cabinet involvement by providing a framework to guide and coordinate the planning and response of the Government of Canada to emergencies. It identifies actions that would need to be considered for implementation in response to a developing or existing emergency, either domestic or international.

- **Network of Interdepartmental Committees** which coordinate the emergency preparedness program at the national level. At the highest level, the Emergency Preparedness Advisory Committee (EPAC) provides program policy guidance and direction. Other multi-sectoral committees include: the Interdepartmental Coordinating Committee (ICC) and the Interdepartmental Exercise Coordinating Committee (IECC). In addition to these, there are a number of sector-specific committees including: industrial production, human resources, strategic minerals, vital points and transportation resources.

- **Non-Government Organizations (NGOs)** Although not federal agencies or part of EPC, these organizations play an indispensable part in the response to disasters and consequently are included as active participants in the development of response plans at the national level. The three NGOs most involved at the federal level of preparedness are: the Salvation Army, the Saint John Ambulance and the Canadian Red Cross. Their expertise and resources are in great demand at the provincial/territorial and local levels where their work in dealing with and caring for people affected directly by a disaster.

- **The Canadian Emergency Preparedness College** in Arnprior, Ontario, offers courses in various aspects of emergency preparedness and response and is administered by EPC. It conducts about 30 courses a year for approximately 3000 officials who come mostly from municipalities.

6.0   EPC Activities

6.1   Vital Points Program

Currently under review, this program was established in 1938 to identify those facilities, manufacturers and services critical to the war effort.

Category I are those deemed critical to the functioning of the nation as a whole. Due to their limited number and unique nature, the Solicitor General is charged with their security.

Category II and III Vital Points are identified by appropriate departmental officials and their proprietors are responsible for their security.

6.2   Business Resumption Planning (BRP)

Business Resumption Planning is defined as planning to ensure the continued availability of essential services, programs and operations, including all resources involved. Business resumption planning prepares government institutions for recovery from contingencies, that may interrupt an operation or affect service or program delivery. Two EPC publications: *Business Resumption Planning – A Guide* and Treasury Board Publication: *Business Resumption Planning – Technical Standards. (See also 5.8)*

6.3   Major Industrial Accidents Council of Canada (MIACC)

In 1984 the world's most devastating chemical accident occurred in Bhopal, India causing over 2000 deaths and tens of thousands of injuries. This even caused the creation, in Canada, of a joint industry/government review committee to examine the potential for a Bhopal-like accident in Canada; to review existing measures taken by industry and government to prevent industrial accidents; and to review the collective ability of industry and government to respond to such accidents.

The committee report, released in 1986, concluded that a possibility of major accident involving hazardous substances did exist, however, the probability and impact could be significantly reduced with certain improvements. One such improvement was the bringing together of experts from all sectors dedicated to promoting excellence in the prevention, preparedness and response to major industrial accidents involving hazardous substances. The organization that evolved was the Major Industrial Accidents Coordinating committee, later renamed MIACC.

MIACC is comprised of four elements: an elected Board comprising members from federal and provincial governments and industry which carry out the decision making and executive functions; an office to handle the administrative tasks of Council; a number of Working Groups to accomplish the detailed work; and, the membership at large which reviews the work of MIACC at the Annual General Meeting.

6.4   Evaluation and Analysis (DEval)

The EPC Directorate of Evaluation and Analysis (DEval) provides scientific consultant services to support EPC decision makers, emergency operations, and staff officers on a wide range of emergency preparedness problems and issues. When appropriate, emergency preparedness projects are also undertaken in conjunction with other government departments or outside agencies who have an interest or responsibility in emergency preparedness.

DEval projects include:

- Participation as Technical Analysis Group facilitators and as evaluators in the CANATEX 2 national earthquake exercise.
- Creation of three database tools for the communication, and/or monitoring, and/or analysis of information on:
- the Joint Emergency Preparedness Program;
- the EPC Digest Index and other emergency information services;
- Canadian disasters.
- Participation and coordination in a Natural Hazards project with the National Atlas Information Service and other government agencies, as well as the Insurance Bureau of Canada. An early phase of this project will create a map illustrating Canada's natural hazards. A later phase will introduce natural hazard representations which can be used by emergency preparedness officials for analysis or policy purposes. The most detailed phase (long-term) will coordinate detailed natural hazard information from a variety of sources for research purposes.

6.5   Public Information from EPC

- *Emergency Preparedness Digest* A quarterly magazine for those in the field of emergency preparedness and response.
- Fact sheets, self-help booklets and videos for the general public on emergency preparedness and response in situations such as: floods, earthquakes, winter storms, winter power failures, tornadoes and other kinds of severe storms.
- Public service announcements on radio and TV on the need to prepare for emergencies.
- The Manual on National Emergency Arrangements on Public Information and an alert/contact list of public information officials in key federal and provincial government agencies is maintained and updated by EPC so the Government can provide timely, consistent, life-saving information and advice to the public in a national crisis.
- SAFEGUARD is a national public recognition program initiated in 1995 by EPC to increase public awareness of emergency preparedness in Canada.

    Some projects resulting from partnerships with governmental, non-governmental and private-sector organizations involved in emergency preparedness and response include: public information booklets, a radio and television public service announcement

campaign and exhibits at conferences and expositions.

- EPC Websites *(see Appendix 3.2 Sources of Assistance: Disaster Planning and Recovery – National, Provincial and Territorial Government Organizations).*

Text adapted and printed by permission of Emergency Preparedness Canada.

Appendix 3:   Resources

Appendix 3: Resources

This appendix covers resources on many aspects of disaster planning, including Canadian providers on a national basis, as well as the United States and a number of international entries. It does not cover local community sources. The appendix is divided into sources of: information; assistance; facilities and services; and, supplies and equipment.

This listing is provided for information, and does not imply endorsement or a recommendation, nor does the omission of a supplier indicate censure. It should be noted that many of the service companies have been involved in disaster recovery for archives, libraries and record centres, and are more likely to understand the specialized requirements of these organizations and their collections.

Internet sources are also provided - users are cautioned about the unmoderated nature of some of this information.

3.1 Sources of Information

The following institutions, organizations, associations and Internet sites provide information on a variety of aspects of disaster planning, prevention, preparedness, response, recovery and rehabilitation. The resources are divided by subject and listed in alphabetical order.

• Armed Conflict

See **Appendix 2: Emergency Preparedness Canada** and **Appendix 3.2 Sources of Assistance: Disaster Planning and Recovery - National, Provincial and Territorial Government Organizations.**

Blue Shield Preparedness and Emergency Response Program
International Council on Monuments and Sites (ICOMOS)
See entry under **3.1 Sources of Information: Conservation and Disasters.**

UNESCO (United Nations Educational, Scientific and Cultural Organization). See entry foe **UNESCO** under **3.1 Sources of Information: Professional Associations.**
Emergency Programme for the Protection of Vital Records in the Event of Armed Conflict
http://mirror-us.unesco.org/webworld.archives/sro-citra/intro.html
Legal Protection for Cultural Heritage
URL: http://mirror-us.unesco.org/culture/legal protection/index.html

• Business Continuity Planning

See **Disaster Planning and Recovery Journals, Education and Training** and **Professional Associations.**

• Conservation and Disasters

See also entries for **Canadian Conservation Institute, National Archives of Canada** and **National Library of Canada** under **3.2 Sources of Assistance: Disasters and Conservation.**

American Institute for Conservation of Historic and Artistic Works (AIC)
See entry for AIC under **Appendix 3.1 Sources of Information: Professional Associations**
- AIC Disaster Recovery Page
URL: http://aic.stanford.edu/disaster
- Foundation of American Institute for Conservation (FAIC) Referral Service
Tel: 202-452-9546
Fax: 202-452-9328
Referral service of conservators.

Blue Shield Preparedness and Emergency Response Program
International Council on Monuments and Sites (ICOMOS)
75 rue de Temple
75005 Paris, France
Tel: 33-1-42773576
Fax: 33-1-42775742
URL: http://www.icomos.org/blue_shield/
Taking its name from the Hague Convention on the protection of cultural property during armed conflict, the international Blue Shield Program covers cultural heritage at risk as a result of any disaster, natural or manmade.

Canadian Association for the Conservation of Cultural Property (CAC) and **Canadian Association of Professional Conservators (CAPC)**
See entries for CAC and CAPC under **Appendix 3.1 Sources of Information: Professional Associations**
Can provide assistance with selecting a conservator. CAPC maintains registry of professional conservators.

Conservation Information Network (CIN)
Canadian Heritage Information Network (CHIN)
Department of Canadian Heritage
Les Terrasses de la Chaudière
15 Eddy Street, 15-4-A
Hull, Québec K1A 0M5
Tel: 1-800-520-2446 (North America)
1-819-994-1200 (International)
Fax: 819-994-9555
E-mail: service@chin.gc.ca
URL: http://www.chin.gc.ca/Resources/Research-Ref/Reference_Info/e_reference.html
Coordinated effort between the Canadian Conservation Institute, Conservation Analytical Laboratory of the Smithsonian Institution, ICCROM, ICOMOS, ICOM, the Getty Conservation Institute and the Canadian Heritage Information Network. Network features three online conservation databases (Bibliographic Conservation Information Network, Materials Conservation Information Network and a suppliers' conservation information network) and an electronic mail system. Access provided on a subscription basis.
CHIN is a special operating agency with the federal Department of Canadian Heritage that collaborates with the heritage community and others to provide heritage services to Canadians.

Conservation OnLine (CoOL)
URL: http://palimpsest.stanford.edu/
Listserv subscription:
consdist-request@lindy.stanford.edu
Most important source of on-line preservation information. Broad coverage of topics pertaining to the preservation and conservation of library, archive and museum materials. Listserv available on subscription basis.
- CoOL Disaster Preparation and Response
URL: http://palimpsest.stanford.edu/bytopic/disasters
Selected reprints from variety of sources.

Getty Conservation Institute (GCI)
1200 Getty Center Drive, Suite 700
Los Angeles, California 90049-1684 U.S.A.
Tel: 310-440-7325
Fax: 310-440-7702
URL: http://www.getty.edu/gci
Operating program of the J. Paul Getty Trust. Seeks to develop, apply and make available appropriate solutions to conservation problems through research, training, field work and the exchange of information.

International Center for the Study of the Preservation and Restoration of Cultural Property (ICCROM)
Via di San Michele 13
I-00153 Rome, Italy
Tel: 39-6-5555531
Fax: 39-6-5553349
URL: http://www.iccrom.org
Autonomous scientific intergovernmental organization representing member states and associate members worldwide. Promotes heritage awareness and the preservation, restoration and preventive conservation of historic buildings, archaeological, sites, museum collections and library and archival material.

International Committee of the Blue Shield (ICBS)
See **Blue Shield Preparedness and Emergency Program** above.
See 1.3.6 for description of the ICBS.

Library of Congress
101 Independence Avenue SE
Washington, D.C. 20540 U.S.A.
Tel: 202-707-5000
URL: http://lcweb.loc.gov/preserv/preserve.html
http://marvel.loc.gov
Serves as the research arm of Congress. Recognized as the national library of the United States.
- National Preservation Program Office
Library of Congress
Room LM-G21
Washington, D.C. 20540 U.S.A.
Tel: 202-707-5213
Fax: 202-707-3434
E-mail: nppo@loc.gov
URL: http://lcweb.loc.gov/preserv/preserve.html
Emergency preparedness:
http://lcweb.loc.gov/preserv/prepare.html
Can provide disaster response and recovery information and advice.

Appendix 3: Resources

National Archives and Records Administration (NARA)
7th & Pennsylvania Avenue N.W.
Washington, D.C. 20408 U.S.A.
Tel: 202-501-5400
URL: http://www.nara.gov/
Government agency responsible for overseeing management of the records of the U.S. federal government.
- NARA Preservation Polices and Services Division
8601 Adephi Road
College Park, Maryland 20740-6001 U.S.A.
Tel: 301-713-6705
Fax: 301-713-6653
URL: http://www.nara.gov/nara/preserva/
Can provide disaster response and recovery information and advice.

National Historical Publications and Records Commission (NHPRC)
National Archives and Records Administration (NARA)
700 Pennsylvania Avenue N.W., Room 106
Washington, D.C. 20408-0001 U.S.A.
Tel: 202-501-5610
Fax: 202-501-5601
E-mail: nhprc@arch1.nara.gov
URL: http://www.nara.gov/nara/nhprc/
Grant-making affiliate of NARA. Federal funding agency assisting with records management, archives and document editing projects.

National Institute for the Conservation of Cultural Property (NIC)
602 - 3299 K Street, NW
Washington, D.C. 20007 U.S.A.
Tel: 202-625-1495
Fax: 202-625-1485
URL: http://www.nic.org
Membership of leading museums, libraries, archives and preservation organizations serves as a national forum for conservation and preservation activities in the U.S. Provides leadership and coordination to promote and facilitate preservation of the nation's heritage.

National Media Laboratory (NML)
3M Center
Building 235-1N-17
St. Paul, Minnesota 55144 U.S.A.
Tel: 612-733-3546
Fax: 612-733-4340
URL: http://www.nml.org/About NTA/About NML/
One of the U.S. National Technology Alliance partners, hosted by 3M. Industry resource supporting the U.S. government in evaluation, development and deployment of advanced storage media and systems.

National Park Service (NPS)
U.S. Department of the Interior
1849 C Street NW
Washington, D.C. 20240 U.S.A.
Tel: 202-208-6843
URL: http://www.nps.gov
Federal bureau responsible for promotion and regulation of national parks, including conservation of scenery and historic objects.

National Trust for Historic Preservation
1785 Massachusetts Avenue, NW
Washington, D.C. 20036 U.S.A.
Tel: 202-588-6000
        1-800-944-6847
URL: http://www.nationaltrust.org/
Non-profit organization responsible for providing leadership, advocacy and education related to historic site preservation. Variety of services provided, i.e. department of historic sites includes preservation programming.

Northeast Document Conservation Center (NDCC)
100 Brickstone Square
Andover, Massachusetts 01810-1494 U.S.A.
Tel: 508-470-1010 (24 hours)
Fax: 508-475-6021
URL: http://www.nedcc.org/
Largest U.S. facility specializing in paper-based conservation. National and international resource for conservation treatment and preservation education. Offers 24 hour/day emergency telephone assistance programme (not generally onsite assistance).

U.S. National Task Force on Emergency Response
602-3299 K Street NW
Washington, D.C. 20007 U.S.A
Tel: 1-888-979-2233
URL: http://www.nic.org/Emergency/Emergency.html
See 1.3.7 for description of the Task Force.

WAAC Newsletter
URL: http://palimpsest.stanford.edu/waac
Articles on disaster prevention, response and mitigation. WAAC (Western Association of Art Conservation) is a non-profit regional membership organization of professional conservators.

• Disaster Planning and Recovery Journals

See also Disaster-Related Periodicals at the Natural Hazards Center at the University of Colorado, Boulder Website
(URL: http://www.Colorado.EDU/hazards/info source2.html)

Contingency Planning & Management (For Business Preparedness and Recovery)
Witter Publishing Corporation
84 Park Avenue
Flemington, New Jersey 08822 U.S.A.
Tel: 908-788-0343
Fax: 908-788-3782
E-mail: WitterPub@aol.com
Dedicated to coverage of all aspects of contingency planning and management, and business continuity.

Disaster Prevention and Management - An International Journal
Emerald
60 -62 Toller Lane
Bradford, West Yorkshire BD8 9YB England
Tel: 44-12-74785202
Fax: 44-12-74785202
Journal dedicated to planning and implementation of effective disaster and loss prevention, damage mitigation and emergency action services in all areas.

Disaster Recovery Journal
Systems Support Group Inc.
P.O. Box 510110
St. Louis, Missouri 63151 U.S.A.
Tel: 314-894-0276
Fax: 314-894-7474
URL: http://www.drj.com/
Journal dedicated to business continuity, with focus on data systems. Also offers other products and services, i.e., disaster recovery videos, disaster recovery directory and directory on-line. Sponsors world's largest business continuity conference.

Emergency Preparedness Digest
Journal published by Emergency Preparedness Canada (EPC) covering whole spectrum of the emergency measures community. EPC is the federal agency operating within the Ministry of National Defense responsible for coordinating civil emergency planning across Canada.
See **Emergency Preparedness Canada** entry under **3.2 Sources of Assistance: Disaster Planning and Recovery.**
See Appendix 2 for details of EPC mandate, services and publications.

• Disaster Planning and Recovery Software

Most available software is directed toward business resumption planning. Modification of an existing software could facilitate the planning process in an archives, library or record centre.

See surveys of PC Based Software and Mainframe Software (*Disaster Recovery Journal* Fall 1996 - available online. See entry in **Appendix 3.1 Sources of Information: Disaster Planning and Recovery Journals**).

• Disaster Planning Standards

See entries for **Canadian Standards Association** and **National Fire Protection Association** (U.S.) under **Appendix 3.1 Sources of Information: Standards.**

• Disaster Resources - General

See also **Appendix 3.1 Sources of Information: Disaster Planning and Recovery Journals.**

British Columbia (BC) Emergency Management Information eXchange
URL: http://hoshi.cic.sfu.ca/bc/index.html
Provides links to BC emergency management organizations, emergency legislation, plans and strategies, etc.

Disaster Management Organizations
URL: gopher: hoshi.cic.sfu.ca...at/oth.int.orgs/int.orgs
Directory of international organizations (non-U.S.) compiled by Natural Hazards Research and Applications Information Center. Private for-profit organizations not included.

Disaster Recovery Yellow Pages
The Systems Audit Group Inc.
25 Ellison Road
Newton, Massachusetts 02159 U.S.A.
Tel: 617-332-3496
Fax: 617-332-4358
URL: http://www.disasterplan.com/yellowpages/
        subscribe.htm
Publication lists wealth of resources for resumption of business operations, with extensive coverage of information technology. Available online and in print. Covers North American sources. Useful for Canadian situation, although primarily U.S. coverage.

Emergency: A Guide to the Emergency Services of the World
URL: http://www.catt.rmit.edu.au/emergency/es-index.html
Non-profit site provides links to emergency services, collections of emergency-related documents and images, etc.

Emergency Resource Directory
URL: http://www.clarknet.com/erd/
Commercial site. Directory of emergency websites.

Emergency Response & Research Institute Emergency Net News Service
URL: http://www.emergency.com/
Commercial site providing 24 hour news, information coverage and analysis of disasters and major emergency events.

EPIX Emergency Management WWW and Gopher Sites
URL: http://hoshi.ccic.sfu.ca/epix/internet_sites.html
Maintained by Emergency Preparedness Information eXchange. Provides extensive links to emergency- and disaster-related internet sites. See entry for EPIX under **Appendix 3.1 Sources of Information: Education and Training**.

Illinois CES (Cooperative Extension Services) Disaster Resources
URL: http://www.ag.uiuc.edu/~disaster/
        disaster.html
Disaster Resources Website at the University of Illinois at Urbana-Champaign. Provides access to information on disaster preparedness and recovery for the State of Illinois and the Internet community.

Internet Alaska Link
URL: http://www.alaska.net/~build/plan.htm
Disaster recovery links.

Internet Disaster Information Network (IDIN)
URL: http://www.disaster.net/index.html
Provided as public service by StarNet and Telekachina Productions. Helps to distribute latest news on disaster situations to the internet community.

Nedsite Disasters
URL: http://www.nedsite.nl/search/disaster.htm
Commercial service. Billed as the most comprehensive search service in the world.

Rothstein Associates
URL: http://rothstein.com/welcome.html
Commercial site on business continuity and disaster recovery. Includes catalog on disaster recovery, articles and links to other resources.

University of Geneva Directory for Disaster Reduction Institutions
URL: http://www.unige_ch/idndr

• Earthquakes

B.C. Earthquake Information
Contact the Insurance Bureau of Canada (Vancouver Office). See **Appendix 3.1 Sources of Information: Insurance.**

Canadian National Earthquake Hazards Program
Geological Survey of Canada (GSC)
Natural Resources Canada
601 Booth Street
Ottawa, Ontario KIA 0E8
Tel: 613-996-3919
Fax: 613-996-9990
URL: http://www.seismo.NRCan.gc.ca/
GSC is the federal agency responsible for geoscientific information and research. Operates Canadian National Seismograph Network - includes detection, automated communication and data analysis. Publishes information i.e. monthly earthquake summaries, hazard estimates for new building design, etc. Makes available subset of Canadian National Earthquake Database epicentre information for Canadian earthquakes since 1980). Five regional offices.
See also **National Earthquake Support Plan for British Columbia**
URL: http://hoshi.cic.sfu.ca/epc/pub/fact-sheets/en_nesp.html

Earthquake Engineering Research Center
University of California at Berkeley
1301 South 46th Street
Richmond, California 94804-4698 U.S.A.
Tel: 510-231-9554
Fax: 510-231-9471
URL: http://nisee.ce.berkeley.edu/
Research Unit of the University of California at Berkeley dedicated to research, education, and dissemination of technical information on earthquake engineering. Serves as world focal point for activities in the field of earthquake hazard mitigation.

Global Earthquake Response Center
URL: http://www.earthquake.com
Links to general earthquake information and specific earthquake data.

United States Geological Survey
National Earthquake Information Center (NEIC)
Box 25046, DFC, MS 967
Denver, Colorado 80225 U.S.A.
Tel: Operations 303-273-8500
        Products 303-272-8418
        Earthquake Info Line 303-273-8516
Fax: 303-273-8450
URL: http://www.neic.cr.usgs.gov/
Determines the location and size of all earthquakes worldwide and disseminates this information. Collects and provides extensive seismic database. National data center and archive for earthquake information. Research program to improve ability to locate earthquakes and their mechanisms. Operates Earthquake Information gopher server (gopher://nisee.CE.Berkeley.EDU:70/00/eqgopher).

World-Wide Earthquake Locator
URL: http://www.geo.ed.ac.uk/quakes/quakes.html
Worldwide earthquake information provided within hours of an earthquake having taken place. System uses earthquake data from the U.S. National Earthquake Information Center. It is processed in Edinburgh and displayed using the Xerox PARC Map Viewer in California.

• Education and Training

See also entries for **Canadian Conservation Institute, National Archives of Canada** and **National Library of Canada** under **3.2 Sources of Assistance.**

Canadian Centre for Emergency Preparedness (CCEP)
P.O. Box 2911
Hamilton, Ontario L8N 3R5
Tel: 905-546-3911
Fax: 905-546-2340
URL: http://www.netaccess.on.ca/~ccep/ccep/
Not-for-profit organization offers training programmes to assist business, industry and government to prepare for, prevent, respond to and recover from all types of disasters. Goal of CCEP is to establish opportunities for collaboration and cooperation and to enhance access to cost-effective training opportunities.

Disaster Recovery Information Exchange (DRIE)
310 - 2175 Sheppard Avenue East
North York, Ontario M2J 1W8
Tel: 416-491-2420
Fax: 416-491-1670
E-mail: info@drie.org
URL: http://www.drie.org/
Non-profit educational foundation dedicated to the exchange of information on disaster recovery planning, business continuity planning, emergency preparedness and crisis management. Affiliated chapters across Canada (DRIE Montreal, DRIE Ottawa, DRIE SW Ontario, DRIE Toronto, DRIE West).

DRI (Disaster Recovery Institute) Canada
P.O. Box 2911
Hamilton, Ontario L8N3R5
Tel: 905-546-2867
Fax: 905-546-2340
URL: http://www.netaccess.on.ca~ccep/ccep/dric.
        shtml
Non-profit corporation created to promote Canadian professionalism in disaster recovery and corporate contingency planning. In partnership with CCEP and Mohawk College for Applied Arts and Technology offers training programmes to assist business, industry and government to prepare for, prevent, respond to and recover from all types of disasters. Dedicated to training and certification of disaster recovery and business continuity professionals in Canada.

DRI (Disaster Recovery Institute) International
111 Park Place
Falls Church, VA 22046-4513
Tel: 703-538-1792
Fax: 703-241-5603
URL: http://www.dr.org/
Founded at Washington University in St. Louis, DRI's purpose is to create common knowledge base for the disaster recovery/business continuity planning field through education, assistance, development of a resource base and professional certification. DRI has established alliances with a number of other organizations including the Canadian Center for Emergency Preparedness.

Appendix 3: Resources

Emergency Preparedness Information eXchange (EPIX)
c/o Centre for Policy Research on Science and Technology
Simon Fraser University (at Harbour Centre)
515 West Hastings Street
Vancouver, B.C. V6B 5K3
Tel: 604-291-5114
Fax: 604-291-5169
URL: http://hoshi.cic.sfu.ca/epix/
SAFEGUARD URL: http://hoshi.cic.sfu.ca/safeguard/
Operated by the Centre for Policy Research on Science and Technology at Simon Fraser University, EPIX aims to enhance the quality and quantity of disaster prevention, preparedness, response and recovery/rehabilitation information available to the emergency management community. Operates as an electronic information and communication server on the Internet. EPIX is not intended to provide assistance during an emergency or disaster.
EPIX operates SAFEGUARD, a national information program aimed at increasing awareness of emergency preparedness in Canada, initiated by Emergency Preparedness Canada. Brings together government, private and voluntary organizations that are part of the emergency planning, response and recovery community. SAFEGUARD NET is intended to become the main Canadian Internet repository of publicly available information on emergency preparedness.

The National Center for Preservation Technology and Training
National Park Service, U.S. Department of the Interior
NSU Box 5682
Natchitoches, Louisiana 71497 U.S.A.
Tel: 318-357-6464
Fax: 318-357-6421
E-mail: ncptt@alpha.nsula.edu
URL: http://www.cr.nps.gov/ncptt/
National interdisiplinary preservation research and development effort. Grants programme funds research and training projects of non-profit preservation organizations, universities and government agencies.

Regional Alliance for Preservation
URL: http://clir.stanford.edu/rap/
Part of a one-year demonstration project to share preservation training resources, including disaster prevention and response. Cooperative initiative of U.S regional field services (The AMIGOS Preservation Service, The Conservation Center for Art and Historic Artifacts, The Northeast Document Conservation Center, The Southeastern Library Network Preservation Services and the Upper Midwest Conservation Association). Support from the Commission on Preservation and Access, Council on Library and Information Resources.

• Emergency Power

Emergency Preparedness Information eXchange: Emergency Power
URL: http://hoshi.cic.sfu.ca/epix/topics/power/power.html

• Environmental Management

See **Appendix 3.1 Sources of Information: Conservation** and **Disasters** and **Professional Associations**.

• Fire

See also **Appendix 3.1 Sources of Information: Professional Associations** and **Standards**.

Arson Information Management System (AIMS)
Software widely used in the U.S. for recording, sharing and tracking incidents of arson. Can be downloaded from
http://www.fema.gov/nfp/arson/aims.htm

Canadian Commission on Building and Fire Codes
Codes Centre
National Research Council of Canada
Building M-24, Montreal Road
Ottawa, Ontario K1A 0R6
Tel: 613-993-9960
Fax: 613-952-4040
E-mail: codes@nrc.ca
URL: http://www.irc.nrc.ca/ccbfc/ccbfc_E.shtml
The National Building Code of Canada is essentially a code of minimum regulations for public health, fire safety and structural sufficiency with respect to the public interest. The National Fire Code of Canada is a model set of technical requirements designed to provide an acceptable level of fire protection and fire prevention within a community. The Code is written in a form suitable for adoption by appropriate legislative authorities in Canada.

Fire Prevention Canada
2425 Don Reid Drive, Unit 1
Ottawa, Ontario K1H 1A4
Tel: 1-800-668-2955
Fax: 613-736-0684
Charitable organization devoted to advancing public awareness of fire safety through education. Developed by partnership of Canadian Association of Fire Marshalls and Fire Commissioners and Canadian Association of Fire Chiefs.

Halon Recycling Corporation (HRC)
See entry for **Halon Alternatives Research Corporation (HARC)** under **3.1 Sources of Information: Professional Associations**.
Tel: 800-258-1283
        703-524-6636
Fax: 703-243-2874
Non-profit information clearinghouse established to assist sellers wishing to dispose of halon in a responsible manner, and to help buyers with critical uses locate supplies for recharge of their systems. Set up by members of the fire protection community and HARC.

United States Fire Administration (USFA)
16825 South Seton Avenue
Emmitsburg, Maryland 21727 U.S.A.
Tel: 301-447-1000
URL: http://www.usfa.fema.gov/
A directorate within the U.S. Federal Emergency Management Agency. Operates the National Fire Academy to advance the professional development of fire service personnel and others engaged in fire prevention and control activities. The National Fire Data Center of the U.S.F.A. is responsible for gathering, analysis, publication and dissemination of data related to prevention, occurrence, control and results of fires of all types. Has established the National Fire Incident Reporting System.

U.S. Environmental Protection Agency: Questions and Answers on Halons and Their Substitutes.
URL: http://www.epa.gov/ozone/title6/snap/hal.html

• Floods

See also **Appendix 3.1 Sources of Information: Weather**.

FEMA Fact Sheet on Flooding
URL: http://www.fema.gov/home/fema/fac104.html

Health and Safety Universal Precautions for Post-Flood Buildings
URL: http:haz1.siri.org/library/flood.html
Information on post-flooding precautions by Matthew Klein and Mark Fleming.

• Health and Safety

See Yellow Pages Directories (Business & Industrial) under Health & Safety-Industrial for industrial hygiene services, occupational health and safety programmes, etc.

See also AIC Health and Safety Guides 1/1, July 1998. *AIC News 23(4)*.
Compilation of U.S. and international health and safety resources related to regulatory, research and toxicological information.

See also **Appendix 3.1 Sources of Information: Standards** and **Human Resources**.

Arts, Crafts and Theatre Safety (ACTS)
181 Thompson Street, No. 23
New York, New York 10012-2586 U.S.A.
Tel: 212-777-0062
URL: http://www.casewb.com/acts
Health and safety data, lectures and training for museums and related organizations.

Canada Safety Council
1020 Spratt Place
Ottawa, Ontario K1G 5L5
Tel: 613-739-1535
Fax: 613-739-1566
E-mail: csc@safety-council.org
URL: http://www.safety.council.org/
Not-for-profit, non-governmental organization dedicated to reducing preventable deaths, injuries and economic loss in the public and private sector on national basis. Variety of services, resources and publications.

Canadian Centre For Occupational Health and Safety (CCOHS)
250 Main Street East
Hamilton, Ontario L8N 1H6
Tel: 905-572-2981
        1-800-668-4284 (Products)
        1-800-263-8466 (Information)
Fax: 905-572-2206
E-mail: custserv@ccohs.ca
URL: http://www.ccohs.ca
Funded by the federal government. Provides occupational health and safety information through its inquiries service, publications and the CCINFO databases.

Center for Safety in the Arts (CSA)
2124 Broadway, P.O. Box 310
New York, N.Y. 10023 U.S.A.
Fax: 212-233-3846
E-mail: csa@artswire.org
URL: http://artswire.org:70/1/csa
Gathers and disseminates information about health hazards encountered by artists, crafts-people, etc. in visual arts, museums and social arts programs.

Environment Canada
Terasses de la Chaudière
10, rue Wellington
Hull (Québec) K1A 0H3
Tel: 819-997-2800
1-800-668-6767
URL: http://www.doe.ca
Federal agency responsible for conducting research and gathering data, providing information and advice, and establishing guidelines and regulations dealing with the environment.

Environmental Protection Agency (EPA)
EPA Headquarters
401 M Street SW
Washington, D.C. 20460 U.S.A.
Tel: 202-260-2090
202-260-2080 (Publications)
Nationwide: 1-800-535-0202
Alaska and D.C.: 703-412-9810
Fax: 202-512-2233
URL: http://www.epa.gov/
SNAP (Significant New Alternatives Policy) Programme:
http://www.epa.gov/ozone/titleo/snap/snap.html
U.S. agency mandated to protect human health and safeguard the natural environment. It is responsible for implementation and enforcement of federal environment laws. Issues regulations and provides publications and advisory services.

Health Canada
Brooke Claxton Building
Tunney's Pasture
120 Parkdale Avenue
Ottawa, Ontario K1A 0K9
Tel: 613-957-2991
Fax: 613-952-7266
URL: http://www.hwc.ca
Principal federal government department focused on health and safety. Provides the fundamental funding and policy for the health care system in Canada. Responsibilities includes health protection and consumer product safety.

National Institute for Occupational Health and Safety (NIOSH)
200 Independence Avenue SW, Room 317B
Washington, D.C. 20210 U.S.A.
Tel: 800-356-4647
Publications 513-533-8326
Databases 513-533-8326
Respirators 304-291-4331
URL: http://www.cdc.gov/niosh/homepage.html
U.S. federal agency that conducts research on various safety and health problems, provides technical assistance to OSHA and recommends standards for OSHA adoption, investigates toxic substances and its development of criteria for use in workplaces.

National Safety Council (NSC)
1121 Spring Lake Drive
Itasca, Illinois 60143-3201 U.S.A.
Tel: 630-285-1121
Fax: 630-285-1315
URL: http://www.nsc.org/
Non-profit, non-governmental, international public service organization dedicated to improving safety, health and environmental well-being of all people. Its library is one of the world's largest sources of safety and health information.

Occupational Safety and Health Administration (OSHA)
U.S. Department of Labour
200 Constitution Avenue N.W.
Washington, D.C. 20210 U.S.A.
Tel: 202-219-8148
URL: http://www.osha.gov
Enforces the U.S. Occupational Safety and Health Act by promulgating health and safety standards, offering training programmes, conducting inspections, and fining violators of OSHA standards.

Workplace Hazardous Materials Information System (WHMIS)
WHMIS is a Canada-wide system designed to provide employers and employees with information on hazardous materials in the workplace.
See: http://www.hs-sc.gc.ca
http://www.ccohs.ca

• **Human Resources**

See also **Appendix 3.1 Sources of Information: Health and Safety.**

American Red Cross Disaster Services
American Red Cross
Public Inquiry Office
6th Floor - 8111 Gatehouse Road
Falls Church, Virginia 22042 U.S.A.
Tel: 703-206-7090
URL: http://www.redcross.org/disaster/
Red Cross offers variety of services related to health and safety, emergency relief and humanitarian aid, national and international. Mission of Disaster Services is to ensure nationwide U.S. disaster planning, preparation, community disaster planning, mitigation and response.

Canadian Red Cross Society
National Headquarters
1800 Alta Vista Drive
Ottawa, Ontario K1G 4J5
Tel: 613-739-3000
Fax: 613-739-2575
E-mail: feedback@redcross.ca
URL: http://www.redcross.ca/
Volunteer-based humanitarian organization with wide range of services. Provides disaster assistance and relief to victims of emergencies in Canada as part of local emergency response plans and partnership arrangements with federal, provincial and municipal governments. Also provides international aid.

Canadian Trauma Stress Network
URL: http://play.psych.mun.ca~dhart/trauma_net/
Canada-wide network of resources. Dedicated to the advancement of trauma-stress services through education, training, public awareness, professional development and research.

Natural Hazards Center at the University of Colorado, Boulder
Campus Box 482
University of Colorado
Boulder, Colorado 80309-0482 U.S.A.
Tel: 303-492-6818
Fax: 303-492-2151
E-mail: hazctr@colorado.edu
URL: http://www.colorado.EDU/hazards/
National and international clearinghouse for information on natural hazards and human adjustments to hazards and disasters. Aim is to increase communication among hazard/disaster researchers and those individuals, agencies, and organizations that are actively working to reduce disaster damage and suffering.

St. John Ambulance Canada
National Headquarters
312 Laurier Avenue East
Ottawa, Ontario K1N 8V4
Tel: 613-236-7461
Fax: 613-236-2425
E-mail: nhq@nhq.sja.ca
URL: http://www.sja.ca
National voluntary, not-for-profit agency. Aim is to enable Canadians to improve, health, safety and quality of life by providing training and community service, i.e., first aid courses and CPR training. Also provide back-up services for emergencies and disaster relief. Offices across Canada.

• **Hurricanes**

See also **Appendix 3.1 Sources of Information: Weather.**

Environment Canada: Canadian Forecasts and Warnings
URL: http://www.ns.ec.gc.ca/weather/index_e.html

Earthwatch Hurricane Imagery
URL: http://www.earthwatch.com
Commercial site where weather watches, warnings and advisories are updated every ten minutes.

Canadian Hurricane Centre
Environment Canada - Atlantic Region
45 Alderney Drive
Queen Square
Dartmouth, Nova Scotia B2Y 2N6
Tel: 902-426-9163
URL: http://www.ns.ec.ca/weather/hurricane
Part of Environment Services Division of Environment Canada. Issues advisories to public and the media.

National (U.S.) Hurricane Center Tropical Prediction Center
11691 SW 17th Street
Miami, Florida 33165-2149 U.S.A.
Tel: 305-229-4470
URL: http://www.nhc.noaa.gov
One of U.S. National Centers for Environmental Protection. Issues watches, warnings, forecasts and analyses of hazardous weather conditions in the tropics.

Appendix 3: Resources

• Industrial Safety

Center for Chemical Process Safety
345 East 47th Street
New York, N.Y. 10017 U.S.A.
Tel: 212-705-7319
Fax: 212-838-8274
E-mail: ccps@aiche.org
URL: http://www.aiche.org/dcos/ccps/
Industry-driven non-profit professional organization affiliated with the American Institute of Chemical Engineers. Committed to development of engineering and management practices to help prevent and mitigate catastrophic accidents involving release of hazardous chemicals and hydrocarbons.

Major Industrial Accidents Council of Canada (MIACC)
600-265 Carling Avenue
Ottawa, Ontario K1S 2E1
Tel: 613-232-4435
Fax: 613-232-4915
E-mail: miacc@globalx.net
URL: http://hoshi.cic.sfu.ca/miacc/index.htnl
Not-for-profit organization of Canadian federal, provincial and municipal governments, industry, industry associations, emergency response organizations, labour, etc. Common interest is to prevent, prepare and respond effectively to major accidents involving hazardous substances.

• Insurance and Risk Management

See also **Appendix 3.1 Sources of Information: Professional Associations**.

The Chubb Corporation: Insurance Library
URL: http://www.chubb.com/library/
Library of insurance information, i.e., policies, claims and procedures.

Insurance Canada
URL: http://www.insurance-canada.ca/insurcan/index.htm
Cooperative venture by organizations in Canadian Insurance industry to provide professionals, business and consumers about insurance-related topics.

Internet Resources for Risk Management and Information Systems
URL: http://rmisweb.com/
Journal articles on risk management and information technology.

RISKweb
URL: http://www.riskweb.com/
Internet mailing list devoted to risk and insurance issues.

Smartsite
URL: http://arkwright.com/
Commercial site on risk management and disaster planning.

• Microreproduction

See also **See also Appendix 3.1 Sources of Information: Standards**.

Canadian Institute for Historical Microreproductions (CIHM)
P.O. Box 2428, Station D
Ottawa, Ontario K1P 5W5
Tel: 613-235-2628
Fax: 613-235-9752
E-mail: cihmicmh@nlo.nlc-bnc.ca
URL: http://www.nlc-bnc.ca/cihm/
National cooperative project established to locate early printed Canadian materials, to preserve their content on microfilm and make the resulting collections available to libraries and archives in Canada and abroad. Website provides searchable database of pre-1990 Canadian titles.

See also **Early Canadiana Online**
(http://www.canadiana.org) - a collaborative research project to provide digital library of primary resources in Canadain history.

• National Disaster Preparedness and Response

Emergency Management Australia (EMA)
P.O. Box 1020
Dickson, ACT 2602
Australia
Tel: 61 2 2665402
Fax: 61 6 2577665
E-mail: ema@ema.gov.au
URL: http://www.ema.gov.au/
Develops, coordinates and supports effective national emergency management arrangements. Provides advice on emergency management matters to commonwealth agencies, States, Territories, industry and the international community. Coordinates material and technical assistance for disasters and emergencies, develops, implements and reviews emergency management policy and planning, develops and delivers emergency management education and training and manages financial assistance through state programs.

Emergency Preparedness Canada (EPC)
See entry under **3.2 Sources of Assistance: Disaster Planning and Recovery**.
See Appendix 2 for details of EPC mandate, services and publications.
Federal agency operating within the Ministry of National Defense responsible for coordinating civil emergency planning across Canada.

Federal Emergency Management Agency (FEMA)
Federal Center Plaza
500 C Street SW
Washington, D.C. 20472 U.S.A.
Tel: 202-646-3923
URL: http://www.fema.gov/
U.S. agency responsible for all federal emergency preparedness, mitigation, response and recovery activities. Works with state and local governments by funding emergency programs and providing technical guidance and training. Extensive set of publications. Has Global Emergency Management System, an online searchable database containing www links on a wide variety of topics related to emergency management.
FEMA is also responsible for national preparedness capabilities, administering the President's Disaster Assistance Program, overseeing the Federal Insurance Administration and serving as a contact for external audiences. FEMA operates out of 10 regional offices across the U.S. FEMA and Emergency Preparedness Canada oversee a number of common issues and interests between the U.S. and Canada.

• Natural Disasters

See also **3.1 Sources of Information: Earthquakes, Hurricanes, Tornadoes** and **Tsunamis**.

Emergency Preparedness Information Center
161-6523 California Avenue SW
Seattle, Washington 98136 U.S.A.
Tel: 206-937-5658
E-mail: bjnelson@TheEpicenter.com
URL: http://TheEpicenter.com/
Commercial site with focus on information and products on how to prepare for natural disasters.

HazardNet
URL: http://hoshi.cic.sfu.ca~hazard/index.html
Experimental IDNDR demonstration project with operational and informational services.

International Decade for Natural Disaster Reduction (IDNDR)
United Nations Department of Humanitarian Affairs
Geneva, Switzerland
URL: http://hoshi.cic.sfu.ca/idndr/index.html
See 1.3.1 for description of IDNDR.

Natural Disaster Reference Database
URL: http://ltpwww.gsfc.nasa.gov/ndrd.html
- **Disaster Finder**
URL: http://ltpwww.gsfc.nasa.gov/ndrd/disaster
Service of NASA and GSFC. Index to "best" disaster websites.

See also **Natural Hazards Center at the University of Colorado, Boulder** under **3.1 Sources of Information: Human Resources**.

• Pest Management

Also check provincial departments of agriculture or environment, local university biology programmes or provincial experimental stations. For health risks, contact industrial hygienists in provincial ministries of labour.

See entry for **Canadian Conservation Institute** under **3.2 Sources of Assistance: Disasters and Conservation**.

See also **Appendix 3.1 Sources of Information: Professional Associations**.

Centre for Land and Biological Resources Research
Biological Resources Division, Research Branch
KW Neatby Building, Room 1015
Ottawa, Ontario K1A 0C6
Tel: 613-759-1772
Fax: 613-759-1924
Provides Canada-wide identification service for fungi.

Integrated Pest Management Information System
British Columbia Ministry of Environment, Land and Parks
URL: http://pupuxl.env.gov.bc.ca/~ipmis/ipmis.html
Electronic library on integrated pest management.

National IPM Network
URL: http://ipmwww.ncsu.edu
Group of U.S. government, educational and commercial organizations dedicated to development and implementation of integrated pest management.

Pest Management Regulatory Agency
Health Canada
59 Camelot Drive
Ottawa, Ontario K1A 0Y9
Tel: 1-800-267-6315
Fax: 613-954-9691
E-mail: pminfoserv@em.agr.ca
URL: http://www.ca/pmra/indexe.html
Federal agency provides service to the public, industry and government on any matters relating to pesticides, including registration, information and publications.

Pestweb
URL: http://www.pestweb.com/
Professional pest control industry-wide website. Information and links to Integrated Pest Management, safety, research, etc.

• Preservation

See also **Appendix 3.1 Sources of Information: Conservation and Disasters.**

Canadian Initiative on Digital Libraries (CIDL)
URL: http://www.nlc-bnc.ca/cidl
Initiative dedicated to promoting, coordinating and facilitating development of digital collections and resources in Canada. Directed by Steering Committee elected from member libraries across the country.

Council on Library and Information Resources (CLIR)
500 - 1755 Massachusetts Avenue N.W.
Washington, D.C. 20036-2188 U.S.A.
Tel: 202-939-4750
Fax: 202-939-4765
E-mail: info@clir.org
URL: http://www.clir.org
Grew out of merger of Commission on Preservation and Access, and Council on Library Resources. CLIR founded to continue support for national information system. The four programme areas include: Commission on Preservation and Access, digital libraries, economics of information and leadership.

European Commission on Preservation and Access (ECPA)
P.O. Box 19121 - 1000 GC
Amsterdam, The Netherlands
Tel: 31 205510839
Fax: 31 206204941
E-mail: ecpa@bureau.knaw.nl
URL: http://www.library.knaw.nl/ecpa/ecpatex/public.htm
Listserv: listserv@nic.surfnet.nl
Website EPIC (European Preservation Information Center) provides gateway for information on preservation of documentary heritage.

Heritage Preservation
566 - 1730 K Street, NW
Washington, D.C. 20006-3836 U.S.A.
Fax: 202-634-1435
URL: http://www.heritagepreservation.org/
Membership organization (museums, libraries, libraries, preservation/conservation organizations, etc.) dedicated to providing leadership and coordination for preservation of cultural heritage in the U.S.

• Professional Associations

Also includes professional societies and industry associations. See also **Standards.**

American Conference of Governmental Industrial Hygienists (ACGIH)
6500 Glenway, Building D-7
Cincinnati, Ohio 45211 U.S.A.
Tel: 513-742-2020
Fax: 513-742-3355
URL: http://www.acgih.org/
Society of professionals employed by official government units responsible for full-time programs of industrial hygiene, educators and others conducting research in industrial hygiene. Promotes standards and exchange of information.

American Industrial Hygiene Association (AIHA)
250 - 2700 Prosperity Avenue
Fairfax, Virginia 22031 U.S.A.
Tel: 703-849-8888
Fax: 703-207-3561
URL: http://www.aiha.org/
Professional society of industrial hygienists that promotes workplace safety by reducing the health risks in the environment.

American Institute for Conservation of Historic and Artistic Works (AIC)
200-1717 K Street NW
Washington, D.C. 20006 U.S.A.
Tel: 202-452-9545
Fax: 202-452-9328
E-mail: infoaic@aol.com
URL: http://aic.stanford.edu/
National organizational of conservation professionals. Advances the practice and promotes the importance of the preservation of cultural property. Establishes and upholds professional standards.

- AIC Book and Paper Group
URL: http://aic.stanford.edu/bpg/

American Library Association (ALA)
Headquarters
50 East Huron Street
Chicago, Illinois 60611 U.S.A.
Tel: 312-280-3215
Fax: 312-944-3897
URL: http://www.ala.org/
Oldest and largest library association in the world. Dedicated to promoting highest quality library and information services. Broad-based programmes of advocacy, public awareness, and professional education and support. Note: Preservation and Reformatting Section of Association for Library Collections and Technical Services Division.

American Society of Heating, Refrigeration and Air Conditioning Engineers (ASHRAE)
1791 Tullie Circle NE
Atlanta, Georgia 30329-2305 U.S.A.
Tel: 404-636-8400
Fax: 404-321-5478
E-mail: techserv@ashrae.org
URL: http://www.ashrae.org
Technical society of heating, ventilating, refrigeration and air-conditioning engineers. Sponsors research and technical programs in cooperation with universities, research laboratories and government agencies.

Antiquarian Booksellers Association of America (ABAA)
National Office
50 Rockefeller Plaza
New York, New York 10020 U.S.A.
Tel: 212-757-9395
Fax: 212-459-0307
E-mail: abaa@panix.com
URL: http://abaa_booknet.com/
Dealer association. Online dissemination of information on stolen books, recoveries and forgeries.

Antiquarian Booksellers Association of Canada (ABAC)
Box 75035, Cambrian Post Office
Calgary, Alberta T2K 6J8
Tel: 403-282-5832
Fax: 403-289-0814
E-mail: Aquila@cadvision.com
URL: http://booknet-international.com/ca/
Dealer association aiming to foster interest in rare books and manuscripts, and maintain high standards in antiquarian book trade.

Association des archivistes du Québec
CP 423 Sillery (Québec) G1T 2R8
Tel: 418-652-2357
Fax: 418-646-0868
E-mail: aaq@microtec.net
URL: http://www.archives.ca/aaq
Provincial association of professional archivists.

Association for Information and Image Management (AIIM)
1100 - 1100 Wayne Avenue
Silver Spring, Maryland 20910-5603 U.S.A.
Tel: 301-587-8202
Fax: 301-587-2711
URL: http://www.aiim.org/
ANSI-accredited standards development association of manufacturers, vendors and individual users of information and management equipment. Principal developer of standards for microforms and other electronic information and storage technologies. Operates resource center and publishes technical reports.

Association for Recorded Sound Collections (ARSC)
P.O. Box 543
Annapolis, Maryland 21404-0543 U.S.A.
Tel: 410-757-0488
Fax: 410-349-0175
Association acts as central information centre for libraries, recording archives and collectors. Promotes professional standards.

Association of Canadian Archivists (ACA)
P.O. Box 2596, Station D
Ottawa, Ontario K1P 5W6
Tel: 613-443-0251
Fax: 613-443-0261
URL: http://www.archives.ca/aca/
Professional organization dedicated to provide regular, informative and scholarly programme of publication; to promote the highest standards in the conduct of archives administration and a code of professional responsibility, to represent the needs of the archives profession, exchange of information (regional, national and international) and to promote public knowledge of archives.

Appendix 3: Resources

Association of College and Research Libraries/Rare Books and Manuscripts Section (ACRL/RBMS) Security Committee
Susan M. Allen, Chair
Director of Libraries and Media Services
Kalamazoo College Library
1200 Academy Street
Kalamazoo, Michigan 49006-3285 U.S.A.
Tel: 616-337-7149
Fax: 616-337-7143
E-mail: sallen@kzoo.edu
Compiles incidents of theft list.

Association of Contingency Planners (ACP)
National Headquarters
c/o Milton G. Wolf, Law Offices
12461 Jacqueline Place
Granada Hills, California 91344 U.S.A.
URL: http://www.acp-international.com/
Non-profit association dedicated to business continuity through information exchange and education on disaster prevention and recovery. Chapters across the U.S.

Association of Records Managers and Administrators, Inc. (ARMA International)
See entry for **ARMA** under **Appendix 3.1 Sources of Information: Standards**.
Chapters around the world.
Toronto Chapter
Unit 15, 5536 Montevideo Road
Mississauga, Ontario L5N 2P4
Tel: 905-812-1761
Fax: 905-812-1763

Association of Specialists in Cleaning and Restoration (ASCR) International
Tel: 301-604-4111
Fax: 301-6-4-4713
URL: http://www.ascr.org/
Trade association (international, non-profit) for cleaning and restoration professionals. Website includes information (including lists of restorers and certified restorers) and links.

Audio Engineering Society Inc. (AES)
International Headquarters
2520 - 60 East 42nd Street
New York, New York 10165-2520 U.S.A.
Tel: 212-661-8528
Fax: 212-682-0477
URL: http://www.aes.org/
Professional society devoted exclusively to audio technology. Technical standards and practices are developed under its auspices.

Canadian Association for the Conservation of Cultural Property (CAC)
P.O. Box 9195
Ottawa, Ontario K1G 3T9
Tel: 819-684-7460
Fax: as above
URL: http://www.archives.ca/cac/index.htm
Non-profit charitable corporation. Aim is to further dissemination of knowledge concerning the conservation of Canada's cultural property.

Canadian Association of Fire Chiefs
National Office
2425 Don Reid Drive, Unit 1
Ottawa, Ontario K1H 1A4
Tel: 613-736-0576
Fax: 613-736-0684
URL: http://www.cafc.ca/
National public service association dedicated to reducing loss of life and property from fire, and advancing science and technology of fire service in Canada. NFPA publications available for purchase.

Canadian Association of Fire Marshals and Fire Commissioners
Current Federal Representative
Mr. P. W. Worona
Director Occupational Safety and Health and Fire Protection
165 Hotel de Ville Street
Phase 2, Place de Portage
Hull (Québec) K1A 0J2
Tel: 819-953-7768
Fax: 819-997-6795
Regulatory body of 13 members (provinces, territories plus federal representative) responsible for fire safety provisions in their particular jurisdictions. Each province and territory has a Fire Marshall or Fire Commissioner.

Canadian Association of Professional Conservators (CAPC)
c/o Canadian Museums Association
400 - 280 Metcalfe Street
Ottawa, Ontario K2P 1R7
Tel: 613-567-0099
Professional non-profit association incorporated to accredit professional conservators in Canada. Founded in 1971, CAPC works to establish and encourage high standards of competence, integrity and ethics in the field of conservation.

Canadian Bookbinders and Book Artists Guild (CBBAG)
220 -35 McCaul Street
Toronto, Ontario M5T 1V7
Tel: 416-581-1071
Fax: 905-851-6029
URL: http:knet.flemingc.on.ca/~rmiller/cbbag
        CBBAGhome.html
Provides contact and support among hand workers in order to promote cooperation, provide access to educational programmes and exhibitions, promote greater awareness of the book arts and standards of excellence.

Canadian Council of Archives (CCA)
1009 - 344 Wellington Street
Ottawa, Ontario K1A 0N3
Tel: 613-995-0210
Fax: 613-947-6662
URL: http://www.CdnCouncilArchives.ca/
Federally-funded national council that provides coordination within the archival community across the country. Responsibilities include identification of national priorities, implementation and management of archival programmes, and communication of archival concerns and needs. Note: Preservation Committee.

Canadian Fire Safety Association
310 - 2175 Sheppard Avenue East
North York, Ontario M2J 1W8
Tel: 416-492-9417
Fax: 416-491-1670
E-mail: taylor@interlog.com
URL: Under development
Association of fire industry professionals in private business and government. Promotes fire safety through training and education.

Canadian Information and Image Management Society (CIIMS)
86 Wilson Street
Oakville, Ontario L6K 3G5
Tel: 905-842-6067
Fax: 905-842-2646
E-mail: ciims@goodmedia.com
URL: http://www.ciims.ca/ciims
Professional organization of information and imaging users dedicated to the promotion of image management and its professional applications.

Canadian Library Association (CLA)
602-200 Elgin Street
Ottawa, Ontario K2P 1L5
Tel: 613-232-9625
Fax: 613-563-9895
URL: http://www.cla.amlibs.ca/
National association dedicated to providing leadership in the provision, development and support of library information services. Note: Preservation/ Conservation Interest Group.

Disaster Preparation and Emergency Response Association, International (DERA)
URL: http://www.disasters.org/weblink.html
Non-profit international service and professional association. Assists communities worldwide in disaster preparation, response and recovery. Professional association linking professionals, volunteers and organizations active in all phases of emergency preparation and management.

Halon Alternatives Research Corporation (HARC)
850 - 2111 Wilson Blvd.
Arlington, Virginia 22201 U.S.A.
Tel: 703-524-6636
Fax: 703-243-2874
URL: http://www.harc.org/
Non-profit trade association formed to promote, develop and approve of environmentally acceptable halon alternatives.

Institute of Paper Conservation (IPC)
Leigh Lodge
Leigh, Worcester WR6 5LB England
Tel: 44-18-86832323
Fax: 44-18-86833688
E-mail: clare:@ipc.org.uk
Leading professional member organization devoted solely to the conservation of paper and related materials. Devoted to increasing the professional awareness of conservation by coordinating exchange of information and facilitating member contact, both nationally and internationally.

Insurance Bureau of Canada (IBC)
Head Office, Ontario Office and Consumer
Information Centre
1800 - 151 Yonge Street
Toronto, Ontario M5C 2W7
Tel: 416-362-2031/9528
         Ontario 800-387-2880
Fax: 416-362-2602
URL: http://www.ibc.ca
National trade association and official voice of
insurance companies (property and casualty)
doing business in Canada. Acts as liaison between
insurers and government, the business world, consumer and other interest groups. Consumer liaison
officers in Toronto and Montreal. Other offices in
major cities across Canada.

**Integrated Pest Management Practitioners
Association (IPMPA)**
P.O. Box 10313
Eugene, Oregon 97440 U.S.A.
Tel: 541-343-6969
Fax: 541-345-2272
URL: http://www.efn.org~ipmpa
Non-profit association founded to facilitate the use
and understanding of integrated pest management in
primarily non-agricultural resource settings. IPM
Access provides networking and information service.

International Association of Arson Investigators
100 - 300 S. Broadway Avenue
St. Louis, Missouri 63102-2808 U.S.A.
Tel: 314-621-1966
Fax: 314-621-5125
URL: http://www.fire.investigators.org/
International association of fire investigators
dedicated to suppression of crime by arson.

International Association of Sound Archives (IASA)
Albrecht Haefner, Secretary General
Svedwestfunk Baden-Baden
Postfach 820 D76522
Baden-Baden, Germany
Tel: 49 7721 9293487
Fax: 49 7221 9292094
URL: http://www.llgc.org.uk/iasa/index.htm
International association dedicated to the preserva-
tion, organization and use of sound recordings, and
co-operation between achives and collectors.

**International City/County Management
Association (ICMA)**
500 - 77 North Capitol Street NE
Washington, D.C. 20002-4201 U.S.A.
Tel: 202-289-4262
Fax: 202-962-3500
URL: http://www.icma.org/
Professional and educational association for admin-
istrators serving cities, counties, other local
governments and regional entities around the world.

International Council of Museums (ICOM)
Maison de l'Unesco
1, rue Miollis
F - 75732 Paris Cedex 15, France
Tel: 33-1-47340500
Fax: 33-1-43067862
URL: http://www.chin.gc/Applications_URL/icom/
Associated with UNESCO; a non-profit, non-gov-
ernmental organization dedicated to the
improvement and advancement of museums and
museum profession. Operates Information
Center which is the world's largest repository of
information on all aspects of museum manage-
ment. Membership in International Committee for
Conservation through affiliated institutions.

- ICOM Canada
400-280 Metcalfe Street
Ottawa, Ontario K2P 1R7
Tel: 613-567-0099
Fax: 613-233-5438

International Council on Archives (ICA)
60, rue des Francs-Bourgeois
F-75003 Paris, France
Tel: 33-1-40276306
Fax: 33-1-42722065
E-mail: 100640.54@compuserve.com
URL: http://www.archives.ca/ica/english.html
Federation of national and international archival
associations, archival institutions and individuals
in more than 150 countries. Encourages preserva-
tion, promotes archival development and
conducts research on descriptive standards and
the impact of information technology on archives.
Note: Preservation Committee.

**International Council on Monuments and Sites
(ICOMOS)**
49-51, rue de la Fédération
75015 Paris, France
Tel: 33-1-5676770
Fax: 33-1-5660622
URL: http://www.icomos.org
Encourages the conservation, protection and
rehabilitation of historic monuments and sites.
Promotes adoption and implementation of inter-
national conventions and recommendations on
conservation. Cooperates in training programs.
Compiles and disseminates information concern-
ing conservation policies and techniques.

ICOMOS CANADA
P.O. Box 737, Station B
Ottawa, Ontario K1P 5R4
Tel: 613-749-0971
Fax: 613-749-2071
E-mail: canada@icomos.org.
URL: http://www.icomos.org/canada

**International Federation of Library Associations
and Institutions (IFLA)**
Postbox 95312
2509 CH The Hague, Netherlands
Tel: 31-70-3140884
Fax: 31-70-3834827
E-mail: IFLA@ifla.org
URL: http://www.nic/bnc.ca/ifla/
Federation of library associations and institutions
in over 150 countries. Promotes international
understanding, cooperation, discussion, research
and development in all fields of library activity.

**IFLA: Preservation and Conservation Core
Programme (PAC)**
Programme dedicated to the preservation activi-
ties and events that support efforts to preserve
materials in the world's libraries and archives.
- International Centre
Bibliothèque nationale de France
2 rue Vivienne
75084 Paris Cedex 02, France
Tel: 33-1-47038726
Fax: 33-1-47037725
E-mail: marie-therese.varlamoff@bnf.fr
- Regional Centre for North America
Library of Congress
Preservation Directorate LM-G21
Washington, D.C. 20540 U.S.A.
Tel: 202-707-5213
Fax: 202-707-3434
E-mail: ator@loc.gov
Other regional centres for Latin America and the
Caribbean, Central and East Asia, etc.

International Institute for Conservation (IIC)
6 Buckingham Street
London WC2N 6BA, United Kingdom
Tel: 44-171-839-5975
Fax: 44-171-976-1564
E-mail: 100731.1565@compuserve.com
International professional body provides a permanent organization for coordinating and
improving the knowledge, methods and working
standards needed to protect and preserve historic and artistic works.

National Computer Security Association
1220 Walnut Bottom Road
Carlisle, Pennsylvania 17013-7635 U.S.A
Tel: 1-800-488-4595
         717-258-1816
E-mail: info@ncsa.com
URL: http://www.ncsa.com/
Organization devoted to computer security
issues in corporations, associations and govern-
ment agencies worldwide.

**National Institute of Disaster Restoration
(NIDR)**
Division of Association of Specialists in
Cleaning and Restoration (ASCR) International
URL: http://www.ascr.org/nidr.htm
International trade association. Authority and
resource on restoration of residential and com-
mercial property as a result of damage from fire,
smoke, vandalism, etc.

Society of American Archivists (SAA)
527 S. Wells, 5th Floor
Chicago, Illinois 60607 U.S.A.
Tel: 312-922-0140
Fax: 312-347-1452
URL: http://www.archivists.org/
Society of individuals and institutions concerned with
the identification, preservation and use of records of
historical value. Note: Preservation Section.

**Society of Motion Picture and Television
Engineers (SMPTE)**
595 Harsdale Avenue
White Plains, New York 10607-1824
Tel: 914-761-1100
Fax: 914-761-3115
URL: http://209.29.37.1661
ANSI-accredited standards developing organi-
zation. Preeminent professional society for
motion picture and television engineers.

Survive!
The Chapel
Royal Victoria Patriotic Building
Fitzhugh Grove, London SW18 3SX
United Kingdom
Tel: 44-181-874-6266
Fax: 44-181-874-6446
E-mail: pbarnes@survive.com
URL: http://www.survive.com/
International, industry-wide user group for busi-
ness continuity planning and disaster recovery
professionals.

Appendix 3: Resources

United Nations Educational, Scientific and Cultural Organization (UNESCO)
7, Place de Fontenoy
F-75700 Paris, France
Tel: 33-1-45681000
Fax: 33-1-45671690
URL: http://unesco.org
Advocates collaboration among nations in the areas of education, science and culture. Strives to protect and preserve mankind's cultural heritage and to instill in member nations a sense of cultural and historic identity.

Memory of the World Programme
URL: http://firewall.unesco.org/webworld/mdm/administ/en/mow_index.html
(See 1.3.5 for description of MOW)

Water Loss Institute (WLI)
Division of Association of Specialists in Cleaning and Restoration (ASCR) International
URL: http://www.aascr.org/wli.htm
International trade association. Authority and resource on restoration of residential and commercial property as a result of water and sewage damage. Website includes information, members and Code of Ethics.

• Records Management

See **Appendix 3.1 Sources of Information: Professional Associations** and **Standards**.

Records Management and Other Related Sites
URL: http://www.flash.net~survivor/websites.htm
Service of Rio Grande Chapter of ARMA.

• Security

See also **Appendix 3.2 Sources of Assistance: Theft.**

Computer Security Administration
URL: http://www.utoronto.ca/security/
Site provides information on all aspects of computer security. Maintained by the University of Toronto Computer Security Administration, Computing and Networking Services.

The Gateway to Information Security Links
URL: http://www.securityserver.com/index.html

The Museum Security Network
URL: http://museum-security.org
Initiative of group of security professionals both in museums and private sector in the Netherlands. Website and mailing list devoted to all aspects of cultural property protection for museums, libraries and galleries.

See **National Computer Security Association** under **Appendix 3.1 Sources of Assistance: Professional Associations**.

RCMP Information Security Branch
URL: http://www.rcmp_grc.gc.ca/html/itsec.htm
IT security bulletins, publications, training, etc.

• Standards

See also **Disaster Standards** and **Professional Associations**.

See Dodson, Suzanne and Johanna Wellheiser, Comps. 1995. *Bibliography of Standards and Standard References Related to Preservation in Libraries.*
URL: http://www.nlc-bnc.ca/resource/presv.eintro.htm#index

American National Standards Institute (ANSI)
11 West 42nd Street, 13th Floor
New York, N.Y. 10036 U.S.A.
Tel: 212-642-4900
Fax: 212-398-0023
URL: http://www.ansi.org/
U.S. representative to ISO and principal national standards organization in the U.S. Private organization that coordinates work of committees and organizations that it has accredited as standards developers. Some, like the ASCs (Accredited Standards Committees), exist solely to develop ANSI standards. Others are technical and professional organizations that develop ANSI standards among many other activities. Provides SID (Standards Information Databases) Service - a reference tool to U.S. national, European regional and International standards.

National Resources for Global Standards
NSSN Services
American National Standards Institute (ANSI)
11 West 42nd Street
New York, New York 10036 U.S.A.
Tel: 212-642-8908
Fax: 212-398-0023
URL: http://www.nssn.org/
Co-operative partnership between ANSI, private sector and international standards organizations, and government agencies. Aims to be most comprehensive data network on standards.

American Society for Testing and Materials (ASTM)
100 Barr Harbor Drive
West Conchohocken, Pennsylvania 19428 U.S.A
Tel: 610-832-9500
Fax: 610-832-9555
URL: http://www.astm.org/
Not-for-profit ANSI-accredited standards developing organization. One of the largest and oldest voluntary standards development organizations in the world. Publishes standard test methods, specifications, practices, guides, classifications and terminology.

Association of Records Managers and Administrators, Inc. (ARMA International)
215 - 4200 Somerset Drive
Prairie Village, Kansas 66208 U.S.A.
Tel: 913-341-3808
Fax: 913-341-3742
URL: http://www.arma.org/hq/
ANSI-accredited standards development association. Principal organization for records and information managers in the U.S. dedicated to efficient records-making and records-keeping.

Bureau de normalisation de Québec
70, rue Dalhousie, bureau 220
Québec (Québec) G1K 4B2
Tel: 418-643-5114
Fax: 418-646-3315
URL: http://www.criq.qc.ca/bnq/english/index html
Canadian National Standards System-accredited standards development organization. Focuses its activities in four areas: the environment, occupational health and safety, construction and public works.

Canadian General Standards Board (CGSB)
Ottawa, Ontario K1A 1G6
Tel: 819-956-0894 (Information)
819-956-0425 (Sales)
1-800-665-CGSB
Fax: 819-956-1634
URL: http://www.pwgsc.gc.ca
Canadian National Standards System-accredited standards development organization. Develops standards and specifications; lists qualified and certified products and services; registers quality systems; and distributes and sells standards. CGSB is part of the Industrial and Commercial Products and Standardization Services Sector of Public Works and Government Services Canada.

Canadian Standards Association (CSA)
178 Rexdale Boulevard
Rexdale (Toronto), Ontario M9W 1R3
Tel: 416-747-4044
Fax: 416-747-2475
URL: http://www.csa.ca/index-t.htm
Note: Other offices across Canada
Canadian National Standards System-accredited standards development organization. Issues safety standards for products in Canada and acts as an advocate for public safety. See *CAN/CSA-Z731-95. 1995. Rev. ed. National Standard of Canada. Emergency Planning for Industry.*

Library Binding Institute (LBI)
321 - Lincoln Drive
Edina, Montana 55436-2703 U.S.A.
Tel: 612-939-0165
Fax: 612-939-0213
Certifies qualified binders after examination of work and investigation of experience in accordance with LBI Standard for Library Binding. Conducts research on binding materials and methods.

Image Permanence Institute (IPI)
Rochester Institute of Technology
70 Lomb Memorial Drive
Rochester, New York 14623-5604 U.S.A.
Tel: 716-475-5199
Fax: 716-475-7230
URL: http://www.rit.edu/
University-based non-profit research laboratory devoted to image preservation, research in stability and preservation of imaging media, training of preservation specialists, development of ANSI and ISO preservation standards, provision of contract testing and consultation services and provision of technical information.

International Organization for Standardization (ISO)
1, rue de Varembe
Case Postale 56
CH - 1211 Genève 20
Switzerland
Tel: 41-22-749-0111
Fax: 41-22-733-3430
E-mail: central@iso.ch
URL: http://www.iso.ch/welcome.html
International standards development organization - federation of national standards bodies united to promote standardization worldwide. Canadian ISO representative is the Standards Council of Canada. U.S. ISO representative is the American National Standards Institute. ISO conducts its work through technical committees that work on specific materials, methods, systems, terminology or technologies.

National Association of Photographic Manufacturers (NAPM)
See Photographic & Imaging Manufacturers Association, Inc. (PIMA).

National Fire Protection Association (NFPA)
1 Batterymarch Park
P.O. Box 9101
Quincy, Massachusetts 02269-9101 U.S.A.
Tel: 1-800-344-3555 (sales)
        617-770-3000
Fax: 617-770-0700
        508-895-8301 (sales)
URL: http://www.nfpa.org
ANSI-accredited standards development organization that promotes fire safety through its research and education programmes. Develops, publishes and disseminates fire prevention, protection, suppression, etc. standards related to structures, testing, equipment, materials, design and systems. Conducts technical training seminars. See *NFPA 1600. 1995. Recommended Practice for Disaster Management.*

National Information Standards Organization (NISO)
300 - 4733 Bethesda Avenue
Bethesda, Maryland 20814 U.S.A.
Tel: 301-975-2814
Fax: 310-869-8071
URL: http://www.niso.org/
Non-profit ANSI-accredited standards developing organization. Principal U.S. standards developer for library-related standards.

National Institute of Standards and Technology (NIST)
Gaithersburg, Maryland 20899 U.S.A.
Tel: 301-975-2000
URL: http://www.nist.gov
Formerly National Bureau of Standards. Principal standards agency within the U.S. federal government. Oversees the development of FIPS (Federal Information Processing Standards) and conducts technical studies for other federal agencies. See **National Technical Information Service.**

National Technical Information Service (NTIS)
U.S. Department of Commerce
Springfield, Virginia 22161 U.S.A.
Tel: 703-487-4650
Fax: 703-321-8547
URL: http://www.fedworld.gov
National clearinghouse for research and development results and other information produced by and for the U.S. government, i.e. NIST reports and FIPS publications. Also leading U.S. government agency in international technical and business information exchange.

Photographic & Imaging Manufacturers Association, Inc. (PIMA)
Formerly NAPM (National Association of Photographic Manufacturers)
307 - 550 Mamaroneck Avenue
Harrison, New York 10528-1612 U.S.A.
Tel: 914-698-7603
Fax: 914-698-7609
URL: http://www.pima.net/
Not-for-profit corporation for manufacturers of image technology products. ANSI-accredited standards developing organization.

Standards Council of Canada (SCC)
1200 - 45 O'Connor Street
Ottawa, Ontario K1P 6N7
Tel: 613-238-3222
        1-800-267-8220 (Sales)
Fax: 613-995-4564
E-mail: info@scc.ca
URL: http://www.scc.ca
National coordinating body for development of standards and ISO representative for Canada. A non-regulatory body which administers the National Standards System (NSS), made up of accredited standards development organizations, accredited certification organizations, accredited testing and certification laboratories, accredited quality systems registration organizations and Canadian committees on national and international standardization. A federation of Canadian governments and organizations that develops standards and tests products.
Offers 5 bilingual databases available 24 hours/day for standards users in Canada and abroad: 1. Canadian Standards; 2. Referenced Standards (Federal); 3. GATT TBT Notifications and Draft European Standards; 4. International Standards; and 5. SCC-Accredited Laboratories in U.S. and Canada.

Underwriters' Laboratories of Canada (ULC)
7 Crouse Road
Scarborough, Ontario M1R 3A9
Tel: 416-757-3611
Fax: 416-757-9540
E-mail: ulcinfo@ulc.ca
URL: http://home.istar.ca/~ulcinfo/
Canadian National Standards System-accredited standards development organization. Maintains and operates laboratories and a certification service for examination, testing and classification of devices, constructions, materials and systems to determine their relation to life, fire and property hazards.

Underwriters Laboratory (UL)
333 Pfingsten Road
Northbrook, Illinois 60062 U.S.A.
Tel: 847-272-8800
URL: http://www.ul.com/
Non-profit ANSI-accredited standards developing organization. Evaluates safety (electrical, fire and mechanical) of wide variety of products. Largest 3rd party certification organization in North America.

• Systems Recovery Planning

See alternate site vendors survey (*Disaster Recovery Journal* 1997. 10(3):63-73).
See consultants survey (*Disaster Recovery Journal* Winter 1997 - available online. See entry in **Appendix 3.1 Sources of Information: Disaster Planning and Recovery Journals**).

• Theft

See also **Appendix 3.1 Sources of Information: Professional Associations** and **Security.**

The AB Bookman's Weekly
P.O. Box AB
Clifton, New Jersey 07015 U.S.A.
Tel: 201-772-0021
Fax: 201-772-9281
Publishes a missing books column free of charge.

Art Loss Register
International Foundation for Art Research (IFAR)
500 - 5th Avenue
New York, N.Y. 10110 U.S.A.
Tel: 212-391-8794
Fax: 212-391-8794
URL: http://www.artloss.com
Largest private computerized database of stolen and missing works of art, antiques and valuables. Operates on international basis to assist law enforcement agencies. Also offices in the U.K. and Germany.

Bookline Alert Missing Books and Manuscripts (BAMBAM)
Katharine and Daniel Leab
P.O. Box 1236
Washington, Connecticut 06793 U.S.A.
Tel: 212-737-2715
Database of missing items privately owned by the Leabs, publishers of American Book Prices Current.

International Institute for the Unification of Private Law (UNIDROIT)
28 Via Panisperna 00184
Rome, Italy
Tel: 39 06 69211
Fax: 39 06 69941394
URL: http://www.unidroit.org
Independent international intergovernmental organization. See 1.3.3 for description of UNIDROIT.

International Trade Law Monitor
URL: http://itl.irv.vit.no/trade_law/

Interpol Stolen Cultural Property Program
U.S. National Central Bureau of INTERPOL
U.S. Department of Justice
Washington, D.C. 20530 U.S.A.
Disseminates information on stolen, seized and/or suspect cultural property worldwide. The U.S. National Central Bureau of INTERPOL maintains a computerized stolen cultural property database. Thefts must be reported through a law enforcement agency.
URL: http:// www.usdoj.gov/usncb/cultprop/ cultureabout.htm

National Stolen Art File
Federal Bureau of Investigation
IT/GRCU, Room 5096
935 Pennsylvania Avenue, NW
Washington, D.C. 20535 U.S.A.
Tel: 202--324-4192
Fax: 202-324-1504
URL: http://www.fbi.gov/majorcases/arttheft/art. htm
Computerized index of stolen art and cultural property as reported to the FBI (U.S. and international). All search requests must be made through a law enforcement agency.

• Tornadoes

See entry for **National (U.S.) Centers for Environmental Prediction (NCEP)** under **Appendix 3.1 Sources of Information: Weather.**

FEMA Tornado Safety Page
URL: http://www.fema.gov/fema/tornadof.html

Appendix 3: Resources

• Tsunamis

See also **Appendix 3.1 Sources of Information: Weather.**

British Columbia Provincial Emergency Programme: BC Tsunami Warning Plan
URL: http://hoshi.cic.sfu.ca/~pep/tsunami.html
General information on tsunamis, explanation of Tsunami Warning System, etc.

FEMA Fact Sheet on Tsunamis
URL: http://www.fema.gov/fema/tsunamif.html

International Tsunami Information Center
Box 50027
Honolulu, Hawaii 96850-4993 U.S.A.
Tel: 808-541-1657/8
Fax: 808-541-1678
E-mail: itic@ptwc.noaa.gov
URL: http://www.geophys.washington.edu/
          tsunami/general/mitigation/itic.html
Maintained by the U.S. NOAA (National Oceanic and Atmospheric Administration) for the Intergovernmental Oceanographic Commission of UNESCO. Carries out public education programmes, assists in maintaining data and descriptive information on tsunamis, and monitors the Tsunami Warning System in the Pacific.

• Volcanos

United States Geological Survey Volcano Hazards Program
URL: http://vulcan.wr.usgs.gov/Vhp/framework.
          html
Description of program, related information and links.

• Weather

See also **Appendix 3.1 Sources of Information: Fire, Floods, Hurricanes, Tornadoes** and **Tsunamis.**

Atmospheric Environment Services Environment Canada
National Headquarters
4905 Dufferin Street
Toronto, Ontario M3H 5T4
Tel: Inquiry 416-739-4826
          1-900-565-1111
          Climate information and publications
          416-739-4826
Fax: 416-739-4521
URL: http://www.tor.ec.gc.ca/
Current Forecasts Across Canada
URL: http://www.tor.ec.gc.ca/forecasts.index.
          html
Regional Forecasts Across Canada
URL: http://www.doe.ca/text/index.html
National service of Environment Canada. Provides meteorological and hydrological warnings and forecasts to reduce risks to life and property of Canadians. Supports and carries out related research.

Emergency Managers Weather Information Network
URL: http://www.nws.noaa.gov/oso/oso1/oso
          /document/enwin.htm

FEMA Links to Weather Information
URL: http://www.gov/fema/weathr.htm

National (U.S.) Centers for Environmental Prediction (NCEP)
URL: http://www.ncep.noaa.gov/
Part of National Oceanic and Atmospheric Administration. Consists of nine centers. National Weather Service provides worldwide forecast guidance products and services.

National Weather Service Warnings
URL: http://win.nws.noaa.gov/iwin/national
          warnings.html
Storm Prediction Center:
URL: http://www.nssi.ouedu/~spc/
Monitors and forecasts severe and non-severe thunderstorms and tornados and other hazardous weather across U.S. 24hours/day.
Tropical Prediction Center - see entry for **National (U.S.) Hurricane Center** under **Appendix 3.1 Sources of Information: Hurricanes.**

Weather Channel
URL: http://www.weather.com

Weather Net
URL: http://cirrus.sprl.umich.edu
Billed as the most popular www site in the world. Provides about hundreds of hyperlinks to other weather sites around the world.

3.2   Sources of Assistance

The following lists institutions and organizations in Canada that can provide not only information, but can provide disaster assistance in the form of advice, aid or service, depending on the circumstances. They are mostly government agencies and are subject divided and listed in alphabetical order.

• Disaster Planning and Recovery - National, Provincial and Territorial Government Organizations

Emergency Preparedness Canada (EPC)
Communications Directorate
122 Bank Street
2nd Floor, Jackson Building
Ottawa, Ontario KIA 0W6
Tel: 613-991-7077
Fax: 613-998-9589
E-mail: communications@epc-pcc.x400.gc.ca
URL: http://hoshi.cic.sfu.ca/epc/
Federal Policy for Emergencies -
          http://hoshi.cic.sfu/epc/POLICY
Disaster Financial Assistance Arrangments -
          http://hoshi.cic.sfu/epc/DFA
Points of Contact -
          http://hoshi.cic.sfu/epc/NTACTS
Joint Emergency Preparedness Program -
          http://hoshi.cic.sfu/epc/JEPP
Federal agency operating within the Ministry of National Defense responsible for coordinating civil emergency planning across Canada.
See Appendix 2 for details of EPC mandate and services.

EPC Regional

- Alberta and Northwest Territories
Emergency Preparedness Canada
9700 Jasper Avenue
Edmonton, Alberta T5J 4C3
Tel: 403-495-3005
Fax: 403-495-4492
E-mail: alb3@jackson.epc.epc-pcc.x400.gc.ca

- British Columbia and Yukon
Emergency Preparedness Canada
P.O. Box 10000
Victoria, B.C. V8Z 6N6
Tel: 604-363-3621
Fax: 604-363-3995
E-mail: bc3@jackson.epc.epc-pcc.x400.gc.ca

- Manitoba
Emergency Preparedness Canada
Suite 403, Macdonald Building
344 Edmonton Street
Winnipeg, Manitoba R3B 2L4
Tel: 204-983-6790
Fax: 204-983-3886
E-mail: man3@jackson.epc.epc-pcc.x400.gc.ca

- New Brunswick
Emergency Preparedness Canada
P.O. Box 534
Fredericton, New Brunswick E3B 5A6
Tel: 506-452-3020
Fax: 506-452-3906
E-mail: nb3@jackson.epc.epc-pcc.x400.gc.ca

- Newfoundland
Emergency Preparedness Canada
Box 73, Atlantic Place, Suite 504
215 Water Street
St. John's, Newfoundland A1°C 6C9
Tel: 709-772-552
Fax: 709-772-4532
E-mail: nfl3@jackson.epc.epc-pcc.x400.gc.ca

- Nova Scotia
Emergency Preparedness Canada
801 - 6009 Quinpool Road
Halifax, Nova Scotia B3K 5J7
Tel: 902-426-2082
Fax: 902-426-2087
E-mail: ns3@jackson.epc.epc-pcc.x400.gc.ca

- Ontario
Emergency Preparedness Canada
205 - 20 Holly Street
Toronto, Ontario M4S 3B1
Tel: 416-973-6343
Fax: 416-973-2362
E-mail: ont3@jackson.epc.epc-pcc.x400.gc.ca

- Prince Edward Island
Emergency Preparedness Canada
P.O. Box 1175
Charlottetown, P.E.I. C1A 7M8
Tel: 902-566-7047
Fax: 902-566-7045
E-mail: pei3@jackson.epc.epc-pcc.x400.gc.ca

- Québec
Emergency Preparedness Canada
250 ouest, Grand-Allée, Suite 700
Québec (Québec) G1R 2H4
Tel: 418-648-3111
Fax: 418-648-4923
E-mail: que3@jackson.epc.epc-pcc.x400.gc.ca

- Saskatchewan
Emergency Preparedness Canada
Suite 850, Avord Tower
2002 Victoria Avenue
Regina, Saskatchewan S4P 0R7
Tel: 306-780-5005
Fax: 306-780-6461
E-mail: sas3@jackson.epc.epc-pcc.x400.gc.ca

Provincial and Territorial Emergency Measures Organizations

- Alberta
Alberta Transportation and Utilities
4999 - 98th Avenue NW
Twin Atria Building, 2nd Floor
Edmonton, Alberta T6B 2X3
Tel: 403-427-8711

- British Columbia
Provincial Emergency Program (PEP)
455 Boleskine Road
Victoria, B.C. V8Z 1E7
Tel: 604-387-5956
Fax: 604-952-4888
URL: http://hoshi.cic.sfu.ca/~pep

- Manitoba
Emergency Management Organization
15th Floor, Woodsworth Building
405 Broadway Avenue
Winnipeg, Manitoba R3C 3L6
Tel: 204-945-4789
URL: http://www.gov.mb.ca/gs/memo/

- New Brunswick
New Brunswick Public Safety Services
Department of Municipalities, Culture and
Housing
P.O. Box 6000
Fredericton, New Brunswick E3B 5H1
Tel: 506-453-2133
Fax: 506-453-5513
URL: http://gov.nb/ca/pss/emo.htm

- Newfoundland
Emergency Measures Division
Department of Municipal Affairs
P.O. Box 8700
St. John's, Newfoundland A1B 4J6
Tel: 709-729-3703

- Northwest Territories
Emergency Measures Department of Municipal
and Community Affairs
Government of Northwest Territories
P.O. Box 1320
Yellowknife, Northwest Territories X1A 2L9
Tel: 403-920-6133

- Nova Scotia
Emergency Measures Organization
P.O. Box 2107
Halifax, Nova Scotia B3J 3B7
Tel: 902-424-5620
Fax: 902-424-5376
URL: http://198.166.215.5/envi/dept/emo/

- Ontario
Emergency Planning Ontario
Ministry of the Solicitor General and
Correctional Services
25 Grosvenor Avenue, 19th Floor
Toronto, Ontario M7A 1Y6
Tel: 416-314-3723
Fax: 416-314-3758
URL: http://hoshi.cic.sfu.ca/ont/index.html

- Prince Edward Island
Emergency Measures Organization
P.O. Box 2063
Summerside, P.E.I. C1A 5L2
Tel: 902-888-8050

- Québec
Direction générale de la Sécurité et de la
prévention
Ministère de la Sécurité publique
2525, boul. Laurier, 2e étage
Sainte-Foy (Québec) G1V 2L2
Tel: 418-643-3256

- Saskatchewan
Emergency Measures Organization
220 - 1855 Victoria Avenue
Regina, Saskatchewan S4P 3V5
Tel: 306-787-9563

- Yukon
Emergency Measures Organization
Department of Community Services and
Transportation Services
Government of Yukon
P.O. Box 2703
Whitehorse, Yukon Y1A 2C6
Tel: 403-667-5220

Industry Canada Emergency Telecommunications
URL: http://hoshi.cic.sfu.ca/ic/
Lists federal government and regional contacts for
emergency telecommunications.

• Disasters and Conservation

See also **Appendix 3.1 Sources of Information:
Professional Associations.**

Canadian Conservation Institute (CCI)
1030 Innes Road
Ottawa, Ontario KIA 0M5
Tel: 613-998-3721 (24 hrs/day)
Fax: 613-998-4721
URL: http://www.pch.gc.ca/cci-icc
Unless otherwise noted, specialists may be contacted as above.
- Disaster Response/Recovery/Training
Deborah Stewart, Senior Assistant Conservator,
or David Tremain, Conservator, Preventive
Conservation Services Division
- Environmental Monitoring
Maureen MacDonald, Assistant Conservation
Scientist, Preventive Conservation Services
Division
- Fire Protection
Paul Baril, Advisor, Fire Protection, Preventive
Conservation Services Division
Tel: 613-745-3760
Fax: 613-745-4519
- Pest Control
Tom Strang, Conservation Scientist, Preventive
Conservation Services Division
- Security
Wayne Kelly, Advisor, Security, Preventive
Conservation Services Division
Tel: 819-827-3714
Fax: 819-827-4514
Special operating agency of the Department of
Canadian Heritage whose mandate is to promote
care and preservation of Canada's moveable cultural property and advance practice, science and
technology of conservation. In the event of emergency such as fire or water damage to collections,
CCI can be contacted at any time, day or night, seven
days a week. In certain situations it may be possible
to send CCI staff to assist with salvage operations.
This service is free of charge to Canadian institutions with publicly owned collections.

National Archives of Canada (NAC)
625, Blvd. du Carrefour
Gatineau (Québec) K1A 0N3
Tel: 819-997-1818
Fax: 819-953-0150
URL: http://www.archives.ca/
Contact: Director, Archives Preservation Division
Tel: 819-953-7701
National archives whose primary functions are
responsibility for archival records in all media,
serving as an administrative arm of the federal
government providing advisory and operational
services in records management, and that of a
leading institution in the Canadian archival and
records management community. Can provide
advice and referrals in the event of emergency.

National Library of Canada (NLC)
395 Wellington Street
Ottawa, Ontario K1A 0N4
Tel: 613-906-1623
Fax: 613-996-7941
URL: http://www.nlc-bnc.ca/
Disaster Response and Training:
Alison Bullock (Manager, Preservation and Copying)
Tel: 613-992-9652
National library whose primary responsibilities are; to collect, preserve and promote access to Canada's published heritage; to foster library development across the country; and to encourage the sharing of resources among libraries. Can provide advice and referrals in the event of emergency.

National Library and National Archives of Canada
Addresses as above.
Disaster Planning:
Carole Beauvais (Chief Special Programs, Management Services Branch) 613-996-2730
Lucie Roy (Administrator, Disaster Control)
Tel: 613-947-0644
Training programme provided under auspices of disaster control programme. Offers basic disaster training and some media-specific workshops, i.e., microforms and sound recordings.

• Theft

See also **Appendix 3.1 Sources of Information: Professional Associations** and **Theft**.

Royal Canadian Mounted Police (RCMP)
National Headquarters
1200 Vanier Parkway
Ottawa, Ontario K1A 0R2
Tel: 613-993-7267 (24hours/day)
URL: http://www.rcmp-grc.gc.ca/html/arttheft.htm
The RCMP is Canada's national police service providing law enforcement services through detachments across the country. And the national central bureau in Canada for Interpol (International Criminal Police Organization). Interpol bureaus worldwide circulate information related to crimes against moveable cultural property.

For information on art theft in Canada,
Contact Alain Lacoursiere, Sergeant Detective, Fraud Division, Montreal Urban Community Police Service
Tel: 514-280-3124

3.3   Sources of Facilities and Services

The following suppliers can provide information and offer a variety of facilities and services to assist with disaster preparedness, as well as response and recovery. Organizations are encouraged to contact these and other businesses to discuss and compare the products and services available. Specific arrangements (credit, delivery, etc.) should be made and verified as part of plan development and revision before a disaster occurs. The disaster plan should also include information specific to your organization and site(s), its services and systems such as those for utilities, fire protection, HVAC, security and information technology.

It is also possible that your organization may be able to obtain services through municipal, regional, provincial or federal governments which do large scale purchasing.

This list focuses on the major providers of facilities and services on a nation-wide basis either from a single site or from locations across Canada. The entries are subject divided and listed in alphabetical order.

• Bookbinding

See Yellow Pages Directories (Business & Industrial) under bookbinders.

Lehmann Bookbinding Ltd.
97 Ardelt Avenue
Kitchener, Ontario N2C 2E1
Tel: 519-570-4444
        1-800-463-3573
Fax: 519-570-4452

Smiths Falls Bookbinding Ltd.
38 Union Street
Smiths Falls, Ontario K7A 5C4
Tel: 613-283-1981
Fax: 613-283-1995

Universal Bindery (MAN) Ltd.
1415 Spruce Street
Winnipeg, Manitoba R3E 2V8
Tel: 204-783-3890
Fax: 204-783-4188

Universal Bindery (SASK) Ltd.
516 A Duchess Street
Saskatoon, Saskatchewan S7K 0R1
Tel: 306-652-8313
Fax: 306-244-2994

Wallaceburg Bookbinding & Mftg. Co. Ltd.
95 Arnold Street
Wallaceburg, Ontario N8A 3P3
Tel: 519-627-3552
Fax: 519-627-6922

• Chemical Spills

Canutec
Transport Canada
Tel: 613-992-4624 (call collect for information)
URL: http://www.tc.gc.ca/canutec/english/main-e.htm
CANUTEC is the Canadian Transport Emergency Centre operated by Transport Canada to assist emergency response personnel in handling dangerous goods emergencies. Can provide information, immediate advice and recommend actions to be taken only by telephone, i.e. health hazards, first aid, protective clothing, evacuation distances, etc. Use of emergency telephone number is free service but requires registration (consignors or manufacturers of dangerous goods).

Environment Canada
See White Pages Telephone Directory under The Blue Pages for numbers for government offices and services. Includes federal, provincial and municipal listings.
See entry under **Appendix 3.1 Sources of Information: Health and Safety**.

• Cleaning Services

See Yellow Pages Directories (Consumer) under Janitorial Service.

Butler Cleaners Inc.
or
Creative Building Maintenance Inc.
Head Offices
4120 Ridgeway Drive, Unit 23
Mississauga, Ontario L5L 5S9
Tel: 905-828-5505
        1-800-668-9695
Fax: 905-828-5634
Service: Includes sterile cleaning
Locations: Across Canada

Modern Building Cleaning
Head Office
811 Islington Avenue
(Islington and Evans Ave. P.O. Box 950 Station U)
Etobicoke, Ontario M8Z 5Y7
Tel: 416-255-1331
Fax: 416-255-4791
Service: Includes sterile cleaning
Locations: Across Canada

• Conservation

See Yellow Pages Directories (Consumer) under Art Restoring.
Check with local institutions and associations who may provide referrals. Contact Canadian Association of Professional Conservators (CAPC) or Canadian Association for Conservation of Cultural Property (CAC) - see entries under **Appendix 3.1 Sources of Information: Professional Associations**.

• Digital Imaging

See Yellow Pages Directories (Consumer) under Imaging Scanning Systems and Service.

Access Document Conversions
Division of Access Systems Ltd.
8 - 333 Wyecroft Road
Oakville, Ontario L2K 2H2
Tel: 905-338-9030
Fax: 905-338-8926
E-mail: accessys@worldchat.com
Service: Electronic imaging services and film-based imaging services. Also do microfilming.

Xebec Imaging Services Inc.
Head Office
2770 - 14th Avenue
Markham, Ontario L3R 0J1
Tel: 905-470-2000
Fax: 905-470-2048
URL: http://www.xebec.ca
Service: Electronic imaging services and film-based imaging services. Also recovery of Kodak microfilm.

• Environmental Control Services

See **3.3 Sources of Facilities and Services: Recovery Services - Full Service.**

• Freeze-Drying Services

See **3.3 Sources of Facilities and Services: Recovery Services - Full Service.**

• Freezing/Cold Storage Facilities and Services

See Yellow Pages Directories (Consumer) under Warehouses - Cold Storage. Many full-service recovery companies will arrange for these services - see **Recovery Services - Full Service.**

Associated Freezers of Canada
Head Office
3691 Weston Road
Toronto, Ontario M9L 1W4
Tel: 416-741-7820
Service: Blast freezing
Locations: Across Canada
Note: At facility, client is responsible for unloading boxes.

• Freezer Trucks

See Yellow Pages Directories (Business & Industrial) under Transport Services and Yellow Pages Directories (Consumer) under Transport Leasing.

Erb Refrigerated Transport Ltd.
Head Office
1889 Britannia Road East
Malton, Ontario L5W 3C3
Tel: 905-670-8490
          1-800-665-COLD
Service: Refrigerated transport across most of Canada.

Ryder Truck Rental Canada Ltd.
Head Office
4255 Weston Road
Toronto, Ontario M9L 1W8
Tel: 416-746-2244
Fax: 416-746-7760
          416-255-2343 For after hours - Service Department
          1-800-667-9337 For truck rental locations
Service: Refrigerated trucks.
Locations: Across Canada

• Pest Management

See Yellow Pages Directories (Consumer) under Pest Control Services.

Abell Pest Control Inc.
Head Office
246 Attwell Drive
Rexdale, Ontario M9W 5B4
Tel: 416-675-1635
          1-888-949-4949
Fax: 416-675-6727
E-mail: ifo@abellgroup.com
URL: http://www.abellgroup.com
Service: Onsite treatment.
Locations: Across Canada.

PCO Services Inc.
Head Office
5840 Falbourne Street
Mississauga, Ontario L5R 3L8
Tel: 905-502-9700
          1-800-726-7324 (24 hours)
Fax: 905-502-9510
URL: http://www.pco.ca
Service: Onsite treatment.
Locations: Across Canada.

Rentokil Initial Canada Ltd.
Head Office
203-3650 Victoria Park Avenue
Willowdale, Ontario M2H 3P7
Tel: 416-492-2633
Fax: 416-492-0194
URL: http://www.rentokil.co.uk/
Service: On-site truck or bubble fumigation.
Locations: Provide service across Canada.

• Records Management

See Yellow Pages Directories (Business & Industrial) under Office Records Stored for companies that provide management and storage services for archive and library information and materials. Most offer disaster planning and recovery programmes.

Archivex Inc.
Head Office
4005, rue Richelieu
Montréal (Québec) H4C 1A1
Tel: 514-935-2493
Fax: 514-935-9379
Service: Full records management services (storage, retrieval, destruction, disaster planning, consulting).
Locations: Across Canada

Pierce Leahy (Formerly Command Records Services Ltd.)
Canadian Head Office
195 Summerlea Road
Brampton, Ontario L6T 4P6
Tel: Information   905-792-7050
          Emergency   1-800-268-5697
Fax: 905-792-1152
URL: http://www.pierceleahy.com/
Service: Include data management, information management software, disaster recovery planning, magnetic media relocations and destruction.
Locations: Across Canada.

Recall Total Information Management
Division of Brambles Canada
Canadian Head Office
P.O. Box 280
Malton, Ontario L4T 3B6
Tel: 1-800-491-2467
Fax: 905-629-3280
URL: http://ca.recall.com/
Service: Comprehensive data storage, protection and recovery services including climate control, pickup and delivery (including emergency service), computerized tracking and management, tape cleaning and verification.
Locations: Toronto, southern Ontario and Quebec.

• Recovery Services - Audio Recordings and Videotape

Note: National Archives of Canada may be able to provide assistance. See **3.2 Sources of Assistance: Disasters and Conservation.**

Graham Newton Digital Audio Restoration
P.O. Box 672
Don Mills, Ontario M3C 2T6
Tel: 416-444-3444
Fax: 416-444-3550
URL: http://www.audio-restoration.com
Service: Transfer and audio restoration of phonograph records or tapes to DAT, CDr, cassette or open reel.

Resources (U.S.) for Transfer and Restoration of Video and Audio Tape
URL: http://www.nta.org/MediaStability/Disaster Recovery/AudioAndVideotapeRecovery Resources

Spec Bros. llc
P.O. Box 5
Richfield Park, New Jersey 07660 U.S.A.
Tel: 201-440-6589
          1-800-852-7732
Fax: 201-440-6588
URL: http://www.crica.com/specs/index.html
Service: Provides full range of services - recovery, restoration, consulting, archive evaluation, etc. - for all audiotape and videotape formats, and some datatape.

Appendix 3: Resources

Vidipax
Headquarters
4th Floor - 450 West 31st Street
New York, N.Y. 10001 U.S.A.
Tel: 1-800-653-8434
         212-563-1999
Fax: 212-563-1994
E-mail: vidipax@panix.com
URL: http://panix-com/~vidipax/index.html
Location: Sales offices in Los Angeles, San
         Francisco and Canada
Service: Provides full range of services -
         restoration, consulting and forensic -
         for all audiotape and videotape for-
         mats, and 16 & 32 mm film.

• Recovery Services - Business

See Yellow Pages Directories (Consumer) under
Computer Repairs, Cleaning & Service.

Comdisco Disaster Recovery Services Canada Ltd.
Canadian Head Office
Royal Bank Plaza, North Tower
Suite 2075, P.O. Box 131
Toronto, Ontario M5J 2L3
Tel: 416-367-4180
Fax: 416-367-5095
URL: http://www.comdisco.com
Service: Full service provider of disaster recov-
         ery and business recovery services
         including hot sites, LAN/PC recovery,
         voice recovery, etc.

Sungard Recovery Services Ltd.
Canadian Head Office
6535 Millcreek Drive, Unit 17
Mississauga, Ontario L5N 2M2
Tel: 905-813-5700
Fax: 905-629-8009
URL: http://recovery/sungard.com.index.html
Service: Specializes in business recovery ser-
         vices especially multi-platform and
         open systems recovery. Hotsites,
         mobile recovery units and data recov-
         ery. Offers consulting services.
Locations: Across Canada

• Recovery Services - Computer Data, Software and Hardware

See Yellow Pages Directories (Consumer) under
Computer Repairs, Cleaning & Service.

Data Recovery Labs
Head Office
100 - 85 Scarsdale Road
Don Mills, Ontario M3B 2R2
Tel: 416-570-6990
         Canada/U.S. 1-800-563-1167
Fax: 416-510-6992
         1-800-563-6979
E-mail: helpme@datarec.com
URL: http://www.datarec.com/
Service: Full service recovery of operating and
         file systems, and data from all magnetic
         and optical storage devices - hard disk
         drives, removable media, optical devices
         and tape. Free evaluations provided.
         Service across Canada, U.S. (office in
         Buffalo, New York) and international.

DataRecovery.ca
590 Alden Road, Unit 105
Markham, Ontario L3R 8N2
Tel: 416-293-2128
         Canada/U.S./International 1-888-481-9501
URL: http://www.datarecovery.ca/
Service: Data recovery from hard drives,
         removable media, tapes and car-
         tridges. Service across Canada and
         international.

Disktek Data Recovery
590 Alden Road, Unit 105
Markham, Ontario L3R 8N2
Tel: 416-984-5388
         Canada/U.S. 1-888-839-0949
E-mail: info@disktek.com
URL: http://www.disktek.com/
Service: Data recovery from high-end network
         systems.

LWG Restoretek Inc.
4444 Eastgate Parkway
Mississauga, Ontario L4W 4T6
Tel: 905-238-1707
Fax: 905-238-8634
Service: Full disaster recovery services for
         computer hardware and software.

Relectronic Remech Inc.
21 - 620 Davenport Road
Waterloo, Ontario N2V 2C2
Tel: 519-884-8665
Fax: 519-884-5721
E-mail: jsutherland@relectronic.com
URL: http://www.relectronic.com
Service: Full service recovery for electronic
         hardware, software and media, either
         onsite or offsite. Provides recommenda-
         tions re viability of recovery.
         Water-based cleaning and decontami-
         nation, convection drying, vacuum
         drying to client's specifications, copying.

Techni-Drives Data Recovery
1 Dean Park Road, Suite 1608
Scarborough, Ontario M1B 2W5
Tel: Emergency hotline 1-888-712-7808
E-mail: sales@techni-drives.com
URL: http://www.techni-drives.com/
Service: Data recovery and hard drive repair.

• Recovery Services - Film and Photo

See Yellow Pages Directories (Consumer) under
Photographic Finishing.

Note: National Archives of Canada may be able
to provide assistance. See **3.2 Sources of
Assistance: Disasters and Conservation**.

See also **Appendix 3.3 Sources of Facilities and
Services: Recovery Services - Full Service**

Data Repro Com Ltd.
Kodak Image Guard Lab
75 Horner Avenue, Unit 12
Toronto, Ontario M8Z 4X5
Tel: 416-251-3721
         1-800-268-2208
Fax: 416-251-4675
Service: Recovery of Kodak microfilm only. No-
         charge reprocessing of Kodak original
         silver gelatin master microfilm.
Locations: Other Kodak Image Guard Labs
         across Canada

Kodak Canada Ltd.
3500 Eglinton Avenue West
Toronto, Ontario M6M 1V3
Tel: 416-760-4565
         1-800-352-8378
Fax: 416-761-4681
URL: http://www.kodak.com/about
         Kodak/regions/kci/engHomePage.shtml
Service: Recovery of Kodak microfilm, fiche or
         aperture cards only. No-charge
         reprocessing of Kodak original silver
         gelatin master microfilm.
         When you use Kodak microfilm, you are
         automatically covered by the Kodak
         Disaster Recovery Program.

MES (Microfilm Equipment Services) Limited
200 Amber Street
Markham, Ontario L3R 3J8
Tel: 905-475-9263
Fax: 416-9494-4079
Service: Recovery of microfilm. If already use
         their film or processing services, dis-
         aster recovery is free. If not, there
         would be a charge.

Restoration House Film Group Inc.
P.O. Box 298
Belleville, Ontario K8N 5A2
Tel: 613-966-4076
Fax: 613-966-8038
Service: Recovery and restoration of all types
         of photographic film and microforms.
         Some treatment of photographic print
         materials.

Xebec Imaging Services Inc.
Head Office
2770 - 14th Avenue
Markham, Ontario L3R 0J1
Tel: 905-470-2000
Fax: 905-470-2048
URL: http://www.xebec.ca
Service: Recovery of Kodak microfilm only.
         No-charge reprocessing of Kodak
         original silver gelatin master micro-
         film. Also digital imaging.

• Recovery Services - Full Service

See Yellow Pages Directories (Consumer) under Fire Damage Restoration and Water Damage Restoration.

Belfor USA (Belfor International)
Home Office
2425 Blue Smoke Court South
Fort Worth, Texas 76105 U.S.A.
Tel: 800-856-3333
Fax: 817-536-1167
URL: http://www.belforusa.com
Service: Full recovery services including appraisal, consulting, dehumidification, smoke odour removal, mold and mildew prevention, structural drying, wet book and document reclamation, magnetic media recovery, etc. across North and South America.

Cromwell Restoration Limited
Head Office
2625 Skeena Avenue
Vancouver, B.C. V5M 4T1
Tel: 604-432-1123
Fax: 604-433-2451
Locations: Other offices in B.C. and Calgary and Winnipeg.
Service: Full service recovery including damage assessment, vacuum freeze-drying, thermal vacuum freeze-drying, ozonation, cleaning, reprocessing, etc.

Document Reprocessors Ltd.
- East Coast
5611 Water Street
Middlesex, N.Y. 14507 U.S.A.
Tel: 716-554-4500
          1-888-4DRYING (437-9464)(24 hours)
Fax: 716-554-4114
- West Coast
1120 - 41 Sutter Street
San Francisco, California 94104 U.S.A.
Tel: 415-362-1290
          1-800-4DRYING (437-9464)(24 hours)
Fax: 415-342-4201
URL: http://www.documentreprocessors.com
Service: Comprehensive recovery services. Includes damage assessment, freeze-drying and vacuum freeze-drying mobile systems for on-site treatment, packout, cleaning, reformatting, etc.

Munters Corp., Moisture Control Services Division
Corporate Headquarters
16 Hunt Road
Amesbury, Massachusetts 01913 U.S.A.
Tel: Emergency 1-800-I-CANDRY (24 hours)
          1-800-388-4900
          508-388-4900
Fax: 508-388-4939
URL: http://www.muntersmcs.com
Service: Comprehensive recovery services as described for Canadian regional office.
Locations: 30 offices across the U.S. and Canada
- Canadian Regional Office
6810 Kitmat Road, Unit 16
Mississauga, Ontario L5N 5M2
Tel: Emergency 905-858-5851 or 1-800-I-CANDRY (24 hours) 1-800-268-1800
Fax: 905-858-9130
Service: Comprehensive recovery services. Includes inspection, damage assessment, emergency extraction of water, dehumidification drying of facilities and collections (onsite or offsite), vacuum freeze-drying, packout, document cleaning, corrosion and odour control and other recovery treatments. Nationwide service.
Locations: Also office in Vancouver
Tel: 604-574-4316
Fax: 604-574-4362

Rosco Document Restoration Inc.
Head Office
225, rue Lindsay
Dorval (Québec) H9P 1C6
Tel: 514-631-7789/931-7789
          1-800-86ROSCO
Fax: 514-931-2494
URL: http://www.roscodoc.com
Service: Full service recovery including inspection, damage assessment, packout, freeze-stabilization, vacuum freeze-drying (1200 cubic foot chamber), desiccant dehumidification of magnetic media, odour control, reproduction services, etc.

Steamatic Canada, Inc.
- Head Office and Services in Québec and the Maritimes
7750 est, rue Jarry
Anjou (Québec) H1J 2M3
Tel: 1-800-215-8621 (24 hour tollfree hotline)
- Ontario and Western Canada Region
31 Saxony Circle
Cambridge, Ontario N1S 4G6
Tel: 1-800-263-5961 (24 hour tollfree hotline)
          1-800-215-8621 (head office 24 hour toll-free hotline)
Fax: 519-624-9431
URL: http://www.locator.ca/on/steamatic/page2.htm
E-mail: johnc@in.on.ca
Services: Provides complete recovery and restoration services including clean-up, damage assessment, recovery recommendations, transportation, freezing, dehumidification drying, vacuum freeze-drying, corrosion and odour control and other recovery treatments. Specializes in data recovery and magnetic media restoration. Linked with response centres across Canada.

Steamatic, Inc.
International Headquarters
303 Arthur Street
Fort Worth, Texas 76107 U.S.A.
Tel: 800-527-1295
          817-332-1575
U.S. Emergency Response Call Center:
          1-888-STEAMATIC (Center will contact location nearest you)
URL: http://www.steamatic.com
Service: Founded by Blackmon and Mooring. Locations across the U.S. Franchises in 20 countries. Provides complete recovery and restoration services as described for Steamatic Canada, Inc.

• Salvage Services

See also **3.3 Sources of Facilities and Services: Recovery Services - Full Service.**
See Yellow Pages Directories (Consumer) under Salvage, Fire Damage Restoration and Water Damage Restoration. Consult with insurance company that handles the policy of the organization, as many work in conjunction with specific salvage companies.

• Space Leasing

See Yellow Pages Directories under Real Estate Brokers and look for listings with office/retail/industrial leasing.

• Storage Services

See entries under **3.3 Sources of Facilities and Services: Records Management.**

• Vacuum-Freeze Drying Services

Check local food processing plants, university research facilities for vacuum freeze-drying operations.

See entries under **3.3 Sources of Facilities and Services: Recovery Services - Full Service.**

Freeze-Dry Foods Inc.
579 Speers Road
Oakville, Ontario L6K 2G4
Tel: 905-844-1471
Fax: 905-844-8140
Service: Vacuum freeze-drying (5,500 square feet)

3.4   Sources of Supplies and Equipment

The following suppliers can provide a variety of supplies and equipment to assist with disaster response, recovery and to a lesser degree rehabilitation. Organizations are encouraged to contact these and local businesses to discuss and compare the products available for purchase or rent. Some supplies should be purchased for emergency supply depots, and others would be acquired on a needs basis. Specific arrangements (credit, delivery, etc.) should be made and verified as part of plan development and revision before a disaster occurs.

Recommended specifications for supplies and equipment are available from: Lucie Roy, Administrator, Disaster Control, National Library and National Archives of Canada, Tel: 613-947-0644.

It is also possible that your organization may be able to obtain supplies through municipal, regional, provincial or federal governments which does large scale purchasing for federal departments.

This list focuses on the major providers of supplies and equipment on a nation-wide basis either from a single site or from locations across Canada. The entries are subject divided and listed in alphabetical order.

• Cleaning and Janitorial Supplies

See Yellow Pages Directories (Consumer) under Janitors' Supplies.

Canadian Mill Supply Co. Ltd.
451 Ellesmere Road
Scarborough, Ontario M1R 4E5
Tel: 416-752-3010
Fax: 416-751-0600
Service: Wiping cloths, paper products and janitorial supplies.

Wood Wyant Inc.
440 Passmore Avenue
Toronto, Ontario M8Z 5M8
Tel: 416-609-9268
Fax: 416-609-9698
Locations: Other locations across Canada.

• Computer Equipment and Supplies

Consult your own computer operations/management information systems departments.
See Yellow Pages Directories (Consumer) under Computer-Renting & Leasing, Computer - Personal-Sales & Service, Computer Supplies and Accessories.

• Conservation Supplies

Archival Conservation Resources
61, rue Cemetary
Norway Bay (Québec) J0X 1G0
Tel: 819-647-1981
Fax: As above
Note: Canadian distributor for Conservation Resources. Wide range of conservation supplies, including absorbent papers, plastic films, storage containers, technical supplies and equipment.

Carr McLean Limited
461 Horner Avenue
Toronto, Ontario M8W 4X2
Tel: 416-252-3371
             1-800-268-2123
Fax: 416-252-9203
Note: Full range of conservation supplies, including absorbent papers, plastic films, spunbonded polyester fabric, storage containers, environmental monitoring equipment, safety supplies, water alarms, dry chemical sponges, cleaning aids, etc. Also sells Protext REACT-PAK and RES-CUBE. See entry for Protext under **3.4 Sources of Supplies and Equipment: Emergency Recovery Supplies.**

University Products of Canada
- Eastern Canada
Division of BFB Sales
6535 Millcreek Drive, Unit #8
Mississauga, Ontario L5N 2M2
Tel: 416-858-7888
             1-800-667-2632
Fax: 905-858-8586
E-mail: bfbsales@aol.com
- Western Canada
Bury Media and Supplies
10 - 3771 North Fraser Way
Burnaby, B.C. 5J 5G5
Tel: 604-431-1964/5
Fax: 604-431-1930
E-mail: info@rbury.com
Note: Full range of conservation supplies, including absorbent papers, plastic films, spunbonded polyester fabric, environmental monitoring equipment, storage containers, safety supplies, water alarms, dry chemical sponges, cleaning aids, etc. Also sells Protext REACT-PAK and RESCUBE. See entry for Protext under **3.4 Sources of Supplies and Equipment: Emergency Recovery Supplies.**

Woolfits Art Enterprises Inc.
1153 Queen Street West
Toronto, Ontario M6J 1J4
Tel: 416-536-7878
             1-800-490-3567
             Gaylord U.S. 1-800-841-5854 and Preservation Hotline 1-800-428-3831
Fax: 416-536-4322
Note: Wide range of conservation supplies, including papers and boards, plastic film, storage containers, etc. Operates bulk order purchase programme. Acts as Canadian distributor for Gaylord in the U.S. - sells Protext REACT-PAK and RES-CUBE. See entry for Protext under **3.4 Sources of Supplies and Equipment: Emergency Recovery Supplies.**

• Containers

See entry for **Carr Mclean** under **3.4 Sources of Supplies and Equipment: Conservation Supplies.**

Bread Trays
See Yellow Pages Directories (Consumers) under Bakers - Wholesale.

Cardboard Boxes
See Yellow Pages Directories (Business & Industrial) under Boxes Corrugated & Fibres.

Colt-Pak Containers Inc.
151 Sterling Road
Toronto, Ontario M6R 2B2
Tel: 416-535-7234
          1-800-249-COLT
Fax: 416-531-5205
Note: Also supplies bubblepack.
Locations: Office also in Montreal.

Domtar Packaging Limited
Head Office
450 Evans Avenue
Etobicoke, Ontario M8W 2T5
Tel: 416-255-8541
Fax: 416-255-5382
Note: Also supplies blank newsprint and bubblepack.

Milk Crates
See Yellow Pages Directories (Consumer) under Dairies.

Plastic Vented Containers
See also **Appendix 3.4 Sources of Supplies and Equipment: Conservation Supplies.**

Norseman Plastics Ltd.
39 Westmore Drive
Rexdale, Ontario M9V 3Y6
Tel: 416-745-6980
Fax: 416-745-1874

Scepter Co. Ltd.
170 Midwest Road
Scarborough, Ontario M1P 3A9
Tel: 416-751-9445
Fax: 416-751-4451

Techstar Plastics
15400 Old Simcoe Road
Port Perry, Ontario L9L 1L8
Tel: 416-439-6111
Fax: 905-985-0264

• Emergency Recovery Supplies

See also **Appendix 3.4 Sources of Supplies and Equipment: Conservation Supplies.**

Emergency Supplies for Collections
P.O. Box 3902
Seattle, Washington 98124-3902 U.S.A.
Tel: 1-800-929-6886
          206-322-4181
Fax: 206-323-4153
E-mail: abconser@halcyon.com
Note: For museums, archives and libraries. Various pre-packaged emergency and disaster supply crates for response and recovery. Supplies can be customized to meet specific needs or purchased individually.

Protext
3515 Leland Street
Bethesda, Maryland 20815 U.S.A.
Tel: 301-718-1659
Note: REACT-PAK (comprehensive disaster recovery supply kit) and RESCUBE (collapsible, vented, high-density polyethylene box for transport of water-damaged materials). Sold in Canada by several companies (see **3.4: Sources of Supplies and Equipment: Conservation Supplies**).

• Environmental Monitoring Equipment

See Yellow Pages Directories (Business & Industrial) under Laboratory Equipment and Safety Supplies & Equipment.

In the event of an emergency, temperature and relative humidity monitoring equipment may be borrowed from another organization. May also be obtained as part of an environmental kit from the Canadian Conservation Institute (see **Disasters and Conservation** under **3.2 Sources of Assistance**). See also listings under **Appendix 3.4 Sources of Supplies and Equipment: Safety Supplies and Equipment.**

Baker Instruments Ltd.
42 Dufflaw Road
Toronto, Ontario M6A 2W1
Tel: 416-781-3500
Fax: 416-781-9484

Cansel Survey Equipment
2414 Holly Lane
Ottawa, Ontario K1V 7P1
Tel: 613-731-4703
Fax: 613-526-0712

Enercorp Instruments Ltd.
25 Shorecliffe Road
Islington, Ontario M9B 3S4
Tel: 416-231-5335
Fax: 416-231-7662

Hoskins Scientific
4210 Morris Drive
Burlington, Ontario L7L 5L6
Tel: 905-333-5510
Fax: 905-333-4976

Labequip Ltd.
330 Esna Park Drive, Units 31-32
Markham, Ontario L3R 1H3
Tel: 905-475-5880
Fax: 905-475-1231

• Equipment - General
Equipment and tools such as dehumidifiers, water pumps, wet and dry vacuum cleaners, generators, fans, saws, scaffolding, etc. can all be rented. As these rental operations are mainly local, check the Yellow Pages Directories (Consumer) under Rental-Equipment & Tools and Rental Services-General. For specific equipment look under the heading for each type of equipment needed.

• Freezers

See Yellow Pages Directories (Business & Industrial) under Laboratory Equipment.

See also entry for **VWR Scientific of Canada** under **3.4 Sources of Supplies and Equipment: Safety Supplies and Equipment.**

Wei T'o Associates Inc.
21750 Main Street, Unit 27
P.O. Drawer 40
Matteson, Illinois U.S.A.
Tel: 708-747-6660
Fax: 708-747-6639
Note: Commercial freezers adapted for drying.

• General Supplies

See Yellow Pages Directories (Consumer) under Hardware-Retail or Building Materials for supplier listings of basic supplies such as sponges, pails, mops, brooms, flashlights, etc. Check White Pages for Home Depot, Business Depot, Canadian Tire, etc.

• Office and Computer Supplies

See Yellow Pages Directories (Consumer) under Office Supplies. Check White Pages for Business Depot, Grand & Toy, etc.

• Paper

See Yellow Pages Directories (Consumer) under Paper Distributors and Paper Manufacturers and Paper Products.

Adelco Glenford Lewis Group
335 Passmore Avenue
Scarborough, Ontario M1V 4B5
Tel: 416-754-2060
Fax: 416-754-0982
Note: Freezer paper, waxed paper, blank newsprint
Service: Across Canada

Buntin Reid Paper
1330 Courtney Park Drive East
Mississauga, Ontario L5T 1K5
Tel: 905-670-1351
Fax: 905-670-6097
Note: Blank newsprint, blotting paper
Locations: Across Canada

See **Colt-Pak Containers Inc.** under **Containers.**
Donohue Recycling Ltd.
123 Eastside Drive
Etobicoke, Ontario M8Z 5S5
Tel: 416-231-7772
Fax: 416-231-1577
Note: Blank newsprint.

Unisource Canada Limited
- Supply System and National Office
1475 Courtney Park Drive
Malton, Ontario L4V 1K3
Tel: 905-795-7400
Fax: 905-795-7491
- Fine Paper Division (Blank newsprint)
Tel: 905-276-8400
- Unisource Industrial
Tel: 905-795-7500 (Wax/freezer paper)

Appendix 3: Resources

• Photographic and Video Equipment

See Yellow Pages Directories (Consumer) under Camera, video recorders rental or purchase.

• Plastic Sheeting

For clear polyester or polyethylene film see Yellow Pages Directories (Consumer) under Polyethylene Materials & Products and Yellow Pages Directories (Business & Industrial) under Plastic-Rods, Tubes, Sheets, etc.

Heavy polyethylene sheeting is available from Canadian Tire, Beaver Lumber, Home Hardware as well as other local hardware and lumber/building supply outlets.

See also **3.4 Sources of Supplies and Equipment: Conservation Supplies.**

Atlantic Packaging Products Ltd.
111 Progress Avenue
Scarborough, Ontario M1P 2Y9
Tel: 416-298-8101
Fax: 416-297-2236

BXL Plastics Ltd.
134 Sunrise Avenue
Toronto, Ontario M4A 1B3
Tel: 416-755-3319. After hours: 416-829-1567
Fax: 416-755-9437

Cadillac Plastics
91 Kelfield Street
Rexdale, Ontario M9W 5A4
Tel: 416-249-83ll
Fax: 416-249-0148
Locations: Across Canada

Commercial Plastics
601 Canarctic Drive
Toronto, Ontario M3J 2P9
Tel: 416-667-7644
        1-800-268-3611
Fax: 416-667-7654
Locations: Across Canada

Transilwrap Plastics
333 Finchdene Square
Scarborough, Ontario M1X 1B9
Tel: 416-292-6000
Fax: 416-292-7399
Locations: Across Canada

• Safety Supplies and Equipment

See Yellow Pages Directories (Consumer) under Safety Equipment & Clothing, and Laboratory and Supplies.

Canadawide Scientific Ltd.
2300 Walkley Road
Ottawa, Ontario K1G 6B1
Tel: 416-283-3269
        1-800-267-2362
Fax: 613-736-0150
        1-800-814-5162

Fisher Scientific
Head Office
112 Colonnade Road
Nepean, Ontario K2E 7L6
Tel: 1-800-234-7437
Fax: 1800-463-2996
URL: http://www.fishersci.ca
Locations: Across Canada

Levitt Safety Limited
Head Office
2872 Bristol Circle
Oakville, Ontario L6H 5T5
Tel: 905-829-3299
Fax: 905-829-2919
Locations: Across Canada

Seton Inc.
56 Leek Crescent
Richmond Hill, Ontario L4B 1H1
Tel: 905-764-1122
        1-800-263-1623
        WHMIS 1-800-663-6852
Fax: 1-800-663-3425
URL: http://www.seton.ca
Services: Across Canada

VWR Scientific of Canada Ltd.
Head Office
2360 Argentia Road
Mississauga, Ontario L5N 5Z7
Tel: 905-813-7377
        1-800-932-5000
Fax: 905-813-5244
URL: http://www.vwrsp.com
Locations: Across Canada

References

These references are intended to serve as chapter footnotes and a select bibliography. Readers should contact individual standards organizations for complete and current standards listings (see Appendix 3: Resources).

General

The following selected references are considered to be comprehensive resources on disaster planning and recovery, or 'classic' case study descriptions or analyses.

Anderson, Hazel and John E. McIntyre. 1985. *Planning Manual for Disaster Control in Scottish Libraries & Record Offices.* Edinburgh: National Library of Scotland.

Baillie, Jeavons, Judith Doig and Cathie Jilovsky. 1994. *Disaster in Libraries: Prevention and Control.* 2nd edition. Melbourne: CAVAL Limited.

Barton, John and Johanna Wellheiser, eds. 1985. *An Ounce of Prevention: A Handbook on Disaster Contingency Planning for Archives, Libraries and Record Centres.* Toronto: Toronto Area Archivists Group Education Foundation.

Bohem, Hilda. 1978. *Disaster Prevention and Disaster Preparedness.* Berkeley, California: University of California.

Buchanan, Sally A. and Philip D. Leighton. 1980. *The Stanford Lockheed-Meyer Flood Report.* Stanford, California: Stanford University Libraries.

Buchanan, Sally A. 1988. *Disaster Planning, Preparedness and Recovery for Libraries and Archives: A RAMP Study with Guidelines.* PGI-88/WS/6. Paris: General Information Programme and UNISIST, United Nations Educational, Scientific and Cultural Organization.

Canadian Standards Association and Major Industrial Accidents Council of Canada (CSA and MIACC). 1995. *CAN/CSA-Z731-95 Emergency Planning for Industry.* Etobicoke, Ontario: Canadian Standards Association.

Cunha, George Martin. 1992. Disaster Planning and a Guide to Recovery Resources. *Library Technology Reports* 28(5):533-624.

DePew, John. 1991. Chapter 8. Disaster Preparedness and Recovery. In *A Library, Media and Archival Preservation Handbook.* Santa Barbara, California: ABC- CLIO. 253-300.

Doig, Judith. 1997. *Disaster Recovery for Archives, Libraries and Records Management Systems in Australia and New Zealand.* Wagga Wagga, New South Wales: Centre for Information Studies, Charles Sturt Libraries.

Drabek, Thomas E., and Gerard J. Hoetmer, eds. 1991. *Emergency Management: Principles and Practice for Local Government.* Washington, D.C.: International City/County Management Association (ICMA).

England, Claire and Karen Evans. 1988. *Disaster Management for Libraries: Planning and Process.* Ottawa: Canadian Library Association.

Eulenberg, Julia Niebuhr. 1986. *Handbook for the Recovery of Water Damaged Business Records.* Prairie Village, Kansas: Association of Records Managers and Administrators, Inc. (ARMA).

FEMA (Federal Emergency Management Agency). 1984. *Objectives for Local Emergency Management.* Publication No. CPG 1-5. Washington, D.C.: FEMA.

Fortson, Judith. 1992. *Disaster Planning and Recovery. A How-To-Do-It Manual for Librarians and Archivists.* Number 21. New York: Neal-Schuman Publishers, Inc.

Howell, Alan, Heather Mansell and Marion Roubos-Bennett, compilers. 1996. *Redefining Disasters: A Decade of Counter-Disaster Planning. Proceedings Wednesday 20-Friday 22 September 1995.* Revised edition. Sydney, Australia: State Library of New South Wales.

Hunter, John E. 1990. Chapter 10. Museum Collections: Emergency Planning. In *National Park Service Museum Handbook, Part I: Museum Collections.* Revised ed. Washington, D.C.: National Park Service:10:1-10:29.

Hunter, John E. 1983. Chapter 11. Museum Disaster Planning. In *Museum, Archive, and Library Security.* Lawrence J. Fennelly, ed. Boston: Butterworths. 235-270.

Kahn, Miriam B. 1998. *Disaster Response and Planning for Libraries.* Chicago: American Library Association.

Martin, John H. 1977. *The Corning Flood: Museum Under Water.* Corning, N.Y.: The Corning Museum of Glass.

Morris, John. 1986. *The Library Disaster Preparedness Handbook.* Chicago and London: American Library Association.

Murray, Toby. 1994. *Basic Guidelines for Disaster Planning in Oklahoma.* Tulsa, Oklahoma: Oklahoma Conservation Congress (OCC).

Society of Archivists (Scottish Region). 1996. *Disaster Preparedness: Guidelines for Archives and Libraries.* London: Society of Archivists (Scottish Region).

Stewart, Deborah and David Tremain. 1994. *Emergency and Disaster Preparedness for Museums.* Canadian Conservation Institute (CCI) Workshop. Revised edition. Ottawa: Department of Canadian Heritage, CCI. (Note: Unavailable. To be revised)

Systems and Procedures Exchange Center (SPEC). 1980. *Preparing for Emergencies and Disasters. SPEC Kit 69.* Washington, D.C.: Association of Research Libraries, Office of Management Studies.

Systems Support Inc. 1996. *Glossary.* Glossary definitions of terms used in the Disaster Recovery Field. Editorial Advisory Board (EAB). http://www.drj.com/gloss.html.

Upton, M.S., and C. Pearson. 1978. *Disaster Planning and Emergency Treatments in Museums, Art Galleries, Libraries, Archives and Allied Institutions.* Canberra: The Institute for the Conservation of Cultural Material, Inc.

Waters, Peter. 1979. *Procedures for Salvage of Water-Damaged Library Materials.* 2nd ed. Washington, D.C.: Library of Congress.

Waters, Peter. 1993. Procedures for Salvage of Water Damaged Library Materials. Extracts from unpublished revised text. In *A Primer on Disaster Preparedness, Management, and Response: Paper-Based Materials.* Selected Reprints issued by the Smithsonian Institution, National Archives and Records Administration, Library of Congress and National Park Service. Distributed by the participating agencies. http://palimpsest.stanford.edu/bytopic/disaster.primer.part4of5.text

Willson, Nancy, ed. 1986. *Proceedings of An Ounce of Prevention: A Symposium on Disaster Contingency Planning for Information Managers in Archives, Libraries and Record Centres.* Toronto: Toronto Area Archivists Group Education Foundation.

References

Selected Bibliographies

Murray, Toby, comp. 1994. *Bibliography on Disasters, Disaster Preparedness and Disaster Recovery.* Revised ed. Tulsa, Oklahoma: Oklahoma Conservation Congress.
This is the most comprehensive bibliography of bibliographies, books, articles and reports. Updated periodically. Send additions and corrections to Toby Murray, McFarlin Library, University of Tulsa, Tulsa, Oklahoma.

Schur, Susan E. 1994. Disaster Prevention, Response and Recovery: A Selected Bibliography - Part I. *Technology and Conservation* Summer:21-32. Literature cited (alphabetically A-Dean) mainly from 1965-1992.

Schur, Susan E. 1995. Disaster Prevention, Response and Recovery: A Selected Bibliography - Part II. *Technology and Conservation* Fall:23-34. Literature cited (alphabetically DeCandido-Kelin) mainly from 1965-1992.

Selected Disaster Plans

CoOL Disaster Plans. Provides links to U.S. library and archive disaster plans.
http://palimpsest.stanford.edu/bytopic/disasters/plans

American Hospital Association Resource Centre Disaster Plan. 1989. Reprinted from 1987 *American Hospital Association.* In *Disaster Planning and Recovery An SLA Information Kit.* Washington, D.C. 169-185.

Canadian National Exhibition (CNE) Archives. 1990. Canadian National Exhibition Archives Disaster Plan. Toronto: CNE.

Concordia University. 1992. *Disaster Plan for the Libraries and the Archives at Concordia University.* Montreal: Concordia University.

Ballard, Mary W. 1984. *Bulletin No. 3: Emergency Planning.* The New York State Conservation Consultancy Bulletin, ed. Konstanze Bachmann New York: Cooper-Hewitt Museum.

J. Paul Getty Museum. 1992. *The J. Paul Getty Museum Emergency Planning Handbook.* Revised. Malibu, California: The J. Paul Getty Museum.

King County Records and Election Division. 1997. *Disaster Plan for King County [Seattle, Washington] Archives and Records Management: Archives and Records Center. DRAFT.* Seattle: King County Records and Election Division.

Lewis, Georgina. 1988. *Recovery Plan for the University of Alberta Library System.* Edmonton: University of Alberta.

Library of Parliament [Canada]. 1994. *Disaster Prevention and Preparedness Plan.* In *Library Disaster Preparedness and Response.* Ottawa: Government of Canada, Council of Federal Libraries.

Metropolitan Toronto Reference Library. 1996. *MTRL Disaster Plan* (under revision). MTRL: Toronto.

National Library of Canada, Council of Federal Libraries. Committee on Conservation/Preservation of Library Materials. Information Kit #8: *Library Disaster Preparedness.*
The kit includes general information on disaster preparedness for libraries. It is intended to provide readers with the basic tools for writing a disaster plan and bringing together the resources needed to respond to an emergency or disaster.

Owens, Brian M. with Paul Leatherdale and Laura Popazzi. 1997. *University of Windsor Archives and Library Disaster Plan.* Windsor: University of Windsor.

Reed Library Disaster Task Force. 1989. *Reed Library Disaster Preparedness and Salvage Plan.* Fredonia, N.Y.: Reed Library State University of New York, College at Fredonia.

Sinclair, Jim, ed. 1995. *State Library of New South Wales. Counter-Disaster Manual.* Revised ed. Sydney, Australia: State Library of New South Wales.

Smithsonian Institution Office of Risk Management. 1993. Smithsonian Institution Staff Disaster Preparedness Procedures. In *A Primer on Disaster Preparedness, Management, and Response: Paper-Based Materials.* Revised edition. Selected Reprints issued by the Smithsonian Institution, National Archives and Records Administration, Library of Congress and National Park Service. Distributed by the participating agencies.
http://palimpsest.stanford.edu/bytopic/disaster/primer.part2of5.txt

Stanford University Libraries. 1992. *Stanford University Libraries Collections Emergency Response Manual.*(under revision).
http://palimpsest.stanford.disaster.plan.txt

Syracuse University Library, Preservation Department. 1995. *Syracuse University Library Manual: Procedures for Recovering Print Materials: Non-Print and Photographic Materials: and Audio Recordings.*
http://libwww.syr.edu/aboutsul/depts/preserve/displan.htm

University of Waterloo Library. 1985. *University of Waterloo Library Emergency Procedures Manual & Disaster Plan.* Waterloo, Ontario: University of Waterloo.

Walsh, Betty and Barry Byers. 1996. British Columbia Archives & Records Service (BCARS) Policy and Procedures Manual, vol. 3: Emergency Preparedness Plans. *BCARS Records Salvage Plan. DRAFT.* Victoria, B.C.: BCARS.

Western New York Library Resources Council. 1994. *Western New York Disaster Preparedness and Recovery Manual for Libraries and Archives.* Revised Edition. Buffalo, New York: Western New York Library Resources Council.

Selected Disaster Case Studies

Armour, Annie. 1994. Learning from Experience: A Trial-and Error Approach to Disaster Planning. *The Southeastern Librarian* 44(2):62-66.
Existing hazards at the University of the South in Sewanee Tennessee make for an environmental disaster involving heat, humidity and moisture and subsequent outbreaks of mould.

Balon, Brett J. and H. Wayne Gardner. 1987. Disaster Contingency Planning: The Basic Elements. *Records Management Quarterly* 21(1):14-16.
Two floods, one natural one caused by construction, prompt the need for a disaster plan. This article is a case study of putting a plan together for Regina, Saskatchewan's City Hall.

Butler, Randall. 1986. The Los Angeles Central Library Fire. *Conservation Administration News* 27:1-2,23,27.
A review and analysis of the 1986 deliberately set fire at the Los Angeles Central Library.

Butler, Randall. 1988. Earthquake! The Experience of Two California Libraries. *Conservation Administration News* 32:1-2, 23-24.
An account of the effects of an 1987 earthquake on the Whittier College and California State University-Los Angeles libraries. Compares the impact on the different types of shelving.

CCI (Canadian Conservation Institute). 1984. *Cultural Emergencies: THE TRIUMPH OF MURPHY'S LAW.* Ottawa: CCI.
A four page paper outlining ten case histories of emergencies that got out of hand and became small scale disasters. Examples are drawn from (unnamed) museums and one library.

Clarke, Reginald. 1996. Construction-Related Threats to Library Collections. *Library Conservation News* 51(Summer):4-5.
Water invades the St. Augustine Library, University of West Indies, Trinidad and fungi infestation results.

George, Susan C. and Cheryl T. Naslund. 1986. Library Disasters: A Learning Experience. *College & Research Library News* (April):251-257.
Account of flooding which occurred eight times at the Kresge Physical Sciences Library, Dartmouth College, U.S.

Green, Kevin. 1993. The Case of the Pilkington Technology Centre Fire. *Aslib Information* 21(2):72-75.
A 1990 fire breaks out on the same floor as a brand new information centre in West Lancashire, England. Five sets of fire doors offer protection, but smoke travelled through the ventilation system and covered everything in sticky black soot. Includes a daily diary of the clean-up.

Henderson, Jane. 1995. Disasters Without Planning: Lessons for Museums. *The Conservator* 19:52-57.
An account of a flood that occurred 1993 in Llandudno, Wales including a diary of the events. The Llandudno Museum was hard hit with its storage in the basement flooded to a depth of over one metre.

Holmes, John. 1986. Disasters Revisited: An Overview of Past Disasters. In *Proceedings of An Ounce of Prevention: A Symposium on Disaster Contingency Planning for Information Managers in Archives, Libraries and Record Centres.* Nancy Willson, ed. Toronto: Toronto Area Archivists Group Education Foundation. 5-15.
International disasters cited include: the 1966 Florence flood and its impact on the National Library; Hurricane Agnes, 1972 and its impact on the Corning Glass Museum; and flooding during construction at Stanford University's Meyer Undergraduate Library in 1978. Canadian disasters cited include: the fire at the University of Toronto's Engineering Library in 1977; the flooding which occurred in 1977 at Old Fort William, Thunder Bay; the 1980 fire at the Perth Public Library and the 1981 fire in Winnipeg involving paper records of two social services agencies.

Hutson, Jennifer. 1994. Disaster Reaction Training at the National Library (or, How not to Panic if the Library is Underwater). *National Library News* 26(7):5.
Disaster training at the National Library of Canada.

Kahn, Miriam. 1994a. Fires, Earthquakes and Floods: How to Prepare Your Library and Staff. *ONLINE* (May):18-24.
This article on disaster preparedness also outlines several case histories of disasters involving information centers and libraries. These include: the bombing of the World Trade Center in New York, 1993, a fire in 1993 at the Banker's Trust and the 1990 power outage which affected the business newspaper, *Journal of Commerce.*

Lundquist, Eric. 1986. *Salvage of Water Damaged Books, Documents, Micrographic and Magnetic Media.* San Francisco: Document Reprocessors.
Recounts treatments involving two case histories: Dalhousie University Law Library and Roanoke Virginia Flood.

Marrelli, Nancy. 1986. Fire in the Concordia University Archives. In *Proceedings of An Ounce of Prevention: A Symposium on Disaster Contingency Planning for Information Managers in Archives, Libraries and Record Centres.* Nancy Willson, ed. Toronto: Toronto Area Archivists Group Education Foundation. 132-144.
Article outlines the anatomy of the 1982 fire and its impact on an archival collection.

Matthews, Fred W. 1989. Dalhousie Fire. Reprinted from 1986 *Canadian Library Journal.* In *Disaster Planning and Recovery. An SLA Information Kit.* Washington, D.C. 139-144.
A chronological account of the 1985 fire at the Dalhousie University's law library. See also Lundquist 1986.

Michaels, Jan. 1994. Standing on the Shoulders of Giants. *National Library News* 26(7):1-4.
Column discusses one year history of incidents at the National Library of Canada and the importance of training to disaster planning.

Mann, Brad. 1993. Lessons Learned From Hurricane Andrew. *Emergency Preparedness Digest* April-June:15-17.
Account of Hurricane Andrew's devastation of South Florida in 1992.

Panone, Carolyn. 1996. In the Face of Adversity. In *Library Conservation News* 51(Summer):3.
Arson in a small library in West Cumbria, England. Article deals with the problems of operating without a facility while still maintaining the services.

Spafford, Sarah and Fiona Graham. 1993. Fire Recovery at the Saskatchewan Museum of Natural History: Part I, Description of Events and Analysis of Recovery. In *ICOM Committee for Conservation. Preprints of the 10th Triennial Meeting, Washington, D.C., U.S.A., 22-27 August 1993.* Volume I. Janet Bridgland, ed. Paris: ICOM Committee for Conservation. 413-419.

Spafford, Sarah and Fiona Graham. 1993. Fire Recovery at the Saskatchewan Museum of Natural History: Part II - Post-Disaster Clean-Up and Soot Removal. In *ICOM Committee for Conservation. Preprints of the 10th Triennial Meeting, Washington, D.C., U.S.A., 22-27 August 1993.* Volume I. Janet Bridgland, ed. Paris: ICOM Committee for Conservation. 420-426.
Account of a fire at the Royal Saskatchewan Museum in 1990 involving modern fire-retardant materials and the subsequent post-disaster clean-up of soot on natural history collections.

Sung, Carolyn Hoover, Valerii Pavlovich Leonov and Peter Waters. 1990. Fire Recovery at the Library of the Academy of Sciences of the USSR. *American Archivist* 53(Spring):298-312.
Three part article outlines recovery following a fire at the Academy of Sciences Library in Leningrad in 1988. Outlines the recovery efforts and puts them in an international context. Description of the on scene activities with a focus on the innovations developed for mass disinfection and drying. Commentary by Waters based on his experience with the Florence flood.

Van Bogart, John W. C. and John Merz. 1996. *St. Thomas Electronic Records Disaster Recovery Effort Technical Report RE0025. National Media Lab.* http://www.nml.org/publications/usvi/usvi.html
In 1995 a hurricane struck the U.S. Virgin Islands affecting paper and electronic records at several government locations. This report describes the recovery of electronic records and computer equipment by National Media Lab personnel.

Wise, Christine. 1995. The Flood and Afterwards: A New Beginning for the Fawcett Library. *Library Conservation News* 48(Autumn):1-2.
A flood occurred at the Fawcett Library, London Guildhall University in 1994 as a result of heavy rains which overtaxed the storm drains. The flood filled the basement to a level of 2-3 inches and required the relocation of collections.

Chapter References

Chapter 1.0   Disaster Planning

Blue Shield Preparedness and Emergency Response Programme
http://www.icomos.org/blue_shield/

Boylan, Patrick J. 1993. *Review of the Convention for the Protection of Cultural Property in the Event of Armed Conflict [The Hague Convention of 1954]. CLT-93/WS/12.* Paris: General Information Programme and UNISIST, United Nations Educational, Scientific and Cultural Organization.

Boylan, Patrick J. 1999. New International Treaty to Strengthen Protection of Cultural Property in the Event of Armed Conflict. *International Prevention News* 19:6-7.

Bumbaru, Dinu. 1996. 1996 Per Guldbeck Memorial Lecture. *IIC-CG Bulletin* 21(3):9-13.

Canadian Standards Association and Major Industrial Accidents Council of Canada (CSA and MIACC). 1995. *CAN/CSA-Z731-95 Emergency Planning for Industry.* Etobicoke, Ontario: Canadian Standards Association.

Clarke, Tony. 1996. Emergency Preparedness in New Zealand: What Has Been Achieved, Where To From Here? In *Redefining Disasters: A Decade of Counter-Disaster Planning. Proceedings Wednesday 20-Friday 22 September 1995.* Revised edition. Alan Howell, Heather Mansell and Marion Roubos-Bennett, Compilers. Sydney, Australia: State Library of New South Wales. 27-40.

Convention for the Protection of Cultural Property in the Event of Armed Conflict [The Hague Convention of 1954]. 1954. UNESCO.
http://mirror-us.unesco.org/culture/laws/haque/html/_eng/page1.htm

Convention on Stolen or Illegally Exported Cultural Objects. 1995. UNIDROIT.
http://www.unidroit.org/english/conventions/c-cult.htm

Convention on the Means of Prohibiting and Preventing the Illicit Import, Export and Transfer of Ownership of Cultural Property. 1970. UNESCO.
http://mirror-us.unesco.org/culture/laws/1970/html_eng/page1.html

Conway, Paul. 1990. Archival Preservation Practice in a Nationwide Context. *American Archivist* 53(2):204-222.

Corelli, Rae. August 5, 1996. Storm Warnings. *Macleans* 109(32):20-25.

Council of Federal Libraries. 1994. *Library Disaster Preparedness and Response.* Ottawa: Government of Canada.

Davenport, Alan G. 1990. Canada and the IDNDR. *Emergency Preparedness Digest* July-September:20-22.

Declaration on Terrorism. Lyon, 27 June 1996. [A declaration by member countries of the G7]. http://www.diplomatie.fr/actual/g7Lyon/Lyon4.gb.html.

DePew, John N. 1989. *Statewide Disaster Preparedness and Recovery Program for Florida Libraries.* Occasional Papers No. 185. Champaign, Illinois: University of Illinois, Graduate School of Library and Information Science.

Donnelly, Helene and Martin Heaney. 1993. Disaster Planning - A Wider Approach. *Aslib Information* 21(2):69-71.

Duguay, Joanne. 1994. Looking Ahead: Emergency Preparedness Training for Canada in the Nineties and Beyond. *Emergency Preparedness Digest* January-March:16-21.

Eden, Paul, John Feather and Graham Matthews. 1994. Preservation *and Library Management: A Reconsideration.* Library Management 15(4):5-11.

Edwards, Susan and Jennifer Reising. 1996. Fortune 1000 Companies Commit to Crisis Management. *Contingency Planning & Management for Business Preparedness and Recovery* 1(2):1,9-11.

Emergency Management Australia. 1996. *IDNDR Briefing Paper Background.*
http://www.ema.gov.au/ema-ido1.html

Emond, Chantal. 1994. *Rapport Final sur l'Évaluation et Les Besoins en Préservation des Services D'Archives Membres du Réseau des Archives du Québec.* Préparé pour Le Comité de préservation du Réseau des archives du Québec.

EPC (Emergency Preparedness Canada). 1996. *A Summary of Federal Emergency Preparedness in Canada.*
http://hoshi.cic.sfu.ca/epc/EPCsum.html.

FEMA (Federal Emergency Management Agency). 1984. *Objectives for Local Emergency Management.* CPG 1-5. Washington, D.C.: FEMA.

Foster, Stephen, Roslyn Russel, Jan Lyall and Duncan Marshall. 1995. *Memory of the World. General Guidelines to Safeguard Documentary Heritage. CII95/WS/11.* Paris: General Information Programme and UNISIST, United Nations Educational, Scientific and Cultural Organization.

Fox, Lisa L. 1989. Management Strategies for Disaster Preparedness. *ALA Yearbook of Library and Information Series* 14:1-6.

George, Susan C. 1994. *Emergency Planning and Management in College Libraries. CLIP Note #17.* Chicago: Association of College and Research Libraries.

Graham, Taylor. 1994. *Disaster and After: The Practicalities of Information Services in Times of War and Other Catastrophes.* London: Taylor Graham Publishing.

Hamilton, Robert M. 1953. The Library of Parliament Fire. *The American Archivist* XVI(2):141-144.

Hawkins, Thomas M. Jr. and Hugh McClees. 1988. Emergency Management. In *Managing Fire Services.* Ronny J. Coleman and John A. Granito, eds. 2nd edition. Washington, D.C.: International City/County Management Association (ICMA). 319-346.

Hunter, John E. 1984a. Outline of the Emergency Planning Process. *Preparing a Museum Disaster Plan.* Omaha, Nebraska: National Park Service.

Hunter, John E. 1984b. Preparing a Museum Disaster Plan: An Outline. In *Selected Readings in Museum Emergency Planning. Seminar on Emergency Planning for Museums, Galleries and Archives. British Columbia Museum (BCM). Victoria, B.C. Canada. October 16 - 19, 1984.* John E. Hunter, compiler. Omaha, Nebraska: National Park Service.

Jablonowski, Mark. 1997. Systematic Disaster Planning. *Disaster Recovery Journal* 10(3):18-21.

Kahn, Miriam. 1993. Mastering Disaster. Emergency Planning for Libraries. *Library Journal* 118(21):73-75.

Long, Jane. 1996. Are We Ready for the Hurricanes?. *AIC News* 21(5):1-3.

MacKenzie, George. 1995. General Assessment of the Situation of the Archives of Bosnia and Herzegovina. http://mirror-us.unesco.org/webworld/en/icadoc.htm

Marrelli, Nancy. 1984. Fire and Flood at Concordia University Archives, January 1982. *Archivaria* 17(Winter 1983-84):266-274.

Marrelli, Nancy. 1991. Les Sinistres: prévention et planifications d'urgences. *Archives* 22(3):3-28.

Matthews, Graham and Paul Eden. 1996a. Disaster Management: Guidelines for Library Managers. In *Redefining Disasters: A Decade of Counter-Disaster Planning. Proceedings Wednesday 20-Friday 22 September 1995.* Alan Howell, Heather Mansell and Marion Roubos-Bennett, compilers. Revised edition. Sydney, Australia: State Library of New South Wales. 137-151.

Matthews, Graham and Paul Eden. 1996b. *Disaster Management in British Libraries. Project Report with Guidelines for Library Managers.* Library and Information Research Report 109. London: The British Library Board.

Matthews, Graham and Paul Eden. 1996c. Guidelines on Disaster Management. *Library Conservation News* 51:1-2.

McIntyre, John E. 1996. Reaction to Realisation. In *Redefining Disasters: A Decade of Counter-Disaster Planning. Proceedings Wednesday 20-Friday 22 September 1995.* Alan Howell, Heather Mansell and Marion Roubos-Bennett, Compilers. Revised edition. Sydney, Australia: State Library of New South Wales. 129-135.

Michaels, Jan. 1994. Standing on the Shoulders of Giants. *National Library News* 26(7):1-4.

Mowat, Ian R. M. 1987. Preservation Problems in Academic Libraries. In *Preserving the Word. The Library Association Conference Proceedings, Harrogate, 1986.* R.E. Palmer, ed. London: The Library Association.

National Fire Protection Association. See **NFPA**.

Nelson, Carl L. 1991. *Protecting the Past from Natural Disasters.* Washington, D.C.: National Trust for Historic Preservation.

NFPA (National Fire Protection Association). 1995. *NFPA 1600 - 95. Recommended Practice for Disaster Management.* Quincy, Massachusetts: NFPA.

Ogden, Sherlyn. 1979. The Impact of the Florence Flood on Library Conservation in the United States of America. A Study of the Literature Published 1956-1976. *Restaurator* 3 (1-2):1-36.

O'Keefe, Patrick J. 1997. *Trade in Antiquities: Reducing Destruction and Theft.* London: Archetype and UNESCO.

Ostiguy, Monique. 1997. *Personal Communication.* January 29, 1997.

Pintus, Sandro and Silvia Messeri, eds. 1996. Thirty Years After the Flood [online exhibition and commentary]. *Mega Review (FAN - Florence ART News)* 2. http://www.mega.it/allu/eng/iocero.htm.

1er Sommet national sur la patrimoine et les mesures d'urgence au Canada - First National Summit on Heritage and Risk Preparedness in Canada. 1996. *Déclaration finale - Final Declaration. 1er Sommet national sur la patrimoine et les mesures d'urgence au Canada -First National Summit on Heritage and Risk Preparedness in Canada.* À Québec le 17 Septembre 1996. (In French, English translation available)

Prince, Samuel. 1920. *Catastrophe and Social Change.* New York: Columbia University Press.

Ready, Chandra, editor-in-chief. To be published spring 2000. Special Issue on Disaster Preparedness and Response. *Journal of the American Institute for Conservation* 39(1).

Resolution on Information as an Instrument for Protection against War Damages to the Cultural Heritage. Stockholm. 1994. http://mirror-us.unesco.org/culture/laws/sweden/html_eng/page1.htm

Roberts, Barbara O. 1992-1993. Establishing a Disaster Prevention/Response Plan: An International Perspective & Assessment. *Technology & Conservation* 4(93):15-17,35-36.

Ruyle, Carol J. and Elizabeth M. Schobernd. 1997. Disaster Recovery Without the Disaster. *Technical Services Quarterly* 14(4):13-26

Saito, Hidetoshi, ed. 1999. *Risk Preparedness for Cultural Properties - Development of Guidelines for Emergency Response, Proceedings of the 1997 Kobe/Tokyo International Symposium, Development Guidelines for Emergency Response.* Tokyo: Chuo-Koron Bijutsu Shuppan.

Sikich, Geary W. 1998. *"All Hazards" Crisis Management Planning.* http://palimpsest. stanford.edu/byauth/sikich/allhz.html

Stasak, Bernard C. 1996. Human Resources. Proper Deployment, Care, and Communication Fortify Team Efforts. *Contingency Planning & Management for Business Preparedness and Recovery* 1(2):29-31.

Stovel, H. 1996. *Premier Sommet Canadien du Bouclier Bleu. Patrimoine et Mesures d'urgence au Canada à Québec, Septembre 1996.* Ottawa: ICOMOS Canada. (In French)

Stovel, Herb. 1998. *Risk Preparedness: A Management Manual for World Cultural Heritage.* Rome: ICCROM.

Technology & Conservation. 1995. On the Road to Recovery... *Technology & Conservation* 12(3):6,8,9,14,36.

The Toronto Star. 1996. Defusing the Terrorist Surge. In *What's Up?* Monday, September 23, 1996. A14.

Toman, Jiri. 1996. *The Protection of Cultural Property in the Event of Armed Conflict.* Hants, England and Paris: Dartmouth Publishing Company Limited and UNESCO.

Tremain, David. 1996. The Blue Shield Programme in Canada. *IIC-CG Bulletin* 21(3):40-42.

UNESCO (United Nations Educational, Scientific and Cultural Organization). 1998. *Emergency Programme for the Protection of Vital Records in the Event of Armed Conflicts.* http://mirror-us.unesco.org/webworld/archives/sro-citra/intro.html

UN General Assembly. 1989. *International Decade for Natural Disaster Reduction Resolution 44/236 Adopted at the Forty-fourth Session of the United Nations General Assembly, 22 December 1989.* gopher://hoshi.cic.sfu.ca:5555/00/epix/idndr/unres/unres 44.236.

van der Hoeven, Hans and Joan van Albada. 1996. *Memory of the World: Lost Memory - Libraries and Archives Destroyed in the Twentieth Century. CII-96/WS/1.* Paris: General Information Programme and UNISIST, United Nations Educational, Scientific and Cultural Organization.

Vossler, Janet L. 1987. The Human Element of Disaster Recovery. *Records Management Quarterly* 21(1):10-12.

Vouglas, Buffy. 1996. Involvement Encouraged for Disaster Reduction Day, Decade. *Contingency Planning & Management for Business Preparedness and Recovery* 1(5):1,5.

Wahle, Thomas and Gregg Beatty. n.d. *Emergency Management Guide for Business & Industry.* Washington, D.C.: Federal Emergency Management Agency (FEMA):1-4. http://www.fema.gov/fema/bizindex.html.

Waters, Peter. 1996. From Florence to St. Petersburg: An Enlightening and Thought-Provoking Experience. A Personal Account of the Past Twenty Nine Years in Pursuit of the Conservation of Library Materials. In *Redefining Disasters: A Decade of Counter-Disaster Planning. Proceedings Wednesday 20-Friday 22 September 1995.* Alan Howell, Heather Mansell and Marion Roubos-Bennett, Compilers. Revised edition. Sydney, Australia: State Library of New South Wales. 237-249.

Wright, Gordon H. 1989. Disaster Management for Libraries: A Management Perspective on Disaster Planning. *Emergency Preparedness Digest* 16(1):14-18.

Chapter 2.0   The Disaster Plan

Anderson, William A. and Shirley Mattingly. 1991. Future Directions. In *Emergency Management: Principles and Practice for Local Government.* Thomas E. Drabek and Gerard J. Hoetmer, eds. Washington, D.C.: International City/County Management Association (ICMA). 311-335.

Armour, Annie. 1994. Learning from Experience: A Trial-and Error Approach to Disaster Planning. *The Southeastern Librarian* 44(2):62-66.

Astle, Deana L. 1989. Disaster Planning for Libraries. Reprinted with permission from *Show-Me-Libraries.* 1982. In *Disaster Planning and Recovery. An SLA Information Kit.* Washington, D.C.: Special Libraries Association. 67-73.

Balon, Brett J. and H. Wayne Gardner. 1987. Disaster Contingency Planning: The Basic Elements. *Records Management Quarterly* 21(1):14-16.

Balon, Brett J. and H. Wayne Gardner. 1988. Disaster Planning for Electronic Records. *Records Management Quarterly* 22(3):20-22,24-25,30.

Bolner, Myrtle Smith. 1993. Designing a Procedures Manual: Benefits and Pitfalls. *LLA Bulletin* 56(1):13-20.

Boyden, Richard. 1996. *Why We Need a Disaster Mutual Assistance Pact.* Presentation for the BAPNet Program (Bay Area Preservation Network). http://palimpsest.stanford.edu/bytopic/disasters/misc/mutual.html

Buchanan, Sally A. 1988. *Disaster Planning, Preparedness and Recovery for Libraries and Archives: A RAMP Study with Guidelines. PGI-88/WS/6.* Paris: General Information Programme and UNISIST, United Nations Educational, Scientific and Cultural Organization.

Buckner Higginbotham, Barbra and Miriam B. Kahn. 1995. Disasters for Directors: The Role of the Library or Archive Director in Disaster Preparedness and Recovery. In *Advances in Preservation and Access.* Vol. 2. Barbra Buckner Higginbotham, ed. Medford, New Jersey: Learned Information Inc. 400-412.

Canadian Conservation Institute. See **CCI.**

CCI (Canadian Conservation Institute). 1984. *Planning for Disaster Management: Introduction. CCI Notes 14/1.* Ottawa: CCI.

CCI 1995. *Emergency Preparedness for Cultural Institutions: Introduction. CCI Notes 14/1.* Ottawa: CCI.

Childress, Schelley. 1994. Planning for the Worst: Disaster Planning in the Library. *The Southeastern Librarian* 44(2):51-55.

Council of Federal Libraries. 1994. *Library Disaster Preparedness and Response.* Ottawa: National Library of Canada.

Cunha, George Martin. 1992. Disaster Planning and a Guide to Recovery Resources. *Library Technology Reports* 28(5):533-624.

References

Daines, Guy E. 1991. Planning, Training and Exercising. In *Emergency Management: Principles and Practices for Local Government.* Thomas E. Drabek and Gerard J. Hoetmer, eds. Washington, D.C.: International City/County Management Association (ICMA). 161-200.

Daley, Wayne. 1991. Business Resumption Planning: An Answer to Surviving a Disaster. *Emergency Preparedness Digest* (July-September):2-5.

DePew, John N. 1991. Chapter 8. Disaster Preparedness and Recovery. In *A Library, Media and Archival Preservation Handbook.* Santa Barbara, California: ABC-CLIO. 253-300.

Donnelly, Helene and Martin Heaney. 1993. Disaster Planning - A Wider Approach. *Aslib Information* 21(2):69-71.

Dorge, Valerie and Sharon Jones. To be published late 1999. *Building an Emergency Plan* Los Angeles: Getty Conservation Institute.

Eden, Paul, John Feather and Graham Matthews. 1994. Preservation and Library Management: A Reconsideration. *Library Management* 15(4):5-11.

Edwards, Susan and Jennifer Reising. 1996. Fortune 1000 Companies Commit to Crisis Management. *Contingency Planning & Management for Business Preparedness and Recovery* 1(2):1, 9-11.

Fennelly, Lawrence J., ed. 1983. *Museum, Archive, and Library Security.* Boston: Butterworths.

Fortson, Judith. 1992. *Disaster Planning and Recovery. A How-To-Do-It Manual for Librarians and Archivists. Number 21.* New York: Neal-Schuman Publishers, Inc.

Fox, Lisa L. 1989. Management Strategies for Disaster Preparedness. *ALA Yearbook of Library and Information Series* 14:1-6.

Fox, Lisa L. 1991. *Contents of a Disaster Plan.* SOLINET Preservation Services. Available on CoOL: http://palimpsest.stanford.edu/solinet/displan.htm.

Haimowitz, Mark. 1996. Don't Assume. *Contingency Planning & Management for Business Preparedness and Recovery* 1(4):13-14.

Hawkins, Thomas M. Jr. and Hugh McClees. 1988. Emergency Management. In *Managing Fire Services.* Ronny J. Coleman and John A. Granito, eds. 2nd edition. Washington, D.C.: International City/County Management Association (ICMA). 319-346.

Henderson, Jane. 1995. Disasters Without Planning: Lessons for Museums. *The Conservator* 19:52-57.

Hosty, John W. 1995. Made in America: Guidelines for Emergency Response Training. *Accident Prevention* March/April:30-33,50.

Hunter, John E. 1983. Chapter 11. Museum Disaster Planning. In *Museum, Archive, and Library Security.* Lawrence J. Fennelly, ed. Butterworths: Boston. 235-270.

Hunter, John E. 1984. *Preparing a Museum Disaster Plan.* Omaha, Nebraska: National Park Service.

Industrial Risk Insurers. 1981. PEPlan: Your People Make It Work!. Hartford, Connecticut: Industrial Risk Insurers. In *Selected Readings in Museum Emergency Planning. Seminar on Emergency Planning for Museums, Galleries and Archives. British Columbia Museum (BCM). Victoria, B.C., Canada. October 16-19, 1984.* John E. Hunter, compiler. Omaha, Nebraska: National Park Service.

Inland Empire Libraries Disaster Response Network (IELDRN). 1990. *The IELDRN Mutual Aid Agreement.* http://palimpsest.stanford.edu/bytopic/disasters/misc/mutual.html

Jablonowski, Mark. 1996. Scenario-Based Planning Proves Practical. *Contingency Planning & Management for Business Preparedness and Recovery* 1(5):9-11.

J. Paul Getty Museum. 1992. *The J. Paul Getty Museum Emergency Planning Handbook.* Revised. Malibu, California: The J. Paul Getty Museum.

Kahn, Miriam. 1993. Mastering Disaster. Emergency Planning for Libraries. *Library Journal* 118(21):73-75.

Knutson, Joan and Ira Bitz. 1991. *Project Management How to Plan and Manage Successful Projects.* New York: American Management Association.

Kreps, Gary A. 1991. Organizing for Emergency Management. In *Emergency Management: Principles and Practice for Local Government.* Thomas E. Drabek and Gerard J. Hoetmer, eds. Washington, D.C.: International City/County Management Association (ICMA). 30-54.

Library of Parliament. 1994. *Disaster Prevention and Preparedness Plan.* Ottawa: Council of Federal Libraries.

Lindblom, Beth C. and Karen Motylewski. 1993. Disaster Planning for Cultural Institutions. AASLH Technical Leaflet No. 183. *History News* 48(1):1-8.

Lopes, Rocky. 1997. Designing Disaster Education Programs. *In Fire Protection Handbook.* 18th ed. Arthur E. Cote, ed. Quincy, Massachusetts: National Fire Protection Association. 2.21-2.29.

Mast, Sharon. 1984. Ripping Off and Ripping Out: Book Theft and Mutilation from Academic Libraries. *Library & Archival Security* 5:31-51.

Matthews, Graham. 1994. Disaster Management: Controlling the Plan. *Managing Information* 1(7/8):24-27.

Miller, R. Bruce. 1988. Libraries and Computers: Disaster Prevention and Recovery. *Information Technology and Libraries.* 7(4):349-358.

Murray, Toby. 1987a. Don't Get Caught With Your Plans Down. *Records Management Quarterly* 21(2):12-14,16-24,26-30,41.

Murray, Toby. 1987b. Preservation Disaster Planning. *The Paper Conservator* 11:87-93.

Murray, Toby. 1994. *Basic Guidelines for Disaster Planning in Oklahoma.* Tulsa, Oklahoma: Oklahoma Conservation Congress (OCC).

NFPA (National Fire Protection Association). 1997. *NFPA 471 - 97. Recommended Practice for Responding to Hazardous Materials Incidents.* Quincy, Massachusetts: NFPA.

NFPA. 1997. *NFPA 472 - 97. Standard for Professional Competence of Responders to Hazardous Materials Incidents.* Quincy, Massachusetts: NFPA.

Paulhus, J. L. (Laurie). 1983. Planning for Safety and Security. In *Planning Our Museums.* Barry Lord and Gail Dexter Lord, eds. Ottawa: National Museums of Canada. 121-134.

Perry, Ronald W. 1991. Managing Disaster Response Operations. In *Emergency Management: Principles and Practice for Local Government.* Thomas E. Drabek and Gerard J. Hoetmer, eds. Washington, D.C.: International City/County Management Association (ICMA). 201-223.

Powell, Pamela A. 1997. Fire and Life Safety Education: Theory and Techniques. *In Fire Protection Handbook.* 18th ed. Arthur E. Cote, ed. Quincy, Massachusetts: National Fire Protection Association. 2.30-2.39.

Powell, Pamela A. and Meri-K Appy. 1997. Fire and Life Safety Education: The State of the Art. *In Fire Protection Handbook.* 18th ed. Arthur E. Cote, ed. Quincy, Massachusetts: National Fire Protection Association. 2.3-2.11.

Rossol, Monona. 1998. Compliance in Recovery: Regulatory Requirements in the Aftermath of Disaster. *AIC News* 23(5):1,4-7.

Rothstein, Philip Jan. 1996. Pitching Preparedness. *Contingency Planning & Management for Business Preparedness and Recovery* 1(1):21-24.

Scanlon, T. Joseph. 1991. Reaching Out: Getting the Community Involved in Preparedness. In *Emergency Management: Principles and Practice for Local Government.* Thomas E. Drabek and Gerard J. Hoetmer, eds. Washington, D.C.: International City/County Management Association (ICMA). 79-100.

Schreider, Tari. 1994. The 10 Most Common Pitfalls in Contingency Planning. *Emergency Preparedness Digest* October-December:22-25.

Stielow, Frederick J. 1993. Disaster Preparedness and Response Manual: A Commonsense Guide to Risk Management. *LLA Bulletin* 56(1):29-33.

Systems and Procedures Exchange Center (SPEC). 1984. *Collection Security in ARL Libraries. SPEC Kit 100.* Washington, D.C.: Association of Research Libraries, Office of Management Studies.

Tregarthen Jenkin, Ian. 1987. *Disaster Planning and Preparedness: An Outline Disaster Control Plan.* British Library Information Guide 5. Cambridge: The British Library.

Tremain, David. 1995. Is There A Need for More Disaster Training for Conservators? *IIC-CG Bulletin* 20(2):15-22.

Tremain, David A. 1996. 'Water, Water, Everywhere, Nor Any Drop to Drink': The Need for More Disaster Training for Conservators. In *Redefining Disasters: A Decade of Counter-Disaster Planning. Proceedings Wednesday 20-Friday 22 September 1995.* Alan Howell, Heather Mansell and Marion Roubos-Bennett, Compilers. Revised edition. Sydney, Australia: State Library of New South Wales. 219-230.

Trinkley, Michael. 1993. *Can You Stand the Heat? A Fire Safety Primer For Libraries, Archives, and Museums.* Atlanta: SOLINET Preservation Program.

U.S. Defence Civil Preparedness Agency. 1978. Civil Preparedness Field Training Manual SM-32.1. Participant Manual for Emergency Planning Workshop for Business and Industry Conferences. Washington, D.C.: Defence Civil Preparedness Agency. In *Selected Readings in Museum Emergency Planning. Seminar on Emergency Planning for Museums, Galleries and Archives. British Columbia Museum (BCM). Victoria, B.C., Canada. October 16-19, 1984.* John E. Hunter, compiler. Omaha, Nebraska: National Park Service.

Waters, Peter. 1996. From Florence to St. Petersburg: An Enlightening and Thought-Provoking Experience. A Personal Account of the Past Twenty Nine Years in Pursuit of the Conservation of Library Materials. In *Redefining Disasters: A Decade of Counter-Disaster Planning. Proceedings Wednesday 20-Friday 22 September 1995.* Alan Howell, Heather Mansell and Marion Roubos-Bennett, Compilers. Revised edition. Sydney, Australia: State Library of New South Wales. 237-249.

Webb, Colin. 1996. The National Library of Australia's 'Clayton's Disaster': a Dry Run in Slowmo, or the Real Thing? In *Redefining Disasters: A Decade of Counter-Disaster Planning. Proceedings. Wednesday 20 - Friday 22 September 1995.* Alan Howell, Heather Mansell and Marion Roubos-Bennett, Compilers. *Revised edition.* State Library of New South Wales. 251-260.

Wright, Gordon H. 1979. Fire! Anguish! Dumb Luck! or Contingency Planning. *Canadian Library Journal* 36(5):254-260.

Wright, Sandra. 1989. Disaster Planning: A Management Success Story. In *Proceedings of Conservation in Archives. International Symposium, Ottawa, Canada. May 10-12, 1988.* Paris: International Council on Archives. 281-290.

Wuorinen, Val. 1986. *Emergency Planning.* Hamilton, Ontario: Canadian Centre for Occupational Health and Safety (CCOHS).

Chapter 3.0 Disaster Prevention Planning

Adcock, Edward P., comp and ed., with assistance of Marie-Thérèse Varlamoff and Virginie Kremp. 1998. *IFLA Principles for the Care and Handling of Library Material. International Preservation Issues No. One.* Paris and Washington: International Federation of Library Associations and Institutions Core Programme on Preservation and Conservation, and Council on Library and Information Resources.

Agbabian, Mihran S., William S. Ginell, Sami F. Masri and Robert L. Nigbor. 1991. Evaluation of Earthquake Damage Mitigation Methods for Museum Objects. *Studies in Conservation* 36:111-120.

Alberta Public Safety Services. 1987. *Tornado, a Report. Edmonton and Strathcona County.* Edmonton: Queen's Printer Publications Services.

American Conference of Governmental Industrial Hygienists (ACGIH). 1995. *ACGIH Industrial Ventilation: A Manual of Recommended Practice.* 22nd edition. Cincinnati: ACGIH.

ANSI/NAPM (American National Standards Institute/National Association of Photographic Manufacturers). 1996. *ANSI/NAPM IT9.13-1996. American National Standard for Imaging Materials - Glossary of Terms Pertaining to Stability.* New York: ANSI.

ANSI/NAPM. 1996. *ANSI/NAPM IT9.21-1996. American National Standard for Life Expectancy of Compact Discs (CD-ROM).* New York: ANSI.

ANSI/NAPM 1993 and **ANSI/ISO** 1997. *ANSI/NAPM IT9.16-1993 and ANSI/ISO 14523: 1997. Joint American National and ISO Standard for Imaging Media - Photographic Activity Test.* New York: ANSI and Geneva: International Organization for Standardization.

ANSI/PIMA (American National Standards Institute/Photographic and Imaging Manufacturers Association). 1998. *ANSI/PIMA IT9.2-1998. American National Standard for Imaging Materials - Photographic Processed Films, Plates and Papers - Filing Enclosures and Storage Containers.* New York: ANSI.

ANSI/PIMA. 1996. *ANSI/PIMA IT9.13-1998. American National Standard for Imaging Materials - Glossary of Terms Pertaining to Stability.* New York: ANSI.

ANSI/PIMA. 1998. *ANSI/PIMA IT9.23-1998. American National Standard for Imaging Materials - Polyester Base Magnetic Tape - Storage.* New York: ANSI.

ANSI/PIMA. 1997. *ANSI/PIMA IT9.25-1997. American National Standard for Imaging Materials - Optical Disc Media - Storage.* New York: ANSI.

American Society of Heating, Refrigerating and Air Conditioning Engineers (ASHRAE). 1989. *ASHRAE 62-1989. Ventilation for Acceptable Air Quality.* Atlanta: ASHRAE.

Appelbaum, Barbara. 1991. *Guide to Environmental Protection of Collections.* Madison, Connecticut: Sound View.

Association of College and Research Libraries/Rare Books and Manuscripts Section Security Committee. 1994. *ACRL Guidelines. Guidelines Regarding Thefts in Libraries.* Chicago: ACRL.

Atabaigi, Robbie. 1996. F.Y.I. - Facts and Stats About Disaster Causing Phenomenas. *Disaster Recovery Journal* 9(2):38-39.

Bahr, Alice Harrison. 1991. Electronic Collection Security Systems Today: Changes and Choices. *Library and Archival Security* 11(1):3-22.

Baillie, Jeavons, Judith Doig and Cathie Jilovsky. 1994. *Disaster in Libraries: Prevention and Control.* 2nd edition. Melbourne: CAVAL Limited.

Baril, Paul. 1995. A Fire Protection Primer. *CCI Newsletter* 15:4-5.

Baril, Paul. 1997. *Personal Communication.* January 1997.

Bennett, Mark. 1997. Red River Rising. *Disaster Recovery Journal* 10(3):52-54.

Bologna, Jack. 1981. *Strategic Planning.* San Francisco: Assets Protection.

Bolt, Bruce A. 1993. *Earthquakes.* Revised edition. New York: W.H. Freeman and Company.

Boss, Richard W. 1999. *Security Technology for Libraries. Library Technology Reports 35, No. 3.* Chicago. American Library Association.

Boston, George, ed. 1998. *Memory of the World Programme. Safeguarding the Documentary Heritage: A Guide to Standards, Recommended Practices and Reference Literature Related to the Preservation of Documents of All Kinds. CII-98/WS/4.* Paris: General Information Programme and UNISIST, United Nations Educational, Scientific and Cultural Organization.

Brand, Marvine. 1984. *Security for Libraries. People, Buildings, Collections.* Chicago: American Library Association.

Brokerhof, Agnes W. 1989. *Control of Fungi and Insects in Objects and Collections of Cultural Value: "A State of the Art".* Amsterdam: Central Research Laboratory for Objects of Art and Science.

Buchanan, Sally A. 1988. *Disaster Planning, Preparedness and Recovery for Libraries and Archives: A RAMP Study with Guidelines. PGI-88/WS/6.* Paris: General Information Programme and UNISIST, United Nations Educational, Scientific and Cultural Organization.

Burke, Robert S. and Sam Adeloye. 1986. *A Manual of Basic Museum Security.* Leicester, England: International Council of Museums.

Bush, Stephen E. and Danny L. McDaniel rev. 1997. Library and Museum Collections. In *Fire Protection Handbook.* 18th ed. Arthur E. Cote, ed. Quincy, Massachusetts: National Fire Protection Association. 9.92 - 9.109.

References

CLA Earthquake Relief Grant Ad Hoc Committee. 1990. *Earthquake Preparedness Manual for California Libraries.* Sacramento: California Library Association.

Campbell-Mahamut, Deanna. 1991. Disaster at the National Library. *National Library News* 23(12):16.

Canadian Conservation Institute See **CCI.**

CCI. (Canadian Conservation Institute. 1988a. *A Light Damage Slide Rule. CCI Notes N2/6.* Ottawa: CCI.

CCI. 1988b. *Daylite Fluro-Spray Floodlight. CCI Notes N2/2.* Ottawa: CCI.

CCI. 1988c. *Planning for Disaster Management: Emergency or Disaster? CCI Notes N14/2.* Ottawa: CCI.

CCI. 1988d. *Planning for Disaster Management: Hazard Analysis. CCI Notes N14/3.* Ottawa: CCI.

CCI. 1992a. *Precautions for Storage Areas. CCI Notes N1/1.* Ottawa: CCI.

CCI. 1992b. *Track Lighting. CCI Notes N2/3.* Ottawa: CCI.

CCI. 1993. *CCI Environmental Monitoring Equipment. CCI Notes N2/4.* Ottawa: CCI.

CCI. 1994. *Ultraviolet Filters. CCI Notes N2/1.* Ottawa: CCI.

CCI. 1995a. *Emergency Preparedness for Cultural Institutions: Introduction. CCI Notes N14/1.* Ottawa: CCI.

CCI. 1995b. *Emergency Preparedness for Cultural Institutions: Identifying and Reducing Hazards. CCI Note N14/2.* Ottawa: CCI.

CCI. 1995c. *Storing Works on Paper. CCI Notes N11/2.* Ottawa: CCI.

CCI. 1996a. *Detecting Infestations: Facility Inspection Procedure and Checklist. CCI Notes N13/2.* Ottawa: CCI.

CCI 1996b. *Preventing Infestations: Control Strategies and Detection Methods. CCI Notes N3/1.* Ottawa: CCI.

CCI. 1997. *Controlling Insect Pests with Low Temperature. CCI Notes N3/3.* Ottawa: CCI.

Canadian Council of Archives. 1990. *Basic Conservation of Archival Materials: A Guide.* Ottawa: Canadian Council of Archives.

Canadian Encyclopedia. 1988. 2nd ed. Vol. IV Sta-Z. James Marsh, ed. Edmonton: Hurtig Publishers.

Canadian Standards Association and Major Industrial Accidents Council of Canada (CSA and MIACC). 1995. *CAN/CSA-Z731-95 Emergency Planning for Industry.* Etobicoke, Ontario: Canadian Standards Association.

Cassar, May. 1995. *Environmental Management Guidelines for Museums and Galleries.* Museums and Galleries Commission Care - Preservation -

Management Programme. Andrew Wheatcroft, Editor in Chief. London: Routledge and Routledge.

Christensen, Carol. 1995. Environmental Standards: Looking Beyond Flatlining? *AIC News* 20(5):1-2, 4-8.

Clarke, Reginald. 1996. Construction-Related Threats to Library Collections. *Library Conservation News* 51:4-5.

Corelli, Rae. August 5, 1996. Storm Warnings. *Macleans* 109(32):20-25.

Cornu, Elisabeth and Lesley Bone. 1991. Seismic Disaster Planning: Preventive Measures Make a Difference. *WAAC Newsletter* 13(3):13-19.

Costain, Charlie. 1994. *Framework for Preservation of Museum Collections.* CCI Newsletter 14(September):1-4.

Craig-Bullen, Catherine. 1996. Guidelines for the Prevention and Treatment of Mould-Damaged Archival and Library Material. *The Archivist* 112: 32-36.

Cunha, George Martin. 1992. Disaster Planning and a Guide to Recovery Resources. *Library Technology Reports* 28(5):533-624.

Dalley, Jane. 1995. *The Conservation Assessment Guide for Archives.* Ottawa: Canadian Council of Archives.

Dawson, John E. Revised by Thomas J. K. Strang. 1991. *Solving Museum Insect Problems: Chemical Control. Technical Bulletin No. 15.* Ottawa: Canadian Conservation Institute.

DePew, John. 1991. Chapter 8. Disaster Preparedness and Recovery. In *A Library, Media and Archival Preservation Handbook.* Santa Barbara, California: ABC-CLIO. 253-300.

DePew, John N. 1994. Lessons From Andrew. *The Southeastern Librarian* 44(2):57-61.

Druzik, James and Paul Banks. 1995. Appropriate Standards for the Indoor Environment. *Conservation Administration News* 62/63:1,3-8.

Duguay, Joanne. 1995. MIACC - Planning for the 21st Century. *Emergency Preparedness Digest* October-December:10-11.

Eastman Kodak Company. 1995. *Safe Handling, Storage, and Destruction of Nitrate-Based Motion Picture Films.* Kodak Publication Number H-182. Rochester, N.Y.: Kodak Environmental Services.

Ebbs, Leslie E. 1995a. Ontario - Making Emergency Preparedness Second Nature. *Emergency Preparedness Digest* July-September:8-10.

Ebbs, Leslie E. 1995b. Waiting for the Wave. *Emergency Preparedness Digest* January-March:7-8.

Ebeling, Walter. 1978. *Urban Entomology.* California: University of California, Division of Agricultural Sciences.

EPC (Emergency Preparedness Canada). *National Earthquake Support Plan for British Columbia.* 1996. Ottawa: Emergency Preparedness Canada. 1-2. http://hoshi.cic.sfu.ca/epc/NESP/english.html

EPC. 1995a. *Expect the Unexpected - Plan for Emergencies.* Ottawa: Ministry of Supply and Services.

EPC. 1995b. *Significant Disasters in Canada.* Ottawa: Ministry of Supply and Services.

Emergency Preparedness Digest. 1992. What Do Canadians Think About Emergency Preparedness? *Emergency Preparedness Digest* January-March:22.

Emergency Preparedness Digest. 1996. Canadian Emergency Preparedness Survey. *Emergency Preparedness Digest* January-March:5.

Erhardt, David and Marion Mecklenberg. 1994. Relative Humidity Re-examined. In *Preventive Conservation: Practice, Theory Research. Preprints of the Contributions to the Ottawa Congress, 12-16 September 1994.* London: International Institute for Conservation. 32-38.

FEMA (Federal Emergency Management Agency). 1984. *Objectives for Local Emergency Management.* CPG 1-5. Washington, D.C.: FEMA.

FEMA. 1990. *Risks and Hazards. A State by State Guide.* Washington, D.C.: FEMA.

FEMA. 1995. *A Guide to Federal Aid in Disasters.* Washington, D.C.: FEMA.

Fennelly, Lawrence J., ed. 1983. *Museum, Archive and Library Security.* Boston: Butterworths.

Fennelly, Lawrence J., ed. 1988. *Handbook of Loss Prevention and Crime Prevention.* 2nd ed. Boston: Butterworths.

Florian, Mary-Lou E. 1993a. Conidial Fungi (Mould, Mildew) Biology: A Basis for Logical Prevention, Eradication and Treatment for Museum and Archival Collections. *Leather Conservation News* 10(1994):1-29.

Florian, Mary-Lou E. 1993b. Conidial Fungi (Mould) Activity on Artifact Materials - A New Look at Prevention, Control and Eradication. In *ICOM Committee for Conservation. Preprints of the 10th Triennial Meeting, Washington, D.C., U.S.A., 22-27 August 1993.* Volume II. Janet Bridgland, ed. Paris: ICOM Committee for Conservation. 868-874.

Florian, Mary-Lou E. 1994. Conidial Fungi (Mould, Mildew) Biology: A Basis for Logical Prevention, Eradication and Treatment for Museum and Archival Collections. *Leather Conservation News* 10:1-29.

Florian, Mary-Lou E. 1997. *Heritage Eaters: Insects and Fungi in Heritage Collections.* London: James and James Science Publishers Ltd.

Fortson, Judith. 1992. *Disaster Planning and Recovery. A How-To-Do-It Manual for Librarians and Archivists. Number 21.* New York: Neal-Schuman Publishers, Inc.

Frens, Dale H. 1993. *Temporary Protection: Specifying Temporary Protection of Historic Interiors During Construction and Repair. Preservation Technical Notes No. 2.* Washington, D.C.: National Park Service.

George, Susan C. and Cheryl T. Naslund. 1986. Library Disasters: A Learning Experience. *College & Research Libraries News* April:251-257.

Glaser, Mary Todd. 1994. Protecting Books and Paper Against Mold. Emergency Management Technical Leaflet. In *Preservation of Library and Archival Materials: A Manual.* Sherelyn Ogden, ed. Revised and expanded edition. Andover, Massachusetts: Northeast Document Conservation Center. 1-6.

Godschalk, David R. 1991. Disaster Mitigation and Hazard Management. In *Emergency Management: Principles and Practice for Local Government.* Thomas E. Drabek and Gerard J. Hoetmer, eds. Washington, D.C.: International City/County Management Association (ICMA). 131-160.

Goldberg, Martin. 1993. The Neverending Saga of Library Theft. *Library and Archival Security* 12(1):87-100.

Goonan, Thomas, rev. 1997. Storage and Handling of Records. In *Fire Protection Handbook.* 18th ed. Arthur E. Cote, ed. Quincy, Massachusetts: National Fire Protection Association. 3.275-3.283.

Gordon, David W. ed. 1994. *Earthquakes & Volcanoes.* Denver: U.S. Geological Survey.

Guaragno, John P. and Clyde L. Monma. 1996. Computer Security in Jeopardy. *Contingency Planning & Management for Business Preparedness and Recovery* 1(5):20-23.

Gwinn, Nancy E. 1992. Politics and Practical Realities: Environmental Issues for the Library Administrator. In *Advances in Preservation and Access.* Vol. I. Barbara Bruckner Higginbotham and Mary E. Jackson, eds. Westport, Connecticut: Meckler Corporation. 135-146.

Hand, Heather. 1993. B.C. Ready for the INEVITABLE. *Emergency Preparedness Digest* January-March:2-6.

Harmon, James D. 1993. *Integrated Pest Management in Museum, Library and Archival Facilities.* Indianapolis: Harmon Preservation Pest Management.

Harvey, Ross. 1993. *Preservation in Libraries: Principles, Strategies and Practices for Librarians.* Topics in Library and Information Studies. London: Bowker-Saur.

Hays, Walter W. 1991. At Risk from Natural Hazards. In *Perspectives on Natural Disaster Mitigation: Papers Presented at 1991 AIC Workshop.* Washington, D.C.: FAIC (Foundation of the American Institute for Conservation of Historic and Artistic Works). 1-8.

Hendley, Norman I. 1996. How Fungi Attack Materials. *Science Journal* January:43-49.

Henry, Walter. 1988. *Outline for Flood Preparedness Exercise.* Stanford University Libraries. http://palimpsest.stanford.edu/bytopic/disasters/misc/disprep.txt

Higgins, John T. 1997. Housekeeping Practices. In *Fire Protection Handbook.* 18th ed. Arthur E. Cote, ed. Quincy, Massachusetts: National Fire Protection Association. 3.364-3.372.

Hodgson, John H. 1965a. Canadian Earthquakes. *Canadian Geographical Journal* 71:30-39.

Hodgson, John H. 1965b. *There Are Earthquake Risks in Canada.* Dominion Observatory Reprint No. 50, National Research Council, Division of Building Research, NRC No. 8546. Ottawa: NRC.

The Home Office. 1994. *Bombs: Protecting People and Property. A Handbook for Managers and Security Officers.* London: Home Office Public Relations Branch.

Hunter, John E. 1983. Chapter 11. Museum Disaster Planning. In *Museum, Archive, and Library Security.* Lawrence J. Fennelly, ed. Boston: Butterworths. 235-270.

Hunter, John E. 1984. Preparing a Museum Disaster Plan: An Outline. In *Selected Readings in Museum Emergency Planning. Seminar on Emergency Planning for Museums, Galleries and Archives. British Columbia Museum (BCM). Victoria, B.C. Canada. October 16-19, 1984.* John E. Hunter, compiler. Omaha, Nebraska: National Park Service.

Hunter, John E. 1986. Museum Disaster Preparedness Planning. In *Protecting Historic Architecture and Museum Collections from Natural Disasters.* Boston: Butterworths. 211-230.

Hutson, Jennifer. 1994. Disaster Reaction Training at the National Library (or, How not to Panic if the Library is Underwater). *National Library News* 26(7):5.

Hyndman, Roy D. 1995. Giant Earthquakes of the Pacific Northwest. *Scientific American* 273(6):68-75.

IASA (International Association of Sound Archives). 1997. *The Safeguarding of the Audio Heritage: Ethics, Principles and Preservation Strategy.* http://www.llgc.org.uk/iasa/0013.htm

Imholte, Thomas J. 1984. *Engineering for Food Safety and Sanitation - A Guide to the Sanitary Design of Food Plants and Food Plant Equipment.* Crystal, Minnesota: Technical Institute of Food Safety.

ISO (International Organization for Standardization). *ISO/DIS 11799. Information and Documentation - Document Storage Requirements for Archive and Library Materials.* Geneva:ISO.

ISO. 1997 *ISO 3897:1997. Photography - Processed Photographic Plates - Storage Practices.* Geneva: ISO.

ISO. 1996. *ISO 5466:1996. Photography - Processed Safety Photographic Films - Storage Practices.* Geneva: ISO.

ISO. 1997. *ISO 6051:1997. Photography - Processed Reflection Prints - Storage Practices.* Geneva: ISO.

ISO. 1991. *ISO 10214:1991. Photography - Processed Photographic Materials - Filing Enclosures for Storage.* Geneva: ISO.

Jervis, Michael. 1990. Tsunami. *Emergency Preparedness Digest* January-March:14-16.

Kelly, Wayne. 1999. *Security Hardware and Security System Planning for Museums. Technical Bulletin No. 19.* Ottawa: Canadian Conservation Institute.

Kenjo, Toshiko. 1997. Preservation Environment in Library Stacks and Anti-Disaster Measures. *International Preservation News* 15(August):20-24.

Kerschner, Richard L. and Jennifer Baker. 1998. *Practical Pest Control: A Selected, Annotated Bibliography.* http://palimpsest.stanford.eu/byauth/kerschner/ccbiblio.html

Knapp, Tony and John E. Hunter. 1990. Chapter 9. Museum Collections Protection: Security and Fire Protection. In *National Park Service Museum Handbook. Part I:Museum Collections.* Revised edition. Washington, D.C.: National Park Service, U.S. Department of the Interior. 9:1-9:33.

Kowalik, Romuald. 1980a. Microbiodeterioration of Library Materials. Part 1: Chapters 1-3. *Restaurator* 4(2):99-114.

Kowalik, Romuald. 1980b. Microbiodeterioration of Library Materials. Part 2: Chapter 4. *Restaurator* 4(3-4):135-219.

Kowalik, Romuald. 1984. Microbiodeterioration of Library Materials. Part 2: Chapter 5-9; Microbiodecomposition of Auxiliary Materials. *Restaurator* 6(1-2):61-115.

Lander, James F. and Patricia A. Lockridge. 1989. *United States Tsunamis (Including United States Possessions) 1690-1988.* National Oceanic and Atmospheric Administration, Publication 41-2.

Lennertz, L. 1995. *Stop Thief! Strategies for Keeping your Collections from Disappearing. Selective Bibliography.* Chicago: American Library Association.

Lincoln, Alan Jay. 1984. *Crime in the Library: A Study of Patterns, Impact and Security.* New York: Bowker.

Lindblom, Beth C. and Karen Motylewski. 1993. Disaster Planning for Cultural Institutions. AASLH Technical Leaflet No. 183. *History News* 48(1):1-8.

Lopes, Rocky. 1997. Designing Disaster Education Programs. In *Fire Protection Handbook.* 18th ed. Arthur E. Cote, ed. Quincy, Massachusetts: National Fire Protection Association. 2.21-2.29.

Lowry, Maynard and Philip M. O'Brien. 1990. Rubble with a Cause: Earthquake Preparedness in California. *College & Research Libraries News* March:192-197.

Lull, William P. with the assistance of Paul N. Banks. 1995. *Conservation Environment Guidelines for Libraries and Archives.* Ottawa: Canadian Council of Archives.

References

Mann, Brad. 1993. Lessons Learned From Hurricane Andrew. *Emergency Preparedness Digest* April-June:15-17.

Mann, Brad. 1994. When the Giant Awakens. *Emergency Preparedness Digest* July-September:5-9.

Marshall, Vanessa. 1995. Assessing and Managing Risks to Your Collections. Report on the Leicester Workshop. *Paper Conservation News* 76:17-18.

Matthews, Fred W. 1986. Dalhousie Fire. *Canadian Library Journal* August:221-226.

McCrady, Ellen. 1994. Mold as a Threat to Human Health. *The Abbey Newsletter* 18(6):1-2.

McCrady, Ellen. 1995. Indoor Environment Standards: A Report on the NYU Symposium. *The Abbey Newsletter* 19(6-7):93-94,96-98.

McCrady, Ellen. 1999. Mold: The Whole Picture. Part 1. *The Abbey Newsletter* 23(4):45,48-50.

McCrady, Ellen. 1999. Mold: The Whole Picture. Part 2, Assessment of Mold Problems. *The Abbey Newsletter* 23(5):61-62,65-67.

McCrady, Ellen. 1999. Mold: The Whole Picture. Part 3, A Neglected Public Health Problem. *The Abbey Newsletter* 23(6):73-74,76-77.

McCrady, Ellen. 1999. Mold: The Whole Picture. Part 4, Effect of Mold on Schools, Homes and Human Begins. *The Abbey Newsletter* 23(7):89-90,92-93.

McFarlane, J.A. (Sandy) and Warren Clements, eds. 1996. *The Globe and Mail Style Book.* 4th ed. Toronto: Penguin.

McIntyre John E. 1996. Managing the Fire Risk: Does the Building Protect or Threaten? In *Redefining Disasters: A Decade of Counter-Disaster Planning. Proceedings. Wednesday 20 - Friday 22 September 1995.* Alan Howell, Heather Mansell and Marion Roubos-Bennett, Compilers. Revised edition. Sydney, Australia: State Library of New South Wales. 115-127.

Merritt, Jane. 1993. Mold and Mildew: Prevention of Microorganism Growth in Museum Collections. Conserve O Gram Number 3/4. July 1993. In *A Primer on Disaster Preparedness, Management, and Response: Paper-Based Materials.* Selected Reprints issued by the Smithsonian Institution, National Archives and Records Administration, Library of Congress and National Park Service. Distributed by the participating agencies.

Metro Corporate Services, The Municipality of Metropolitan Toronto. 1994. *Policies and Principles for the Management of Records, Data and Information Technology Security. March 18, 1994.* Toronto: The Municipality of Metropolitan Toronto.

Michalski, Stefan. 1993. Relative Humidity: A Discussion of Correct/Incorrect Values. In *ICOM Committee for Conservation: 10th Triennial Meeting, Washington, D.C., U.S.A., 22-27 August, 1993, Preprints,* ed. J.Bridgland, Vol. 2. Paris: ICOM Committee for Conservation. 624-629.

Michalski, Stefan. 1994. Relative Humidity and Temperature Guidelines: What's Happening? *CCI Newsletter* 14 (September):6-8.

Miller, Charles. 1993. *Information Technology Security Handbook.* Ottawa: Ministry of Government Services.

Morris, John. 1979. *Managing the Library Fire Risk.* 2nd ed. Berkeley: University of California.

Morris, John. 1987. Los Angeles Library Fire - Learning the Hard Way. *Canadian Library Journal* 44(4):217-221.

Motylewski, Karen. 1994. Protecting Collections During Renovation. Emergency Management Technical Leaflet. In *Preservation of Library and Archival Materials: A Manual.* Sherelyn Ogden, ed. Revised and expanded edition. Andover, Massachusetts: Northeast Document Conservation Center. 1-7.

Murray, Toby. 1987a. Don't Get Caught With Your Plans Down. *Records Management Quarterly* 21(2):12-14,16-24,26-30,41.

Murray, Toby. 1987b. Preservation Disaster Planning. *The Paper Conservator* 11:87-93.

Murray, Toby. 1994. *Basic Guidelines for Disaster Planning in Oklahoma.* Tulsa, Oklahoma: Oklahoma Conservation Congress (OCC).

National Archives of Canada (Conservation Treatment Division). 1996. *Precautionary Measures for Dealing with Mould Contamination of Archival and Library Collections and Locally Contaminated Buildings (Internal Procedures Document).*

National Media Lab. 1997. *Recommended Storage Conditions for Magnetic Tape.* http://www.nta.org/MediaStability/StorageAndHandling/TapeStorage Recommendations.

NFPA. (National Fire Protection Association). 1997. *NFPA 40 - 97. Standard for the Storage and Handling of Cellulose Nitrate Motion Picture Film.* Quincy, Massachusetts: NFPA.

NFPA. 1997. *NFPA 909-97. Standard for the Protection of Cultural Resources including Museums, Libraries, Places of Worship and Historic Properties.* Quincy, Massachusetts: NFPA.

NFPA. 1994. *NFPA 914-94. Recommended Practice for Fire Protection in Historic Structures.* Quincy, Massachusetts: NFPA.

Nelson, Carl L. 1991. *Protecting the Past from Natural Disasters.* Washington, D.C.: National Trust for Historic Preservation.

NISO (National Information Standards Organization). 1994. *ANSI/NISO Z39.73-1994. Single-Tier Steel Bracket Library Shelving.* Bethesda, Maryland: NISO Press.

Nyberg, Sandra. 1987. *The Invasion of the Giant Spore.* Solinet Preservation Program Leaflet 5. Atlanta, Georgia: SOLINET Preservation Program.

O'Connell, Mildred. 1983. Disaster Planning: Writing & Implementing Plans for Collections-Holding Institutions. *Technology and Conservation* 8(2):18-24.

O'Connell, Mildred. 1996. The New Museum Climate: Standards and Technologies. *The Abbey Newsletter* 20(4-5):58-60.

Olcott Price, Lois. 1994. *Mold - Managing a Mold Invasion: Guidelines for Disaster Response.* Technical Series No. 1. Philadelphia: Conservation Center for Art and Historic Artifacts.

Ontario Management Board of Cabinet. 1991. *Information Technology Security: A Managers Guide. Ontario Management Board of Cabinet Guideline 7:3.* Toronto: The Queen's Printer.

Ontario Ministry of Labour, Occupational Health and Safety Division. 1995. *Workplace Hazardous Materials Information System: A Guide to the Legislation. (WHMIS).* Toronto: Ministry of Labour.

Padfield, Tim. 1988. Climate Control in Libraries and Archives. *Australian Institute for the Conservation of Cultural Material Bulletin* 14(1/2):49-68.

Padfield, Tim. 1998. *An Introduction to the Physics of the Museum Environment.* http://www.natmus.min.dk/cons/tp/index/htm

Parker, Thomas A. 1988. *Study on Integrated Pest Management for Libraries and Archives.* Paris: General Information Programme and UNISIST, UNESCO.

Paulhus, J. L. (Laurie). 1983. Planning for Safety and Security. In *Planning Our Museums.* Barry Lord and Gail Dexter Lord, eds. Ottawa: National Museums of Canada. 121-134.

Pearce, Robert J. 1997. Protection of Electronic Equipment. In *Fire Protection Handbook.* 18th ed. Arthur E. Cote, ed. Quincy, Massachusetts: National Fire Protection Association. 9.205 - 9.208.

PEP Provincial Emergency Program. 1996. *Prepare Now for an Earthquake in British Columbia.* http://hoshi.cic.sfu.ca/~pep/prepare.html.

Pest Control Canada. 1996. *Pest Control Canada. A Reference Manual.* 11th edition. Hensall, Ontario: PCC and North American Compendiums Limited.

Powell, Pamela A. 1997. Fire and Life Safety Education: Theory and Techniques. *In Fire Protection Handbook.* 18th ed. Arthur E. Cote, ed. Quincy, Massachusetts: National Fire Protection Association. 2.30-2.39.

Powell, Pamela A. and Meri-K Appy. 1997. Fire and Life Safety Education: The State of the Art. *In Fire Protection Handbook.* 18th ed. Arthur E. Cote, ed. Quincy, Massachusetts: National Fire Protection Association. 2.3-2.11.

Prevention Committee, President's Council on Integrity and Efficiency. 1986. *Computers: Crimes, Clues and Controls. A Management Guide.* Washington, D.C: publisher unknown.

Provost, Lynne. 1992. Lessons from the PAST. *Emergency Preparedness Digest* January-March:17-19.

Reilly, James M. 1993. *IPI Storage Guide for Acetate Film.* Rochester, N.Y.: Image Permanence Institute, Rochester Institute of Technology.

Reilly, James M., Peter Z. Adelstein and Douglas W. Nishimura. 1991. *Preservation of Safety Film.* Final Report to the Office of Preservation, National Endowment for the Humanities, Grant #PS-20159-88. Rochester, N.Y.: Image Permanence Institute, Rochester Institute of Technology.

Reilly, James M., Peter Z. Adelstein, Douglas Nishimura and Catherine Erbland. 1994. *New Approaches To Safety Film Preservation.* Final Report NEH Grant PS-20445-91. Rochester, N.Y.: Image Permanence Institute, Rochester Institute of Technology.

Reilly, James M., Douglas Nishimura and Edward Zinn. 1995. *New Tools for Preservation: Assessing Long-Term Environmental Effects on Library and Archives Collections.* Washington, D.C.: The Commission on Preservation and Access.

Reimer, Chris R. and Milton R. Shefter. 1994. Clean-Agent Fire Suppression Alternatives. *SMPTE Journal* 103(8):523-527.

Ritzenthaler, Mary Lynn. 1993. *Preserving Archives and Manuscripts: Conservation.* SAA Archival Fundamentals Series. Chicago: Society of American Archivists.

R. R. Donnelley and Sons. 1967. *Florence Rises from the Flood.* Chicago: R.R. Donnelley and Sons Co.

Ruffman, Alan. 1996. Lessons from the 1929 Newfoundland Tsunami. *Emergency Preparedness Digest* January-March:25-28.

Saunders, M. 1993. How a Library Picked up the Pieces after the IRA Blast. *Library Association Record* 95(2):100-101.

Schreider, Tari. 1994. The 10 Most Common Pitfalls in Contingency Planning. *Emergency Preparedness Digest* October-December:22-25.

Sebera, Donald K. 1994. *Isoperms: An Environmental Management Tool.* Washington, D.C.: The Commission on Preservation and Access.

Shaw, James R. 1991. Fire Retardant and Flame Resistant Treatment of Cellulosic Materials. In *Fire Protection Handbook.* 17th ed. Arthur E. Cote, ed. Quincy, Massachusetts: National Fire Protection Association. 3.174-3.183.

Shelton, John A. 1990. *Seismic Safety Standards for Library Shelving.* California State Library Manual of Recommended Practice. Sacramento: California State Library Foundation.

Silverman, Richard M. 1993. A Mandate for Change in the Library Environment. *Library Administration & Management* 7(3):145-152.

Skepastianu, Maria with the assistance of Jean I. Whiffin. 1995. *Library Disaster Planning.* The Hague: IFLA Section on Conservation and Preservation.

Smith, Richard D. 1992. Disaster Recovery: Problems and Procedures. *IFLA Journal* 18(1):13-23.

Snyder, Janice. 1992. A Threat Erupts. *Emergency Preparedness Digest* January-March: 20-21.

Society of Archivists (Scottish Region). 1996. *Disaster Preparedness: Guidelines for Archives and Libraries.* London: Society of Archivists (Scottish Region).

Society of Motion Picture and Television Engineers (SMPTE). 1994. Proposed SMPTE Recommended Practice. RP 103 (Revision of RP 103-1982. Care, Storage. Operation, Handling and Shipping of Magnetic Recording Tape for Television. *SMPTE Journal (October 1994):* 693-695.

Spafford, Sarah and Fiona Graham. 1993a. Fire Recovery at the Saskatchewan Museum of Natural History: Part I, Description of Events and Analysis of Recovery. In *ICOM Committee for Conservation. Preprints of the 10th Triennial Meeting, Washington, D.C., U.S.A., 22-27 August 1993.* Volume I. Janet Bridgland, ed. Paris: ICOM Committee for Conservation. 413-419.

Spafford, Sarah and Fiona Graham. 1993b. Fire Recovery at the Saskatchewan Museum of Natural History: Part II - Post-Disaster Clean-Up and Soot Removal. In *ICOM Committee for Conservation. Preprints of the 10th Triennial Meeting, Washington, D.C., U.S.A., 22-27 August 1993.* Volume I. Janet Bridgland, ed. Paris: ICOM Committee for Conservation. 420-426.

Spielmann, Nicole and Robert Benoît. 1995. Estimating Damage: A Vital Part of Emergency Planning. *Emergency Preparedness Digest* July-September:20-21.

Schwanke, Harriet. 1994. Hurricane Andrew: Community Information Services Disaster Relief - CIS to the Rescue. *The Southeastern Librarian* 44(2):69-71.

Stewart, Deborah and David Tremain. 1994. *Emergency and Disaster Preparedness for Museums.* Canadian Conservation Institute (CCI) Workshop. Revised edition. Ottawa: Department of Canadian Heritage, CCI. (Note: Unavailable. To be revised.)

Story, Keith O. 1985. *Approaches to Pest Management in Museums.* Suitland, Maryland: Conservation Analytical Laboratory, Smithsonian Institute.

Stowlow, Nathan. 1966. The Action of Environment on Museum Objects. Part II: Light. *Curator* 9:298-306.

Strang, Thomas J. K. and John E. Dawson. 1991a. *Controlling Museum Fungal Problems. Technical Bulletin No. 12.* Ottawa: Canadian Conservation Institute.

Strang, Thomas J. K. and John E. Dawson. 1991b. *Controlling Vertebrate Pests in Museums. Technical Bulletin No. 13.* Ottawa:Canadian Conservation Institute.

Strang, Tom. 1994. Reducing the Risk to Collections from Pests. *CCI Newsletter* 14 (September):8-10.

Tétreault, Jean. 1998. *Personal Communication.* December 10, 1998.

Tétreault, Jean. 1999. *Coatings for Display and Storage in Museums. Technical Bulletin No. 21.* Ottawa: Canadian Conservation Institute.

Thomson, Garry. 1986. *The Museum Environment.* 2nd ed. Butterworth Series on Conservation in the Arts, Archaeology and Architecture. London: Butterworths.

Trinkaus-Randall, Gregor. 1995. *Protecting Your Collections A Manual of Archival Security.* Chicago: SAA The Society of American Archivists.

Trinkley, Michael. 1993a. *Can You Stand the Heat? A Fire Safety Primer For Libraries, Archives, and Museums.* Atlanta: SOLINET Preservation Program.

Trinkley, Michael. 1993b. *Hurricane! Surviving the Big One: A Primer for Libraries, Museums and Archives.* Atlanta: SOLINET.

Trinkley, Michael. 1998. *Protecting Your Institution From Wild Fires: Planning Not to Burn and Learning to Recover.* http://palimpsest.stanford.edu/byauth/trinkley/wildfire.html

United States Department of the Interior. 1994. *Earthquakes and Volcanoes.* 25(2):60-108.

Van Bogart, John W. C. 1995. *Magnetic Tape Storage and Handling: A Guide for Libraries and Archives.* Washington, D.C.: The Commission on Preservation and Access and The National Media Laboratory.

Vouglas, Buffy. 1996. Studies Tap Into Computer Crime Problem, Prevention. *Contingency Planning & Management for Business Preparedness and Recovery* 1(4):1,5.

Walch, Timothy. 1977. *Archives and Manuscripts: Security.* Chicago: The Society of American Archivists.

Washizuka, Hiromitsu. 1985. Protection Against Earthquakes in Japan. *Museum* 37(2):119-122.

Watt, Marcia A. 1994. 2200 Gallons of Water. *The Southeastern Librarian* 44(2):67-68.

Weber, David C. 1990. *Library Buildings and the Loma Prieta Earthquake Experience of October 1989.* Sacramento: California State Library Foundation.

Weintraub, Steven. 1996. Revisiting the RH Battlefield: Analysis of Risk and Cost. *WAAC Newsletter* 18(3):22-23.

Wellheiser, Johanna. 1992. *Nonchemical Treatment Processes for Disinfestation of Insects and Fungi in Library Collections.* IFLA Publication 60. Munchen: KG Saur.

Wessel, Carl J. 1970. Environmental Factors Affecting the Permanence of Library Materials. In *Deterioration and Preservation of Library Materials.* The Thirty-fourth Annual Conference of the Graduate Library School, August 4-6, 1969. H.W. Winger and R.D. Smith, eds. Chicago: University of Chicago Press.

Western New York Library Resources Council. 1994. *Western New York Disaster Preparedness and Recovery Manual for Libraries and Archives.* Revised ed. Buffalo: Western New York Library Resources Council.

Wilson, J. Tuzo. 1983. Earthquake. *The Toronto Star.* November 5, 1983:B1.

Wilson, William K. 1995. *Environmental Guidelines for the Storage of Paper Records. NISO Technical Report: 1. NISO-TR01-1995.* Bethesda, Maryland: NISO Press.

References

Wise, Christine. 1995. The Flood and Afterwards: A New Beginning for the Fawcett Library, London Guildhall University. *Library Conservation News* 48 (Autumn):1-2.

Wood, Dr. Robert Muir. 1987. *Earthquakes and Volcanoes*. A Mitchell Beazley Earth Science Handbook. New York: Weidenfeld & Nicolson.

Wood Lee, Mary. 1988. *Prevention and Treatment of Mold in Library Collections with an Emphasis on Tropical Climates; A RAMP Study. PGI-88/WS/9*. Paris: General Information Programme and UNISIST: United Nations Educational, Scientific and Cultural Organization.

Wuorinen, Val. 1986. *Emergency Planning*. Hamilton, Ontario: Canadian Centre for Occupational Health and Safety.

Yatcom Communications, Inc. 1995a. *All About Hurricanes — What Is a Hurricane*. http://www.yatcom.com/neworl/weather/whatis.html

Yatcom Communications, Inc. 1995b. *All About Hurricanes — Preparing for a Hurricane*. http://www.yatcom.com/neworl/weather/prepare.html

Yatcom Communications, Inc. 1995c. *All About Hurricanes — Evacuation versus "Riding the Storm Out"*. http://www.yatcom.com/neworl/weather/evacduate.html

Yatcom Communications, Inc. 1995d. *All About Hurricanes — After the Hurricane Passes*. http://www.yatcom.com/neworl/weather/aftermath.html

Yatcom Communications, Inc. 1995e. *All About Hurricanes — Tornadoes*. http://www.yatcom.com/neworl/weather/tornado.html

Zycherman, Lynda A. and J. Richard Schrock, eds. 1988. *A Guide to Museum Pest Control*. Washington, D.C.: Foundation of the American Institute for Conservation of Historic and Artistic Works and Association of Systematics Collections.

Zyska, Bronislaw. 1997. Fungi Isolated from Library Materials: A Review of the Literature. *International Biodeterioration and Biodegradation* 40 (1):43-51.

Chapter 4.0   Disaster Protection Planning

Artim, Nicholas. 1993. Cultural Heritage Fire Suppression Systems: Alternative to Halon 1301. *WAAC Newsletter* 15(2):34-36.

Artim, Nicholas. 1994. An Introduction to Automatic Fire Sprinklers, Part I. *WAAC Newsletter* 16(3):20-27.

Artim, Nicholas. 1995. An Introduction to Automatic Fire Sprinklers, Part II. *WAAC Newsletter* 17(2):23-28.

Baril, Paul. 1991. Fire Protection. In *Art Gallery Handbook*. Vol. II. W. McAllister Johnson and Frances W. Smith, eds. Toronto: Ontario Association of Art Galleries. 39-46.

Baril, Paul. 1995. A Fire Protection Primer. *CCI Newsletter* 15:4-5.

Baril, Paul. 1996. *Personal Communication*. October 8, 1996.

Baril, Paul. 1997. Fire Prevention Programmes for Museums. *Technical Bulletin No. 18*. Ottawa:Canadian Conservation Institute.

Buchanan, Sally A. 1988. *Disaster Planning, Preparedness and Recovery for Libraries and Archives: A RAMP Study with Guidelines. PGI-88/WS/6*. Paris: General Information Programme and UNISIST, United Nations Educational, Scientific and Cultural Organization.

Bullock, Alison. 1997. *Personal Communication*. Feb. 12, 1997.

Bush, Stephen E. rev. 1991. Library and Museum Collections. In *Fire Protection Handbook*. 17th ed. Arthur E. Cote, ed. Quincy, Massachusetts: National Fire Protection Association. 8.61-8.73

Bush, Stephen E. and Danny L. McDaniel rev. 1997. Library and Museum Collections. In *Fire Protection Handbook*. 18th ed. Arthur E. Cote, ed. Quincy, Massachusetts: National Fire Protection Association. 9.92-9.109

Butler, Randall. 1986a. The Los Angeles Central Library Fire. *Conservation Administration News* 27:1-2,23,27.

Butler, Randall. 1986b. *The Los Angeles Central Library Fire: A Review and Analysis of a Disaster*. Unpublished paper.

Butler, Randall. 1988. Earthquake! The Experience of Two California Libraries. *Conservation Administration News* 32:1-2, 23-24.

Caldararo, Niccolo. 1993. The Solander Box: Its Varieties and Its Role as an Archival Unit of Storage for Prints and Drawings in a Museum, Archive or Gallery. *Museum Management and Curatorship* 12(4):387-400.

Canadian Commission on Building and Fire Codes, National Research Council of Canada (NRC). Revised 1995. *National Building Code of Canada 1990*. Ottawa: NRC.

Canadian Commission on Building and Fire Codes, National Research Council of Canada (NRC). Revised 1995. *National Fire Code of Canada 1990*. Ottawa: NRC.

CCI (Canadian Conservation Institute). 1995. *Storing Works on Paper. CCI Notes N11/2*. Ottawa: CCI.

CCI (Canadian Conservation Institute). 1996. *Making Protective Enclosures for Books and Paper Artifacts. CCI Note N11/1*. Ottawa: CCI.

Canadian Standards Association. 1994. *1994 Canadian Electrical Code, Part I*. 17th edition. Rexdale (Toronto): CSA.

CAN/ULC. 1987. *CAN/ULC - S529-M87. Standard for Smoke Detectors for Fire Alarm Systems*. Toronto: ULC.

CAN/ULC. 1991. *CAN/ULC - S524-M91. Standard for the Installation of Fire Alarm Systems*. Toronto: ULC.

CAN/ULC. 1992. *CAN/ULC - S536-M86. Amended 1992. Standard for the Inspection and Testing of Fire Alarm Systems*. Toronto: ULC.

CLA Earthquake Relief Grant Ad Hoc Committee. 1990. *Earthquake Preparedness Manual for California Libraries*. Sacramento: California Library Association.

Colby, Karen. 1992. A Suggested Exhibition Policy for Works of Art on Paper. *Journal of the International Institute for Conservation - Canadian Group* 17:3-11.

Conroy, Mark. 1996. Readers' Forum: The Word on Halons. *Contingency Planning & Management for Business Preparedness and Recovery* 1(5):8.

Cote, Arthur E., ed. 1991. *Fire Protection Handbook*. 17th ed. Quincy, Massachusetts: National Fire Protection Association.

Cote, Arthur. E. and Russell P. Fleming. 1997. Fast Response Sprinkler Technology. In *Fire Protection Handbook*. 18th ed. Arthur E. Cote, ed. Quincy, Massachusetts: National Fire Protection Association. 6.181-6.197.

DePew, John. 1991. Chapter 8. Disaster Preparedness and Recovery. In *A Library, Media and Archival Preservation Handbook*. Santa Barbara, California: ABC-CLIO. 253-300.

DiNemo, Philip. 1997. Direct Halon Replacement Agents and Systems. In *Fire Protection Handbook*. 18th ed. Arthur E. Cote, ed. Quincy, Massachusetts: National Fire Protection Association. 6.297-6.330.

Environmental Protection Agency (EPA). 1997. *Halon Substitutes Under SNAP as of June 3, 1997*. http://www.epa.gov/ozone/title6/snap/snaplift.html (see Fire Suppression and Explosion Protection).

Fortson, Judith. 1992. *Disaster Planning and Recovery. A How-To-Do-It Manual for Librarians and Archivists. Number 21*. New York: Neal-Schuman Publishers, Inc.

General Services Administration (GSA). 1977. *Protecting Federal Records Centers and Archives from Fire. Report of the General Services Administration Advisory Committee on the Protection of Archives and Record Centers.* Washington, D.C.: GSA.

Goonan, Thomas, rev. 1997. Storage and Handling of Records. In *Fire Protection Handbook.* 18th ed. Arthur E. Cote, ed. Quincy, Massachusetts: National Fire Protection Association. 3.275-3.283.

Hawkins, Thomas M. Jr. and Hugh McClees. 1988. Emergency Management. In *Managing Fire Services.* Ronny J. Coleman and John A. Granito, eds. 2nd edition. Washington, D.C.: International City/County Management Association (ICMA). 319-346.

Higgins, John T. 1997. Housekeeping Practices. In *Fire Protection Handbook.* 18th ed. Arthur E. Cote, ed. Quincy, Massachusetts: National Fire Protection Association. 3.364-3.372.

Hunter, John E. 1993a. Filing Cabinets and Safes for Protection of Paper Records, Computer Media, and Photographic Records from Fire Damage. *CRM Bulletin Supplement* 16(5):1-8.

Hunter, John E. 1993b. Protecting Paper Records and Computer Media from Fire. *GRIST* 37(4):37-41.

Kahn, Miriam. 1994. *Disaster Response and Prevention for Computers and Data.* Columbus, Ohio: MBK Consulting.

Keafer, Yvonne M. 1998. Protection Without Halon: What are the Alternatives? *Disaster Recovery Journal* 11(3): 38, 40-44.

Knapp, Tony and John E. Hunter. 1990. Chapter 9. Museum Collections Protection: Security and Fire Protection. In *National Park Service Museum Handbook. Part I: Museum Collections.* Revised edition. Washington, D.C.: National Park Service, U.S. Department of the Interior. 9:1-9:33.

Kulka, Edward. 1993. *National Archives of Canada: Textual Containerization Project.* Ottawa: National Archives of Canada.

Kulka, Edward. 1995. *Archival Enclosures: A Guide.* Ottawa: Canadian Council of Archives.

Lee, B. M. 1996. Fire Protection for Libraries; A Technology Update. In *Redefining Disasters: A Decade of Counter-Disaster Planning. Proceedings. Wednesday 20 - Friday 22 September 1995.* Alan Howell, Heather Mansell and Marion Roubos-Bennett, Compilers. Revised edition. Sydney, Australia: State Library of New South Wales. 97-106.

Lopes, Rocky. 1997. Designing Disaster Education Programs. *In Fire Protection Handbook.* 18th ed. Arthur E. Cote, ed. Quincy, Massachusetts: National Fire Protection Association. 2.21-2.29.

Lougheed, G.D., J.R. Mawhinney and J. O'Neill. 1994. Full-Scale Fire Tests and the Development of Design Criteria for Sprinkler Protection of Mobile Shelving Units. *Fire Technology* 30(first quarter):98-133.

Macwhinney, Jack R. and Robert Solomon. 1997. Water Mist Suppression Systems. In *Fire Protection Handbook.* 18th ed. Arthur E. Cote, ed. Quincy, Massachusetts: National Fire Protection Association. 6.216-6.248.

Metcalf, Keyes DeWitt. 1986. *Planning Academic and Research Library Buildings.* 2nd ed. Philip D. Leighton and David C. Weber. Chicago: American Library Association.

Moore, Wayne D., rev. 1997. Automatic Fire Detectors. In *Fire Protection Handbook.* 18th ed. Arthur E. Cote, ed. Quincy, Massachusetts: National Fire Protection Association. 5.12-5.23.

Morris, John. 1979. *Managing the Library Fire Risk.* 2nd ed. Berkeley: University of California.

Morris, John. 1986. *The Library Disaster Preparedness Handbook.* Chicago and London: American Library Association.

Murray, Toby. 1994. *Basic Guidelines for Disaster Planning in Oklahoma.* Tulsa, Oklahoma: Oklahoma Conservation Congress (OCC).

NFPA (National Fire Protection Association). 1999. *National Electrical Code.* Quincy, Massachusetts: NFPA.

NFPA. 1997. *NFPA 1-97. Fire Prevention Code.* Quincy, Massachusetts: NFPA.

NFPA. 1998. *NFPA 10 - 98. Standard for Portable Fire Extinguishers.* Quincy, Massachusetts: NFPA.

NFPA. 1997. *NFPA 12A-97. Standard on Halon 1301 Fire Extinguishing Systems.* Quincy, Massachusetts: NFPA.

NFPA. 1999. *NFPA 13 - 99. Standard for Installation of Sprinkler Systems.* Quincy, Massachusetts: NFPA.

NFPA. 1996. *NFPA 14 - 96. Standard for Installation of Standpipe and Hose Systems.* Quincy, Massachusetts: NFPA.

NFPA. 1996. *NFPA 15 - 96. Standard for Water Spray Fixed Systems for Fire Protection.* Quincy, Massachusetts: NFPA.

NFPA. 1999. *NFPA 72 - 99. National Fire Alarm Code.* Massachusetts: NFPA.

NFPA. 1999. *NFPA 75 - 99. Standard for Protection of Electronic Computer/Data Processing Equipment.* Quincy, Massachusetts: NFPA.

NFPA. 1996. *NFPA 92A - 96. Recommended Practice for Smoke-Control Systems.* Quincy, Massachusetts: NFPA.

NFPA. 1997. *NFPA 101-97. Life Safety Code.* Quincy, Massachusetts: NFPA

NFPA. 1998. *NFPA 101A-98. Guide on Alternatives to Life Safety.* Quincy, Massachusetts, NFPA.

NFPA. 1998. *NFPA 231 - 98. Standard for General Storage.* Quincy, Massachusetts: NFPA.

NFPA. 1998. *NFPA 231C - 98. Standard for Rack Storage of Materials.* Quincy, Massachusetts: NFPA.

NFPA. 1995. *NFPA 232 - 95. Standard for Protection of Records.* Quincy, Massachusetts: NFPA.

NFPA. 1995. *NFPA 232A - 95. Guide for Fire Protection for Archives and Record Centres.* Quincy, Massachusetts: NFPA.

NFPA. 1998. *NFPA 318-98. Standard for the Protection of Cleanrooms.* Quincy, Massachusetts: NFPA.

NFPA. 1995. *NFPA 550 - 95. Guide to the Fire Safety Concepts Tree.* Quincy, Massachusetts: NFPA.

NFPA. 1996. *NFPA 601-96. Standard for Security Services in Fire Loss Prevention.* Quincy, Massachusetts: NFPA.

NFPA. 1996. *NFPA 750 - 96. Standard for the Installation of Water Mist Fire Protection Systems.* Quincy, Massachusetts: NFPA.

NFPA. 1997. *NFPA 909-97. Standard for the Protection of Cultural Resources including Museums, Libraries, Places of Worship and Historic Properties.* Quincy, Massachusetts: NFPA.

NFPA. 1994. *NFPA 914-94. Recommended Practice for Fire Protection in Historic Structures.* Quincy, Massachusetts: NFPA.

NFPA. 1995. *NFPA 1600 - 95. Recommended Practice for Disaster Management.* Quincy, Massachusetts: NFPA.

NFPA. 1996. *NFPA 2001 - 96. Standard on Clean Agent Fire Extinguishing Systems.* Quincy, Massachusetts: NFPA.

NISO (National Information Standards Organization). 1994. *ANSI/NISO Z39.73-1994. Single-Tier Steel Bracket Library Shelving.* Bethesda, Maryland: NISO Press.

Novak, Gloria. 1999. *Mobile Systems for Compact Storage. Library Technology Reports 35, No. 5.* Chicago. American Library Association.

Pacey, Antony. 1991. Halon Gas and Library Fire Prevention. *Canadian Library Journal* 48(1):33-36.

Panone, Carolyn. 1996. In the Face of Adversity. *Library Conservation News* 51:3.

Pearce, Robert J., rev. 1997. Chapter 28. Protection of Electronic Equipment. In *Fire Protection Handbook.* 18th ed. Arthur E. Cote, ed. Quincy, Massachusetts: National Fire Protection Association. 9.205-9.208.

Powell, Pamela A. 1997. Fire and Life Safety Education: Theory and Techniques. *In Fire Protection Handbook.* 18th ed. Arthur E. Cote, ed. Quincy, Massachusetts: National Fire Protection Association. 2.30-2.39.

Powell, Pamela A. and Meri-K Appy. 1997. Fire and Life Safety Education: The State of the Art. In *Fire Protection Handbook.* 18th ed. Arthur E. Cote, ed. Quincy, Massachusetts: National Fire Protection Association. 2.3-2.11.

References

Schmidt, William A. 1997. Air Conditioning and Ventilating Systems. In *Fire Prevention Handbook*. 18th ed. Arthur E. Cote, ed. Quincy, Massachusetts: National Fire Protection Association. 7.175-7.181.

Schreider, Tari. 1994. The 10 Most Common Pitfalls in Contingency Planning. *Emergency Preparedness Digest* October-December:22-25.

Shelton, John A. 1990. *Seismic Safety Standards for Library Shelving*. California State Library Manual of Recommended Practice. Sacramento: California State Library Foundation.

Shepilova, Irina. G., prep. 1992. *Main Principles of Fire Protection in Libraries and Archives: A RAMP Study. PGI-92/WS/14*. Thomas, Adrienne G., ed. Paris: General Information Programme and UNISIST, United Nations Educational, Scientific and Cultural Organization.

Society of Archivists (Scottish Region). 1996. *Disaster Preparedness: Guidelines for Archives and Libraries*. London: Society of Archivists (Scottish Region).

Solomon, Robert E. 1994. *Automatic Sprinkler Systems Handbook*. 6th ed. Quincy, Massachusetts: National Fire Protection Association.

Solomon, Robert E., rev. 1997. Automatic Sprinkler Systems. In *Fire Protection Handbook*. 18th ed. Arthur E. Cote, ed. Quincy, Massachusetts: National Fire Protection Association. 6.136-6.164.

Sung, Carolyn Hoover, Valerii Pavlovich Leonov and Peter Waters. 1990. Fire Recovery at the Library of Sciences of the USSR. *American Archivist* 53(Spring):298-312.

Swartzburg, Susan Garretson and Holly Bussey with Frank Garretson. 1991. *Libraries and Archives: Design and Renovation with a Preservation Perspective*. Metuchen, N.J.: Scarecrow Press.

Taylor, Gary M., rev. 1997. Halongenated Agents and Systems. In *Fire Protection Handbook*. 18th ed. Arthur E. Cote, ed. Quincy, Massachusetts: National Fire Protection Association. 6.281-6.296.

Tremain, David. 1996. *Halon and Cellular Phone*. Dec. 16, 1996. Available CoOL DistList Archives.

Trinkley, Michael. 1993. *Can You Stand the Heat? A Fire Safety Primer For Libraries, Archives, and Museums*. Atlanta: SOLINET Preservation Program.

ULC (Underwriters' Laboratories of Canada.) See **CAN/ULC.**

UL (Underwriters' Laboratory). 1995. *UL 72 - 1995. Test for Fire Resistance of Record Protection Equipment*. Northbrook, Illinois: UL.

UL. 1995. *UL 155 - 1995. Tests for Fire Resistance of Vault and File Room Doors*. Northbrook, Illinois: UL.

Weber, David C. 1990. *Library Buildings and the Loma Prieta Earthquake Experience of October 1989*. Sacramento: California State Library Foundation.

Wilson, J. Andrew. 1989. Fire Fighters. *Museum News* Nov/Dec:68-72.

Chapter 5.0   Disaster Preparedness Planning

(AASLH) American Association for State and Local History. Technical Leaflet No. 183. *Disaster Planning for Cultural Institutions*. Nashville, Tennessee: AASLH.

Baker, Ed, Greg Van Hise and Steve Luko. 1997. Performance Hierarchy of Disaster Recovery Solutions. *Disaster Recovery Journal* 10(3):13-16.

Balon, Brett J. and H. Wayne Gardner. 1987. Disaster Contingency Planning: The Basic Elements. *Records Management Quarterly* 21(1):14-16.

Barber, David. 1994. Mass Storage Systems for Digital Data, with Strategies for Increasing Capacity and Improving Speed and Economy. *Library Technology Reports* 30(4):451-534.

Bates, Regis J. 1992. *Disaster Recovery Planning: Networks, Telecommunications, and Data Communications*. U.S.A.: McGraw-Hill, Inc.

Bates, Regis J. 1994. *Disaster Recovery for LANs: A Planning and Action Guide*. U.S.A.: McGraw-Hill, Inc.

Buckland, John, ed. 1991. *Disaster Recovery Handbook*. Blue Ridge Summit, Pennsylvania: Chantico Publishing Company, Inc.

CCI (Canadian Conservation Institute). 1995. *Emergency Preparedness for Cultural Institutions: Introduction. CCI Note N14/1*. Ottawa: CCI.

CCI. 1995. *Emergency Preparedness for Cultural Institutions: Identifying and Reducing Hazards. CCI Note N14/2*. Ottawa: CCI.

Canadian General Standards Board. 1993. *CAN/CGSB-72.11-93. Microfilm and Electronic Images as Documentary Evidence*. Ottawa: Canadian General Standards Board (CGSB).

Cornell, Camilla. August 3, 1996. Insure Yourself Against Mother Nature. *Toronto: The Globe and Mail.*

Cunha, George Martin. 1992. Disaster Planning and a Guide to Recovery Resources. *Library Technology Reports* 28(5):533-624.

Daines, Guy E. 1991. Planning, Training and Exercising. In *Emergency Management: Principles and Practice for Local Government*. Thomas E. Drabek and Gerard J. Hoetmer, eds. Washington, D.C.: International City/County Management Association (ICMA). 161-200.

Daley, Wayne. 1991. Business Resumption Planning: An Answer to Surviving a Disaster. *Emergency Preparedness Digest* (July-September):2-5.

Davies, J. Eric. 1994. Locks, Bolts and Bars - Real and Virtual: Computer Security. *Aslib Managing Information* 1(7/8):28-32.

Deeney, Marian. 1989. Disasters: Are You Ready If One Should Strike Your Library? Reprinted from the *Southeastern Librarian* (Summer) 1985. In *Disaster Planning and Recovery An SLA Information Kit*. Washington, D.C.: Special Libraries Association. 62-66.

Dean Witter. 1996. Progress Report. *Contingency Planning & Management for Business Preparedness and Recovery* 1(2):18.

DeLuca, Frank. 1996. Recovery Has Its Place. *Contingency Planning & Management for Business Preparedness and Recovery* 1(4):21-24.

DePew, John N. 1991a. Chapter 8. Disaster Preparedness and Recovery. In *A Library, Media, and Archival Preservation Handbook*. Santa Barbara: ABC-CLIO. 253-300.

DePew, John N. 1991b. Chapter 8G. Insurance. In *A Library, Media, and Archival Preservation Handbook*. Santa Barbara: ABC-CLIO. 288-300.

Donaldson, Richard C. 1983. Protecting the Business from Disaster. *Records Management Quarterly* January:33-41.

Doten, Neal. 1996. Mitigation: Pay Now or Pay More Later. *Contingency Planning & Management for Business Preparedness and Recovery* 1(2):13-18.

Drewes, Jeanne. 1989. Computers: Planning for Disaster. *Law Library Journal* 81:103-116.

Drewes, Jeanne. 1998. Bibliography of Insurance Information Sources and Library Insurance Bibliography. http://milton.mse.jhu.edu:8001/library/pres/insso urces.htm

EPC (Emergency Preparedness Canada). 1987. *Guide to the Preservation of Essential Records*. Ottawa: Ministry of Supply and Services Canada.

EPC. 1991. *Information Technology Security: A Manager's Guide*. Ottawa: Minister of Supply and Services.

EPC. 1995. *Business Resumption Planning. A Guide*. Ottawa: Ministry of Supply and Services Canada in consultation with The Disaster Recovery Information Exchange (DRIE).

EPC. 1996. *The Preservation of Essential Records. A Guide for Governments, Organizations, Institutions and Businesses*. Ottawa: Minister of Supply and Services Canada.

England, Claire and Karen Evans. 1988. Chapter 5: Insurance for the Library Collection. In *Disaster Management for Libraries: Planning and Process*. Ottawa: Canadian Library Association. 59-70.

English, Dick. 1986. Insurance. In *Proceedings of An Ounce of Prevention: A Symposium on Disaster Contingency Planning for Information Managers in Archives, Libraries and Record Centres*. Nancy Willson, ed. Toronto: Toronto Area Archivists Group Education Foundation. 90-98.

FEMA (Federal Emergency Management Agency). 1984. *Objectives for Local Emergency Management. CPG 1-5*. Washington, D.C.: FEMA.

Fortson, Judith. 1992. *Disaster Planning and Recovery. A How-To-Do-It Manual for Librarians and Archivists. Number 21.* New York: Neal-Schuman Publishers, Inc.

Foster, Al. 1996. Prepare to Compare. *Contingency Planning & Management for Business Preparedness and Recovery* 1(2):33.

Fox, Lisa L. 1989. Management Strategies for Disaster Preparedness. *ALA Yearbook of Library and Information Series* 14:1-6.

Greene, Harlan. 1994. Build It and They Will Come: Libraries and Disaster Preparedness. *North Carolina Libraries* 52(1):6-7.

Guaragno, John P and Clyde L. Monma. 1996. Computer Security in Jeopardy. *Contingency Planning & Management for Business Preparedness and Recovery* 1(5):20-23.

Haimowitz, Mark. 1996. Don't Assume. *Contingency Planning & Management for Business Preparedness and Recovery* 1(4):13-14.

Henderson, Jane. 1995. Disasters Without Planning: Lessons for Museums. *The Conservator* 19:52-57.

Hunter, John E. 1983. Chapter 11. Museum Disaster Planning. In *Museum, Archive, and Library Security.* Lawrence J. Fennelly, ed. Boston: Butterworths. 235-270.

Hunter, John E. 1984. *Preparing a Museum Disaster Plan.* Omaha, Nebraska: National Park Service.

Hunter, John E. 1990. Chapter 10. Museum Collections: Emergency Planning. In *National Park Service Museum Handbook. Part I: Museum Collections.* Revised edition. Washington, D.C.: National Park Service. 10:1-10:29.

ISO (International Organization for Standardization). 1990. *ISO/TR 10200:1990 Legal Admissibility of Microforms. Technical Report.* Geneva: ISO.

ISO/IEC. 1997. *ISO/IEC TR 13335-2:1997. Information Technology - Guidelines for the Management of IT Security - Part 2: Managing and Planning IT Security.* Geneva: ISO.

Ives, David, J. 1996. Security Management Strategies for Protecting Your Library's Network. *Computers in Libraries* 16(2):36-42.

Kahn, Miriam. 1994a. Fires, Earthquakes and Floods: How to Prepare Your Library and Staff. *ONLINE* (May):18-24.

Kahn, Miriam. 1994b. *Disaster Response and Prevention for Computers and Data.* Columbus, Ohio: MBK Consulting.

Lewis, Steve, ed. 1996. *Disaster Recovery Yellow Pages.* 5th ed. Newton, Massachusetts: The Systems Audit Group Inc.

Luongo, Rich. 1996. Insurance Assurance. *Contingency Planning & Management for Business Preparedness and Recovery* 1(2):15.

Maedke, W.O., M.F. Robek and G.F. Brown. 1981. *Information and Records Management.* 2nd edition. Encino, California: Glencoe Publishing Co. Inc.

Marrelli, Nancy. 1986. Fire in the Concordia University Archives. In *Proceedings of An Ounce of Prevention: A Symposium on Disaster Contingency Planning for Information Managers in Archives, Libraries and Record Centres.* Nancy Willson, ed. Toronto: Toronto Area Archivists Group Education Foundation. 132-144.

Marrelli, Nancy. 1996. *Personal Communication.* August 1996.

Matthews, Graham. 1994. Disaster Management: Controlling the Plan. *Managing Information* 1(7/8):24-27.

Matthews, Joseph R. and Mark R. Parker. 1995. Local Area Networks and Wide Area Networks for Libraries. *Library Technology Reports* 31(1):7-110.

Metro Corporate Services, The Municipality of Metropolitan Toronto. 1994. *Policies and Principles for the Management of Records, Data and Information Technology Security.* March 18, 1994. Toronto: The Municipality of Metropolitan Toronto.

Miller, R. Bruce. 1988. Libraries and Computers: Disaster Prevention and Recovery. *Information Technology and Libraries* 7(4):349-358.

Miller, Charles. 1993. *Information Technology Security Handbook.* Ottawa: Ministry of Government Services.

Moore, Pat. 1997. Vital Records Protection Issues. *Disaster Recovery Journal* 10(3):26-28.

Murray, Toby. 1987. Preservation Disaster Planning. *The Paper Conservator* 11:87-93

Murray, Toby. 1994. *Basic Guidelines for Disaster Planning in Oklahoma.* Tulsa, Oklahoma: Oklahoma Conservation Congress (OCC).

Myers, Gerald E. 1977. *Insurance Manual for Libraries.* Chicago: American Library Association.

Myers, Marcia J., comp. 1991. *Insuring Library Collections and Buildings. SPEC Kit 178.* Washington, D.C.: Association of Research Libraries, Office of Management Studies.

National Archives and Records Administration (NARA). 1996. *Vital Records and Records Disaster Mitigation and Recovery. An Instructional Guide.* Maryland: NARA, Office of Records Administration. Available on Conservation Online.

National Archives and Records Service. 1982. *Intrinsic Value in Archival Material. National Archives and Records Service Staff Information Paper No. 21.* Washington, D.C.: National Archives and Records Service, General Services Administration.

NFPA (National Fire Protection Association). 1995. *NFPA 232 - 95 Protection of Records.* Quincy, Massachusetts: NFPA.

Ogorchock, Jim. 1996. Data Back-Up Technologies for Any Occasion. *Contingency Planning & Management for Business Preparedness and Recovery* 1(5):17-18.

Ontario Management Board of Cabinet. 1991. *Information Technology Security: A Manager's Guide. Ontario Management Board of Cabinet Guideline 7:3.* Toronto: The Queen's Printer.

Ontario Ministry of Citizenship and Culture, Heritage Administration Branch. 1983. *Museum Notes for Community Museums in Ontario, Number 5 Museum Insurance.* MCC: Toronto.

Ontario Ministry of Culture, Tourism and Recreation (MCTR) and Archives of Ontario. 1994. *RIM Fact Sheet #5 (Recorded Information Management). Electronic Records: Some Key Challenges.* Toronto: MCTR.

Penn, Ira A., Gail Pennix, Anne Morddel and Kelvin Smith. 1989. *Records Management Handbook.* Brookfield, Vermont: Gower Publishing Company.

Pickren, Ann. 1997. Business Continuity Planning: New Choices in Alternate Site Selection. *Disaster Recovery Journal* 10(3):10-12.

Poulter, Alan and Graham Matthews. 1993. Mixed-Media Disaster Control Planning. *Records Management Bulletin* 54:21-22.

Prevention Committee, President's Council on Integrity and Efficiency. 1986. *Computers: Crimes, Clues and Controls. A Management Guide.* Washington, D.C: publisher unknown.

Price, Laura and Abby Smith. 2000. *Managing Cultural Resources from a Business Perspective.* Washington, D.C.: Council on Library and Information Resources in cooperation with the Library of Congress.

Rossol, Monona. 1998. Compliance in Recovery: Regulatory Requirements in the Aftermath of Disaster. *AIC News* 23(5):1,4-7.

Schreider, Tari. 1994. The 10 Most Common Pitfalls in Contingency Planning. *Emergency Preparedness Digest* October-December:22-25.

Scott, Jude. 1985. *Museum & Archival Supplies Handbook.* Third revised edition. Toronto: Ontario Museum Association & The Toronto Area Archivists Group.

Seal, Robert A. 1989a. Insurance for Libraries: Part I. *Reprinted from Conservation Administration News* 1984, 19(8). In Disaster Planning and Recovery. An SLA Information Kit. Washington, D.C.: SLA. 57-58.

Seal, Robert A. 1989b. Insurance for Libraries: Part II. *Reprinted from Conservation Administration News* 1985, 20(10). In Disaster Planning and Recovery. An SLA Information Kit. Washington, D.C.: SLA. 59-61.

Siebert, Ann. 1996. *Emergency Preparedness for Library of Congress Collections.* http://palimpsest.stanford.edu/bytopic/disasters

Skepastianu, Maria with the assistance of Jean I. Whiffin. 1995. *Library Disaster Planning.* The Hague: IFLA Section on Conservation and Preservation.

Smith, Richard D. 1992. Disaster Recovery: Problems and Procedures. *IFLA Journal* 18(1):13-23.

References

Stasak, Bernard C. 1996. Human Resources. Proper Deployment, Care, and Communication Fortify Team Efforts. *Contingency Planning & Management for Business Preparedness and Recovery* 1(2):29-31.

Stewart, Deborah and David Tremain. 1994. *Emergency and Disaster Preparedness for Museums.* Canadian Conservation Institute (CCI) Workshop. Revised edition. Ottawa: Department of Canadian Heritage, CCI. (Note: Unavailable. To be revised.)

Takemura, Robert. 1996. Recovery Strategies Mirror the Times. Cited in Lee Tydlaska's What's Behind Your Back-Up Plan? *Contingency Planning & Management for Business Preparedness and Recovery* 1(2):23.

Toigo, Jon William. 1989. *Disaster Recovery Planning. Managing Risk And Catastrophe in Information Systems.* Englewood Cliffs, New Jersey. Yourdon Press.

Turner, Rollo. 1994. Computers and Disasters: Putting Your PC in the Recovery Position. *Aslib Managing Information* 1(7/8):38-40.

Tydlaska, Lee. 1996. What's Behind Your Back-up Plan? *Contingency Planning & Management for Business Preparedness and Recovery.* 1(2):22-28.

Ungarelli, Donald L. 1984. Insurance and Prevention: Why and How? *Library Trends* (Summer):57-67.

Vouglas, Buffy. 1996. Records Storage Providers Have the Answers. *Contingency Planning & Management for Business Preparedness and Recovery* 1(4):25-26.

Wright, Gordon H. 1979. Fire! Anguish! Dumb Luck! or Contingency Planning. *Canadian Library Journal* 36(5):254-260.

Wuorinen, Val. 1986. *Emergency Planning.* Hamilton, Ontario: Canadian Centre for Occupational Health and Safety (CCOHS).

Chapter 6.0   Disaster Response Planning

Brown, Robert D. Jr. 1994. Lessons Reaffirmed, Extended or Revealed. *Earthquakes & Volcanoes* 25(2):103-106.

Buchanan, Sally A. 1988. *Disaster Planning, Preparedness and Recovery for Libraries and Archives: A RAMP Study with Guidelines. PGI-88/WS/6.* Paris: General Information Programme and UNISIST, United Nations Educational, Scientific and Cultural Organization.

Buckland, John, ed. 1991. *Disaster Recovery Handbook.* Blue Ridge Summit, Pennsylvania: Chantico Publishing Company, Inc.

Craig-Bullen, Catherine. 1996. Guidelines for the Prevention and Treatment of Mould-Damaged Archival and Library Material. *The Archivist* 112:32-36.

Cunha, George Martin. 1992. Disaster Planning and a Guide to Recovery Resources. *Library Technology Reports* 28(5):533-624.

DeLuca, Frank. 1996. Recovery Has Its Place. *Contingency Planning & Management for Business Preparedness and Recovery* 1(4):21-24.

DePew, John. 1991. Chapter 8. Disaster Preparedness and Recovery. In *A Library, Media and Archival Preservation Handbook.* Santa Barbara, California: ABC-CLIO. 253-300.

Drabek, Thomas E., and Gerard J. Hoetmer, eds. 1991. *Emergency Management: Principles and Practice for Local Government.* Washington, D.C.: International City/County Management Association (ICMA).

Environment Canada, The Crisis Management Division of the Conservation and Protection Branch. 1993. Guide for Crisis Management Planning. *Emergency Preparedness Digest* April-June:23-26.

EPC (Emergency Preparedness Canada). *National Earthquake Support Plan for British Columbia.* 1996. Ottawa: Emergency Preparedness Canada.1-2. http://hoshi.cic.sfu.ca/epc/NESP/english.html.

FEMA (Federal Emergency Management Agency). 1984. *Objectives for Local Emergency Management* CPG 1-5. Washington, D.C.: FEMA.

FEMA (Federal Emergency Management Agency). 1990. *Risks and Hazards. A State by State Guide.* Washington, D.C.: FEMA.

Florian, Mary-Lou. 1993. Conidial Fungi (Mould) Activity on Artifact Materials - A New Look at Prevention, Control and Eradication. In *ICOM Committee for Conservation. Preprints of the 10th Triennial Meeting, Washington, D.C., U.S.A., 22-27 August 1993.* Volume II. Janet Bridgland, ed. Paris: ICOM Committee for Conservation. 868-874.

Florian, Mary-Lou E. 1997. *Heritage Eaters: Insects and Fungi in Heritage Collections.* London: James and James Science Publishers Ltd.

Fortson, Judith. 1992. *Disaster Planning and Recovery. A How-To-Do-It Manual for Librarians and Archivists. Number 21.* New York: Neal-Schuman Publishers, Inc.

Gavitt, Sharon. 1995. Observations on the Effect of Freezing and Thawing Microfilm. In *Advances in Preservation and Access.* Vol. 2. Barbra Buckner Higginbotham, ed. Medford, New Jersey: Learned Information Inc. 268-279.

Hand, Heather. 1993. B.C. Ready for the INEVITABLE. *Emergency Preparedness Digest.* January-March:2-6.

Henderson, Jane. 1995. Disasters Without Planning: Lessons for Museums. *The Conservator* 19:52-57.

Hunter, John E. 1984. *Preparing a Museum Disaster Plan.* Omaha, Nebraska: National Park Service.

Hyndman, Roy D. 1995. Giant Earthquakes of the Pacific Northwest. *Scientific American* 273(6):68-75.

ICOM International Committee for Conservation. 1994. Report of the 10th Triennial Meeting. *Control of Biodeterioration Newsletter* 1(January):1-7.

Kahn, Miriam. 1994. Fires, Earthquakes and Floods: How to Prepare Your Library and Staff. *ONLINE* May:18-24.

Kahn, Miriam B. 1998. *Disaster Response and Planning for Libraries.* Chicago: American Library Association.

Lyall, Jan. 1995. *Disaster Planning for Libraries and Archives: Understanding the Essential Issues.* Canberra: National Library of Australia. http://www.nla.gov.au/3/npo/pubs/papers/jlyall/disaster.html.

Mann, Brad. 1994. Straight Talk: The Value of Effective Disaster Communications. *Emergency Preparedness Digest* April-June:2-6.

Matthai, R. A. 1979. *Protection of Cultural Properties during Energy Emergencies and Energy Conservation and Historic Preservation.* Washington, D.C.: U.S. Department of Commerce.

McFarlane, J.A. (Sandy) and Warren Clements, eds. 1996. *The Globe and Mail Style Book.* 4th ed. Toronto: Penguin.

Munters Corp., Moisture Control Services Division and MBK Consulting. 1996. *Document Restoration Manual.* Internal Training Document.

Murray, Toby. 1994. *Basic Guidelines for Disaster Planning in Oklahoma.* Tulsa, Oklahoma: Oklahoma Conservation Congress (OCC).

National Archives of Canada (Conservation Treatment Division). 1996. *Precautionary Measures for Dealing with Mould Contamination of Archival and Library Collections and Locally Contaminated Buildings (Internal Procedures Document).* Ottawa: National Archives of Canada.

Nelson, Carl L. 1991. *Protecting the Past from Natural Disasters.* Washington, D.C.: National Trust for Historic Preservation.

Palmer Eldridge, Betsy. 1999. Natural Freeze Drying: A Viable Option. In **The Book and Paper Group Annual** 17, 1998. Robert Espinosa, compiler and managing editor. Washington, D.C.: American Institute for Conservation of Historic and Artistic Works. 1- 4.

Parker, A.E. 1989. The Freeze-Drying Process. *Library Conservation News* 23(April):4-6,8.

Parker, A.E. 1991. Freeze-Drying of Vellum. *Library Conservation News* 33(5):4-6.

Parker, A.E. 1993. Freeze-Drying Vellum Archival Materials. *Journal of the Society of Archivists* 14(2):175-185.

PEP (Provincial Emergency Program). 1995. *Prepare Now For an Earthquake in British Columbia. A Guide for B.C. Families and Individuals to Prepare for Surviving a Major Earthquake.* Victoria, B.C.: PEP. 1-10. http://hoshi.cic.sfu.ca/~pep/prepare.html.

Perry, Ronald W. 1991. Managing Disaster Response Operations. In *Emergency Management: Principles and Practice for Local Government.* Thomas E. Drabek and Gerard J. Hoetmer, eds. Washington, D.C.: International City/County Management Association (ICMA). 201-223.

Rossol, Monona. 1998. Compliance in Recovery: Regulatory Requirements in the Aftermath of Disaster. *AIC News* 23(5):1,4-7.

Scanlon, T. Joseph. 1991. Reaching Out: Getting the Community Involved in Preparedness. In *Emergency Management: Principles and Practice for Local Government.* Thomas E. Drabek and Gerard J. Hoetmer, eds. Washington, D.C.: International City/County Management Association (ICMA). 79-100.

Shapinka, Larissa B. et al. 1991. New Technologies from the U.S.S.R.: Restoring Book Paper and Drying Water Wetted Books. In *Book and Paper Group Annual.* Vol. 10. Robert Espinosa, compiler. Washington, D.C.: American Institute for Conservation for Historic and Artistic Works.

Smith, Richard D. 1984. The Use of Redesigned and Mechanically Modified Commercial Freezers to Dry Water-Wetted Books and Exterminate Insects. *Restaurator* 6(3-4):165-190.

Smith, Richard D. 1992. Disaster Recovery: Problems and Procedures. *IFLA Journal* 18(1):13-23.

Smithsonian Institution. 1993. In *A Primer on Disaster Preparedness, Management, and Response: Paper-Based Materials.* Selected Reprints issued by the Smithsonian Institution, National Archives and Records Administration, Library of Congress and National Park Service. 9-10. Distributed by the participating agencies. http://palimpsest.stanford.edu/bytopic/disaster.primer.part4of5.text

Stewart, Deborah and David Tremain. 1994. *Emergency and Disaster Preparedness for Museums.* Canadian Conservation Institute (CCI) Workshop. Revised edition. Ottawa: Department of Canadian Heritage, CCI. (Note: Unavailable. To be revised.)

Syracuse University Library, Preservation Department. 1995. *Syracuse University Library Manual: Procedures for Recovering Print Materials: Non-Print and Photographic Materials: and Audio Recordings.* http://libwww.syr.edu/aboutsul/depts/preserve/displan.htm

Thorburn, Georgine. 1993. Library Fire and Flood - Successful Salvage, But Beware the Cowboy. *Aslib Information* 21(2):76-78.

Tremain, David. 1997. Books With Blocked Pages. December 8, 1997. Available *CoOL DistList Archives.*

Tremain, David. 1998. **Notes on Emergency Drying of Coated Papers Damaged by Water.** http://palimpsest.stanford.edu/byauth/tremain/coated.html

Trinkley, Michael. 1993. *Can You Stand the Heat? A Fire Safety Primer For Libraries, Archives, and Museums.* Atlanta: SOLINET Preservation Program.

U.S. Defence Civil Preparedness Agency. 1978. Civil Preparedness Field Training Manual SM-32.1. Participant Manual for Emergency Planning Workshop for Business and Industry Conferences. Washington, D.C.: Defence Civil Preparedness Agency. In *Selected Readings in Museum Emergency Planning. Seminar on Emergency Planning for Museums, Galleries and Archives. British Columbia Museum (BCM). Victoria, B.C., Canada. October 16-19, 1984.* John E. Hunter, compiler. Omaha, Nebraska: National Park Service.

Van Bogart, John W. C. 1996a. *Recovery of Damaged Magnetic Tape and Optical Disk Media. Part 1: Recovery from Improper Storage.* Presented at "Emergency Preparedness and Disaster Recovery of Audio, Film and Video Materials". A Library of Congress Symposium - September 21, 1995. http://www.nml.org/presentations/disaster_recovery/lc_disaster_recovery.html

Van Bogart, John W. C. 1996b. *Recovery of Damaged Magnetic Tape and Optical Disk Media. Part 2: Recovery from Disasters.* Presented at "Emergency Preparedness and Disaster Recovery of Audio, Film and Video Materials". A Library of Congress Symposium - September 21, 1995. http://www.nml.org/presentations/disaster_recovery/lc_disaster_recovery.html

Ward, Alan and Peter Copeland. 1992. Freeze-Drying of Tapes. *Library Conservation News* 34(7):4-5.

Waters, Peter. 1979. *Procedures for Salvage of Water-Damaged Library Materials.* 2nd ed. Washington, D.C.: Library of Congress.

Waters, Peter. 1993. Procedures for Salvage of Water Damaged Library Materials. Extracts from unpublished revised text. In *A Primer on Disaster Preparedness, Management, and Response: Paper-Based Materials.* Selected Reprints issued by the Smithsonian Institution, National Archives and Records Administration, Library of Congress and National Park Service. Distributed by the participating agencies. http://palimpsest.stanford.edu/bytopic/disaster.primer.part4of5.text

Waters, Peter. 1996. From Florence to St. Petersburg: An Enlightening and Thought-Provoking Experience. A Personal Account of the Past Twenty Nine Years in Pursuit of the Conservation of Library Materials. In *Redefining Disasters: A Decade of Counter-Disaster Planning. Proceedings. Wednesday 20 - Friday 22 September 1995.* Alan Howell, Heather Mansell and Marion Roubos-Bennett, Compilers. Revised edition. Sydney, Australia: State Library of New South Wales. 237-249.

Watson, A.L. 1984. Quake, Rattle, and Roll: or the Day the Coalinga Library Stood Still and Everything Else Moved. *Library and Archival Security* 6(1984):1-5.

Weber, David C. 1990. *Library Buildings and the Loma Prieta Earthquake Experience of October 1989.* Sacramento: California State Library Foundation.

Wessel, Carl J. 1970. Environmental Factors Affecting the Permanence of Library Materials. *Deterioration and Preservation of Library Materials.* Chicago: University of Chicago Press.

Western New York Library Resources Council. 1994. *Western New York Disaster Preparedness and Recovery Manual for Libraries and Archives.* Revised Edition. Buffalo, New York: Western New York Library Resources Council.

Wright, Gordon H. 1979. Fire! Anguish! Dumb Luck! or Contingency Planning. *Canadian Library Journal* 36(5):254-260.

Yatcom Communications, Inc. 1995a. *All About Hurricanes — What Is a Hurricane.* http://www.yatcom.com/neworl/weather/whatis.html

Yatcom Communications, Inc. 1995b. *All About Hurricanes — Preparing for a Hurricane.* http://www.yatcom.com/neworl/weather/prepare.html

Yatcom Communications, Inc. 1995c. *All About Hurricanes — Evacuation versus "Riding the Storm Out".* http://www.yatcom.com/neworl/weather/evacuate.html

Yatcom Communications, Inc. 1995d. *All About Hurricanes — After the Hurricane Passes.* http://www.yatcom.com/neworl/weather/aftermath.html

Yatcom Communications, Inc. 1995e. *All About Hurricanes — Tornadoes.* http://www.yatcom.com/neworl/weather/tornado.html

References

Chapter 7.0 Disaster Recovery Planning for Collections and Records

ARMA International Standards Disaster Recovery Task Force. 1987. *Magnetic Diskettes Recovery Procedures - A Guideline.* Prairie Village, Kansas: Association of Records Managers and Administrators Inc.

Atwood, Catharine. 1999. The Aftermath of Arson: Packing a Freezer Trailer and other Tidbits. In *The Book and Paper Group Annual 17, 1998.* Robert Espinosa, compiler and managing editor. Washington, D.C.: American Institute for Conservation of Historic and Artistic Works. 1-4.

Banik, Gerhard. 1990. Conservation of Water Damaged Museum Archival Documents. In *ICOM Committee for Conservation. 9th Triennial Meeting. Dresden, German Demcratic Repiblic, 26-31 August 1990. Preprints.* Kirsten Grimstad ed. Paris and Marina del Ray California: ICOM and the Getty Conservation Institute.

Barton, John and Johanna Wellheiser, eds. 1985. *An Ounce of Prevention: A Handbook on Disaster Contingency Planning for Archives, Libraries and Record Centres.* Toronto: Toronto Area Archivists Group Education Foundation.

Buchanan, Sally A. 1988. *Disaster Planning, Preparedness and Recovery for Libraries and Archives: A RAMP Study with Guidelines. PGI-88/WS/6.* Paris: General Information Programme and UNISIST, United Nations Educational, Scientific and Cultural Organization.

CCI (Canadian Conservation Institute). 1989. *Emergency Treatment for Water-Damaged Paintings on Canvas. CCI Note N10/5.* Ottawa: CCI.

CCI. 1996. *Emergency Treatment for Water-Damaged Paintings on Canvas. CCI Note 10/5.* Revised. Ottawa: CCI. Unpublished.

CCI. 1999. *Research and Development Projects, Canadian Conservation Institute, 1999-2000, Draft.* Ottawa: CCI. 28.

Cuddihy, Edward F. 1994. Storage, Preservation and Recovery of Magnetic Recording Tape. In *Environnement et Conservation de L'Écrire, de L'Image et du Son. Actes des Deuxièmes Journées Internationales D'Études de l'ARSAG. Paris 16 au 20 mai 1994.* Paris: Association pour la Recherche Scientifique sur les Arts Graphiques (ARSAG). 182-186.

Cunha, George Martin. 1992. Disaster Planning and a Guide to Recovery Resources. *Library Technology Reports* 28(5):533-624.

DePew, John. 1991. Chapter 8. Disaster Preparedness and Recovery. In *A Library, Media and Archival Preservation Handbook.* Santa Barbara, California: ABC-CLIO. 253-300.

Doig, Judith. 1997. *Disaster Recovery for Archives, Libraries and Records Management Systems in Australia and New Zealand.* Wagga Wagga, New South Wales: Centre for Information Studies.

Eastman Kodak. 1985. *Conservation of Photographs.* Kodak Publication No. F-40. Rochester, N.Y.: Eastman Kodak Co.

Eulenberg, Julia Niebuhr. 1986. *Handbook for the Recovery of Water Damaged Business Records.* Prairie Village, Kansas. ARMA (Association of Records Managers and Administrators, Inc.).

Fischer, Mark, W.A. 1996. Vacuum Freeze-Drying of Paper-Based Materials. In *Redefining Disasters: A Decade of Counter-Disaster Planning. Proceedings. Wednesday 20 - Friday 22 September 1995.* Alan Howell, Heather Mansell and Marion Roubos-Bennett, Compilers. Revised edition. Sydney, Australia: State Library of New South Wales. 65-67.

Fleider, Françoise, Françoise Leclerc and Claire Chahine. 1978. *Effet de la lyophilisation sur le comportement mécanique et chimique du papier, du cuir et du parchemin.* Comité pour la conservation de l'ICOM (Paris), 5ème réunion, triennale, Zagreb. 5-6.

Fortson, Judith. 1992. *Disaster Planning and Recovery. A How-To-Do-It Manual for Librarians and Archivists. Number 21.* New York: Neal-Schuman Publishers, Inc.

Geller, Sidney B. 1983. *Care and Handling of Computer Magnetic Storage Media. NBS Special Publication 500-101.* Washington, D.C.: National Bureau of Standards. 34-35.

Harvey, Christopher. 1995. The Treatment of Flood-Damaged Photographic Material at the Perth Museum and Art Gallery. *Paper Conservation News* 76:8-12.

Henderson, Jane. 1995. Disasters Without Planning: Lessons for Museums. *The Conservator* 19:52-57.

Hendriks, Klaus B. 1986. Rehabilitation of Salvaged Material Photography & Film. In *Proceedings of An Ounce of Prevention.* Nancy Willson, ed. Toronto: Toronto Area Archivists Group Education Foundation. 157-168.

Hendriks, Klaus B. 1991. Recovery of Photograph Collections Following a Flood. In *Sauvegarde et Conservation des Photographies, Dessins, Imprimes et Manuscrits. Actes des Journées Internationales D'Études de l'ARSAG. Paris, 30 septembre au 4 octobre 1991.* Paris: Association pour la Recherche Scientifique sur les Arts Graphiques (ARSAG). 15-20.

Hendriks, Klaus B. and Brian Lesser. 1983. Disaster Preparedness and Recovery: Photographic Materials. *American Archivist* 46(1):52-68.

Hendriks, Klaus B., Brian Thurgood, Joe Iraci, Brian Lesser and Greg Hill. 1991. 9.4 Emergency and Disaster Preparedness Procedures. In *Fundamentals of Photograph Conservation: A Study Guide.* Toronto: Lugus Publications in cooperation with The National Archives of Canada and Supply and Services Canada. 423-427

Hess Norris, Debbie. 1996. Air-drying of Water-soaked Photographic Materials: Observations and Recommendations. In *ICOM Committee for Conservation 11th Triennial Meeting Edinburgh, Scotland 1-6 September 1996, Preprints, Volume II.* Janet Bridgland, ed. London: James & James. 601-608.

Hutson, Jennifer. 1996. *Personal Communication.* September 1996.

Ibsen, Soren. 1998. Conservation and Restoration of Water-Damaged Books. *Paper Conservation News* 87(September): 12-13.

IIC-CG and CAPC. 1989. *Code of Ethics and Guidance for Practice for Those Involved in the Conservation of Cultural Property in Canada.* Second edition. Ottawa: International Institute for Conservation - Canadian Group (now CAC) - Canadian Association for the Conservation of Cultural Property (currently under revision).

Kahn, Miriam. 1994a. *Disaster Response and Prevention for Computers and Data.* Columbus, Ohio: MBK Consulting.

Kahn, Miriam. 1994b. *First Steps for Handling & Drying Water-Damaged Materials.* Columbus, Ohio: MBK Consulting.

Kahn, Miriam B. 1998. *Disaster Response and Planning for Libraries.* Chicago: American Library Association.

Keck, Caroline K. 1972. On Conservation Instructions for Emergency Treatment of Water Damage. *Museum News* 50(10):13.

Kopperl, D.F. and C.C. Bard. 1985. *Freeze-Thaw Cycling of Motion-Pictures Films. SMPTE Journal* 94 (8) : 826-827.

Lyall, Jan. 1995. *Disaster Planning for Libraries and Archives: Understanding the Essential Issues.* Canberra: National Library of Australia. http://www.nla.gov.au/3/npo/pubs/papers/jlyall/disaster.html.

Macgregor, Colin, A. 1996. The Effects of Freezing and Freeze-Drying of Waterlogged Photographic Materials: An Interim Report. In *Redefining Disasters: A Decade of Counter-Disaster Planning. Proceedings. Wednesday 20 - Friday 22 September 1995.* Alan Howell, Heather Mansell and Marion Roubos-Bennett, Compilers. Revised edition. Sydney, Australia: State Library of New South Wales. 107-110.

McDaniel, D. Dave. 1996. *Disaster Preparedness. Protecting Your Vital Records.* Paper presented at the 8th International Disaster Recovery Symposium and Exhibition, Atlanta, Georgia, September 9, 1996.

Moor, Ian L. and Angela Moor. 1987. Fire and Flood: Criteria for the Recovery of Photographic Materials. In *Recent Advances in the Conservation and Analysis of Artifacts.* James Black, comp. London: University of London, Institute of Archaeology.

Munters Corp., Moisture Control Services Division and MBK Consulting. 1996. *Document Restoration Manual.* Internal Training Document.

Murray, Toby. 1994. *Basic Guidelines for Disaster Planning in Oklahoma.* Tulsa, Oklahoma: Oklahoma Conservation Congress (OCC).

Olson, Nancy B. 1986. Hanging Your Software Up To Dry. *College & Research Libraries News* 47(10):634-636.

Osborne, Larry N. 1989. Those (In)destructible Disks; or, Another Myth Exploded. *Library Hi Tech* 7(3):7-10,28.

Paine, Shelley Reisman. n.d. *Protocol for Emergencies* (developed for international exhibition of paintings). http://palimpsest.stanford.edu/byauth/paine. protocol.html.

Parker, A.E. 1989. The Freeze-Drying Process. *Library Conservation News* 23(April):4-6,8.

Parker, A.E. 1991. Freeze-Drying of Vellum. *Library Conservation News* 33(5):4-6.

Parker, A.E. 1993. Freeze-Drying Vellum Archival Materials. *Journal of the Society of Archivists* 14(2):175-185.

Smith, Richard D. 1984. The Use of Redesigned and Mechanically Modified Commercial Freezers to Dry Water-Wetted Books and Exterminate Insects. *Restaurator* 6(3-4):165-190.

Smithsonian Institution. 1993. *A Primer on Disaster Preparedness, Management, and Response: Paper-Based Materials.* Selected Reprints issued by the Smithsonian Institution, National Archives and Records Administration, Library of Congress and National Park Service. Distributed by the participating agencies. http://palimpsest.stanford.edu/bytopic/disaster.p rimer.part4of5.text

St-Laurent, Gilles. 1991. *The Care and Handling of Recorded Sound Materials.* Washington, D.C.: Commission on Preservation and Access.

Stewart, Deborah and David Tremain. 1994. *Emergency and Disaster Preparedness for Museums.* Canadian Conservation Institute (CCI) Workshop. Revised edition. Ottawa: Department of Canadian Heritage, CCI. (Note: Unavailable. To be revised)

Syracuse University Library, Preservation Department. 1995. *Syracuse University Library Manual: Procedures for Recovering Print Materials: Non-Print and Photographic Materials: and Audio Recordings.* http://libwww.syr.edu/aboutsul/depts/preserve/di splan.htm

Tremain, David. 1998. **Notes on Emergency Drying of Coated Papers Damaged by Water.** http://palimpsest.stanford.edu/byauth/tremain/c oated.html

Van Bogart, John W. C. 1996a. *Recovery of Damaged Magnetic Tape and Optical Disk Media. Part 1: Recovery from Improper Storage.* Presented at "Emergency Preparedness and Disaster Recovery of Audio, Film and Video Materials". A Library of Congress Symposium - September 21, 1995. http://www.nml.org/presentations/disaster_reco very/lc_disaster_recovery.html

Van Bogart, John W. C. 1996b. *Recovery of Damaged Magnetic Tape and Optical Disk Media. Part 2: Recovery from Disasters.* Presented at "Emergency Preparedness and Disaster Recovery of Audio, Film and Video Materials". A Library of Congress Symposium - September 21, 1995. http://www.nml.org/presentations/disaster_reco very/lc_disaster_recovery.html

Van Bogart, John W. C. and John Merz. 1996. *St. Thomas Electronic Records Disaster Recovery Effort Technical Report RE0025. National Media Lab.* http://www.nml.org/publications/usvi.html

Walsh, Betty. 1988. Salvage Operations for Water-Damaged Archival Collections: Salvage at a Glance. *WAAC Newsletter* 10(2):2-5.

Walsh, Betty. 1996. *Personal Communication.* August 22, 1996.

Walsh, Betty. 1997. Salvage Operations for Water Damaged Archival Collections: A Second Glance. *WAAC Newsletter* 19(2):12-23.

Ward, Alan and Peter Copeland. 1992. Freeze-Drying of Tapes. *Library Conservation News* 34(7):4-5.

Waters, Peter. 1993. Procedures for Salvage of Water Damaged Library Materials. Extracts from unpublished revised text. In *A Primer on Disaster Preparedness, Management, and Response: Paper-Based Materials.* Selected Reprints issued by the Smithsonian Institution, National Archives and Records Administration, Library of Congress and National Park Service. Distributed by the participating agencies. http://palimpsest.stanford.edu/bytopic/disaster.p rimer.part4of5.text

Waters, Peter. 1996. From Florence to St. Petersburg: An Enlightening and Thought-Provoking Experience. A Personal Account of the Past Twenty Nine Years in Pursuit of the Conservation of Library Materials. In *Redefining Disasters: A Decade of Counter-Disaster Planning. Proceedings. Wednesday 20 - Friday 22 September 1995.* Alan Howell, Heather Mansell and Marion Roubos-Bennett, Compilers. Revised edition. Sydney, Australia: State Library of New South Wales. 237-249.

Weidner, Marilyn Kemp. 1974. Instructions on How to Unframe Wet Prints. *Ontario Museum Association Newsletter* 3(2):36-39.

Western New York Library Resources Council. 1994. *Western New York Disaster Preparedness and Recovery Manual for Libraries and Archives.* Revised Edition. Buffalo, New York: Western New York Library Resources Council.

Wright, Gordon H. 1979. Fire! Anguish! Dumb Luck! or Contingency Planning. *Canadian Library Journal* 36(5):254-260.

Chapter 8.0 Disaster Rehabilitation Planning for Collections and Records

ANSI/NISO/LBI (American National Standards Institute/National Information Standards Organization/Library Binding Institute). 2000. *ANSI/NISO/LBI Z39. 78-2000. American National Standard for Library Binding.* Annapolis Junction, Maryland: NISO.

ANSI/NISO. 1997. *ANSI/NISO Z39.48-1992. Revised 1997. American National Standard for Permanence of Paper for Publications and Documents in Libraries and Archives.* Bethesda, Maryland: NISO Press.

ANSI/NISO. 1992. *ANSI/NISO Z39.66-1992. American National Standard for Durable Hardcover Binding for Books.* Bethesda, Maryland: NISO Press.

ANSI/NISO. 1996. *ANSI/NISO Z39.76-1996. American National Standard for Data Elements for Binding Library Materials.* Bethesda, Maryland: NISO Press.

Buchanan, Sally A. 1988. *Disaster Planning, Preparedness and Recovery for Libraries and Archives: A RAMP Study with Guidelines. PGI-88/WS/6.* Paris: General Information Programme and UNISIST, United Nations Educational, Scientific and Cultural Organization.

Canadian Co-operative Preservation Project. 1993. *Guidelines for Preservation Microfilming in Canadian Libraries.* Ottawa: National Library of Canada.

Collins, Grant. 1996. Salvage of Fire-Damaged Collections. In *Redefining Disasters: A Decade of Counter-Disaster Planning. Proceedings. Wednesday 20 - Friday 22 September 1995.* Alan Howell, Heather Mansell and Marion Roubos-Bennett, Compilers. Revised edition. Sydney, Australia: State Library of New South Wales. 41-46.

Conway, Paul. 1996. *Preservation in the Digital World.* Washington: Commission on Preservation and Access.

Elkington, Nancy E., ed. 1994. *Archives Microfilming Manual.* Mountainview, California: Research Libraries Group.

Fortson, Judith. 1992. *Disaster Planning and Recovery. A How-To-Do-It Manual for Librarians and Archivists. Number 21.* New York: Neal-Schuman Publishers, Inc.

Fox, Lisa L. ed. 1996. *Preservation Microfilming: A Guide for Librarians and Archivists.* Chicago and London: American Library Association.

Ibsen, Soren. 1998. Conservation and Restoration of Water-Damaged Books. *Paper Conservation News* 87(September): 12-13.

ISO (International Organization for Standardization). *ISO/DIS 144.16. Information and Documentation - Requirements for Binding of Books, Periodicals, Serials and Other Paper Documents for Archive and Library Use - Methods and Materials.* Geneva: ISO.

References

ISO. 1994. *ISO 9706:1994. Information and Documentation - Paper for Documents - Requirements for Permanence.* Geneva: ISO.

ISO. 1996. *ISO 11108:1996. Information and Documentation - Archival Paper - Requirements for Permanence and Durability.* Geneva: ISO.

Kahn, Miriam. 1994a. Fires, Earthquakes and Floods: How to Prepare Your Library and Staff. *ONLINE* (May):18-24.

Kahn, Miriam. 1994b. *Disaster Response and Prevention for Computers and Data.* Columbus, Ohio: MBK Consulting.

Kenney, Anne R. and Stephen Chapman. 1996. *Digital Imaging for Libraries and Archives.* Ithaca, New York: Cornell University.

Lundquist, Eric. 1986. *Salvage of Water Damaged Books, Documents, Micrographic and Magnetic Media.* San Francisco: Document Reprocessors.

Matthews, Fred W. 1986. Dalhousie Fire. *Canadian Library Journal* August:221-226.

Miller, R. Bruce. 1988. Libraries and Computers: Disaster Prevention and Recovery. *Information Technology and Libraries* 7(4):349-358.

Moffat, Elizabeth. 1992. Analysis of "Chemical" Sponges Used by the Commercial Fire Clean-Up Industry to Remove Soot From Various Surfaces. *IIC-CG Bulletin* 17(3)September:9-10.

Moffat, Elizabeth. 1986. Smoke-Off. *ARS Report No. 2445. January 24, 1986.* Ottawa: Canadian Conservation Institute.

Moffat, Elizabeth. 1991. Analysis of a Sponge for Cleaning Fire-Damaged Documents. *ARS Report No. 2928. January 25, 1991.* Ottawa: Canadian Conservation Institute.

Moffat, Elizabeth. 1992. Analysis of a Wallmaster Chemical Sponge and a Quality Rubber Sponge. *ARS Report No. 4000. July 20, 1992.* Ottawa: Canadian Conservation Institute.

Munters Corp., Moisture Control Services Division and MBK Consulting. 1996. *Document Restoration Manual.* Internal Training Document.

NISO (National Information Standards Organization). 2000. *NISO Z39.77-2000. Guidelines for Information about Preservation Products.* Annapolis Junction Maryland: NISO.

Olcott Price, Lois. 1994. *Mould - Managing a Mould Invasion: Guidelines for Disaster Response.* Technical Series No. 1. Philadelphia: Conservation Center for Art and Historic Artifacts.

Page, Julie. 1998. Mold. December 17, 1998. Available Co01 DistList Archives.

Preusser, Frank D. 1994. UV/Ozone and Mold. *Conservation OnLine Distlist.* May 26, 1994.

Spafford, Sarah and Fiona Graham. 1993a. Fire Recovery at the Saskatchewan Museum of Natural History: Part I, Description of Events and Analysis of Recovery. In *ICOM Committee for Conservation. Preprints of the 10th Triennial Meeting, Washington, D.C., U.S.A., 22-27 August 1993.* Volume I. Janet Bridgland, ed. Paris: ICOM Committee for Conservation. 413-419.

Spafford, Sarah and Fiona Graham. 1993b. Fire Recovery at the Saskatchewan Museum of Natural History: Part II - Post-Disaster Clean-Up and Soot Removal. In *ICOM Committee for Conservation. Preprints of the 10th Triennial Meeting, Washington, D.C., U.S.A., 22-27 August 1993.* Volume I. Janet Bridgland, ed. Paris: ICOM Committee for Conservation. 420-426.

Van Bogart, John W. C. 1996a. *Recovery of Damaged Magnetic Tape and Optical Disk Media. Part 1: Recovery from Improper Storage.* Presented at "Emergency Preparedness and Disaster Recovery of Audio, Film and Video Materials". A Library of Congress Symposium - September 21, 1995. http://www.nml.org/presentations/disaster_recovery/lc_disaster_recovery.html

Van Bogart, John W. C. 1996b. *Recovery of Damaged Magnetic Tape and Optical Disk Media. Part 2: Recovery from Disasters.* Presented at "Emergency Preparedness and Disaster Recovery of Audio, Film and Video Materials". A Library of Congress Symposium - September 21, 1995. http://www.nml.org/presentations/disaster_recovery/lc_disaster_recovery.html

Van Bogart, John W. C. and John Merz. 1996. *St. Thomas Electronic Records Disaster Recovery Effort Technical Report RE0025. National Media Lab.* http://www.nml.org/publications/usvi.html

Waters, Peter. 1993. Procedures for Salvage of Water Damaged Library Materials. Extracts from unpublished revised text. In *A Primer on Disaster Preparedness, Management, and Response: Paper-Based Materials.* Selected Reprints issued by the Smithsonian Institution, National Archives and Records Administration, Library of Congress and National Park Service. Distributed by the participating agencies. http://palimpsest.stanford.edu/bytopic/disaster.primer.part4of5.text.

Western New York Library Resources Council. 1994. *Western New York Disaster Preparedness and Recovery Manual for Libraries and Archives.* Revised Edition. Buffalo, New York: Western New York Library Resources Council.

Wood Lee, Mary. 1988. *Prevention and Treatment of Mold in Library Collections with an Emphasis on Tropical Climates: A RAMP Study. PGI-88/WS/9.* Paris: General Information Programme and UNISIST, UNESCO.

Wright, Sandra. 1989. Disaster Planning: A Management Success Story. In *Proceedings of Conservation in Archives. International Symposium, Ottawa, Canada, May 10-12, 1988.* Paris: International Council on Archives. 281-290.

Chapter 9.0   Disaster Recovery and Rehabilitation Planning for Facilities and Systems

Anderson, William A. and Shirley Mattingly. 1991. Future Directions. In *Emergency Management: Principles and Practice for Local Government.* Thomas E. Drabek and Gerard J. Hoetmer, eds. Washington, D.C.: International City/County Management Association (ICMA). 311-335.

Boyd, John. 1994. Disaster Recovery Plans. The Nottinghamshire Experience. *Aslib Information* 1(7/8):33-35.

Cesa, Rebecca. 1996. Don't Let Disaster Linger. Eliminating Odor Makes Sense. *Contingency Planning & Management for Business Preparedness and Recovery* 1(2):19-21.

Cunha, George Martin. 1992. Disaster Planning and a Guide to Recovery Resources. *Library Technology Reports* 28(5):533-624.

Drabek, Thomas E. 1991. The Evolution of Emergency Management. In *Emergency Management: Principles and Practice for Local Government.* Thomas E. Drabek and Gerard J. Hoetmer, eds. Washington, D.C.: International City/County Management Association (ICMA). 3-29.

Environment Canada, The Crisis Management Division of the Conservation and Protection Branch. 1993. Guide for Crisis Management Planning. *Emergency Preparedness Digest* April-June:23-26.

Fischer, Mark, W.A. 1996. Salvage and Recovery of Water, Fire and Smoke Damaged Library Buildings and Their Contents. In *Redefining Disasters: A Decade of Counter-Disaster Planning. Proceedings. Wednesday 20 - Friday 22 September 1995.* Alan Howell, Heather Mansell and Marion Roubos-Bennett, Compilers. Revised edition. Sydney, Australia: State Library of New South Wales. 59-64.

Gordon, Roger, P. 1994. The First 24 Hours Post-Disaster. *Disaster Recovery Journal* 7(3):70-72.

Hays, Walter W. 1991. At Risk from Natural Hazards. In *Perspectives on Natural Disaster Mitigation: Papers Presented at 1991 AIC Workshop.* Washington, D.C.: FAIC (Foundation of the American Institute for Conservation of Historic and Artistic Works). 1-8.

Kahn, Miriam. 1994a. *Disaster Response and Prevention for Computers and Data.* Columbus, Ohio: MBK Consulting.

Kahn, Miriam. 1994b. Fires, Earthquakes and Floods. How to Prepare Your Library and Staff. *ONLINE* (May):18, 20-24.

Moore, Pat. 1996. Damage Done: Assessment to Come. *Contingency Planning & Management for Business Preparedness and Recovery* 1(3):17-21.

Munters Corp., Moisture Control Services Division. n.d. *Disaster Recovery Plan [name of organization].* Information and promotional literature package. Amesbury, Massachusetts: Munters MCS.

National Park Service, Preservation Assistance Division. 1995. *After the Flood: Emergency Stabilization and Conservation Measures.* http://palimpsest.stanford.edu/bytopic/disaster/misc/nps.after.the.flood.

Nelson, Carl L. 1991. *Protecting the Past from Natural Disasters.* Washington, D.C.: National Trust for Historic Preservation.

Rubin, Claire B. 1991. Recovery From Disaster. In *Emergency Management: Principles and Practice for Local Government.* Thomas E. Drabek and Gerard J. Hoetmer, eds. Washington, D.C: International City/County Management Association (ICMA). 224-259.

Spafford, Sarah and Fiona Graham. 1993a. Fire Recovery at the Saskatchewan Museum of Natural History: Part I, Description of Events and Analysis of Recovery. In *ICOM Committee for Conservation. Preprints of the 10th Triennial Meeting, Washington, D.C., U.S.A., 22-27 August 1993.* Volume I. Janet Bridgland, ed. Paris: ICOM Committee for Conservation. 413-419.

Spafford, Sarah and Fiona Graham. 1993b. Fire Recovery at the Saskatchewan Museum of Natural History: Part II - Post-Disaster Clean-Up and Soot Removal. In *ICOM Committee for Conservation. Preprints of the 10th Triennial Meeting, Washington, D.C., U.S.A., 22-27 August 1993.* Volume I. Janet Bridgland, ed. Paris: ICOM Committee for Conservation. 420-426.

Chapter 10.0   Post-Disaster Planning

Anderson, William A. and Shirley Mattingly. 1991. Future Directions. In *Emergency Management: Principles and Practices for Local Government.* Thomas E. Drabek and Gerard J. Hoetmer, eds. Washington, D.C.: International City/County Management Association (ICMA). 311-335.

Blythe, Bruce. 1996. Mental Health Plan. Trauma Intervention Supports Company Well-Being. *Contingency Planning & Management for Business Preparedness and Recovery* 1(4):15-20.

Buckland, John, ed. 1991. *Disaster Recovery Handbook.* Blue Ridge Summit, Pennsylvania: Chantico Publishing Company. Inc.

Clouse, Monty and Killorin Riddell. 1996. Plan for, Recognize, and Respond to "First Wave" Trauma. In Mental Health Plan. Trauma Intervention Supports Company Well-Being by Bruce Blyth. *Contingency Planning & Management for Business Preparedness and Recovery* 1(4):20.

Drabek, Thomas E. 1991. The Events of An Emergency. In *Perspectives on Natural Disaster Mitigation: Papers Presented at 1991 AIC Workshop.* Washington, D.C.: FAIC (Foundation of the American Institute for Conservation of Historic and Artistic Works). 31-36.

England, Claire and Karen Evans. 1988. Chapter 5: Insurance for the Library Collection. In *Disaster Management for Libraries: Planning and Process.* Ottawa: Canadian Library Association. 59-70.

Environment Canada, The Crisis Management Division of the Conservation and Protection Branch. 1993. Guide for Crisis Management Planning. *Emergency Preparedness Digest* April-June:23-26.

Hunter, John, E. 1983. Chapter 11. Museum Disaster Planning. In *Museum, Archive, and Library Security.* Lawrence J. Fennelly, ed. Boston: Butterworths. 235-270.

Hunter, John E. 1990. Chapter 10. Museum Collections: Emergency Planning. In *National Park Service Museum Handbook. Part I: Museum Collections.* Revised edition. Washington, D.C.: National Park Service:10:1-10:29.

J. Paul Getty Museum. 1992. *The J. Paul Getty Museum Emergency Planning Handbook.* Revised. Malibu, California: The J. Paul Getty Museum.

Lyall, Jan. 1995. *Disaster Planning for Libraries and Archives: Understanding the Essential Issues.* Canberra: National Library of Australia. http://www.nla.gov.au/3/npo/pubs/papers/jlyall/disaster.html.

Lystad, Mary, H. 1991. People in Emergencies. In *Perspectives on Natural Disaster Mitigation: Papers Presented at 1991 AIC Workshop.* Washington, D.C.: Foundation of the American Institute for Conservation of Historic and Artistic Works. 17-25.

Matthews, Graham. 1994. Disaster Management: Controlling the Plan. *Managing Information* 1(7/8):24-27.

Mutton, David. 1996. Critical Incident Stress. In *Redefining Disasters: A Decade of Counter-Disaster Planning. Proceedings. Wednesday 20 - Friday 22 September 1995.* Alan Howell, Heather Mansell and Marion Roubos-Bennett, Compilers. Revised edition. Sydney, Australia: State Library of New South Wales. 169-180.

Nelson, Carl L. 1991. *Protecting the Past from Natural Disasters.* Washington, D.C.: National Trust for Historic Preservation.

Paulhus, J. L. (Laurie). 1983. Planning for Safety and Security. In *Planning Our Museums.* Barry Lord and Gail Dexter Lord, eds. Ottawa: National Museums of Canada.

Pember, Margaret E. 1996. The Psycho-Social (P-S) Factor in Counter-Disaster Planning: The Human Element. In *Redefining Disasters: A Decade of Counter-Disaster Planning. Proceedings. Wednesday 20 - Friday 22 September 1995.* Alan Howell, Heather Mansell and Marion Roubos-Bennett, Compilers. Revised edition. Sydney, Australia: State Library of New South Wales. 199-206.

Rubin, Claire B. 1991. Recovery From Disaster. In *Emergency Management: Principles and Practice for Local Government.* Thomas E. Drabek and Gerard J. Hoetmer, eds. Washington, D.C.: International City/County Management Association (ICMA). 224-259.

Stasak, Bernard C. 1996. Human Resources. Proper Deployment, Care, and Communication Fortify Team Efforts. *Contingency Planning & Management for Business Preparedness and Recovery* 1(2):29-31.

Vossler, Janet L. 1987. The Human Element of Disaster Recovery. *Records Management Quarterly* 21(1):10-12.

Wright, Gordon H. 1979. Fire! Anguish! Dumb Luck! or Contingency Planning. *Canadian Library Journal* 36(5):254-260.

Index

About the Authors

Johanna Wellheiser is the manager of preservation and digitization services for the Toronto Public Library. She co-edited the first edition of *An Ounce of Prevention*, winner of the Society of American Archivists' Gifford Leland Award, and among other works, authored *Nonchemical Treatment Processes for Disinfestation of Insects and Fungi in Library Collections*. She is a member of the Standing Committee of the International Federation of Library Associations' Section on Preservation and Conservation.

Jude Scott is a writer and researcher specializing in projects for the Canadian heritage and cultural sectors. Among other works, she is author and editor of the *Museum and Archival Supplies Handbook (MASH)*, which received an Award of Merit from the American Association of State and Local History, the *Historic Sites Supplies Handbook* and a book on literacy publishing.